MW01195542

METALLIC CARTRIDGE RELOADING

3rd Edition

By M.L. McPherson

DBI BOOKS, INC.

STAFF

SENIOR STAFF EDITORS
Harold A. Murtz
Ray Ordorica

PRODUCTION MANAGER
John L. Duoba

EDITORIAL/PRODUCTION ASSOCIATE
Laura M. Mielzynski

ELECTRONIC PUBLISHING MANAGER
Nancy J. Mellem

ELECTRONIC PUBLISHING ASSOCIATE
Larry Levine

COVER PHOTOGRAPHY
John Hanusin

MANAGING EDITOR
Pamela J. Johnson

PUBLISHER
Sheldon L. Factor

About The Cover

Building safe, tack-driving, high-performance handloads doesn't require a lot of equipment, but it does demand the best that the industry has to offer. Featured on our covers are three of the leading manufacturers of high-quality reloading tools and components—Lapua, Redding and VihtaVuori Oy.

At center stage is reloading equipment from Redding. In its 50th year, **Redding** continues to be one of the oldest and most respected names in precision reloading tools. The Boss O-type press, a cast-iron brute offering great strength yet sensitivity for seating primers, provides a 36-degree frame offset for good visibility and access to reloading operations.

Left of the press is Redding's deluxe die set. Made of the finest alloy steels, these dies are meticulously machined, knurled and hand-polished so they'll last a lifetime. The other die is Redding's new Benchrest Competition bullet seating die, a straight-line seater with micrometer adjustment and very precise alignment.

Also shown are Redding's No. 2 Master powder and bullet scale with 505-grain capacity, $1/_{10}$-grain accuracy, and simple two counterpoise system; their No. 5 Powder Trickler; and Redding's Original Formula Case Lube for tough resizing and forming operations.

Lapua, the Finnish sporting ammunition and components maker, is perhaps best known for their high-quality match ammunition used to win numerous gold medals in World Championships, Olympic Games and other national and international shooting competitions since 1923.

That same commitment to Olympic-quality products is being offered in reloading brass, both rifle and handgun, the most notable of which is the 220 Russian. This fabulously accurate round is the basis of many match-winning rifle/cartridge combinations that are rewriting the record books.

There is also an interesting line of bullets of their own design, for a variety of purposes: Mega is a flatpoint big game bullet; Scenar, a hollowpoint boattail target and benchrest bullet; Lock Base is a patented long-range boattail target and benchrest design; D46 is a FMJBT that's made to the tightest tolerances and is a record setter; and Forex, a special-construction, softpoint, hollow-base, ribbed big game bullet. Lapua is a name shooters will be seeing more of in the coming years. Keng's Firearm Specialty, Inc. is the source.

Another Finnlander, one already making a big splash on the American market, is **VihtaVuori Oy**. Founded in 1922, the company is a leader in explosive technology for the military, mining and construction industries.

VihtaVuori's wide variety of smokeless powders meet nearly any reloading chore, from 17-caliber up to 50 BMG, and from 25 ACP to 454 Casull in handguns. The N100 series are primarily rifle powders, with ten speeds currently offered. The N160 shown here is a relatively slow powder ideally suited to many magnum and standard rounds like the 243, 25-06, 264 Winchester Magnum, 30-06 and 375 H&H. Handgun powders include the N300 series. The 3N37 shown at right is specially designed for high-velocity rimfire cartridges, but has good application in 9mm Parabellum, 38 Super, 357 Magnum, 44 Magnum and others.

VihtaVuori also offers a high-energy line of five powders, catagorized as N500s. N560, a traditional single-base powder with nitroglycerine added to boost energy, is designed for use with 270 Winchester, 6.5x55 Swede, 300 Winchester Magnum, 30-06 and 220 Swift loads. VihtaVuori's *Reloading Manual*, 2nd Edition, covers the full range of VihtaVuori powder applications in great detail with exhaustively tested data.

Photo by John Hanusin.

Copyright © MCMXCVI by DBI Books, Inc., 4092 Commercial Ave., Northbrook, IL 60062. Printed in the United States of America. All rights reserved. No part of this book may be reproduced, stored in a retrieval system, or transmitted in any form or by any means, electronic, mechanical, photocopying, recording or otherwise, without prior written permission of the publisher.

The views and opinions of the author expressed herein are not necessarily those of the publisher, and no responsibility for such views will be assumed.

Arms and Armour Press, London, G.B., exclusive licensees and distributor in Britain and Europe, India and Pakistan; Book Services International, Sandton, Transvaal, exclusive distributor in South Africa and Zimbabwe. Forrester Books N.Z. Limited, Auckland, exclusive distributor in New Zealand.

CAUTION: The load data presented here inevitably reflects individual experience with particular equipment and components under specific circumstances the reader cannot duplicate exactly. Such data presentations therefore should be used for guidance only and with caution.

Since the author, editors and publisher have no control over the components, assembly of the ammunition, arms it is to be fired in, the degree of knowledge involved or how the resulting ammunition may be used, no responsibility, either implied or expressed, is assumed for the use of any of the loading data in this book.

ISBN 0-87349-180-7   Library of Congress Catalog Card #81-70996

ACKNOWLEDGEMENTS

IN PREPARING THE 3rd Edition of METALLIC CARTRIDGE RELOADING, we have drawn upon many sources for information of many types. Without the kind assistance of numerous fellow handloaders, the compilation of these handloading concepts and data would never have been possible.

We must specifically credit those companies whose kind consent facilitated incorporating the data herein. The investment in time and money represented by their original compilation of data for the more than 100 cartridges and 10,000 loads we have reproduced here is difficult to imagine.

These efforts were of enormous magnitude. Consider the following facts. The facilities required for pressure testing cost several tens of thousands of dollars. The basic pressure-testing equipment necessary costs about $10,000. Each different pressure barrel costs several hundred dollars. Each load (bullet and powder type for one cartridge) requires many hours work and about $10 worth of components.

Specifically, we would like to thank the following companies for their permission to use proprietary data, and these individuals for their help in ensuring that we have accurately represented that data.

Accurate Arms, Mr. William Falin, Jr.
Hodgdon Powder Company, Mr. Ron Reiber
VihtaVuori Oy/Kaltron-Pettibone, Mr. Vince Tunzi
Winchester Div., Olin Corp., Mr. Mike Jordan

Similarly, many companies and individuals have provided expert advice and assistance regarding various handloading concepts detailed in this text. These folks have answered numerous questions about the various tools described herein. Without this assistance, this text would never have been possible.

We would like to thank the following companies and individuals:
Barnes Bullets, Inc., Jessica Harrison
Black Hills Ammunition, Jeff Hoffman
Forster Products, Bob Ruch
4-D Custom Die Co., Dave Davidson
Hart & Son, Inc., Bob Hart
Hoch Custom Bullet Moulds, Dave Farmer
Hornady Mfg. Co., Doug Engh and Bob Palmer
K&M Services, Ken Markle
L.E. Wilson, Inc., John Morrison
Lee Precision, Inc., John Lee
Lyman Products Corporation, Ed Schmidt
Magma Engineering Co., Paul B. Moore
Midway Arms, Inc., John Branch
MTM Molded Products Co., Inc., Carol Stebbins
NECO, Roger Johnston
Oehler Research, Inc., Ken Oehler and James Bohls
RCBS, Art Peters
Redding Reloading Equipment, Patrick Ryan
Shooting Chrony, Inc., Peter Trnkoczy
Sinclair International, Inc., Bill Gravatt
Speer Products, Allen Jones
Star Machine Works, George Rainbolt
Stoney Point Products, Inc., Tom Peterson
Finally, we would like to thank the following companies for their general assistance: G96 Products Co., Inc.; Hoppes Div., Birchwood Laboratories, Inc.; Iosso Products; Outers Laboratories; Penguin Industries, Inc.

This listing is certainly not complete. Many other individuals and companies have contributed in many ways. For all of their contributions, both small and large, our heartfelt thanks.

Mic McPherson

CONTENTS

CONTENTS

Pistol Data 271

Specialty Handgun Data 332

Manufacturers' Directory of the Reloading Trade 350

FOREWORD

IN SETTING OUT to update METALLIC CARTRIDGE RELOADING for this, the 3rd edition, we recognized the need for an advanced handloading book, one that could answer questions experienced handloaders might have, yet be interesting and useful for the novice. This book is intended to be a single source for detailed information on advanced handloading issues, while offering a wide variety of loading data. In the latter effort, we have certainly succeeded. We have listed more than 10,000 loads covering more than 125 rifle and handgun cartridges. For most of these cartridges, you will find more data right here than in any other single source.

While we will assume a certain amount of fundamental handloading knowledge, even the less experienced reloader should be able to follow our discussions and, at the very least, gain an understanding of the advanced techniques he might employ to improve the quality of his handloaded ammunition. Helping interested readers understand the "why" of important handloading issues is one of our goals. It seems too many sources offer the "what, where and how" without explaining the "why." It is our belief that handloaders who understand the "why" will be more apt to enjoy the fruits of safe handloading practices.

For those interested in a more detailed background study of handloading fundamentals, we can heartily recommend *ABC's of Reloading, 5th Edition*; *Hornady Handbook of Cartridge Reloading, 4th Edition*; or the *Speer Reloading Manual, 12th Edition*. This is certainly not an exhaustive listing, but it does cover the author's favorites. For those interested in more thorough, and even esoteric, discussions of advanced topics, we can highly recommend *Precision Shooting's Reloading Guide*.

While we will be discussing specific handloading tools, this is not a catalog. Those interested in learning what tools are currently available should refer to the most recent edition of *Handloader's Digest*. This one source manages to offer more information than seems possible.

It is our fervent hope that this 3rd Edition of METALLIC CARTRIDGE RELOADING will be valuable to all handloaders who are interested in improving their understanding of what they are doing and how to do it better.

Safety

As in all aspects of the shooting sports, never forget that when handloading ammunition you are dealing with energetic materials and devices capable of bringing great harm and destruction.

I am constantly reminded of the dangers primers present. One regional ammunition manufacturer formerly demonstrated this fact to all new employees at the company's annual picnic. At 200 yards, he would set up two targets: one was a company coffee cup with 200 primers in it; the other, two sticks of dynamite hidden behind a similar cup. He would then explode each target with precisely placed shots from his 308 Winchester-chambered target rifle. The question the group was to answer: "Which was which..?" And the answer was not obvious!

Yes, primers are dangerous. They definitely deserve your utmost attention in safe handling. Follow all safety precautions listed on the box and those packaged with all priming tools. Always keep primers in their original containers until you are ready to use them, and never leave unused primers unattended.

Powder is our most obvious safety concern, and with good cause. Should you ever have the misfortune of igniting a large quantity of any smokeless powder, blackpowder or blackpowder substitute in any enclosed space, you might survive long enough to gain new respect for what seems to be such a harmless substance.

Consider the plight of a fellow handloader who recently succeeded in igniting a nearly full and open 8-pound can of Red Dot powder in his handloading-specific outbuilding. He managed to escape. The resulting inferno destroyed the building along with thousands of dollars worth of equipment. Had he hesitated in his departure, or had the door opened inward or had it been bolted, he would not have survived the incident.

More commonly, we are concerned with powder safety from the aspect of handloading. Inadvertent use of the wrong type or wrong amount of powder in a handload is the most likely source of catastrophic gun failure. Develop unwavering powder handling habits. *Never, ever* allow two types of powder to be within reach on your loading bench at the same time. Otherwise, rest assured, it is only a matter of time before you either use the wrong powder or return excess powder to the wrong canister. Always double-check to make absolutely certain you are using the intended powder and correct charge for the handloads you are producing.

Besides personal lead contamination, bullet handling has other pitfalls. It is entirely possible to seat wrong-diameter bullets in certain cartridges. Several are genuine lookalikes. Many .257"/.264", .277"/.284" and .308"/.311" pairs are visually indistinguishable, and a gun with a slightly loose throat might chamber your error. The combination of an oversize bullet mistakenly loaded in the wrong cartridge has wrecked many a gun. The danger? The case neck might not have the necessary room to expand away from the bullet. If the case cannot expand efficiently, it cannot properly release the bullet. This can lead to devastating pressures.

In the first two of the above-noted similar-size pairs, guns intended for the smaller bullet will not normally allow a cartridge loaded with the larger, oversize bullet to freely chamber. However, if a particular gun's throat does happen to be large enough to allow chambering of a cartridge loaded with such an oversize bullet, it is a practical certainty that the chamber throat will be very tight around the case mouth. This is a sure road to disaster—and it has happened. With the latter pair of lookalikes, many .308" chambered guns will allow cartridges loaded with .311" bullets to chamber normally. Here the danger of a chambered case loaded with an oversize bullet not having sufficient neck clearance to properly release the bullet is somewhat less. Nevertheless, potentially dangerous excess pressures are still a likely consequence.

Keep your bullets in their original boxes and keep those boxes closed when not in use. Also, keep bullet boxes segregated according to diameter. A roll of drafting tape is useful for resealing opened bullet boxes and is cheap insurance. When you are buying bullets, off the shelf, insist your retailer prevents tampering—the urge to examine bullets is great. If you are ever in doubt, measure each bullet's diameter and weigh it before use.

The list of potential hazards is endless. Over-length cases can lead to pressure troubles. The tapered portion of the chamber throat can crimp an over-length case mouth into the bullet as the bolt drives the case into the chamber. Also, over-length loads can jam bullets into the rifling. This can significantly raise pressures. Excessive charges of powder will obviously raise pressure, potentially beyond any safe level. Use of the wrong powder is surprisingly common. Trust us here, if you use the wrong powder, you have about a 50/50 chance of not destroying something. If the powder used happens to be a slower burner than the intended powder, you will have been very lucky.

Use common sense and develop the habit of staying as safe as possible rather than getting as close to danger as possible. If you really must take chances, do all the rest of us shooters and handloaders a genuine favor—take up untethered mountain climbing or some other similar sport.

A quick word on pressure safety: I am still young and enthusiastic enough to want to get all the ballistic performance out of my handloads as is safely feasible. However, for target work, the only meaningful criterion is accuracy. For all other loads, delivered energy takes precedence, and that is where pressure concerns come to the forefront of the discussion.

There is no trick to creating handloads that surpass factory-load ballistics: Anyone can do it, by simply loading to higher pressures than the factories do! Right here I will paraphrase Ken Oehler (Oehler Ballistics Labs), dean of pressure measurement: "High-performance handloads *often* generate pressures exceeding factory proof loads. When you are handloading like that, you are seeing how close you can skate to the thin edge, not seeing how far you can stay away from it."

The trick? Develop handloads that beat factory loads without increasing pressure. This is not easy. You must understand that the factories have access to every type of powder you do and many types you do not. If Remington, or any other major manufacturer, so chooses, they can have a powder with any burning rate they want made up and delivered, no problem.

Here we do not intend to suggest one cannot sometimes beat factory ballistics without increasing pressure. Sometimes one can. The point is, do not set velocity as your primary goal. Your goal should be to create ammunition that fulfills your needs better than factory ammunition, when used in your gun. That is a goal you can always strive toward without sacrificing your margin of safety—and happily one can usually achieve this goal.

Accuracy and Functionality

To paraphrase the late Colonel Townsend Whelen: "The only interesting gun is an accurate gun, and the only interesting handload is an accurate handload." Almost anyone interested in guns can manufacture ammunition. This is an absorbing and rewarding hobby that can lead to money savings and increased opportunities, but it offers so much more.

What separates usable reloads from high-performance handloads is not the velocity generated, but, rather, how well each load functions in any given gun, the load's accuracy potential and the ballistic uniformity it delivers. In certain applications, other factors are also critical.

An obvious example is hunting ammunition, where terminal performance is a major consideration. At least one person has died after his "super" reloads failed him in an encounter of the worst kind. In one instance, the bullet in an unfired round pulled out of the case and locked up a revolver. With his powerful revolver reduced to an expensive and awkward club, our hapless hunter died when a wounded grizzly bear came right down on top of him. He had failed to verify that his hunting loads would work every time, and he paid the ultimate price. His load delivered a good bullet with plenty of energy, but it failed the ultimate test—functionality.

Generally, it should be possible for any handloader, who is willing to make the effort, you create handloads that deliver superior accuracy in any given gun. This is most true in rifles, but even in handguns there is hope of improving on factory load accuracy and performance. This is simple enough to understand: Factories have to manufacture ammunition to tolerances that ensure every round will chamber in any commercial gun ever made for that cartridge. Since there are manufacturing tolerances involved, what universal functionality usually means is that any factory cartridge will be a somewhat loose fit in any particular gun.

On the other hand, you can tailor your handloads to fit more closely in your gun's chamber. This close fit results in better case and bullet-to-bore alignment. It also improves ignition uniformity since the firing pin (striker) doesn't waste as much energy moving the case around in the chamber. Better alignment between the cartridge and the bore is the primary feature separating the best benchrest ammunition and guns from your trusty old hunting rifle. Generally, the tighter you can fit your cartridges, the better they will shoot—regardless of the type of gun. However, in all ammunition, except that used strictly for target shooting, this goal—accuracy—is always subservient to functionality.

The factories keep making strides, and they are gaining. While it used to be a simple matter to surpass the accuracy of factory fodder, this is no longer the situation. If you want to beat the "Big Boys," you had better know what you are doing and you had better concentrate on doing it well. We dedicate this book to helping you do it well.

Here we have another consideration that is rather important. How can one tell if any given load is more accurate than some other similar load? The only method I know of that makes any sense is to sit down at a bench, rest the gun and carefully fire shots through paper for groups.

Regardless of the type of gun or the type of shooting involved, benchtesting is the definitive method used to measure the accuracy of the load and gun combination. The idea is to minimize variables. As an example, if you are shooting a hunting rifle, equip it with a good riflescope so that your ability to see does not limit your ability to shoot—generally, you cannot deliberately hit what you cannot see! Then rest the gun on some sort of cradle that will support it the same way for each shot while providing a steady platform so that you do not have to hold the rifle on target. Make sure that you hold the gun the same way for each shot. Gently squeeze the trigger until the gun fires. Ensure that you can do this without disturbing the gun's alignment on target. The bottom line? Make sure your shooting ability and technique is not limiting your ability to measure the intrinsic accuracy of the gun and load.

Chapter 1

CASE INSPECTION

THE CARTRIDGE CASE has two functions: containment of the components necessary to make the cartridge work; and sealing the chamber from the high pressure gases generated when the cartridge is fired. Brass, aluminum or steel have been the materials most commonly used in the manufacture of cartridge cases, but because of handloading equipment and safety concerns our discussion will be limited to brass cartridge cases.

The brass case has not changed much since the late 1800s. While quality varies, all such cases are similar in design and composition. The basic brass alloy is 70 percent copper and 30 percent zinc with impurities kept to an absolute minimum. This brass alloy has several advantages: its ductility facilitates manufacture; its high lubricity minimizes frictional wear of tools and gun chambers; its resistance to corrosion minimizes storage concerns; it is work-hardening which allows the use of very high chamber pressures; it is heat-annealable to allow softening of the case neck and body to facilitate loading and chamber sealing; and it is relatively inexpensive which keeps ammunition affordable.

Brass cases are sometimes nickel-plated to prevent corrosion in leather cartridge loops or to enhance appearance. This plating can lead to increased chamber pressures in some applications because it increases bullet-to-neck friction. For this reason, the handloader is wise to avoid nickel-plated cases for rifle loads or, at the very least, reduce charges a few percent whenever using them.

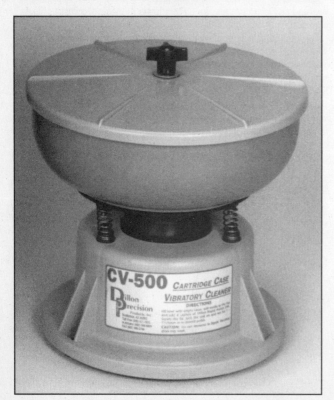

Vibratory or rotary case tumbler case cleaners are a welcome addition to the handloader's workbench.

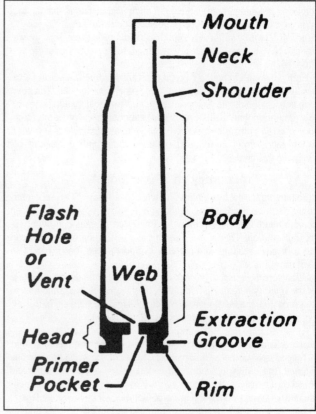

Initial Case Inspection

You might consider cleaning dirty or tarnished cases before beginning your inspection. Clean cases are easier to examine and can definitely add to "pride in ownership."

Many have advocated never using cartridge cases of unknown history. It is prudent to follow that advice. The safest approach is to only add to your case inventory factory-new cases or cases from factory ammunition you have fired.

However, if you find a case of unknown history in your inventory, it should be tested for hardness. Although unlikely, cases exposed to sufficient heat to anneal the brass sometimes exhibit no significant visual evidence. Hardness testers are available and can easily do a proper job. However, you can judge the hardness of a case head quite adequately by comparing it to a case of known adequate hardness. Simply press the edge of the rim of the known good case against the flat part of the head of the questionable case and, while maintaining as much pressure as you can muster by hand, slide the two past each other. If this action results in a significant gouge in the case you are testing, assume that case is faulty—it is unsafe for handloading.

The first step when working with any batch of cartridge cases—whether the cases are factory fresh or from some other source—is to examine each case for structural problems, either manufacturing flaws or problems resulting from being fired. Find an area with good light and use a small magnifying glass, especially if your eyesight is not as

(Left) These cases are all headed for retirement (left to right): 45 Colt, 44 Special, 308 Winchester converted to 358 Winchester—all have split necks that cannot properly hold a bullet in place; 30 Carbine—body split might prevent proper chamber sealing and thereby allow a dangerous gas escape, similar less-obvious splits are much more dangerous because they might not be recognized; 30-30 Winchester—partial case head separation, incipient separations are also dangerous.

(Below) These cases should be destroyed (left to right): 30-30 Winchester, partial separation; dissected 30-30 Winchester, incipient separation evidenced; 7mm Mauser, partial separation (the result of firing in a 270 Winchester chambered rifle!); 280 Remington, bright band on case evidences excessive thinning. These cases show ample evidence of thinning at the web and body juncture.

good as it once was. The OptiVisor, from Brownells, provides $2^{1}/_{2}$x magnification and eye protection. I've found this product useful for case inspection as well as a safety aid during bullet casting and primer seating.

On unprimed cases, look at the flash hole. If it is not properly centered, destroy and discard the case. Doing so will save you the inconvenience of a broken decapping pin, at the very least. Some experts conjecture that off-center flash holes are detrimental to accuracy. Since this condition is so rare, there is no good reason to use any case with such a flaw.

Incipient Separations and Body Cracking

It may come as a surprise to many experienced handloaders that a good deal of case stretching, historically attributed to full-length sizing and the firing of hot loads, is really the result of the striker shoving the case so far and so hard into the chamber that the case shoulder is pushed back. This, combined with a similar effect caused by the detonation of the primer, can move the case forward considerably. Then, as the powder burns, chamber pressure builds, and this eventually locks the case walls to the chamber. Finally, when chamber pressure exceeds the strength of the case walls to resist stretching, it forces the case head back against the bolt. Chamber pressure compresses the bolt and stretches the receiver; other pieces of the gun also undergo elastic deformation.

With the case body locked in place and the case head pushing back out of the chamber, is it any wonder the case stretches at the juncture of the web and the body? When chamber pressure falls, the bolt presses the case back into the chamber, setting the shoulder back, lengthening the neck and assuring easy extraction.

This understanding also makes it obvious why straight-bodied, sharp-shouldered cases exhibit less stretching, compared to more tapered cases with gentler shoulders. Cases with the former design are better able to resist striker- and primer-induced headspace changes because of their wider and sharper shoulders, which naturally resist being moved back better than those with narrow sloping shoulders.

As noted, action flexing also contributes to case stretching. More pronounced in rear-locking guns, action flexing occurs to varying degrees in all action types. The stress created by increasing peak chamber pressures or case-head diameter additionally promotes action flexing. Similarly, because of inertial effects, the longer chamber pressure is applied, the more action flexing takes place. A large capacity case can stress an action more than a small capacity case, even when peak chamber pressure and case head diameter are identical, because the larger slower burning charge of powder it uses applies pressure for more time.

However, regardless of action type or case design, all rifle cases, with the exception of the truly low pressure numbers, stretch with every firing. Eventually, enough brass flows forward from the web of the case that the area becomes critically thin. At that point, the case becomes unsafe, subject to separation at the juncture of the web and body.

The lesson is that cases can and do stretch, and stretching will eventually lead to case separations.

A bright ring around the case head, just ahead of the solid portion of the web, is one sign of excessive stretching. Any suggestion of a crack in this area of the case requires its destruction.

If you see no obvious outward sign of case wall thinning, you can measure case wall thickness using RCBS' Case Master or NECO's case gauge. Both have attachments which will accurately assess thinning at the juncture of case body and solid web. If thinning has reduced case wall thickness at the juncture to less than about 60 percent of the thickest portion of the case body wall, in front of the thinned region, destroy and discard the case.

Also, carefully examine the case body, shoulder and neck for cracks. Any evidence of cracking suggests destroying and discarding the case. Neck cracks can destroy a cartridge's accuracy potential and lead to inadequate bullet containment.

Excess Pressure Signs

The case is the only thing standing between the shooter and the enormous pressure contained in a gun's chamber every time a cartridge is fired. The case can give clues that your loads might exceed safe and prudent pressure levels. If anything seems out of the ordinary when a shot is fired or when a case is extracted, give the brass, the gun's action, and the barrel a careful examination before you consider firing another shot.

With all previously fired cases, check the case head for any signs of excessive pressure, softness or headspace problems. Excessive headspace in low- or moderate-pressure cartridges is characterized by odd, excessively flattened primers or primers that extend beyond flush with the head of the case. This is a common condition in rifles such as the 30-30. It can also develop in any gun that delivers an excessively heavy striker blow or when a full-length reloading die excessively moves the shoulder on a rimless cartridge designed to headspace on the case shoulder.

I am no fan of using primer appearance as a means of monitoring pressure. There are too many pitfalls. First, primer cup thickness and hardness vary from brand to brand and from lot to lot, and primer cup hardness and thickness controls the amount of flattening that any given chamber pressure will generate. Also, headspace variations can alter the amount of flattening with identical pressures—more headspace, more flattening. Further, in many cartridges, safe and sensible pressures simply do not create *any* primer flattening. And finally, primer cratering is more dependent on striker-to-bolt fit and striker shape than peak pressure; very mild loads can pierce primers and patently dangerous overloads might not show any evidence of primer cratering. Even leaking primers do not prove all that much! During case manufacture, primer pockets sometimes acquire longitudinal scratches on the sides. Those scratches can lead to insignificant leakage that will, nevertheless, leave a small amount of smoky residue. Conversely, I have seen intense overloads that opened case heads until the primer fell out of the case, and in spite of such obviously excessive pressure, there was still zero evidence of any gas having leaked past the primer! Unless you are completely familiar with the gun and the primers used, never suspect you can look at the primer in a fired case and make any reasonable or useful pressure judgments based on any visible characteristic of that primer.

Another area to examine for signs of excess pressure, and one that is a bit more universal and useful, is the head of the case. If you see any evidence the case head was disturbed by features of the bolt, typically bright spots or lines on the case headstamp area, be concerned. Any case showing any of those signs was probably subjected to excessive

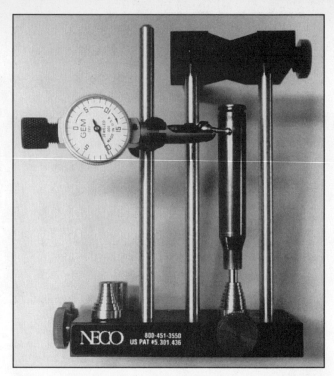

With NECO's case gauge, one can easily and accurately measure thinning at the case web and body juncture (RCBS offers a similar tool). This case shows a total thinning at the juncture of about 0.010″—not dangerous, nonetheless such a case should be retired for safety's sake.

pressure in a previous use. If case head deformation is significant, destroy and discard the case.

Keep in mind, though, that cases just a tad on the soft side may exhibit case head markings even with normal loads. In that instance, such marks do not necessarily indicate a ruined case, but they do warrant further monitoring, as when seating the next primer. If the primer seats with undue ease, destroy and discard the case or permanently mark it and relegate it to use as a gauging tool. It is not particularly uncommon for new cases to be comparatively soft. Two commercial manufacturers, Norma and Federal, seem to produce cases that are commonly somewhat softer than those made by either Remington or Winchester. Military cases are also often softer than commercial cases. Usually after the first loading, the heads of these softer cases will work-harden sufficiently so that further case head marking and deformation will stop—so long as factory pressure levels are not exceeded.

If, after firing your loads, you note any new marks on the heads of previously used cases, back the charge down about 5 percent. If you cannot live with that, try to find a harder batch of cases for your top loads.

Measurable case head expansion after the initial firing is probably a good indication that the load is too hot. Generally, such loads will soon open the primer pockets. Until that happens, unless one bothers to measure case head diameter both before and after shooting any given load, this excess pressure sign can easily go unnoticed. If you have any questions about your loads, measure the diameter of the case immediately in front of the rim and compare that figure with the one given in the dimensional drawing in the load data section of this book.

Never forget this salient fact: That piece of brass is the only thing standing between you and certain disaster; when you see it reacting to your loads by exhibiting permanent case-head deformation, you are seeing *proof* that your loads are pushing that case right up against the ragged edge of complete failure. You might have done this thousands of times without incident. If so, that fact only suggests that you are long past due for an accident—if it is fair to call such an incident an "accident." This really is like rolling dice with your life on the line; sooner or later you will shoot craps.

When pressure exceeds the case's strength, bad things happen! With a bit more pressure, this failure could have been catastrophic.

CASE PREPARATION

NEW OR ONCE-FIRED CASES can benefit from any of various types of preparation techniques. These include techniques intended to make all cases in a group as similar as possible. Doing so will improve accuracy and consistency of the resulting handloads and are necessary steps with all cases.

This chapter covers case preparation procedures from the mundane to the esoteric, from trimming to uniform length to outside neck turning. Which of these steps is important to you will depend on what you intend to do with the ammunition you produce. However, an understanding of each procedure can be beneficial, regardless of your goal.

Assuming you have purchased new cases, or are working with once-fired cases, there are several steps you should consider in your quest to produce superior handloads. Base your decision to perform any of these steps on an analysis of your goals and the benefits you feel each operation might garner. Since none will harm the accuracy or functionality of your loads, we recommend you perform as many as you feel comfortable doing. Of those presented here, only trimming to length and neck turning are necessary from a safety standpoint.

Several of these steps require case sizing be performed first. A detailed discussion of the various types and methods of case sizing can be found in Chapter 4.

File-type dies are readily available. These are simple, slow and boring to use.

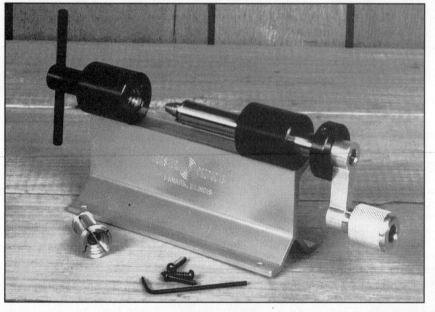

Lathe-type case trimming tools, like this Forster model, are handy for trimming cases to uniform length. They can be adapted to many other functions.

Case Trimming to Proper Length

Most rifle cartridge cases and some handgun cases lengthen with each use. When cases get too long, they can bear against the front end of the chamber and cause difficult, or impossible, closing of the action. More importantly, a case that is overly long cannot properly expand to release the bullet, which results in increased chamber pressure. The amount of lengthening in any given firing depends on a plethora of gun, cartridge and load characteristics. To assure proper chamber clearance and maintain uniform cartridge performance, case necks must be periodically trimmed to a uniform, proper length.

There are three basic systems to maintain proper case length. First is the inexpensive and specially hardened file-type trim die offered by RCBS, among others. These are available in many calibers. Using this system, simply screw the trim die into your standard reloading press and run the sized case all the way into the die by raising the press' ram until the shellholder touches the die. Then file off the protruding portion of the case mouth. Simple, tedious and slow.

The second system involves a lathe-type tool, either manual or power driven. Since these gadgets can be used for several jobs, they are a wise investment. If you are working with large batches of cases, we highly recommend one of the powered models.

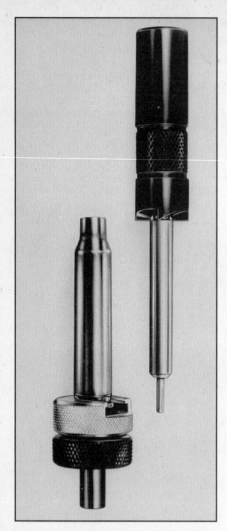

(Left) Similar (functionally identical) deburring tools are offered by a number of companies. These tools all do a good job of deburring the inside of the case neck, but all leave a wire of brass inside the case neck. For accurate loads, this has to be removed.

(Below) The RCBS Trim Mate can be accessorized to deburr, uniform flash holes, uniform primer pockets, remove crimped primer pockets, brush case necks, etc—a very handy addition to the loading bench.

Lee's Case Trimmer-2 is affordable, easy to use and fast. It eliminates the need to measure anything! Simply choose the correct tool and go to work.

Using one of the manual lathe-type tools requires installing the proper shellholder, or collet, and case neck pilot, adjusting the tool by trial and error until it trims the sized case to the proper length, and then locking the length-controlling set screw. Several turns of the handle, while applying moderate pressure, gets the job done. These tools are faster than trim dies, but still a bit time-consuming.

Power trimmers are much faster and somewhat easier to adjust. One favorite power-driven alternative is RCBS's Pro Power Case Trimmer. Among the simplest, quickest and easiest lathe-type case trimmers to use, it offers quick shellholder changes, even quicker shell changes and allows indexed 0.001″ incremental changes in trimmed case length.

Another tool designed for trimming large volumes of cases is Lee Precision's simple, affordable and practically foolproof Lee Case Trimmer. Here, you chuck the shellholder base into your drill press or hand drill clamped to a vise. With the drill running, push the proper cutter head into the case. When the cutter's built-in stop passes through the flash hole and abuts against the shellholder base, the case is properly trimmed.

Like the file-type trim die, these units are cartridge-specific, so they eliminate the need to measure anything. To some users, this is a significant advantage and it does eliminate one potential source for error.

Note, however, that variations in chambers are rather significant. Many guns will safely allow the use of much longer cases than suggested by the "Maximum Case Length," listed in this manual. To test your chamber, purchase the proper Chamber Length Gauge from Sinclair. For about $5, this tool will tell you exactly how long cases can safely lengthen and yet function properly in a specific gun. Often the maximum length allowed by the chamber is several tenths-of-an-inch greater than the "maximum" listed length. Longer case necks can be conducive to accuracy, and obviously, one would prefer to avoid spending time trimming case necks unnecessarily short. The only caveat is that you must provide the necessary safeguards to ensure that any gun-specific over-length cases are never chambered in any other gun. Such an occurrence is likely to result in a major disaster.

Whether using manual or power-driven case trimming tools, the cutter will eventually require sharpening. When it no longer removes excess brass easily and quickly, consider replacing it or having it sharpened. All manufacturers offer this service. Most charge a nominal fee; some provide this service for free. Most offer spare cutters at a modest price. By keeping a spare cutter on hand, one can return a dulled unit for sharpening while suffering no interruption of tool availability.

Mouth Chamfering

Once you have reduced all cases to the recommended "trim-to" length, you need to deburr both the inside and the outside of the case mouths. Seating bullets into cases with burrs inside the mouth will result in damaged bullets, and these burrs can also interfere with proper crimping. Burrs on the outside of the case mouth can interfere with chambering the loaded round and could increase chamber pressures.

New cases will often have rough case necks, so plan on deburring them before the first loading.

The typical deburring tool is a simple hand-operated two-ended 60-degree reamer. Lee Precision makes the most compact deburring tool I know of.

When deburring, you want to remove only the burrs and bevel the inside of the case mouth ever so slightly. However, the inside deburring cutter often leaves a "wire" of brass inside the case neck, and it is important to remove this wire. K&M Services makes a handy tool that can perform this operation with a quick flick of the wrist. The current model only works with 22- through 30-caliber cases, but the precise 4-degree controlled depth bevel it provides is the ultimate in precision and repeatability. You can also use one of the legs of the outside deburring end of a standard tool or a small knife blade to remove the "wire" edge from inside the beveled case neck. Insert the cutting edge of the tool in the case and, holding it almost parallel with the neck, give the case a quick turn while pressing the blade lightly against the case. Take the time to learn how to consistently perform this simple operation; it is important.

Flash Hole Deburring

The flash holes of standard cartridge cases are formed during manufacture by pushing a special punch through the web of the case from the primer pocket side. This operation leaves bent and rough burrs on the inside of the case that can interfere with uniform and consistent primer-flash propagation, which is critical to consistent powder ignition. To maximize shot-to-shot velocity uniformity and accuracy, one should deburr and uniform all flash holes. Fortunately, this is a simple, one-time-only process.

Typical flash hole tools feature built-in stops to ensure flash holes are uniform in diameter and length, and have a uniform chamfer on the exit side. K&M Services and RCBS offer simple useful tools that do a good job.

It must be noted that flash hole length and variation of that length differs from case to case and case lot to case lot. Fortunately, tests have shown that these variations are usually minor and result in minor ballistic differences. However, to minimize deleterious effects, the best practice is to keep cases segregated by lots.

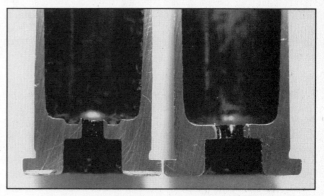

Stock and deburred flash hole comparison.

The K&M Services Controlled Depth Tapered Case Mouth Reamer, a wonderful 4° inside neck deburring tool, works with 22- to 30-caliber cases. Adjustable for depth of cut, this tool leaves no accuracy-destroying "wire" of brass inside the case neck.

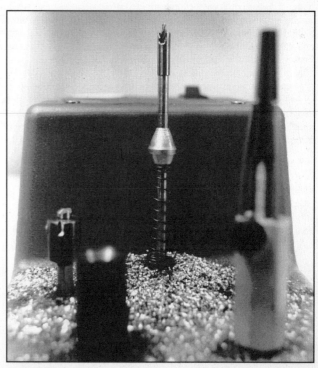

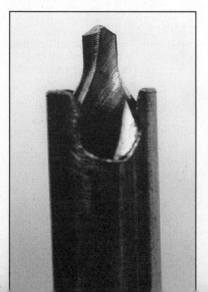

This close-up shows a modification of K&M Services' Flash Hole Uniformer. This alteration is necessary so cuttings do not jam the tip.

This K&M Services' Flash Hole Uniformer is modified so that cuttings automatically fall out. It is also adapted for use on the RCBS Trim Mate Power Tool.

When using any of these tools, clear the chips from the tool often and expect limited tool life. Here you have a hardened steel cutter working against brass that has been work-hardened to the maximum degree possible. Because it has been additionally worked, the burr inside the case is considerably harder than the case head! However, since this is a "once in a case's lifetime" operation, these tools will last most shooters a very long time. The K&M tool I am now using has processed thousands of cases and is still going strong.

Many of these tools can be power-driven to ease one's work. If you are doing a large batch of cases, this is a significant advantage. However, be certain you do not turn the tool faster than a few hundred rpm. The speed of most hand-held power screwdrivers is about perfect. Slow-speed operation prevents overheating and prolongs tool life. Also, by the nature of these cutters, they work best when mounted almost horizontally with the cutting end pointing down slightly. With this orientation, cuttings tend to fall clear instead of jamming the tool.

I have modified my K&M flash hole uniformer and deburring tool to work on RCBS's power driven Trim Mate. This required only threading the driven end to fit the Trim Mate and the addition of a spring to push the centering flange into the case neck. Since the Trim Mate orients the tool vertically, a further modification is necessary to prevent cuttings from jamming the tip. This latter modification involves drilling holes in the cutter jacket and filing channels to allow cuttings to fall out of the tool.

Primer Pocket Uniforming

Machining primer pockets to a uniform depth and squaring the pocket bottom facilitates seating primers to a uniform depth and, thereby, improves ignition uniformity. This makes sense in theory, even if field data does not support that this step garners much, if any, improvement in ballistic uniformity.

Another little-studied aspect concerns the conformation of the flash hole entrance. Squaring off the base of the primer pocket will certainly improve uniformity within any group of cases. Stock flash holes are always somewhat beveled on the entrance side, the amount of bevel and exact height of the entrance varying from case to case and around the perimeter of each hole. Squaring the primer pocket bottom provides a consistent floor for the primer's anvil to seat against, which improves the uniformity of the primer's reaction to the striker's blow. While this might not manifest in a reduction of shot-to-shot velocity variation, it could improve the consistency of ignition lag time and reduce shot-to-shot variations in gun vibration. For these reasons alone, this step *should* improve accuracy.

Finally, in rare instances, primer pockets can be too shallow. Sooner or later, you could come across a combination of cases and primers that make seating the face of the primer past flush with the case head practically impossible without crushing the primer beyond all hope of proper function. This analysis reflects bad experiences from earlier

decades. In truth, the quality of today's primers and cases renders this possibility truly ephemeral.

Nevertheless, primer-pocket uniforming is a real can of worms. Some advise doing it every time a case is handloaded. Others suggest it is of no value to the non-target shooter and of precious little value to most target shooters. I suspect the truth is somewhere in the middle. Likely, there is some value in terms of accuracy potential, and it does ease the task of seating primers uniformly. Perhaps most important, it affords the fastest and simplest way to completely clean primer residues from the primer pocket.

I have recently decided this extra step is worthwhile for all my rifle cases, regardless of the load's intended use. The initial cut shows me which primer pockets are off-center or significantly out of square with the case head, either condition sufficient cause to relegate the case to plinking or gauging use. Even when the initial cut shows the pocket to be adequately centered and square, I can still spot widely varying pocket depths and excessively deep pockets.

If primer pocket depth varies significantly among individual cases from one lot, you might become a bit suspicious about the overall quality of that lot of cases. However, such variation by itself is not cause to remove any case from your "best-load" group. After all, this step is intended to square the bottoms of all primer pockets and cut all to a uniform, acceptable depth. However, if you should happen upon cases with pockets that are so deep the cutter will not cut completely around the bottom of the pocket, you should consider using those for plinking loads.

Several companies offer primer pocket uniformers with carbide or hardened-steel cutters. Some are adjustable, and others feature a proper fixed depth. Three general sizes are available: Large Rifle, Large Pistol and Small Rifle/Pistol. Since these tools will be cutting through primer residue that contains glass, and then into the hardest portion of the case, tools with carbide cutters are by far the best choice. Haydon, K&M, Sinclair, RCBS and others all offer perfectly acceptable tools.

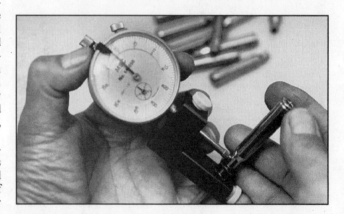

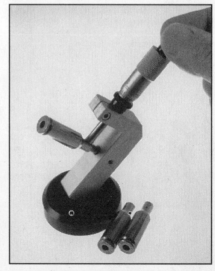

(Above and left) Sinclair offers these two precision tools for accurately measuring neck wall thickness: one a .001″ dial indicator, the other a .0001″ Vernier micrometer.

The Sinclair Primer Pocket Uniformer, among others, provides precisely uniform primer pocket depth and configuration with either power or hand operation.

We do not recommend adjusting cutting depth on primer pocket uniforming tools unless you know how to do the job properly. Depth is factory set and should be left alone. Periodically check to make sure the cutter-locking set-screw is tight. With the vibrations and heat generated in long-term continuous use, that screw can work loose. I have had it happen! This occurrence forces one to reset the depth and retighten the screw. Since this cutter should be set to an accuracy of +/- 0.0005″ this is no simple task. Lacking proper tools and gauging equipment, the only easy way to do this, and this is not particularly precise, is to use a properly cut primer pocket as a gauge. Extend the cutter from the tool somewhat beyond the proper setting, tighten the set screw just enough so that moderate pressure is required to push the cutter into the tool. Insert the cutter into a properly cut primer pocket until the tool bottoms against the case head, then tighten the set screw. If carefully done, the tool should still just touch and barely cut against the bottom of the gauging primer pocket when one applies considerable pressure. Best bet: Keep the set-screw tight.

Many of these tools can be chucked into power drills. Here, again, make certain you do not turn the tool faster than about 1000 rpm; slower is better. This will allow you to feel what is going on and will prevent generating excess heat which could destroy the tool and the case! Also note that running the tool too slow can lead to tool chatter. Find a speed that discourages chatter and thereby produces a smooth cut in the bottom of the primer pocket.

Outside-Neck Turning and Reaming

Outside neck turning is a simple, albeit precise, operation that requires fairly expensive tools and considerable skill, or at least patience, to do correctly.

As with case trimming, this step requires full-length case sizing as a preliminary step. There are several reasons why reaming the inside or removing brass from the outside of a case's neck can be beneficial or necessary. If the neck of any chambered case is too thick to allow clearance for expansion and bullet release, the case neck must be thinned before loading the case. Also, don't forget gun-to-gun variations. It is possible that loads with very tight neck-to-chamber tolerances for one gun might be too tight in another. This situation often results when case forming—shortening one type of case to convert it into some other type, like converting 30-06 Springfield cases to 8mm Mauser. Case stretching can also result in necks that are too thick. As cases stretch at the web and body juncture, brass that formerly made up the case shoulder flows to the neck.

Usually such cases are inside-neck reamed after the outside of the neck is sized to a specific diameter. This operation is easy to do with any lathe-type case trimming tool equipped with the proper inside neck reaming attachment. The disadvantage of inside-neck reaming is that the process does nothing to ensure the resulting case neck is concentric, that is, uniform in thickness from end to end and around its perimeter. Outside-neck turning is an obvious choice in any effort to add uniformity and accuracy potential to ammunition. I recommend it for any situation where increased accuracy might be beneficial, and from my perspective, that seems to cover the gambit of all shooting!

Outside-turned case necks also offer the possibility of precisely matching neck-to-bullet tension in a group of cases. If case necks are not uniform in thickness, from one case to another, how can we ever hope to achieve uniform bullet pull? Loads with varying amounts of bullet pull are notoriously inaccurate.

The importance of uniform bullet pull to ballistic uniformity and accuracy has to do with the consistency of the delay after the primer flash occurs and before the bullet starts moving. Powder ignition is not instantaneous. It takes time for the pressure generated by the burning powder to build. The longer the bullet stays in place, the higher the chamber pressure pushing on the bullet as it breaks free of the case. If bullet pull varies considerably, this delay will also vary and, thus, the pressure accelerating the bullet will not be uniform. Such variation will always result in inconsistent barrel times and muzzle velocity. Barrel vibrations and external ballistic effects ensure that such loads will exhibit lousy grouping consistency. Conversely, when case necks are concentric and properly annealed, load-to-load bullet pull can be extremely precise and consistent.

One novice NRA High Power competitor recently proved this the hard way. A combination of loading factors—chiefly, varying amounts of lubrication between the bullet and the case neck—led to a situation where his ammunition had wildly varying bullet pull. He was hard-pressed to keep his shots inside 3″ at 100 yards! With a change to a milder primer, which did not dislodge *some* of the bullets before the powder ignited, his groups shrank to under 1″. The problem was not fundamentally with the primer used, but rather the varying bullet pull. In some loads, the blast from the hotter primer moved the bullet into the rifling, while in other loads the bullet remained in the case until the pressure from the burning powder was sufficient to dislodge it. Obviously, ballistics were different in the two instances. Solving the root problem, varying neck-to-bullet friction, is certain to further improve his groups.

The best reason to outside-neck turn a case is to provide accurate bullet-to-chamber alignment. When the neck of the case is concentric and the case is properly centered in the chamber, the bullet is automatically centered and aligned to the bore. In some instances, it makes a significant difference in a load's accuracy potential.

This is the main reason why benchrest guns and loads excel. Ammunition and chambers are consistent and precise. Tolerances are so tight that benchrest ammunition is gun specific.

There are those who argue that excessive neck turning is generally ill-advised; others suggest that only about 60 percent of the neck's area be trimmed, as evidenced by exposure of bright new brass; still others believe deeper cutting only increases case neck working in subsequent loading and firing cycles.

All of these arguments sound reasonable if the only consideration is that a thinner case neck has to expand farther before the chamber confines it. However, if you happen to be using conventional sizing dies, this is a meaningless consequence. Consider the action of a sizing die on a case neck. The sizing die returns all case necks to the same outside diameter. The expander ball then expands the neck's inside diameter to the proper size to hold a bullet. These two steps are necessary because case neck thickness varies from case to case. The actual amount the neck is sized down is the same for both thick- and thin-necked cases. However, for thinner case necks, the expander ball does not have to expand the neck as much. The result is a wash: The thicker-necked case expands less in the chamber but more in the die; the thinner-necked case expands more in the chamber but less in the die. The differences exactly equalize. The total amount of neck working with each shooting and reloading cycle is identical for both regardless of neck-wall thickness.

However, slightly thinner neck walls can lead to cases that are truer. Since the case neck is thinner, it requires less expansion and is, therefore, easier to expand. For this reason, the conventional resizing die expander does not pull as hard on the case neck. With less expander ball pull, thinner case necks are less apt to bend out of alignment with the case body. However, for reasons of functionality and sufficient case neck tension, never cut case necks any thinner than necessary to achieve proper clearance, concentricity and case-to-case uniformity. I prefer to set the cutting depth to the point where almost all cases from any given lot show at least some cutting on almost every portion of the case neck. At least 75 percent, preferably 90 percent, of the neck perimeter should come out bright and shiny. Those few cases, in any group, showing evidence of significantly thinner case necks are culled for other uses.

In any event, never thin the neck any more than necessary to achieve this result unless you have a specific need to do so. Additional thinning might be necessary in a tight-chambered target rifle or when using converted cases. In those instances, reduce neck thickness until the diameter with a seated bullet of the proper diameter is at least 0.002″ smaller than the chamber throat diameter. Even this amount of clearance is calling things very close. If you use such tight tolerances, you will have to maintain a constant vigil to keep your rifle's chamber and the loads you use in it very clean. Benchrest shooters loading

Several lathe-type case trimmers are easily adapted to outside case neck turning, like this RCBS Outside Neck Turner adapted to the RCBS Trim Pro trimmer. While probably not as precise as the dedicated (hand-held) units, these conversions are generally less expensive and are somewhat easier to use.

(Below) This properly turned case neck shows about "90% turning."

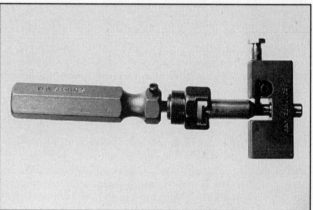

This K&M Services Micro-Adjustable Case Neck Turning Tool offers precision adjustments to 0.0001″ accuracy! Results are repeatable.

ammunition for a specific gun sometimes use even tighter tolerances, but the tighter the fit, the more cautious the handloader has to be.

To verify chamber dimensions to this level of accuracy you will need one of the following: chambering dimensions, several cases fired in that gun using full-power loads, or an accurate chamber casting. A product called Cerrosafe is commercially available through Brownells. It's easy to use, and it can provide an accurate chamber casting. If you intend to work with such close tolerances, this is a good place to start.

Several manufacturers offer outside-neck turning attachments for their lathe-type case trimming tools. Forster and RCBS both feature mechanisms on their case trimmers to control cutter feed rate. With the Forster unit, one has to have enough dexterity to turn two things at the same time and do so at the proper rates. I prefer RCBS's system for overall ease of use. However, I suspect Forster's collet-type shellholder provides more accurate case alignment. Consistent case alignment could improve accuracy of the outside-neck turning operation.

The RCBS system includes a pilot that slightly reams and removes any high spots from the inside of the case neck before the cutter goes to work on the outside, a useful feature. Lathe-type turners rely on the

shoulder-to-head case dimension for uniformity and properly turn the neck on sized cases regardless of variations in case neck length.

The various hand-held, dedicated outside-neck turning tools are somewhat more precise and can provide more accurate results. Several offer neck wall thickness adjustment with almost incredible precision. K&M Services' tool is easily, accurately and repeatedly adjustable to 0.0001″ increments. While expensive, these tools are affordable for the serious shooter and adjust to work with cases of most popular target sizes through 35-caliber. To use these tools, one has to start with full-length-sized cases trimmed to uniform length. A special mandrel is run through the case neck to open it to fit the tool's mandrel very snugly, but not too tightly. You cannot skip this step. Working with a neck that is too tight or too loose guarantees poor results. Before beginning, lightly lubricate the inside of the neck or the cutter mandrel. Imperial die wax works well.

To cut case necks to the proper thickness, simply keep closing the cutter toward the guide shank until it touches most of the case neck. It'll leave a bright shiny surface, as it progresses.

Adjusting these tools for the proper length of cut on the case neck is

These cases, from the same lot of 280 Remington brass, were painted with a permanent marker before outside-neck turning. These show three extreme instances: Entire neck was thick enough to be thinned by the cutter, all is now shiny; about 90% of neck was thinned, almost all is now shiny; only about 50% of neck was thinned, this case will be culled from the group.

This close-up shows the variation in apparent height of the cut where the outside case neck turner cuts into the case neck. This apparent variation in cut distance, up the case shoulder, results from the cutter actually cutting deeper into the neck on the thick side of the case. This case neck is cut to the proper stopping point—cutting further will weaken or destroy the case; cutting less will create an off-center case neck, chamber and bullet condition that is worse than no neck turning at all!

not easy. All hand-held tools provide an adjustment to lock-in the length of neck the cutter will turn, but getting the tool correctly adjusted is difficult although extremely critical. Cutting too far into the case shoulder will destroy the case. Not cutting far enough into the shoulder can be worse than not turning the case neck at all, because failure to trim the entire length of the neck can exacerbate bullet and case misalignment in the chamber.

Cut the entire length of the neck until the cutter just bumps into the case shoulder. To get this length perfect, you might want to use a magnifying glass to examine the area where the cut ends. The shiny cut surface should extend up the shoulder of the case just a very little bit and all the way around the case. On case necks far from concentric, the distance the cut appears to extend up the case shoulder will vary considerably from the thin side of the case to the thick side.

Though you can do this process entirely by hand, I prefer to use a variable-speed power drill. K&M Services' tool is ideal because the shellholder easily chucks in the drill. I mount the drill in my bench vise and lock the trigger "on" with the drill running at a very slow speed. A drill press will work, but might not be as handy to use. It is critical that the cutting tool is free to wobble, which is necessary for it to stay in proper alignment with the case neck. The case head and neck are almost never perfectly aligned.

With a power tool, one can concentrate on advancing the cutter at a slow and constant rate. But first you have to get the tool properly adjusted. Follow the manufacturer's instructions here. Each system has unique idiosyncrasies and, as these are precision tools, you have to learn to use each properly.

Once you've determined the length of neck to be turned and amount of thinning required, lock those settings in. Now, it is time to really slow down the operation. Start the case spinning at a slow speed and ever so slowly advance the cutter until it bottoms out, then ever so slowly withdraw the cutter. Done correctly, you should see the outside of the case neck become shiny almost everywhere with new brass exposed and no high spots. Better to advance too slowly than too fast.

Some suggest a final polish with 000 or 0000 steel wool, and this step cannot hurt. Simply leave the case spinning and grab the case neck with a layer of steel wool between your thumb and forefinger. Apply moderate pressure for a few seconds. This cuts away any burrs and leaves the outside of the case neck picture-perfect.

If improving accuracy is your goal and you are considering skimping on the effort you put into this operation, don't bother to do it; results will be worse than doing nothing at all.

Case Forming

Though outside the realm of typical case preparation operations, case forming has certain advantages. Forming can sometimes be used to make cases that are otherwise unavailable or cases that better fit a gun's chamber. An example is conversion of 375 Winchester cases for use in a 30-30 Winchester chamber.

Forming these thicker-walled cases down to 30-30 Winchester dimensions creates a thick case neck. By turning the necks a specified consistent amount, it is possible to create benchrest-quality cases with significantly reduced case-neck-to-chamber clearance. You could mimic the benefits of a benchrest- (tight) chambered gun and still be able to shoot standard handloads or factory ammunition.

Similar conversions are possible for a plethora of chamberings. But the handloader must take measures with any such special ammunition to prevent possible use in any other gun, where adequate chamber clearance might not exist. For example, you can form 308 Winchester from 30-06 or 8x57mm cases. With proper neck reaming and turning, you could make cases with benchrest fit in almost any sporting chamber. Many such conversions use nothing more complicated than the correct progression of sizing dies that one might already have on hand.

Taking our 375 Winchester example, first size the case neck to about 35-caliber using a 38 Special bullet seating die. The large radius on this die should begin the necking operation quite easily. Follow this with a pass through a 38 Special carbide sizer. Then, if you happen to have one, switch to a 32 Special seating die, then to a 32 Special sizing die sans decapping stem. Finally, size normally in a 30-30 sizing die, expand the neck as necessary to use the neck turning tool, and proceed to turn the neck to a uniform, albeit greater than normal, concentric thickness. (Since the 30-30 normally headspaces on the rim, excess neck length is not a serious concern—just get it long enough.)

Compare the neck of the loaded case to a chamber cast or a case fired in that gun's chamber to ensure it has sufficient clearance. Generally, you should measure a minimum of 0.002″ difference in chamber neck and loaded round neck diameter. If necessary, turn the case neck thinner to achieve adequate clearance. As noted, for safety reasons, segregate such cases for use only in the gun they were sized to fit. The increased accuracy potential can be worth the effort.

Certain case conversions are not feasible without proper forming dies, and in some instances, it might not be possible to come up with a conversion that would offer thicker case necks. However, if you are serious about making your stock-chambered hunting rifle into a serious varminter, you might want to consider this approach.

Chapter 3

CASE SORTING

AFTER PERFORMING ANY initial case preparation steps one deems necessary or useful, there are two sorting steps the advanced handloader can take to enhance the accuracy of any loads produced. One is to separate cases into weight groups, which helps minimize shot-to-shot velocity variations resulting from differences in internal case volume. The other is to measure cases for crookedness, called "indexing," to facilitate consistent chambering of crooked cartridges, which can enhance accuracy.

Sorting by Weight

Like so many things in the shooting world, cartridge cases are an industrial marvel. Considering raw materials, manufacturing, handling and transporting costs, it seems miraculous that retailers can sell these things for pennies apiece. It is a tribute to economies of scale and efficient manufacturing processes, more than anything else.

Serious shooters often sort cases that weigh more than 100 grains each into categories ranging in 1-grain increments, plus or minus 0.5-grain. Really serious competitors often carry this to plus or minus 0.1-grain precision. That represents an accuracy of one part per thousand or less.

When you consider all the vagaries that can contribute to case weight variations, differences of one or two percent—typical as-produced ranges—seem very close tolerances, indeed. However, a few percent is not good enough for the most ardent shooters.

Our concern with weight variation centers on the belief, correct or not, that weight variation can reflect internal volume variation. When loaded and fired, cartridges with varying internal volume will manifest pressure and velocity differences, in spite of otherwise identical loading parameters. We should realize that some of the weight variance can result from external case differences, such as rim and case head dimensional variations, but we assume that cases of similar weight from the same lot of manufacture will share similar external case head dimensions. Though this latter assumption might not be true, it is our best speculation. If external case head dimensions are reasonably similar, then we know that differences in case weight reflect differences in internal case volume. Internal case volume (boiler room) directly affects chamber pressure and velocity, so it is important to accuracy.

The problem is, we have no particularly accurate means to measure the internal volume of a case. We could load and fire new cases, weigh those with the fired primers in place, then fill each case with water and reweigh. Although this would be time-consuming, it sounds like the perfect solution because we would be measuring only the internal case volume. With a good scale and good technique, we could measure that value quite accurately. Unfortunately, there are several problems with this approach.

First, all cases are springy. This means that they come out of the gun's chamber a bit smaller than when they filled the chamber. If all cases were equally springy, this would be of no consequence, but—alas, even when brand new—all cases are not equally springy. For instance, just the sort of variations in case dimensions we are trying to measure can affect the amount of side-wall and shoulder spring-back any given case exhibits. The result? This sophisticated system of measuring case volume only succeeds in adding one more unknown to a list of variables we are simultaneously measuring.

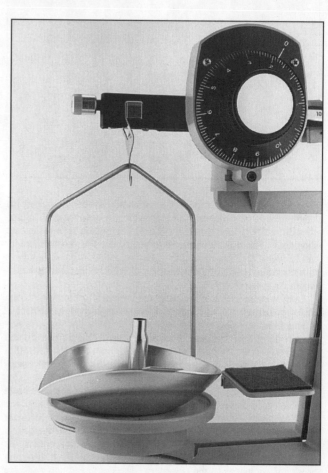

A beam scale is perfectly acceptable for weighing bullets or powder charges. However, this type of scale—even the most advanced—is no pleasure when sorting hundreds of cases or cast bullets into weight categories.

A second problem is that it is rather difficult to get all the air out of any case when filling it with water. Perhaps we could use a wetter fluid, such as alcohol, but this is still a messy system and requires thoroughly drying the cases afterward. If such a system gave perfect volume measurements, it would no doubt be worth the effort for certain dedicated target shooters. Since it does not give perfect volume measurements, it does not seem to be worthwhile to anyone, certainly not to me! Evidently, weighing cases is our best means of estimating usable capacity, but how best to do this?

This is an area where a little mental work comes in to play, because you have to decide the parameter for sorting your cases. You'll also have to decide which advanced case preparation steps to incorporate into each lot of cases and complete all of those steps before separating cases into weight groups.

As a hypothetical example, assume you have bought a new Mountain Eagle 280 Remington and your interests include both varmint and big game hunting. Most would argue that for big game hunting pur-

(Above) This close-up of weight-coded case heads shows the single indentations located in various areas. Each represents a certain weight group in the author's coding system.

(Left) The RCBS Powder Pro can accurately weigh as much as 1500 grains. It is very fast for weighing cases. An electronic digital scale simplifies and speeds the process of accurately separating cases into weight groupings.

The large MTM loading blocks are a real convenience for case weight sorting. I apply weight-range labels on drafting tape (which easily peels off later). Cases are weighed and then placed in the proper area. With five blocks, I can usually sort 200 cases without confusion (each block holds 100 cases—insert cases in different ways, neck down or base down.)

poses extraordinary accuracy steps are not necessary; however, for varmint hunting, you want to wring out the last measure of accuracy from this fine Krieger-barreled Sako action.

You shoot one box of factory fodder through your new rifle, are impressed with the accuracy and suspect it has potential as a real shooter. Evidently, the gun is worthy of your efforts in accurizing and precision loading. You decide to do all the other little things that can improve box-stock accuracy potential, like lapping the locking lugs, adjusting the trigger mechanism, fire lapping the gun's bore and even, perhaps, Cryo treating (controlled-rate deep freezing) the barrel. Having decided to go the extra mile with the rifle, it now makes sense to contemplate how far along the accuracy road you are willing to go with your handloads.

Remember, though, that all the load tinkering in the world cannot cure accuracy problems in the gun. About half of the intrinsic accuracy equation is in the load; the other half is in the gun. The most accurate rifle in the world will not shoot lousy ammo into world-class groups; equally, the most accurate ammunition in the world will not shoot one-hole groups when fired from a bad rifle.

Figuring you can get in a considerable amount of varmint shooting on a good weekend, you plan to buy several hundred cases in bulk, at a good price. This seems a reasonable plan. The main advantage of a bulk purchase is that it gives you a large batch of cases manufactured in the same lot—therefore, more likely to be similar in dimension and performance. Once you have worked up your loads, you can be sure all your cases will function well with your final working load. If you used cases from several manufacturing lots, you might have to alter the charge weight to maintain similar velocity and pressure because of significant lot-to-lot variations in case weight.

OK, you own 200 same-lot cases and you've invested in specialty handloading tools, now what do you do?

First, run each case through a full-length sizing die. Then, trim every case to a uniform length and deburr the necks. There can be surprising variation in overall length among new cases from the same lot. Further, case mouths are often bent during polishing and shipping/handling, and they have to be straightened. In addition, factory-fresh case mouths are always rough, and these require deburring regardless of other processing. After sizing, trimming and deburring, your cases are all the same length. You could now load them if you didn't want to go through additional case uniforming steps.

Assuming you want to go further, we recommend the following order and priority. First, turn case necks. Second, deburr and uniform primer flash holes. Finally, uniform and square primer pockets. If you plan to do all three steps, this sequence is of no great consequence.

Don't plan on doing all this work in one sitting. Most handloaders will find it easier to proceed in steps and use these operations as distractions from other work on the rifle, like while waiting for the epoxy to cure.

After you have fully prepped all the cases, you are ready to sort them into weight groups. But you still have a decision or two to make. To what degree of weight uniformity do you want to sort this batch of cases?

For a 280 Remington-chambered sporter, plus-or-minus 1-grain seems sufficient. If you are dealing with a serious varmint or target-grade rifle, you will probably want to sort to plus-or-minus 1/2-grain, or closer, increments. In the big magnums, plus-or-minus 2 grains is generally sufficiently consistent.

The uniformity of the particular lot of cases could influence your decision. You don't really want to end up with fifty different weight groupings any more than you want to have excessive weight variation within any given grouping. As a preliminary step, you might choose to weigh some or all the cases to get an idea of weight variation in the lot before making any decision on group boundaries.

It is useful to establish permanent weight groups for any given type of case. For example, I have established 184-grain +/- 2 grains as my standard W-W 30-06-family case weight for all hunting loads.

If the maximum weight variation of twenty randomly sampled cases is 2 grains or less, you should consider buying more cases from the same lot since those are unusually consistent. In this instance, you might want to sort to +/- 0.5-grain groupings for convenience.

The type of scale you use becomes an issue here. This is one operation where an electronic digital scale makes a world of difference. A beam scale makes this operation rather time-consuming. You either have to adjust the scale for the weight of each case the first time through—a procedure bound to lead to errors—or you must weigh each case many times—very time-consuming and also error prone. However, if a beam scale is all you have, I've developed a procedure to speed the process. I begin by finding all cases that are heavier than the lightest boundary of the heaviest acceptable group, a weight you have to determine before starting. Having separated all the cases, I set the scale to the bottom weight of the next-lighter group. All cases that are heavier than that setting become members of the next to heaviest group. I repeat this process until all cases are sorted by weight. Finally, I reweigh all members of the heaviest group to ensure none are heavier than the upper weight boundary of that group and then all members of the lightest group to ensure none are lighter than the lower weight boundary of that group.

Now using Dillon's D-Terminator or RCBS's Powder Pro digital scale, I can weigh each case to the nearest tenth-grain in less than five seconds. Regardless of the system you use, keep several loading blocks at hand and mark sections with labeled masking tape to properly identify each case by weight.

The next decision is how to go about marking or segregating cases to keep them permanently identifiable. I prefer to permanently mark each case rather than simply sorting cases into different ammunition boxes. With the latter system, you have to maintain eternal vigilance to prevent inadvertently remixing carefully sorted cases. I use an automatic center punch to permanently mark cases. This handy device costs only a few dollars and can be used to rapidly mark case heads with an identifying code via an indentation. For most weight groups, I use one punch mark somewhere on the headstamp area of each case head, the location signifying the case's weight group. A dent before or after the numerical portion of the headstamp, in the manufacturer's name or in other areas, distinctly designates five weight group classes, each easily identified at a glance. I go the extra mile and note the codes on the labels associated with the load and include the case weight group in the "Case Make" area of my reloader's label.

As a final identifying method, it is worthwhile to include the manufacturing lot number (if available) and which case preparation steps you have performed on that group of cases. For example, "Midway lot purchase, 1993, fully prepped."

With an electronic scale and several loading blocks, it is a simple matter to initially group all cases to $\frac{1}{2}$-grain groups. After completing this operation, choose grouping boundaries and reload the group with the largest number of cases—unless, of course, you have chosen to establish permanent standard-weight groupings. You might then relegate the three or four heaviest and lightest cases in the group to duty and die adjustment use, as gauging rounds or for initial load development work. If the weight groups are somewhat evenly distributed, you might choose to increase the weight variation boundaries, thus giving you more cases in each group; a more practical approach, but less precise. The decision is yours.

My choice for big game hunting loads is to use almost all cases in a group except the lightest and heaviest few. For those, I simply adjust the powder charge to compensate for variations in capacity. I don't intermix loads from different case weight groups during any shooting session; all the loads in the magazine and in reserve are from the same weight group. For all rifle cartridges using near case capacity charges, I adjust the powder charge 0.6-grain for each 10 grains of case weight variation (see table). If I switch to 5-grain heavier cases, I reduce the

NECO's Concentricity, Wall Thickness and Runout Gauge is a handy and precise tool that quickly measures case and cartridge concentricity. It also allows precise measurement of case-wall thickness—valuable for checking for incipient case separations at the web and body juncture, and for predicting cases that will bend when fired.

charge by 0.3-grain and am certain to get nearly identical velocity and very similar pressure. In loads using 50-percent loading density, I use a 0.3-grain load adjustment for each 10 grains of case weight. The relationship between loading density and appropriate adjustments of powder charge to compensate for variations in case weight should be obvious: If the case is heavier, reduce the powder charge; if the case is lighter, increase the powder charge.

Powder Charge Adjustments

Case Weight +/-	Charge Adjustment		
	Loading Density 100%	Loading Density 75%	Loading Density 50%
1 grain	0.06	0.045	0.03
2 grains	0.12	0.090	0.06
3 grains	0.18	0.135	0.09
4 grains	0.24	0.180	0.12
5 grains	0.30	0.225	0.15
6 grains	0.36	0.270	0.18
7 grains	0.42	0.315	0.21
8 grains	0.48	0.360	0.24
9 grains	0.54	0.405	0.27

Of course, it is neither practical nor reasonable to make very fine adjustments in powder charges. This table should help you understand how much effect a variation in case weight will have on velocity. Compare the suggested charge adjustments to load data for the cartridge.

If the suggested powder adjustment in the chart is 0.18 grains and in the data a 2-grain increase in powder charge increases velocity in the given load by 120 fps, this difference in case weight will generate about 11 fps difference in muzzle velocity—$(120 \div 2) \times 0.18 = 10.8$. This table also suggests approximate compensating charge adjustments that should allow cases of different weights to shoot to the same point of impact at long range, an important consideration for the hunter.

Case Indexing

If the bullet in a chambered cartridge does not line up with the barrel, the bullet could be asymmetrically deformed when it hits the rifling. This would ruin the bullet's balance, and unbalanced bullets are not accurate. There are two common causes of bullet-to-bore misalignment: Non-concentric case necks and bent cartridges. We discussed the former in Chapter 2; we will cover the latter condition here. Since bent ammunition can ruin a group or a shot, both serious target competitors and varmint hunters can benefit from testing their cases and loads for straightness.

When a bullet jacket is not concentric, the center of gravity of the bullet will not coincide with the center of rotation as the bullet travels through the bore. When such a bullet exits the bore, it will begin rotating around its center of gravity, disrupting the bullet's ballistic flight. Instead of following a simple ballistic parabola, the bullet will begin traveling in an ever widening spiral superimposed on that basic ballistic parabola.

The width of that spiral, and the distance the bullet misses its mark, is directly proportional to the bullet's imbalance. Since the degree of perfection of bullet-jacket concentricity varies, imbalance varies. Also, the width of the spiral is a function of the length of time the bullet has been in ballistic flight. Therefore, the size of the spiral at any given range depends upon how perfect the bullet is and how long it has been in flight. Imperfect bullets shoot somewhat erratically. Group dispersion will depend on the level of imperfection and muzzle-velocity variations, both unknowns before the shot is fired.

In recent decades, manufacturers have improved the quality of most jacketed bullets to the point where bullet quality is no longer a significant consideration for most shooters under most conditions. However, there is another factor that can upset a bullet's balance and significantly affect accuracy.

Bullets not aligned with, and centered in, the gun's bore when the cartridge is fired will strike the beginning of the rifling off-center, or tilted out of alignment with the barrel, or both off-center and tilted. When this happens, one side of the bullet contacts the rifling first. Depending on variables in bullet construction and materials, and upon how fast the bullet is moving when it hits the rifling, such an impact can asymmetrically deform the bullet. Any such deformation will almost certainly destroy the bullet's balance, and it will no longer revolve around its center of gravity as it moves through the barrel. Upon exiting the bore, it will begin a spiral flight despite having been initially balanced and symetrical. Further, off-center and unsquare impacts on the rifling cause asymmetric vibrations in the gun's barrel, which will certainly affect where the barrel happens to be pointing when the bullet exits. As with initially unbalanced bullets, the resulting variations will tend to be unpredictable.

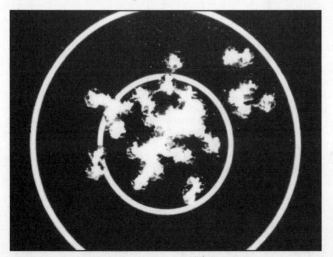

This sixty-shot 300-meter group would make any varmint hunter happy! To achieve this kind of consistency for long shot strings, everything has to be just right.

However, there is a way to judge such misalignments before firing the shot and, surprisingly, to minimize these effects. We will discuss those methods shortly, but first we will review an old method of improving bullet-to-bore alignment. By neck-sizing only, a technique practiced by handloaders for decades, we can improve the centering of the bullet in the chamber. However, regardless of the type of dies used, neck-sizing does not necessarily ensure proper bullet-to-bore alignment. The problem is that cartridge cases often become bent when fired, and bent cases tend to stay bent even after resizing. Also, during the heat-treating phase of the manufacturing process, some sizing dies become bent; such dies can bend the case's body as it is sized.

Regardless how closely the round fits the chamber, a bent case body or neck will force the bullet into misalignment. Tighter chambering tolerances minimize this effect, but they do not eliminate it. Obviously, random insertion of the cartridge in the chamber can leave the bullet in a bent case tipped in any direction. Now let us consider what happens when this bullet is launched down the barrel.

As the bullet impacts the rifling, it will very likely be deformed asymmetrically. The degree of deformation will depend on how much the bullet tilts, on rifling leade design (the area of the throat that tapers into the rifling), on the type of load used and on bullet variables. How far, and in which direction, the bullet might hit from the nominal group center depends on the degree of asymmetric deformation, on which direction the bullet was tipped in the chamber and on where any unusual barrel vibrations might leave the barrel pointing the instant the bullet exits. Obviously, we would like to eliminate or control as many of these variables as possible.

One thing we can measure is which direction the bullet is tipped and to what degree it is tipped. Formerly, the standard means of testing for bent cases was to fire the loads! Target shooters assumed accurate loads suggested good, straight cases. Conversely, unexplained fliers suggested crooked cases. There is a better way. Before firing a shot you can easily measure the concentricity of the load. Further, you can mark all bent cases and segregate them into groups, thereby significantly reducing the accuracy variables this problem might introduce.

The idea is very simple. Place the fired case or loaded cartridge in a supporting fixture and, while rolling the case, measure the runout. RCBS's Case Master features a pair of adjustable "V" blocks to hold the case. Position these blocks near the head and shoulder of the case. NECO's Concentricity Gauge features a "V" block for support near the case head and an arbor to support the case mouth (near the bullet tip on loaded rounds).

To measure a bent case, locate the dial indicator on the case body at a point about midway along the body. Slowly roll the case in the blocks. If the case is not true, the indicator shows the amount of runout. This also indicates which direction the case is bent—the high side.

Unfired cases are usually straight, but upon firing, most bend some amount. To determine a new case's propensity for bending, measure the concentricity of case wall thickness at a point about 0.5″ below the case shoulder. Cases stretch more on the thin side. The greater the difference in thickness between the thin and thick side, the greater the resulting differential stretching and bending. The thin side becomes the high side of the case. Either of the above-mentioned gauges make these case-body concentricity measurements.

To measure bent cartridge necks using RCBS's gauge, locate the dial indicator midway along the bullet's ogive and roll the case. If the high side of the bullet is not opposite the high side of the case body the neck is bent out of alignment with the rest of the case. Using NECO's gauge, measure for runout near the base of the case neck. If the low side is not opposite the high side of the case, the neck is bent out of alignment with the rest of the case. Bent case necks likely suggest one's bullet seating equipment or techniques are damaging the loads.

Marking bent cases to allow chambering of loaded rounds with the bullets tipped in the same direction each time is likely to improve the accuracy of the ammunition. The benchrest technique is to mark the high side of the case by filing a small notch in the case rim. This mark becomes a permanent identifier because bent cases tend to stay bent the same way (unless a bent sizing die is bending the case). For the best groups, chamber indexed loads that are similarly bent in a consistent orientation.

Chapter 4

CASE MAINTENANCE

BRASS CASES WON'T last forever. The number of times any case can be reloaded safely is finite. However, armed with a good working knowledge of headspace and its effects upon the case, and advanced case preparation techniques, the average reloader can achieve optimum accuracy and prolonged case life from his reloads.

In this chapter, we'll explore full-length and neck resizing, case neck annealing, and bullet pull and neck tension adjustments. These techniques increase life expectancy of your brass and improve the accuracy potential, dependability and safety of your loads.

Understanding Headspace

One aspect of the cartridge case is of greatest concern to the handloader, and that is its shape, insofar as that characteristic influences how the cartridge headspaces in the gun's chamber. For our purposes, we will define headspace as that distance a chambered cartridge can freely move forward and backward. If there were not some amount of play (positive headspace), it would be difficult or impossible to chamber the cartridge. However, if headspace is grossly excessive, the round might not fire or the case might separate upon firing. Either result could have devastating consequences. And between these two extremes lies the importance of headspace to any reloader—accuracy.

Accuracy requires consistency. If we can control headspace to the point where the fit of the cartridge to the chamber is just right, then each round will seat in the chamber in the same fashion each time, which is just one more variable we've removed or minimized.

There are four basic types of cases, and headspace is controlled in different ways for each: belted, rimmed, rimless, and rimless pistol-type.

Let's consider the belted magnum case as a rimmed type. Rimmed (or belted) cartridges are designed to headspace on the rim (or belt). Manufacturers are supposed to tightly control rim thickness and the depth of the rim cut in the gun's chamber. For various reasons, either or both of these dimensions can and do vary excessively from nominal values. Thin rims and excessively deep rim cuts in the chamber are common, and both of these conditions generate excessive headspace, which is too much freeplay fore and aft.

With rimmed cartridges, you can see, and perhaps measure, excessive headspace by simply chambering a primed empty case and firing the primer. A fired primer protruding more than a few thousandths of an inch (0.002″-0.004″) from the head of the case suggests excessive headspace.

In bottlenecked rimmed and belted cases, the handloader can eliminate excessive headspace by moving headspace control to the case shoulder. You only need to adjust the full-length sizing die correctly, as discussed later in the text. This technique can achieve reduced and uniform headspace for any given load used in any given gun. However, such loads might not fit another gun chambered for the same cartridge.

Case length controls headspace in straight or tapered rimless or semi-rimmed cartridges; the case mouth abuts against a sharp shoulder in the chamber. Obviously, case length is critical. Trimming these cases more than about 0.005″ shorter than maximum design length compromises headspace and functionality.

All other case design types headspace on the shoulder, and this class includes the majority of rifle cartridges. Excess headspace is common.

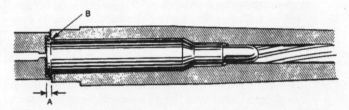

Rimmed Cartridge. Headspace **(A)** is measured from bolt face to front edge of rim. Rim **(B)** holds cartridge in place and stops the travel of the case into the chamber.

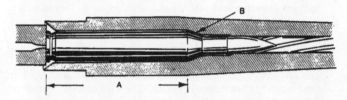

Rimless Cartridge. Headspace **(A)**, the distance between the bolt face and case head, is determined by the case shoulder. On rimless cartridges, the shoulder of the case **(B)** stops travel of the cartridge into the chamber.

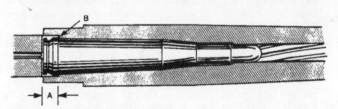

Belted Cartridge. Headspace **(A)** is measured from bolt face to front edge of belt. The belt on the case **(B)** seats against a shoulder in the chamber and stops travel of the cartridge into the chamber.

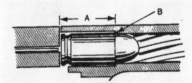

Rimless Pistol. Headspace **(A)** for rimless pistol cartridges is measured from bolt face to edge of case mouth **(B)**, which seats against shoulder in the chamber and stops travel of the cartridge into the chamber.

Copyright 1973 George C. Nonte, Jr.

You can accurately measure the effective headspace with tools from RCBS, Stoney Point and Sinclair, and this measurement will allow you to build safe, consistent reloads for each gun.

Full-Length Sizing for Proper Headspace

Before performing several of the case uniforming steps discussed in Chapter 2, we assumed an initial full-length sizing of our batch of cases. Unless we are working with factory loads fired in our gun, full-

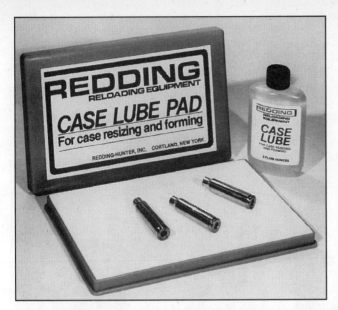

Redding, and others, offer case lube pads and lubricants. These speed case lubrication with liquid products. Various aerosol and pump-actuated sprays are also available; Spray-Dry from E.A. Brown is a favorite. Imperial Die Wax and Hornady Unique are favorite solid products. When properly used, any of these provide adequate lubrication for full-length case sizing.

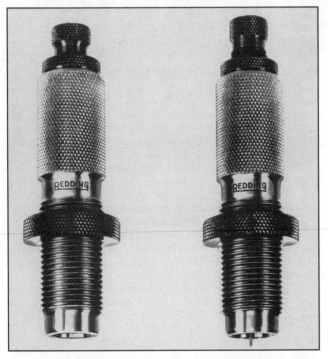

Standard and deluxe threaded full-length sizing dies are available from many manufacturers. All are of high-quality, but standards and features do vary. Redding's standard two-die set is typical of bottleneck cartridge loading dies offered by all mainline die manufacturers.

length sizing is a necessary step before we can properly accomplish any other case processing step.

Full-length resizing ensures the case will fit in any like-chambered gun, but it also reduces case body diameter and pushes the case shoulder back enough so that the case will be a somewhat sloppy fit in our gun's chamber. Normal sizing excessively works the case neck, first making it smaller than necessary and then enlarging it to properly accept a bullet. This eases bullet seating and assures adequate neck-to-bullet tension. All of this is as it should be for ammunition used for big game hunting or self-defense.

For almost all target and varmint ammunition, and to some extent for big game hunting ammunition, we can do better. We will return to this discussion, but first a few comments on proper full-length sizing.

Three main subjects come to mind. First is proper die adjustment for headspace control; second, proper die alignment for concentricity; third, proper and consistent case lubrication to equalize friction.

Theoretically, manufacturers make full-length sizing dies and shellholders to automatically maintain "proper" headspace. The nominal adjustment procedure is to simply screw the die into the press until it contacts the shellholder hard at the top of the ram's stroke.

This is all fine and good, providing the die and shellholder are of proper dimensions and the press is sufficiently rigid. However, even if all those criteria are met, this procedure still introduces a measure of excess headspace that ensures all full-length resized cases will fit into all guns chambered for that cartridge. Typically, die makers aim to set the case shoulder back about 0.002" past SAAMI's minimum chambering specification. This assures easy chambering in any so-chambered gun.

Should your gun have a 0.002" longer than minimum chamber, which is typical, you are now loading cases with 0.004" headspace. In truth, built-in tolerances more often add up to about 0.006". This amount of headspace is not dangerous, but it shortens case life and limits potential accuracy of the resulting loads.

Things are often worse with bottlenecked belted magnum cases. These headspace on the belt, which is nothing more than a wide rim with a groove cut in it. For this reason, manufacturers have played fast and loose with case and chamber dimensions in these numbers. In the past, it was commonly found that manufacturers cut the base-to-shoulder length in gun chambers on the long side, and in sizing dies on the short side. In a typical rifle, it is not at all unusual for the shoulder of normally full-length-sized belted magnum cases to be an astounding 0.040" short of touching the chamber shoulder. *Also, very often both belted case-chambered guns and belted ammunition exhibit poor control of nominal headspacing dimensions. Note that the chamber pressures normally employed in belted magnum cases are typically among the highest encountered in commercial cartridges.*

Since the belt nominally controls headspace, excess clearance between the case shoulder and chamber does not necessarily create an imminent safety problem. Upon firing, chamber pressure simply blows the case shoulder forward until it contacts the chamber shoulder. This fireforming process is not in itself dangerous. However, this action also shoves the case walls forward, stretching the case body back near the solid web of the head. Combined with the excess true headspace these guns and cases often exhibit, the result can be a tremendous amount of stretching near the base of the case body. I have seen belted magnum rifles that would separate cases on the third reloading. Allen Jones of Speer reports on one gun and one lot of *factory new* ammunition that caused partial case separations upon firing. That, my friends, *is* a recipe for disaster.

Fortunately, this problem is easy to solve. With the belted magnum or the rimmed bottleneck case, it is both easy and desirable to move headspace control to the case shoulder. This alteration improves accuracy and case life, and certainly increases the safety factor.

The solution is to adjust the sizing die so that it just barely touches the fired case's shoulder, moving it back only about 0.001". Cases sized in this manner will generally only work in that one gun. The cases will last considerably longer, and the cartridges will chamber and align with the bore more consistently, which means better accuracy. Such loads will work perfectly in the rifle they are specifically loaded for—providing chamber and loads are kept properly clean. Because of variations in chamber length and diameter, due to manufacturing tolerances, you can't count on these loads to chamber properly in any other rifle.

One suggested method of decreasing excessive headspace is to slightly back the die out of the press. Considering the extremely coarse threads on standard sizing dies (14 turns equals 1" of die travel), it is difficult to adjust dies to reduce shoulder setback by only a few thousandths of an inch. If the threads are perfect, each 5-degree of die rotation will correspond to 0.001" of vertical movement, i.e., headspace adjustment. However, 5 degrees is only $\frac{1}{72}$ of one complete revolu-

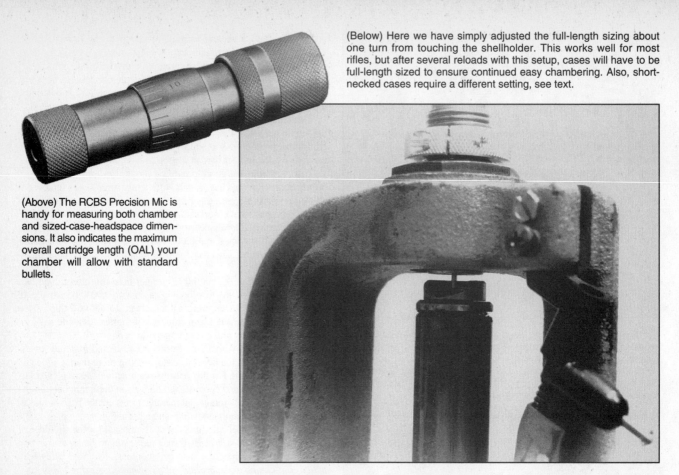

(Below) Here we have simply adjusted the full-length sizing about one turn from touching the shellholder. This works well for most rifles, but after several reloads with this setup, cases will have to be full-length sized to ensure continued easy chambering. Also, short-necked cases require a different setting, see text.

(Above) The RCBS Precision Mic is handy for measuring both chamber and sized-case-headspace dimensions. It also indicates the maximum overall cartridge length (OAL) your chamber will allow with standard bullets.

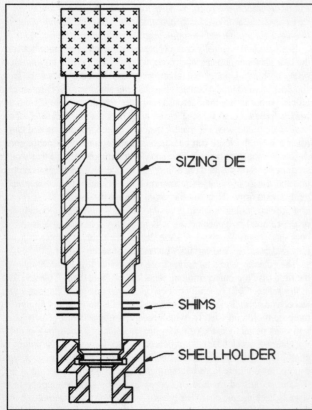

SIZING DIE

SHIMS

SHELLHOLDER

This represents one good method of preventing full-length sizing from driving the case shoulder back too far. Precise thickness shims interpose shellholder and die to create tight, consistent headspace between full-length-sized case and chamber.

tion of the die, about 0.043″ rotation at the outside of a 1″ diameter die body. Few of us are particularly good at judging such small increments. Worse, the flex in a typical press can exceed 0.010″ during full-length sizing operations and is quite variable. Variations in case hardness or lubrication will significantly alter the amount any press flexes and, therefore, effective headspace when the die does not solidly contact the shellholder.

One way out of this problem is to make shims that can be glued to the bottom end of the full-length sizing die. Screw the die tightly down against the raised shellholder, with 0.002-0.003″ of shims between the bottom of the die and the top of the shellholder. Size a case fully and try it in your rifle. If the bolt closes freely, add more shims and size another fired case. Keep on adding shims and trying a fully sized case in your rifle until the bolt won't close freely, indicating zero headspace. Remove 0.002″ worth of shims and you have set that sizing die to give exactly 0.002″ of headspace *in that rifle*.

If you are working with a belted magnum with wildly excessive shoulder setback, you will need several thicker shims to get close to the correct initial sizing dimension. Since we will be adjusting the sizing die so that rimmed or belted cases also headspace on the shoulder, we will henceforth refer to case-head-to-shoulder length as headspace, regardless of case type and nominal headspace design.

In setting up actual headspace, begin by stoning the top of the shellholder and the bottom of the sizing die to a smooth finish using a very fine sharpening stone. All you want to do here is remove burrs or high spots, nothing more. We are assuming the shellholder and die are initially square and true. Quality counts. Keep the polished shellholder and die together as a team.

Working to tolerances closer than 0.002″ is meaningless. Brass varies in springiness. In fact, you might find that as you repeatedly reload your cases and they work-harden, or when you switch to a different lot of cases, you will have to remove 0.001″ or 0.002″ of shim thickness to maintain free chambering of resized cases.

Note that a Remington-style plunger-type ejector makes it very difficult, perhaps impossible, to feel the exact point of case fit. In this design, the ejector pushes the case away from the bolt face, and you will likely feel the ejector spring instead of case fit. To properly do this operation in this type of rifle, temporarily remove the plunger from the bolt. This is neither a simple nor an easy task, but most reasonably skilled tinkerers can do this with only a vise, punch and a small hammer. This step is necessary to achieve proper sizing die adjustment. Before reassembly, you might consider slightly shortening the plunger spring. A shorter, weaker spring that still provides positive ejection is beneficial because it reduces the amount of canting force on the chambered case. If this gun will be used to hunt dangerous game, don't shorten the spring because it might impair rapid and dependable case ejection.

RCBS makes a tool called the Precision Mic (pronounced mike, as in *mic*rometer) that speeds up this process. If you have many rifles to check, in any given caliber, this is a worthwhile investment. RCBS's instructions are very easy to follow. This tool gives you a measure of the total shim thickness that you can add between the shellholder and die body, just as with the above trial and error procedure.

The problem is that this procedure leads to a sizing die adjusted to work properly with only one gun. If you have several guns chambered for the same cartridge, this is less than perfect, because it is unlikely two or more of your guns will be identical. You can, however, add the amount of shimming the shortest chambered gun will allow. This will improve your ammunition fit in all of your like-chambered guns. Of course, you could simply buy a full-length die to match to each gun, which is not an insurmountable expense.

Now that you have determined the proper shim thickness for this die, shellholder and gun combo, grind or cut the shims into circles with an outside diameter of about 0.725″ with ⁹⁄₁₆″ holes centered. Remove any burrs from the ground edges and degrease the base of the die. Apply a dab of automotive adhesive silicone to the flat area of the base of the die and spread it to a uniform thin layer. Thoroughly clean the shims, apply silicon to them, and attach the shims to the die, centered over the end.

Install the shellholder on the press ram and lightly oil the top of the shellholder. Turn the die all the way into the press, then raise the ram until the shellholder contacts the shims with moderate force. The weight of the press's handle will provide plenty of pressure. Let this assembly dry for a few hours. As the adhesive cures, periodically lift the ram handle and turn the shellholder about a half turn. This will ensure uniform pressure all the way around the shims, eliminating any thick spots. After the glue has cured for several days, adjust the die until the ram bumps it hard while you are sizing properly lubricated cases. With this setup, you will be properly and uniformly sizing every case to headspace correctly in your rifle.

Other systems of full-length sizing die adjustments do not account for inevitable variations in the amount of press springing that can come from variations in lubrication and case hardness. These variations will alter the amount of headspace for each case, which are certain to produce loads that are inconsistent (read inaccurate).

We also advise the installation of a rubber O-ring between the press and the die adjustment ring. This provides a springy platform and might allow the die to achieve better alignment with the shellholder, thereby minimizing the possibility of getting case heads out of square with the case body.

If all this seems like too much work, you have several options. First, you might choose to have a custom sizing die made to fit your rifle's chamber—costly but effective. Second, you could simply adjust the die back from contacting the shellholder by some portion of one revolution, which is inconsistent but generally effective. Third, you could simply adjust the die until the shellholder hits it solidly. With this latter method, you know you are shortening case life and hindering accuracy, but you also know you are dimensioning every case almost identically. Round-to-round consistency can be more important to accuracy than a tight chamber fit.

Adjusting Neck Tension and Bullet Pull

We have not yet discussed the important issue of bullet pull. This is a fancy term for the amount of friction generated by case neck tension against the bullet. For hunting and self-defense ammunition, bullet pull

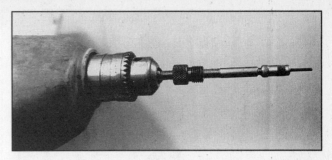

(Above) This RCBS expander-rod is chucked in a vised hand drill for polishing the expander with 660-grit emery cloth. The mirror-finish thus afforded markedly reduces neck expansion friction and case scarring. (Below) Expander diameter can be reduced 0.0001″ or more, which will generally increase case-neck-to-bullet friction. This can improve functionality.

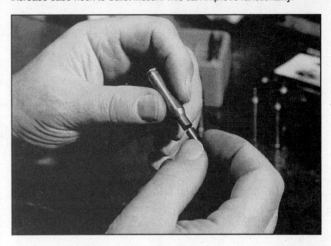

is a paramount consideration because it relates to cartridge durability and dependability.

Most full-length sizing dies have expander balls that do a very good job of assuring adequate neck tension. The only alteration I suggest for steel neck-expander balls is a good polishing with 660-grit emery cloth. This operation is easy with most types of sizing dies. Simply remove the decapper/expander stem from the die body and chuck it with its attached expander ball into a hand drill clamped into a vise. With the drill running at moderate speed, a few minutes of light pressure with a very fine grade of emery cloth will polish the expander to a mirror finish. This will let the expander slip out of the case neck more easily.

Unless you have reason to believe you need to increase neck tension, this is the only alteration I suggest for the expander ball. Generally, you shouldn't remove more than a few ten-thousandths of the expander's diameter in this process. I measure before and during polishing with a 0.0001″ micrometer. I have found no harm in reducing the diameter as much as 0.0005″.

Some pistol loads with slow-burning ball powders can benefit markedly by tightening case necks considerably. In some instances, removal of 0.002″ or more from the expander ball is beneficial. For dangerous game loads, rifle ammunition might benefit from a similar reduction in expander diameter. Decreasing the sized inside neck diameter can increase the amount of force required to move the bullet, which helps prevent bullets from moving during mishandling or recoil while in the magazine.

Don't even try to alter carbide or hard-surfaced expanders. Should you need a smaller one of these, call the die manufacturer.

Partial or Neck Sizing

Target and varmint loads get a slightly different treatment. After we have the full-length die properly adjusted and have sized all our fired brass to give minimum headspace, set that die aside. We may want to use our customized full-length die every fifth firing or so, to keep our cases chambering easily. We'll want to use it for all hunting loads.

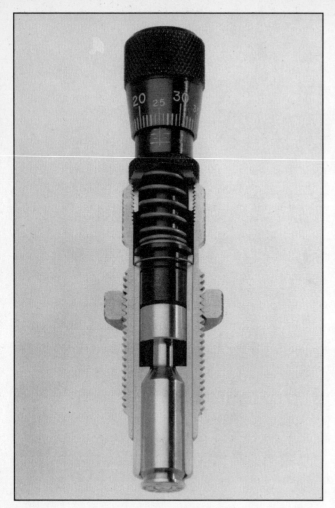

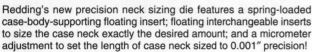

Redding's new precision neck sizing die features a spring-loaded case-body-supporting floating insert; floating interchangeable inserts to size the case neck exactly the desired amount; and a micrometer adjustment to set the length of case neck sized to 0.001″ precision!

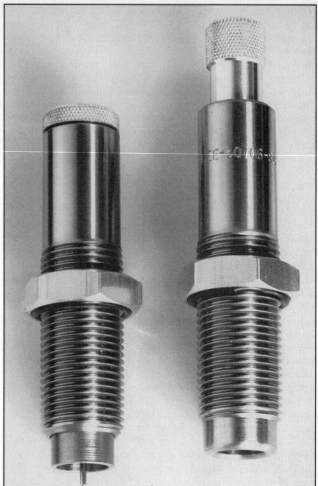

Lee's Collet Die can provide world-class accuracy. It is not a full-length sizing die and cannot be used for that purpose.

However, for the best accuracy in target and varmint work, it is desirable to re-size only the neck. To accomplish this, you can use a standard full-length sizing die by simply screwing it out from the press about one turn. This will *still partially resize the case body,* perhaps easing rechambering, and it will only size part of the case neck. However, the latter effect can be beneficial to accuracy since this will leave a portion of the case neck fitting the chamber's throat very accurately. This will hold the front of the case centered in the chamber, especially if we turned the outside of the case neck for concentricity. Since the base of the case will also be nearly unsized, the entire case should chamber with a good degree of alignment. With short-necked cases such as the 243 Winchester, 7mm Remington Magnum, 300 Savage and 300 Winchester Magnum, screwing the sizer die back more than about half a turn could significantly reduce bullet pull and might compromise functionality.

Several manufacturers offer neck-size-only dies. These work just like a standard full-length sizing die, but only size the case neck. However, just as is true with full-length sizing dies, standard neck-sizing dies work case necks more than necessary. This shortens case life.

Adjustable neck-sizing dies are a major step up in precision. These have interchangeable inserts to size the case neck to any degree desired. Neil Jones and Redding offer these dies. In Redding's die, a spring-loaded sliding section centers and supports the case body before neck-sizing occurs. Interchangeable titanium nitrite-coated neck-sizing inserts, requiring no lubrication, size the neck. To use these dies, the necks must be of a uniform and consistent thickness, i.e., turned pre-

cisely. Normally, these don't use an expander button because they size the neck only the necessary amount. However, Redding offers a carbide kit that allows you to size the neck slightly smaller than necessary and then expand it to proper size for bullet seating.

By adjusting any such die to limit the length of case neck that is sized, the handloader can assure precise alignment of the case in the gun's chamber. Just as noted above, this leaves a portion of the case neck fitting the gun's throat very precisely.

Next up the scale is Lee's Collet and mandrel-style neck-sizing die. Properly adjusted, this die does nothing but squeeze the case neck closed just enough so that it will hold a bullet adequately for normal cartridge handling. Slight changes in die body adjustment or reducing mandrel size will change the amount of neck-to-bullet tension. This die system has several advantages. First, because it requires absolutely no lubrication, it eliminates concerns about properly lubricating and degreasing cases. Second, it leaves the body of the case completely unaltered; assuming your gun's chamber is square and true, the cases will align and center in the chamber as perfectly as is possible. Third, this system works the case the least of *any* die system on the market; there is almost no pulling or pushing on the neck as the collet squeezes it to the proper size to hold a bullet. It is even possible that Lee's Collet Die might straighten bent case necks. For this reason, Lee recommends sizing the case, withdrawing it from the die, rotating it 180° and sizing it again.

Arbor press neck-sizing dies are another option, and they also use interchangeable sizing rings. This allows the inside neck diameter to be

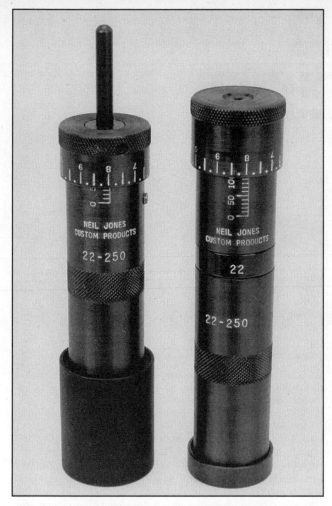

Hand sizing dies, actually designed for use with arbor presses, offer the ultimate in precision for dedicated accuracy applications. One thing these dies do better than Lee's affordable Collet Die is allow precise neck size adjustments to alter bullet pull.

controlled exactly, assuming uniformly turned necks. Here, too, there is no need for the expander ball. This system reduces neck pull, minimizes neck working and can leave cases squarer than standard dies. It also allows precise incremental neck-sizing to adjust bullet pull, which often improves the accuracy of benchrest loads. However, for loads used in most sporting rifles, these dies offer no obvious advantage over Lee's inexpensive Collet Die.

With any of the dies using interchangeable sizing inserts, you can easily adjust bullet pull. If you have worked up a good load using one of these dies, try experimenting with both smaller and larger inserts. See what happens to your groups. Sometimes minor adjustments in bullet pull can result in large changes in accuracy. As with all other load development, the only way to find out is to experiment.

Neck Annealing

We've talked about the importance of consistent neck tension, and this is a good place to suggest methods and explain reasons for adjusting it. With each loading and firing, case necks are work-hardened. This happens regardless of the type of sizing dies used, but it's more pronounced with standard dies. Even with benchrest cartridges fired in a very tight chamber and resized in special dies, reloading involves reducing the case neck several thousandths of an inch, and firing expands it several thousandths. Eventually, the brass will work-harden sufficiently to alter the performance of the load.

Cases used in "typical" chambers and reloaded with "typical" dies experience considerably more squeezing and swelling during each shooting/reloading cycle. Since the neck undergoes more working than any other portion of the case, it hardens faster than any other portion of the case. Without annealing, it will eventually fail.

As case necks get particularly hard, several things may occur. First, the necks can split upon firing or during loading operations. Second, loaded rounds can spontaneously split their necks after an extended period of holding a bullet or upon firing. Third, hard case necks make sizing and bullet seating difficult. Finally, accumulated variations in neck tension lead to differences in bullet pull, which give shot-to-shot velocity variations and enlarged groups.

As the case neck hardens, it holds the bullet more tightly, retarding its release. This increases chamber pressure and velocity, which alters external ballistics and point of impact on target. Obviously, consistent accuracy and varying neck tension are unlikely companions.

Here, neck annealing comes into play. This process can lengthen case life. Assuming a case has not thinned significantly at the head to body juncture or developed a loose primer pocket, periodic annealing can extend case life indefinitely. After reloading a batch of cases perhaps ten times, you should consider annealing the necks. This will soften the brass and prevent splitting, easing full-length sizing. Properly done, neck annealing minimizes variations in bullet pull.

The most popular method of neck annealing is to stand unprimed cases in a pan of water that reaches about halfway up the case bodies. Apply the flame from a propane torch to each neck until the neck glows dull red. This operation should be performed in a dimly lit room. When the color looks "right," tip the case over into the water by gently pushing it with the torch tip. The trouble with this method is that it relies on you to do a good job of repeating the rate of heating, the maximum temperature reached, and the time of heating. With practice and a good eye, you can do this with reasonable consistency. Nevertheless, I don't like this method because it is so hard to control the variables. It is also apt to result in differential annealing because one side of the neck will get hotter for a longer time. Given brass's high rate of thermal conduction, this difference is slight, but it still exists.

A much better method involves your trusty bullet-casting lead pot. Near good ventilation, position the pot on a standard workbench and place a large bucket of water within reach, but well below the bench top. Fill the pot full of bullet metal and bring it up to no more than 850°F. (Lead alloys exceeding 850°F give off invisible, odorless and toxic fumes.)

With the lead up to temperature, hold a decapped case by the head between your index and middle finger and your thumb. It is important that you do not wear a glove. Insert the mouth of the case straight down into the molten lead, submerging only the neck and perhaps a portion of the shoulder. Hold the case in that position until you begin to feel uncomfortable heat against your fingers. Remove the case from the molten lead and immediately drop it into the water bath. Be very careful not to splash water into the lead pot or get water on your hand, which might then drop into the molten lead. A drop of water could cause the lead to erupt out of the pot.

Regardless of which method of annealing you use, the water is absolutely essential, not because the quick cooling softens the brass, but because it prevents the case head from getting too hot. Should you somehow manage to heat the head of a cartridge case to only a few hundred degrees, Fahrenheit (actually about 400°F), the brass will spontaneously anneal. Thus softened, the head loses all ability to control chamber pressure, and with any normal load it would expand uselessly, allowing powder gases to escape from the chamber, possibly destroying the gun and perhaps injuring the shooter and bystanders. Use extreme caution here.

Neck annealing does require a bit of time and skill to do right, but it offers the opportunity to establish virtually identical neck tension from case to case, and it can extend case life significantly. Considering all the other work you have done to produce uniform cases, this small effort promises significant rewards. Many handloaders and even benchrest competitors do not fully appreciate the potential benefit proper case neck annealing affords.

Chapter 5

BOXER PRIMERS

THERE ARE TWO types of reloadable primers, Boxer and Berdan. The latter is less popular in the United States and requires special tools for handling. Our concern here is the Boxer primer and its proper use and handling. The four sizes of Boxer primers in current handloading use are small (rifle and pistol); large pistol; large rifle and 50 BMG.

Both small rifle and pistol cases use a 0.175″ diameter primer. The two primers are dimensionally interchangeable, but the cups and chemical pellets are different. Both large pistol and large rifle primers are 0.210″ in diameter, but the latter have slightly longer cups and normally will not seat correctly in pistol cases. The 50 BMG uses a much larger (0.3165″) primer that has no other handloading application.

Manufacturers design pistol primers to work at lower pressures because handguns generally use lower pressure loads. These primers have thinner and softer cups and will properly detonate with a milder striker impact, compared to rifle primers. Since pistol cartridges generally use smaller quantities of powder that are easier to ignite, the primers designed for them generally produce a milder ignition blast. Because pistol primers have softer cups, they are generally not safe for use in rifle loads.

Similarly, although small rifle primers will fit small handgun cases, their use is not recommended because the cups are harder, and adequate striker energy might not be available. More importantly, the hotter flash from rifle primers can sometimes create extremely high pressures with pistol powders. Accurate Arms has shown that substitutions of different kinds of small pistol primers can lead to devastating pressures in certain handgun loads using certain powders. Where a load specifies a particular primer, the only safe course is to stick with *only* that primer.

The Boxer-primed case (left) is easily reloaded. The Berdan-primed case (right) has a built-in primer anvil, but requires a special decapping tool, and these are seldom reloaded in the United States.

Magnum primers generally offer a hotter and more voluminous flame. The design purpose is to properly ignite large charges of slow-burning powders, even in very cold temperatures. The use of magnum primers in standard loads usually increases pressure somewhat and often degrades accuracy. Again, the only safe course is to stick with the recommended primer.

Benchrest or match-grade primers are generally similar to standard primers and are therefore interchangeable. Manufacture of these primers involves higher quality control standards and more precise techniques.

Primers are powerful devices. They should always be handled with utmost care. These pictured flame columns are about 18″ high (from left): Remington 7½, Remington 9½, Alcan Large Rifle Magnum, Winchester Large Rifle Magnum.

When using automatic primer tubes, primer flipper trays are an asset. With careful use, these tools help keep primers clean—a tiny amount of penetrating oil can kill a primer. This MTM and similar trays might not be large enough for convenient use with modern primer packages. If your primer flipper is smaller than the primer box, consider getting a new, larger unit.

Primer Safety

If there is one area of deep concern, it is the safe handling of primers. I don't understand how it happens, but people are always finding ways to set off a primer unintentionally. Stories abound of handloaders, managing to mass explode them. These incidents often involve hand-held priming tools or automatic primer feeds using a tube of stacked primers.

The handloader can treat primers with all manner of disrespect, but sooner or later he will pop a primer unintentionally. If that primer happens to be intimately associated with a large group of primers, the results can be devastating. Even one primer by itself can inflict a severe wound—one handloader had a primer cup driven completely through his finger.

Certain brands of primers might be unsafe to use in some priming tools like Lee's AutoPrime because of the potential for mass detonation. With these tools, should an operator detonate one primer, as can happen when a handloader tries to seat one primer on top of another, the detonation subjects other primers in the tray to a shock and an incandescent flash. If this shock and flash can detonate a second primer, there is the potential that most or all (perhaps 100 or more) primers in the tray might all detonate *en masse*. Such a simultaneous detonation would be a disaster.

Lee has tested all available primers and, excepting CCI and Winchester, all brands produce an unacceptable number of mass explosions when the primer being seated is forced to detonate (by heating in a remote explosion-proof box). By comparing Federal and CCI primers, we can gain some understanding why brands vary in this regard. Federal primers do not have a foil covering over the primer pellet; an application of a type of paint replaces the foil. That sealant is easily ignited and highly flammable, possessing a very low kindling temperature. These are beneficial characteristics; among other things, they help reduce combustion residues. However, use of this pellet sealant makes these primers very easy to ignite. Exposure of the open front of the cup to the flash from an adjacent primer easily does the job! Conversely, CCI primers have a paper foil almost completely covering the front of the pellet. This foil deters pellet ignition because it is only moderately combustible and has a relatively high kindling temperature. A short duration flash from a primer is unlikely to ignite the foil or penetrate through it to ignite the pellet underneath.

Here is a good place to warn against one potential hazard you might not have considered. Let's assume you have just completed seating a bullet in a cartridge and you notice, that you failed to properly seat the primer. "No problem," you say, "I'll simply run the case back through my priming tool." **Do not do it.** You now have a loaded round complete with powder and bullet. There is very likely a reason the primer did not seat properly the first time around. There might also now be powder granules down in the primer pocket (most ball-type and many tubular powders can easily fall through the flash hole). Both factors are good reasons to suspect that attempting to reseat the primer could cause it to go "pop." If that happens, you are quite certain to have problems. The case will almost certainly rupture and burning powder and the bullet will all be expelled at unpleasant velocities.

About the only scenario that could be worse would be in a press system where one inserts the loaded cartridge in an enclosed die as the primer is reseated. With that combination, you have all the ingredients for a bomb, and you are trying to trigger it.

RCBS and CCI have collaborated on a new priming system called APS, for Advanced Priming System. The system makes priming cases easier and faster, but more importantly it makes priming safer.

The key to this system is that the primers come prepackaged into plastic strips, twenty-five per strip. The strips can be connected end to end for continuous feed into the special bench- or press-mounted priming tool.

Since the primers are horizontally rather than vertically oriented and separated from each other in the strips, there is little chance of sympathetic detonation should one go off in the priming tool. In addition, since you don't have to handle the primers (fill a feed tube, flip the ones that refuse to turn over on the tray, or pick up strays from the floor), there is little chance of primer contamination.

The APS system is likely to revolutionize handloading, and RCBS expects to have a new progressive press equipped with this system on the market in a year or so.

The RCBS/CCI Automatic Priming System is poised to revolutionize handloading! The tool and color-coded primer strips absolutely eliminate primer handling and vastly reduce the possibility of confusing one type of primer for another. The only thing lacking are adapters for the various progressive presses.

Handle primers with the respect these little bombs deserve and follow *all* safety precautions provided by the manufacturers. Always wear safety glasses when handling primers.

Primer Production

Modern primers are a manufacturing miracle, perhaps second only to the 22 LR cartridge. Sophistication of production techniques and quality control boggles the mind. Consider this question: When was the last time you had a primer fail to function properly, and it was not your fault? We can trace the vast majority of primer failures to one of the following areas: contamination of the pellet with some type of oil, failure to seat the primer to the bottom of the primer pocket, a too-light striker or firing pin fall, or excessive cartridge headspace. None of these in any way suggests a faulty primer.

A typical primer production line makes primer cups and anvils in groups of six, meaning that at each step six separate tool heads process one of these pieces. Initially, a press punches the primer cup and the anvil from sheets of brass. Precise control of thickness, composition and hardness of this sheet stock is a fundamental component of primer quality. A series of stamping steps works each punched-out piece until it reaches final configuration. Rows of formed cups are passed under a machine where primer pellets are inserted. Surprisingly, a skilled operator *manually* controls the amount of compound in these pellets. After that, either a paper insulating disk (called a foil disk) or a layer of special cellulose-based paint is applied over the pellet. The last steps include installation of the anvil in the cup and final sizing. Finished primers are boxed and shipped for our pleasure. Everyone profits and we can buy these little industrial marvels for less than the cost of a stick of gum! That's rather amazing.

Primer Chemistry

The modern primer pellet is, in itself, a minor miracle. It starts life as a group of relatively harmless chemicals, most of which are dry. The main ingredient is either lead styphnate or basic lead styphnate, a chemical derivation of the same impact-sensitive substance. Various other components include additional fuels, oxidizers, abraders and binders.

The fuels and oxidizers increase the total heat generated without increasing the brisance (explosive force) of the primer, as would happen if one simply used more lead styphnate. The abraders act to cut through the difficult-to-ignite surface of the powder granules, thereby facilitating ignition. The binders act as a glue to hold the pellet together during manufacturing, seating, striker impact and combustion.

Each company has a proprietary formulation for each type of primer it produces, and each formulation has peculiar advantages. Further, specific types of primers use different amounts and mixes of priming compound. Those who suspect one primer brand and type will work well for all their shooting needs across a wide spectrum of loads are liable to be disappointed.

It might be noteworthy that, strictly speaking, modern primers do not explode. The technical term is conflagration, which is a particularly rapid form of combustion. This is simply a process of very rapid self-contained burning; just like a true explosion, the reacting product contains both fuel and oxidizer. However, you and I cannot tell the difference between what a primer does and a true explosion. If it looks like an explosion, sounds like an explosion and acts like an explosion, we had better treat it like an explosion.

Technically, an explosion is a chemical reaction where propagation of the boundary between the unaltered product and the reacting product exceeds the speed of a shock wave traveling through the reacting substance (the speed of sound in that substance). A conflagration is a chemical reaction where propagation of the boundary between the unaltered product and the reacting product is slower than the speed of a shock wave traveling through the reacting substance.

A little reflection will suggest the effective difference in these two types of reaction. If you could view either at a large enough scale to see what was happening, you'd see distinct features and results. In an explosion, any areas beyond the propagating front would remain completely unaffected until the propagating front arrived. Thereafter, the area would begin chemically reacting. In a conflagration, shock waves and associated physical disruptions would affect areas beyond the propagating reaction front. Sometime thereafter—when the propagating reaction front arrived—those areas would begin chemically reacting.

As a practical matter, explosions are more efficient at converting available fuel into reaction products because all intimately associated material will fully react. Also, because the reaction propagates faster, explosions generally create a more shattering release of energy, compared to conflagrations.

Effectively, since the reaction products of a conflagration are subject to disruption before they enter into the reaction process, vagaries of confinement can have a profound effect upon the efficiency of the reaction. Increased confinement increases the conversion of reactants into reaction byproducts and energy. For this reason, it is important to control primer pocket depth and flash hole geometry.

This might also be one of the reasons benchrest shooters have found that smaller flash holes increase the consistency of their best loads. By increasing containment, the smaller flash hole decreases precombustion disruption of the primer pellet, thereby increasing total energy release and consistency thereof. Another advantage of a smaller flash hole might be the generation of a longer lasting blast of primer flash, but with less maximum pressure and, therefore, less chance of dislodging the bullet.

Primer Selection

In recent years, all manufacturers have made great strides toward improving the overall quality and consistency of their primers. One area of improvement that is immediately obvious is dimensional control and beveling of the primer cup's outside open end. For example, CCI primers made after 1989 are much more consistent in size and are overall much easier to seat than those of years past.

Also, in recent decades, makers have changed priming mix formulations. Generally, they've been striving toward primers that can provide more consistent velocity. They have also tried to design any new formulations so that the old and new primers are ballistically interchangeable. However, should you have an old load that used an old primer and was right against the edge of the safety envelope, you might keep the following bit of commonsense logic well in mind: *similar is not identical*. Treat any change to a significantly newer primer just as a change to a different brand or type of powder. An initial charge reduction and new load development are fully in order.

You can set up your own tests of different primer makes and types, but no such test can suggest the ballistic effects of changing primers. A milder appearing primer can generate more pressure with certain powders or bullets. This is one area where you simply cannot outguess the gun, so stay with the recommended primer. If you switch primer types for any reason, remember that you are dealing with a *new load*, and you need to work it up all over again.

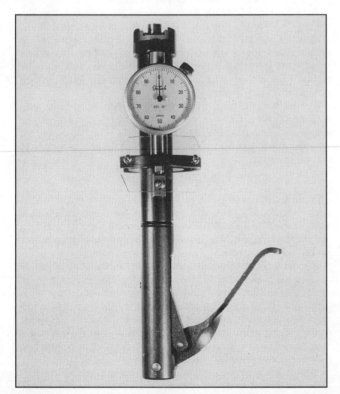

The K&M Services Priming Tool/Gauge is equipped with a dial indicator. This tool allows precise primer seating to an almost exact primer-pellet preload—regardless of vagaries of primer pocket, primer or alignment of the planets!

Within the sphere of target rifle competition, no facet has been more discussed than primer selection. The trouble is, the only way you can prove which primer works best in your load and your gun is to experiment. Assuming you have settled on a good basic test load that delivers good accuracy, you have several choices. For most varmint and target loads, non-magnum primers are likely to offer the best accuracy, and with these you have many options. First, there are four brands commonly stocked in any good handloading supply store and you can special order several other makes. Then, there is the question of the premium Match or Benchrest primers. In addition, there's the possibility of using pistol primers in low-pressure lever-action rifle loads. Here a softer primer cup compensates for the low striker energy so often exhibited in such guns. However, don't ever try to use pistol primers in any medium- to high-pressure rifle load. Loads not exceeding factory 30-30 pressure levels and using relatively fast powders can use magnum pistol primers—CCI's 350 primers seem to work splendidly.

At CCI's plant, the production of the "Benchrest" line of primers is straight forward. The output of one of each of the six simultaneous production lines that produce cups and anvils is diverted so that all primers from that lot are as dimensionally identical as possible—each anvil and cup in the lot was produced on the same set of tools. The primer pellets are made from a specially controlled mix by the operator who has shown the ability to produce the most consisient pellets. Finally, foil and anvils are installed, and all primers are processed through the finishing operations on one single production line. The keyword is consistency.

For this reason, Benchrest primers might offer a consistency advantage in non-bolt-action guns that is all out of proportion. In these action types, striker energy is both low and, potentially, inconsistent, and the increased uniformity of Benchrest primers can mitigate this disadvantage. I have seen significant improvements in shot-to-shot uniformity from their use.

Primer Seating Tools

If you want to see disagreement among the world's best precision handloaders, simply ask any small group about the best method of seating primers! Opinions vary from: "It doesn't make a lick of difference how you seat primers as long as you do it about the same way each time and don't completely crush them," to, "You absolutely must ensure that you preload the priming pellet exactly 0.003″ on each and every primer." Every opinion in-between these extremes seems well represented, too.

For what it might be worth, most target shooters agree that, as long as the tool seats the primers reasonably square and allows the operator to feel the primer bottoming in the primer pocket, the tool will do the job. The only thing the operator has to do is practice reasonable care in seating all primers sufficiently deep. There are even good arguments that applying varying amounts of excess pressure after fully seating the primer does little, if any, harm to the ballistic uniformity of the loaded round.

If you simply must have perfection, K&M Services makes a tool that will allow you to precisely seat each and every primer to exactly the same pellet preload, regardless of vagaries in pocket depth or primer height. This tool is expensive and comparatively slow to use, and for accurate results, you must square and clean the primer pocket. However, it allows you to seat primers precisely beyond all evident need of perfection, and it does offer exquisite feel. Both K&M Services and Sinclair offer similar tools without a dial indicator. They allow seating depth to be controlled accurately because they afford precise feel.

After using many of the available tools, I have come to favor Lee's simple and affordable AutoPrime for its ease of use and because it is reasonably ambidextrous. RCBS's similar tool appears to have both safety and precision advantages, but it is definitely designed for right-handed users. RCBS's bench-mounted tool works very well and might appeal to handloaders particularly concerned with primer safety because it holds primers in a metal tube well away from the priming

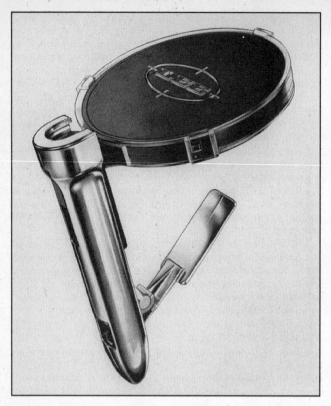

Lee's affordable Auto Prime is the fastest and most convenient hand-held priming tool on the market, particularly for those who are left-handed (about 11 percent of all handloaders).

This RCBS Hand Priming Tool offers safety advantages and uses standard shellholders. However, it is not convenient for left-handed operators and will not accept oversize shellholders for cartridges such as the 45-70.

George and Roy's Primer Sealant will also seal case necks. Primer sealing (and bullet sealing) is strongly advised for those who might be hunting in extremely humid environments, for ammunition that might be stored for several years, or for ammunition that might be subjected to incautious handling—as with most ammunition destined for safari use.

operation and the operator. It also provides plenty of feel, but is not as precise for me as the various hand-held units.

Note that Lee specifically cautions against use of Federal, Remington, RWS or Fiocchi primers in the AutoPrime—use *only* CCI and Winchester primers in this tool. This prohibition also applies to the primer feeds in the various Lee progressive presses. Lee will continue to retest the proscribed primers, and as formulations and processes change, some of those might eventually be sanctioned for use in their Automatic Priming Systems.

Compared to the hand-held variety, press-mounted priming tools are generally not as fast or sensitive, though I have loaded very precise ammunition on a progressive press. Typically, with press-mounted systems, you do give up a great deal of feel as the primer bottoms in the primer pocket.

Primer Sealing

Ammunition that might be used in areas of extreme weather conditions, and especially where atmospheric humidity is extremely high, is always subject to the infiltration of moisture into the primer and the powder. You can eliminate this problem simply by sealing the primer pocket and the case neck.

A more serious concern for most of us is the possibility of gun oil reaching the primer pellet. This sort of contamination can lead to duds, squib loads and hangfires. In a dangerous-game or self-defense situation, any of these outcomes could be quite lethal. A worst-case scenario is a squib load that leaves a bullet stuck in the barrel. This would render the gun worse than useless! In the heat of battle, you might chamber and fire another round, and with a bullet stuck in the barrel the results are inescapable—a violent barrel burst.

George & Roy's primer sealant can easily prevent this problem. Providing that primers are not contaminated before seating, and that the cases and bullets are free of oil, a simple application of this product leaves a loaded round completely resistant to water, either from humidity or in the liquid form, as well as penetrating oils and almost any other common chemical. It's inexpensive, easy to use and excellent insurance.

SMOKELESS POWDERS

THE CHARACTERISTICS AND qualities of smokeless powders are related to granule shape and size, and also to porosity. The burn rate is related to all of those, and also to the chemical makeup of the basic granule and to the nature and amount of deterrent modifiers adsorbed into the surface.

There are two common shapes of handloader smokeless powders: ball (or spherical) and extruded, which includes tubular and flake. Diamond-shaped cut-flake powders are common in Europe, but are not generally available in the United States.

It is all too easy for handloaders to become complacent about handling powder. However, your safety and that of others depends on your handling powders with care.

Never allow more than one type of powder to be on your loading bench or within reach of your loading position at any time. Never allow any kind of propellant powder to come into contact with any source of heat, sparks or open flame. Never use any powder of uncertain origin or condition. Always follow all recommended powder handling safety precautions, copies of which are available from all major powder distributors and are printed on the powder container. Before proceeding with any handloading, always double-check yourself to ensure you are using the powder you think you are using.

Powder Types

Ball powder granules are generally spherical in shape. The size of the granule and the type and amount of deterrent coating are the primary controls of any powder's burn rate. Manufacturers commonly adjust ball-type powder burn rate by partially flattening some or all of the granules. Flattening increases surface area and, thereby, burn rate.

Ball powders have several advantages over tubular powders. Generally, ball powder burns at a lower temperature, which can extend barrel life. These powders can give increased packing density, so compared to tubular powders, one can sometimes use a heavier charge of a slower burning ball powder. For this reason, and because these powders can have a higher per-grain energy content, one can sometimes produce more velocity with a ball powder. Ball powders have superior metering characteristics, which makes it easier to load consis-

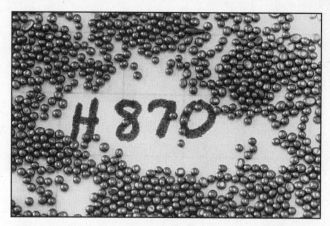

Hodgdon's H870 is a typical ball-type powder. Note that some granules are flattened. This powder contains 10% nitroglycerine.

Alliant's Unique is a typical porous-flake powder. Note the rough texture. This powder is 20% nitroglycerine.

IMR's SR4759 is a short tubular-granular powder. Note large axial holes.

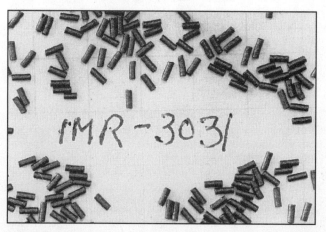

IMR's 3031 is a typical tubular-granule powder. This powder also features an axial hole.

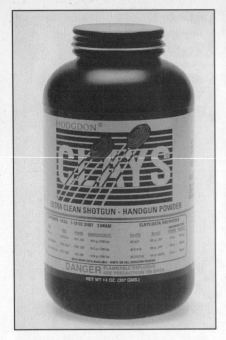

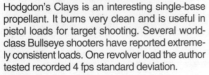

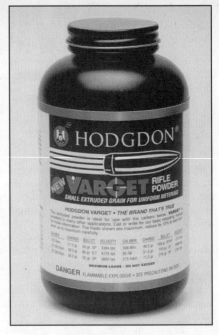

Hodgdon's Clays is an interesting single-base propellant. It burns very clean and is useful in pistol loads for target shooting. Several world-class Bullseye shooters have reported extremely consistent loads. One revolver load the author tested recorded 4 fps standard deviation.

VihtaVuori offers an entire line of powders, several of which have application in Action Pistol competition. Others are noted for high-performance results in all manner of rifle loads.

Hodgdon's VarGet is poised to capture a considerable share of the market. It is clean burning and consistent. In a plethora of applications, this powder delivers more velocity than any other. However, its claim to fame is the accuracy it can deliver.

tent charges from either handloading tools or automated equipment. However, ball-type powders have one significant disadvantage: They are dirty-burning and generate more barrel fouling. For this reason, target shooters seldom use them.

Manufacturers produce ball and extruded powders in porous-based form. During the manufacturing process, solvents leach out a certain controlled percentage of each granule, making them porous. Raising the porosity decreases density, while increasing compressibility and burn rate. Decreasing density is beneficial where a small charge of fast-burning powder is desirable, such as in 38 Special target loads. Low-density powders fill more of the available space and, therefore, provide improved ballistic uniformity and decreased sensitivity to powder position. Increased compressibility is most desirable in shotshell loading, where differing loads must all fit in a shell of a specific size. Increased burn rate is beneficial because this eliminates the need to create powders with unusually fine granules to achieve particularly fast burn rates. Such powders would be hard to manufacture and use.

The most common handloader powders are tubular. These powders range from very thin tubular flakes that are many times larger in diameter than they are long to tubes that are several times longer than they are wide. Commonly, such powders feature one lengthwise perforation. Granule size, length-to-width ratio, and the amount and type of deterrent coatings control burn rate. As with ball powders, adjusting porosity creates powders with faster burn rates, lower density and increased compressibility.

Coatings

Deterrent coatings are not painted onto the surface of the granules. Rather, the granules adsorb these chemicals into their surface. The difference is similar to comparing latex and oil-based finishes applied to wood. The oil finish soaks into and bonds with the wood, much as the deterrent bonds with the granules.

In some instances, a coating of one or more flame-suppressing chemicals is applied to the granules. These chemicals can drastically alter the muzzleflash. However, they do have disadvantages, not the least of which is an increased corrosive effect.

A final coating of graphite, generally between one part per thousand

and five parts per thousand by weight, is applied to the surface of the granules in a glazing process. This application is necessary to eliminate the potential buildup of static electricity between moving granules. A static spark could ignite the powder. This coating also helps the powder flow through your powder measure. Moreover, the graphite coating slightly slows combustion. Manufacturers sometimes make minor adjustments to burn rate by slightly altering the amount of graphite used. Graphite has an affinity for the surface of the powder granules, so it stays in place quite well.

Powder Chemistry

Smokeless powders available to handloaders come in two basic chemical compositions: single-base and double-base. Composition, by weight, of single-base powders is generally between 97 and 99 percent nitrocellulose [$(C_{12}H_{14}N_6O_{22})_x$, density 1.66]. Various deterrents, flash suppressants and the graphite safety coating compose the additional 1-3 percent. These powders derive all of their energy from nitrocellulose, a progressive burning substance. Progressive burning means the greater the pressure, the faster the burn.

The composition of double-based powders is nitrocellulose and nitroglycerin [$O_2NOCH_2CH(ONO_2)CH_2ONO_2$, density 1.59]. Nitroglycerin can make up as much as 40 percent of the total weight. Various deterrents, flash suppressants and the graphite safety coating compose, as with single-base powder, about 1-3 percent. Double-base powders are also progressive burning substances, but do have a somewhat higher per-grain energy content.

We should also mention that the nitroglycerin is absorbed into the nitrocellulose. While the two substances are not chemically bound, they cannot be separated by any physical means. The intimate nature of the relationship explains why the nitroglycerin is stabilized and will not normally explode. It is also interesting to note that nitroglycerin-impregnated nitrocellulose is not necessarily any less dense than pure nitrocellulose. The effect is somewhat like mixing one pint of pure water with one pint of pure ethyl alcohol: one does not get one quart of liquid.

Compared to single-base powders, double-base powders are less sensitive to spontaneous hydration—taking on water from the air—perhaps because the crystalline interstices are already filled. Depending upon storage and environmental conditions, single-base powders can vary significantly in moisture content. Hydration significantly alters density and burn rate. Increasing moisture content slows the burn rate, sometimes dramatically.

Burn Rate

Smokeless powder burn rate is controlled by the various aforementioned characteristics of the individual granules and by the amount of confining pressure the powder is subjected to as it burns. This explains why one powder type can be considered a fast-burning number in one application while considered a slow-burning number in another application.

For example: When used in a 44 Magnum with a 240-grain bullet, H4227 is among the slowest of usable powders. When used in the 30-30 with a 150-grain bullet, H4227 is among the fastest of usable powders. (Actually, handloaders seldom use H4227 in the 30-30 because slower powders generally give better results.)

In the 44 Magnum, a somewhat compressed load generates perfectly normal pressure. In the 30-30, full normal pressure results from a case filled to only two-thirds capacity. In both instances, the charge used and the peak pressure generated are similar. The main difference is that in the 44 Magnum the bullet offers less resistance to the burning gases.

As another example, consider the 44 Magnum and the 444 Marlin. These cartridges have about the same SAAMI pressure specification and use identical bullets; they differ only in length and usable case capacity. The 444 can hold almost exactly twice as much powder.

In the 44 Magnum, Accurate's No. 9 is one of the better powders. A load of 21.3 grains pushes a 240-grain jacketed bullet at 1625 fps from a 20″ barrel while generating 40,000 CUP. In the 444 Marlin, A2230 is one of the better powders, and 54.2 grains pushes a 240-grain jacketed bullet at 2181 fps while generating 40,000 CUP. Accurate No. 9 is entirely too fast to produce acceptable ballistics in the 444 Marlin, and A2230 is entirely too slow for useful loads in the 44 Magnum. Here the *only* difference is usable case capacity.

As a final example, consider the 9mm Luger and the 35 Remington. These 35-caliber cartridges work at very similar pressures. Powders that are entirely too slow for use in the tiny 9mm case (11.4 grains of usable capacity with a 100-grain bullet seated normally) are entirely too fast for any normal load in the 35 Remington (44.0 grains of usable capacity with a 200-grain bullet). Conversely, the fastest usable powders in the 35 Remington are entirely too slow for use in the 9mm Luger.

The point of importance here is that many variables—bore diameter, usable pressure, bullet weight and case capacity—influence a powder's burning rate in any given application. Powders that are considered slow in one application can be dangerously fast in another. When it comes to smokeless powder, "slow" and "fast" are completely relative terms.

The absolute difference in controlled test (closed bomb) burning rates between the fastest and slowest handloader powders is about twelve times. This number has no value to the handloader except as a safety flag; clearly, *use of the wrong powder can generate gun-destroying pressures and could easily lead to loss of life and limb.*

Powder Selection

Handloader powders are currently provided by the following companies in the listed variety: **Accurate Arms:** Czech Republic-manufactured double-base ball (11 types), flake (1 type) and tubular (1 type); single-base tubular (4 types) and flake (3 types). **Alliant** (formerly Hercules): U.S.-manufactured double-base flake (7 types) and German-manufactured double-base tubular (5 types). **Hodgdon:** U.S.-manufactured double-base ball (10 types) and Australian-manufactured single-base flake (3 types) and tubular (9 types). **IMR:** Canadian-manufactured double-base flake (5 types) and single-base tubular (10 types). **Olin/Winchester:** U.S.-manufactured double-base ball (11 types). **Vihtavuori Oy:** Finland-manufactured single-base flake and tubular (17 types) and double-base tubular (3 types).

Additionally, the following companies list powders, though domestic distribution is currently limited: **Norma** of Sweden manufactures tubular (7 types). **Thunderbird Cartridge Company** of the U.S. offers double-base ball (4 types). This totals to 111 types, plenty of variety for most handloading.

In choosing likely powders for your handloading requirements, you should consider and compare your needs. If you intend to shoot competitively, you will want to talk with other competitors using similar cartridges. The powders they are using will certainly be a good place to start. Those interested only in hunting loads might have some choices different from those interested in competition or self-defense.

Here are some considerations that might make it easier to pick the best powder for your application.

Traditional handgun events require mild recoil, consistent velocity, clean burning and, in some events, maximum possible energy. Typically, handloaders produce ammunition for handgun target shooting using progressive presses that automatically measure and dump the powder charge into the sized and primed case. Despite the automatic nature of these presses, consistent operator technique can add to load uniformity.

Conversely, handloaders usually produce ammunition for target rifle competition using conventional presses. However, there is no reason a careful handloader cannot produce top-quality rifle ammunition using a progressive press. Many progressive presses afford the option of separate powder charging. For some types of competition, handloaders carefully weigh the powder charge; for other competitions, they carefully measure the charge. Regardless of the system used, operator skill, patience, attention to detail and consistency are important to the production of quality ammunition.

Handgun Competition

Traditional handgun target shooting such as NRA Bullseye uses cartridges and loads with low to moderate case capacity, e.g., 38 Special, 45 ACP, and similar chamberings. This is most beneficial because it is easier to develop good consistent loads with small capacity cases, especially when working at low pressures. Traditional powders for these types of loads are usually fast-burning, low-density, flake and double-base such as Bullseye, Red Dot, Green Dot, 700-X, SR7625, PB, Nitro100, No. 2, R1, HP38 and W231. Newer offerings that might find utility include Clays, N310, N320, and Scot1000.

One bit of advice in choosing a powder for such loads: Look for a combination that nearly fills the available powder space and generates only the velocity you need. If you are looking at powders that don't fill the available powder space, stay with double-base powders because these tend to be less sensitive to powder position. Additionally, in any type of load where the powder does not substantially fill the available powder space, pay critical attention to how you handle the gun between shots. Powder position effects can be extremely significant.

Some of the best loads for NRA Bullseye use so little powder that a double charge can easily fit in the case. Take every precaution to guard against this.

Action Pistol (IPSC) Competition

Action shooters also need consistent velocity and clean loads. However, these folks need to achieve the required power levels. This means handgun IPSC (International Practical Shooting Confederation) competitors typically use slower powders where the load nearly fills the case and generates significantly higher pressure, compared to Bullseye shooters. These factors make it easier to achieve ballistic uniformity, and powder position effects are less of a concern. A wide choice of powders have potential application in Action Pistol loads. Typical powders include No. 7, Blue Dot, HS6, HS7, N340, N350, 3N37, 800-X, SR4756, WSF, WAP and Unique.

Silhouette Pistol Competition

Silhouette pistol shooters generally shoot magnum revolver cartridges or small-capacity rifle cartridges. Most magnum revolver loads work best with these powders: N110, W296, H110, 2400, IMR4227,

H4227 and A1680. Small rifle-type cartridges fired from short barrels also work well with these same powders. For this latter application, other good choices include SR4759, SC4198, H4198, IMR4198, RL-7, N130 and N133. In some applications, slower powders might offer higher velocity potential, but generally at the expense of a large increase in recoil and muzzleblast, and with a significant loss of ballistic uniformity.

Benchrest Competition

In benchrest competition, accuracy is the only criterion. Benchrest shooters will try anything to achieve any small improvement in accuracy. Current benchrest cartridges tend to be of small capacity and work at moderately high pressures. This configuration gives up considerable velocity potential for a measure of increased consistency. Another thing benchrest shooters can give up is fouling control. Typically, they clean the bore after firing eleven or twelve shots—one or two foulers plus ten for group.

Powders that have been used successfully or show promise in benchrest competition include H322, A2015BR, H4198, IMR4198, RL-7, N130 and N133. The nature of this game is such that no powder is considered unsuitable. If Pyrodex-P or cannon-grade blackpowder shot smaller groups, rest assured, you would see plenty of smoke at benchrest events!

With continued reductions in benchrest cartridge case capacities, faster and faster powders come into the running. Again, if the powder and charge you happen to settle on does not completely fill the available powder space, pay particular attention to gun handling so as to maintain consistent shot-to-shot powder position.

Most benchresters dump measured powder charges directly from the measure into the cartridge case. Consistent charging is determined by the measure used and the operator's technique.

NRA High Power Competition

Long-range competitors have a completely different set of considerations and an entirely different perspective. First, they are concerned with finding a load that will shoot good groups consistently over a long string of shots and without the necessity of cleaning the gun. Second, they are much more concerned about maximizing velocity, minimizing extreme velocity spread and wind drift, and using the most efficient bullet. These issues get important when one is shooting beyond 200 yards. Finally, since these competitors do a passel of shooting in a season, they look for combinations that offer any possibility of extending barrel life.

NRA High Power competitors look for powders that minimize bore fouling and erosion, while providing high, consistent velocities. Curiously, this is one area where normal statistical analysis fails to provide useful information. Normally, we can say that standard velocity deviation, a measure of expected variation around a load's mean velocity, is the most useful measure of a load's consistency. However, in long-range target shooting, the most important measure of ballistic consistency is extreme spread.

At long ranges, large changes in muzzle velocity result in large changes in vertical impact and wind drift. If long-range target shooting is to be your game, look for a powder that can deliver shot after shot within the narrowest velocity window possible. Forget standard deviation. Concentrate on *minimizing* extreme velocity spread.

Historically, traditional IMR powders, especially 4895, 4064 and 4350, have faired extremely well in this sport. These are still a good place to start. Newer numbers with great promise include VarGet, N140, N150, N160, N165, RL-19 and RL-22. Vihtavuori's 500 series of powders might have potential, but that remains to be proven.

Big Game Hunting

The hunter has a different set of criteria than the formal target shooter. Generally, hunters are more concerned with delivered energy than any other factor. I, like many nimrods, simply try to find the powder that safely delivers the highest velocity while achieving the necessary level of accuracy—my personal big game criterion is consistent 1.5 minute of angle (MOA) 300-yard three-shot groups. Barrel fouling, extended shot-string accuracy, component cost and equipment cost are

When the game is a trophy like this mule deer, taken by the author's brother in 1965, delivered energy is of critical concern, as is terminal bullet performance. Nevertheless, both factors are subservient to the necessity of precise shot placement, which depends on the shooter, the gun and the load.

not important considerations for the big game hunter; however, for the varmint hunter, they often are.

Opinions vary about what a powder should do in a hunting load. I contend that only two powder factors really matter to the hunter: shot placement and delivered energy. Obviously, the load generating more velocity delivers the most energy.

Regarding shot placement, for a big game hunting load (rifle or pistol), accuracy needs to be judged based on the first shot from a cold barrel and, perhaps, one or two additional shots. I prefer to gather data from many three-shot groups as a measure of a hunting rifle and load's potential.

Most important is that the first shot goes where the shooter intends. If a shot is pulled or a twig gets in the way and prevents that first shot from doing its intended job, then follow-up shots can be important, but it is ever so unlikely that accuracy after the third shot will ever matter to the big game hunter. Measuring a hunting rifle's useful accuracy using five-shot or, worse, ten-shot groups makes little sense. It is better to fire many three-shot groups from a clean cold barrel under differing atmospheric conditions. Fire three-shot groups from a fouled barrel under different atmospheric conditions. Fire three-shot groups at 100 yards and then at 300 yards. But always fire three-shot groups. When you find a powder that delivers good velocity and always keeps such three-shot groups near one minute of angle (MOA), then you have found a good powder for your big game hunting load.

There is no way anyone can predict what powder will give the best performance in any hunting gun. In some instances, writers offer suggestions in the text associated with specific cartridges, and this can be a useful indicator. Generally, look for a load developing good velocity with a safe charge that nearly fills the available powder space or is somewhat compressed. Avoid lightly compressed loads.

Varmint Hunting

Varminters often shoot many shots without cleaning the barrel, so they look for a powder that minimizes fouling. They shoot at long and short range, and at unknown ranges. For these reasons, velocity is particularly important. Somewhere on their wish list will be the desire for a powder that minimizes barrel erosion.

Absolute accuracy is important, but varmint hunters don't really care much if their pet load throws an occasional flier. As long as most shots are similar in velocity and shoot to the same point of aim, the load will do the job. Varmint shooting, by its very nature, includes a considerable number of missed shots. Varmint hunters will view any powder that increases the number of good shots in any string, or decreases barrel fouling, as beneficial.

These 38-40 cases are all level, and each contains the same 5.0-grain charge of Bullseye. Obviously such a powder charge can settle anywhere in the case. This can drastically affect ballistics.

There are several new powders on the market that show promise for this sport. Hodgdon's VarGet is one. It has less than one-tenth the graphite coating of typical smokeless powders and, therefore, generates considerably less fouling. Because of the unique chemistry of the deterrent coating used, VarGet also shows considerably less sensitivity to temperature variations. Vihtavuori's powders evidently use very clean raw materials because they are also unusually clean burning.

Conversely, although they are noted for increased barrel fouling, the various ball powders also burn cooler and might, thereby, extend barrel life. Ball-type powders have another significant advantage, ease of loading. When one might fire hundreds of rounds a day for several days on an extended weekend, this is a significant consideration.

Be that as it may, most varmint hunters look first at velocity and then at accuracy. One should test the accuracy produced with the powder offering the highest velocity before testing any other powders. The reason? Shots at unknown ranges place a premium on the flattest possible trajectory. If two powders offer similar velocity, the one that offers the best *average* accuracy is preferred. If two powders offer similar velocity and accuracy, the cleanest is preferred. If two powders offer similar velocity, accuracy and cleanliness, the one that might reduce bore erosion, i.e., overall shooting costs, is preferred.

Low-Pressure and Large-Capacity Cartridges

Cartridges such as the 25-20, 32-20, 38-40, 44-40, 45 Colt, 32-40, 38-55, 45-70, 50-70, 50-90 and 50-140 were originally designed for blackpowder. They are commonly reloaded to operate at blackpowder pressure levels. Most standard and magnum revolver cartridges and many rifle cartridges can be included here if the load chosen happens to develop relatively low pressure. These cartridges offer a special challenge to the handloader.

Generally, these numbers have relatively large capacity. This suggests these cartridges can generate good velocity at low pressure, which is a useful quality. The problem is that smokeless powders which work consistently at low pressure often do not significantly fill the usable case capacity in these cartridges. With considerable unused powder space, powder position effects can be significant.

Slower powders that do significantly fill the case often don't work consistently at these low pressures. This really is a "catch-22." Intermediate powders, rather than solving either problem, typically offer the worst of both worlds.

For low-pressure revolver loads, try to maximize bullet pull by using a smaller diameter neck expander and a heavy roll crimp. This practice can dramatically improve shot-to-shot uniformity because it helps keep the bullet in place longer as the powder ignites. Stay with porous double-base flake powders—Bullseye, 700-X and Nitro100 are hard to beat. These powders minimize the considerable powder-position ballistic effects, perhaps because they occupy more of the available space and tend to ignite faster.

If you can tolerate a lot of powder residue and smoke, try Unique or similar moderate-burning-rate double-base flake powders. Avoid light bullets. The primer's blast can dislodge these more easily. Light bullets also leave more unused space for the powder to move around in. Remember to handle the gun in such a way as to minimize variation in powder position before firing each shot. The same general plan is useful for high-capacity low-pressure rifle loads. Stay with the faster powders and avoid ball powders. Reloder-7 might be the all-time sleeper for these cartridges, but the various 4198s and 4227s have been widely used, and both SR4759 and XMP5744 offer exceptionally good results.

As an example, consider the 38-40 Winchester. This is perhaps the worst of the lot. Besides being handicapped with a comparatively large usable case capacity and a very low working pressure, this cartridge also features a thin, short case neck and uses comparatively light bullets. Factory 38-40 loads and most handloads are extremely sensitive to powder position. Even at their best, 38-40 loads typically exhibit more than 100 fps difference in velocity with only minor variations in gun handling. Shots fired deliberately at a steep angle, either up or down, demonstrate dramatic variations in recoil.

Both MTM and Midway offer eminently useful logbooks. These three-ring binders contain matching target and log pages, making it simple to keep all handloading and shooting records in one place.

If one chooses a powder that fills, or nearly fills, the 38-40's available powder space, and yet produces safe 38-40 pressure, the powder is generally very difficult to ignite and does not burn consistently. This results in a load that leaves lots of unburned powder, typically produces considerable smoke and seldom demonstrates reasonable shot-to-shot uniformity.

If one chooses a fast powder, which ignites and burns properly at safe 38-40 pressure levels, the proper charge will fill only about one-third of the available powder space. When faced with this dilemma, in this and other cartridges, some handloaders have used case fillers to keep the powder in place against the primer. However, the potential ballistic effects of this practice are not properly understood and we cannot suggest this practice.

To demonstrate the magnitude of powder-position effects, consider a recent test done by Ken Oehler of Oehler Ballistics Labs. In that test, Mr. Oehler loaded 38 Special cases with a charge of Unique powder that filled about 70 percent of the available powder space. He seated Speer's 110 JHP bullets on top of that, in Remington cases. The pressure gun was a 10″ T/C Contender connected to Oehler's Model 43 Personal Ballistics Lab.

With the powder settled against the bullet, these loads averaged 1110 fps with an average peak pressure of 15,000 psi—perfectly normal 38 Special numbers. Loads from the same batch fired with the powder settled against the primer produced an average velocity of 1393 fps with an average pressure of 26,100 psi. The industry-standard pressure for 38 Special +P *proof* loads is 27,000 psi.

Currently, there are no perfect smokeless powders for these applications. If we can just get some manufacturer to introduce a double-base flake propellant line offering a bulk density of about 0.25 (one-quarter the density of water, about one-half the density of the lightest currently available propellant), we would likely see vastly improved ballistic uniformity in many such loads. Three such powders—one similar in burn rate to Bullseye, one similar to Blue Dot and one similar to 4198—would go a long way toward providing useful loads for these cartridges. Such a load should be clean-burning and could offer reasonable ballistic consistency—something that has, heretofore, been unavailable with smokeless loads in these cartridges.

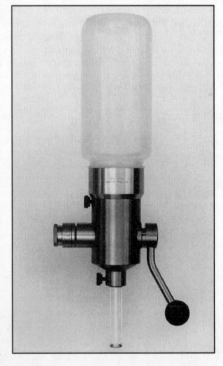

A wide variety of powder measures are available like the Redding Master Model 3 (left), Lee Auto-Disk (center), and Neil Jones Micro Measure (right). Many are adaptable to progressive presses and can do an admirable job of dispensing substantially consistent charges of many types of powders.

VibraShine's Electric Powder Trickler eases this tedious operation, making quick and accurate work of bringing the charge to weight. For coarse-granulated tubular powders, it's best to dispense approximate charges with a powder measure, then add the last grain or so with this powder trickler.

Many manufacturers offer loading blocks. Midway produces fine close-fitting wood blocks that are a pleasure to own and use, and MTM's compact Loading Trays are particularly handy for charging cases with powder dropped from a measure.

Charge Selection

After you have settled on one or a few powders to try, the next step is to determine the best charge to use. Here, meticulous record-keeping is particularly important.

If you're looking for the best accuracy, once you have demonstrated that your chosen load produces safe pressure, test various charges of the selected powder while holding all other variables constant. Look for the safe charge that gives the smallest group. For a discussion of how to determine the safety of the charge, refer to Chapter 9 on pressure.

It is an interesting study to watch a group change in character as one varies the charge weight in, say, half-grain increments. I once worked up a load in a Remington pump chambered in 270 Winchester using Nosler's 160-grain Partition bullet. As I increased the charge in half-grain steps, my 100-yard three-shot groups changed from $1^1/_2''$ vertical strings to $1^1/_2''$ horizontal strings to $1''$ vertical strings and finally to $^3/_4''$ clusters. Happily, this closure occurred at the maximum load, a perfect—and fortuitous—combination.

Such a result is not uncommon in a hunting rifle. The "stringing" has to do with complicated barrel vibrations. The secret to good accuracy is to find a load combination that launches the bullet from the barrel with the barrel vibrated into the same orientation each time.

Almost every load combination has a "sweet spot." Even after one has settled on the powder one wants to use, one might find tinkering with the charge to be worthwhile.

Measuring Charges

Almost all benchrest competitors and most pistol shooters throw charges directly into the case using a powder measure. Most benchrest competitors do quite well at maintaining uniform charges by using proper and consistent techniques. However, the technique that works for one type of powder might not work for another.

The powder measuring system recommended by many benchrest competitors is to fill the powder hopper with the powder of choice, then dump about ten charges and return those to the reservoir. This eliminates the excess packing that occurs near the base of the powder column while filling the hopper. This process also settles the entire hopper volume to a more uniform packing scheme.

To drop consistent charges, use a steady, deliberate and repeatable motion. Move the handle until the measuring cavity fills and the handle stops. Move the handle the other way about one inch, reverse and return the handle to the stop. This repeated motion should fill the measuring cavity with a more uniformly packed volume, and hence a more uniform weight, of powder. Hold a case under the outlet. Move the handle the other way until it stops. This action dumps the charge into the waiting case. Again start the handle back. Move it about one inch and reverse until the handle again stops. This motion helps settle the powder in the hopper directly over the drum. This prepares a more consistent charge to fill the hopper the next time. Repeat this process until you have charged all the cases.

For non-benchrest loads, I have found that with most ball powders the extra effort of reversing the motion of the handle at both ends of the stroke is of little or no value. To get uniform charges, I raise and drop the handle at a moderate and consistent speed, bumping the drum against the stops at both ends of its travel. However, to each his own. Practice several methods and use whatever technique your tests show works best for you. Above all, be consistent.

If you want to use a measure with tubular powders, drop a few dozen charges using your best technique and weigh them to see how consistent they are. Direct metering from a good powder measure is a handy method of charging cases.

Weighing Charges

Most long-range competitors and handloading hunters *weigh* their powder charges, but not because they enjoy it.

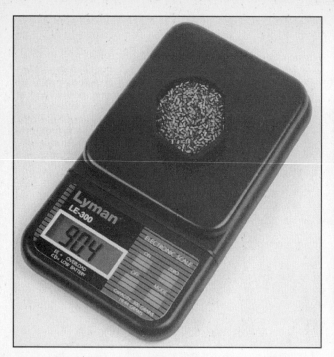

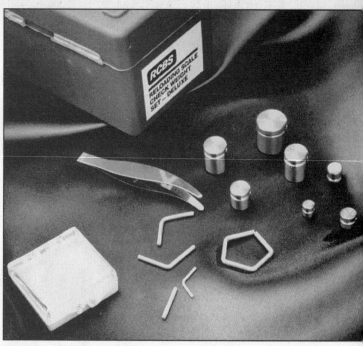

Completely portable, Lyman's LE-300, with ±0.1-grain accuracy, is a real boon to the handloader who prefers to load in the field. With 300-grain capacity, this scale is useful for weighing bullets, cases and powder charges.

RCBS' Deluxe Scale Check Weight Set is valuable for the reloader concerned with precise measurements, and that should include all serious handloaders.

Some reloading hunters don't even own a powder measure because they use tubular powders that don't meter well. Where only a few rounds a year might be fired at game, weighing charges seems a minor inconvenience.

Long-range target shooters have found that the powders that produce the most accurate extended shot strings are all coarse-granuled tubular-types. These simply cannot be metered with sufficient consis-

Lyman's Autoscale is the answer to a handloader's dream. This unit automatically dispenses weighed charges of tubular powders with ±0.1-grain accuracy. Most charges can be accurately dispensed in less than six seconds.

tently to give the uniform performance required for shooting at 600 yards and beyond.

With a good beam balance or a digital electronic scale, it's no trick to consistently and repeatedly weigh charges to an accuracy of less than ±0.1 grain. One needs to practice good scale-operation techniques for consistent results. Every time you readjust the weight setting on a beam scale, you should lightly bump the pointer end of the beam down to ensure the beam and weights settle properly into their bearing grooves. After turning on any electronic scale, wait until it has fully warmed up, perhaps fifteen minutes, and then calibrate it. After doing these things, go to handloading. With very little effort, anyone should be able to weigh charges with more precision than is necessary for any type of shooting.

Unfortunately, no technique works particularly well for dropping consistent measured charges of tubular powders. The factories use vibration to minimize variation. To see how well this works, pull a few bullets from factory loads that use tubular powders and weigh the charges.... The newer short-cut granules and several of the smaller-granuled tubular powders seem to measure reasonably consistently. However, I still don't trust any powder measure to meter weights of any tubular powder as consistently as a scale. When using a scale, a powder trickler can speed things considerably.

Lyman's new Autoscale offers a fast, accurate way to weigh tubular powder charges. In less than ten seconds, this handy tool can dispense an accurate charge of any tubular powder (it will not work with ball-type powders). With proper adjustment and careful operation, one can easily achieve charge weights within 0.1-grain of the desired weight. The Autoscale is slightly slower to use than a measure. However, the repeatability and accuracy are worth the minor delay.

Slightly Compressed Charges

Try to avoid powder charges that result in a slight compression of the as-dumped powder charge. Some slightly compressed charges might spontaneously settle, most likely from vibrations during transportation. If this happens to some of the loads, they will shoot to a different point of impact. The folks at Alliant have studied this effect in

The same powder charge in 7mm Remington Magnum cases (from left): as-dumped and settled by vibration. Whether you pre-settle or not, when you seat a 175-grain bullet on this charge, the packing scheme is locked in.

Forster's Blue Ribbon extended drop tube funnel is extremely useful for installing powder charges that might otherwise slightly overfill the case.

This 270 case has a 170-grain Speer bullet seated on 65.6 grains of H570 (long discontinued). OAL is about 3.3″. This powder charge is not about to spontaneously adjust itself to some other packing scheme!

some detail and have found it to be significant. In moderately to highly compressed charges, the powder granules are pressed together so tightly that spontaneous settling can't occur.

Highly Compressed Charges

Assume you have finalized a load that shoots like a house afire and shows very good ballistic uniformity; however, it is a compressed charge. Such loads are not at all uncommon. The only thing unique about a compressed-charge load is that seating the bullet locks the as-charged granule packing scheme into the powder charge. Packing schemes and as-loaded density can both influence internal ballistics, so one must be very careful to assemble all compressed-charge loads as consistently as possible. This is a subject that has received little, if any, attention.

In a recent test, I charged forty fully prepped 30-30 cases with a charge of VarGet that nearly filled the case. I charged twenty of the cases by simply pouring the charge into a standard powder funnel. I filled the other twenty by pouring the powder so that the granules fell against the side of the funnel's cone. Because of this, the charge swirled as it passed through the spout. In both instances, the charge filled the case to the middle of the neck—the charged cases were indistinguishable. Seating a 150-grain bullet substantially compressed the powder charge. Every effort was made to ensure the ammunition was otherwise exactly alike.

There was, however, a substantial difference when I fired those rounds for velocity. The first group, where the powder was simply dumped into the cases, produced slightly more than 18 fps standard deviation. The swirl-charged group produced slightly less than 12 fps standard deviation.

There is nothing wrong with compressed powder charges, and many loads that offer superior performance are highly compressed charges of relatively slow-burning powders. As long as one can seat the bullet on top of the powder charge without deforming the case or the bullet, and without the bullet being pushed back out of the case by the stressed powder, and assuming the resulting load does not create unsafe pressure, compressed charges are perfectly safe. They are often particularly good loads. However, use special care to assure consistent powder charging.

To gain some understanding as to how important powder charging technique might be, consider this: Benchrest competitors long ago ceased using scales to weigh individual powder charges. They found that charges dropped into their cases from their powder measures produced more consistent results.

Those dumped charges don't deliver more consistent results because they are more consistent in weight. Compared to weighed charges, dropped charges are introduced into the case with a greater level of *consistency*. The more consistent packing scheme, from one round to the next, turns out to be more important than keeping charges exactly uniform in weight.

Compressed-charge loads are sometimes difficult to get into the case. They can also cause difficulties in bullet seating. If necessary, use a long drop tube when installing these loads. Simply pour the charge into the extended funnel at a slow and constant rate. If the charge requires further settling, tap the case against the bench as the powder is settling in place. Another method that works splendidly is to use a small hand-held vibratory sander to settle the charge. After dumping the powder through the funnel, and with the funnel still in place, lightly press the vibrating felt pad of the sander against the body of the case. A bit of trial and error will show the technique that provides the maximum amount of powder settling—as much as 6 percent with certain powders.

SMOKELESS POWDER—COMPOSITION AND BURN RATE
From Fastest Burning to Slowest (Approximate)

Manuf.	Powder	Granule Shape	Nitroglyc. %	Bulk Density	Suggested Primers	Primary Uses
Hodg.	Clays	Flake	P	0.475	Standard Pistol	Shotgun/Targ. Pistol
Norma	R1	—	2	—	Standard Pistol	Targ. Pistol
Scott	Red Diam.	Diamond	22	—	Standard Pistol	Shotgun/Light Pistol
Vihta.	N310	Porous base cylin.	0	0.45	Standard Pistol	Targ. Pistol
Herc.	Red Dot	Flake	20	0.480	Standard Pistol	Shotgun/Light Pistol
Herc.	Bullseye	Flake	40	0.620	Standard Pistol	Light to Med. Pistol
Vihta.	N312	Porous base	0	0.435	Standard Pistol	Special Blank Powder
Win.	230*	Sphere	UN	0.715	Standard Pistol	Light Pistol
Scott	1000	Flake	0	—	Standard Pistol	Light to Med. Pistol/Shotgun
Vihta.	N318	Porous base flake	0	0.430	—	Shotgun
Scott	Nitro100	Flake	27	0.510	Standard Pistol	Shotgun/Light Pistol
IMR	700-X	Flake	29	0.500	Standard Pistol	Shotgun/Light Pistol
Win.	452AA*	Sphere	13	0.555	Standard Pistol	Shotgun/Light Pistol
Scott	453	Sphere	13	0.555	Standard Pistol	Shotgun/Light Pistol
Vihta.	N319	Porous base flake	0	0.430	—	Shotgun
Accur.	AA2	Sphere	24	0.750	Standard Pistol	Light to Mod. Pistol
Vihta.	N320	Porous base cylin.	0	0.500	Standard Pistol	Shotgun/Light to Mod. Pistol
Scott	Royal D	—	0	—	Standard Pistol	Shotgun/Light to Mod. Pistol
Vihta.	N321	Porous base flake	0	0.450	—	Shotgun
Win.	231	Sphere	22.5	0.700	Standard Pistol	Light to Mod. Pistol
Vihta.	N322	Porous base flake	0	0.430	—	Shotgun
Hodg.	HP38	Sphere	P	0.635	Standard Pistol	Light to Mod. Pistol
Vihta.	N324	Porous base flake	0	0.470	—	Shotgun
Vihta.	N325	Porous base flake	0	0.520	—	Shotgun
Win.	WST	Sphere	20	0.535	Standard Pistol	Shotgun/Targ. Pistol
Vihta.	N326	Porous base flake	0	0.520	—	Shotgun
Hodg.	Int'l Clays	Flake	P	0.525	—	Shotgun
Vihta.	N328	Porous base flake	0	0.500	—	Shotgun
Herc.	Green Dot	Flake	20	0.515	—	Shotgun
Vihta.	N330	Porous base cylin.	0	0.600	Standard Pistol	Light to Mod. Pistol
IMR	7625	Flake	0	0.640	Standard Pistol	Shotgun/Pistol
IMR	PB	Porous base	0	0.555	Standard Pistol	Shotgun/Light Pistol
Vihta.	N331	Porous base cylin.	0	0.680	Standard Pistol	9mm Luger/Light to Mod. Pistol
Scott	Pearl	—	0	—	Standard Pistol	Shotgun/Mod. Pistol
Win.	WSL	Sphere	34	0.765	Standard Pistol	Shotgun/Targ. Pistol
Hodg.	Univ. Clays	Flake	P	0.650	Standard Pistol	Shotgun/Pistol
Win.	473AA*	Sphere	UN	0.665	—	Shotgun
Herc.	Unique	Flake	20	0.610	Standard Pistol	Mod.-Heavy Pistol/Light Cast-Bullet Rifle
Win.	WAP	Sphere	15	—	Standard Pistol	Pistol
Vihta.	N338	Porous base cylin.	0	0.540	—	Blanks/Shotgun
Accur.	AA5	Sphere	17	0.950	Standard Pistol	Sub-Sonic 9mm Luger/Mod. Pistol
Win.	WSF	Sphere	34	0.770	Standard Pistol	Shotgun/Mod. Pistol
Vihta.	N340	Porous base cylin.	0	0.560	Standard Pistol	Mod. to Heavy Pistol
Win.	540	Sphere	21	0.950	Standard Pistol	Shotgun/Pistol
Vihta.	N342	Porous base cylin.	0	0.560	Standard Pistol	Shotgun/Pistol
Herc.	Herco	Flake	20	0.570	Standard Pistol	Shotgun/Mod. Pistol
Hodg.	HS6	Sphere	P	0.945	Standard Pistol	Mod. to Heavy Pistol/Shotgun
Vihta.	N344	Porous base flake	0	0.520	—	Shotgun
IMR	4756	Flake	0	0.610	Standard Pistol	Shotgun/Pistol
Vihta.	N347	Porous base flake	0	0.540	—	Shotgun
Scott	1250	Flake	0	—	Standard Pistol	Shotgun/Mod. Pistol

SMOKELESS POWDER—COMPOSITION AND BURN RATE
From Fastest Burning to Slowest (Approximate)

Manuf.	Powder	Granule Shape	Nitroglyc. %	Bulk Density	Suggested Primers	Primary Uses
Vihta.	3N37	Porous base cylin.	0	0.640	Standard Pistol	High Vel. 22 RF/Pistol/Shotgun
Vihta.	3N17	Porous base cylin.	0	0.520	Standard Pistol	22 Rimfire
Vihta.	3N36	Porous base cylin.	0	0.500	Standard Pistol	22 Rimfire
IMR	800-X	Flake	29	—	—	Shotgun
Scott	1500	Flake	0	—	Standard or Mag. Pistol	Mod. to Heavy Pistol
Vihta.	N350	Porous base cylin.	0	0.570	Standard Pistol	Mod. to Heavy Pistol/Shotgun
Hodg.	HS7	Sphere	P	0.990	Standard Pistol	Shotgun/Heavy Pistol
Herc.	Blue Dot	Flake	20	0.780	Standard or Mag. Pistol	Mod. to Heavy Pistol/Shotgun
Accur.	AA7	Sphere	10.5	0.985	Standard or Mag. Pistol	9mm Luger/10mm/Mod. to Heavy Pistol
Win.	571	Sphere	21	0.955	—	Shotgun
Win.	630*	Sphere	UN	0.965	Mag. Pistol	Heavy Pistol
Herc.	2400	Tubular	15	0.870	Standard or Mag. Pistol	Heavy and Mag. Pistol
Vihta.	N110	Tubular	0	0.760	Standard or Mag. Pistol	Heavy and Mag. Pistol
Norma	R123	—	0	—	Standard or Mag. Pistol	Heavy and Mag. Pistol
Accur.	AA9	Sphere	10	0.975	Mag. Pistol	Mag. Pistol/30 Carb/410
Hodg.	110	Sphere	P	0.975	Mag. Pistol	Mag. Pistol/30 Carb/410
Win.	296	Sphere	11	0.975	Mag. Pistol	Mag. Pistol/30 Carb/410
IMR	4759	Tubular	0	0.675	Standard/BR Only	Heavy Pistol and Light Cast-Bullet Rifle
Vihta.	N120	Tubular	0	0.820	Standard Rifle	Light Bullets in 22 Varmint Loads
IMR	4227	Tubular	0	0.870	Standard/BR Only	Heavy Pistol/Light Cast-Bullet Rifle
Vihta.	N125	Tubular	0	0.850	Standard Rifle	7.62X39
Hodg.	4227	Tubular	0	0.870	Standard/BR Only	Heavy Pistol/Light Cast-Bullet Rifle
Vihta.	N130	Tubular	0	0.850	Standard Rifle	Factory 22 & 6mm PPC
Win.	680*	Sphere	10	0.950	Mag. Only	454 Casull/Small Rifle Cases
Accur.	1680	Sphere	10	0.950	Mag. Only	454 Casull/Small Rifle Cases
T-Bird	680	Sphere	10	0.950	Mag. Only	454 Casull/Small Rifle Cases
Vihta.	N132	Tubular	0	0.860	Standard Rifle	5.56 Tracer/Limited Application
Norma	200	Tubular	0	—	Standard Rifle	Small Capacity Rifle
Vihta.	N133	Tubular	0	0.860	Standard Rifle	222, 223 & 45-70
IMR	4198	Tubular	0	0.850	Standard Rifle	Excellent Cast-Bullet Rifle
Scott**	4197	Tubular	0	0.850	Standard Rifle	Excellent Cast-Bullet Rifle
Hodg.	4198	Tubular	0	0.850	Standard Rifle	Excellent Cast-Bullet Rifle
Hodg.	4198SC	Tubular	0	0.880†	Standard Rifle	Excellent Cast-Bullet Rifle
B-West	BW36	Tubular	0	—	Standard Rifle	Mod. Capacity Rifle
Herc.	RL-7	Tubular	7	0.890	Standard Rifle	Mod. Capacity Rifle
Vihta.	N134	Tubular	0	0.860	Standard Rifle	7.62mm NATO Tracer
Accur.	2015BR	Tubular	0	0.900	Std./BR/Mag. Rifle	Mod. Capacity Rifle
Scott**	3032	Tubular	0	0.880	Standard Rifle	Mod. Capacity Rifle
IMR	3031	Tubular	0	0.880	Standard Rifle	Mod. Capacity Rifle
Norma	201	Tubular	0	—	Standard Rifle	Mod. Capacity Rifle
Hodg.	322	Tubular	0	0.920†	Standard Rifle	Mod. Capacity Rifle
Scott**	322	Tubular	0	0.920†	Standard Rifle	Mod. Capacity Rifle
B-West	IMR8208	Tubular	—	—	Standard Rifle	Mod. Capacity Rifle
Accur.	2230	Sphere	10	—	Std./BR/Mag. Rifle	.223/Mod. Capacity Rifle
Win.	748	Sphere	10	0.995	Std./BR/Mag. Rifle	Mod. to Large Rifle
Hodg.	335	Sphere	P	1.035	Mag. Rifle	Mod. to Large Rifle
Hodg.	BL-C(2)	Sphere	P	1.035	Mag. Rifle	Mod. to Large Rifle
Accur.	2460	Sphere	10	0.975	Std./BR/Mag. Rifle	Mod. Capacity Rifle
IMR	4895	Tubular	0	0.920	Standard Rifle	Versatile/Gd. Cast Bullet & Reduced Lds.
Hodg.	4895	Tubular	0	0.920	Standard Rifle	Versatile/Gd. Cast Bullet & Reduced Lds.
Herc.	RL-12	Tubular	7	1.000	Standard Rifle	Mod. Capacity Rifle

SMOKELESS POWDER—COMPOSITION AND BURN RATE
From Fastest Burning to Slowest (Approximate)

Manuf.	Powder	Granule Shape	Nitroglyc. %	Bulk Density	Suggested Primers	Primary Uses
Vihta.	N135	Tubular	0	0.860	Standard Rifle	7.62 Ball/Mod. Capacity Rifle
IMR	4064	Tubular	0	0.905	Standard Rifle	Mod. Capacity Rifle
Scott**	4065	Tubular	0	0.905	Standard Rifle	Mod. Capacity Rifle
Accur.	2520	Sphere	10	0.970	Std./BR/Mag. Rifle	Mod. Capacity Rifle
IMR	4320	Tubular	0	0.935	Standard Rifle	Mod. to Large Rifle
Norma	202	Tubular	0	—	Standard Rifle	Mod. to Large Rifle
Vihta.	N140	Tubular	0	0.860	Standard Rifle	Mod. to Large Rifle
Vihta.	N540	Tubular	P	0.860	Standard Rifle	Mod. to Large Rifle
Accur.	2700	Sphere	10	0.960	Std./BR/Mag. Rifle	Mod. to Large Rifle
Herc.	RL-15	Tubular	7.5	0.920	Standard Rifle	Mod. Capacity Rifle
Hodg.	380	Sphere	P	0.967	Mag. Rifle	Mod. to Large Rifle
Scott**	4351	Tubular	0	0.910	Std./BR/Mag. Rifle	Large Rifle
Win.	760	Sphere	10	1.000	Std./BR/Mag. Rifle	Large Rifle
Hodg.	414	Sphere	P	0.995	Mag. Rifle	Large Rifle
Vihta.	N150	Tubular	0	0.850	Std./BR/Mag. Rifle	Large Rifle
Vihta.	N550	Tubular	P	0.850	Std./BR/Mag. Rifle	Large Rifle
Accur.	4350	Tubular	0	0.910	Std./BR/Mag. Rifle	Large & Mag. Rifle
IMR	4350	Tubular	0	0.910	Std./BR/Mag. Rifle	Large & Mag. Rifle
Hodg.	4350	Tubular	0	0.910	Std./BR/Mag. Rifle	Large & Mag. Rifle
Hodg.	4350SC	Tubular	0	0.945†	Std./BR/Mag. Rifle	Large & Mag. Rifle
Vihta.	24N64	Tubular	0	—	Mag. Rifle	Large & Mag. Rifle
Norma	204	Tubular	0	0.990	Std./BR/Mag. Rifle	Large & Mag. Rifle
Herc.	RL-19	Tubular	11.5	0.890	Std./BR/Mag. Rifle	Large & Mag. Rifle
Vihta.	N160	Tubular	0	0.900	Mag. Rifle	Large & Mag. Rifle
Vihta.	N560	Tubular	P	0.900	Mag. Rifle	Large & Mag. Rifle
IMR	4831	Tubular	0	0.930†	Std./BR/Mag. Lg. Rifle	Large & Mag. Rifle
Hodg.	450	Tubular	P	0.990	Mag. Lg. Rifle	Large & Mag. Rifle
Hodg.	4831	Tubular	0	0.930	Std./BR/Mag. Lg. Rifle	Large & Mag. Rifle
Hodg.	4831SC	Tubular	0	0.960	Std./BR/Mag. Lg. Rifle	Large & Mag. Rifle
Scott**	4831	Tubular	0	0.930	Std./BR/Mag. Lg. Rifle	Large & Mag. Rifle
IMR	7828	Tubular	0	0.910†	Mag. Lg. Rifle/Fed. 215	Large & Mag. Rifle
Accur.	3100	Tubular	0	0.945***	Std./BR/Mag. Lg. Rifle	Large & Mag. Rifle
Win.	785*	Sphere	—	1.015	Mag. Lg. Rifle	Large & Mag. Rifle
Norma	MRP	Tubular	0	1.000†	Std./BR/Mag. Lg. Rifle	Large & Mag. Rifle
Norma	205*	Tubular	0	1.000	Std./BR/Mag. Lg. Rifle	Large & Mag. Rifle
Vihta.	N165	Tubular	0	0.900	Mag. Lg. Rifle	Large & Mag. Rifle
Herc.	RL-22	Tubular	11.5	0.890	Std./BR/Mag. Lg. Rifle	Large & Mag. Rifle
Win.	WMR	Sphere	13.5	1.000	Mag. Lg. Rifle	Large & Mag. Rifle
Hodg.	1000	Tubular	0	—	Fed-215/Mag. Lg. Rifle	Mag. Rifle
Vihta.	170	Tubular	0	0.900†	Fed-215	Mag. Rifle/50 BMG
T-Bird	5020	Sphere	—	0.965	Fed-215	Mag. Rifle/50 BMG
Hodg.	570*	Tubular	0	0.945	Mag. Lg. Rifle/Fed-215	Mag. Rifle/50 BMG
Hodg.	870	Sphere	P	0.965	Fed-215	Mag. Rifle/50 BMG
Accur.	8700	Sphere	10	0.960	Fed-215	Mag. Rifle/50 BMG
T-Bird	870	Sphere	10	0.965	Fed-215	Mag. Rifle/50 BMG
Hodg.	5010*	Tubular	0	0.910	Fed-215	Mag. Rifle/50 BMG
T-Bird	5070	Sphere	—	0.965	Fed-215	Mag. Rifle/50 BMG

UN = % unavailable; P = % proprietary; * = Obsolete; ** = Recently Discontinued; *** = Conflicting density data from various sources; † = Estimated VihtaVuori Oy data was included for completeness but VihtaVuori Oy rankings were based solely on information from their catalogue. Evidently VihtaVuori Oy uses shotgun pressures to compare *all* powders that are intended primarily for use in shotshell loading. Because of the lower pressures involved—compared to the pistol pressures all other powders in this table are compared at—VihtaVuori Oy's rankings for shotgun/pistol type powders differ considerably from those shown here.

MEASURED POWDER DENSITY
1″ High Circular Column

—Powder— Name	Type	Listed Bulk Density	Container Dia. (ins.)	Standard Funnel	6″ Drop Tube	Max.	830 psi During	830 psi After	3320 psi During	3320 psi After
Accurate/Scot—										
N100	F	—	.357	0.445	0.497	0.550	54.3	53	—	—
			.410	0.477	0.509	0.543				
			.452	0.493	0.521	0.533				
#2 Imp.	B	—	.357	0.650	0.658	0.695	13.1	8	33.7	28
			.410	0.663	0.676	0.707				
			.452	0.677	0.691	0.715				
S1000	F	—	.357	0.450	0.486	0.497	34.3	23	52.3	45
			.410	0.469	0.489	0.497				
			.452	0.465	0.483	0.488				
Scot D	F	—	.357	0.460	0.470	0.501	29.4	15	48.1	40
			.410	0.483	0.509	0.531				
			.452	0.472	0.517	0.528				
453	B	0.555	.357	0.624	0.656	0.658	14.8	8	37.8	33
			.410	0.631	0.656	0.690				
			.452	0.634	0.660	0.686				
#5	B	0.950	.357	0.893	0.897	0.920	19.6	10	34.3	28
			.410	0.861	0.943	0.955				
			.452	0.875	0.943	0.974				
#7	B	0.985	.357	0.457	1.006	1.047	7.7	2	17.3	8
			.410	0.969	1.037	1.063				
			.452	0.965	1.019	1.064				
#9	B	0.975	.357	0.931	0.950	0.987	8.5	2	18.6	10
			.410	0.937	0.963	0.986				
			.452	0.946	0.967	0.988				
1680	B	0.950	.357	0.976	1.009	1.047	7.5	2	17.7	10
			.410	0.972	1.026	1.060				
			.452	0.979	1.038	1.061				
Hercules—										
Bullseye	F	0.620	.357	0.607	0.609	0.658	44.9	43	—	—
			.410	0.605	0.656	0.707				
			.452	0.608	0.667	0.689				
Red Dot	F	0.480	.357	0.400	0.447	0.467	54.9	50	—	—
			.410	0.409	0.455	0.477				
			.452	0.417	0.474	0.485				
Green Dot	F	0.515	.357	0.434	0.486	0.520	50.6	46	—	—
			.410	0.469	0.517	0.528				
			.452	0.488	0.514	0.533				
Unique	F	0.610	.357	0.497	0.542	0.568	43.4	43	—	—
			.410	0.514	0.554	0.565				
			.452	0.542	0.578	0.587				
Herco	F	0.570	.357	0.482	0.538	0.550	41.9	35	—	—
			.410	0.503	0.545	0.562				
			.452	0.505	0.564	0.571				
Blue Dot	F	0.780	.357	0.665	0.755	0.759	25.4	15	44.0	40
			.410	0.707	0.744	0.766				
			.452	0.708	0.764	0.783				
2400	F	0.870	.357	0.837	0.871	0.901	17.1	13	34.1	30
			.410	0.844	0.898	0.909				
			.452	0.842	0.901	0.910				
Hodgdon—										
Clays	F	0.475	.357	0.407	0.464	0.475	39.0	35	—	—
			.410	0.449	0.486	0.494				
			.452	0.451	0.498	0.503				
HP38	B	0.635	.357	0.639	0.725	0.748	27.4	20	45.3	40
			.410	0.687	0.724	0.735				
			.452	0.693	0.731	0.757				
Inter	F	0.525	.357	0.479	0.538	0.557	36.4	30	—	—
			.410	0.506	0.548	0.554				
			.452	0.509	0.554	0.559				

MEASURED POWDER DENSITY
1" High Circular Column

—Powder— Name	Type	Listed Bulk Density	Container Dia. (ins.)	Standard Funnel	6" Drop Tube	Max.	—Reduction in Volume— 830 psi During	After	3320 psi During	After
Hodgdon—										
Univ	F	0.650	.357	0.591	0.624	0.658	23.6	15	41.9	36
			.410	0.608	0.670	0.682				
			.452	0.618	0.672	0.684				
HS6	F	0.945	.357	0.893	0.957	1.002	12.3	5	27.0	18
			.410	0.901	0.952	0.997				
			.452	0.903	0.974	1.004				
HS7	B	0.990	.357	0.897	0.972	1.021	12.3	5	24.4	20
			.410	0.937	0.947	1.031				
			.452	0.915	1.000	1.040				
H4227	B	0.870	.357	0.811	0.879	0.897	11.8	6	24.0	15
			.410	0.827	0.889	0.898				
			.452	0.837	.0899	0.908				
H110	B	0.975	.357	0.987	1.034	1.084	6.8	1	17.7	5
			.410	0.994	1.054	1.088				
			.452	0.995	1.057	1.090				
IMR—										
PB	F	0.555	.357	0.512	0.583	0.607	20.1	13	41.5	33
			.410	0.537	0.594	0.611				
			.452	0.535	0.594	0.614				
700-X	F	0.500	.357	0.471	0.523	0.583	56.0	48	—	—
			.410	0.483	0.528	0.585				
			.452	0.488	0.554	0.583				
800-X	F	—	.357	0.572	0.647	0.692	49.8	45	—	—
			.410	0.594	0.653	0.705				
			.452	0.587	0.660	0.712				
SR4756	F	0.610	.357	0.587	0.665	0.684	18.6	8	38.1	25
			.410	0.611	0.670	0.682				
			.452	0.606	0.670	0.679				
IMR4227	T[1]	0.870	.357	0.852	0.879	0.931	10.6	4	21.5	10
			.410	0.869	0.946	0.955				
			.452	0.875	0.934	0.946				
Winchester—										
WST	B	0.535	.357	0.516	0.564	0.602	26.4	18	47.1	40
			.410	0.545	0.574	0.619				
			.452	0.542	0.580	0.620				
WSL	B	0.765	.357	0.680	0.781	0.826	36.0	34	—	—
			.410	0.722	0.770	0.815				
			.452	0.712	0.776	0.815				
231	B	0.700	.357	0.645	0.714	0.748	28.4	20	45.5	40
			.410	0.690	0.724	0.756				
			.452	0.691	0.733	0.750				
WSF	B	0.770	.357	0.707	0.781	0.821	32.3	30	46.6	40
			.410	0.736	0.770	0.824				
			.452	0.731	0.792	0.833				
WAP	B	—	.357	0.800	0.841	0.875	12.8	2	28.0	15
			.410	0.815	0.855	0.889				
			.452	0.811	0.856	0.882				
540	B	0.950	.357	0.893	0.961	0.998	14.5	4	29.2	20
			.410	0.920	0.972	1.009				
			.452	0.920	0.995	1.017				
571	B	0.955	.357	0.905	0.968	1.021	14.1	4	28.4	19
			.410	0.929	0.991	1.020				
			.452	0.941	1.007	1.031				
296	B	0.975	.357	0.964	1.024	1.054	8.2	1	18.3	5
			.410	0.983	1.045	1.068				
			.452	0.982	1.054	1.073				

MEASURED POWDER DENSITY
Specified Case, Level Full

—Powder— Name	Type	Listed Bulk Density	Container Dia. (ins.)	Standard Funnel	6" Drop Tube	Max.	830 psi During	After	3320 psi During	After
Accurate/Scott—										
1680	B	0.950	222 Rem.	0.998	1.030	1.058	6.4	1.5	17.0	7.5
			308 Win.	0.984	1.026	1.054	6.4	1.5	17.0	7.5
			7mm Rem. Mag.	0.986	1.041	1.053	6.4	1.5	17.0	7.5
2230	B	—	222 Rem.	0.998	1.041	1.062	8.1	2.0	20.7	8.5
			308 Win.	1.011	1.047	1.065	8.1	2.0	20.7	8.5
			7mm Rem. Mag.	1.022	1.058	1.071	8.1	2.0	20.7	8.5
2460	B	0.975	222 Rem.	0.928	0.965	0.991	8.3	3.0	21.2	12.0
			308 Win.	0.928	0.965	0.977	8.3	3.0	21.2	12.0
			7mm Rem. Mag.	0.943	0.978	0.993	8.3	3.0	21.2	12.0
2495BR	T1	—	222 Rem.	0.839	0.871	0.885	9.4	2.0	20.9	10.5
			308 Win.	0.876	0.910	0.913	9.4	2.0	20.9	10.5
			7mm Rem. Mag.	0.887	0.918	0.929	9.4	2.0	20.9	10.5
2520	B	0.970	222 Rem.	0.945	0.988	1.012	7.7	1.5	20.0	12.0
			308 Win.	0.963	1.009	1.023	7.7	1.5	20.0	12.0
			7mm Rem. Mag.	0.968	1.025	1.029	7.7	1.5	20.0	12.0
2700	B	0.960	222 Rem.	0.938	0.963	0.988	8.2	1.5	20.2	10.0
			308 Win.	0.954	0.982	1.002	8.2	1.5	20.2	10.0
			7mm Rem. Mag.	0.956	1.004	1.018	8.2	1.5	20.2	10.0
4350	T2	0.950	222 Rem.	0.850	0.878	0.896	10.4	4.0	22.9	12.0
			308 Win.	0.888	0.916	0.929	10.4	4.0	22.9	12.0
			7mm Rem. Mag.	0.905	0.925	0.938	10.4	4.0	22.9	12.0
3100	T2	0.945	222 Rem.	0.853	0.896	0.903	8.8	2.5	20.2	9.0
			308 Win.	0.893	0.921	0.930	8.8	2.5	20.2	9.0
			7mm Rem. Mag.	0.915	0.935	0.942	8.8	2.5	20.2	9.0
8700	B	0.960	222 Rem.	0.924	0.977	1.019	7.8	2.0	20.4	10.0
			308 Win.	0.942	1.002	1.035	7.8	2.0	20.4	10.0
			7mm Rem. Mag.	0.958	1.006	1.041	7.8	2.0	20.4	10.0
Hercules—										
2400	F	0.870	222 Rem.	0.846	0.878	0.910	16.3	9.0	32.5	26.0
			308 Win.	0.846	0.890	0.933	16.3	9.0	32.5	26.0
			7mm Rem. Mag.	0.854	0.909	0.936	16.3	9.0	32.5	26.0
RL-7	T3	0.890	222 Rem.	0.843	0.899	0.917	10.5	3.0	22.9	14.0
			308 Win.	0.879	0.923	0.937	10.5	3.0	22.9	14.0
			7mm Rem. Mag.	0.889	0.935	0.950	10.5	3.0	22.9	14.0
RL-12	T3	1.000	222 Rem.	0.889	0.928	0.956	9.5	2.0	21.2	10.5
			308 Win.	0.916	0.960	0.977	9.5	2.0	21.2	10.5
			7mm Rem. Mag.	0.940	0.979	0.991	9.5	2.0	21.2	10.5
RL-15	T3	0.920	222 Rem.	0.867	0.913	0.935	10.6	5.0	22.3	12.0
			308 Win.	0.911	0.951	0.956	10.6	5.0	22.3	12.0
			7mm Rem. Mag.	0.920	6.949	0.959	10.6	5.0	22.3	12.0
RL-19	T2	0.890	222 Rem.	0.864	0.903	0.917	13.3	7.0	26.5	17.5
			308 Win.	0.895	0.940	0.951	13.3	7.0	26.5	17.5
			7mm Rem. Mag.	0.920	0.945	0.957	13.3	7.0	26.5	17.5
RL-22	T2	0.890	222 Rem.	0.871	0.896	0.928	13.0	7.5	25.9	18.0
			308 Win.	0.907	0.940	0.947	13.0	7.5	25.9	18.0
			7mm Rem. Mag.	0.923	0.946	0.959	13.0	7.5	25.9	18.0
Hodgdon—										
H4227	T3	0.870	222 Rem.	0.818	0.871	0.882	11.8	6.0	24.0	15.0
			308 Win.	0.837	0.876	0.890	11.8	6.0	24.0	15.0
			7mm Rem. Mag.	0.843	0.887	0.898	11.8	6.0	24.0	15.0
H110	B	0.975	222 Rem.	0.995	1.027	1.069	6.8	1.0	17.7	5.0
			308 Win.	1.009	1.046	1.084	6.8	1.0	17.7	5.0
			7mm Rem. Mag.	1.006	1.058	1.090	6.8	1.0	17.7	5.0
H4198	T1	0.880	222 Rem.	0.776	0.814	0.822	10.8	2.5	24.1	10.0
			308 Win.	0.807	0.844	0.849	10.8	2.5	24.1	10.0
			7mm Rem. Mag.	0.820	0.847	0.854	10.8	2.5	24.1	10.0
H4198SC	T2	—	222 Rem.	0.850	0.896	0.906	9.5	2.5	20.3	10.0
			308 Win.	0.890	0.923	0.930	9.5	2.5	20.3	10.0
			7mm Rem. Mag.	0.892	0.933	0.946	9.5	2.5	20.3	10.0

MEASURED POWDER DENSITY
Specified Case, Level Full

—Powder— Name	Type	Listed Bulk Density	Container Dia. (ins.)	Standard Funnel	6" Drop Tube	Max.	830 psi During	830 psi After	3320 psi During	3320 psi After
Hodgdon—										
H322	T3	—	222 Rem.	0.885	0.917	0.931	9.4	3.0	18.6	8.0
			308 Win.	0.897	0.942	0.953	9.4	3.0	18.6	8.0
			7mm Rem. Mag.	0.906	0.959	0.968	9.4	3.0	18.6	8.0
BL-C2	B	1.035	222 Rem.	0.991	1.041	1.065	6.5	1.5	16.3	6.0
			308 Win.	1.016	1.056	1.081	6.5	1.5	16.3	6.0
			7mm Rem. Mag.	1.020	1.064	1.084	6.5	1.5	16.3	6.0
H335	B	1.035	222 Rem.	0.991	1.037	1.058	6.3	1.5	15.7	5.5
			308 Win.	1.005	1.035	1.070	6.3	1.5	15.7	5.5
			7mm Rem. Mag.	1.011	1.055	1.076	6.3	1.5	15.7	5.5
H4895	T2	0.920	222 Rem.	0.878	0.913	0.924	9.5	3.5	19.1	10.5
			308 Win.	0.898	0.942	0.947	9.5	3.5	19.1	10.5
			7mm Rem. Mag.	0.913	0.949	0.959	9.5	3.5	19.1	10.5
H380	B	0.967	222 Rem.	0.917	0.952	0.981	6.9	1.5	17.4	5.5
			308 Win.	0.944	0.974	1.007	6.9	1.5	17.4	5.5
			7mm Rem. Mag.	0.951	0.981	1.008	6.9	1.5	17.4	5.5
H414	B	0.995	222 Rem.	0.935	0.988	1.027	6.8	1.5	17.0	7.0
			308 Win.	0.951	1.004	1.040	6.8	1.5	17.0	7.0
			7mm Rem. Mag.	0.957	1.018	1.049	6.8	1.5	17.0	7.0
H4350SC	T3	—	222 Rem.	0.899	0.935	0.945	8.9	3.0	20.2	10.0
			308 Win.	0.926	0.963	0.969	8.9	3.0	20.2	10.0
			7mm Rem. Mag.	0.940	0.982	0.988	8.9	3.0	20.2	10.0
H450	B	0.990	222 Rem.	0.928	0.963	0.981	7.9	1.5	19.0	8.5
			308 Win.	0.944	0.981	1.002	7.9	1.5	19.0	8.5
			7mm Rem. Mag.	0.947	1.001	1.014	7.9	1.5	19.0	8.5
H4831	T2	0.930	222 Rem.	0.892	0.913	0.928	8.6	2.0	20.0	9.0
			308 Win.	0.930	0.953	0.964	8.6	2.0	20.0	9.0
			7mm Rem. Mag.	0.945	0.964	0.974	8.6	2.0	20.0	9.0
H4831SC	T3	—	222 Rem.	0.906	0.928	0.945	9.0	2.5	19.7	9.5
			308 Win.	0.940	0.958	0.976	9.0	2.5	19.7	9.5
			7mm Rem. Mag.	0.952	0.982	0.992	9.0	2.5	19.7	9.5
H1000	T3	—	222 Rem.	0.889	0.942	0.952	8.8	3.0	19.2	10.0
			308 Win.	0.937	0.965	0.981	8.8	3.0	19.2	10.0
			7mm Rem. Mag.	0.947	0.985	0.992	8.8	3.0	19.2	10.0
H570	T3	—	222 Rem.	0.857	0.899	0.917	8.2	1.5	19.5	7.5
			308 Win.	0.912	0.939	0.947	8.2	1.5	19.5	7.5
			7mm Rem. Mag.	0.927	0.959	0.972	8.2	1.5	19.5	7.5
H870	B	0.965	222 Rem.	0.942	0.984	0.998	9.8	2.0	18.6	6.5
			308 Win.	0.958	1.005	1.023	9.8	2.0	18.6	6.5
			7mm Rem. Mag.	0.964	1.020	1.030	9.8	2.0	18.6	6.5
IMR—										
IMR4227	T3	0.870	222 Rem.	0.860	0.910	0.928	10.6	4.0	21.5	10.0
			308 Win.	0.883	0.940	0.942	10.6	4.0	21.5	10.0
			7mm Rem. Mag.	0.884	0.946	0.961	10.6	4.0	21.5	10.0
IMR4198	T1	0.850	222 Rem.	0.793	0.832	0.850	10.6	2.5	23.6	11.5
			308 Win.	0.833	0.874	0.884	10.6	2.5	23.6	11.5
			7mm Rem. Mag.	0.844	0.884	0.891	10.6	2.5	23.6	11.5
IMR3031	T2	0.880	222 Rem.	0.814	0.860	0.885	10.2	2.5	23.9	12.5
			308 Win.	0.853	0.893	0.902	10.2	2.5	23.9	12.5
			7mm Rem. Mag.	0.858	0.894	0.904	10.2	2.5	23.9	12.5
IMR4895	T2	0.920	222 Rem.	0.882	0.924	0.942	8.8	2.5	19.6	9.0
			308 Win.	0.907	0.949	0.961	8.8	2.5	19.6	9.0
			7mm Rem. Mag.	0.929	0.965	0.972	8.8	2.5	19.6	9.0
IMR4064	T1	0.905	222 Rem.	0.829	0.871	0.885	9.9	3.0	22.3	10.5
			308 Win.	0.872	0.905	0.920	9.9	3.0	22.3	10.5
			7mm Rem. Mag.	0.885	0.923	0.930	9.9	3.0	22.3	10.5
IMR4320	T3	0.935	222 Rem.	0.903	0.942	0.952	8.3	2.0	18.5	8.0
			308 Win.	0.923	0.974	0.981	8.3	2.0	18.5	8.0
			7mm Rem. Mag.	0.942	0.979	0.992	8.3	2.0	18.5	8.0

MEASURED POWDER DENSITY
Specified Case, Level Full

—Powder— Name	Type	Listed Bulk Density	Container Dia. (ins.)	Standard Funnel	6″ Drop Tube	Max.	—Reduction in Volume— 830 psi During	After	3320 psi During	After
IMR—										
IMR4350	T2	0.910	222 Rem.	0.853	0.885	0.899	9.3	2.5	21.1	13.0
			308 Win.	0.890	0.930	0.942	9.3	2.5	21.1	13.0
			7mm Rem. Mag.	0.910	0.932	0.949	9.3	2.5	21.1	13.0
IMR4831	T2	0.930	222 Rem.	0.864	0.889	0.910	8.8	2.5	20.0	8.0
			308 Win.	0.898	0.926	0.939	8.8	2.5	20.0	8.0
			7mm Rem. Mag.	0.917	0.946	0.958	8.8	2.5	20.0	8.0
IMR7828	T2	—	222 Rem.	0.857	0.896	0.913	9.8	4.0	20.8	10.0
			308 Win.	0.900	0.937	0.953	9.8	4.0	20.8	10.0
			7mm Rem. Mag.	0.913	0.953	0.964	9.8	4.0	20.8	10.0
Norma—										
N205	T2	—	222 Rem.	0.928	0.975	0.995	9.3	3.0	20.2	8.0
			308 Win.	0.975	1.012	1.018	9.3	3.0	20.2	8.0
			7mm Rem. Mag.	0.981	1.025	1.034	9.3	3.0	20.2	8.0
VihtaVuori—										
N133	T3	0.88	222 Rem.	0.853	0.896	0.927	9.1	2.0	18.8	8.0
			308 Win.	0.883	0.923	0.944	9.1	2.0	18.8	8.0
			7mm Rem. Mag.	0.887	0.930	0.950	9.1	2.0	18.8	8.0
N140	T3	0.92	222 Rem.	0.867	0.919	0.935	9.3	2.0	19.2	8.0
			308 Win.	0.902	0.951	0.972	9.3	2.0	19.2	8.0
			7mm Rem. Mag.	0.924	0.961	0.975	9.3	2.0	19.2	8.0
N150	T3	0.91	222 Rem.	0.860	0.882	0.920	8.6	2.0	18.5	6.0
			308 Win.	0.902	0.940	0.956	8.6	2.0	18.5	6.0
			7mm Rem. Mag.	0.915	0.943	0.954	8.6	2.0	18.5	6.0
N160	T3	0.94	222 Rem.	0.885	0.935	0.952	8.8	2.0	19.0	7.0
			308 Win.	0.919	0.961	0.972	8.8	2.0	19.0	7.0
			7mm Rem. Mag.	0.939	0.971	0.984	8.8	2.0	19.0	7.0
N170	T3	—	222 Rem.	0.896	0.935	0.953	8.6	2.0	19.0	7.0
			308 Win.	0.939	0.977	0.991	8.6	2.0	19.0	7.0
			7mm Rem. Mag.	0.961	0.985	0.995	8.6	2.0	19.0	7.0
24N64	T3	0.84	222 Rem.	0.818	0.867	0.889	9.0	2.0	20.1	7.0
			308 Win.	0.882	0.905	0.918	9.0	2.0	20.1	7.0
			7mm Rem. Mag.	0.895	0.905	0.924	9.0	2.0	20.1	7.0
Winchester—										
296	B	0.975	222 Rem.	0.963	0.991	1.062	8.2	1.0	18.3	5.0
			308 Win.	0.984	1.026	1.068	8.2	1.0	18.3	5.0
			7mm Rem. Mag.	0.985	1.023	1.069	8.2	1.0	18.3	5.0
748	B	0.995	222 Rem.	0.956	0.984	1.051	7.1	1.5	17.2	8.0
			308 Win.	0.975	1.019	1.067	7.1	1.5	17.2	8.0
			7mm Rem. Mag.	0.972	1.044	1.074	7.1	1.5	17.2	8.0
760	B	1.000	222 Rem.	0.931	0.984	1.035	7.3	1.5	17.8	7.5
			308 Win.	0.944	0.995	1.044	7.3	1.5	17.8	7.5
			7mm Rem. Mag.	0.963	1.000	1.044	7.3	1.5	17.8	7.5
WMR	B	—	222 Rem.	0.889	0.942	0.988	7.6	2.0	18.7	9.5
			308 Win.	0.921	0.965	0.998	7.6	2.0	18.7	9.5
			7mm Rem. Mag.	0.926	0.970	1.011	7.6	2.0	18.7	9.5

Listed Bulk Density: As advertised or otherwise estimated, in grams per cubic centimeter (water is 1.00); Reduction in Volume: Percent Reduction in total column volume after listed pressure was applied long enough so that further change was minimal. Pressure was applied to the open top of a cylindrical column of presettled powder; During: Volume loss while pressure applied; After: Stable loss of volume after pressure removed; Experimental Density (measured in listed case or in circular column about 1″ high and of specified diameter): Standard Funnel = Powder dumped through standard handloader's funnel, excess struck off even with top of case; 6″ Drop Tube = Powder dumped through 6″ drop tube, excess struck off even with top of case; Maximum = Powder settled via vibrations as much as possible, excess struck off even with top of case

B = Ball Type (may include any combination of spheres and flattened spheres and may also be porous); PB = Porous Base (porous disks); F = Flake or very short disks (disks: may have one central perforation, may be porous and may be non-flat); T1 = Short tubular granules (Diameter similar to length); T2 = Medium tubular granules (Diameter about one-half length); T3 = Long tubular granules (Diameter less than one-half length)

Chapter 7

BULLET TYPES & PERFORMANCE

WHILE THERE ARE many types of bullets in common use, all share the same basic functions. First, bullets have to obturate the bore, that is, seal against the pressure of propellant gases. Second, bullets must be strong enough to withstand the accelerating forces that engender muzzle velocity and rotation. Third, to provide accuracy, bullets have to be balanced and aerodynamically stable. Finally, bullets have to perform properly upon impact.

Composition, Construction and Characteristics

Bullets available to handloaders are most often made of copper and lead alloys. Most are either homogeneous (composed entirely of one of these alloys), or have a thin jacket of copper alloy partially or totally enclosing a lead or lead-alloy core.

There are two basic types of homogeneous bullets. The most common is simply cast or swaged from either pure lead or an alloy composed of lead, antimony and possibly tin. Shooters have been using these for hundreds of years. More recent are bullets of copper or bronze. These are either swaged, hammer-forged or lathe-turned.

Homogeneous hard bronze bullets are non-expanding designs, called solids. Sophisticated design features allow one type of solid copper bullet, the Barnes-X, to provide dependable controlled expansion. Soft lead-alloy bullets with a hollow point are designed to provide expansion.

Hard copper-alloy (bronze) bullets are so durable that they can dependably withstand impact with almost any bone on any animal without deforming or fracturing. However, these bullets are so tough that they shouldn't be used in extremely thin barrels such as commonly found on British double rifles.

Soft copper bullets can be designed and constructed to deliver controlled expansion. Both Barnes-X and Winchester FS (Fail Safe) hunting bullets are essentially pure copper. Winchester's FS bullets have a complicated base cavity that contains steel, lead and brass inserts, but these components do not directly enter into the bullet's terminal performance. Both the X and the FS offer nearly 100-percent weight retention, dependable expansion across a wide range of impact velocities, and deep penetration with superior wounding potential.

Cast bullets are widely available from regional manufacturers, but with the proper equipment you can easily make them at home. This approach offers an almost limitless variety of designs, using standard or custom moulds. Affordability is the biggest advantage of cast bullets, but in certain applications these are also the most accurate.

Swaged lead bullets are usually made of pure lead. Many regional and national bullet makers offer swaged bullets, typically in target designs. With the proper (expensive) equipment and supplies, you can swage solid lead or jacketed bullets at home. The potential advantages of swaged bullets include low cost and superior accuracy.

Jacketed bullets also come in several varieties. Designs include non-expanding, controlled-expanding and fragmenting. Typical bullet jackets are 0.010″-0.040″ thick, and the manufacturers control jacket thickness and other characteristics to achieve desired terminal performance.

The usual jacket material is gilding metal, an alloy of 95-percent copper and 5-percent zinc. This highly malleable and inexpensive metal reduces friction between bullet and barrel, limiting metal fouling in

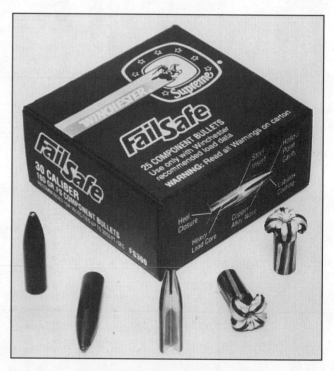

Winchester's Fail Safe bullets feature a pressure and fouling reducing coating and other sophisticated design characteristics.

the bore. It is strong enough to withstand high pressure and velocity without stripping in the rifling or significantly deforming under the stresses of acceleration as the cartridge is fired.

Several bullet makers use pure copper jackets for high-performance expanding bullets. Compared to gilding metal, copper is more ductile and resistant to fragmentation. However, copper generates considerably more friction and, thus, more bore fouling. Other copper alloys, steel and aluminum are also sometimes used for bullet jackets.

Non-expanding jacketed bullets often use a very thick copper-alloy jacket or a copper-clad steel jacket. This latter type allows the combination of a strong steel jacket to support the weak lead core without subjecting the gun's bore to the abrasive effects of steel.

Non-expanding bullets fall into two general categories of intended use. Those for which terminal performance is not a consideration, like target bullets, have comparatively thin jackets of gliding metal and are sometimes closed at the front and open at the back (FMJ). When a bullet has to withstand the stresses of impact without suffering significant deformation, especially when used on dangerous game, the jacket is usually very thick and can be of copper, gliding metal or copper-clad steel. These are also FMJ designs, but the jacket is usually partially folded over the core, locking it in place.

Controlled-expansion bullets typically have gilding-metal jackets. Some have plastic or metal inserts in the nose (Nosler's Ballistic Tip and Remington's Bronze Point) that resist deformation from handling and recoil and, in some instances, facilitate expansion. Controlled

Like all target bullets, this 174-grain .311″ Sierra Match King (above) is not designed for hunting. Terminal performance cannot be counted on to cleanly bag your game.

This Sierra hunting bullet (below), 125-grain .311″, is designed to provide dependable terminal performance. It is intended for use in hunting small species of big game.

expansion is desirable for most big game hunting and self-defense bullets. Various jacket features are used to control the rate and degree of expansion.

Fragmenting bullets usually have thin jackets of gilding metal. These, too, sometimes have a plastic insert in the nose, like Hornady's V-Max and Nosler's Ballistic Tip. Fragmenting bullets are particularly desirable for varmint hunting because they lessen the chance of ricochet and help to ensure a quick kill.

Lead-alloy bullet cores are the most common because they are affordable, ductile and dense. Use of this material in bullet manufacture is so common that it has long been named "bullet metal," and it is a variable alloy of lead, antimony and, sometimes, tin. Composition is usually 91- to 98.5-percent lead with 1.5- or 6-percent antimony and, sometimes, 1- to 3-percent tin added. Though rarely used, adding about 1-percent silver improves bullet metal's casting characteristics. A bullet's terminal performance can be altered by adjusting various characteristics of the bullet core. Alloy composition affects core hardness and ductility. So does heat-treating, hollow-pointing and cutting.

Pure lead is the material of choice for the cores of several high-performance jacketed controlled-expansion bullets, typically those with pure copper jackets. Lead is more ductile and resists fragmentation better than lead alloy.

To ensure that the jacket supports the very ductile pure lead core of these high-performance bullets and that they stay together after impact, manufacturers often bond the core and jacket together. Soldering is a common method. In Swift's A-Frame bullet, for example, the bullet's nose core is inserted into the clean and fluxed opening at the front of the copper jacket. A propane flame then heats this assembly, melting the core and making a complete bond. This process also anneals both

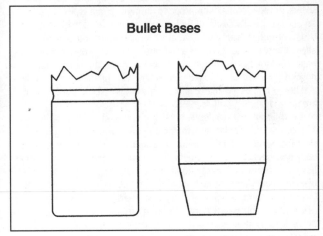

Bullet Bases

(Above) Bullet bases are generally of two types, flat base and boattail. The flat base is easier and less expensive to manufacture. The boattail shape cuts air drag, which helps the bullet retain its velocity.

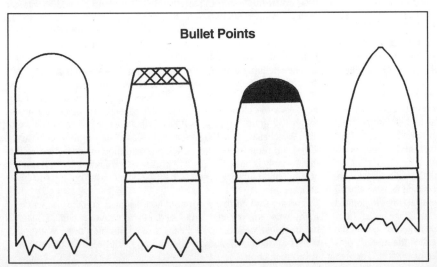

Bullet Points

Four common nose shapes (left to right): round- or blunt-nosed solid, commonly used in the hunting of large dangerous game. Bullets of this type are made of homogeneous bronze or covered with a full jacket of gilding-clad steel. Next is a flat-nosed softpoint, a design used in tubular-magazine rifles, such as Marlin's lever actions. The flat point won't set off the primer of the round in front of it. Third is a round-nose softpoint, used in low-velocity cartridges. Fourth is a spirepoint, shown full-metal-cased, typical of military bullets. This is the most common hunting bullet shape.

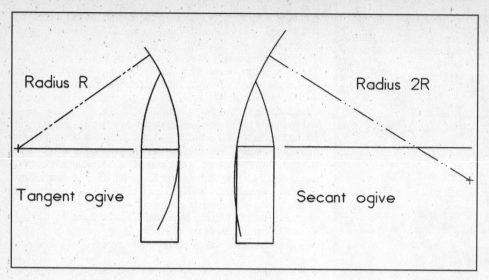

The nose of the bullet is called the "ogive," an architectural term meaning pointed arch. The two most common types are the tangent ogive (left) and the secant ogive. The center of the arc forming the nose profile of the tangent ogive is exactly lined up with the end of the bullet shank, and therefore the bullet nose tangentially meets the shank and smoothly blends into it. In the secant ogive, the arc center forming the nose profile is behind the shank shoulder, and the arc thus generated meets the bullet shank at an angle. The radius of the arc is also longer, typically twice as long, resulting in a more pointed nose. This design tends to lengthen the bullet shank, which might make the resultant bullets more accurate.

core and jacket, ensuring maximum malleability and minimizing fragmentation.

Totally jacketed, non-expanding bullets are growing in popularity. Combined with the use of lead-free primers, they can eliminate airborne lead contamination at indoor target ranges. These bullets have a lead-core with an electroplated copper jacket, typically about 0.010" thick, that covers the bullet's entire surface.

Bullet Shape

We can classify most bullets as either blunt, round-nosed or pointed. These include special short-range target designs, long-range target designs, shapes intended to function properly through certain types of guns, and several specifically designed for hunting or self-defense purposes.

Blunt bullets come in several styles. Made of either lead or lead alloy, the wadcutter (WC) is a flat-pointed bullet used for short-range handgun target competition and practice. When the sharp edge at the nose of a wadcutter hits a paper target, it cuts out a clean circular hole. At shorter ranges, you can easily see the holes in the target. Wadcutters are non-expanding bullets.

Lead-alloy semi-wadcutters (SWC) are another blunt bullet style. These are very popular for handgun hunting, target shooting and target practice. Semi-wadcutters combine a sharp shoulder with a truncated-cone nose section. These bullets also cut nice round holes on paper targets and shoot accurately to intermediate ranges. SWCs are also effective handgun hunting bullets and are generally non-expanding.

A third blunt bullet growing in popularity is the truncated cone (TC). These are popular in both handgun and rifle use, and can be either lead, lead alloy or jacketed. When used in semi-automatic pistols, TCs can offer the superior feeding characteristics of round-nose bullets, but often have superior terminal ballistics. These, too, are non-expanding bullets.

The round nose (RN) bullet is commonly used in semi-automatic pistols because it can provide superior functioning and dependability. Typical construction is lead, lead alloy or jacketed. These are non-expanding bullets.

Pointed bullets fit a wide variety of applications, and manufacturers usually design varmint and big game hunting bullets to combine several features. Important considerations include dependable expansion, a relatively flat trajectory and minimal wind drift. Typically, these bullets are jacketed, sharp-pointed and, often, boat-tailed (taper-based).

Manufacturers use various nose shapes on pointed bullets. These are all generally referred to as spitzers or semi-spitzers (spitzer is a German term that means pointed). There are two important variables in pointed bullet shape. First is the length of the pointed portion of the bullet, from the beginning of the ogive to the bullet's tip. Second is the size of the flat portion of the bullet's tip (this flat area is called the meplat, pronouced *meh-play*). There are two common styles of spitzers. The first

uses what is called a tangent ogive radius; the second uses what is called a secant ogive radius; see the nearby illustration.

Improving a bullet's ability to pass through the air without losing velocity is beneficial, and this is accomplished by increasing the weight and adding a sharper point. The technical term for this measure of ballistic efficiency is ballistic coefficient (BC).

Ballistic coefficient is a measure of how little velocity a bullet will lose as it travels through the air. A *higher* BC indicates *less* velocity loss. Increasing BC allows the bullet to reach the target faster (less flight time), which reduces drop, crosswind deflection and the necessary lead on a moving target. In addition, the bullet is traveling faster; this increases delivered energy and momentum.

This leads us to a continuing misconception among hunters—that of the "brush-buster" cartridge. Contrary to popular belief, there is no such thing as a brush-buster cartridge or bullet type. Should a branch or twig get in the way of a shot, a high-velocity spitzer has exactly the same chance of reaching the target as a low-velocity round-nose bullet—very little. Regardless of folklore to the contrary, the 243 Winchester is just as likely to get the job done as the 45-70 Government, and testing has borne this out. For every example where the large low-velocity round-nosed bullet penetrated and found the target (rare) and the high-velocity spitzer failed to reach the target (very common), there was a counter-example of the opposite happening.

It is possible that certain bullet shapes might have a comparative advantage for certain types of impacts with certain types of obstacles. For example, a round-nosed bullet might be deflected less than a sharply pointed bullet by an impact grazing the edge of a small branch. Equally, a sharp-pointed bullet might be deflected less than a round-nose bullet by an impact more nearly centered on a somewhat larger branch. In any random shot fired through a maze of branches, it would be impossible to guess which bullet shape might be deflected the least. However, we can say that any encounter with a branch is almost certain to deflect any bullet enough to ensure that it will miss the target.

The one thing that seems constant in the tests was that heavily constructed bullets always stay on course better than more fragile bullets. This is not exactly a surprise, but it does suggest a surprising prediction. As a so-called brush-buster, a 270 Winchester shooting Barnes' tough 130-grain X bullet would likely be a better choice than either a 308 Winchester or a 300 Magnum loaded with a lightly constructed 220-grain round-nose. Nevertheless, the important point here is that there simply is no such thing as a brush-buster. Consequently, it makes absolutely no sense to choose a hunting bullet based on any such misconception.

Having said all this, I am no doubt destined to incur the wrath of many who "know better." As I said, testing proves me out. If you do not trust that, please, by all means, make your own tests. With a few weeks of dedicated study, you should be able to prove this result to your satisfaction.

Varmint Bullets

The basic idea behind a varmint bullet is to deliver the maximum amount of energy upon impact, and designing the bullet to disintegrate as rapidly as possible after impact is the best way to achieve this goal. As a useful by-product, most varmint bullets disintegrate when they hit any target at any reasonable range, which almost completely prevents ricochets.

Choosing which varmint bullet to use requires consideration of maximum rated velocity, if the bullet has one. After that, we recommend looking to the bullet that offers the flattest trajectory across the usable hunting range of the cartridge in question. That analysis requires comparison of ballistic coefficients (BC) and achievable muzzle velocities. In many instances, a lighter bullet with a lower BC will shoot flatter because it can achieve a higher initial velocity. Conversely, a heavier bullet often provides better performance at maximum range because it holds its velocity better. Bullets in the middle of the available weight range are usually the best choice.

An additional consideration is wind drift. When wind conditions include anything other than dead calm, it might be better to give up a bit of flatness in trajectory to significantly reduce potential wind drift errors. It is a fact that heavier bullets with higher BCs can exhibit less wind drift in reaching the same target under the same crosswind conditions, even when they take longer to reach the target. The most important factor is the bullet's BC. Wind drift is most closely related to the amount of velocity the bullet loses.

Historically, ranging errors have been a major consideration for varminters. Because of this, varminters have always placed a premium on muzzle velocity to keep bullet drop to a minimum. With the advent of affordable, portable and accurate laser rangefinders, this situation will almost certainly pass. Anyone who can afford to spend nearly $1000 on a proper long-range varmint-hunting rig will likely find little problem spending a few hundred dollars to own a device that can tell the exact range separating him from a tiny target. Accurate range information combined with accurate external ballistics data can virtually eliminate hold-over errors.

When accurate rangefinders become commonplace, we will likely see a shift toward heavier varmint bullets. Owing to higher BCs, heavier bullets can buck a crosswind better and will often reach distant targets carrying more velocity, in spite of an initial velocity handicap. Meanwhile, typical varmint loads invariably use the bullet weight that shoots flattest across the cartridge's usable range. For the same reason, bullet profile is a big factor.

In a sense, the final consideration for any varmint hunter is the accuracy the bullet can deliver. Regardless of other considerations, if the bullet will not provide the accuracy the shooter requires, it is the wrong choice. Figure out the best bullet from the trajectory and wind-drift perspective and then try that bullet for accuracy. If you can't find a load that shoots that bullet well enough in your rifle, try another. Typically there will be several very similar bullets from which to choose.

Hunters using a 222 Remington might find that Nosler's efficient 40-grain Ballistic Tip is their best choice among current bullets, based strictly on ballistic considerations. The 22-250 shooter would likely step up to bullets in the 50- to 55-grain range, and the 220 Swift shooter might find that 60-grain bullets garner the best overall results. For the varmint shooter, "best overall results" translates very simply to the fewest missed shots. It makes no difference why the shot missed—windage errors, range-estimation errors, alignment of the planets—in this game one judges all misses equally.

The pattern is similar in other calibers. The more muzzle velocity the chambering can offer, the heavier the bullet that is likely to give the best results. If you happen to run across a serious varmint hunter using her trusty 300 Magnum, it is almost a sure bet she will *not* be shooting 110-grain bullets! In that chambering, 125- or 130-grain bullets can shoot flatter with less wind drift across the usable varminting range. Therefore, heavier bullets are the better choice.

Keep in mind that various makers offer bullets designed specifical-ly for varminting, often with "speed limits" on the velocity. These bullets are designed to disintegrate on contact with anything other than air. Before choosing one of these lightly constructed bullets, consider its velocity limitation. If your rifle can drive a bullet of that weight faster than the speed limit, you will either have to step up to a similar but thicker-jacketed counterpart (where available) or load down to the velocity limit. Driving these bullets too fast will result in poor accuracy or in-flight disintegration. Also note that a faster-than-normal rifling twist can make a big difference here. Expect fragile varmint bullets to fail at several hundred fps below the nominal maximum-rated velocity when used in a quick-twist barrel.

Judging the varmint accuracy of a given bullet is simple. Go to the range on a calm day and fire a series of groups on paper at 300 yards. Keep shooting until your results convince you the load can deliver almost every shot into a group that measures no larger than 1 to 1½ MOA. Occasional fliers are meaningless. A reasonable test group should include no fewer than twenty shots.

What should you look for in these groups? Think of it this way: Would you rather have a load that prints twenty bullets inside 4″ at 300 yards with a uniform pattern density or an otherwise similar load that will print eighteen out of twenty bullets inside 2½″ at 300 yards with two fliers that open the group to 7″? Remember, you are trying to maximize your percentage of solid hits.

The varmint hunter is a different breed. It is not uncommon for these shooters to fire hundreds of rounds through a prized rifle in the course of a good afternoon's shooting. The thought of taking a break from the action for bore cleaning—to improve accuracy or to extend barrel life—or to let the barrel cool down is furthest from the average varminter's mind. Because of the extended shot strings involved, the varmint hunter can find benefits in the use of moly-plated bullets, which reduce fouling. NECO can treat your bullets or provide a kit so you can do it yourself. Besides reducing fouling, many users report accuracy and trajectory advantages, and there is even evidence that using moly-plated bullets can significantly extend barrel life.

Similarly, these hunters should consider either BlackStar's barrel-treating process or NECO's Pressure Lapping system. Shooters report that barrels treated with either of these exhibit vastly less fouling and usually an increase in accuracy.

If you want to do terminal ballistics testing with varmint bullets, look for complete bullet disintegration in saturated telephone books with about 4″ of penetration. Remember, the less penetration, the better. The only reliable method is to test full-power loads at the range of your longest anticipated shots.

Big Game Bullets

Hypothetically, consider a small group of elk hunters sitting around the campfire the night before the big hunt. Ask each hunter what chambering he considers minimum for elk hunting and what bullet weight he recommends. Unless a fight breaks out in the meantime, you are likely to eventually get as many answers as there are faces staring back at you. And believe me, they will be staring.

When considering what constitutes an adequate energy level and proper bullet choice for hunting other species, opinions might not vary too much. Nevertheless, rest assured, opinions will always vary some. Above all, in considering this subject, the one fundamental tenet that too many so-called experts all too often disregard is that if you can't place your shot properly, no amount of "bigger gun" can possibly compensate.

Any hunter's first priority—some consider this an obligation—is to place every shot where it was intended to go. To put this very bluntly, a 60-grain Hornady HP from a 22-250 fired into the lungs of a big bull elk, broadside at 300 yards, will absolutely bag that animal more *humanely* than a 500-grain round-nose fired from a 460 Weatherby Magnum, broadside through the guts. That is a fact.

The priorities, in order, are correct shot placement, proper terminal bullet performance, and adequate *delivered* energy.

As for accuracy, for the big game hunter, I strongly advocate testing with three-shot groups. Choose a calm day and decide at what range

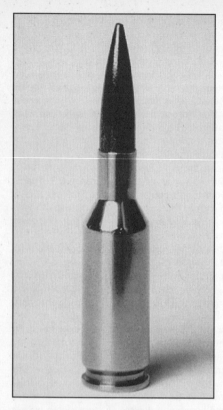

This is Norma's new Diamond line 6mm BR Norma loading. Featuring a moly-plated bullet (under license from NECO), this represents factory ammunition of superior quality. The handloader has to work hard to surpass the quality of today's best factory loads. Moly-plating reduces fouling and has myriad other benefits.

PRESSURE (FIRE) LAPPING™

INSTRUCTION MANUAL

NECO LAP™

Laboratory Grade Abrasive

Polish #1200

Post Office Box 427
Lafayette, CA 94549
Telephone: 510-450-0420

NECO's moly-plated bullets and their Pressure (Fire) Lapping kits are a team effort. Both were designed to substantially reduce fouling, and they deliver. Moly-plated bullets yield a profusion of other advantages.

you want to know what the load will do. If you often hunt where long shots are possible, you should try to find a place to set up targets at 300 yards.

During your tests, keep good records of how your loads perform. Fire a lot of three-shot groups from a cold barrel, then fire a few groups from a warm barrel; try a clean, cold barrel, and then a few from a barrel that has had a dozen rounds through it without cleaning. Then shoot groups in the crisp early morning air and in the warm afternoon after the gun has been lying in the sun for an hour. The compilation of the results will suggest what you can expect of your rifle and your load in the real world of hunting. Who cares what a hunting load and gun will do with ten-shot groups? If you have time to fire ten, or even five, shots at a game animal, you certainly will have had time to have properly placed your first shot.

Later, in this chapter, we will discuss a simple method anyone can use to compare terminal performance of various big game hunting bullets. This testing is worthwhile to any serious hunter.

Bullets for Thin-Skinned Game

For hunting lighter, or non-dangerous and thin-skinned, species of big game, the arguments are very much the same as for the varmint hunter. First, consider the applications intended for the bullet. Since this is among the most popular types of hunting, all major bullet producers and many of the custom bullet makers cater heavily to this field.

Obviously, except in large-caliber handguns, non-expanding bullets are a poor choice, and hunting with them is also illegal in many jurisdictions. To provide dependably quick kills, non-expanding bullets require shots to the brain or spine. Equally, you can't count on varmint bullets to anchor big game unless the shot happens to enter directly into the rib cage.

Hunters hold wildly varying opinions about what constitutes a proper big game bullet. One of the reasons for such disparity has to do with the variety of hunting habitats. If you find yourself working the thick brush and heavy timber, where you might only have a few seconds as your trophy moves through a clearing, you will certainly want a cannon-grade rifle delivering a heavy bullet that will absolutely break heavy bones and leave a gaping exit wound. Such a combination is almost certain to generate a good blood trail and prevent your trophy from traveling far.

This is the argument that Elmer Keith made. I suspect the conditions he encountered in the areas he habitually hunted had a lot to do with his beliefs on what constituted a proper elk rifle and load. As near as I can decipher the matter, based on our correspondence, Elmer believed the 338-378 Keith-Thompson Magnum, a cartridge capable of shooting a 250-grain bullet at about 3000 fps, was just about right for mule deer.

Conversely, if you are hunting the open parklands and sparse aspen groves, such as we find here in Western Colorado, you might feel completely confident using a 270 Winchester shooting 130-grain bullets of proper construction. I know three hunters who have collectively taken close to one hundred animals with similar load combinations and have yet to lose any animal they have shot. What is necessary to properly get the job done depends a great deal on the hunter's skill and the terrain hunted.

Jack O'Connor felt perfectly confident hunting elk with his 270 Winchester. He normally practiced an entirely different style of hunting in more open country, compared to Elmer Keith's country. In their day, folks generally viewed the controversy as a question of personality. However, I suspect the type of hunting each man practiced had more to do with their opinions as to what constituted a proper gun and load than any other factor. Certainly, both were expert hunters, and both collected more than a fair measure of game animals using their personal choice of equipment. Viewed from that perspective, both were right.

As to the question of what constitutes proper terminal performance, that depends. If you are hunting tall timber, you had better choose a bullet that you can be absolutely certain will achieve 100-percent pen-

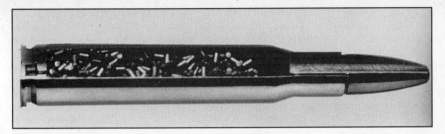

Speer's Grand Slam is an example of an exotic jacketed softpoint that can provide impressive terminal performance. Although it loses more energy getting to distant targets, compared to the best spitzer boattail hunting bullets, it holds together better at the far end—it can thereby deliver more dependable results. Here it is shown in a cutaway of Speer's new Nitrex load.

These various Barnes bullets are representative of an entire genre of premium-quality hunting bullets. These can provide terminal performance that vastly surpasses what standard jacketed softpoints or solids can deliver. Many makers—Barnes, Nosler and Speer, not to mention a host of specialty bullet producers—offer bullets promising superior big game performance. The expanded Barnes-X bullet should make the case very clear. X bullets deliver incredible performance. Penetration is all out of proportion to weight, and compared to a typical mushroomed JSP bullet, they do more damage as they penetrate.

etration. This increases the chances of a good blood trail. If you are hunting open country, a lighter bullet that will open up and deliver 100 percent of its energy into the vitals of the target will likely serve you better because it may generate a quicker kill and will have a flatter trajectory. You have to decide what your needs are and proceed from there.

What is our best advice? Choose the most powerful gun you can *properly* handle and practice with. Then, select a bullet that provides the appropriate terminal performance, taking into consideration the species you will be hunting and the conditions in your area. Lighter and more ballistically efficient bullets are a better choice, if they can do the job at the target. This is where premium-style designs shine, because they can allow use of a lighter and flatter shooting bullet that generates less recoil.

Having chosen the proper bullet *type*, next consider the general *quality* in regard to terminal performance characteristics. There are significant differences. Those concerned with "taking their best shot" will often choose one of the more expensive, premium-grade bullets, such as those offered by A-Square, Speer, Nosler, Barnes, Winchester and Swift. Premium-grade bullets can deliver much better terminal performance and usually cost only a few cents more apiece than conventional bullets. Compared to the cost of a hunt, this is insignificant.

This argument is especially meaningful when considering species bigger than mule deer. Here, delivered bullet energy per pound of animal is significantly limited. This fact suggests that the use of appropriate premium-grade bullets makes especially good sense. A slight increase in terminal performance might make all the difference in the instance of a bad hit or a shot taken from a bad angle. However, these bullets are generally not necessary for the lightest species of big game where it is possible to deliver substantial energy per pound of animal weight. Also, certain types of premium bullets don't offer as high a BC as more common big game bullets. This is a significant consideration if you anticipate shots at longer ranges.

We should also note that pronghorn hunters have special needs. First, owing to the extended unknown ranges often encountered,

pronghorn hunters should choose a bullet that can deliver the flattest possible trajectory. Second, since these are small animals that offer little resistance to a bullet and because of the long ranges involved (which considerably compromise impact velocities), look for a rapidly expanding bullet that can quickly transfer a great deal of energy. Lighter bullets of adequate caliber, designed to expand quickly, are in order for this game.

Obviously, appropriate bullet weight depends on the species one will hunt, but many have overrated this factor. For example, I have long preferred Sierra's 150-grain SBT for hunting both mule deer and elk with the 270 Winchester. Compared to the 130-grain Sierra SBT, the heavier bullet destroys much less meat on deer and seems to be a better choice for elk hunting. Long-range trajectory is very similar, and delivered energy at the extreme usable range is significantly higher with the 150-grainer. However, when hunting pronghorn, or the smallest species of deer, it is important not to choose a too-hard bullet—here, Sierra's 150 SBT would not likely be the best choice.

Once you have established a group of bullets you feel will provide acceptable terminal performance, look at the bullet's ballistic coefficient (BC). Most experts consider this a critically important characteristic in longer-range shooting. All other things being equal, regardless of range, a higher BC is always preferable.

Unlike the varminter, big game hunters are concerned with delivered energy. It is often desirable to give up a measure of trajectory flatness to deliver more energy at long range. Obviously, a bullet that can deliver 20-percent more energy at the reasonable maximum range the hunter might shoot would be a superior choice, even if it has a few inches more drop.

Before spending too much time on other considerations, it is a good idea to see if the selected bullet will offer the accuracy you feel you need. I like to see three-shot groups consistently under 1″ at 100 yards for my hunting rifles. Given the opportunity, I like to do my testing at 300 yards. If my load can keep three shots inside 4.5″ at that range, I figure the gun and load are not limiting my ability to place the shot properly for deer or elk hunting.

If you perform terminal ballistics testing with controlled-expansion hunting bullets, look for penetration of about 12″ to 18″ (less is acceptable for pronghorn hunting). Bullets performing at the lower end deliver more energy to the vitals, while those at the upper end will likely provide a better exit wound. Weight retention should be no less than 60 percent (premium bullets will approach 100 percent). Expanded bullet diameter should exceed 1.5 times the diameter of the original bullet, and typically the diameter will almost double.

We have to mention that the Winchester Fail Safe and Barnes-X are both capable of penetration all out of proportion to their weight. For this reason, many hunters who might be unfamiliar with these bullets will choose an entirely too-heavy FS or X for the job at hand. Keep in mind that, regardless of impact velocity, these bullets retain virtually 100 percent of their weight and generally penetrate farther than typical jacketed or even premium-quality jacketed bullets that might have weighed 50-percent more before impact.

Bullets for Heavy Non-Dangerous Game

Those hunting the heavier species of non-dangerous North American game—elk, and especially bison and moose—are well advised to consider using Barnes-X, Winchester Fail Safe or heavier premium-grade controlled-expansion bullets. When hunting one of these big critters, most folks don't want to carry or shoot the type of gun capable of

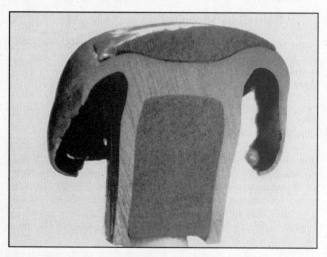

After a moderately high-velocity impact with saturated telephone books, Nosler's Partition typically looks like this. The expansion demonstrated here is representative of impacts at typical hunting ranges using typical cartridges.

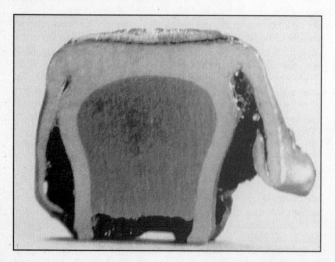

After a high-velocity impact with saturated telephone books. Nosler's Partition typically looks like this. The expansion demonstrated here is representative of impacts at very close range or with magnum cartridge velocities and moderate hunting ranges.

delivering sufficient energy to cause instant death unless the brain or spine is hit. These animals are simply too big.

I like to make a comparison based on energy delivered per pound of animal weight, which reasonably assesses a load's capability to stop an animal with any given hit. Comparing the 30-30 against mule deer with the 460 Weatherby Magnum against elk, and assuming the bullets stop in the animals, on this "energy per pound" basis the results are very similar. In rough figures, the 30-30 gives about 5 foot-pounds of energy per pound of deer; the 460 Weatherby about 6.5 foot-pounds for elk.

Any moose hunter is in a situation somewhat similar to the average Texas whitetail deer hunter using a 22 WMR—sure, it'll get the job done if the shot is well placed, but it certainly is not going to bowl the animal over unless the brain or spine is hit. Moose hunters can't deliver truly devastating energy to such a large target with any gun they could carry and shoot from the shoulder. The solution is to choose a solidly constructed bullet, preferably one that offers superior weight retention and penetration.

In the unusual circumstance where a long shot presents itself, if the target is among the largest species, good advice suggests the hunter refrain from taking the shot.

We strongly advise terminal ballistics testing of any load used in this type of hunting. Look for a minimum penetration of 15″ and bullets that give around 75-percent weight retention at realistic impact velocities. Diameter of the expanded bullet should be 1.5 times original bullet diameter and probably should not exceed 2 times.

Bullets for Thick-Skinned Dangerous Game

Thick-skinned dangerous game like elephant, rhino, Cape buffalo and hippo present entirely different problems. First, you should not try a shot unless you can guarantee proper placement, and target motion should carefully be considered. Second, like the moose, these thick-skinned animals are all quite large, they can bite back, and it takes a big gun to kill them quickly.

Used against a small elephant, the vaunted 700 Nitro Express (or any of the proprietary big chamberings producing in the neighborhood of 9000 foot-pounds of muzzle energy) would deliver about 1 foot-pound of energy per pound of animal. On a per-pound basis, that is just about what the 17 Remington would deliver to a good-sized bull elk, at point-blank range. To get into the *energy* range typically accepted for effective big game performance, the elephant hunter would have to at least *triple* the energy of the 700 Nitro—just about double what the 50 Browning Machine Gun cartridge delivers! Within acceptable recoil limits, such a gun would be simply too heavy to carry into the field, and few among us could possibly bring it to bear when the opportunity to use it presented itself.

Obviously, energy is not the whole story, but the common solution is to target the brain or spine with any shot, unless the range involved guarantees sufficient time for the hunter to safely use a heart or lung shot. Since all the animals in this class can easily survive long enough to travel a very great distance after a mortal wound is delivered to the thorax, the merit of such a shot seems highly questionable unless major bones are broken.

These animals have very tough and heavy hide, thick fat, thick and dense muscles, and heavy bone structures. For this reason, some professional dangerous game hunters and guides favor non-expanding bullets for use against all such game. One type of solid advocated by outdoor writer, experimenter and serious African hunter Karl Bosslemann is the flat-pointed style. His theory is that such bullets will break heavy bone without as much deflection as round-nosed solids. Bosslemann has been most successful using his personally modified solids. Trophy Bonded is now offering such a design.

As noted elsewhere in the text, do not use homogeneous bronze solids in any thin-barreled, double rifle. Investigation has linked this practice with the failure of several such rifles. Evidently, those bullets simply over-stress the thin portion of the bore, thereby rupturing the barrel.

Even the smallest carnivore is nothing to be trifled with! Choose a proper bullet to get the job done. Here, a bullet's ability to break heavy bone and still penetrate can be more important than expansion.

For hunting thick-skinned dangerous game, accuracy is no less important than for the varmint shooter. The target area might be very small, and a shot that misses the proper area can be more than just a bit embarrassing—all of these critters have a propensity for stomping two-legged animate objects into pancakes—especially those that have given them a headache.

Test three-shot groups fired from a clean and then a dirty barrel. If both you and the gun can do it, 1-inch three-shot groups at 50 yards seem completely adequate. Again, the important consideration is how close the first shot from a cold barrel goes to the point of aim.

Again, we strongly advise terminal ballistics testing. However, in this instance, the test is pure simplicity. Fire bullets into stacks of dry telephone books to see if the bullet deforms. Solids should not deform at all. If a recovered bullet shows any evidence of deformation, its performance is suspect. Do at least three tests with each bullet. With heavier solids at higher velocities, it might take many feet of dry paper to stop the bullet.

Bullets for Thin-Skinned Dangerous Game

Here we are considering the bigger species of cats, bears and wild boar. Smaller species can be plenty dangerous, but any reasonably powerful big game gun loaded with a controlled-expansion bullet of reasonable weight should do the job, given proper shot placement.

Wounded cats have mauled or killed many an otherwise cautious hunter because he used the wrong bullet. In several well-studied cases, it appears the first shot would have anchored the cat if the hunter had used a properly expanding bullet.

I have studied the accounts of four lion maulings. Three of those began when the hunter wounded the cat with a non-expanding bullet. The fourth was the result of a hit with an expanding bullet that failed to hold together properly. As always, what counts is shot placement, bullet performance and, finally, delivered energy.

For hunting any of these species, use of anything other than a premium-quality controlled-expansion bullet seems truly foolish. There is a fundamental difference between a ruined hunt caused by a failed bullet resulting in a lost trophy and what could happen if that trophy were to take a hankering toward biting back. I've been charged by a big,

wounded mule deer buck, and I want no part of any charging animal, wounded or not, especially one with claws and fangs!

The best choice here is a gun launching a big, heavy, controlled-expansion slug delivered properly to break major bones. Using such a bullet, even if it misses heavy bones, you should expect plenty of damage and a devastating blow.

We strongly suggest terminal ballistics testing. Providing the bullet holds together properly, exceptionally deep penetration is not particularly critical. It is a rare lion that weighs 500 pounds, and very few boars are anywhere near that big. Look for about 18″ of penetration. These are tough animals to stop, and for this reason we strongly recommend premium bullets demonstrating more than 75-percent weight retention at realistic impact velocities. Test bullet integrity by firing into stacks of dry telephone books, and look for bullets that hold together when tested in this medium.

When talking about the biggest of bears, bullet weight and the ability of the bullet to hold together are even more critical. There is no doubt that a 130-grain 270 Winchester bullet will dispatch the largest of bears, if properly placed—broadside into the lungs. But how long will it take for the bear to realize it is dead? A grizzly bear can cover rough, dead-tree- and brush-covered ground faster than a thoroughbred can negotiate Churchill Downs. With that in mind, do you really want to try to find out just how small a gun will do the job? On the other hand, remember that unless you hit the brain or spine, the chances of instantly stopping any big bear are virtually zero, regardless of the gun used. To stop the fight, you will have to hit a nerve center or do considerable other damage.

Again, we highly recommend terminal ballistics testing. The biggest bears can weigh more than 1000 pounds and are exceptionally sturdy. Look for no less than 18″ of penetration. Premium bullets demonstrating more than 75-percent weight retention at realistic impact velocities are strongly recommended. Also, test bullet integrity by firing into stacks of dry telephone books; select bullets that will not disintegrate.

Accuracy is no less important here than for non-dangerous big game, and vital shot placement is ever more critical. Fire three-shot groups from a clean barrel and from a dirty barrel because you might get a shot after bagging another game animal. How close the first shot comes to where it should hit is the critical issue in this analysis.

Testing a Bullet's Terminal Performance

Terminal ballistics testing involves the evaluation a bullet's performance after it impacts any given substance at a given angle while traveling at some particular velocity. All manner of variables can complicate this testing. When measuring a bullet's overall performance, ballisticians often have to evaluate the consequences of various types of impacts with more than one substance.

These tests can include firing at various combinations of glass, sheet

metal, armor plating (both soft and hard), fabric and other substances, and evaluation would measure penetration, weight retention and expansion characteristics of the bullet.

While laboratories use ballistic gelatin for all comparisons intended to suggest a bullet's performance in flesh, this is not necessarily the best substance for the purpose. We handloaders have a better choice. We can use exactly two substances to answer all our questions. The first is paper, and the second is wet paper. We only need to test a bullet's penetration, expansion and weight retention. Comparison of one bullet's performance to that of another can be most revealing. Also, comparison at different impact velocities is useful.

Saturated telephone books contain water, cellulose and clay in proportions that are reasonably similar to living flesh, especially regarding how the substance interacts with a bullet. Nothing is a substitute for living flesh, blood and bone, but wet phone books comes a lot closer than ballistic gelatin or clay. Further, telephone books are easy to get and provide repeatable results. Finally, almost anyone interested in terminal ballistics can prepare and use this substance. That is not true of ballistic gelatin; even the best laboratories have trouble with that stuff.

To mimic heavy bone, writer Finn Aagaard suggests placing about 1″ of saturated phone books in front of about 4″ of dry phone books followed by another 18″ of saturated phone books. This simulates impacts into the heavy shoulder bones of large big game animals. However, a simple stack of saturated phone books satisfies my needs for most testing.

When I am concerned about the structural integrity of an expanding bullet, I shoot it into a 12″ stack of dry telephone books. Any bullet that can hold together in that test is apt to fare well against the most solid of bones. This also provides a handy performance comparison for different bullets.

For the standard test, saturate about 9″ of dry book, which will swell to about 12″ thickness. Remove the books from the water bath after about 24 hours. Remove excess water by placing the stack face up and pressing with about 50 pounds of force for about 30 seconds. Tie the bundle together with heavy monofilament fishing line wrapped near each edge or across the center from both the sides and the ends. Keep the ties in the same location for all stacks and avoid shooting through the strings. Interestingly, a bullet hitting a tie string completely fouls the test results. Also, for consistent results, remove all shiny pages.

To begin, fire into the stacks at close range. For most cartridges up to 30-06 class, you can use each stack for at least six shots. I sometimes crowd nine or more low-powered handgun shots into one stack.

This is all one needs to do an expansion/penetration test. Simply saturate the phone books overnight, then tie 12″ stacks with fishing line. Few pistol bullets penetrate that far, but I double the stacks just in case. For expanding-bullet rifle loads, two such stacks are necessary and adequate. Shots can be within a few inches of each other—closer with low-powered pistols, farther with high-velocity rifles.

Here, Winchester's 180-grain Fail Safe was compared to Hornady's 190-grain BTSP with similar impact velocity in dry telephone books. Note how much faster the BTSP expanded. This harsh test strained the Hornady bullet, but the Fail Safe expanded normally with 100% weight retention. This type of test is critical for dangerous game bullet evaluation.

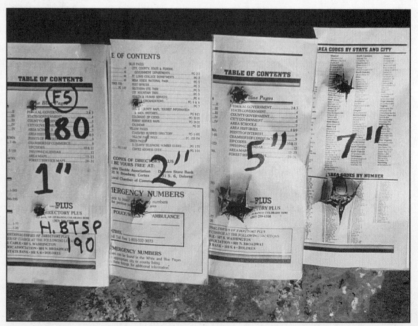

However, with too many shots, it becomes difficult to keep the "wound" channels sorted out. For the biggest cartridges, four shots per stack is about maximum. You can visually separate the books into four quarters to get your "targets." Finally, be certain to fire your shots parallel to the stack so that bullets don't come out one of the sides or intersect each other's paths.

For hunting most thin-skinned animals, 12″ of penetration with a bullet that holds together suggests the bullet will perform adequately on game. For heavier game, 18″ is generally sufficient. A bullet that fails to maintain significant integrity is a poor choice for anything except varmint hunting, especially where close shots are anticipated. I like to see at least 60-percent weight retention.

You can *approximate*, but not duplicate, long-range shots by firing into these stacks with reduced loads. My opinion is that these are worthwhile tests when considering a new hunting bullet. Use a ballistics program or published data to estimate the bullet's impact velocity at the far end of the useful hunting range for the gun, shooter and load. Work up a load launching the bullet to that velocity. If you can't find such a load listed herein, try Lyman's manual, which offers a considerable number of excellent reduced-velocity loads.

However, reduced loads at close range fall short of accurately representing actual long-range performance for several important reasons. First, bullets will not be spinning at the same rate as in actual full-power shots impacting at long range. This can affect stability after impact and will certainly dramatically reduce rotational forces, which contribute to expansion. Second, such loads don't stress bullets the same way as full-power loads. Finally, such bullets are not at as high a temperature upon impact. All these effects can alter terminal results.

To properly mimic actual long-range results, set up saturated phone book stacks at the range in question and fire into them with your actual hunting load. This takes some work, but the results are most interesting and are certainly worthwhile. If a bullet fails to expand properly in this medium at any given distance, you can be certain it is a poor hunting choice.

Examining the bullet and measuring the distance it penetrated offers good information that you can easily use to compare various bullets. None of this *proves* anything about hunting effectiveness, but it does compare the performance of various bullets. These results are *suggestive* of actual hunting performance. The three things to look at are percentage of retained bullet weight, the frontal area of the expanded bullet and the distance the bullet penetrated. Comparison of similar bullets will soon suggest which offers the greatest chance of providing the best terminal performance.

For those who might be thinking such a simple system just can't be all that useful, consider that many experts employed in ballistics laboratories, who routinely work with ballistic gelatin, choose saturated telephone books for their personal work. Why? Because it is easier to use and gives more representative results for hunting-bullet performance.

Bullet Safety

Always be sure the bullet you are loading is the bullet you *think* you are loading. For example, it is possible to load .284″ diameter bullets into 270 Weatherby Magnum cases, instead of the correct .277″. You might not notice the slight increase in bullet seating resistance.

Usually, such a cartridge will not properly chamber in a 270 Weatherby, but it might. If it does, it is almost a sure bet that the case neck won't have enough room to expand and release the bullet. This will result in skyrocketing pressure, perhaps enough to destroy the gun.

A second concern is that all similarly designed, equal-weight bullets of any given diameter will not generate the same pressure with any given load. We recently completed a series of tests at Accurate Arms' ballistic laboratory, involving the 270 Winchester and thirteen commonly available 150-grain .277″ bullets. With otherwise identical loads, pressures varied from 54,700 psi to 72,400 psi, a difference of 32.4 percent. This is approximately the difference between a standard load and a proof load.

As a general rule for all metallic cartridge handloading, if a load calls for a specific bullet, you can't substitute other bullets. Hodgdon gets around this problem by choosing to do their testing with the bullet that creates the highest pressure among standard bullets of that weight and caliber. That explains the lack of bullet-specific requirements in loads based on Hodgdon data.

Never, for any reason, seat any Barnes-X, Winchester Fail Safe or any other homogeneous solid bullet closer than 0.050″ to the rifling in any load. These bullets can raise pressures drastically if seated too close to the rifling because they need a running start to properly engrave the rifling and enter the barrel. Further, as noted previously, never use any homogeneous copper or copper-alloy bullet in any double rifle. The thin barrels common on these guns cannot withstand the stresses such bullets impose.

Keep in mind that manufacturers are continuously offering new bullets, and unless the maker specifically states that a new bullet is safe for use with existing data, do not use any data in this guide, or any other, for loading that bullet. Ask the manufacturer for load recommendations.

Homogeneous copper or copper-alloy bullets like these Barnes-Xs need a running start at the rifling. Seating any homogeneous (copper or copper-alloy) bullet too close to the rifling can skyrocket pressures, *so don't do it!* Give these bullets a full .050″ jump, minimum. Also, do not use these bullets in any low-pressure double rifle or similar gun—violent barrel ruptures have occurred.

Chapter 8

SEATING BULLETS

IN THIS CHAPTER, we will consider various aspects of bullet seating to achieve the correct cartridge overall length and the effects of varying neck tension and crimping. We'll also discuss how each of these relates to functioning, accuracy and dependability. This chapter chiefly addresses hunting ammunition, but many of these concepts apply to target and plinking loads.

Determining Maximum Usable Cartridge Length

In many types of loads, static parameters tightly control either bullet seating depth (how far the bullet is driven into the case) or cartridge overall length (OAL). Examples of the former include bullets which have crimping grooves (cannelures) intended for typical revolver and tubular-magazine rifle loads. Here, seating depth is predetermined. One must push these bullets into the case until the cannelure lines up with the case mouth so that the crimp is in the right place.

In some guns, short magazines, ejection ports or other features restrict overall cartridge length. For this reason, you may not be able to alter the bullet-seating depth. You must seat the bullet so that the cartridge is just short enough to fit the magazine and function through the action.

However, in many guns, the chamber (not the magazine or other features of the gun) limits cartridge overall length. One example is the typical single shot rifle. With these, and with many bolt actions, you can tinker with bullet-seating depth to improve accuracy. Sometimes changing the OAL of a load just a few thousandths of an inch can produce a startling increase in accuracy.

Using several of the OAL gauges on the market, you can accurately determine the cartridge OAL where the bullet hits the rifling. Examples include RCBS's simple-to-use Precision Mic, Stoney Point's Chamber-All OAL Gauge and similar tools from Sinclair International, Inc., and others.

The Precision Mic chamber gauge resembles a cartridge, but features a friction-loaded sliding nose section, or "bullet." This tool is chambered into the gun being measured. As one closes the bolt, the sliding "bullet" eventually contacts the rifling and stops. The bolt continues to push the body section forward until the bolt closes fully. One then carefully extracts this chamber gauge (friction holds the sliding "bullet" in place). A two-piece calibrated gauge is then assembled over this chamber gauge, screwed together on a micrometer thread until the top half *just* touches the "bullet." A scale on the calibrated gauge gives a reading of the specific length of that combination. Thereafter, you can use the same reading to load any bullet for that gun and set the bullet the precise distance you want it from the rifling.

The Precision Mic measures the overall length based on where a typical bullet's ogive hits the rifling. This measurement does not depend upon vagaries of bullet design. Though this measurement is not exactly precise when comparing bullets of significantly different nose shapes, these minor errors are of little consequence. Stoney Point's handy and affordable Chamber-All OAL Gauge works differently, but achieves the same goal.

An old method of testing OAL requires no special tools, is inexpensive and adequately accurate for hunting loads, but is time consuming. Load up a dummy round using a sized case with no powder or primer. Seat the bullet just deep enough to ensure that the dummy will fit into the gun's magazine.

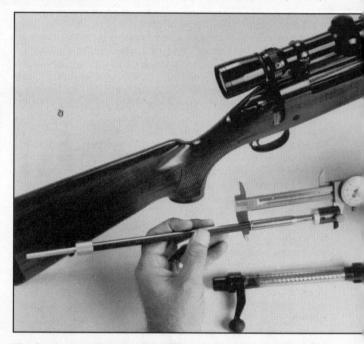

The Stoney Point Comparator and OAL Gauge, with modified case, is extremely easy to use. A similar model designed for lever, pump and semi-auto guns is also available.

Assuming the magazine length limits the cartridge overall length, turn in the seating stem of your seating die to position the bullet in the dummy round about 0.035″ deeper than the magazine length. Magazine length minus about 0.035″ seems to be about the greatest OAL that will assure proper functioning. Before chambering this dummy round in a Remington pump, or in any other rifle with a limited-length ejection port, ensure the round is short enough to eject.

Then, light a small candle and hold the bullet in the flame, close enough to blacken the bullet jacket. If the gun features controlled feed, carefully insert this dummy in the magazine, then begin to close the bolt. If the gun is not a controlled-feed action, simply insert the dummy into the chamber and begin to close the bolt. In the latter instance, when the bolt stops, use just enough force to snap the extractor over the case rim.

This magazine-length dummy will often be too long to allow the bolt to travel far enough forward to begin to lock. If this happens, remove the dummy and observe the bullet. It should have shiny marks where the rifling touched the bullet and marred the candle blacking. Seat the bullet deeper, reblack the bullet and repeat the test.

Determine the maximum OAL, by trial-and-error, that will just allow the bolt to lock fully. Be aware that the camming force provided by the locking lugs is sufficient to allow the bolt to easily lock, whether the bullet is hitting the rifling or not. As you gently lower the bolt handle toward the fully locked position, feel for any increase in resistance. Such an increase suggests the bullet is hitting the rifling.

Continue shortening the round and reblacking the bullet until the bolt fully closes without any evidence of increased resistance. The bullet's ogive should exhibit no shiny marks from the rifling. Pull the old bullet and insert a new one. The test process may have damaged the old bullet, so it can no longer give precise results. Blacken this new bullet and again chamber the dummy, then extract it and carefully examine the bullet's ogive. If it shows only a slight marring from the rifling, the measurement is close enough. If carefully done, this measurement can be very precise.

If the new bullet shows no marring, unscrew the seating stem about 0.002″, pull the bullet slightly from the case, reseat the bullet, reblack and rechamber. Keep doing this until you arrive at an OAL that just barely shows a slight marring where the rifling hits the bullet.

When you are satisfied with the measurement, check this finished dummy carefully for proper and consistent functioning through the action. Measure the overall length and write all pertinent information on the case body using a permanent marker (Sanford's Sharpie fine point works well). Record all important data: gun tested, bullet make and style, OAL information.

Adjusting Seating Depth for Accuracy

Once we have determined the maximum OAL for the gun and bullet, we can look to adjusting bullet-seating depth as a method of improving accuracy.* Seating a bullet the proper distance from the rifling can profoundly affect accuracy. There are several reasons for this. One is how the bullet responds to the primer blast before the burning powder has time to generate enough gas pressure to move it. Another is how fast the bullet is traveling when it hits the rifling (the farther it moves, the faster it will be going). Although an analysis of these questions is beyond the scope of this book, we can state that most loads give the best accuracy with a specific amount of bullet jump.

Before tinkering with your cartridge length, remember that, in hunting loads, accuracy is often subordinate to functionality.

I recently encountered a problem with a Remington pump-action rifle chambered for the 280 Remington. My handloads used 130-grain Barnes-X boattail bullets.

I had a good safe load, but wanted to improve its accuracy. I carefully measured the gun's chamber using Stoney Point's handy OAL

---

*For practical purposes, you can't improve the accuracy of loads for free-bored rifles, such as Weatherbys, by altering bullet seating depth. The bullet-to-rifling jump is long enough that any slight alteration of seating depth is unlikely to improve accuracy. However, such guns might be particularly sensitive to variations in case neck tension and crimping. See the appropriate sections on those subjects.

gauge system. I found that the maximum-length cartridge that would fit in that gun's magazine left the bullet 0.080″ off the rifling. I loaded a batch of cartridges at this maximum usable length, as limited by the magazine.

With some of those cartridges inserted into the three magazines I carry when hunting and a few rounds loose in my pockets, I went to the range, shot those rounds and zeroed my new hunting scope, and functioning was flawless. The cartridges fed into the chamber smoothly, and the groups were very impressive. However, I should have been a bit more observant.

A few days later, after a hard day's hunting, I tried to eject an unfired cartridge and found that unfired cartridges don't clear the ejection port. I never noticed this at the range because I never ejected an unfired cartridge.

I had to remove the magazine and do a bit of digital gymnastics to get that round out of the receiver. I have since solved this problem with a bit of judicious filing on the rifle's ejection port. However, the standard cure is simply to seat the bullets deep enough to avoid this problem in the first place.

This points out a serious concern of hunters and competitive target shooters alike. Make absolutely certain the loads you concoct function through your gun under all conditions. If you fail to do this, you will eventually discover the exception, and most likely, it will occur at the most inconvenient time. As a practical matter, it is much better to sacrifice a bit of accuracy in order to be sure your loads work properly every time.

Now let's adjust our seating depth to improve accuracy. With standard seating dies, one achieves the best bullet-seating results by adjusting the die body about one-half turn from the point where it either begins to apply a crimp (in those dies so designed) or almost touches the shellholder.

I prefer to use Lee Precision's die-body locking rings for locking the position of all threaded dies. These work with a rubber "O" ring that allows the die body to center in and align with the press. I install a rubber "O" ring between the die body and the locking nut of the bullet seating stem. This allows the stem to align with the case, thereby reducing the chances of bending the case neck during the bullet-seating operation. I use the same system for the neck expander stem on the sizing die.

Assuming you have established a safe load that fulfills your needs and the maximum OAL for that load in your gun, hold all other variables as close to the same as possible and load groups of cartridges with varying seating-depth settings. For preliminary work, ten rounds at each setting will suffice.

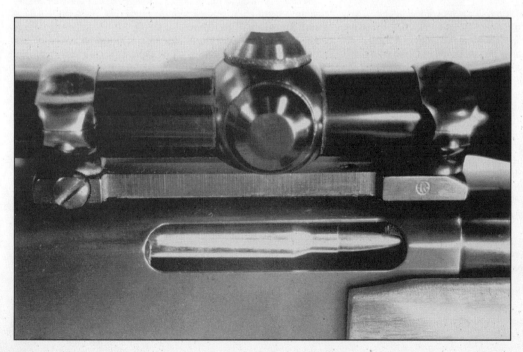

This is an embarrassment you want to avoid! Although this cartridge is otherwise safe, accurate and powerful—equipped with a serious terminal-performance bullet (Barnes 130-grain XBT)—this round fails the ultimate hunting cartridge test...functionality! By shortening this load a few thousandths of an inch or, better, making a minor alteration of the rifle's ejection port, this problem is solved. (Other than this "little glitch," the load functions perfectly in this rifle.)

For hunting guns with jacketed bullet loads, a good plan is to test with bullets seated at about 0.040″, 0.030″, 0.020″ and 0.015″ from the rifling. The exact values are not critical, but don't seat jacketed bullets any closer than 0.015″ from the rifling, or pressure can rise dramatically. In most instances, one can safely seat *cast* bullets closer.

For hunting loads using solid copper, copper-alloy or Winchester Fail Safe bullets, test your loads in the 0.075″ to 0.050″ bullet-jump range. Loads with less bullet jump will generate much higher pressures. Further, these bullets generally require that much jump to achieve the best accuracy.

In target guns or varmint rifles with special chambers, begin testing your loads with the bullet almost touching the rifling. Some use loads with the bullet jammed into the rifling quite firmly; however, none of the data listed in this manual is appropriate for such loads, because this technique can create significant pressure increases. Consider a hypothetical load "X." Assume you have worked up load "X" using current data, and it shows no signs of excess pressure. Load "X" chronographs at 3600 fps when the OAL allows 0.020″ bullet-to-rifling jump. Suppose you test a load with a 10-percent reduction in powder charge, but with the bullet seated to just touch the rifling. Call this load "X-20." Suppose "X-20" also chronographs at 3600 fps. Since the velocities of "X" and "X-20" are identical, you might be tempted to assume they produce similar pressures. You might be very wrong. First, the very fact that 10-percent less powder is generating the same velocity suggests that peak pressure is almost certainly higher. This is analogous to using a 10-percent faster powder to achieve the same velocity in an otherwise identical load. Most handloaders understand that a faster powder has to generate more peak pressure to achieve the same velocity (the pressure curve is narrower). Second, accelerating a bullet and engraving the rifling simultaneously will likely increase the bullet-to-bore friction. With more friction, more energy is transferred to the barrel. If more energy is transferred to the barrel and the bullet's muzzle energy (velocity) is the same, more energy will have to have been created by the powder. The only way for less of the same powder to create more energy is to burn at a higher pressure. This fact falls directly from a fundamental law of thermodynamics.

The point of the foregoing discussion is that it's impossible to predict the pressure consequences of seating a bullet into the rifling. In target and varmint rifles, you can often achieve the best accuracy by locating the bullet nearer the rifling, rather than farther from it; hence the temptation to seat a bullet against the rifling might be strong. Generally, unless you are a very sophisticated handloader, this is a temptation best denied.

Be aware that variations exist from lot to lot with all bullets. If you have established an accurate load using one lot of bullets, then run out of that lot and buy more from a different lot (all target and some hunting bullets come with a lot number printed on the box), the nose shape might be just different enough that your loads will now touch the rifling. Pressure could escalate, and you'll be in trouble.

If you want to put together a large batch of hunting loads, for example, you're better off making sure that your OAL puts the bullet a good distance from the rifling, even if that costs you a bit of accuracy. That way your future reloads with different lots of bullets won't give you problems.

To test these various-length loads for accuracy, five-shot groups are appropriate. Begin with the shortest loads. As the loads get longer, accuracy will likely increase. If it *decreases* with the longest loads, try loads that split the difference between the two most accurate lengths tested until you get the best length. Often differences as small as 0.005″ can affect group size.

If you find the most accurate load tested was the shortest load, go back and test even shorter loads. In rare instances, jacketed bullets may perform best with jumps as great as 0.060″ or thereabouts.

Seating for Proper Function

For typical hunting loads, bullet seating consists of simply inserting a bullet in the sized, primed and charged case. Many handloaders never give the matter a second thought.

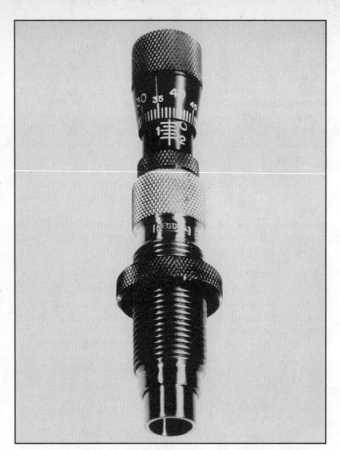

Redding's Competition Bullet Seating Die features infinite micrometer-adjustable bullet-seating depth and a spring-loaded case body chamber. Forster offers a similar die under the Bench Rest banner.

Serious target shooters use entirely different methods and achieve vastly superior control of the overall length and concentricity of their finished rounds. There is an in-between ground where better tools and techniques can provide superior results to any handloader. This is one area where serious hunters and informal target shooters can easily improve their ammunition.

Several die manufacturers offer various styles of improved bullet-seating systems with standard press-mounted dies. Forster offers their Bench Rest die set. This features two specific advantages worth noting. First, this sizing die uses an elevated neck-expander ball. With proper adjustment, this feature allows you to expand the case neck to proper inside diameter while the neck-sizing portion of the die is still partially supporting the case neck. This design also affords much more leverage. Compared to standard dies, neck expansion effort is typically only about one-third as much.

I have modified standard RCBS-style expander stems so that I can install Hornady's after-market carbide expander button higher on the stem. (The carbide button eliminates the need for inside neck lubricants.) Properly modified, this system allows me to adjust the height of the expander button so that most of the neck expansion occurs while the neck-sizing portion of the die is still partially supporting the case neck. As with the Forster Bench Rest dies, this minimizes the possibility of bending the case neck out of alignment. The elevated Hornady carbide expander button reduces friction and effort to an absolute minimum. With this set-up, inside neck lubes are never required. I will not further detail this modification here, but I can provide this information, upon request.

Another feature of Forster Bench Rest dies that I find most beneficial is the sliding spring-loaded case-alignment body within the seating die. As the ram raises the bullet and case into this die, the sliding sleeve fully supports and centers the case body. A separate, floating stem cen-

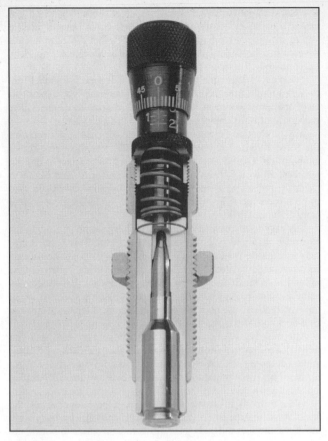

Redding's Competition Seating Die. As this cutaway shows, this seating die has a plethora of advanced features.

RCBS' Competition Seating die offers micrometer (0.001″ detent) seating-stem adjustment and easy bullet insertion. With this die, precise bullet seating is a snap.

ters and supports the bullet. In this manner, case and bullet are aligned with each other before the seating stem reaches its stop and begins pushing the bullet into the case. This system virtually eliminates lateral forces on the bullet or case neck as the bullet is being seated. This minimizes the possibility of bending the case neck.

Hornady (New Dimension), Redding (Competition), RCBS and others offer improved seating dies that allow easier and more precise bullet insertion. All are designed for use in standard presses.

Neil Jones, Wilson and others offer hand dies with similar features. These give precise control over the bullet seating depth and reduce the chance of bullet distortion or case neck bending. All are worth considering, and most are extremely easy to adjust and use. These special dies are designed for use with an arbor press.

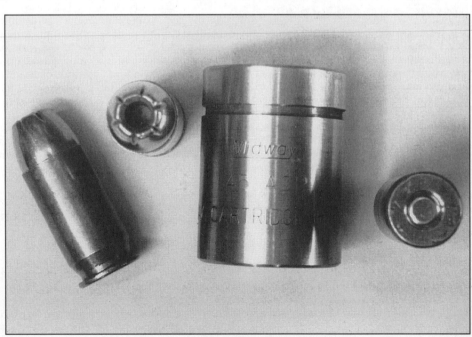

Midway's Max Cartridge Gauge (pistol or revolver) measures all facets of a loaded round. If your handloads will not easily fully chamber in the proper gauge (without the bullets protruding out of the front), they might not work properly in your gun; conversely, if they do, they will!

The wide selection of precision bullet-seating dies available suggests the importance of doing this step properly. Shown here is Wilson's Hand Die with Sinclair International, Inc.'s Micrometer Adjustable Seating Stem.

Bullet Pull

In previous chapters, we explored the importance of consistent case neck tension in some detail. Benchrest competitors and serious varmint hunters often vary the case neck tension of their loads in an effort to find that final measure of accuracy. Sometimes the slight additional delay that results from increasing bullet pull will improve accuracy. Perhaps the bullet seals the bore sooner. If chamber pressure is higher when the bullet starts moving, it will more quickly reach the level necessary to swell the bullet before the bullet moves as far into the barrel. Bullet pull can have a serious effect on accuracy.

Handloaders can use several methods to adjust case-neck tension. With neck-sizing dies using interchangeable inserts, one can install a smaller insert to expand the neck less. A 0.001″ reduction in neck size adds significantly to bullet pull. If sizing the neck 0.001″ smaller increases bullet pull too much, compensate by sizing less of the case neck so that it holds less of the bullet. This affords very fine adjustments to bullet pull.

If your best load is one with very little case-neck tension, you can use it for extreme-accuracy shooting. You can get away with this because you'll be able to handle your ammunition with kid gloves and feed cartridges one by one into the chamber. These loads won't work in the field because you may dislodge the bullet. For target shooting, though, the amount of case-neck tension used is based solely on accuracy considerations.

Hunters of dangerous game have different needs. A jammed gun caused by a bullet that dislodged in the case doesn't matter much if you're shooting at a prairie dog. However, as many African hunters have learned the hard way, a jammed gun can be life-threatening. Here, bullet pull must be secure to avoid jams.

Two factors determine bullet pull. The first is neck-to-bullet friction. This results from the interference fit created when you force a bullet of one diameter into an elastic case neck of a smaller diameter. The second factor is the crimp, and we'll get to that a bit later.

Any lubrication between the bullet and the case neck decreases the force required to dislodge the bullet. For most low-recoil ammunition, a small amount of graphite in the case neck is of little concern. However, keep the lubrication uniform from round to round. For absolute security with dangerous-game cartridges used in high-recoiling rifles, the case neck and the bullet must be free from all lubrication.

It is easy to increase case-neck tension by simply removing the expander stem and polishing the expander ball. This process also reduces expander-to-neck friction, which lessens the possibility of case deformation during neck expansion. For hunting loads, I often turn the expanders as much as 0.001″ smaller than standard. For dangerous-game and high-recoil loads, a reduction of as much as 0.002″ is sometimes advisable. Case-neck thickness and hardness limits the ultimate case-neck-to-bullet tension.

After repeated reloadings, case necks can get very hard, and you might notice that their necks are harder to expand than less-used cases. Although more neck tension can be desirable, an excessively work-hardened case neck might spontaneously split at any time after seating the bullet and before firing the round. A split case neck cannot properly hold a bullet. If this happens, either discard the cases or anneal the necks. Assuming the primer pocket is still tight and the case body is not too thin at the web and body juncture, there is no reason to discard the case just because its neck is too hard. Annealing makes sense for the handloader who might have spent hours preparing a few boxes of brass to a state of near-perfection.

If you suspect your case necks are not providing sufficient tension, or if you suspect that increasing neck tension might improve accuracy, you can easily work-harden them. Lubricate the case inside and out, and run the case fully into your full-length sizing die. This will size the neck smaller. Withdraw the case until the expander button expands the neck larger. This work-hardens the neck. Repeat the above cycle enough times to provide the hardness you need.

Deliberately hardening case necks adds measurably to the force it takes to move a bullet into or out of the case, and this force is a measure of a cartridge's dependability. An example of an instance where increasing bullet pull might be worthwhile is the 358 Winchester.

Normal powder charges in the 358 Winchester are often extremely compressed. A compressed mass of powder can generate a lot of elastic force. In the case of the 358, the powder is pushing against a large bullet base. If neck tension is insufficient, the powder will push the bullet out of the case. If this happens in the gun's magazine, it can jam the action.

If potential bullet movement is a concern, be certain both bullet and case-neck interior are free of lubricant. Settle any compressed charge as much as possible before seating the bullet. Make every effort to provide maximum case-neck tension in all loads by sanding the neck expander button as much as 0.001″-0.002″ smaller than stock and work-hardening the case necks.

Crimping

A heavy crimp alone won't hold a bullet in the case with a revolver that generates heavy recoil. Anyone who thinks it will is welcome to reprime a batch of 44 Magnum cases *without sizing*. Then, drop in your favorite heavy charge, seat the bullet in place and apply the heaviest crimp your tools can muster.

After one or two shots, the gun will jam from bullets jumping the crimp and protruding from the front of the cylinder. Bullet-to-case friction, not the crimp, holds bullets in place. To prove that fact, you can

(Above) Taper-crimp dies are designed to turn any belling of the case mouth back straight and to slightly crimp the case into the side of the bullet, if one desires. These dies are necessary for proper semi-automatic pistol loads that headspace on the case mouth.

(Left) The Redding Profile Crimp Die delivers a superior roll crimp for rimmed revolver loads.

do a similar experiment with normally sized cases loaded with no crimp. They will shoot fine. A proper crimp adds only a small amount of resistance. However, if improperly done, a crimp can actually decrease the friction.

The purpose of a crimp is to add a measure of security and dependability to a load. A crimp can also improve ballistic uniformity in revolver loads. A good roll crimp into a deep cannelure can mechanically lock the bullet against *deeper* seating, in spite of an otherwise loose neck-to-bullet fit. This effect is beneficial for ammunition used in magazine rifles where the battering associated with heavy or repeated recoil might otherwise drive the bullet into the case. In this situation, a load having a compressed powder charge can also help keep the bullet in place.

Ammunition used in many types of guns can *require* a crimp. Some examples are high-recoil box-magazine rifles, heavy-caliber double rifles, rifles with tubular magazines, revolvers and pistols.

Where a non-cannelured bullet is used, consider the possibility of using either a taper-crimp die or Lee's Factory Crimp Die (FCD) to slightly crimp the case mouth into the bullet. With soft jacketed bullets, one can often use the FCD to simultaneously swage a crimping groove and apply a crimp. The FCD does this easily without damaging the case.

In all loads where the case mouth was belled to facilitate bullet seating, such as with cast bullet loading and most pistol and revolver loads, one must make the case mouth straight again after seating the bullet. This is necessary to assure proper chambering. Crimping automatically accomplishes this task. Many standard bullet-seating dies allow the option of crimping the case as you seat the bullet.

Don't use a roll crimp on any ammunition that headspaces on the case mouth. Here you must use a taper crimp. This process involves a taper-crimp die that simply pushes the case against the bullet. You can adjust a taper-crimp die to push the case slightly into the surface of the bullet to lock it against deeper seating. This is beneficial in semi-automatic pistols to prevent bullet movement during chambering.

Many have denigrated crimping as always detrimental to rifle accuracy, but this is not necessarily so. When properly applied to cases of uniform length, a crimp will have no effect on accuracy. In some instances, the slight added bullet pull can help accuracy.

Standard crimping dies will either apply no crimp, insufficient crimp, a perfect crimp, or mangle the cartridge, depending upon case length. Worse, in cartridges with fragile and springy case bodies, such as the 30-30, this characteristic can make it almost impossible to

Lee's Factory Crimp Die for rifle loads: These are not sensitive to precise case length and can even crimp into soft bullets lacking a cannelure or crimping groove. A similar Carbide Factory Crimp Die for cylindrical handgun cases provides final resizing after the bullet is seated. A bad crimp will be ironed out, and the cartridge will still chamber.

achieve a perfect crimp, even when one has carefully trimmed all the cases to a uniform length. Through its design, Lee's Factory Crimp Die solves all these problems because it is not sensitive to case length.

With standard dies, to achieve the best crimp results, you must trim cases to uniform length. You'll get better and more uniform crimps if you crimp as a separate step, after the bullets are seated. Trying to seat a bullet and apply a crimp in the same step is frustrating at best.

Chapter 9

INTERNAL BALLISTICS

BALLISTICS IS THE study of projectiles in free flight, but the term also has come to include what happens within the gun after the firing pin falls—called internal ballistics—and what happens to the bullet after it strikes the target—called terminal ballistics. In this chapter, we'll discuss internal ballistics.

Largely, the handloader's only internal ballistics concern is *pressure*. Previously, we have discussed other internal ballistic effects such as everything that happens to the shooter, the gun, the cartridge, and each of its components after the striker hits the primer, but before the bullet has left the barrel.

The Weak Link

The most important reason to discuss internal ballistics is *safety*, not pressure. Pressure is what makes a gun work, and in this sense, pressure is our friend. *Control* of pressure is the issue here. With pressure under control, there is no danger whatsoever in placing your face a few inches from a rifle chamber that contains as much as 65,000 psi. However, if we lose that control, our rifle can become a bomb.

In every cartridge gun there is a "chain" of safety separating the shooter from injury. As with any other kind of chain, there is one weakest link.

In most modern bolt-action rifles, the weak link is the cartridge case. In some lever-action and other rear-locking rifles, the weak link might be the action itself. In many revolvers, the weak link is the cylinder. In some pistols, the weak link may be that portion of the chamber that leaves part of the cartridge case unsupported. In other pistols, it might be the barrel itself or the locking lugs in the frame.

In modern rifles with locking lugs located at the front of the action, the gun is usually strong enough to control any pressure the brass cartridge case is capable of withstanding. Assuming a properly fitting striker in a properly sized hole in the bolt face, the hardness of the case head determines how much pressure the gun and cartridge case can safely contain.

Many believe a thicker case head is a stronger case head, but that's not true. A harder case head is *stronger*, even if the softer case head is twice as thick but only 5 percent softer. In modern solid-head cases, the *hardness* of the brass is the only factor that determines how much pressure the case can withstand before undergoing plastic deformation.

When chamber pressure exceeds the elastic limit of the case, the brass will begin to deform, acting just like bubble gum. It will swell and expand into any deformations or holes in the bolt face, and this deformation will be permanent. If the pressure remains high enough for long enough, and if the case head finds enough room to expand, a dangerous gas leak could develop.

At still higher pressure, the case will begin to act like water. The brass case head will simply liquefy. The 100,000 psi or so of pressure pushing on it will then blow it through any minute openings in the action.

Either situation typically results in the destruction of the rifle. It is a lucky shooter who can survive such a high-pressure encounter of the worst kind unscathed.

Case-head failure can occur even with normal loads. A case that has been exposed to temperatures exceeding about 400°F (≈200°C) has been annealed and will no longer be able to withstand pressure exceed-

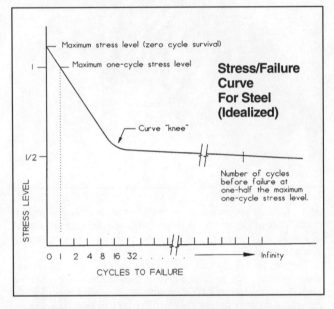

Stress/Failure Curve For Steel (Idealized)

ing about 10,000 psi. For this reason, never use any case of unknown history if you can't measure the hardness of the case head. Similarly, "hot" loads that do not cause case-head expansion in one brand or lot of cases can cause failure in other, softer cases.

It has often been said that if the case can hold the pressure, the load is perfectly safe for use in front-locking guns. However, that is not necessarily true. Continuous use of "hot" loads in particularly hard cases is not prudent. Such loads might be stressing the action past the knee of the life-cycle curve (see the associated graph). Because this is an important safety concept, we'll discuss it a bit further.

Steel has the physical characteristics that, if a part made of it can withstand a specific stress level one time without failing, that part can withstand half that stress level millions of times without failing.

All types of steel, regardless of heat-treatment, have similar-shaped stress/failure (fatigue life) curves. When the applied stress causes the part to fail on the first cycle, that level of stress is the ultimate, or zero-cycle, failure point. The amount of stress that causes failure on the second cycle will be considerably less. Similarly, the amount of stress that causes failure on the fourth cycle will be considerably less, still. This process continues. These points form a more-or-less straight line (refer to the graph, left-hand side).

Long before the applied stress drops to one-half of the zero-cycle failure level, the curve flattens. Small decreases in applied stress lead to huge increases in life cycles (refer to the graph, right-hand side).

This is the basis of all proper *proof testing*. A proof load stresses the gun sufficiently so that if the gun survives intact, we automatically know that the gun will safely withstand an almost unlimited number of normal-pressure loads. This also explains the folly of using hot handloads. If the hot loads significantly exceed standard pressure, we can no longer assume the gun will safely endure an infinite number of shots. All too often, hot handloads are actually equivalent to proof loads.

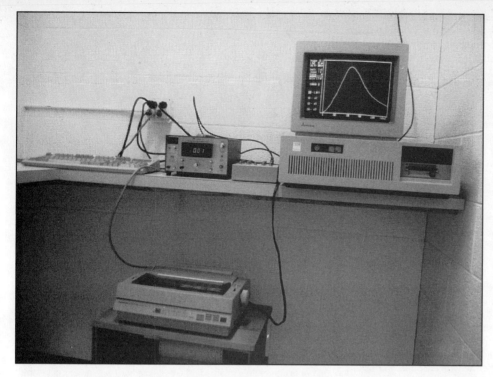

Accurate Arms' pressure instrumentation features a black box with three-digit display giving pressure in hundreds of psi. The monitor is displaying a memorized graph of the previous shot. The printer allows the reproduction of a hard copy of the pressure curve. The computer records each shot and its associated information.

An IPSC competitive shooter who was using hot 38 Super handloads had his gun come apart recently. Although he suffered no permanent damage, those who saw him immediately after the blowup said his general appearance was rather tattered. This event could very easily have killed him. For your health and well-being, *don't use hot loads!*

In rear-locking actions, the cartridge case might not be the weak link in the safety chain. In these guns, the fired case head pushes against the bolt and compresses it. At the same time, the bolt pushes against the locking lugs, compressing them. The lugs then push against the receiver, stretching it. (This process also occurs in front-locking guns, but the total movement of the bolt face is not great enough to matter on any one shot.)

When a cartridge fires, chamber pressure locks the case body to the chamber walls and the case head moves back, following the retreating bolt head.

In rear-locking rifles, a modestly high-pressure load that shows none of the classic pressure signs—primer flattening, case-head expansion, difficult extraction—can, nevertheless, cause catastrophic failure of the rifle. This is not the fault of the case. A stronger case, in the sense that the head is harder, will not help here. A case with thicker case walls at the body-to-web juncture can provide additional safety because it can stretch more before separation occurs. This is why Winchester makes the body of their 375 Winchester brass thicker than that of 30-30 Winchester cases. Normal loads in the 375 Winchester generate significantly higher pressures and, therefore, place more strain on the receiver. Thicker case walls add a significant margin of safety. Generally, if your handloads show more stretching than factory loads exhibit (in your rear-locking gun), the pressure is probably too high. Reduce your load until case stretching is similar to that seen in factory loads. (The chamber and case must be free of lubricant.)

Remember that all rifle cases stretch with every firing cycle, regardless of the action type. That stretching results in case-wall thinning, and with repeated reloadings, that will eventually result in a case-head separation. If that separation occurs while there is still significant chamber pressure, containment is lost, and both gun and shooter can be injured or destroyed.

Such separations can occur after the bullet leaves the muzzle, when chamber pressure has dropped to near zero. Inertial effects can continue to stretch the case after chamber pressure stops pushing back the case head.

Be sure to examine your cases before each reloading. Destroy and discard any that show significant thinning at the body-and-web junc-ture. The classic symptom of excess thinning is a shiny ring around the outside of the case body, visible just ahead of the solid case web. Any case showing such a band is suspect. If you cannot measure the actual thinning using a case gauge such as the RCBS or NECO, the only safe course is to discard that case.

In some pistols, a portion of the cartridge case body wall is unsupported by the chamber in the area where the feed ramp leads into the chamber. Variations in the feed ramps among individual pistols combined with lot-to-lot variations of case-web thickness can leave a significant portion of the case wall unsupported. Pressure containment in such a situation relies entirely on the strength of the brass. Its strength is usually more than adequate for any standard pistol load. However, some enthusiastic shooter might work up a hot load for such a gun and then substitute a batch of cases with thinner walls or a shorter web, or try his hot loads in a gun with a longer feed ramp. Such a situation could result in a ruptured case. This typically swells the grip frame, blows off the grip panels, and violently ejects the destroyed magazine. The opportunity for injury is rather significant.

Further, just as with rifles, such hot loads might be stressing the pistol's action beyond the design level. Such loads might cause a catastrophic action failure after some arbitrary small number of shots.

Revolvers are a different situation entirely. Long before pressures reach the level that would swell the case head or stretch the frame enough to allow case-head separation, the cylinder can fail. Usually the top of the fired cylinder separates, shearing through the webs separating the fired chamber from those adjacent to it, and breaking the outside of the cylinder over those two adjacent chambers. This violently rupturing cylinder often completely shears the topstrap off the gun, making for at least three pieces of scrap metal flying off in all directions at great velocity, which should help make my point: Avoid any kind of overload in revolvers.

The classic example of a revolver overload is the double charge, where one case gets two charges of a fast and dense powder. Such a load creates *four times* the intended pressure.

All handloaders have a responsibility to identify and understand the weak link in the chain of safety of any gun they might be loading for. Shooters who don't understand how to estimate pressure by looking at primers, measuring case-head expansion or even just noting extraction effort can find themselves in trouble.

In one instance, a novice was interested in learning to handload. He owned a highly touted European-manufactured 243 rifle and had been shooting 80-grain Remington ammunition in it with acceptable results. We loaded up several boxes of handloads using his once-fired cases. Some of our loads were with 85-grain bullets and others with 100-grainers. We loaded the 85-grain bullet to about the same cartridge OAL as the 80-grain factory load and the 100-grain bullets to about the maximum OAL listed, *a much longer setting*. Because he had only a few boxes of brass to work with, he purchased a box of 100-grain factory loads to take to the range.

Both of the handloads chosen should have been mild and should have generated relatively low pressure.

At the range, we started our testing by firing the 85-grain handloads and the remaining few 80-grain factory loads, and I was pleased to see our handloads shooting smaller groups than the factory load. Everything seemed completely normal. The loads grouped acceptably, and there were no untoward pressure signs.

Then we switched to the 100-grain handloads. The first few shots seemed normal, but the bullets were impacting all over the paper. Examination of the primers suggested severe pressures. The shooter said the bolt handle was a bit hard to lift.

I suggested he stop shooting those loads and try the 100-grain factory loads. I stood there, staring at the head of a case that clearly indicated excess pressure, trying to comprehend what could possibly have gone wrong with my carefully planned handloads. Then he touched off one of the factory loads! Let's just say that smoke rolled out of the action.

Neither he nor the gun was hurt, but the case head had failed enough to allow a considerable gas leak. After he wrenched the bolt handle open, he knew enough to quit right then and there.

What had happened? We finally ascertained that the barrel in question was about 0.005″ smaller than nominal minimum diameter in both bore and groove diameters, and that the leade was both highly tapered and extremely short. The 80-grain factory and 85-grain handloads worked safely because they both had a running start at the rifling, and both were *very* soft and easily swaged bullets. Conversely, both the factory and the handloaded 100-grain cartridges placed the bullets *into* the rifling upon chambering, and those bullets were comparatively hard and would not swage down so easily.

The moral of the story: Know your gun and always look for indications of excessive pressure, regardless of the ammunition used.

Revolvers and other low-pressure guns are potentially the worst offenders here. How can one know if the pressures are safe when even a proof load for the gun might not visibly alter the primer, swell the case head measurably or cause any extraction difficulty? The only answer I can offer is to look at the velocity. If you're getting velocities significantly higher than similar factory loads, or higher than the loading data suggests you should get, you might have a problem. All else being equal, the only way to increase velocity is to increase pressure. This is a classic example of the prudence of sticking with *modern* published loads. I add the word modern because some early published loads were potentially overloads. For your safety, don't use those!

Measuring Pressure

Sir Alfred Nobel—benefactor of the Nobel prize—invented the first commercially successful method of measuring chamber pressures in firearms. His system used a simple arrangement of a movable piston fitted to a hole in the gun's chamber. When chamber pressure pushed on one end of this piston, the other end pushed on one end of a lead cylinder. A rigid anvil attached to the barrel supported the other end of this lead cylinder. By adjusting pressure-piston and lead-cylinder size, this system was useful for interpreting pressure in the normal black-powder range. However, this system was not particularly useful for comparing pressures in the normal smokeless-powder range.

The simple substitution of copper cylinders for the lead cylinders solved this problem. When properly annealed, pure copper proved to be useful for comparing pressures from the top end of the lead crusher range through modern smokeless proof-load pressures.

Both of these systems suffer from significant errors related to inertial effects. We will return to this subject later. The other problem with

Primer appearance can sometime suggest the relative pressure generated by a load (from left to right and top to bottom): Increasing pressure is suggested by the increasing amount of flat area on the base of each primer. However, these were different brands of primers and different loads. The large flat area of the lower right primer is completely misleading—that was fired with a very mild load! The lack of cratering around the firing pin suggests lower pressure, compared to the adjacent rounds.

these systems is that this technique requires considerable finesse. Different operators can and do get substantially different readings when measuring the same loads with the same equipment.

Originally, ballisticians applied this pressure-measuring method to muzzle-loading guns and then to cartridge guns. For many decades, laboratory cartridge-pressure-testing procedure called for drilling a hole in the case so that chamber pressure would have direct access to the pressure piston. With the adoption of copper for higher-pressure smokeless loads, laboratories adopted this same procedure. However, because case drilling was so time-consuming, ballistics laboratories in the United States eventually omitted this step. However, the Europeans maintained it—a prescient decision.

Evidently, some ballisticians assumed that omitting the case-drilling step would make little difference when testing cartridges generating sufficient chamber pressure to easily rupture the case wall. Perhaps they assumed that once the case wall ruptured, full chamber pressure would press against the piston, and the piston would therefore crush the copper just as it would have crushed the copper had a drilled case been used. The problem was that this analysis ignored some rather significant inertial effects. (Inertia is the measure of mass in motion.)

The cartridge case wall could support many thousands of pounds of chamber pressure before it ruptured. Therefore, when the case wall did rupture, an almost instantaneous blast of many thousands of pounds pressure hit the piston. The net result was that an undrilled case usually generated much greater crusher-flattening than a drilled case, when testing an otherwise identical load.

Worse, depending upon load variables, two loads that showed identical pressures with drilled cases often showed vastly different pressures with undrilled cases. This should have been a significant clue that this system was not actually measuring chamber pressure at all. Inertial effects were corrupting the data, regardless of drilled cases or not. One could only count on these results for comparing pressures generated by different loads in the most general of ways.

Today, we have something better. This new pressure-testing standard relies on computers and sophisticated electronics, but it gives a very close approximation of an actual chamber pressure measurement. Ballisticians now refer to the numbers generated by this newer system as psi (Pounds per Square Inch). They now refer to the old crusher

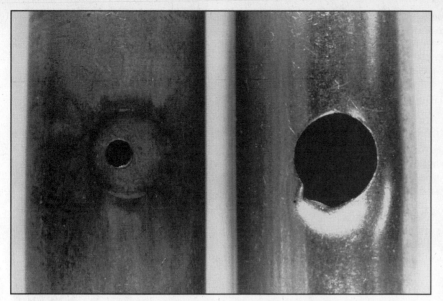

The drilled case (small hole) represents the old CUP system and provided more accurate results than the more recent system, which allows the case to retain pressure until the case wall ruptures. Here, the undrilled case shows a hole the size of the hole in the pressure barrel. Note that the case wall had been bent back in (where the ruptured wall had been partially attached). This facilitated removing the case from the pressure-testing barrel.

You might be able to just discern the slightly raised area of this case. This is where the conformal transducer is located when the case is chambered.

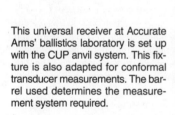

This universal receiver at Accurate Arms' ballistics laboratory is set up with the CUP anvil system. This fixture is also adapted for conformal transducer measurements. The barrel used determines the measurement system required.

method as CUP or LUP (Copper Units of Pressure or Lead Units of Pressure). The important thing to remember here is that there is no proper conversion from one system to the other. CUP is still in use, but is rapidly being replaced by the simpler, cheaper to use and more accurate psi method for most cartridges. (The CUP and LUP systems will continue in use indefinitely because obsolete cartridges can never be evaluated for estimation of a proper psi standard, because no reference ammunition exists.)

The British have a unique pressure-measuring method, and in some instances, the Europeans are still using the drilled CUP pressure-measuring method. Formula-based conversion of data from any one of these systems to any other of these systems is impossible.

The psi method uses a conformal transducer to measure the force of

the case body pushing out on the chamber wall. A portion of the gauge exactly replaces the chamber wall—it conforms to the contour of the chamber wall, whence the name. As the case pushes on the conformal portion of the gauge, this compresses a piezoelectric cell a very small amount. Compressing this cell modifies its electrical properties.

The electronics connected to the gauge measure this change, and a computer records chamber pressure on a continuous, real-time basis. For the first time, we have an opportunity to examine a representation of chamber pressure that includes almost the entire pressure history (this system cannot record the pressure before the case expands enough to press against the chamber walls). Conformal transducer systems can be extremely accurate and are comparatively simple to use and maintain.

You might have noted we stated that this system gives a very close approximation of an actual chamber-pressure measurement. Since no system can measure pressure without any movement of anything, and since chamber pressure is dynamic, it is fundamentally impossible to measure exact pressure at any given instant. Nevertheless, this system can come acceptably close. Assuming a properly calibrated system, the difference in actual peak pressure and measured peak pressure is of no consequence.

Pressure-Measuring Methods for the Handloader

Average handloaders do not have access to any "official" system of pressure measurement. However, they can and should observe various pressure manifestations. This is all about *safety*. Understanding how to observe pressure signs and what those signs can mean is most important.

Beginning at the low end of the pressure scale, let us consider the revolver shooter. Excepting the magnums and a few other high-pressure numbers (357 Magnum, 357 Maximum, 375 Supermag, 41 and 44 Magnums, 445 Supermag, and the 454 Casull), revolver loads don't generate enough pressure to create any signs of pressure on the case or primer. Even high-pressure revolvers offer little in the way of clues.

In some instances, loads that exceed normal pressures might exhibit a slight resistance to extraction. However, you can't rely on this. In these low-pressure chamberings, the handloader's only option is to stay within recommendations in this reloading manual.

Should any load generate any sign of difficult extraction, immediately discontinue using that load, assuming the gun's chambers are clean and smooth.

Recently, the author tested an imported Colt replica revolver chambered in 38-40 Winchester. In that gun, mild factory loads produced difficult extraction. Evidently, the reamer used to cut those chambers was in very bad repair, because those chambers all exhibited visible grooves. I solved the extraction problem by polishing away the high spots. If you suspect rough chambers are causing difficult extraction, have a competent gunsmith examine the gun. If necessary, a simple chamber polishing job is often worthwhile.

The high-pressure revolver chamberings mentioned earlier work at pressures twice as high as pressures reached in the 38 Special. Still, the only sign of excess pressure will be difficult extraction. Even that will be lacking in guns with highly polished chambers. Only the 454 Casull works at pressures that show notable primer flattening. As one works up a 454 Casull load, one can observe the primer getting flatter and flatter. With certain types of primers, this

When all is said and done, it still comes down to this! The only way to know what a load will do is to test it on paper. Here, Bill Falin of Accurate Arms is in the process of shooting a near-MOA 300-yard group.

might also be manifest in the other high-pressure revolver chamberings, but you can't count on it.

Semi-auto pistol cartridges, just like most revolver loadings, work at a pressure level that leaves absolutely no objective evidence. The only advice we can give is to stick with loads recommended in this reloading manual. If such a load gives any suggestion of excess pressure, stop using the gun and consult a gunsmith. Chamber roughness or other mechanical problems with the gun can cause problems such as bent or torn rims or scratched cases, even with loads generating normal pressures.

Rifle cartridges come in two basic pressure categories—those that can show evidence of excessive pressure and those that do not. Many old, low-pressure cartridges such as the 30-30 Winchester exhibit no signs of pressure variations to differentiate normal loads from dangerous ones. Generally, long before pressures reach a level that would cause primer flattening, case-head expansion or difficult extraction, pressure has exceeded the safe working limit of the gun.

In guns chambered for low-pressure cartridges, generally rear-locking lever-action rifles, any sign of primer flattening, case-head expansion or difficult extraction is ample reason to discontinue using the load. The best course is to use only loads suggested in this manual.

Rear-locking guns do offer one means of comparing pressures that is reasonably reliable: In these guns, loads working at normal pressures generally cause a few thousandths of an inch stretch in the case with each firing. Top loads often exceed 0.010" stretch on each shot. On rimmed cartridges, one can establish a reasonable baseline using factory loads.

Measure the case length of several factory cartridges and fire those clean, dry cases in a clean, dry chamber. One can use the average lengthening of that group of cases as a baseline. If your reloads *in the same cases* generate similar case stretching, they are generating similar pressures and should, therefore, be safe. Of course, both the reloads and the gun's chamber must be clean and dry.

The prudent handloader will not reload cases used in rear-locking guns as many times as those used in a front-locking gun. It's a good

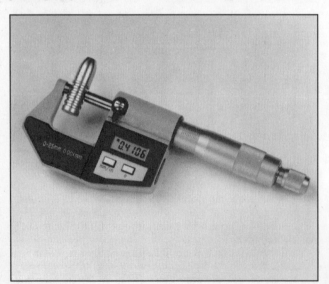

This Lyman digital 0.001" micrometer is an impressive tool. This is much faster and easier to use than a Vernier scale micrometer. It has a zero feature for comparing pieces.

Oehler's Model 43 Ballistic Laboratory

For the first time in history, the serious handloader can measure the relative pressure of any given load in his gun and without destroying the gun to do so. The Oehler Model 43 Ballistic Laboratory is an affordable system that will give real-time pressure data for almost any load fired from almost any type of rifle and rifle-type handgun. This system is not particularly suited to revolvers or auto pistols.

The Model 43 is not inexpensive. Its cost is similar to a typical high-performance scoped rifle, and it requires a portable computer. The Oehler Model 43 works by measuring the strain on the gun's chamber when one fires a cartridge. A special strain gauge is glued over the chamber, and the Model 43 measures the change in electrical properties as this gauge stretches in response to chamber pressure.

The Model 43 does not measure actual chamber pressure, it *compares* pressures. The pressure curve printouts can show the consistency of any particular load. The Model 43 allows you to measure and record all important load parameters simultaneously. With each shot, you get the pressure curve, muzzle velocity, velocity at the target and ballistic coefficient, target impact point, and distance from group center.

If you are serious about handloading, consider Oehler's Model 43. This sophisticated machine offers the serious handloader, target shooter and hunter information ballisticians a generation back could only dream of.

Here we see a Model 97 Winchester shotgun with attached strain gauge and the leads connected. This is the heart of Oehler's Model 43 system.

Forensic scientist Luke Haag puts the Model 43 through its paces, testing his own handloads in Ken Oehler's 30-06. With every shot, the computer records a real-time pressure curve for the cartridge; simultaneously, the bullet's muzzle velocity, target velocity, target impact point and ballistic coefficient are recorded. Within seconds, all of this information is displayed on the computer screen.

idea to keep careful records of the number of times each group of cases has been reloaded.

Most high-pressure rifle cartridges can show several signs of excess pressure. Typically, primer flattening increases as the load pressure increases. Eventually, the normally rounded primer becomes a large flat surface. If you stay with the same brand, type and lot number of primers, flattening can be a reasonably good indicator of relative pressure. However, there are vast differences between brands of primers. Lot-to-lot differences can also be significant. Comparing the pressure of your handloads to factory ammunition based upon the appearance of the fired primers is generally meaningless and can be downright dangerous.

Another means of comparing pressures is to measure case-head expansion. If your handloads in *new* cases generate case-head expansion similar to factory loads fired in the same gun and using the same brand of cases, you can reasonably assume that the two loads generate similar pressure.

Measuring case-head expansion is very simple. On rimless and belted cases, measure the diameter of the unfired case across the rim of the case head, using a 0.0001″ accuracy micrometer. Take this reading measuring from the first letter in the brand stamp (as in the R in R-P) to the opposite side. The the important point is to be certain to measure the same place before and after firing the round, and to avoid extractor scars on the rim.

On rimmed cases, take this measurement directly ahead of the rim, preferably with a blade micrometer capable of accurately reading to 0.0001″. The micrometer has to be capable of measuring across the narrow solid-web portion of the case in front of the rim and behind the hollow body of the case. If you don't have such a micrometer, measure across the rim just as with the rimless cartridges. You lose a measure of accuracy, but the data is still useful. After firing the cartridge and allowing the case to return to ambient temperature, remeasure the diameter.

On new cases, it is common for rifle-pressure loads to cause 0.001″ to 0.0015″ case-head expansion. However, in the most intense chamberings such as the 22-250, 220 Swift, 6mm Remington, 25-06, 6.5 Remington Magnum, 264 Winchester Magnum, 270 Winchester, all of the 300 magnums, 8mm Remington Magnum, 338 Winchester Magnum, 350 Remington Magnum, 375 H&H Magnum, 416 Remington Magnum, 458 Winchester Magnum and all of the Weatherby magnums, initial case-head expansion often exceeds 0.002″.

Handloads in new cases that produce expansion similar to factory loads will generally fall within industry pressure guidelines. Further, on subsequent similar loadings, case-head expansion will not occur or will be minimal. Primer pockets will not loosen with repeated reloading. You can be reasonably certain such handloads do not exceed established pressure limits for the cartridge. Remember that cases work-harden, so never use the *lack* of expansion as justification for exceeding published loads.

If your handloads cause primer pockets to loosen after repeated reloadings, the pressure is too high for those cases and might exceed acceptable pressure for the gun. Reduce the powder charge a few percent. The increased safety factor should more than compensate for any loss of velocity, and you might also see an improvement in accuracy.

Always use reputable, currently recommended loading data. Always start your load development at or near the minimum suggested load. Always watch for any obvious pressure signs. *Never exceed the maximum listed load!*

EXTERNAL BALLISTICS

WHILE THE STUDY of external ballistics includes many aspects of projectiles in free flight, only a few of those concern the average handloader. The path a bullet takes after leaving a gun's muzzle depends primarily upon how fast the bullet is going and how rapidly it slows down in response to wind resistance. The most significant additional complications result from crosswinds.

In order to estimate a bullet's drop at any given range, its energy at that range, the wind drift at that range and the correct lead on a moving target at that range, one must know how fast the bullet was moving when it left the barrel and how fast it loses velocity as it travels toward the target.

Affordable chronographs now allow the handloader to measure a bullet's velocity at almost any range to an accuracy of better than one part per thousand. One can estimate how fast any given bullet will slow down by referring to the Ballistic Coefficient (BC) value for that bullet. All major bullet manufacturers publish these values for their bullets.

However, the concept of projectile ballistic coefficient deserves a bit of explanation. (The following is an idealized account.) Early on in the study of ballistics, which matured about a hundred years ago, ballisticians recognized that the adoption of standard references would make their lives a whole lot less hectic. The idea was to establish a standard measure of ballistic efficiency with which to compare all bullets. This is similar to having any other standard—for example, our standard measure of velocity: feet traveled per second (fps). This realization presaged the development of the "standard bullet." That bullet's ballistic properties were measured. Specifically, ballisticians determined how fast a bullet of the standard size, weight and shape lost velocity as it traveled through the air while traveling at any given velocity.

This one quantity, velocity loss, was comparatively easy to measure, even in the days before electro-wizardry. One can measure a bullet's velocity by firing it into a ballistic pendulum. In this device, a bob weight attached to a string stops the bullet. The bullet's momentum is thereby transferred to the bob, which swings in a pendulum arc. The height the bob travels in the resulting arc provides all the data necessary to calculate the bullet's impact velocity.

One can easily back-calculate from the height the bob reached to find the velocity it started moving at, in response to the bullet's impact. From initial bob velocity, one can easily calculate the bullet's impact velocity. The modern chronograph is a lot easier to use and can also measure the bullet's velocity without interfering with the bullet's ballistic flight.

To ascertain this standard bullet's rate of velocity loss as a function of velocity, ballisticians fired many duplicate standard bullets, loaded to as constant a muzzle velocity as was possible, into ballistic pendulums at various ranges. The average value recorded for many shots at each range gave a very close estimate to the real velocity for an ideal standard bullet at that range.

Consider two target ranges, say, 100 yards and 200 yards. Subtracting the velocity measured at 200 yards from the velocity measured at 100 yards gave the standard bullet's rate of velocity loss across 100 yards. If the standard bullet was traveling at 2585 fps at 100 yards and 2515 fps at 200 yards, it could be said that in the velocity range near 2550 fps the standard bullet lost about 70 fps in traveling 100 yards.

With tests made at many distances, the standard bullet's velocity loss was measured across a wide velocity range, including ranges where it was traveling fast (near the muzzle) and those where it was traveling slowly (at long distance), and everything in between.

It was also necessary to load the standard bullet to a lower muzzle velocity to get data for very low velocities. (There were several reasons for this complication. Bullets that drop to subsonic velocity at long range can become unstable and tumble. Testing errors become more common with increasing range. Targets are progressively harder to hit at longer range.) *Eventually*, calculations revealed the expected rate of velocity loss for the standard bullet at any velocity between a few hundred feet per second and something over 4000 fps.

There are complications, however. Not all bullets match the standard bullet regarding the rate of change of their velocity loss with dif-

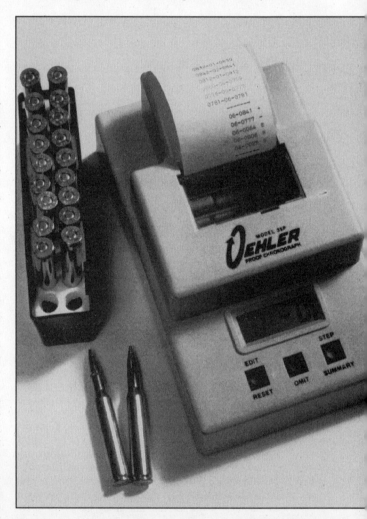

Oehler's 35P is the premier chronograph for the hobbyist and serious shooter alike. With adequate screen spacing and careful use, it can provide accuracy beyond any feasible requirement. The chronograph is the basis of all efforts toward scientifically achieving accurate handloads.

ferences in velocity. Compared to the standard bullet, one bullet might hold its velocity better at high speeds, but lose its velocity faster at slow speeds. This is a common situation determined by the particular shape of the bullet nose, shank and base. For this reason, ballisticians eventually adopted several standards to try to accurately cover most basic bullet shapes. However, for sporting ammunition, we can generally ignore this complication.

Well, now that we have a standard bullet to compare to, what do we do with it? First, we assign the standard bullet a ballistic coefficient of 1.00 (BC=1.00). Thereafter, we can calculate the ballistic properties of any other bullet (tested) by making one comparison of the tested bullet's rate of velocity loss with the rate of velocity loss for the standard bullet. Though the following explanation is not *technically* correct, it is essentially correct and is much easier to follow than any similar textbook discussion.

Consider bullets launched at the same muzzle velocity. If the standard bullet (BC=1.00) could travel 100 yards while losing 100 fps, a bullet that traveled only 50 yards before losing 100 fps would have a BC rating of 0.50. Similarly, a bullet that traveled 200 yards before losing 100 fps would have a BC rating of 2.00. The higher the BC, the less velocity the bullet loses in covering any given distance. Most sporting rifle bullets have BCs in the range from about 0.10 to about 0.70.

Increasing the BC allows any given bullet to deliver more energy to distant targets and to get to those targets with less drop. A higher BC also means that a bullet gets to a distant target faster and will, therefore, require less lead on a moving target.

Increasing the BC also allows a bullet to reach a distant target with less deflection resulting from any intervening crosswind. The amount of deflection exhibited by a bullet in a crosswind is more closely related to how much velocity the bullet lost in reaching that target than it is to how long the bullet took to reach that target. This counter-intuitive fact is well proven. The best example comes from 22 rimfire target shooting. Manufacturers always load 22 rimfire match ammo to about 1050 fps muzzle velocity (the speed of sound is about 1120 fps). Conversely, manufacturers load 22 high-speed ammo to about 1250 fps muzzle velocity. Obviously, high-speed bullets reach the target faster. However, these bullets are supersonic until they have traveled about 50 yards. Supersonic bullets slow down much faster than subsonic bullets. Air "cannot get out of the way" of a supersonic bullet, therefore, a high-pressure wave builds in front of any supersonic bullet. Effectively, supersonic bullets "feel" more resistance just as if they were traveling through thicker air.

The result is that, in crossing 100 yards, a high-speed 22 rimfire bullet loses about 240 fps, while an otherwise identical subsonic 22 rimfire bullet loses only about 150 fps. In a 10 mph crosswind, the high-speed bullet drifts about 5.5″, while the subsonic match bullet drifts only about 4.1″. This is in spite of the fact that the high-speed bullet covers the 100 yards 10 percent faster, 0.27 versus 0.30 seconds. This effect holds true for all bullets. A slower bullet with a higher BC can exhibit less wind drift despite having taken longer to reach the target.

We will touch briefly on the effects of shooting uphill or downhill at any angle. For all practical purposes, one can simply envision the problem thus: When estimating holdover, it is not the distance to the target that matters but, rather, the horizontal distance to the target. If one were to shoot uphill at a 60-degree angle at a target 1000 yards distant with the proper holdover, the bullet would only cover 500 actual horizontal yards. Drop would be very similar to the drop for a bullet fired level at a target that was 500 yards distant.

There are errors in this statement associated with decreasing air pressure as the bullet rises through the atmosphere and with the energy the bullet loses in working against gravity, but these two largely cancel each other. The results of shooting downhill are analogous. However, wind drift, delivered energy and target lead still relate to the actual horizontal distance the bullet travels. In the end, less holdover than one would expect is required when shooting up or down hill.

Chronographs

The serious handloader should consider the purchase of a chronograph. The less expensive units are useful, and the better units provide a degree of accuracy beyond what most handloaders could ever use. The chronograph measures the velocity of each shot. By comparing a string of same-load shots, handloaders can better understand the quality of their loads.

One can use this information to assess the potential accuracy of any given load. Loads with particularly low velocity variations generally are good candidates for further accuracy development. Though exceptions do occur, loads with relatively high shot-to-shot velocity variations do not generally shoot accurately, even at short range.

One can also use the chronograph to simply compare loads and to determine which load might work best in one's gun.

Finally, the chronograph can point out potential problems. Loads that fall far outside published ballistics are always suspect. Remember, the only way to substantially increase the velocity of any given bullet is to push on it substantially harder or longer. A load that generates higher velocity than normal most likely generates higher pressure than normal. Equally, a gun that always produces significantly lower-than-normal velocities might have a problem, such as a worn chamber throat.

The chronograph is a valuable tool for the handloader, and with proper record keeping, it can become an important part of any trip to the range. It also gives one a means of evaluating the progressive erosion of one's barrel—generally, as the bore erodes, the same load will generate progressively less velocity.

Several makers offer top-quality chronographs, and two of the best are the P.A.C.T. Professional and the Oehler 35P. My experience is

Shooting Chrony offers an affordable line of feature-packed chronographs. All are fully suitable for both novice handloaders and serious target shooters on a budget. Note the large "window" in these skyscreens.

The old and the new! Even revolver shooters can learn something from computer ballistics programs.

with the Oehler 35P, and I consider it the "Cadillac" of personal chronographs. This machine offers a level of precision and repeatability that is truly outstanding. With its attached printer, the 35P is most useful in the field. One can set up and shoot targets without the interruptions that might otherwise be necessary for immediate record keeping.

Shooting Chrony, Inc., offers an inexpensive line of units that are useful for the shooter who requires a simple setup and uncomplicated use. All Chrony units provide acceptable accuracy. The top-end units also feature erasable permanent memory. One can connect these to a personal computer for further load analysis without the need of manually entering shooting data. In my opinion, both are features Oehler's 35P could use. Chrony packages their top-end unit, the Gamma, with a computer ballistics program (ADC's excellent PC-Bullet).

Setting up the Chrony for recording velocities takes only minutes, and a sturdy tripod is the best method for mounting it. Once you have positioned it, you can fire shot strings on several targets without leaving the shooting bench. The skyscreen window is large enough to allow one to shoot at several targets without repositioning. The more expensive Chrony units include a remote button that allows reviewing of the group and switching to a new group without leaving the shooting bench—most convenient. Ultimate accuracy is not as good as is provided by Oehler's 35P, but it is generally adequate, and results are repeatable.

Most Chrony units, Oehler's 35P and most other chronographs provide built-in statistical analysis of shot strings. Values typically reported for a shot string include the velocity for each shot, the spread between the highest and lowest velocity, the standard deviation, the average velocity and the number of shots fired.

External Ballistics Programs

The advent of the personal computer has given shooters the opportunity to include external ballistics programs in their handloading repertoire. Several companies offer useful programs. Oehler and ADC (PC-Bullet) offer good software adapted to use with chronographs. Also, these programs allow a shooter to compare downrange performance of various loads.

These and other programs are user-friendly and allow the shooter to easily learn more about his pet load than he could hope to know based on any reasonable amount of actual shooting. Many of these programs are currently available only in the DOS format, but Windows versions are appearing. Cost is reasonable, and many offer load and component library options that give any shooter a ready and convenient source of information on ballistics of factory loads and on handloading components that are available.

Examples of uses for these programs cover almost all types of serious shooting. The varmint hunter can easily compare various potential loads (particularly bullet weights) to see which might be the best for any particular shooting conditions, such as differing wind conditions and elevations. The hunter can see what happens to his load's trajectory with significant changes in shooting altitudes—a rifle sighted to properly zero at, say, 300 yards near sea level can shoot much differently at 9000 feet. The target shooter can prepare for re-zeroing a rifle at a different range and elevation, instead of having to zero the gun on the fly, so to speak.

The documentation features of these programs are significant. These programs record all important handloading data, internal and external ballistics data, and accuracy results—all in one place. The graph printouts offered are handy, too. One can carry these in the field and use this information to estimate bullet drop or wind drift at the locale of the hunt or target match.

We have to mention that no ballistics program can substitute for actual shooting. First, one cannot know the bullet's true BC using any method other than firing it and measuring its actual performance. Second, firing the bullet alters its shape so that its BC in flight will be a function of the gun used (variations in rifling deformation of the bullet's jacket, for example). Third, no ballistics program can exactly account for all the real-world variables involved. No doubt we could expound other important reasons.

When it is all said and done, even the Big Boys measure BC by testing. This applies to bullets and space shuttles alike! Nevertheless, since ballistics programs can provide a reasonably accurate first-approximation estimate of actual performance, you might want one for your computer.

BULLET MAKING

UNLIKE OTHER AMMUNITION components, handloaders can still make their own bullets. Whether cast or swaged, almost every aspect of a homemade bullet can be controlled. Lead or lead alloy is the material of choice for both types, but that is just about the only common ground they share.

Generally, the cast bullet is seen as a means of generating inexpensive bullets at home. It is also used to produce bullet styles that can't be purchased commercially, like a 500-grain full wadcutter 454 Casull slug. Also, the caster can adjust bullet hardness and thereby improve accuracy and terminal performance.

The swaged bullet is generally a purely esoteric endeavor. Equipment costs are so high that the only real justification for swaging is the satisfaction of one's ego. There is nothing wrong with this, and we highly praise those with such incentive, and such a budget.

Bullet casting involves various equipment to heat and handle the various alloys of lead, antimony and tin, and to transfer that material to a bullet mould. Other equipment can include sizing and lubricating tools and supplies. In some instances, the kitchen oven can be handy for hardening bullets.

The basic process involves melting the metal and pouring it into a bullet-shaped mould, sizing the bullet to the proper size to fit the gun's bore (not always required) and lubricating the bullet to minimize leading.

We must point out one thing before proceeding with a discussion of casting: Bullet casting is very much an art, so don't expect to learn how to make perfect cast bullets in one afternoon. Practice makes perfect. Read and follow the instructions that come with the your equipment and don't be afraid to ask for expert advice. Each type of mould has unique idiosyncrasies, so you should always heed the mould maker's instructions.

The cast bullet harks to the earliest days of shooting, at a time when all guns were custom muzzleloaders. Until long after that era ended, manufacturers included one or more bullet moulds with any new gun. Without these "accessories," the shooter had no source for proper bullets because there were no standards. Each barrel was unique and therefore required unique bullets.

Modern bullet casters choose to cast bullets either because they have more time than money or because they want to shoot a particular type of bullet that is unavailable commercially. William Falin of Accurate Arms Co. provides a classic example of this. He casts a particular 44 Magnum bullet only because he can't buy it commercially.

Falin makes these bullets using Lyman's #429650 mould. Though nominally a 300-grain mould, when cast of his (not-too-hard) alloy, the bullets weigh about 325 grains. They also cast large enough in diameter to properly fill the somewhat oversize cylinder throats in Falin's S&W Model 29 revolver. No commercially available bullet offers those two features.

Falin loads those bullets over 17 grains of Accurate No. 9 with a CCI 350 primer. The long-range accuracy these loads deliver is nothing less than astounding. As a big game hunting load, this combination would be hard to beat, especially where one prefers a non-expanding bullet.

For an excellent discussion of the techniques required to produce match-grade cast bullets, we suggest the *Precision Shooting Reloading Guide*. Mr. Clouser's article on pages 237-261 is a *tour de force* in

A large-capacity bottom-pour lead pot is a great aid in bullet casting, and Magma's high-capacity lead pot is equipped with an accurate, calibrated thermostat.

the art of making *precision* cast bullets. Those who do not believe cast bullets can be accurate should refer to the 1000-yard records of the 1880s, and the 200-yard records of the early part of the 1900s. Those cast bullet records were unsurpassed, in some instances, for many decades. Never underestimate the cast bullet, or blackpowder, for that matter.

Alloy Hardness and Heat-Treating

By altering the alloy, you can change the pressure range within which cast bullets properly work. Alternately, bullet metal alloys made of lead, tin and antimony that contain a smidgen of arsenic (which is almost ubiquitous in such alloys) can be heat-treated. But, two lead bullet problems can occur: Chamber pressure can damage a too-soft cast bullet while accelerating it through the bore's rifling, and a too-hard cast bullet will not swell up to properly obturate (seal against pressure) the bore and gas cutting will result. Either situation will result in excessive bore leading and loss of accuracy.

Bullets that are either too soft or too hard can lead the bore and be inaccurate, so you have to vary other load parameters to determine the condition. If a cast bullet shoots properly with one load and leads when fired with an increased powder charge, it seems rather obvious that the bullet is too soft for use at the pressure level of the hotter load. In such a situation, either use a slower powder to achieve the increased velocity (with less pressure) or add a bit of antimony to the bullet metal to harden it.

Conversely, a very mild load that creates significant barrel leading might be *too* mild. Try a faster-burning powder to generate more pressure to achieve the same velocity, or add lead to the bullet metal to soften it. The biggest problem in the entire subject of cast bullet hardness seems to be that almost everyone "knows" that barrel leading is indisputable evidence that the bullet is *too soft*. "Experts" have been preaching this for decades. However, with the good-quality commercial cast bullets and the good casting alloys now available, barrel leading or poor accuracy are very often the result of using a bullet that is *too hard!* Again, if peak pressure is not sufficient, a too-hard bullet will not expand to properly seal the bore. The hot high-pressure gasses leaking past such a bullet will melt its surface, and that melted lead will be deposited in the bore.

To see what is happening with your loads, simply fire a few bullets into a 12″ to 24″ stack of saturated telephone books. A too-soft bullet will show evidence of bullet stripping in the rifling. Its surface will generally be visibly mangled. A too-hard bullet will show evidence of gas cutting. This will show up on the area that filled the bore's grooves and will look like little worm tracks progressing from the bullet's base toward its nose.

Determining any necessary adjustment in bullet hardness is very much a trial-and-error process. Fortunately, most bullets cast of typical bullet alloy will work properly. There are exceptions, but with a little thought one can generally figure out why a bullet and load is causing *undue* leading.

A tiny bit of leading is almost inevitable when shooting any lead bullets. However, you should be able to fire hundreds of shots before leading measurably interferes with accuracy. Obviously, the rougher the bore, the faster the build-up of this "baseline" leading.

Saeco (Redding) offers a hardness tester for the serious bullet caster. This simple, albeit precise and expensive, device allows one to easily compare the hardness of any lead-alloy bullet or bullet-metal source material to a standard. Saeco's Lead Hardness Tester reports hardness on a Vernier scale. Most lead alloys will measure in the range from 0 to about 13.

Saeco includes a chart that relates "Saeco hardness" to Brinell Hardness Number (BHN), an industry standard used for measuring the relative hardness of all manner of soft metals.

The folks at Lead Bullet Technology (LBT) offer a similar scale that measures in Brinell Hardness from pure lead (6) to annealed pure copper (40). This tool is somewhat less expensive than Saeco's, but it is certainly a worthwhile addition to any caster's tool room.

If you happen to know the approximate peak pressure of the load you're using, you can very easily calculate the maximum Brinell Hardness that will allow bullet obturation. Various sources quote different versions of the following formula, but we believe the easiest to remember involves the Gregorian year of Columbus' famous voyage, 1492. Simply divide peak chamber pressure in CUP by 1492! (In the pressure range typical of cast bullet loads, CUP and psi are reasonably similar and for this discussion we can use these interchangeably.) This divisor is not the correct number, but it is close enough, especially considering that there is no way anyone can know the *exact* peak pressure level of any load in any gun.

For example, assume you're loading for the 30-30 Winchester with a slow-burning powder using a 173-grain cast bullet. Published data suggests the load is generating a peak chamber pressure of about 30,000. The proper bullet Brinell Hardness will be somewhat less than about 30,000 ÷ 1492, which is about 20. According to Saeco, a Brinell hardness of 20 relates to a Saeco hardness of about 9.5.

What this means is that, if your bullets measure 10 on Saeco's scale (22 on LBT's scale), obturation is suspect and both barrel leading and accuracy problems are almost inevitable. Conversely, if your bullets measure about 9 on Saeco's scale (about 19 on LBT's scale) your load should work very well. If your bullets are significantly softer, leading might occur. In that instance, you will need to choose a lower-pressure loading or use harder bullets.

Adding more antimony and tin to the basic alloy makes cast bullets harder. Here we are considering antimony in the range from 1 to 6 percent. Increasing the antimony 1 percent will typically harden bullet alloy several Saeco points. The degree of hardening generated by a 1-percent increase decreases as the total antimony content increases. The standard method of increasing the antimony content is to add harder alloy to the too-soft alloy until the hardness of a cast test sample is correct.

Adding 1 to 3 percent of tin adds a small measure of hardness, but it chiefly improves castability and is necessary with high-antimony alloys, those with more than about 3-percent antimony. However, since tin is comparatively expensive, casters try to keep tin content to the minimum level that provides good casting. Alloys with 1-percent silver are particularly fluid and tend to cast very good bullets. The silver in such an alloy adds one to two cents to the cost of a typical bullet.

If your tests suggest your bullets are too hard, simply add pure lead to your alloy. As a starting point, try mixing one part pure lead with three parts of your original bullet metal.

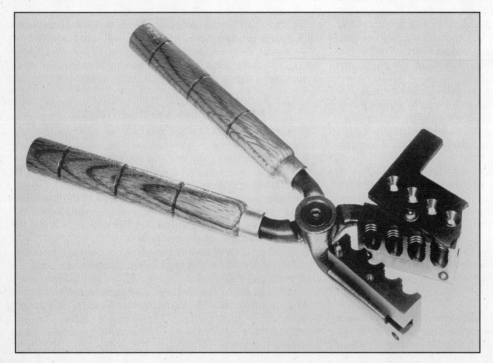

Bullet moulds, as supplied with most early guns, bore little resemblance to this modern Saeco four-cavity revolver bullet mould.

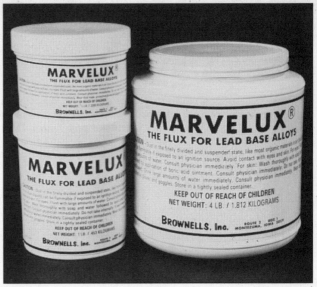

Accurate bullet casting requires proper control of bullet metal temperature; a thermometer is valuable, if not necessary. This unit, available from Brownells, is affordable, accurate and easy to use. Under no circumstance allow bullet metal to exceed about 850°F—above about 900°F, invisible and odorless toxic fumes are generated!

Just as important as using clean alloy in the first place, a quality flux can help keep your bottom-pour lead pot in good repair. Commercial casters use sawdust, which can even help refine the alloy!

Another method of hardening that works for many alloys is heat-treating. Simply heat low-alloy tin/antimony/lead bullets in an oven to about 464°F. Optimal temperature depends upon the actual alloy used, but it should be as near to the point where melting begins to occur as is feasible. The closer you can get the bullets to their melting temperature, the better the results will be. For this work, we highly recommend a lead casting thermometer. These are available from Sinclair International, Inc., and others. Do a test sample to ascertain exactly how hot you can set the oven.

We are not aware of any ready-made accessories designed to allow easy cast-bullet oven-hardening. For this, you will have to make several things. The basic idea is to have a pan that will fit in the oven and allow you to stand bullets close enough that they almost touch. This pan must have a perforated bottom. When placing this pan in the oven, put it above a solid pan. This will prevent radiant heat from the burner or electric elements from overheating and melting the bullets. This second pan will also act as a trap in the unfortunate event of melted bullets. Finally, never use the top element (broiler) to heat the oven while bullets are in it. The perforated bullet pan should also have a handle so you can pick it up and carry it. The second needed item is a larger pan that you can fill with *cold* water (the colder the better, and 32°F is ideal) and *that* will hold the first pan.

Let the unlubed bullets stand in the oven at about 464°F for thirty minutes or longer. Remove the bullets and *immediately* (the sooner the better, *instantly* would be ideal!) quench the batch in cold water. After you have fully submerged the bullets, repeatedly agitate the bullet pan by lifting and lowering it a few inches at a reasonably fast rate, thereby keeping the coolest water possible in contact with the bullets. Do not remove the quenched bullets too soon. Lead is not that good of a conductor of heat. Give the water a long count of five to fully cool the bullets all the way to the interior. If you intend to heat-treat bullets that will require sizing, do the sizing first, then heat-treat and finally lubricate the bullets, after a thorough drying. Sizing heat-treated bullets will return the surface to the original hardness! The same thing happens when one shoots the bullets. However, the softening that results from deformation requires several minutes to occur.

Depending upon the alloy and quality of the heat-treating operation, this process can harden bullets to two to three times the Brinell Hardness of the as-cast bullets. With correct heat-treating, bullets of

the proper alloy (generally about 6-percent antimony) will be substantially harder than bullets cast from the hardest bullet metal alloys.

Assuming they are cast of heat-treatable alloy, all cast bullets are heat-treated to some degree. The question is only how fast they are cooled. As cast, they cool very slowly in the mould and then only slightly faster when removed from the mould. The hardest bullets possible are cast and then dumped directly into ice water. This method is inconsistent, because one cannot dump all bullets into the water at exactly the same temperature. It's also dangerous because it's easy to get water into the lead pot.

Heat-treatable alloy bullets will spontaneously harden over a period of several months after casting. This additional hardening occurs whether or not the bullets are deliberately heat-treated in a separate step. However, after several years of exposure to normal temperatures, heat-treated bullets begin to soften.

After about five years (perhaps sooner), the hardness of heat-treated and unheat-treated bullets will be identical. If you want to maintain the hardness of heat-treated bullets indefinitely, keep them in your freezer. At -20°F, they will maintain almost a full measure of their maximum hardness for decades.

Lyman and other sources offer discussions of this process, although, they are not particularly complete. On page 60 of the January 1995 issue of *Precision Shooting Magazine,* Roger Johnson explored bullet heat-treating in some detail, and we highly recommend his article for detailed information on this subject.

Basic Equipment

You can spend a little or a lot on basic casting equipment. My personal choice is to follow a middle road, so to speak. Lee's Pro 20 bottom-pour lead pot is affordable. For the shooter who might only need to cast a few thousand bullets a year, this is a fine choice. For the serious shooter, Lyman, Magma and RCBS offer fine bottom-pour pots that can last a lifetime, even for the serious user. A casting thermometer is a good addition, as proper flux.

Moulds are commonly available in two basic types: iron alloy and aluminum alloy. Each has its pundits and certain advantages. The novice caster might find aluminum moulds a bit easier to use. Iron moulds are somewhat more robust and are less susceptible to damage from handling, but they are harder for most novices to master.

This difference revolves around getting the blocks up to proper temperature. Aluminum moulds can be preheated by simply holding a corner of the mould block in the molten bullet metal. The only safe way to bring iron blocks up to the proper temperature is to cast bullets. This process takes a few minutes and the bullets cast in the "cold" blocks won't be usable, but they can simply be returned to the pot.

The variety of commercial moulds is staggering, and custom moulds are available at usually reasonable prices. If you simply have to have a multi-cavity 500-grain wadcutter 454 Casull mould, Dave Farmer at Hoch Custom Bullets can certainly produce one for you. In fact, like several other mould makers, he specializes in custom moulds to fulfill the wildest dreams of shooters.

For those who simply want to cast bullets from lead scrap such as wheelweights, a mould for a bullet similar in style and weight to an original factory number is a good choice. Such moulds are available from Lee Precision, Lyman, RCBS, Saeco and others. Using a mould that casts a bullet of typical weight for the application, you can usually make bullets shoot very accurately and without barrel leading. Simply choose the appropriate powder and velocity level necessary to match the bullet's as-cast hardness to the pressure level.

The secret here is to spend the money necessary to get a proper hardness tester. With a tester, when you have to switch to a different alloy, you can determine how to soften or harden it to get it to shoot properly with the same loads. This can be worthwhile since bullets made from scrap alloys can be very inexpensive.

The casting process is pure simplicity: You pour molten lead into the mould. The difficulties come in the details. What is the proper temperature for the alloy? How fast should you pour the melt into the mould? How much extra lead should you pour on top of the sprue plate? How long does it take for the bullet to solidify? How long should you wait before filling the mould for the next bullet?

We can only offer the most basic of guidelines here. If the alloy fills the properly warmed mould fully and forms good, sharp corners on the bullets, it is hot enough. The sprue plate should have sufficient excess lead covering it so the bullet doesn't have a hole where the sprue was cut off. You should pour the melt as fast as the hole in the sprue plate will allow without undue amounts of melt running off the plate. If the sprue plate wipes lead across the top of the blocks as it's moved, wait a bit longer. If the bullets look frosted, let the mould cool longer before refilling or reduce the alloy temperature (the preferable choice, when possible).

By trial and error, almost anyone can learn to cast good bullets in a matter of hours. However, you must have a good understanding of the basic principles. The best time to get that knowledge is *before* starting!

Lubricating and Sizing

Lubricating and sizing also runs the gambit. If the as-cast bullets are close to the proper diameter for the gun, typically within about 0.0005″ of throat diameter, you can lubricate and use them as-cast. For this, Lee's Liquid Alox works very well.

A simple method is to simply stand the bullets in a shallow pan, melt the necessary amount of your favorite bullet lube and pour it into the pan so the grease grooves are covered. After the lube cools, punch the bullets out individually. This will leave the lube in the grease grooves.

Bullets cast to fit the gun properly without sizing are generally more accurate, because sizing both distorts and softens them. If your bullets come out of the mould more than 0.002″ larger than necessary to fit the bore—generally, groove diameter or 0.001″ larger—consider adjusting the alloy or casting temperature to get bullets that cast closer to groove diameter. Reduction of tin and antimony content will allow the bullet to shrink more, and casting at a higher temperature will (usually) result in smaller bullets. However, in some instances, it is not feasible to cast to the proper diameter, and sizing then becomes necessary.

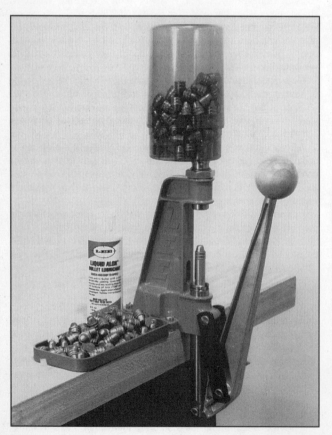

Lee's Sizer Lubricator is affordable. It does an eminently good job. Use the recommended Liquid Alox or pan-lube bullets with regular lube before sizing.

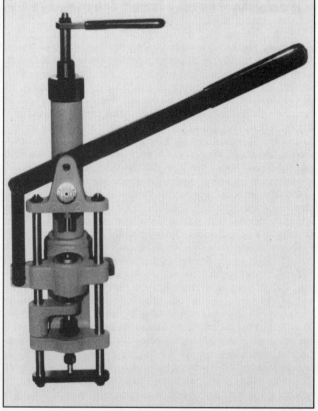

Saeco (Redding), RCBS and Lyman all offer similar lubricator/sizers for low- to moderate-volume bullet sizing and lubricating. These also apply gas checks (where applicable).

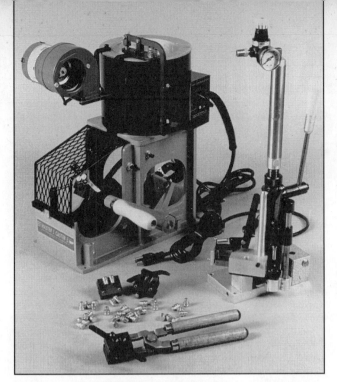

Magma's Master Caster and the Magma-accessorized Star lubricator/sizer are a good investment for the small club or shooting team. One can produce top-quality cast bullets of almost any imaginable design and not spend much time in the process. Production rates on the order of 800 bullets per hour are typical.

You can size bullets very inexpensively using Lee's press-mounted Lube and Sizing Kit. This unit is very fast to operate, and results are most impressive. The only limitation is that you can't easily use standard bullet lubes. However, you can use the above-mentioned pan-lube method before the sizing step. Alternatively, Liquid Alox lube can be used, but this leaves the bullets a bit messy. However, it does an impressive job of limiting barrel leading.

Standard lubricator/sizers available from RCBS, Lyman and Saeco are all easy to use. Each does a smart job of properly lubricating and sizing the bullet, and also provides a means of attaching a gas check to the base of bullets designed to accept them. Copper gas checks allow increased velocity, help reduce leading and can also improve accuracy.

All of these lubri-sizers use stick lubes which are available from many suppliers. Find one you like and enjoy. We couldn't possibly make any recommendation, because the one that works best for your purpose might not be optimum for the next person. Generally, we prefer the harder lubes that require moderate heating to properly apply. Bullets lubed with these are cleaner to handle, and the lube isn't apt to melt in a loaded round that might get particularly hot, as when the load is exposed to the sun or the ammunition is left in the car trunk in summer. Melted lube might infiltrate into the powder, which could alter the load's ballistics or even kill the primer.

These lubes require the use of a heater. These thermostatically controlled electric units typically bolt under the lubri-sizer and are easily adjusted to get the proper temperature.

Paper-Patched Bullets

Buffalo hunters and target shooters of the 1800s often used paper-patched bullets. These are cast or swaged lead-alloy bullets with a cylindrical shank portion and, usually, a slightly hollow base. Specially treated and sized paper is wrapped around the bullet's shank and folded into the base. Paper-patch bullets are still being shot. Moulds and paper are both commercially available. The reason these bullets were once so popular and are still with us is simple to understand—they work.

Originally, paper-patched bullets were used because they reduced barrel fouling, a considerable concern in blackpowder days. Shooters soon learned that these also offered distinct accuracy and long-range trajectory advantages.

The paper-patched bullet is more aerodynamic than the standard grooved and greased bullet. The stresses of internal ballistics are also less apt to deform such a bullet. Finally, these bullets can achieve extremely high velocities without barrel leading. Modern shooters often exceed 3000 fps with smokeless-powder paper-patch loads with no metallic barrel fouling—something no lead or jacketed bullet can claim.

For the blackpowder shooter, paper-patched bullets can deliver more energy to long range and shoot flatter while providing extended shot strings without the necessity of bore cleaning. This was something the buffalo hunters appreciated tremendously. Since it is less susceptible to fouling, this design can provide supersior target accuracy.

Paper-patch-style bullet moulds are available from Colorado Shooters Supply and many others. Custom moulds are available in almost any imaginable length and nose profile, and often include very heavy full-spitzer designs. These bullets must be cast appropriately smaller than bore diameter to compensate for the thickness of the patch. Typically, they are patched as-cast and don't require sizing, providing the mould size is correct and both alloy composition and casting temperature are correct.

Pre-cut and treated paper patches for 40- and 45-caliber guns are available from Yesteryear Armory. These are made from 100-percent rag paper. One can easily make patches from any high-quality thin rag paper. The basic process involves tightly wrapping the bullet shank to the proper thickness and wax-sealing the paper in place. An excess length of just over one-half of bullet diameter is left behind the bullet to be folded into the hollow cavity in the bullet's base. The process sounds a bit daunting, but is actually rather easy to master.

Our forebears used to do this entire process in the field, both when hunting and at the target range. We encourage interested shooters to try paper-patched bullets for the many benefits they offer.

Swaged Jacketed Bullets

Bullet swaging (pronounced "sway-jing") involves the pressure forming of cold lead into a specific shape. This process begins with swaging a lead wire to the proper diameter and then cutting it to the proper length. Lubing or crimping grooves could be added, or the bullet could be swaged to the correct finished size for use as a paper-patch bullet. In either instance, it would be a finished bullet.

Often, however, this semi-formed lead core is inserted into a commercially produced, semi-finished gilding metal jacket for further processing. This involves swaging-up the core so that it stretches the jacket, necessary since this is the only way to maintain intimate contact between the elastic bullet jacket and the ductile core. This jacket and core unit are then final sized to a *slightly* smaller outside diameter, and the base and nose of the bullet are formed in one or more additional swaging steps.

The materials for swaging jacketed bullets are all expensive. The tools are *very* expensive. Even the most dedicated shooter would have a hard time justifying the process for economy's sake. Further, the best standard and custom commercial bullets offer levels of quality that would be difficult or impossible for any hobbyist to match. Nevertheless, swaging does have certain appeal. Those interested in doing for themselves as much of "it" as possible are the major group interested in bullet swaging.

Those willing to invest the price of a very good custom rifle can set themselves up in the bullet swaging business. We must note that each new bullet one wants to make requires a *considerable* additional investment in swaging dies. Nevertheless, just like casting, swaging offers considerable latitude in bullet design, and custom dies are available. If you simply must have a 300-grain 30-caliber spitzer boattail to shoot from your 1:6-twist custom-barreled super varmint special rifle, swaging is the only game in town.

Space limitations prevent our discussion of this process in any greater detail. Swaging tools are well represented in *Handloader's Digest*, and the folks at Corbin Manufacturing & Supply, Inc., among others, are always willing to offer advice and references.

12

RELOADING PRESSES

A QUICK COUNT shows that today's handloader has close to fifty presses from which to choose. There are portable presses that can be used at the range, affordable single-stage presses, compound-leverage presses that can crush a rock, progressive presses that allow loading hundreds of rounds of quality ammunition an hour, power-driven progressives that might appeal to the small gun club or shooting team, and arbor presses for loading the most precise ammunition in the world. (Note: One should never use any normal arbor press for full-length case sizing). For a good review of many of these, refer to *Handloader's Digest*. Here, we can afford only a short discussion.

You need a place to work, and it can be small or large, simple or complicated. To be comfortable while handloading, most of us need a special area dedicated to our hobby.

Progressive Presses

Throughout this text we have discussed various tools that experienced handloaders might want to consider adding to their workbenches. The one subject we have not heretofore discussed is the reloading press. With the recent innovations involving progressive presses, we feel that we should point out some of what is available, why the advanced handloader might be interested in upgrading to one of these newer presses and how one uses a progressive press.

Most handloaders started out with a single-stage press, and many have already stepped up to progressive units. Progressives are not appropriate for all types of loading. Generally, one can do a better job loading the largest rifle cartridges on a single-stage press. One should keep a good, heavy-duty press—such as the RCBS Rock Chucker or Redding's impressive Ultramag—around for case forming and other heavy-duty operations. However, for loading any of the classic handgun cartridges and rifle cartridges up to at least 30-06 size, the progressive press can be a genuine joy to own and use.

Several manufacturers offer perfectly useful units, but two stand out from the crowd in my experience. Lee has priced their Load-Master very affordably. This sophisticated press offers five positions, automatic indexing, automatic case feeding, automatic bullet feeding and the simplest primer feeding system of any metallic cartridge loading press on the market. This press does require a bit of patience to set up properly. We do not recommend the Load-Master for those who might be intimidated by sophisticated mechanisms. Our only special comment on the usage of this press is that one should limit primer choice to those produced by CCI after 1990. In our experience, these are the only primers that work properly and dependably in this press.

The Load-Master's best purpose is loading conventional pistol and revolver cartridges, but it also does a fine job with rifle cartridges through 30-06 case size. However, it will not automatically feed cases or bullets for rifle calibers. The handloader who is not afraid to do a bit of tinkering to get this machine working perfectly, and who wants to load a mountain of handgun ammunition in a hurry, will find this press a joy to own. Quick-change removable toolheads and shellplates allow for very quick caliber conversions, on the order of one minute or so.

Hornady's Projector is conceptually on the other side of the aisle. This press does not come with all the bells and whistles offered by Lee's top-of-the-line press. The Projector offers five positions, auto-matic indexing, automatic priming and the option of automatic powder dispensing. The operator has to feed cases and bullets individually. Also, the Projector lacks an interchangeable toolhead. This author believes that is a fundamental oversight that Hornady should address. This makes the Projector a bit slower and considerably more awkward for caliber changes, compared to progressive presses that have this feature. There is no better place to store one's dies than in a toolhead. That way they won't become separated and misplaced, and adjustments remain fixed.

On the other hand, the Projector is fully capable for loading any standard rifle cartridge. It also provides the most positive priming system of any progressive press with which I am familiar. Positive and correct priming is the biggest problem with any progressive press. Per-

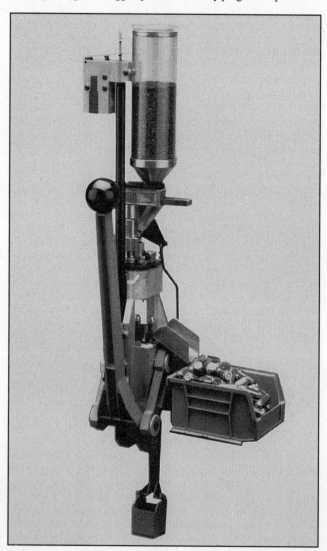

Dillon's Square Deal B is affordable, easy to use and will produce high-quality pistol or revolver ammunition in a hurry (350 per hour).

haps most important, Hornady builds the Projector to standards of fit and quality that are absolutely astounding. This press is a pleasure to use. There is no reason a careful operator could not use the Projector to turn out any kind of metallic cartridge ammunition to topmost quality. About the only limitation is the need to use ball-type powders for rifle loads, in order to achieve good dropped-charge consistency.

This is a limitation all progressive presses share with regard to rifle loads. However, one can simply omit the automatic powder dispensing step and fill the case with a weighed charge when the case is at the correct location. This will slow the loading process somewhat, but is not a major problem. Combining Lyman's Auto Flo powder dispensing system with the use of a progressive press, one could produce loaded rounds of belted magnum ammunition at the approximate rate of 360 per hour. This presumes only that the cases have been lubed and that you forgo primer pocket cleaning.

Dillon Precision Products, Inc., has introduced more progressive presses than anyone else to the market. These include the Square Deal B, a revolver- and pistol-specific press that uses unique Dillon dies. This press provides automatic priming, powder feeding and shellholder indexing. All the operator has to do is feed in a new case, insert a bullet, stroke the handle, and fill the primer tube and powder hopper as required.

The Dillon 550B is a versatile affordable unit that is equally useful for loading all common handgun and rifle cartridges. With four die positions, interchangeable toolheads and quick-change shellholders,

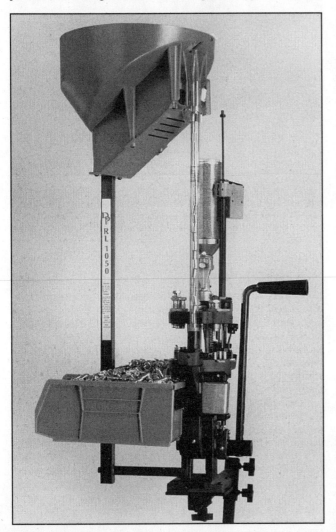

For those who do a lot of shooting (teams or clubs), Dillon's RL 1050 brings commercial-scale production to the reloading bench. Top-quality pistol, revolver and short rifle cartridges can be punched out at 1000 rounds per hour.

one can swap from loading 45 Colt ammunition for a Cowboy Action Shooting event to loading 6mm BR ammunition for an important benchrest event, in a matter of minutes.

The 550B, like the Projector, is fully capable of loading to the highest level of accuracy. To achieve this goal: Use the proper dies—for example, Redding's Competition dies; follow the guidelines in this book regarding die adjustment, case preparation, case maintenance and other loading details; practice consistent press manipulation. Many serious rifle competitors have already learned that a progressive press is fully capable, given the correct dies and technique, of delivering match-grade ammunition.

The 550B does not feature automatic shellholder indexing. This is by design. Omission of this feature allows the operator to advance the shellholder at his leisure, which can be beneficial. However, this does add to the opportunity for error. To prevent double charges, always make certain you turn the shellholder after charging a case. In reality, manual indexing is no big handicap. One has plenty of time to advance the shellholder while bringing a new case to position one. This press is both fast and dependable.

The only problems I have found with the Dillon 550B are primer-related. It sometimes ejects a spent primer that fails to land in the primer catcher, no big deal. It also sometimes fails to feed a primer correctly, and this is a problem. Choosing a different primer type can sometimes improve primer-feed dependability.

Dillon's XL 650 offers five die stations and adds auto-indexing to the repertoire. The fifth die position is a boon. This allows installation of the Dillon powder level alarm, without forgoing separate bullet seating and crimping stages. This alarm produces a piercing audible warning when it senses any case not charged with the proper amount of powder. The auto-indexing feature is most useful if you equip the XL 650 with the optional electric pistol-case feeder. With this option, you have only to work the handle, feed bullets and keep the basic supplies stocked. Ammunition production rates are most impressive. This press will process most common handgun and rifle cartridges.

The RL 1050 is altogether a different breed. Rather than detail everything the RL 1050 will do, we will just note that it includes eight die stations and automatic case feeding. The additional die stations allow you to specially process cases (for example, swaging out the military crimp). With the proper conversion kits, this machine will load all common handgun cartridges and the 223 and 7.62x39 rifle cartridges. Small-scale ammunition manufacturers often use this press to produce tens of thousands of rounds every week. Enough said!

When using a progressive press, you don't handle each case to perform each separate loading operation. With a typical progressive press, you simply insert a case into the shellholder at position one and a bullet at position three. When you lower the press handle, the following things happen automatically: The case at position one is full-length sized; the case at position two is neck expanded and bell-mouthed (if necessary), and has a powder charge dumped in; the case at position three has the bullet seated (and perhaps crimped); the case at position four has the bullet crimped (if desired).

When one raises the handle, the press automatically installs a primer into the newly sized case at position one. Then, the press rotates the shellholder plate automatically, or the operator rotates it manually to the next position. When the shellholder plate rotates, the press ejects a completed cartridge and the first position is ready to accept another case. Progressive press systems vary in actual layout and operation, but this scenario generally explains what happens.

Compared to a single-stage press, case handling and the number of handle strokes per loaded round are drastically reduced. We might add that the opportunities for errors are entirely different. The use of a progressive press reduces the opportunities for handling-related errors, but it increases the opportunity for processing errors. As an example of a most serious processing error, it is quite possible to stop the ram stroke part way down and then return it to the top. If you're employing automatic powder dispensing, this act is likely to result in a double-charge of powder in a case.

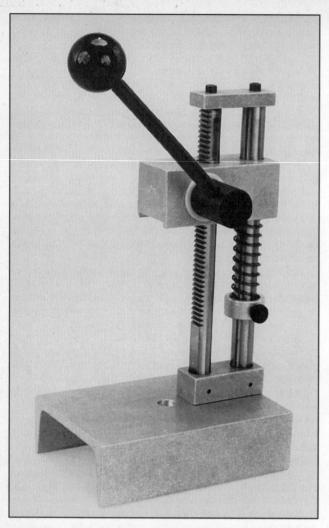

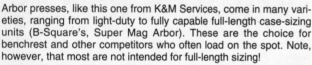

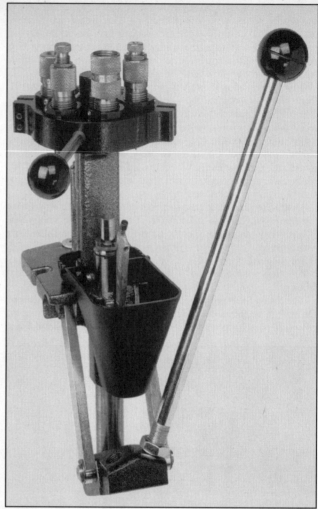

Arbor presses, like this one from K&M Services, come in many varieties, ranging from light-duty to fully capable full-length case-sizing units (B-Square's, Super Mag Arbor). These are the choice for benchrest and other competitors who often load on the spot. Note, however, that most are not intended for full-length sizing!

The safe use of any progressive press requires the operator to maintain great concentration, compared to a single-stage press. The handloader must observe one cardinal safety rule religiously: Once the ram on any progressive press starts moving either up or down, always complete the stroke without changing directions. If some problem prevents your completing a stroke, make sure that you don't get a double-charged case, a case with no powder, one with no primer or one that is in any other way defective or incomplete.

Turret Presses

The turret press is an old design. While not a progressive press, this design allows quick die changes. This is useful for those who don't want a progressive press, but who do want their loading to go a bit faster without so many distractions. Some turret presses also feature interchangeable toolheads. Most toolheads hold six dies, so one can load several calibers without any interruption for die changes. Extra turrets also provide a convenient place to store your dies.

Use of a turret press is no different from a single-stage press except that one can choose to load ammunition sequentially. Size and prime, turn the toolhead, charge the case, turn the toolhead, and seat a bullet. While this process is possible, it does not seem feasible except for load development work where one is loading only a few rounds. However, for that use it is most handy. One can mount a powder measure in one of the positions and use it for standard manual case charging. This keeps the powder measure handy and out of the way at the same time.

Turret presses represent a step up from single-stage presses. Lyman's full-featured T-Mag II offers almost instantaneous die selection. Toolheads can be interchanged in seconds. This allows quick caliber conversions for as many calibers as the handloader might require.

Arbor Presses

Various makers offer arbor presses (most are not intended for full-length sizing) for use with the various hand dies—discussed throughout this text. We can divide these into three groups. First, we have the lightweight units intended for ease of transport. These are appropriate for neck sizing and bullet seating with hand dies. Second, we have standard models, handier and more precise in operation. Their purpose is the same as the lightweight units. Third are heavy-duty units—tough enough and with the gearing necessary to allow full-length sizing of many rifle cartridge cases.

Besides portability, these presses provide a simple means of neck sizing cases and seating bullets. Their use requires special dies, and they are most appropriate to benchrest shooting where loading is often done at the shooting bench between rounds of competition.

You do not have to own an arbor press to use hand dies, but these presses certainly do ease the chore. An arbor press is a good investment for those interested in loading the most precise ammunition possible. Operation is pure simplicity. To neck size a case, insert the case into the open end of the die, then set the die in a die base with the case head up. Crank the handle to lower the ram. This pushes the case fully into the die and completes the neck-sizing operation. Release the spring-loaded crank, which will raise the ram automatically. Turn the die over in the base. Crank the handle a second time. The ram will drive the case out of the die and then decap it.

Introduction To Loading Data

HANDLOADING DATA IS presented in many different formats—each a compromise. In an ideal world, all load data would be gathered in a ballistics laboratory using pressure barrels. Each load would be fired in at least three nominally identical pressure barrels fitted with conformal transducers and the results averaged to represent "nominal pressure barrel datum." Tenth-grain charge increments would be tested in each barrel until the next increment pushed peak pressure over the SAAMI maximum average pressure (MAP) limit. The resulting charges for the three barrels would be averaged, rounded down to the nearest tenth-grain and then listed as the "maximum recommended charge." The pressures generated with the rounded-down average charge would be averaged and listed as maximum recommended charge "test pressure." The velocities generated with the rounded-down average charge would also be averaged and listed as maximum recommended charge "test velocity." Similarly, a minimum recommended charge would be listed with both the average velocity generated and average pressure generated along with the standard deviations of all test barrel data (both pressure and velocity).

In an ideal world, only fully prepped cases of uniform nominal weight with consistent nominal flash holes and uniform case-neck-to-bullet tension would be used in the testing. Ten cartridges would be loaded for each powder and bullet combination with each of three lots of the same powder, three lots of the same bullet, three lots of the same case and three lots of the same primer—810 cartridges for each powder and bullet combination. And of course, *perfect* testing techniques and procedures would be maintained at all times, and all suspect tests would be repeated. Using this ideal method, it would take one week to load and fire any one cartridge/bullet/powder combination. To test all the data represented in this book would have taken over 200 years.

Obviously, this "perfect" system is totally unfeasible. The above discussion was intended only to demonstrate why all ballistics testing laboratories make compromises. They do so not because they want to, but, rather, because they have to. In presenting this data, we will make compromises, too. Wherever feasible, we will explain our compromises.

First, you must understand explicitly that the data listed here was generated by other ballistics laboratories. We are, therefore, constrained by the compromises those laboratories chose to make while generating their data. In some instances, we will impose additional compromises in order to present safe, meaningful and comparable data that is easy to use.

We have made every effort to present the data in a format that is both useful and concise. Each cartridge is accompanied by a actual-size photograph of the loaded round, a cross-sectional dimensional drawing of the case, cartridge specific information, a brief write-up on the history and performance characteristics of the cartridge and, finally, the load data itself.

The case drawings list nominal case dimensions that are either of primary importance or interest to the handloader. The dimensions normally shown include rim thickness, if the case type headspaces on the case rim; head-to-shoulder length; head-to-base-of-neck length; mouth case length; head-to-mouth case length; maximum nominal case length; rim diameter; body diameter immediately ahead of the rim (where not given the case is essentially cylindrical, e.g., 375 Mag.); body diameter at the shoulder; neck diameter at base of neck, if significantly different from diameter at mouth of case; neck diameter at mouth; shoulder angle, if applicable.

In some instances, the dimensional numbers vary in the third decimal place from SAAMI specifications or similar drawings found in other reference sources. The dimensions given for non-SAAMI cartridges, when compared to other sources, will demonstrate the variation in opinion regarding nominal dimensions. Also, very old cartridges can show significant differences in shoulder-angle data.

The dimensional drawing is followed by load specific information for the data: case, primer, barrel, bullet diameter, maximum case length, trim to length, maximum cartridge OAL; minimum cartridge OAL. Under "Barrel" we list one or more barrel lengths along with the companies who provided data for that cartridge. If the firearm is not specified, then the barrel used was a test barrel.

In some instances, you might find that the original data used a different make of case than we suggest. In such instances, we have chosen to suggest the lightest case commonly available. If the original load used a heavier case, the only harm is that your load will generate *slightly* less velocity and pressure. Should you choose to use a brand of case that is heavier than the one we suggest, employ the following simple system to ensure you will create a safe load that falls within SAAMI maximum allowable pressure specifications. For normal rifle and large handgun cases, reduce your maximum powder charge by 0.6-grain for each 10 grains of increased case weight; for 5 grains increased case weight, decrease the charge by 0.3-grain. For a more thorough analysis, see Chapter 4; however, the above formula is sufficiently accurate to ensure the safety of the resulting load. If your cases are less than 5 grains heavier than the cases we list, you can use our data with no alterations. For the smaller pistol and revolver cases, generally those smaller in capacity than the 45 Automatic, one cannot account for capacity differences by tenth-grain powder increments! No charge alteration is necessary.

The load data tables offer several interesting features. First, loads were developed in full-grain increments, 100 fps velocity increments, or tenth-grain increments. This is because many ballistics laboratories load in full-grain increments and stop at the greatest full-grain increment that does not violate SAAMI's maximum average pressure standard; others load in 100 fps increments and stop at the highest 100 fps increment that falls short of SAAMI's MAP standard; still others increase their charges by tenth-grain increments until reaching the maximum tenth-grain increment that does not exceed the SAAMI MAP.

While the latter method is likely most informative, it, too, is a compromise since it assumes all testing variables were nominal, which they are not. Since we have gleaned the best data from many sources, the user will note the existence of all three methodologies used in the data. It would be a happy coincidence if all the incremental maximum loads were incrementally remote from SAAMI's maximum pressure, but, alas, this is not the situation. By simple statistical analysis, we know that a certain percentage of all such loads fall arbitrarily near SAAMI's maximum pressure limit. For this reason, you cannot blithely assume it is OK to increase these even-full-grain or even-100-fps maximum charges by *any* amount; the load listed might already fall right on SAAMI's maximum pressure limit. Abide by common sense and stay within the guidelines of this manual. Any minor ballistic improvement you might be able to achieve can only come at the expense of increased pressure. And increased pressure can only reduce your margin of personal safety!

Warning

Where the data calls for a specific primer and/or bullet in the "Comments" column, substitutions are not allowable. You must stay with that bullet or primer. Substitutions can change peak pressure dramatically. If you must use a bullet other than that specified, then choose a load using a powder that does not require a specific bullet. Those powders were tested with all common bullets of the described weight.

Primer substitutions are even worse! If the cartridge heading specifies a primer by make and number, use that primer for all loads except where the "Comments" column specifies a different primer. If the "Comments" column specifies a certain primer, never substitute any other make or type. There are instances where seemingly innocent primer substitutions such as one brand of small pistol standard primer for another brand of small pistol standard primer have generated greater than 30 percent increases in chamber pressures! Certain fast-burning porous-base powders and ball powders are extremely sensitive to primer characteristic.

When the maximum/minimum cartridge overall length is not specified, you should seat a rifle bullet a minimum of 0.0625" clear of the rifling. In no instance should you use this data with any load where the bullet is touching the rifling or with any load using a copper or copper alloy bullet that is closer to the rifling than 0.050".

For pistol and revolver loads, seat the bullet as close as possible to specified OAL. Deep-seating pistol and revolver bullets will raise pressures dramatically. In cartridges such as the 38 Special, seating a bullet 0.10" deeper can double chamber pressure!

The load data is presented in muzzle velocity order from highest fps in a maximum charge to lowest for each bullet weight. For cast or swaged lead bullets, the bullet-weight heading will specify "Lead" then the bullet weight and other bullet information such as the mould manufacturer and mould number in the case of cast bullets.

In a seven-column format for each bullet weight or weight range, we list the powder, its starting charge in grains, starting charge muzzle velocity, maximum charge, maximum charge muzzle velocity, maximum charge chamber pressure and pertinent comments.

The "Comments" column contains specific bullet, OAL, primer and other important information. A blank column indicates no datum was necessary.

In some instances, we have not listed a starting charge because the information was not available. For those, you must reduce the maximum charge by 5 to 10 percent for your starting load.

In the "Pressure" column, a "C" after the pressure signifies copper units of pressure and indicates copper crusher testing; a "p" signifies psi units and indicates conformal transducer testing.

The abbreviations found in the "Comments" column are explained in a key which accompanies each two-page spread in the data section. Abbreviations not spelled out in the key are common proprietary bullet configuration acronyms.

All data for Accurate's powders were tested at Accurate Arms' ballistic laboratory. These powders are N100, No. 2, No. 5, No. 7, No. 9, A1680, A2015BR, A2230, A2460, A2495BR, A2520, A2700, A4350, A3100 and A8700.

All data for Vihtavuori powders were tested at Vihtavuori's ballistic laboratory. These powders are N310, N320, N330, N340, N350, 3N37, N110, N120, N130, N133, N135, N140, N150, N160, N165, 24N64 and 24N41.

Some data for the Winchester powders were tested at Winchester's ballistic laboratory. These powders are WAP, WMR, W231, W748 and W760. Winchester-tested loads are indicated by a separate barrel length listing for Winchester and, usually, by the existence of any comment in the "Comments" column for that Winchester powder.

All data for the various other powders were tested at Hodgdon's ballistic laboratory. The Hodgdon powders are H4198, H322, BLC(2), H335, H4895, H380, H414, H4350, H450, H4831, H1000, H870, HP38, Clays, HS6, HS7, H110, H4227, Trap100 and Universal. IMR powders include IMR4227, IMR4198, IMR4895, IMR4064, IMR4320, SR4759, IMR4350, IMR4831, IMR3031, IMR7828, IMRPB, SR4756, 700-X, 800-X and SR7625. Hercules (now Alliant) powders represented are Blue Dot, Red Dot, Green Dot, Herco, Unique, Bullseye, Her2400, RL-7, RL-12, RL-15, RL-19 and RL-22. Winchester powders are W748, W760, W231 and W296.

Caution: Technical data presented here inevitably reflects individual experience with particular equipment and components under specific circumstances the reader cannot duplicate exactly. Such data presentations, therefore, should be used for guidance only, and then only with caution.

CASE CAPACITY FOR CARTRIDGES FIRED IN SPORTING CHAMBERS

Max. CC Grs.Water	Make	Bullet Wgt.Grs.	Type	Cart. OAL	Usable CC Grs.Water	Primer+Case Wgt.Grs.	Cartridge
Rifle Cartridges							
28.4	H	25	SP	2.15	26.5	92.1	17 Rem.
14.9	Si	45	S	1.72+	12.2	54.9	22 Hornet
17.9	Si	45	S	1.68	15.5	78.6	218 Bee
28.6	Si	52	HP	2.13	26.0	95.1	222 Rem.
31.1	Si	52	HP	2.26	28.8	100.5	223 Rem.
31.8	Si	52	HP	2.28	29.2	98.7	222 Rem. Mag.
42.0	Si	52	HP	2.50	40.6	148.8	225 Win.
44.9	Si	52	HP	2.35	42.5	169.4	22-250
51.1	Si	52	HP	2.68	49.0	163.5	220 Swift
56.7	Si	100	S	2.71	52.8	162.2	243 Win.
58.4	Si	100	S	2.82+	53.7	173.9	6mm Rem/244 Rem
23.0	Sp	60	S	1.59	18.1	83.6	256 Win Mag
39.0	R	117	FP	2.55	33.0	133.3	25-35 Win
48.2	Si	100	S	2.51+	43.2	156.3	250 Sav
58.1	Si	100	S	2.78	53.2	180.6	257 Rob/257 Rob+P
69.1	R	120	S	3.25	64.0	197.3	25-06 Rem
58.8	Si	100	S	2.90	56.8	188.2	6.5x55 Swed. Mauser
72.0	R	120	S	2.80	66.0	218.5	6.5mm Rem Mag
85.8	W	120	S	3.34	81.7	242.1	264 Win Mag
69.2	Si	130	SBT	3.34	65.4	195.2	270 Win
57.3	Sp	145	SBT	2.80	51.2	165.5	7mm-08
61.5	Sp	145	SBT	3.06+	56.8	182.9	7mm Mauser
69.6	Sp	145	SBT	2.80	61.3	200.3	284 Win
73.2	Sp	145	SBT	3.33	67.7	191.0	280 Rem
85.9	Sp	145	SBT	3.28	80.8	223.6	7mm Wby Mag
86.7	Sp	145	SBT	3.29	81.3	239.7	7mm Rem Mag
20.9	H	110	FMJ	1.68	15.5	75.5	30 Carb
46.7	Sp	170	FSP	2.55	37.8	137.8	30-30 Win
47.0	Sp	170	FSP	2.52+	37.4	131.2	30 Rem
55.7	H	150	SPBT	2.60	49.1	155.3	300 Sav
57.6	Sp	170	FSP	2.56	49.2	188.6	307 Win
58.0	H	150	SPBT	2.81	52.9	167.4	308 Win
57.1	H	150	SPBT	2.81	52.0	181.9	308 Win (Mil)
59.6	H	150	SPBT	3.09-	53.8	195.2	30-40 Krag
70.6	H	150	SPBT	3.34	67.6	190.4	30-06 Sprg
88.0	H	150	SPBT	3.60	82.2	255.4	300 H&H Mag
90.9	H	165	SPBT	3.30	80.0	249.6	308 Norma Mag
93.4	H	150	SPBT	3.34	86.8	242.8	300 Win Mag
105.7	H	150	SPBT	3.56	98.8	229.3	300 Wby Mag
35.9	H	130	SP	2.20	31.4	108[1]	7.62x39
50	Sp	170	FSP	2.52	40.4	142.6	303 Sav
21.4	W	86	LRN	1.59+	17.1	74.1	32-20 Win
58.8	H	150	SP	2.99	50.6	164.4	303 Brit
47.2	Sp	170	FP	2.50	38.1	131.0	32 Rem
48.3	Sp	170	FSP	2.56+	39.2	137.3	32 Win Spl
64.4	H	170	RN	2.81	56.9	179.7	8mm
99.3	H	150	SP	3.6	93.9	259.7	8mm Rem Mag
88.3	H	225	SP	3.34	78.3	237.9	338 Win Mag
101.9	H	225	SP	3.69	91.0	251.8	340 Wby Mag[2]
106.4	H	225	SP	3.69	95.4	224.8	340 Wby Mag
78.2	W	200	RN	2.78	66.7	257.6	348 Win
25.0	W	180	RN	1.90	20.2	89.4	351 Win SL
52.0	R	200	RN	2.52	44.0	156.6	35 Rem
58.1	W	250	FP	2.56	44.9	187.1	356 Win
59.2	Sp	250	S	2.78	47.4	175.6	358 Win

IN THE INTRODUCTORY text for most of the cartridge data listed here, we have included mention of usable case capacity in grains of water. We specify a certain type and weight of bullet, and that the bullet is seated normally. That information is based on the adjacent chart. Usable case capacity represents the amount of water (in grains) that the fired case can hold when the specified bullet is seated to a typical overall length (*usually* maximum OAL). In gathering the data for this chart, we chose a bullet weight and type that is commonly used in each cartridge. This chart also lists additional information on the case and bullet used.

"Maximum Case Capacity in Grains of Water" (Max. CC Grs. Water) represents how much water the case will hold after firing in a standard sporting chamber. This information—combined with bulk powder density information (listed in the Measured Powder Density Chart in Chapter 6, pages 47-49—allows the handloader to calculate how much powder a given case will hold.

For example: A fired 30-06 case will hold 70.6 grains of water; H870 has an as-dumped bulk density of about 0.96 (96% of that of water). This suggests that it might be possible to dump about 68 grains (70.6 x 0.96) of H870 into a fired 30-06 case. Experience shows that full-length-sized cases typically hold about 5% less powder than fired cases. Therefore, we would expect that loading more than about 64 grains (68 x 0.95) of H870 would require special powder settling techniques, which is just what we observe in practice.

While this information cannot be used for any other purpose, it will tell the handloader if a suggested load is liable to require the use of powder settling techniques for proper charge installation without spilling.

Similarly, "Usable Case Capacity in Grains of Water" (Usable CC Grs. Water) can be used to determine if a suggested load is liable to create a slightly compressed charge. Simply multiply the usable capacity by the as-dumped bulk density for the powder of interest.

When using a different-weight bullet from that listed here, estimate actual usable case capacity in the following manner: When a heavier bullet is used, reduce listed usable powder capacity by about 1 grain for each additional 10 grains of bullet weight; when a lighter bullet is used, increase listed usable powder capacity by about 1 grain for each 10 grains of difference.

Obviously, variations in bullet nose profile and cartridge overall length will also affect actual usable powder capacity, sometimes drastically. If seated to the same overall length, typical spitzer (Sptz) versus round nose (RN) bullets alter actual usable capacity as shown in the following chart (spitzer-bulleted loads will have less actual usable case capacity); similarly, changing cartridge overall length (OAL) will also alter actual usable capacity (shorter cartridges have less actual usable case capacity). Use this chart to estimate the usable case capacity when affected by these variables:

Estimating Usable Case Capacity

Bullet Dia. (ins.)	RN vs. Sptz. ±grs. of CC	±0.01" OAL ±grs. of CC
.224	1.0	1.0
.243	1.3	1.2
.257	1.5	1.3
.264	1.6	1.4
.277	1.9	1.5
.284	2.0	1.6
.308	2.6	1.9
.311	2.7	1.9
.323	3.0	2.1
.338	3.5	2.3
.348	3.8	2.4
.358	4.1	2.5
.366	4.4	2.7
.375	4.7	2.8
.401	5.8	3.2
.416	6.4	3.4
.429	7.1	3.6
.458	8.6	4.2
.510	11.9	5.2

Whenever a load might result in a slightly compressed powder charge, consider using powder settling techniques to fully settle the powder before seating the bullets. Ensure that none of the resulting loads actually leave the powder charge slightly compressed. Slightly compressed powder charges might spontaneously settle. When *some* of the loads in any given group have spontaneously settled, two kind of loads are produced: Those with slightly compressed charges and those with settled and non-compressed charges. Those two types of loads will produce different mean velocities and shoot to different points of impact!

CASE CAPACITY FOR CARTRIDGES FIRED IN SPORTING CHAMBERS

Max. CC Grs.Water	Make	Bullet Wgt.Grs.	Type	Cart. OAL	Usable CC Grs.Water	Primer+Case Wgt.Grs.	Cartridge
72.7	—	—	—	—	—	223.6	350 Rem Mag
73.3	Sp	250	S	3.34	63.6	189.1	35 Whelen
51.1	H	220	FSP	2.56	40.5	150.8	375 Win
95.3	Sp	235	SS	3.60	86.5	258.2	375 H&H Mag
51.9	H	220	FSP	2.51	40.2	137.9	38-55 Win
41.0	CAST	180	FP	1.59+	32.9	97.7	38-40 Win
107.4	—	—	—	—	—	261.2	416 Rem Mag
130.5	—	—	—	—	—	337.2	416 Rigby
42.8	CAST	200	FP	1.59+	32	96.4	44-40 Win
40.2		240	JHP	1.61	25.2	113.3	44 Rem Mag
69.3	R	240	JSP	2.57	51.2	199.0	444 Mar
76.5	H	300	JHP	2.55	62.7	201.0	45-70 Govt
95.5	H	500	RN	3.34	74.7	229.9	458 Win Mag
149.3	—	—	—	—	—	321.6	470 NE
260	—	—	—	—	—	829	50 BMG

Pistol and Revolver Cartridges

Max. CC Grs.Water	Make	Bullet Wgt.Grs.	Type	Cart. OAL	Usable CC Grs.Water	Primer+Case Wgt.Grs.	Cartridge
18.9	H	45	SP	1.65	16.2	75.3	22 Rem Jet Mag
23.7	Si	45	S	1.83	22.0	85.0	221 Rem Fireball
5.8	FAC	50	FMJ	0.91	4.4	28.4	25 Auto
23.0	Sp?	60	S	1.59	18.1	83.6	256 Win Mag
38.9	Si	120	S	2.18	33.7	136.8	7mm BR-Rem
9.8	H	71	FMJ	0.98+	7.0	39.3	32 Auto
9.3	W	86	LRN	0.93	6.2	B-29.1	32 S&W
12.1	H	71	FMJ	1.23	12.1	48.0	32 CNP/32 S&WL
13.8	W	86	LRN	1.35	14.8	58.0	32 H&R Mag
13.7	FAC	100	JSP	1.17-	11.4	62.6	9mm Luger/+P
18.7	FAC	100	JSP	1.28	15.5	60.1	38 Auto/+P
22.4	FAC	100	JSP	1.57	20.4	81.0	9mm Win Mag
11.1	FAC	100	FMJ	0.98+	7.5	52.4	380 Auto/Super Auto +P
21.5	CAST	148	WC	1.36	14.8	64.3	38 LC
24.5	CAST	148	WC	1.55	20	67.6	38 Spc Match
24.5	H	158	JHP	1.55	18.2	67.6	38 Spc/+P
26.7	H	158	JHP	1.59	17.8	84.0	357 Mag
34.5	H	158	JHP	1.99	27.7	96.9	357 Rem Max
15.1	CAST	148	WC	1.24	9.5	58.5	38 CNP/38 S&W
20.2	CAST	180	RNFP	1.13+	10.6	68.3	40 S&W
24.7	CAST	180	RNFP	1.26	14.6	74.0	10mm Auto
35.6	Si	210	JHP	1.59	20.8	105.9	41 Rem Mag
21.6	Cast	180	RNFP	1.15+	12.3	76.3	41 AE
35.9	—	240	JHP	1.61+	25.9	95.5	44 S&W Spc
40.2	—	240	JHP	1.61	25.2	113.3	44 Rem Mag
27.1	W	230	FMJ	1.27+	17.6	84.8	45 Auto (+P/Match)
31.0	W	230	FMJ	1.27+	21.5	72.4*	45 Auto Rim
42.0	H	250	JHP	1.60	29.8	117.4	45 Colt
47.4	H	250	JHP	1.60	35.2	87.2*	45 Colt*
38.8	H	250	JHP	1.57+	29.3	109.1	45 Win Mag
46.8	H	250	JHP	1.72+	33.8	132.8	454 Casull*
50.0	IMI	300	JHP	1.59	35.4	168.7	50 AE

* = Semi-Balloon Head case
[1] 340 Wby. Mag. made from Win. 375 H&H case.
[2] Steel Berdan primed case.

H = Hornady; Si = Sierra; Sp = Speer; R = Remington; W = Winchester; FAC = Unknown factory bullet; SP = Spire Point; S = Spitzer; HP = Hollowpoint; FP = Flatpoint; SBT = Spitzer Boattail; FMJ = Full Metal Jacket; FSP = Flat-Softpoint; SPBT = Softpoint Boattail; LRN = Lead Round-nose; RN = Jacketed Round-nose; JHP = Jacketed Hollowpoint; JSP = Jacketed Softpoint; WC = Wadcutter; RNFP = Round-nose Flatpoint

Maximum Case Capacity is the volume of entire case interior in grains of water
Usable Case Capacity is the volume of entire case interior minus volume occupied by seated bullet
Cartridge OverAll Length is the length of cartridge with bullet seated normally.

Introduction To Rifle Data

IN THIS SECTION, we list the largest selection of data compiled and published into one source for 101 popular rifle cartridges. There are certainly dozens of other cartridges that are reasonable, common and being handloaded, but besides the obvious constraints of space, the non-availability of pressure-tested data precluded their inclusion.

You will notice many loads listed here do not include pressure data. Where that occurs, we did have comparative pressure data, thereby gaining a measure of security in the reasonableness of those loads. This necessary compromise allowed us to list significant data for many popular chamberings.

Since the test barrels used to create the load data were all reasonably similar in length, all the data for each bullet weight or weight range was melded into a single heading (a compromise to keep the data reasonably usable). Where test barrels differ in length, the attending velocities for the shorter barrels are lower. It would have been interesting and perhaps useful to interpolate velocity so that all data reflected the same barrel length. We chose not to do this because that process adds one more variable with an attendant loss of accuracy.

However, you can estimate barrel-length velocity variations with sufficient accuracy to judge which powder might give the highest velocity in any given barrel length. First, to determine which barrel length was used for a given load refer to page 83 to determine the source of the data. Then use the Barrel Length vs. Velocity chart to make your adjustments. For example, if your barrel is 2″ longer than the specified test barrel and the working velocity range of the load you want to use is in the 2000-2250 fps range, your barrel will generate 16 fps more velocity. Conversely, if your barrel is 2″ shorter than the test barrel, it will generate 16 fps less. The nearby chart is sufficiently accurate for that purpose, but is only applicable for normal-length rifle barrels.

Barrel Length vs. Velocity

Listed Range (fps)	Per Inch of Barrel Length Velocity Change (fps)
<2000	5
2000-2250	8
2250-2500	12
2500-2750	17
2750-3000	22
3000-3500	27
3250-3500	32
3500-3750	38
3750-4000	43
4000-4250	48

Caution: The maximum charge for your firearms will depend, in part, on the specific components you use, and your specific assembly methods and equipment, as well as your specific firearm.

In that neither the publisher nor the author has any control over the manufacture, assembly, and storage of components, or the method of assembling a handload, the condition of the firearm in which it is used, or the degree of knowledge of the handloader, we cannot assume any responsibility, either expressed or implied, for the use of this data. While this data was safe in the original test firearm, it could prove otherwise in your gun with your components. Use of this data is entirely at the risk of the handloader.

No warranty or guarantee is expressed or implied. The publisher and author assume no responsibility for any use of this data. It is offered solely as a comparison to other such data.

RIFLE CARTRIDGE DATA

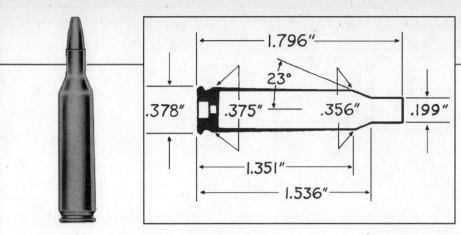

Case: Remington
Primer: Small Rifle
Barrel: 24″ Accurate
  24″ Hodgdon
  22″ Vihtavuori

Bullet Diameter: 0.172″
Maximum Case Length: 1.796″
Trim to Length: 1.786″
Maximum Cartridge OAL: 2.150″
Minimum Cartridge OAL: 2.090″

Remington standardized this chambering in 1971 after a flurry of 17-caliber activity in the custom and wildcatting arena. Only bolt-action rifles are factory chambered in 17 Remington.

Originally, cases were formed by necking down the 222 Remington Magnum and driving back that case's shoulder. Cases can be formed from 223 Remington brass, but doing so results in shorter-than-standard case necks. Such cases might require neck turning to reduce excessive thickness, to give proper chamber clearance for safety. Finally, capacity of such cases might be significantly different from commercial 17 Remington cases. Should you choose to make such conversion cases, weigh them and adjust loads accordingly. If the diameter of the neck of loaded rounds exceeds 0.199″, neck turning is advisable.

Offering over 4000 fps muzzle velocity with a 25-grain bullet, the 17 Remington can be depended on to give spectacular varmint performance to reasonable ranges. Recoil is practically non-existent. However, these tiny bullets do suffer extremely fast velocity loss. Further, even the slightest breeze will push them far off target across normal varmint shooting ranges. Finally, bore fouling is often rapid and soon destroys accuracy, even with the best of loads.

One other factor has limited the popularity of this cartridge among handloaders. . . all 17 bore chamberings are generally extremely sensitive to slight variations in powder charge. Use due caution in developing loads and weigh or measure charges with exceptional care.

With a standard 25-grain bullet, seated normally, usable case capacity is about 26.5 grains of water. IMR4320, H380 and H4895 have been suggested as good performers in the 17 Remington. Several newer Vihtavuori and Accurate Arms powders would seem to offer genuine promise and Hodgdon's VarGet will likely prove a superior choice as data becomes available.

17 REMINGTON LOADING DATA

Powder	STARTING Grs.	MV (fps)	MAXIMUM Grs.	MV (fps)	Press. (CUP/psi)	Comments
25						
A2700	25.7	3838	27.0	4083	49,900C	Hdy/2.17″
A2495BR	20.7	3569	23.0	4056	51,100C	Hdy/2.17″
N135			22.8	4040	52,214p	Rem 7½
A2520	20.4	3496	22.7	3973	51,600C	Hdy/2.17″
A2460	19.8	3489	22.0	3965	49,600C	Hdy/2.17″
W760	24.5	3760	26.0	3962		
W748	21.5	3640	23.0	3917		
A2015BR	18.0	3442	20.0	3911	48,400C	Hdy/2.17″
A2230	19.4	3412	21.5	3877	47,900C	Hdy/2.17″
H414	23.5	3439	25.5	3845		
IMR4320	22.0	3575	24.0	3840		
H450	26.0	3580	27.5	3794		
BL-C(2)	20.5	3557	22.0	3772		
H335	20.0	3514	21.5	3749		
H380	22.5	3525	24.0	3744		

Powder	STARTING Grs.	MV (fps)	MAXIMUM Grs.	MV (fps)	Press. (CUP/psi)	Comments
25 con't						
IMR4064	20.5	3514	22.5	3727		
RL-7	18.0	3638	19.0	3724		
H4895	20.5	3500	21.5	3719		
IMR3031	19.0	3502	21.0	3718		
IMR4895	20.0	3484	22.0	3709		
IMR4350	22.0	3419	24.0	3550		

Caution: Loads exceeding SAAMI OAL Maximum must be verified for bullet-to-rifling clearance and magazine functioning. Where a specific primer or bullet is indicated those components must be used, no substitutions! Where only a maximum load is shown, reduce starting load 10%, unless otherwise specified.

Key: (C) = compressed charge; C = CUP; p = psi; Plink = Plinker; Bns = Barnes; Hdy = Hornady; Lap = Lapua; Nos = Nosler; Rem = Remington; Sra = Sierra; Spr = Speer; Win = Winchester.

Never exceed maximum load nor use any load exhibiting signs of excessive pressure. Begin at suggested starting load and work up carefully.

22
Hornet

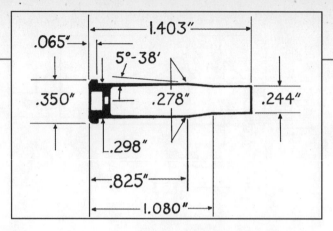

Dimensions: 1.403″, .065″, 5°-38′, .350″, .278″, .244″, .298″, .825″, 1.080″

Case: Winchester
Primer: Small Rifle
Barrel: 24″ Accurate
    20″ Hodgdon
    23½″ Vihtavuori

Bullet Diameter: 0.223″-0.224″
Maximum Case Length: 1.403″
Trim to Length: 1.393″
OAL Maximum: 1.723″
OAL Minimum: 1.660″

This circa 1920s cartridge was derived from the black-powder 22 Winchester Centerfire, introduced in 1885. Names like Wotkyns and Whelen figure in the domestic development of this cartridge. However, the Europeans beat these men to the punch. A modernized version of the 22 WCF was introduced there several years earlier. The 22 Veirling is practically interchangeable with the 22 Hornet.

To its credit, and one of the reasons the Hornet maintains considerable popularity, recoil and muzzle blast are much milder than with higher-performance 22 chamberings. The Hornet also provides almost unlimited barrel life, where cartridges in the 22-250 class can burn out a barrel in a good year's varmint shooting!

Winchester produced the first commercial factory ammunition in 1930. Standard chambering for the Hornet has always been in bolt-action and single shot guns—to which it is well adapted. Original bores used 0.223″ bullets—the same as the 22 rimfire. Most modern guns are bored to use standard 0.224″ bullets. Because both sizes are common, most bullet manufacturers offer bullets in both diameters. It is well worthwhile to slug your gun's bore to determine which bullet to use. Correct diameter bullets will certainly shoot better.

Owing to limited velocity potential, best results are usually obtained with lighter bullets of the rapid-expansion variety. There is currently a paucity of powders that perform optimally in the Hornet. We have listed the best here.

With a standard 45-grain bullet, seated normally, usable case capacity is about 12.2 grains of water. W680 (obsolete), IMR4227, A1680, W296, H110, H4227 and N110 are the best choices for loading the Hornet.

22 HORNET LOADING DATA

Powder	Grs.	MV (fps)	Grs.	MV (fps)	Press. (CUP/psi)	Comments
Lead 44 Lyman 225438						
A1680	10.4	2069	11.5	2351	31,100C	1.665″
A2015BR	11.3	1801	12.5	2047	29,700C	1.665″
Nitro100	2.7	1349	3.0	1533	32,600C	1.665″
40						
H110	10.0	2719	11.0	2845		
W296	10.0	2721	11.0	2840		
A1680	12.6	2451	14.0	2785	43,000C	Sra Hornet/1.715″
W680	11.5	2540	12.0	2664		
H4227	9.5	2562	10.5	2653		
IMR4227	9.5	2539	10.5	2611		
Her2400	8.5	2414	9.5	2604		
IMR4198	10.5	2370	11.5	2560		
H4198	10.5	2152	11.5	2462		
A2015BR	11.3	1762	12.5	2002	26,900C	Sra Hornet/1.715″/(C)

Powder	Grs.	MV (fps)	Grs.	MV (fps)	Press. (CUP/psi)	Comments
45						
H110	9.0	2488	10.0	2623		
W296	9.0	2490	10.0	2616		
W680	10.5	2362	11.5	2575		
Her2400	8.0	2325	9.0	2552		
N110			9.6	2530	37,710p	Sako SP 104
H4227	9.0	2378	10.0	2494		
A1680	11.1	2194	12.3	2493	40,700C	Nos Hornet/1.72″/CCI 500
IMR4227	9.0	2352	10.0	2444		
H4198	10.5	2191	11.5	2402		
IMR4198	10.5	2191	11.5	2387		
N110	7.2	2107	8.8	2371	39,200p	1.713″/Spr Sptz/Rem 7½
A2015BR	11.3	1829	12.5	2078	32,100C	(C)

Never exceed maximum load nor use any load exhibiting signs of excessive pressure. Begin at suggested starting load and work up carefully.

Powder	—STARTING— Grs.	MV (fps)	—MAXIMUM— Grs.	MV (fps)	Press. (CUP/psi)	Comments
50						
H4198	10.5	2229	11.5	2461		
IMR4198	10.5	2189	11.5	2455		
H110	8.5	2285	9.5	2430		
W296	8.5	2249	9.5	2420		
Her2400	7.5	2162	8.5	2409		
A1680	10.4	2105	11.5	2392	42,400C	Hdy SX/1.78"/CCI 500
W680	10.0	2218	11.0	2390		
H4227	8.5	2078	9.5	2366		
IMR4227	8.5	2104	9.5	2361		
N120	9.3	1961	10.7	2237	37,700p	Spr Sptz/1.713"/Rem 7½
A2015BR	10.8	1780	12.0	2023	35,000C	Hdy SX/1.78"/CCI 500
53						
W680	10.0	2198	11.0	2357		
H110	8.0	2142	9.0	2316		
W296	8.0	2133	9.0	2304		
H4227	8.0	2016	9.0	2278		
IMR4227	8.0	2024	9.0	2269		
Her2400	7.0	2041	8.0	2254		
IMR4198	10.0	2077	11.0	2222		
H4198	10.0	2086	11.0	2219		

Powder	—STARTING— Grs.	MV (fps)	—MAXIMUM— Grs.	MV (fps)	Press. (CUP/psi)	Comments
55						
W680	9.5	2109	10.5	2289		
H4198	10.0	2002	11.0	2259		
IMR4198	10.0	2029	11.0	2230		
Her2400	7.0	2004	8.0	2210		
IMR4227	7.5	1934	8.5	2191		
H110	7.5	2037	8.5	2188		
W296	7.5	2049	8.5	2180		
H4227	7.5	1929	8.5	2168		
N120	8.8	1840	10.3	2142	39,200p	Spr Sptz/1.713"/Rem 7½

Caution: Loads exceeding SAAMI OAL Maximum must be verified for bullet-to-rifling clearance and magazine functioning. Where a specific primer or bullet is indicated those components must be used, no substitutions! Where only a maximum load is shown, reduce starting load 10%, unless otherwise specified.

Key: (C) = compressed charge; C = CUP; p = psi; Plink = Plinker; Bns = Barnes; Hdy = Hornady; Lap = Lapua; Nos = Nosler; Rem = Remington; Sra = Sierra; Spr = Speer; Win = Winchester.

218 Bee

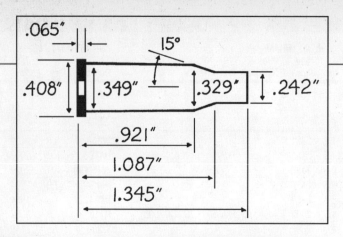

Case: Winchester
Primer: Small Rifle
Barrel: 24″ Accurate/26″ Hodgdon
Bullet Diameter: 0.223″-0.224″

Maximum Case Length: 1.345″
Trim to Length: 1.335″
Maximum Cartridge OAL: 1.680″
Minimum Cartridge OAL: 1.645″

The 218 Bee was designed specifically to produce 22 Hornet performance in a lever-action rifle. The base cartridge was the circa-1873 32-20 Winchester. Original chambering was in Winchester's Model 65 lever action introduced in 1938. The Model 65 was a modernized version of John M. Browning's Model 1892 Winchester.

Evidently, Winchester should have put more care into the production of these rifles and the 218 Bee ammunition made expressly for them. In spite of considerable enthusiasm following the announcement of this handy new varmint chambering and rifle combination, sales were never more than dismal. The problem seems to have been a matter of accuracy.

The lever-action rifle design has always been blamed for this problem. Most authors agree that in a good rifle, good 218 Bee ammunition shoots as good as any similar load.

However, the fact is, in the better lever-action rifles, good 218 Bee ammunition can shoot better than necessary for its original intended purpose—varmint and small-game hunting to about 150 yards.

The other factor limiting the Bee's performance and success was the necessity of using blunt bullets, in deference to safety requirements in tubular magazines. Never use pointed bullets in a tubular magazine.

Regardless of these limitations, in one of the better quality guns, the Bee can be loaded to provide what Winchester had intended—150-yard varmint and small-game accuracy and performance.

With a standard 46-grain bullet, seated normally, usable case capacity is about 15.5 grains of water. H110, H4198 and A1680 are both good choices for loading the little Bee.

218 BEE LOADING DATA

Lead 44 Lyman 225438

Powder	STARTING Grs.	MV (fps)	MAXIMUM Grs.	MV (fps)	Press. (CUP/psi)	Comments
A1680	9.9	1976	11.0	2246	30,100C	1.615″/CCI 400

40

Powder	Grs.	MV (fps)	Grs.	MV (fps)	Press. (CUP/psi)	Comments
A1680	13.5	2463	15.0	2799	34,700C	Sra Hornet*/1.76″/CCI 400
H4198			14.0	2792		
H4227			12.0	2760		

45

Powder	Grs.	MV (fps)	Grs.	MV (fps)	Press. (CUP/psi)	Comments
H4198			14.0	2779		
A1680	12.6	2350	14.0	2670	39,800C	Hdy HP Bee/1.61″/CCI 400
A1680	11.7	2165	13.0	2460	36,600C	Hdy SX*/1.78″/CCI 400
H110			9.0	2294		

* Note: Not for use in tubular magazine firearms.

46

Powder	Grs.	MV (fps)	Grs.	MV (fps)	Press. (CUP/psi)	Comments
A1680	12.6	2339	14.0	2658	38,600C	Spr FN/1.67″/CCI 400

50

Powder	Grs.	MV (fps)	Grs.	MV (fps)	Press. (CUP/psi)	Comments
H4198			13.5	2582		
A1680			13.0	2460	36,600C	Hdy SX*/1.78″/CCI 400
H4198			11.0	2414		

55

Powder	Grs.	MV (fps)	Grs.	MV (fps)	Press. (CUP/psi)	Comments
H4198			13.5	2567		

* Note: Not for use in tubular magazine firearms.

Never exceed maximum load nor use any load exhibiting signs of excessive pressure. Begin at suggested starting load and work up carefully.

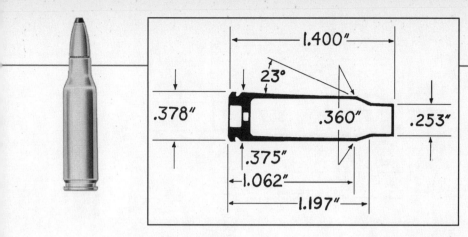

Case: Remington
Primer: Remington 7½
Barrel: 24″ Accurate
Bullet Diameter: 0.224″

Maximum Case Length: 1.40″
Trim to Length: 1.39″
Maximum Cartridge OAL: 1.83″
Minimum Cartridge OAL: 1.78″

Developed more than a decade after its parent cartridge—the 222 Remington—the Fireball was designed specifically to give optimal 22-caliber performance from the XP-100, with consideration given to that pistol's limited 10¹³/₁₆″ barrel. Using about 30 percent less powder and working at somewhat higher pressures than the 222 Remington, the Fireball produces 95 percent of the velocity of the 222—despite its substantially smaller capacity.

(In the "Improved" configuration, with a sharper shoulder and reduced body taper, the Fireball very nearly duplicates 222 performance.)

An efficient cartridge, the Fireball has a shorter powder column than similar standard chamberings offering "middle of the road performance" and can, therefore, be suggested as a superior choice for varmint hunting at intermediate ranges—to perhaps 250 yards.

With a 52-grain bullet, seated normally, usable case capacity is about 22.0 grains of water. There is currently a genuine paucity of powder choices, only A1680 has been noted as an excellent performer.

221 REMINGTON FIREBALL LOADING DATA

Powder	—STARTING— Grs.	MV (fps)	—MAXIMUM— Grs.	MV (fps)	Press. (CUP/psi)	Comments
45						
A1680	16.5	2819	18.3	3203	51,300C	Nos SP/1.765″
A2015BR	18.0	2659	20.0	3022	47,100C	Nos SP/1.765″/(C)
A2230	18.9	2600	21.0	2955	49,500C	Nos SP/1.765″/(C)
50						
A1680	16.0	2691	17.8	3058	51,500C	Hdy SX/1.825″
A2015BR	17.6	2557	19.5	2906	45,600C	Hdy SX/1.825″/(C)
A2230	18.9	2556	21.0	2905	49,500C	Hdy SX/1.825″/(C)

Powder	—STARTING— Grs.	MV (fps)	—MAXIMUM— Grs.	MV (fps)	Press. (CUP/psi)	Comments
55						
A1680	15.3	2600	17.0	2950	52,000C	Nos SBT/1.85″
A2015BR	17.1	2498	19.0	2839	48,700C	Nos SBT/1.85″/Case Full
A2230	18.0	2431	20.0	2763	51,600C	Nos SBT/1.85″/(C)

> **Caution:** Loads exceeding SAAMI OAL Maximum must be verified for bullet-to-rifling clearance and magazine functioning. Where a specific primer or bullet is indicated those components must be used, no substitutions! Where only a maximum load is shown, reduce starting load 10%, unless otherwise specified.
>
> **Key:** (C) = compressed charge; C = CUP; p = psi; Plink = Plinker; Bns = Barnes; Hdy = Hornady; Lap = Lapua; Nos = Nosler; Rem = Remington; Sra = Sierra; Spr = Speer; Win = Winchester.

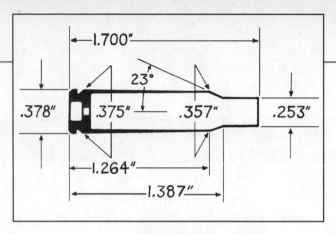

Case: Winchester
Primer: Small Rifle
Barrel: 24″ Accurate
26″ Hodgdon
23″ Vihtavuori

Bullet Diameter: 0.224″
Maximum Case Length: 1.70″
Trim to Length: 1.69″
Maximum Cartridge OAL: 2.13″
Minimum Cartridge OAL: 2.04″

If ever any factory research and development effort ever got anything right, the 222 Remington is a shining example! Introduced in 1950 in the Model 722 rifle—and still available in the Model 700—the "triple deuce" was an instant success. Within only a few years, it began to dominate benchrest competition, holding that post for decades. Newer developments have displaced it from that lofty position, but it is still perhaps the most accurate factory load and rifle combination commonly available.

With careful handloading, or with any of the better factory loadings, this cartridge will deliver all the accuracy necessary to cleanly dispatch any varmint to 250 yards—perhaps a bit

farther in especially competent hands. In the field, it easily outshoots most shooters, even on their best days.

Moderate pressure and case capacity combine to offer long barrel life, compared to hotter numbers that can offer 50 to 100 yards more useful range. Most shooters find such longer shots intrinsically too difficult anyway. That fact likely explains the 222's continued popularity among varmint hunters.

With a 52-grain bullet, seated normally, usable case capacity is about 26.0 grains of water. H322, IMR4198, BL-C(2), H335, H4198 and RL-7 have all been noted as excellent choices for loading the 222 Remington.

222 REMINGTON LOADING DATA

Powder	STARTING Grs.	MV (fps)	MAXIMUM Grs.	MV (fps)	Press. (CUP/psi)	Comments
40						
H4198	19.5	3259	21.5	3566	48,000C	
RL-7	20.0	3309	22.0	3554	47,600C	
IMR4198	19.0	3217	21.0	3524	48,400C	
N130	21.6	3191	23.2	3435	44,962p	Spr SP
IMR3031	22.0	3182	24.0	3389	47,800C	
N120	20.1	3251	20.8	3373	45,542p	Sra SP
IMR4320	23.0	3060	25.0	3323	43,400C	
N133			23.9	3284	38,435p	Sra SP
IMR4895	22.0	2919	24.0	3272	45,800C	
IMR4064	22.0	2889	24.0	3222	42,600C	
H4227	13.5	2862	14.5	3019	47,100C	
45						
H4198	18.5	3118	20.5	3452	50,200C	
A2230	24.3	3033	27.0	3447	47,400p	Nos SB/2.065″/ Rem 7½/(C)
A2460	24.3	2996	27.0	3405	45,900p	Nos SB/2.065″/ Rem 7½/(C)
IMR4198	18.5	3091	20.5	3393	49,600C	

Powder	STARTING Grs.	MV (fps)	MAXIMUM Grs.	MV (fps)	Press. (CUP/psi)	Comments
45 con't						
A2015BR	22.1	2978	24.5	3384	49,300p	Nos SB/2.065″/Rem 7½
RL-7	19.0	3110	21.0	3362	46,000C	
N130	21.8	3120	23.2	3340	44,962p	Hdy SP Hornet
BL-C(2)	22.5	2957	24.5	3305	45,900C	
A1680	18.9	2901	21.0	3297	48,500p	Nos SB/2.065″/Rem 7½
W748	22.5	2944	24.5	3288	46,000C	
N133			23.9	3284	44,236p	Sra SMP
IMR3031	21.0	2927	23.0	3281	48,200C	
N120			19.8	3260	46,412p	Sako FMJ 103G
IMR4320	23.0	2951	25.0	3203	46,000C	
A2520	22.5	2777	25.0	3156	34,200p	Nos SB/2.065″/ Rem 7½/(C)
A2495BR	21.6	2776	24.0	3154	39,900p	Nos SB/2.065″/ Rem 7½/(C)
IMR4895	21.5	2819	23.5	3150	46,100C	
H4895	21.5	2801	23.5	3140	45,100C	
IMR4064	21.5	2799	23.5	3140	45,800C	

Never exceed maximum load nor use any load exhibiting signs of excessive pressure. Begin at suggested starting load and work up carefully.

Powder	—STARTING— Grs.	MV (fps)	—MAXIMUM— Grs.	MV (fps)	Press. (CUP/psi)	Comments

50

Powder	Grs.	MV (fps)	Grs.	MV (fps)	Press. (CUP/psi)	Comments
H4198	18.0	3018	20.0	3306	50,200C	
RL-7	19.0	2880	21.0	3271	48,000C	
N120			19.3	3250	46,412p	Sako FMJ 105G
A2230	22.1	2840	24.5	3227	48,200C	Hdy SX/2.15"/Rem 7½/(C)
N133			23.5	3220	46,412p	Sako FMJ 105G
N133	22.2	2969	24.0	3215	45,000C	Hdy SX/2.118"/Rem 7½
A2015BR	21.2	2823	23.5	3208	45,800C	Hdy SX/2.15"/Rem 7½
BL-C(2)	22.0	2927	24.0	3206	49,600C	
A2460	22.1	2820	24.5	3204	46,000C	Hdy SX/2.15"/Rem 7½/(C)
W748	22.0	2901	24.0	3197	49,500C	
H322	20.5	2880	22.5	3167	50,700C	
IMR3031	20.5	2910	22.5	3144	50,000C	
N130	20.5	2918	22.1	3142	44,962p	Hdy SP
VarGet			25.0	3114	40,600C	
A2520	22.5	2711	25.0	3081	38,300C	Hdy SX/2.15"/Rem 7½/(C)
A2495BR	21.6	2678	24.0	3043	41,100C	Hdy SX/2.15"/Rem 7½/(C)
A1680	16.6	2648	18.5	3009	50,000C	Hdy SX/2.15"/Rem 7½

52-53

Powder	Grs.	MV (fps)	Grs.	MV (fps)	Press. (CUP/psi)	Comments
A2015BR	21.1	2811	23.5	3194	50,000C	Hdy HP/2.19"/Rem 7½
A2230	22.1	2746	24.5	3120	46,400C	Hdy HP/2.19"/Rem 7½/(C)
RL-7	18.0	2769	20.0	3117	46,400C	
A2460	22.1	2738	24.5	3111	45,500C	Hdy HP/2.19"/Rem 7½/(C)
VarGet			25.0	3097	42,700C	
A2520	22.5	2712	25.0	3082	40,900p	Hdy HP/2.19"/Rem 7½/(C)
BL-C(2)	21.5	2837	23.5	3075	47,600C	
A2495BR	21.6	2702	24.0	3071	46,300C	Hdy HP/2.19"/Rem 7½/(C)
W748	21.5	2798	23.5	3066	47,400C	
H322	20.0	2834	22.0	3059	48,000C	
IMR3031	20.0	2822	22.0	3047	49,600C	(53-gr.)
H335	21.0	2709	23.0	3042	46,300C	
IMR4064	21.0	2616	23.0	3030	45,600C	(53-gr.)
H4895	21.0	2672	23.0	3020	46,500C	
IMR4895	21.0	2641	23.0	3009	46,700C	(53-gr.)

55

Powder	Grs.	MV (fps)	Grs.	MV (fps)	Press. (CUP/psi)	Comments
A2230	22.1	2733	24.5	3106	46,200p	Nos SB/2.155"/Rem 7½
VarGet			25.0	3095	43,000C	
A2460	22.1	2720	24.5	3091	45,000p	Nos SB/2.155"/Rem 7½
RL-7	17.5	2737	19.5	3069	46,200C	
H4198	17.0	2840	19.0	3051	48,500C	
N133			22.4	3050	46,412p	Sako SP 110G
A2015BR	20.3	2681	22.5	3047	46,100C	Nos SB/2.155"/Rem 7½
IMR4198	17.0	2829	19.0	3027	49,400C	
N130	20.0	2803	21.4	3025	44,962p	Hdy BTSP
IMR3031	19.5	2779	21.5	3018	49,400C	
H322	19.5	2796	21.5	3010	47,400C	
BL-C(2)	21.0	2794	23.0	3004	45,900C	
W748	21.0	2774	23.0	2994	46,000C	
N120			18.5	2970	46,412p	Hdy SP
A2520	22.1	2607	24.5	2962	36,300p	Nos SB/2.155"/Rem 7½/(C)
H335	20.5	2692	22.5	2960	45,600C	

55 con't

Powder	Grs.	MV (fps)	Grs.	MV (fps)	Press. (CUP/psi)	Comments
A2495BR	21.2	2570	23.5	2920	42,100p	Nos SB/2.155"/Rem 7½/(C)
A1680	17.1	2548	19.0	2896	44,200p	Nos SB/2.155"/Rem 7½
IMR4064	21.0	2570	23.0	2884	45,800C	

60-64

Powder	Grs.	MV (fps)	Grs.	MV (fps)	Press. (CUP/psi)	Comments
N135			23.1	3100	46,412p	Hdy SP
A2230	21.6	2592	24.0	2945	48,100p	Hdy SP/2.2"/Rem 7½
A2015BR	20.0	2588	22.2	2941	47,800p	Hdy SP/2.2"/Rem 7½
A2460	21.5	2586	23.9	2939	46,100p	Hdy SP/2.2"/Rem 7½
A2520	22.1	2583	24.5	2935	43,900p	Hdy SP/2.2"/Rem 7½/(C)
A2495BR	21.2	2582	23.5	2934	49,400p	Hdy SP/2.2"/Rem 7½/(C)
N130	19.2	2640	21.1	2877	44,962p	Hdy HP
BL-C(2)	20.5	2682	22.0	2856	45,600C	
N133			21.8	2850	46,412p	Hdy SP
H4198	16.5	2685	18.5	2843	48,500C	
IMR4198	16.5	2674	18.5	2841	48,300C	
W748	20.5	2676	22.0	2839	45,600C	
H322	18.5	2505	20.5	2805	46,900C	
A1680	17.1	2467	19.0	2803	50,000p	Hdy SP/2.2"/Rem 7½
IMR3031	19.0	2580	21.0	2779	47,800C	
H380	22.0	2601	24.0	2771	43,500C	
H335	19.5	2539	21.0	2720	44,200C	
IMR4064	20.0	2489	22.0	2717	44,800C	
RL-7	16.5	2449	18.5	2714	45,800C	

70

Powder	Grs.	MV (fps)	Grs.	MV (fps)	Press. (CUP/psi)	Comments
N540	22.7	2592	24.3	2809	45,000p	Sra HPBT (69-gr.)/ 2.126"/Rem 7½
N140	22.2	2554	23.7	2748	45,000p	Sra HPBT (69-gr.)/ 2.126"/Rem 7½
H380	22.0	2477	23.0	2646	45,300C	
N130	18.1	2456	19.5	2641	44,962p	Sra MK (69-gr.)
IMR4064	20.0	2461	21.0	2640	47,400C	
IMR4320	20.0	2414	22.0	2630	48,000C	
BL-C(2)	19.5	2377	21.0	2623	44,700C	
H322	17.5	2365	19.5	2621	46,900C	
IMR3031	17.5	2340	19.5	2606	47,000C	
RL-7	15.0	2343	17.0	2594	44,400C	
W748	19.5	2370	21.0	2590	44,500C	
H335	19.0	2359	20.5	2577	44,200C	
H4895	19.0	2328	20.5	2573	45,700C	
IMR4350	21.5	2248	23.5	2491	39,400C	
H4350	21.5	2226	23.5	2472	37,200C	

Caution: Loads exceeding SAAMI OAL Maximum must be verified for bullet-to-rifling clearance and magazine functioning. Where a specific primer or bullet is indicated those components must be used, no substitutions! Where only a maximum load is shown, reduce starting load 10%, unless otherwise specified.

Key: (C) = compressed charge; C = CUP; p = psi; Plink-er; Bns = Barnes; Hdy = Hornady; Lap = Lapua; Nos = Nosler; Rem = Remington; Sra = Sierra; Spr = Speer; Win = Winchester.

Never exceed maximum load nor use any load exhibiting signs of excessive pressure. Begin at suggested starting load and work up carefully.

223 Remington

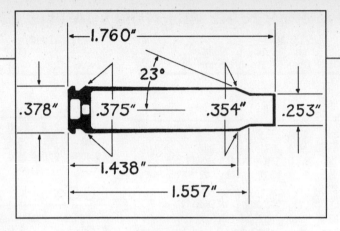

Dimensions: 1.760″, 23°, .378″, .375″, .354″, .253″, 1.438″, 1.557″

Case: Remington
Primer: Small Rifle
Barrel: 24″ Accurate
　　　　 26″ Hodgdon
　　　　 25″ Vihtavuori

Bullet Diameter: 0.224″
Maximum Case Length: 1.76″
Trim to Length: 1.75″
Maximum Cartridge OAL: 2.26″
Minimum Cartridge OAL: 2.16″

After considerable research and development by several of the NATO allies, the 5.56mm Ball Cartridge M193 was adopted in 1964 for standardization by all NATO forces. Since this cartridge is nothing more than a lengthened 222 Remington, at a somewhat higher pressure, it was natural for Remington to commercialize it as the 223 Remington.

We have to note that military chambers do not necessarily meet current SAAMI chamber specifications, also military 5.56mm Ball ammunition does not necessarily meet current SAAMI ammo specs. So, we advise against firing any military ammunition in any commercial chamber. Further, we strongly caution against using commercial ammunition or handloads in military chambers. Use extreme caution.

Military cases are common and inexpensive, so their use is inevitable. If you use these thicker and softer cases, we recommend reduction of charge by a full 10 percent. Such loads will produce nearly the same velocity as the listed loads, which were developed in commercial cases. Using full listed loads in military cases can result in dangerous pressures.

With fast-twist barrels, the 223 is gaining acceptance in long-range target competition. In those sports, special bullets of 69 grains, and heavier, are delivering impressive results.

One special caution is in order here: Remington developed the 222 Remington Magnum in the search for a cartridge satisfying NATO requirements. Ultimately, NATO opted for a slightly shorter version of that experimental cartridge. Meanwhile Remington had already commercialized the 222 Remington Magnum as a standard chambering...223 ammunition will freely chamber and fire in a 222 Remington Magnum chamber. The problem is that such a combination results in an excess headspace condition of about 0.026″, just enough to almost guarantee a separated case head, a wrecked gun and perhaps a wrecked shooter. DON'T DO IT! Often the extractor will hold the case against the firing pin's impact. When that happens, the case might not rupture. Nevertheless, sooner or later the extractor will fail to hold the cartridge, and case head and body separation will almost certainly result. It simply is not worth the gamble. If you happen to own guns chambered in both the 223 and the 222 Remington Magnum, use extreme caution.

With a 52-grain bullet, seated normally, usable case capacity is about 28.8 grains of water. H322, BL-C(2), H335, RL-15 and VarGet are noted 223 performers.

223 REMINGTON LOADING DATA

Powder	STARTING Grs.	MV (fps)	MAXIMUM Grs.	MV (fps)	Press. (CUP/psi)	Comments
40						
N130	24.4	3399	26.3	3685	52,214p	Spr SP
BL-C(2)	26.5	3368	28.5	3612	45,400C	
N120	22.1	3445	23.0	3609	50,763p	Sra SP
H4198	20.5	3247	22.5	3601	49,600C	
H322	23.5	3376	25.5	3574	48,000C	
H335	26.0	3299	28.0	3572	44,600C	
IMR4198	20.0	3019	22.0	3361	44,400C	
IMR3031	23.5	2990	25.5	3244	42,000C	
IMR4320	25.0	2964	27.0	3204	38,900C	
H414			29.0	3184	34,800C	
H4895	24.0	2972	26.0	3174	31,200C	

Powder	STARTING Grs.	MV (fps)	MAXIMUM Grs.	MV (fps)	Press. (CUP/psi)	Comments
40 con't						
IMR4064	24.0	2969	26.0	3170	41,800C	
IMR4895	24.0	2951	26.0	3169	38,600C	

Caution: Loads exceeding SAAMI OAL Maximum must be verified for bullet-to-rifling clearance and magazine functioning. Where a specific primer or bullet is indicated those components must be used, no substitutions! Where only a maximum load is shown, reduce starting load 10%, unless otherwise specified.

Key: (C) = compressed charge; C = CUP; p = psi; Plink = Plinker; Bns = Barnes; Hdy = Hornady; Lap = Lapua; Nos = Nosler; Rem = Remington; Sra = Sierra; Spr = Speer; Win = Winchester.

Never exceed maximum load nor use any load exhibiting signs of excessive pressure. Begin at suggested starting load and work up carefully.

45

Powder	—STARTING— Grs.	MV (fps)	—MAXIMUM— Grs.	MV (fps)	Press. (CUP/psi)	Comments
N133	24.9	3245	27.0	3565	52,200p	Spr Sptz/2.126"/Rem 7½
BL-C(2)	26.5	3266	28.5	3559	48,000C	
A2015BR	23.4	3120	26.0	3546	49,100C	Nos SP/2.115"/Rem 7½
N130	23.5	3235	25.6	3511	52,214p	Spr Sptz
RL-7	22.0	3292	24.0	3510	45,800C	
RL-12	26.0	3277	28.0	3508	47,500C	
A2460	24.8	3059	27.5	3476	49,300C	Nos SP/2.115"/Rem 7½
A2230	24.3	3041	27.0	3456	50,500C	Nos SP/2.115"/Rem 7½
RL-15	25.0	3111	27.0	3438	39,800C	
A2495BR	23.9	3023	26.5	3435	47,000C	Nos SP/2.115"/Rem 7½/(C)
N133	23.9	3248	25.3	3428	50,763p	Sra SP
A2520	25.7	3013	28.5	3424	42,000C	Nos SP/2.115"/Rem 7½/(C)
H322	23.0	3164	25.0	3424	47,400C	
IMR4198	20.0	3089	22.0	3393	49,900C	
N120	21.1	3215	22.1	3379	50,763p	Sra SP
IMR3031	23.0	3080	25.0	3322	43,800C	
A1680	18.5	2906	20.5	3302	48,200C	Nos SP/2.115"/Rem 7½
H4895	24.0	2944	26.0	3219	37,800C	
IMR4895	24.0	2939	26.0	3210	39,000C	
IMR4064	24.0	2944	26.0	3184	42,100C	
H414			29.0	3181	35,400C	
IMR4320	25.0	2981	27.0	3172	42,600C	

50

Powder	—STARTING— Grs.	MV (fps)	—MAXIMUM— Grs.	MV (fps)	Press. (CUP/psi)	Comments
BL-C(2)	26.0	3187	28.0	3428	47,100C	
N133	24.6	3113	26.2	3398	52,200p	Spr TNT/2.244"/Rem 7½
H335	24.0	3166	26.0	3393	51,700C	
RL-12	25.0	3180	27.0	3390	47,000C	
A2015BR	23.0	2981	25.5	3387	46,400C	Spr TNT/2.235"/Rem 7½
VarGet			27.5	3383	44,800C	
N130	23.0	3097	24.9	3368	52,214p	Spr TNT
RL-15	25.0	3074	27.0	3351	41,500C	
N133			25.9	3350	52,214p	Sako FMJ 105G
A2520	25.7	2944	28.5	3346	42,200C	Spr TNT/2.235"/Rem 7½/(C)
A2230	23.4	2941	26.0	3342	49,800C	Spr TNT/2.235"/Rem 7½
RL-7	21.5	3011	23.5	3340	48,600C	
A2460	23.4	2930	26.0	3329	47,100C	Spr TNT/2.235"/Rem 7½
H322	22.0	3018	24.0	3301	49,300C	
A2495BR	23.9	2888	26.5	3282	44,400C	Spr TNT/2.235"/Rem 7½/(C)
N120			22.1	3280	52,214p	Sako FMJ 105G
IMR4320	25.0	2920	27.0	3161	47,400C	
H414			29.0	3153	36,600C	
IMR4064	24.0	2890	26.0	3147	44,100C	
A1680	18.5	2768	20.5	3146	47,900C	Spr TNT/2.235"/Rem 7½

52-53

Powder	—STARTING— Grs.	MV (fps)	—MAXIMUM— Grs.	MV (fps)	Press. (CUP/psi)	Comments
RL-15	25.0	3131	27.0	3403	47,000C	
BL-C(2)	26.0	3090	28.0	3328	47,600C	
H335	24.0	3060	26.0	3300	52,000C	
W748	26.0	3088	28.0	3296	47,400C	
RL-12	24.0	2963	26.0	3286	48,500C	
A2015BR	22.1	2876	24.5	3268	47,800C	Hdy MHP/2.225"/Rem 7½
A2495BR	23.4	2874	26.0	3266	48,800C	Hdy MHP/2.225"/Rem 7½/(C)
A2230	23.4	2862	26.0	3252	49,900C	Hdy MHP/2.225"/Rem 7½
A2520	24.8	2847	27.5	3235	43,200C	Hdy MHP/2.225"/Rem 7½/(C)
A2460	23.0	2846	25.5	3234	47,300C	Hdy MHP/2.225"/Rem 7½
H4198	19.5	2986	21.5	3188	46,700C	
H322	21.5	2912	23.5	3183	48,900C	
IMR3031	22.0	2899	24.0	3180	49,000C	
RL-7	21.0	2981	23.0	3179	47,900C	
IMR4198	19.0	2971	21.0	3149	48,800C	
H380	26.5	2853	28.5	3133	37,200C	
H414			28.5	3131	38,400C	
IMR4064	24.0	2876	26.0	3130	44,900C	
A1680	18.0	2681	20.0	3047	49,600C	Hdy MHP/2.225"/Rem 7½

55

Powder	—STARTING— Grs.	MV (fps)	—MAXIMUM— Grs.	MV (fps)	Press. (CUP/psi)	Comments
VarGet			27.5	3384	49,700C	
RL-15	25.0	3045	26.5	3342	48,500C	
BL-C(2)	25.5	3069	27.5	3313	48,500C	
W748	25.5	3051	27.5	3309	48,400C	
A2015BR	22.5	2887	25.0	3281	49,800C	Nos SPBT/2.23"/Rem 7½
A2495BR	23.6	2878	26.2	3271	51,100C	Nos SPBT/2.23"/Rem 7½/(C)
A2460	23.9	2843	26.5	3231	49,200C	Nos SPBT/2.23"/Rem 7½
A2520	24.8	2837	27.5	3224	43,300C	Nos SPBT/2.23"/Rem 7½/(C)
N133			24.8	3220	52,214p	Lapua SP E372
N130	22.1	2931	24.1	3217	52,214p	Hdy FMJ BT
A2230	23.4	2830	26.0	3216	50,300C	Nos SPBT/2.23"/Rem 7½
RL-12	23.5	2896	25.5	3191	46,000C	
N135			26.4	3180	52,214p	Sako SP 110G
RL-7	20.5	2960	22.5	3152	47,100C	
H4198	19.0	2847	21.0	3150	47,600C	
N120			21.3	3130	52,214p	Sako SP 110
H414			28.5	3123	40,800C	
H322	21.0	2841	23.0	3106	48,900C	
IMR4064	23.5	2896	25.5	3101	49,800C	
H4895	24.0	2893	26.0	3099	46,400C	
H380	26.5	2821	28.5	3082	37,800C	
IMR3031	21.0	2840	23.0	3080	48,200C	
IMR4895	23.5	2877	25.5	3062	48,200C	
A1680	18.5	2691	20.5	3058	50,000C	Nos SPBT/2.23"/Rem 7½
IMR4198	18.5	2797	20.5	3041	48,600C	

>>>>>>>>>>>>>>>>>>>>>>>>>>>>>>>>>>>>>

Never exceed maximum load nor use any load exhibiting signs of excessive pressure. Begin at suggested starting load and work up carefully.

60-64

Powder	Grs.	MV (fps)	Grs.	MV (fps)	Press. (CUP/psi)	Comments
N540	26.5	2930	29.0	3266	52,200p	Hdy HP/Rem 7½
VarGet			26.4	3199	50,700C	
A2520	24.8	2776	27.5	3154	45,600C	Hdy SP/2.235"/ Rem 7½/(C)
RL-15	23.5	2839	25.5	3141	48,000C	
A2015BR	21.6	2752	24.0	3127	49,100C	Hdy SP/2.235"/ Rem 7½
A2230	22.1	2717	24.5	3087	49,200C	Hdy SP/2.235"/ Rem 7½
H4895	23.5	2831	25.5	3078	50,000C	
A2460	22.7	2706	25.2	3075	49,400C	Hdy SP/2.235"/ Rem 7½
N135			25.8	3070	52,939p	Hdy SP
N130	21.4	2796	23.7	3063	52,214p	Hdy HP
BL-C(2)	24.0	2847	26.0	3054	46,300C	
H335	22.5	2820	25.0	3051	50,000C	
W748	24.0	2839	26.0	3050	46,400C	
N133			24.5	3050	53,664p	Hdy SP
A2495BR	22.2	2680	24.7	3046	46,300C	Hdy SP/2.235"/ Rem 7½/100% Density
IMR4895	23.0	2806	25.0	3039	49,100C	
RL-12	23.0	2816	25.0	3036	47,000C	
IMR4320	24.0	2770	26.0	3012	49,600C	
IMR4064	23.0	2796	25.0	3009	49,400C	
H380	26.0	2710	28.0	2983	38,400C	
H322	20.0	2672	22.0	2862	48,400C	
IMR3031	20.0	2670	22.0	2851	48,200C	
RL-7	19.5	2674	21.5	2847	46,900C	
H4198	18.0	2680	20.0	2846	44,600C	
IMR4198	18.0	2661	20.0	2820	45,600C	
H4350	24.5	2474	26.5	2691	37,800C	
H4831			26.5	2625	31,600C	

69-70

Powder	Grs.	MV (fps)	Grs.	MV (fps)	Press. (CUP/psi)	Comments
A2520	24.3	2679	27.0	3044	48,200C	Sra HPBT/2.25"/ Rem 7½
N540	24.9	2736	27.3	3039	52,200p	Sra HPBT/2.244"/ Rem 7½
RL-15	23.0	2795	25.0	2994	47,500C	(70-gr.)
VarGet			25.5	2993	47,700C	(70-gr.)
A2460	22.2	2632	24.7	2991	51,800C	Sra HPBT/2.25"/ Rem 7½
A2495BR	22.5	2608	25.0	2964	49,800C	Sra HPBT/2.25"/ Rem 7½
A2230	22.1	2578	24.5	2929	51,300C	Sra HPBT/2.25"/ Rem 7½
N140	23.6	2633	26.4	2922	52,800p	Sra HPBT/2.244"/ Rem 7½
A2015BR	20.7	2567	23.0	2917	48,400C	Sra HPBT/2.25"/ Rem 7½
H335	21.0	2603	23.5	2825	51,900C	(70-gr.)
RL-12	20.5	2490	23.0	2797	49,500C	(70-gr.)
BL-C(2)	21.5	2537	23.5	2753	48,400C	(70-gr.)
H380	26.0	2614	27.0	2742	41,800C	(70-gr.)
IMR4320	23.0	2515	25.0	2717	49,800C	(70-gr.)
H4895	21.0	2548	23.0	2679	48,900C	(70-gr.)
H414	27.0	2585	28.0	2674	43,700C	(70-gr.)
H322	19.0	2441	21.0	2673	48,900C	(70-gr.)
W760	27.0	2587	28.0	2666	44,400C	(70-gr.)
IMR4064	21.0	2490	23.0	2660	49,000C	(70-gr.)
IMR4895	21.0	2525	23.0	2650	49,200C	(70-gr.)
IMR3031	19.0	2430	21.0	2647	49,600C	(70-gr.)
RL-7	18.0	2429	20.0	2634	47,200C	(70-gr.)
H4350	24.0	2239	26.0	2432	38,200C	(70-gr.)
IMR4350	23.0	2240	25.0	2430	39,800C	(70-gr.)
H4831	25.0	2228	26.0	2297	32,000C	(70-gr.)

80

Powder	Grs.	MV (fps)	Grs.	MV (fps)	Press. (CUP/psi)	Comments
A2520	22.5	2460	25.0	2796	49,700C	Sra HPBT/2.45"
A2460	21.6	2453	24.0	2788	49,500C	Sra HPBT/2.45"/ Rem 7½
A2495BR	21.2	2453	23.5	2788	51,600C	Sra HPBT/2.45"/ Rem 7½
A2230	21.2	2424	23.5	2754	49,100C	Sra HPBT/2.45"/ Rem 7½
A2015BR	19.8	2382	22.0	2707	49,000C	Sra HPBT/2.45"/ Rem 7½

Caution: **Loads exceeding SAAMI OAL Maximum must be verified for bullet-to-rifling clearance and magazine functioning. Where a specific primer or bullet is indicated those components must be used, no substitutions! Where only a maximum load is shown, reduce starting load 10%, unless otherwise specified.**

Key: (C) = compressed charge; C = CUP; p = psi; Plink = Plinker; Bns = Barnes; Hdy = Hornady; Lap = Lapua; Nos = Nosler; Rem = Remington; Sra = Sierra; Spr = Speer; Win = Winchester.

Never exceed maximum load nor use any load exhibiting signs of excessive pressure. Begin at suggested starting load and work up carefully.

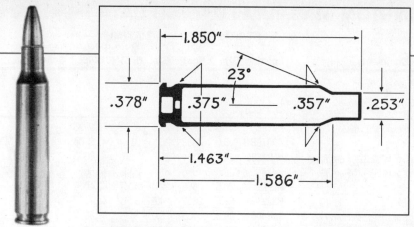

Case: Winchester
Primer: Small Rifle
Barrel: 24″ Accurate
      26″ Hodgdon
      23″ Vihtavuori

Bullet Diameter: 0.224″
Maximum Case Length: 1.850″
Trim to Length: 1.84″
Maximum Cartridge OAL: 2.28″
Minimum Cartridge OAL: 2.22″

On the road to a successful bid to produce a new NATO chambering, Remington lengthened the 222 Remington to provide the requisite performance. Remington was so impressed with this design that they offered it as a standard commercial chambering in 1958. Working at the same pressure as the 222 Remington, the lengthened "Magnum" version offers several hundred feet per second velocity advantage and considerably more useful range for those who can shoot that well.

Later, NATO opted for a slightly shorter cartridge that worked at a higher pressure, which was commercialized as the 223 in 1964. Since the more compact 223 is both a military chambering and delivers the same performance as the 222 Remington Magnum, the 222 Remington Magnum was instantly doomed. While ammunition is still available, this cartridge is long-since on the way to obsolescence.

Regardless, this is a fine intermediate varmint cartridge, and there is no compelling reason for anyone owning such a rifle to feel the necessity of another chambering. Even the hottest of 22s do not offer much in the way of increased range, and they do so only at the expense of much increased muzzle blast and reduced barrel life.

Only with the most carefully loaded ammunition, fired from the best of rifles, by the best of shooters, and only then when shooting conditions are just right, can the increased performance of hotter numbers be fully realized.

With a 52-grain bullet, seated normally, usable case capacity is about 29.2 grains of water. H335, W748, A2460, IMR4895, BL-C(2), H4895 and IMR3031 are all good choices.

222 REMINGTON MAGNUM LOADING DATA

Powder	STARTING Grs.	MV (fps)	MAXIMUM Grs.	MV (fps)	Press. (CUP/psi)	Comments
40						
BL-C(2)	27.5	3513	30.0	3818	49,200C	
H335	27.5	3532	30.0	3803	47,800C	
H4198	23.0	3592	24.5	3760	49,100C	
W748	27.0	3484	29.0	3744	48,800C	
IMR4198	22.0	3444	24.0	3714	49,600C	
H322	25.0	3318	27.0	3622	48,400C	
IMR3031	25.0	3384	27.0	3616	48,600C	
RL-7	22.0	3367	24.0	3542	47,200C	
IMR4320	26.0	3384	28.0	3540	47,400C	
IMR4064	26.0	3271	28.0	3494	45,400C	
H4895	26.5	3363	29.0	3490	45,400C	
IMR4895	26.0	3339	28.0	3414	45,000C	
H414			31.0	3142	28,000C	
H4227	15.5	2714	17.0	3062	36,600C	
45						
BL-C(2)	26.0	3302	28.0	3664	50,100C	
W748	26.0	3334	28.0	3651	49,800C	
45 con't						
H335	26.0	3343	28.0	3647	49,600C	
H4198	22.0	3392	24.0	3641	50,200C	
A2460	26.4	3150	29.3	3579	49,400p	Nos Hornet/2.22″/Rem 7½
A2230	25.8	3122	28.7	3548	47,500p	Nos Hornet/2.22″/Rem 7½
H322	24.5	3159	26.5	3532	50,300C	
A2015BR	24.3	3098	27.0	3521	47,200p	Nos Hornet/2.22″/Rem 7½
A2520	26.1	3057	29.0	3474	43,900p	Nos Hornet/2.22″/Rem 7½
IMR4198	21.0	3194	23.0	3464	49,800C	
H4895	26.5	3314	29.0	3442	49,700C	
IMR4320	26.0	3272	28.0	3439	49,800C	
IMR4895	26.0	3294	28.0	3434	49,400C	
RL-7	21.0	3177	23.0	3414	47,000C	
IMR3031	24.0	3179	26.0	3384	47,400C	
IMR4064	25.0	3169	27.0	3291	46,100C	
H414	28.5	2946	31.0	3199	33,000C	
A2700	27.6	2922	29.0	3109	33,900p	Nos Hornet/2.22″/Rem 7½

▶▶▶▶▶▶▶▶▶▶▶▶▶▶▶▶▶▶▶▶▶▶▶▶▶

Never exceed maximum load nor use any load exhibiting signs of excessive pressure. Begin at suggested starting load and work up carefully.

50

Powder	STARTING Grs.	MV (fps)	MAXIMUM Grs.	MV (fps)	Press. (CUP/psi)	Comments
N133			27.6	3510	52,214p	Sako FMJ 105G
H335	25.0	3232	27.0	3476	48,200C	
A2230	25.4	3047	28.2	3462	51,700p	Spr HP/2.32"/Rem 7½
A2460	25.5	3032	28.3	3445	50,600C	Spr HP/2.32"/Rem 7½
BL-C(2)	25.0	3212	27.0	3433	47,300C	
W748	25.0	3209	27.0	3419	47,400C	
A2520	26.1	2994	29.0	3402	46,900p	Spr HP/2.32"/Rem 7½
A2015BR	23.9	2991	26.5	3399	49,100p	Spr HP/2.32"/Rem 7½
H322	24.0	3128	26.0	3385	49,300C	
H4198	21.5	3147	23.5	3379	45,400C	
IMR3031	24.0	3164	26.0	3349	49,400C	
IMR4064	25.0	3132	27.0	3318	49,000C	
H4895	26.0	3166	28.5	3306	45,900C	
IMR4895	25.0	3128	27.0	3300	48,800C	
N120			21.6	3300	50,763p	Sako SP 106G
IMR4198	20.0	3108	22.0	3294	48,800C	
RL-7	20.5	2955	22.5	3264	46,800C	
H414	28.5	2888	31.0	3123	34,800C	
W760	29.0	2910	31.0	3100	35,000C	

52-53

Powder	STARTING Grs.	MV (fps)	MAXIMUM Grs.	MV (fps)	Press. (CUP/psi)	Comments
N133			26.7	3400	50,763p	Hdy HP
A2460	25.5	2982	28.3	3389	50,000p	Nos HP/2.295"/Rem 7½
A2230	24.9	2981	27.7	3388	52,400p	Nos HP/2.295"/Rem 7½
A2015BR	23.2	2942	25.8	3343	49,900p	Nos HP/2.295"/Rem 7½
H335	25.0	3089	27.0	3340	47,600C	
BL-C(2)	25.0	3074	27.0	3313	47,800C	
IMR3031	24.0	3127	26.0	3309	49,800C	(53-gr.)
W748	25.0	3071	27.0	3296	47,600C	
H322	23.0	3014	25.0	3285	49,800C	
H4198	21.0	3076	23.0	3282	45,900C	
IMR4064	25.0	3101	27.0	3274	49,800C	(53-gr.)
H4895	25.5	3137	28.0	3272	48,500C	
IMR4895	25.0	3110	27.0	3261	49,200C	(53-gr.)
IMR4320	25.0	3092	27.0	3251	48,400C	(53-gr.)
IMR4198	20.0	3079	22.0	3239	49,000C	(53-gr.)
RL-7	20.0	2909	22.0	3224	46,600C	
H380	28.5	3067	30.0	3181	44,700C	
H414	28.5	2903	31.0	3155	40,800C	
W760	29.0	2927	31.0	3141	40,700C	
A2520	26.1	2673	29.0	3037	45,400p	Nos HP/2.295"/Rem 7½

55

Powder	STARTING Grs.	MV (fps)	MAXIMUM Grs.	MV (fps)	Press. (CUP/psi)	Comments
N140			29.0	3410	49,313p	Sako SP 110G
N133			26.2	3330	52,214p	Sako SP 110G
H335	24.0	3086	26.0	3294	48,100C	
A2460	24.9	2896	27.7	3291	50,900p	Nos SBT/2.31"/Rem 7½
A2520	25.8	2884	28.7	3277	46,800C	Nos SBT/2.31"/Rem 7½
N120			22.7	3260	50,763p	Sako SP 110G
H4895	25.5	3121	28.0	3257	48,900C	
A2230	24.3	2861	27.0	3251	49,200p	Nos SBT/2.31"/Rem 7½
BL-C(2)	24.5	3021	26.5	3240	46,800C	

55 con't

Powder	STARTING Grs.	MV (fps)	MAXIMUM Grs.	MV (fps)	Press. (CUP/psi)	Comments
H4198	21.0	3024	23.0	3222	46,300C	
A2015BR	23.0	2833	25.5	3219	47,200p	Nos SBT/2.31"/Rem 7½
IMR4895	24.5	3061	26.5	3210	49,800C	
H414	28.5	2968	31.0	3209	44,600C	
RL-7	20.0	2888	22.0	3207	47,400C	
H322	22.5	2867	24.5	3191	49,300C	
IMR4064	24.0	3039	26.0	3174	49,200C	
IMR3031	22.5	3039	24.5	3158	48,900C	
H380	28.5	2952	31.0	3136	44,900C	
IMR4198	18.5	2840	20.5	3116	48,400C	

60-64

Powder	STARTING Grs.	MV (fps)	MAXIMUM Grs.	MV (fps)	Press. (CUP/psi)	Comments
N140			27.9	3180	52,214p	Hdy SP
N135			25.9	3150	43,511p	Hdy SP
A2520	24.9	2772	27.7	3150	48,800C	Nos/2.33"/Rem 7½
A2460	24.0	2752	26.7	3127	49,100p	Nos/2.33"/Rem 7½
IMR4064	23.0	2881	25.0	3110	48,600C	
A2230	23.4	2717	26.0	3088	49,300p	Nos/2.33"/Rem 7½
A2015BR	22.1	2716	24.5	3086	48,800p	Nos/2.33"/Rem 7½
H414	27.5	2786	30.0	3085	45,400C	
W760	28.0	2804	30.0	3079	45,800C	
BL-C(2)	24.0	2913	26.0	3078	49,600C	
A2015BR	22.3	2700	24.8	3068	50,300p	Sra SP/2.28"/Rem 7½
W748	24.0	2904	26.0	3066	49,500C	
IMR4895	23.0	2818	25.0	3061	47,800C	
H335	23.5	2910	25.5	3057	49,100C	
H4895	24.5	2869	26.5	3046	48,400C	
IMR4320	23.0	2814	25.0	3037	47,600C	
H4198	18.5	2845	20.5	3019	47,800C	
A2520	24.3	2646	27.0	3007	45,600p	Sra SP/2.28"/Rem 7½
A2460	23.0	2644	25.5	3005	47,000C	Sra SP/2.28"/Rem 7½
H380	27.5	2839p	30.0	2977	45,200C	
RL-7	19.0	2755	21.0	2974	47,800C	
A2230	22.5	2606	25.0	2961	48,700p	Sra SP/2.28"/Rem 7½
IMR4198	17.5	2740	19.5	2941	48,800C	
H322	21.5	2763	23.5	2934	48,900C	
IMR3031	21.0	2739	23.0	2924	47,900C	
A2700	26.6	2668	28.0	2838	37,700p	Nos/2.33"/Rem 7½
A2700	25.2	2452	28.0	2786	38,600p	Sra SP/2.28"/Rem 7½

70

Powder	STARTING Grs.	MV (fps)	MAXIMUM Grs.	MV (fps)	Press. (CUP/psi)	Comments
H414	27.0	2714	29.0	2864	47,400C	
W760	27.0	2710	29.0	2851	47,600C	
H380	26.0	2671	28.0	2811	46,900C	
IMR4895	22.0	2630	24.0	2788	49,600C	
H4895	22.5	2639	24.5	2785	49,800C	
IMR4320	22.0	2600	24.0	2764	48,800C	
H322	20.5	2528	22.5	2753	48,400C	
H335	21.5	2575	23.5	2744	48,600C	
BL-C(2)	22.0	2591	24.0	2734	46,900C	
W748	22.0	2577	24.0	2729	47,000C	
RL-7	18.0	2509	20.0	2717	48,000C	

Never exceed maximum load nor use any load exhibiting signs of excessive pressure. Begin at suggested starting load and work up carefully.

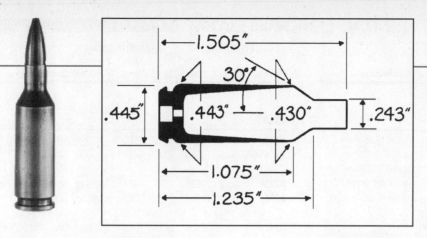

Case: Sako
Primer: Small Rifle
Barrel: 24″ Accurate
　　　　 24″ Hodgdon
　　　　 24″ Vihtavuori

Bullet Diameter: 0.224″
Maximum Case Length: 1.505″
Trim to Length: 1.495″
Maximum Cartridge OAL: 1.960″
Minimum Cartridge OAL: Bullet Dependent

The history of this wildcat chambering begins with the 7.62x39mm case. That cartridge was modified by Russian designers for use in international accuracy competition events as the 220 Russian. Benchrest shooters, Dr. Lou Palmisano and Ferris Pindell, further modified that Russian designed 0.220″ bulleted cartridge to develop, first, the 6mm PPC, then the 22 PPC. Sako currently offers factory cases.

A caution is in order: Since such guns are primarily designed and used in benchrest competition, custom chambers are the norm. It is entirely possible that you could find a combination of bullet, case and chamber that did not allow sufficient room for the case mouth to expand away from the bullet to release it upon firing. Such a situation could result in devastating pressures.

The safest approach is to make a proper chamber cast and measure the barrel's throat. If the necks of your loaded rounds

do not measure at least 0.002″ smaller than the chamber's throat, you must turn the case necks until such clearance is achieved, see Chapter 2 for a discussion on outside neck turning.

Further, this data was developed in a "standard" throated chamber. Use of this data in a tight-chambered gun will necessarily increase pressure somewhat. If you have a tight-chambered gun, reduce starting loads an additional 5 percent and work up for accuracy, watching carefully for signs of excess pressure.

The 22 PPC offers startling performance for a cartridge of such limited capacity. Considering the accuracy available, this cartridge is hard to beat for an all-around varmint chambering.

Usable case capacity depends on bullet and case used and on actual chamber dimensions, but is typically about 32.0 grains of water. A2460 and A2520 are known performers in the 22 PPC.

22 PPC LOADING DATA

Powder	STARTING Grs.	MV (fps)	MAXIMUM Grs.	MV (fps)	Press. (CUP/psi)	Comments
40						
VarGet			29.5	3560	45,700C	

Powder	STARTING Grs.	MV (fps)	MAXIMUM Grs.	MV (fps)	Press. (CUP/psi)	Comments
45						
A2460	26.7	3259	29.7	3703	51,100p	Nos Hornet/1.89″/Rem 7½
A2230	26.3	3255	29.2	3699	54,500p	Nos Hornet/1.89″/Rem 7½
A2015BR	23.9	3160	26.5	3591	51,600p	Nos Hornet/1.89″/Rem 7½
A2495BR	25.2	3153	28.0	3583	48,300p	Nos Hornet/1.89″/Rem 7½/(C)
A2520	26.1	3129	29.0	3556	43,600p	Nos Hornet/1.89″/Rem 7½/(C)

Caution: Loads exceeding SAAMI OAL Maximum must be verified for bullet-to-rifling clearance and magazine functioning. Where a specific primer or bullet is indicated those components must be used, no substitutions! Where only a maximum load is shown, reduce starting load 10%, unless otherwise specified.

Key: (C) = compressed charge; C = CUP; p = psi; Plink = Plinker; Bns = Barnes; Hdy = Hornady; Lap = Lapua; Nos = Nosler; Rem = Remington; Sra = Sierra; Spr = Speer; Win = Winchester.

>>>>>>>>>>>>>>>>>>>>>>>>>

Never exceed maximum load nor use any load exhibiting signs of excessive pressure. Begin at suggested starting load and work up carefully.

101

50

Powder	—STARTING— Grs.	MV (fps)	—MAXIMUM— Grs.	MV (fps)	Press. (CUP/psi)	Comments
A2230	26.1	3183	29.0	3617	54,600p	Spr HP/2.0"/Rem 7½
A2460	26.1	3148	29.0	3577	54,800p	Spr HP/2.0"/Rem 7½
A2495BR	25.2	3083	28.0	3503	53,800p	Spr HP/2.0"/Rem 7½/(C)
A2520	26.1	3050	29.0	3466	48,000p	Spr HP/2.0"/Rem 7½/(C)
A2015BR	23.4	3047	26.0	3462	51,300p	Spr HP/2.0"/Rem 7½
H335	26.0	3183	28.0	3418	50,000C	
RL-12	28.0	3249	30.0	3417	49,000C	
H322	25.0	3204	26.0	3385	48,000C	
RL-15	27.0	3145	29.0	3369	44,000C	
RL-7	23.0	3135	25.0	3352	48,000C	
H4895	26.0	2989	28.0	3347	46,500C	
BL-C(2)	29.0	3210	30.5	3316	47,000C	
W748	28.5	3184	30.0	3284	46,500C	

52-53

Powder	—STARTING— Grs.	MV (fps)	—MAXIMUM— Grs.	MV (fps)	Press. (CUP/psi)	Comments
A2460	26.1	3107	29.0	3531	53,200p	Hdy HP/1.975"/Rem 7½
A2495BR	25.2	3084	28.0	3504	57,200p	Hdy HP/1.975"/Rem 7½/(C)
A2230	25.7	3078	28.5	3498	53,000p	Hdy HP/1.975"/Rem 7½
N135	25.1	3130	27.8	3443	49,300p	Sra HPBTM
A2520	26.1	3019	29.0	3431	47,700p	Hdy HP/1.975"/Rem 7½/(C)
N133	23.1	3085	25.8	3380	49,300p	Sra HPBTM
A2015BR	23.0	2969	25.5	3374	51,900p	Hdy HP/1.975"/Rem 7½
VarGet			28.5	3363	48,900C	
RL-12	27.0	3072	29.0	3359	50,000C	
RL-15	27.0	3102	29.0	3345	47,000C	
H335	25.5	3107	27.5	3344	49,000C	
N130	21.6	3027	24.3	3335	49,300p	Sra HPBTM
H322	24.0	3046	26.0	3333	48,500C	
H4895	26.0	3079	28.0	3321	49,000C	
RL-7	22.5	3096	24.5	3291	50,000C	
BL-C(2)	29.0	3152	30.5	3288	48,000C	
W748	28.5	3141	30.0	3260	47,500C	
N120	21.9	3171	22.7	3254	49,300p	Sra HPBTM

55

Powder	—STARTING— Grs.	MV (fps)	—MAXIMUM— Grs.	MV (fps)	Press. (CUP/psi)	Comments
N135	25.5	3091	28.3	3435	49,300p	Spr SP
A2495BR	24.8	3010	27.6	3421	56,400p	Nos SP/1.96"/Rem 7½/(C)
A2230	25.2	2996	28.0	3404	55,300p	Nos SP/1.96"/Rem 7½
A2520	26.1	2962	29.0	3366	50,900p	Nos SP/1.96"/Rem 7½/(C)
A2460	25.2	2960	28.0	3364	51,200p	Nos SP/1.96"/Rem 7½
RL-15	27.0	3137	29.0	3359	48,000C	
H4895	26.0	3047	28.0	3346	50,000C	
VarGet			28.5	3317	47,800C	
H322	24.0	3052	26.0	3306	50,000C	
BL-C(2)	28.5	3091	30.0	3285	50,000C	
A2015BR	22.5	2885	25.0	3278	53,200p	Nos SP/1.96"/Rem 7½
W748	28.0	3101	29.5	3249	48,000C	
RL-12	26.0	2975	28.0	3248	48,000C	
N133	22.8	2996	25.4	3232	49,300p	Spr SP
H335	24.5	2951	26.5	3216	47,500C	
N130	21.6	2946	24.3	3202	49,300p	Spr SP
RL-7	22.0	2977	24.0	3186	49,000C	

60-64

Powder	—STARTING— Grs.	MV (fps)	—MAXIMUM— Grs.	MV (fps)	Press. (CUP/psi)	Comments
A2460	25.2	2948	28.0	3350	56,200p	Hdy HP/1.985"/Rem 7½
A2520	26.1	2944	29.0	3345	54,300p	Hdy HP/1.985"/Rem 7½/(C)
A2230	24.8	2920	27.5	3318	54,600p	Hdy HP/1.985"/Rem 7½
A2495BR	23.9	2878	26.5	3270	56,400p	Hdy HP/1.985"/Rem 7½
A2015BR	22.5	2834	25.0	3220	54,800p	Hdy HP/1.985"/Rem 7½
H4895	24.5	2873	26.5	3127	48,500C	
H322	23.5	2875	25.5	3118	50,000C	
H335	24.0	2935	26.0	3110	49,500C	
RL-12	25.0	2850	27.0	3110	50,000C	
RL-15	25.5	2895	27.5	3109	48,000C	
BL-C(2)	27.0	2846	29.0	3068	48,000C	
W748	27.0	2828	28.5	3052	48,500C	
RL-7	21.0	2805	23.0	3037	50,000C	

68-70

Powder	—STARTING— Grs.	MV (fps)	—MAXIMUM— Grs.	MV (fps)	Press. (CUP/psi)	Comments
BL-C(2)	26.0	2758	28.0	2985	49,500C	
W748	25.5	2719	27.5	2957	49,000C	
H4895	23.0	2718	25.0	2919	48,500C	
RL-15	24.0	2730	26.0	2911	49,500C	
H335	22.5	2702	24.5	2908	48,500C	
RL-12	23.5	2707	25.5	2898	50,000C	
H322	22.0	2688	24.0	2876	50,000C	

Caution: Loads exceeding SAAMI OAL Maximum must be verified for bullet-to-rifling clearance and magazine functioning. Where a specific primer or bullet is indicated those components must be used, no substitutions! Where only a maximum load is shown, reduce starting load 10%, unless otherwise specified.

Key: (C) = compressed charge; C = CUP; p = psi; Plink = Plinker; Bns = Barnes; Hdy = Hornady; Lap = Lapua; Nos = Nosler; Rem = Remington; Sra = Sierra; Spr = Speer; Win = Winchester.

Never exceed maximum load nor use any load exhibiting signs of excessive pressure. Begin at suggested starting load and work up carefully.

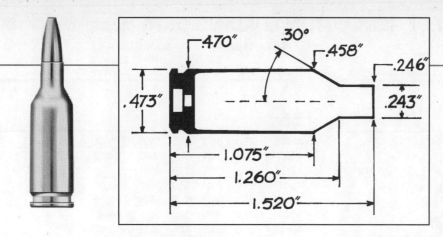

Case: Remington
Primer: Remington 7½
Barrel: 26″ Accurate
      24″ Hodgdon
Bullet Diameter: 0.224″

Maximum Case Length: 1.520″
Trim to Length: 1.515″
Maximum Cartridge OAL: Gun Dependent
Minimum Cartridge OAL: Bullet Dependent

The origin of the 22 BR Remington harks back to the 7mm BR Remington, which was originally fashioned from a special 308 Winchester case made by Remington designed to use small primers. This thin-walled case was designed especially for easy conversion to other, shorter designs. Like the 22 PPC, the 22 BR takes advantage of a small primer and a shorter powder column to generate surprisingly consistent velocities. The 22 BR is widely used in the benchrest shooting game.

Few would guess that this cartridge, although nearly 1-inch shorter, produces virtually identical velocity to the 22-250 Remington! Performance is so good that it can be highly recommended to those interested in a near-maximum-range custom 22 varmint rifle.

Several cautions are in order. First, cases for these loads were produced from the basic BR case. One must not attempt to use standard thick-walled, large-primer cases to fashion any of the BR series of cartridges. Doing so creates a case with considerably less usable capacity, using primers that are generally hotter. We cannot advise on any "safe" approach to working up safe loads for such cases.

Also, since BR cartridge chambered guns are primarily designed and used in benchrest competition, many have custom chambers. It is entirely possible that you could find a combination of bullet, case and chamber that did not allow sufficient room for the case mouth to expand away from the bullet and release it upon firing. Such a situation could result in devastating pressures.

The safest approach is to make a proper chamber cast to measure the barrel's throat. If the necks of your loaded rounds do not measure at least 0.002″ smaller than the chamber throat, you must turn the case necks until such clearance is achieved. See the discussion on outside neck turning in Chapter 2.

Further, this data was developed in a "standard" throated chamber. Use of this data in a tight-chambered gun will necessarily increase pressures somewhat. If you have a tight-chambered gun, reduce starting loads about 5 percent and work up for accuracy, watching carefully for signs of excess pressure.

Usable case capacity depends on bullet and case used and on actual chamber dimensions, but is typically about 35.0 grains of water. The powder, *de rigor*, for the 22 BR is H322.

There is also a shorter version of the BR family of cartridges currently gaining favor—ensure you are not loading one of those with standard BR data! Results could be disastrous.

22 BENCHREST REMINGTON LOADING DATA (22 BR)

Powder	—STARTING— Grs.	MV (fps)	—MAXIMUM— Grs.	MV (fps)	Press. (CUP/psi)	Comments
40						
XMP5744			26.5	3843		Nos BT
45						
A2460	30.6	3443	34.0	3913	57,600p	Nos Hornet/1.895″
A2520	30.9	3428	34.3	3896	55,300p	Nos Hornet/1.895″/(C)
A2230	30.2	3417	33.5	3883	57,400p	Nos Hornet/1.895″
A2015BR	27.5	3356	30.5	3814	57,000p	Nos Hornet/1.895″
H4895	30.0	3429	32.5	3768	49,000C	
H335	31.0	3441	33.0	3759	48,600C	
RL-12	32.0	3490	34.5	3759	48,900C	

Powder	—STARTING— Grs.	MV (fps)	—MAXIMUM— Grs.	MV (fps)	Press. (CUP/psi)	Comments
45 con't						
BL-C(2)	34.0	3369	36.0	3746	48,000C	
H322	29.0	3409	31.5	3741	49,400C	
A2495BR	29.3	3281	32.5	3728	48,100p	Nos Hornet/1.895″/(C)
W748	33.5	3427	35.5	3717	47,400C	
IMR3031	29.0	3493	31.0	3714	48,800C	
IMR4320	30.0	3422	33.5	3682	48,400C	
IMR4064	29.5	3404	32.5	3667	47,000C	
IMR4895	29.0	3440	32.5	3660	48,800C	
RL-7	26.5	3392	28.5	3612	46,900C	
A2700	33.7	3359	35.5	3573	46,700p	Nos Hornet/1.895″/(C)

Never exceed maximum load nor use any load exhibiting signs of excessive pressure. Begin at suggested starting load and work up carefully.

50

Powder	STARTING Grs.	MV (fps)	MAXIMUM Grs.	MV (fps)	Press. (CUP/psi)	Comments
A2230	30.0	3313	33.3	3765	56,000p	Spr TNT/2.0"
A2460	30.2	3311	33.5	3762	54,900p	Spr TNT/2.0"
A2520	30.3	3301	33.7	3751	54,900p	Spr TNT/2.0"/(C)
A2015BR	27.5	3282	30.5	3729	55,900p	Spr TNT/2.0"
RL-12	31.5	3421	34.0	3676	49,000C	
BL-C(2)	33.5	3440	35.5	3649	49,000C	
H322	28.0	3292	30.5	3637	50,000C	
H335	30.0	3419	32.0	3628	48,800C	
W748	33.0	3414	35.0	3624	48,800C	
IMR4064	30.0	3430	32.5	3612	48,800C	
H4895	29.5	3404	32.0	3606	48,000C	
IMR4895	29.5	3366	32.0	3600	49,400C	
IMR3031	28.5	3324	30.0	3589	48,000C	
IMR4320	30.0	3362	33.0	3574	47,400C	
XMP5744			26.0	3563		Spr TNT
A2495BR	28.8	3132	32.0	3559	45,400p	Spr TNT/2.0"/(C)
RL-7	26.0	3322	28.0	3516	47,500C	
A2700	33.3	3267	35.0	3476	46,900p	Spr TNT/2.0"/(C)

52-53

Powder	STARTING Grs.	MV (fps)	MAXIMUM Grs.	MV (fps)	Press. (CUP/psi)	Comments
A2460	29.5	3215	32.8	3653	57,300p	Hdy HP/1.985"
A2520	29.5	3186	32.8	3620	56,400p	Hdy HP/1.985"
A2230	29.0	3183	32.2	3617	57,900p	Hdy HP/1.985"
BL-C(2)	32.5	3403	35.0	3592	48,800C	
IMR4064	29.5	3389	32.0	3587	48,200C	
H335	29.5	3371	31.5	3587	49,200C	
W748	32.5	3404	35.0	3586	49,100C	
A2015BR	26.6	3150	29.5	3579	56,600p	Hdy HP/1.985"
RL-12	31.0	3339	33.5	3576	49,800C	
H4895	29.5	3377	31.5	3566	49,000C	
IMR4895	29.5	3370	31.5	3559	49,400C	
IMR4320	29.5	3329	32.5	3556	50,000C	
H322	28.0	3270	30.0	3544	48,400C	
A2495BR	28.4	3116	31.5	3541	52,400p	Hdy HP/1.985"
IMR3031	28.0	3240	29.8	3515	47,700C	
RL-7	25.5	3302	27.5	3463	49,800C	
XMP5744			25.0	3443		Hdy HP
A2700	33.3	3111	35.0	3310	46,600p	Hdy HP/1.985"/(C)

55

Powder	STARTING Grs.	MV (fps)	MAXIMUM Grs.	MV (fps)	Press. (CUP/psi)	Comments
A2460	29.3	3172	32.5	3605	59,900p	Nos SBT/1.97"
A2520	29.4	3159	32.7	3590	57,400p	Nos SBT/1.97"/(C)
A2230	28.8	3138	32.0	3566	55,700p	Nos SBT/1.97"
RL-12	31.0	3304	33.0	3560	50,300C	
BL-C(2)	32.5	3329	34.5	3531	48,200C	
W748	32.0	3299	34.5	3519	48,400C	
IMR4064	29.0	3320	31.5	3512	49,000C	
A2015BR	26.1	3071	29.0	3490	56,500p	Nos SBT/1.97"
H335	29.5	3269	31.5	3489	49,800C	
H4895	29.0	3212	31.0	3478	49,400C	
IMR3031	27.0	3202	29.5	3473	47,500C	
IMR4320	29.0	3210	32.0	3460	50,000C	
IMR4895	28.0	3204	31.0	3454	49,600C	
A2495BR	27.9	3033	31.0	3447	49,600C	Nos SBT/1.97"/(C)
H322	28.0	3219	30.0	3439	48,800C	
RL-7	25.5	3269	27.5	3439	50,300C	
A2700	32.3	3156	34.0	3357	47,600p	Nos SBT/1.97"/(C)
XMP5744			24.5	3335		Nos SBT

60-64

Powder	STARTING Grs.	MV (fps)	MAXIMUM Grs.	MV (fps)	Press. (CUP/psi)	Comments
A2460	28.5	3040	31.7	3455	56,900p	Hdy HP/1.99"
A2495BR	27.9	3021	31.0	3433	56,700p	Hdy HP/1.99"/(C)
A2230	28.1	3005	31.2	3415	55,700p	Hdy HP/1.99"
A2520	28.4	2995	31.5	3403	56,000p	Hdy HP/1.99"
A2015BR	25.7	2965	28.5	3369	55,800p	Hdy HP/1.99"
A2700	32.3	3122	34.0	3321	51,900p	Hdy HP/1.99"/(C)
BL-C(2)	31.0	3049	33.0	3298	48,400C	
H335	26.5	3032	29.0	3290	49,900C	
RL-12	29.0	3090	31.0	3286	50,400C	
W748	30.5	3004	32.5	3271	48,600C	
IMR4320	28.0	3044	30.5	3241	50,000C	
IMR4064	27.5	3034	29.0	3240	50,100C	
H4895	26.0	2994	28.0	3146	49,400C	
XMP5744			24.0	3211		Hdy HP
IMR4895	27.0	2988	28.0	3142	49,400C	
H322	24.0	2962	26.5	3120	48,800C	
IMR3031	24.0	2927	26.5	3100	46,800C	

70

Powder	STARTING Grs.	MV (fps)	MAXIMUM Grs.	MV (fps)	Press. (CUP/psi)	Comments
BL-C(2)	26.5	2811	28.5	3009	49,500C	
IMR4320	26.0	2810	28.0	2986	48,500C	
IMR4064	25.0	2830	26.5	2970	48,900C	
H335	24.0	2740	26.0	2959	49,900C	
W748	26.0	2777	28.0	2944	49,100C	
IMR4895	23.0	2744	25.5	2940	49,900C	
RL-12	24.5	2820	26.5	2937	48,900C	
H322	22.0	2696	24.0	2889	49,900C	
H4895	23.0	2707	24.5	2845	50,000C	

WARNING: Cases formed from 6mm BR or 7mm BR are always neck reamed. Dangerous pressures might occur if cases are not properly neck reamed.

Caution: Loads exceeding SAAMI OAL Maximum must be verified for bullet-to-rifling clearance and magazine functioning. Where a specific primer or bullet is indicated those components must be used, no substitutions! Where only a maximum load is shown, reduce starting load 10%, unless otherwise specified.

Key: (C) = compressed charge; C = CUP; p = psi; Plink = Plinker; Bns = Barnes; Hdy = Hornady; Lap = Lapua; Nos = Nosler; Rem = Remington; Sra = Sierra; Spr = Speer; Win = Winchester.

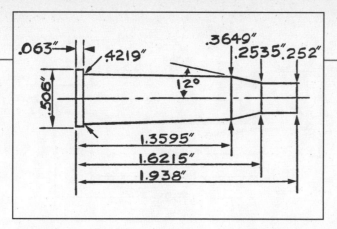

Case: Winchester
Primer: Large Rifle
Barrel: 26″ Accurate
Bullet Diameter: 0.224″

Maximum Case Length: 1.938″
Trim to Length: 1.928″
Maximum Cartridge OAL: 2.260″
Minimum Cartridge OAL: Bullet Dependent

In a parallel development to the 218 Bee, Winchester modernized and modified John M. Browning's Model 94 Winchester, as the Model 64, and designed a varmint cartridge to chamber in it—the 219 Zipper.

Entirely similar to the earlier 22 Savage High Power, the Zipper was loaded with standard diameter and lighter 22-caliber bullets to higher velocity, compared to Savage's development. Where Savage saw their 30-30-based 22 Savage High Power as a combination small- and big-game hunting cartridge, Winchester developed the Zipper strictly for varmint and small-game hunting.

Evidently Winchester should have spent more time, and money, carefully producing rifles and ammunition in this caliber. This combination soon garnered a reputation for erratic and inadequate accuracy. Here we had a cartridge that could launch bullets sufficiently fast to suggest 200-yard-plus shots on vermin, but accuracy was seldom sufficient to deliver the bullet to the target at such ranges.

Historically the blame has been almost universally laid at the feet of the rifle. Considering actual testing with high-quality ammunition in the best of these rifles, this seems unfair. Good ammunition in a good Model 64 can deliver the bullet to about 250 yards with all the accuracy necessary for the job Winchester's engineers had intended.

However, there was another significant problem. The Model 64 did not present itself for easy or useful adaptation to telescopic sights. Those who did adapt such a sight on the side of the receiver found they had rendered the gun useless as a "beater". . . a gun they could just toss in the old pickup, in case they saw a varmint while doing farm or ranch chores. However, without a scope sight, few could use the gun for shots on varmints past about 100 yards!

Nevertheless, the 219 Zipper is a good performer, capable of impressive accuracy and velocity, when chambered in the right gun and with careful loading.

Usable case capacity depends on bullet and case used, but will typically be about 34.0 grains of water.

Never use pointed bullets in any centerfire cartridge used in a tubular magazine.

219 ZIPPER LOADING DATA

Powder	STARTING Grs.	MV (fps)	MAXIMUM Grs.	MV (fps)	Press. (CUP/psi)	Comments
46						
A2495BR	24.3	2930	27.0	3300	42,000p	Spr FN/2.255″/CCI 200
A2520	24.8	2892	27.5	3286	38,500p	Spr FN/2.255″/CCI 200
A2460	23.4	2842	26.0	3230	38,700p	Spr FN/2.255″/CCI 200
A2700	27.9	2840	31.0	3227	40,000p	Spr FN/2.255″/CCI 200
A2230	23.0	2834	25.5	3220	39,800p	Spr FN/2.255″/CCI 200
A2015BR	21.6	2797	24.0	3178	39,400p	Spr FN/2.255″/CCI 200
50						
A2495BR	25.2	2913	28.0	3310	42,000p	Hdy SX/2.35″/CCI 200
A2015BR	23.4	2844	26.0	3232	40,800p	Hdy SX/2.35″/CCI 200
A2520	24.3	2814	27.0	3198	38,400p	Hdy SX/2.35″/CCI 200
50 con't						
A2230	23.4	2811	26.0	3194	40,800p	Hdy SX/2.35″/CCI 200
A2460	23.4	2778	26.0	3157	37,900p	Hdy SX/2.35″/CCI 200
A2700	27.0	2700	30.0	3068	36,300p	Hdy SX/2.35″/CCI 200
55						
A2460	23.9	2740	26.5	3114	41,700p	Nos SBT/2.375″/CCI 200
A2495BR	23.9	2728	26.5	3100	40,000p	Nos SBT/2.375″/CCI 200
A2230	23.4	2725	26.0	3097	41,800p	Nos SBT/2.375″/CCI 200
A2015BR	22.5	2716	25.0	3086	40,800p	Nos SBT/2.375″/CCI 200
A2520	23.9	2696	26.5	3064	37,100p	Nos SBT/2.375″/CCI 200
A2700	27.0	2696	30.0	3064	42,000p	Nos SBT/2.375″/CCI 200

Never exceed maximum load nor use any load exhibiting signs of excessive pressure. Begin at suggested starting load and work up carefully.

219
Donaldson Wasp

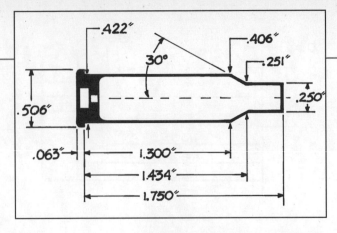

Case: Winchester
(Converted from 7-30)
Primer: Large Rifle
Barrel: 28″ Hodgdon
Bullet Diameter: 0.224″

Maximum Case Length: 1.750″
Trim to Length: 1.74″
Maximum Cartridge OAL: Gun Dependent
Minimum Cartridge OAL: Bullet Dependent

Designed by Harvey Donaldson in 1937, the Wasp was created by shortening the 219 Zipper and then fireforming it to a sharper shoulder with less body taper. Mr. Donaldson intended the Wasp to work at bolt-action cartridge pressures. Evidently, he well understood the benefits of reduced case capacity and high working pressures because the Wasp, chambered in single shot and turn-bolt guns, soon found favor among the benchrest fraternity.

Through the years preceding the introduction of the 222 Remington, the Wasp won more than its share of benchrest competitions. Even by today's standards, it is a fine car-tridge, and those interested in converting a single shot rifle to a high-performance 22-caliber chambering should consider it.

Case-forming was originally done with 219 Zipper or 25-35 Winchester cases. Today cases are formed from other 30-30-family cases, and neck-wall thickness might, therefore, be excessive; use caution. It might be necessary to turn the necks to achieve adequate chamber clearance.

Usable case capacity depends on bullet and case used, but will typically be about 30.0 grains of water.

219 DONALDSON WASP LOADING DATA

Powder	STARTING Grs.	MV (fps)	MAXIMUM Grs.	MV (fps)	Press. (CUP/psi)	Comments
40						
H4895			28.0	3312		

Powder	STARTING Grs.	MV (fps)	MAXIMUM Grs.	MV (fps)	Press. (CUP/psi)	Comments
55						
H4895			28.0	3501		

Caution: Loads exceeding SAAMI OAL Maximum must be verified for bullet-to-rifling clearance and magazine functioning. Where a specific primer or bullet is indicated those components must be used, no substitutions! Where only a maximum load is shown, reduce starting load 10%, unless otherwise specified.

Key: (C) = compressed charge; C = CUP; p = psi; Plink = Plinker; Bns = Barnes; Hdy = Hornady; Lap = Lapua; Nos = Nosler; Rem = Remington; Sra = Sierra; Spr = Speer; Win = Winchester.

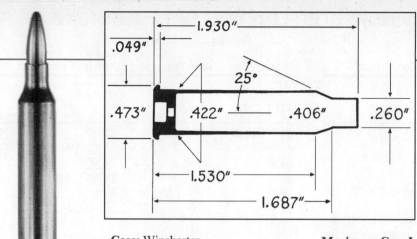

Case: Winchester
Primer: Large Rifle
Barrel: 24″ Accurate/26″ Hodgdon
Bullet Diameter: 0.224″

Maximum Case Length: 1.930″
Trim to Length: 1.92″
Maximum Cartridge OAL: 2.50″
Minimum Cartridge OAL: 2.42″

When Winchester paradoxically decided to discontinue the 220 Swift—"Fastest commercial chambering ever produced!"—in 1964, they immediately introduced a "replacement." By slightly reducing the rim diameter of the basic 30-30 case, Winchester engineers adapted this rimmed cartridge to work with a standard 30-06 bolt face. While they were at it, they moved the shoulder forward and reduced the body taper, while necking the case to 22-caliber.

When loaded to typical bolt-action cartridge pressures, velocities are only about 10 percent under top 220 Swift loads, not far behind the 22-250. Nevertheless, the 225 Winchester never gained any significant degree of popularity. A likely explanation is that it just does not offer much that other larger or smaller numbers do not.

Nevertheless, there is nothing wrong with the 225, and it is fully capable as a top-end 22 varminter cartridge. It is easily adapted to single shot guns and offers plenty of velocity for all but the very longest of shots. With a 52-grain bullet, seated normally, usable case capacity is about 42.5 grains of water. BL-C(2), A2495BR and H414 are good 225 choices.

225 WINCHESTER LOADING DATA

Powder	Grs.	MV (fps)	Grs.	MV (fps)	Press. (CUP/psi)	Comments
40						
BL-C(2)	33.0	3772	36.0	4020	49,200C	
W748	33.0	3660	36.0	3910	49,700C	
H322	28.0	3628	31.0	3896	49,800C	
IMR4895	31.0	3569	33.0	3864	48,400C	
IMR3031	29.0	3554	31.0	3839	50,000C	
H414	36.0	3404	39.0	3829	43,300C	
IMR4064	31.0	3515	33.0	3821	49,000C	
H4895	31.5	3583	34.0	3811	48,200C	
IMR4320	32.0	3594	34.0	3717	49,900C	
45						
BL-C(2)	32.0	3535	35.0	3890	47,300C	
W748	33.0	3560	35.0	3871	47,600C	
H380	34.0	3451	37.0	3749	47,300C	
H4895	31.0	3504	33.5	3736	49,300C	
H414	35.5	3473	38.5	3698	45,400C	
H322	27.0	3303	30.0	3685	50,000C	
W760	36.0	3469	37.0	3645	45,900C	
IMR4320	31.0	3480	33.0	3629	49,100C	
IMR4895	30.0	3444	32.0	3591	48,400C	
IMR4064	30.0	3431	32.0	3519	48,000C	
IMR3031	28.0	3290	30.0	3447	48,200C	

Powder	Grs.	MV (fps)	Grs.	MV (fps)	Press. (CUP/psi)	Comments
50						
BL-C(2)	32.0	3342	35.0	3768	49,300C	
H4895	31.0	3330	34.0	3722	48,400C	
H335	31.5	3337	34.5	3721	49,100C	
W748	32.0	3349	34.0	3707	48,800C	
H414	35.5	3389	38.5	3702	47,600C	
H380	33.0	3394	36.0	3659	47,300C	
A2495BR	28.6	3218	31.8	3657	57,400p	Spr SP/2.4″/CCI 200
A2015BR	27.9	3206	31.0	3643	57,200p	Spr SP/2.4″/CCI 200
A2520	30.0	3206	33.3	3643	57,800p	Spr SP/2.4″/CCI 200
A2460	29.3	3200	32.5	3636	56,100p	Spr SP/2.4″/CCI 200
A2230	28.8	3191	32.0	3626	57,300p	Spr SP/2.4″/CCI 200
W760	34.0	3360	36.0	3601	47,400C	
A2700	35.6	3348	37.5	3562	51,500p	Spr SP/2.4″/CCI 200/(C)
IMR4320	30.0	3366	32.0	3519	48,700C	
IMR4064	30.0	3331	32.0	3509	48,600C	
IMR4895	30.0	3304	32.0	3496	48,800C	
IMR3031	28.0	3274	30.0	3452	49,000C	
H322	26.0	3164	29.0	3401	48,900C	

>>>>>>>>>>>>>>>>>>>>>>>>>>>>>>

Never exceed maximum load nor use any load exhibiting signs of excessive pressure. Begin at suggested starting load and work up carefully.

107

52-53

Powder	Grs.	MV (fps)	Grs.	MV (fps)	Press. (CUP/psi)	Comments
H414	35.5	3334	38.5	3662	49,600C	
H335	31.5	3271	34.0	3662	50,000C	
BL-C(2)	31.5	3282	34.0	3656	50,100C	
W748	32.0	3310	34.0	3649	49,900C	
A2495BR	28.4	3197	31.6	3633	60,700p	Hdy HP/2.415"/CCI 200
W760	34.0	3444	36.0	3580	47,700C	
A2015BR	27.7	3148	30.8	3577	58,400p	Hdy HP/2.415"/CCI 200
A2520	29.8	3130	33.1	3557	58,100p	Hdy HP/2.415"/CCI 200
H380	32.5	3316	35.0	3542	49,600C	
A2460	29.1	3115	32.3	3540	56,800p	Hdy HP/2.415"/CCI 200
A2230	28.6	3088	31.8	3509	55,800p	Hdy HP/2.415"/CCI 200
IMR4320	30.0	3282	32.0	3480	48,900C	
A2700	35.6	3264	37.5	3472	51,600p	Hdy HP/2.415"/ CCI 200/(C)
H4895	29.5	3239	32.0	3463	49,600C	
IMR4895	29.0	3229	31.0	3451	48,600C	
IMR4064	29.0	3188	31.0	3411	48,000C	
H322	26.0	3128	28.5	3333	48,000C	
IMR3031	27.0	3084	29.0	3327	48,200C	

55

Powder	Grs.	MV (fps)	Grs.	MV (fps)	Press. (CUP/psi)	Comments
BL-C(2)	31.5	3220	34.0	3643	49,400C	
H335	31.0	3192	33.5	3601	48,700C	
H414	35.0	3287	38.0	3596	47,600C	
W748	31.0	3200	33.0	3590	48,700C	
A2460	29.5	3111	32.8	3535	57,600p	Nos BT/2.425"/CCI 200
A2230	29.3	3098	32.6	3520	57,000p	Nos BT/2.425"/CCI 200
A2520	29.9	3096	33.2	3518	57,600p	Nos BT/2.425"/CCI 200
A2495BR	28.1	3089	31.2	3510	57,900p	Nos BT/2.425"/CCI 200
A2015BR	27.5	3076	30.5	3495	58,500p	Nos BT/2.425"/CCI 200
H380	32.5	3196	35.0	3493	46,900C	
H4895	29.5	3159	32.0	3476	48,000C	
IMR4320	30.0	3249	32.0	3460	49,400C	
A2700	35.2	3227	37.0	3433	51,700p	Nos BT/2.425"/ CCI 200/Case Full
IMR4895	29.0	3171	31.0	3429	48,800C	
IMR4064	29.0	3140	31.0	3390	48,200C	
IMR3031	27.0	3041	29.0	3309	48,800C	
H322	25.5	3052	28.0	3283	48,900C	
IMR4350	34.0	3019	36.0	3239	48,200C	
H4350	35.0	2970	37.0	3189	46,000C	
H4831	35.0	2860	37.0	3112	39,500C	

60-64

Powder	Grs.	MV (fps)	Grs.	MV (fps)	Press. (CUP/psi)	Comments
BL-C(2)	30.5	3235	33.0	3428	48,700C	
A2495BR	27.9	3003	31.0	3413	59,000p	Hdy HP/2.425"/CCI 200
A2520	29.3	3000	32.5	3409	59,600p	Hdy HP/2.425"/CCI 200
H414	34.0	3124	37.0	3408	49,100C	
H335	30.0	3197	32.5	3404	48,000C	
A2460	28.8	2989	32.0	3397	56,400p	Hdy HP/2.425"/CCI 200
H4895	29.0	3125	32.0	3396	49,000C	
H380	32.0	3133	35.0	3387	48,500C	
A2230	28.1	2966	31.2	3370	58,100p	Hdy HP/2.425"/CCI 200
A2015BR	27.0	2966	30.0	3370	58,700p	Hdy HP/2.425"/CCI 200
IMR4320	29.0	3109	31.0	3357	49,200C	
W760	33.0	3079	35.0	3350	48,100C	
A2700	34.7	3131	36.5	3331	51,000p	Hdy HP/2.425"/ CCI 200/Case Full
IMR4064	28.0	3079	30.0	3311	48,800C	
IMR4895	28.0	3091	30.0	3290	49,000C	
IMR3031	26.0	2880	28.0	3219	49,400C	
H4350	34.0	2911	36.0	3120	44,400C	
IMR4350	33.0	2940	35.0	3110	46,800C	
H4831	34.0	2779	36.0	3068	40,600C	

70

Powder	Grs.	MV (fps)	Grs.	MV (fps)	Press. (CUP/psi)	Comments
IMR4350	32.0	2717	34.0	2960	48,000C	
H4350	32.0	2696	35.0	2949	47,800C	
H414	31.5	2759	33.5	2940	47,200C	
W760	31.0	2761	33.0	2932	47,000C	
IMR4320	27.0	2616	29.0	2889	49,600C	
IMR4064	26.0	2610	28.0	2884	49,600C	
IMR4895	26.0	2589	28.0	2870	49,900C	
IMR4831	33.0	2710	35.0	2860	44,400C	
H4831	33.0	2599	35.0	2831	40,800C	

Caution: Loads exceeding SAAMI OAL Maximum must be verified for bullet-to-rifling clearance and magazine functioning. Where a specific primer or bullet is indicated those components must be used, no substitutions! Where only a maximum load is shown, reduce starting load 10%, unless otherwise specified.

Key: (C) = compressed charge; C = CUP; p = psi; Plink = Plinker; Bns = Barnes; Hdy = Hornady; Lap = Lapua; Nos = Nosler; Rem = Remington; Sra = Sierra; Spr = Speer; Win = Winchester.

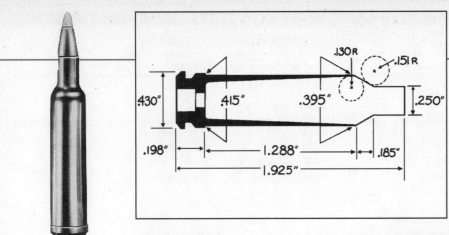

Case: Weatherby
Primer: Large Rifle
Barrel: 26″ Accurate/23″ Hodgdon
Bullet Diameter: 0.224″

Maximum Case Length: 1.925″
Trim to Length: 1.915″
Maximum Cartridge OAL: 2.375″ (Recommended)
Minimum Cartridge OAL: Bullet Dependent

Introduced in 1963 in the Weatherby Mark V rifle, the 224 Weatherby offers performance nearly duplicating the 22-250 Remington. Frankly, the only justification for this cartridge's existence is to appease those who feel a belt adds something to a cartridge's performance and who would not buy a fine Weatherby rifle chambered for any cartridge that did not feature this sex symbol.

This case is not based on any previous design and cannot be formed from any other case.

In direct contradiction to all previous Weatherby designs,

this chambering did not compete with the hottest 22s then available. In fact it falls considerably short of matching 220 Swift performance, a 1935 development. However, performance is still impressive, and Weatherby's 22 hot-rod is fully capable for use in long-range varmint shooting.

With a 52-grain bullet, seated normally, usable case capacity is about 40.0 grains of water. H414, H4895, A2460 and H335 are all good choices in the "Varmintmaster." Slower powders seldom perform well in free-bored barrels.

224 WEATHERBY MAGNUM LOADING DATA

Powder	STARTING Grs.	MV (fps)	MAXIMUM Grs.	MV (fps)	Press. (CUP/psi)	Comments
45						
H335	29.5	3447	32.0	3865		
H4895	29.5	3419	32.0	3861		
BL-C(2)	29.5	3457	32.0	3808		
H380	32.0	3425	35.0	3731		
H414	34.5	3420	36.5	3631		
50						
BL-C(2)	29.0	3427	31.5	3723		
H380	31.0	3232	34.0	3705		
H4895	28.5	3199	31.0	3648		
A2460	29.3	3191	32.5	3626	51,500p	Spr HP/2.375″/ Rem 9½
H335	28.5	3298	31.0	3607		
H414	34.0	3415	36.0	3602		
A2015BR	27.5	3139	30.5	3567	50,900p	Spr HP/2.375″/ Rem 9½
A2230	28.4	3129	31.5	3556	52,700p	Spr HP/2.375″/ Rem 9½
A2520	29.7	3060	33.0	3477	45,400p	Spr HP/2.375″/ Rem 9½/(C)
A2495BR	28.8	2981	32.0	3387	41,800p	Spr HP/2.375″/ Rem 9½/(C)

Powder	STARTING Grs.	MV (fps)	MAXIMUM Grs.	MV (fps)	Press. (CUP/psi)	Comments
52-53						
H414	33.5	3352	35.5	3525		
H4895	27.5	3032	30.0	3522		
BL-C(2)	26.5	2945	29.0	3493		
H380	29.5	3111	32.0	3482		
H335	26.0	2894	28.5	3462		
55						
H4895	27.5	2971	30.0	3503		
H414	33.0	3242	35.0	3497		
H380	29.5	3045	32.0	3461		
A2460	28.8	3016	32.0	3427	50,000p	Nos SBT/2.37″/Rem 9½
A2015BR	27.0	3015	30.0	3426	52,400p	Nos SBT/2.37″/Rem 9½
A2230	28.4	3005	31.5	3415	51,100p	Nos SBT/2.37″/Rem 9½
A2520	29.7	2988	33.0	3395	48,900p	Nos SBT/2.37″/ Rem 9½/(C)
A2495BR	28.8	2964	32.0	3368	47,900p	Nos SBT/2.37″/ Rem 9½/(C)
H335	27.5	3033	29.0	3367		
BL-C(2)	26.5	2910	28.0	3341		
H4350	32.0	2879	34.0	3240		
H4831	31.5	2834	34.0	3200		

▶▶▶▶▶▶▶▶▶▶▶▶▶▶▶▶▶▶▶▶▶▶▶▶▶▶

Never exceed maximum load nor use any load exhibiting signs of excessive pressure. Begin at suggested starting load and work up carefully.

60-64

Powder	—STARTING— Grs.	MV (fps)	—MAXIMUM— Grs.	MV (fps)	Press. (CUP/psi)	Comments
A2460	28.8	2963	32.0	3367	54,700p	Hdy SP/2.375"/ Rem 9½
A2230	28.4	2920	31.5	3318	53,500p	Hdy SP/2.375"/ Rem 9½
A2520	29.7	2917	33.0	3315	50,900p	Hdy SP/2.375"/ Rem 9½/(C)
A2015BR	26.6	2910	29.5	3307	54,000p	Hdy SP/2.375"/ Rem 9½
A2495BR	28.8	2904	32.0	3300	51,000p	Hdy SP/2.375"/ Rem 9½/(C)
H380	28.5	2931	31.0	3281		
H414	31.0	2958	33.0	3245		
H4350	31.0	2832	34.0	3240		
H4895	26.0	2792	28.0	3205		
BL-C(2)	26.0	2894	28.0	3178		
H335	26.0	2873	28.0	3147		
H4831	31.0	2781	33.5	3041		

70

Powder	—STARTING— Grs.	MV (fps)	—MAXIMUM— Grs.	MV (fps)	Press. (CUP/psi)	Comments
H414	29.0	2847	31.0	2969		
H380	27.0	2804	29.0	2914		
H4350	30.0	2644	32.0	2777		
H4831	30.0	2395	32.0	2486		

Caution: **Loads exceeding SAAMI OAL Maximum must be verified for bullet-to-rifling clearance and magazine functioning. Where a specific primer or bullet is indicated those components must be used, no substitutions! Where only a maximum load is shown, reduce starting load 10%, unless otherwise specified.**

Key: (C) = compressed charge; C = CUP; p = psi; Plinker; Bns = Barnes; Hdy = Hornady; Lap = Lapua; Nos = Nosler; Rem = Remington; Sra = Sierra; Spr = Speer; Win = Winchester.

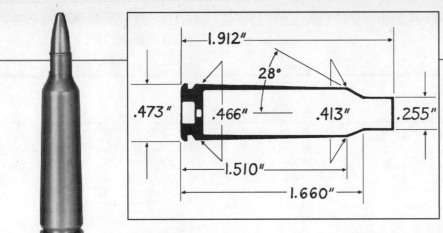

22-250 Remington

Case: Remington
Primer: Large Rifle
Barrel: 24″ Accurate
26″ Hodgdon
22″ Vihtavuori

Bullet Diameter: 0.224″
Maximum Case Length: 1.912″
Trim to Length: 1.902″
Maximum Cartridge OAL: 2.350″
Minimum Cartridge OAL: 2.315″

As a wildcat cartridge based on Charles Newton's 250-3000, the 22-250 has been around and has been one of the most popular wildcat chamberings since the mid-1930s. It has been known as the Wotkyns Original Swift and the Varminter, but the moniker 22-250 has always been the most popular. In 1965, Remington standardized this chambering under their name, 22-250 Remington.

Performance is reasonably close to the Swift, and this chambering is available from almost every major sporting rifle manufacturer. Case capacity is somewhat less than the

Swift, but still considerable. Working pressure is right up there with the Swift and a handful of other hot numbers. The 22-250 is considered by many to be a better balanced varmint cartridge than the Swift and can provide almost as much usable range under most conditions.

Rifles equipped with "fast-twist" barrels can take advantage of the heavier bullets now available. With a standard 52-grain bullet, seated normally, usable case capacity is about 42.5 grains of water. H380, VarGet, N550 and RL-15 are good powders for the Varminter.

22-250 REMINGTON LOADING DATA

Powder	STARTING Grs.	MV (fps)	MAXIMUM Grs.	MV (fps)	Press. (CUP/psi)	Comments
40						
VarGet			39.5	4135	51,100C	
A2460	34.2	3600	38.0	4091	61,600p	Sra SP/2.26″/CCI 200
H4895	34.0	3750	37.0	4060	48,700C	
A2230	33.3	3560	37.0	4045	60,000p	Sra SP/2.26″/CCI 200
A2520	34.7	3555	38.5	4040	58,500p	Sra SP/2.26″/CCI 200
IMR4320	35.0	3722	37.0	3988	49,900C	
H380	36.5	3697	39.5	3984	48,700C	
A2015BR	31.1	3494	34.5	3971	57,600p	Sra SP/2.26″/CCI 200
W748	33.0	3790	35.0	3962	48,900C	
IMR4895	34.0	3742	36.0	3943	49,400C	
H414	38.0	3644	41.0	3933	47,100C	
W760	38.0	3630	41.0	3920	47,200C	
IMR4064	34.0	3690	36.0	3904	48,800C	
IMR3031	32.0	3617	34.0	3871	48,900C	
RL-7	29.0	3529	31.0	3757	48,000C	
RL-12	32.0	3577	35.5	3749	47,800C	
A4350	36.0	3081	40.0	3501	38,900p	Sra SP/2.26″/ CCI 200/(C)
A3100	36.0	2688	40.0	3055	28,400p	Sra SP/2.26″/ CCI 200/(C)
45						
N140	36.6	3576	40.1	3941	49,300p	Spr Sptz/2.319″/Rem 9½
BL-C(2)	32.0	3612	35.0	3928	49,100C	
H4895	34.0	3660	37.0	3918	49,100C	
H335	31.5	3593	34.5	3908	48,500C	
H414	38.0	3537	41.0	3899	47,600C	
IMR4320	34.0	3631	36.0	3894	49,400C	
W748	33.0	3700	35.0	3894	49,400C	
A2700	40.4	3660	42.5	3894	60,400p	Nos Horn./2.305″/CCI 200
W760	38.0	3530	41.0	3879	48,800C	
A2520	33.8	3412	37.5	3877	58,800p	Nos Hom./2.305″/CCI 200
A2230	32.0	3410	35.5	3875	59,700p	Nos Hom./2.305″/CCI 200
H380	36.0	3595	39.0	3856	48,400C	
A2460	32.4	3392	36.0	3854	58,800p	Nos Hom./2.305″/CCI 200
IMR4895	34.0	3613	36.0	3846	50,800C	
IMR4064	34.0	3598	36.0	3839	49,400C	
A2015BR	29.7	3354	33.0	3811	58,500p	Nos Hom./2.305″/CCI 200
RL-15	32.0	3588	36.5	3741	46,500C	
H322	31.0	3490	32.5	3720	48,500C	
RL-12	32.0	3498	35.0	3699	48,400C	
RL-7	28.0	3467	30.0	3690	49,400C	
IMR3031	32.0	3539	34.0	3690	49,600C	

▶▶▶▶▶▶▶▶▶▶▶▶▶▶▶▶▶▶▶▶▶▶▶▶▶▶▶▶

50

Powder	Starting Grs.	Starting MV (fps)	Max Grs.	Max MV (fps)	Press. (CUP/psi)	Comments
N135			35.8	3840	53,664Cp	Sako SP 106G
VarGet			37.5	3834	50,400C	
A2460	32.9	3371	36.5	3831	61,900p	Nos SP/2.35"/CCI 200
H4895	33.5	3530	36.5	3827	50,200C	
A2520	33.3	3361	37.0	3819	63,100p	Nos SP/2.35"/CCI 200
A2230	32.4	3344	36.0	3800	61,400p	Nos SP/2.35"/CCI 200
A2015BR	30.6	3335	34.0	3790	60,700p	Nos SP/2.35"/CCI 200
RL-15	34.0	3629	36.0	3780	50,500C	
N140			37.0	3770	53,664Cp	Sako FJ 105G
H414	37.0	3494	40.0	3765	48,600C	
H335	31.5	3519	34.5	3753	48,700C	
W760	37.0	3489	40.0	3744	49,000C	
BL-C(2)	31.5	3506	34.5	3740	48,400C	
IMR4895	33.0	3510	35.0	3729	50,200C	
H380	35.0	3499	38.0	3719	48,900C	
W748	31.0	3491	34.0	3711	48,200C	
A2700	39.0	3461	41.0	3682	56,000p	Nos SP/2.35"/CCI 200
IMR4320	34.0	3494	36.0	3680	50,900C	
IMR4064	33.0	3448	35.0	3669	49,800C	
H322	30.0	3441	32.0	3628	50,300C	
RL-12	31.0	3441	34.0	3594	49,800C	
RL-7	27.0	3393	29.0	3590	48,900C	
N140	32.1	3133	37.2	3588	49,300p	Spr Sptz/2.346"/Rem 9½
H4350	39.0	3410	42.0	3579	48,900C	
RL-19	39.0	3388	41.0	3577	51,000C	
IMR3031	31.0	3387	33.0	3557	48,900C	
H450	40.0	3386	43.0	3552	45,400C	
IMR4350	38.0	3391	40.0	3540	47,400C	
A4350	36.0	3107	40.0	3531	49,200p	Nos SP/2.35"/CCI 200/(C)
H4831	39.0	3301	42.0	3473	41,000C	
A3100	36.0	2789	40.0	3169	37,100p	Nos SP/2.35"/CCI 200/(C)

52-53

Powder	Starting Grs.	Starting MV (fps)	Max Grs.	Max MV (fps)	Press. (CUP/psi)	Comments
H4895	32.5	3467	35.5	3729	49,600C	
H380	35.0	3458	38.0	3709	50,100C	
BL-C(2)	31.0	3461	34.0	3702	49,700C	
W748	31.0	3446	34.0	3694	49,500C	
H414	37.0	3461	40.0	3692	48,900C	
W760	37.0	3454	40.0	3682	49,200C	
A2015BR	30.2	3220	33.5	3659	61,200p	Hdy HP/2.38"/CCI 200
H335	31.0	3417	33.5	3657	49,200C	
IMR4895	33.0	3474	35.0	3650	50,900C	
RL-15	33.5	3519	35.0	3641	50,000C	
IMR3031	31.0	3341	33.0	3636	49,700C	
A2460	31.5	3194	35.0	3629	58,600p	Hdy HP/2.38"/CCI 200
IMR4064	33.0	3417	35.0	3626	50,400C	
A2700	39.0	3404	41.0	3621	59,300p	Hdy HP/2.38"/CCI 200
IMR4320	34.0	3429	36.0	3606	51,800C	
A2520	32.0	3167	35.5	3599	56,400p	Hdy HP/2.38"/CCI 200
RL-7	27.0	3380	29.0	3597	47,700C	

52-53 con't

Powder	Starting Grs.	Starting MV (fps)	Max Grs.	Max MV (fps)	Press. (CUP/psi)	Comments
RL-12	31.0	3422	33.5	3588	48,800C	
A2230	30.6	3154	34.0	3584	59,200p	Hdy HP/2.38"/CCI 200
H450	40.0	3358	43.0	3559	47,600C	
H4350	39.0	3402	41.0	3557	49,400C	
IMR4350	38.0	3377	40.0	3541	48,000C	
RL-19	38.0	3360	40.0	3512	50,000C	
A4350	36.0	3084	40.0	3505	51,600p	Hdy HP/2.38"/CCI 200/(C)
H322	29.0	3379	31.0	3498	48,000C	
H4831	39.0	3237	42.0	3486	42,600C	
A3100	36.0	2739	40.0	3112	37,900p	Hdy HP/2.38"/CCI 200/(C)

55

Powder	Starting Grs.	Starting MV (fps)	Max Grs.	Max MV (fps)	Press. (CUP/psi)	Comments
N550			38.0	3750	58,800p	Hdy SP Rem 9½
H4895	32.5	3446	35.5	3670	49,300C	
A2460	32.4	3230	36.0	3670	62,300p	Nos SBT/2.37"/CCI 200
VarGet			36.5	3664	50,400C	
A2700	38.0	3436	40.0	3655	60,700p	Nos SBT/2.37"/CCI 200
H380	34.5	3416	37.0	3654	50,400C	
N140			36.4	3630	53,664p	Sako SP 110G
N135			35.2	3610	53,664p	Sako SP 110G
N150			36.5	3610	58,500p	Sako SP
A2230	31.5	3176	35.0	3609	59,700p	Nos SBT/2.37"/CCI 200
BL-C(2)	31.0	3410	34.0	3606	49,600C	
A2520	32.4	3172	36.0	3605	59,700p	Nos SBT/2.37"/CCI 200
A2015BR	29.7	3166	33.0	3598	59,600p	Nos SBT/2.37"/CCI 200
W748	31.0	3414	34.0	3597	49,900C	
H335	30.5	3400	33.0	3589	51,100C	
H414	36.0	3324	39.0	3582	46,700C	
W760	36.0	3320	39.0	3580	46,800C	
IMR4320	33.0	3360	35.0	3544	50,500C	
RL-15	32.0	3424	34.0	3541	50,000C	
IMR4064	32.0	3380	34.0	3540	50,200C	
IMR4895	32.0	3392	34.0	3536	50,400C	
IMR4350	37.0	3341	39.0	3525	48,000C	
H450	39.5	3321	42.5	3521	47,600C	
N150	34.4	3189	38.1	3521	49,300p	Spr Sptz/2.346"/Rem 9½
N160			42.4	3510	50,763p	Sako SP 110G
RL-12	30.0	3357	33.0	3498	48,800C	
H4350	37.0	3296	39.0	3490	47,800C	
H322	28.0	3339	30.0	3480	49,800C	
RL-19	37.5	3240	39.5	3473	50,500C	
H4831	39.0	3184	42.0	3472	43,500C	
IMR3031	30.0	3288	32.0	3472	48,400C	
A4350	36.0	3050	40.0	3466	51,500p	Nos SBT/2.37"/CCI 200/(C)
RL-7	26.5	3329	28.5	3412	47,600C	
A3100	36.0	2699	40.0	3067	37,400p	Nos SBT/2.37"/CCI 200/(C)

Never exceed maximum load nor use any load exhibiting signs of excessive pressure. Begin at suggested starting load and work up carefully.

60-64

Powder	Starting Grs.	MV (fps)	Maximum Grs.	MV (fps)	Press. (CUP/psi)	Comments
N550			37.5	3630	58,800p	Hdy SP/Rem 9½
N150			36.0	3520	59,500p	Hdy HP
A2520	32.4	3091	36.0	3512	62,300p	Hdy HP/2.4"/CCI 200
A2015BR	29.7	3077	33.0	3497	61,500p	Hdy HP/2.4"/CCI 200
H4895	31.5	3317	34.0	3486	50,400C	
A2700	36.1	3269	38.0	3478	61,100p	Hdy HP/2.4"/CCI 200
IMR4831	38.0	3240	40.0	3470	50,100C	
IMR4895	31.0	3261	33.0	3445	50,400C	
H4831	38.0	3169	41.0	3441	48,100C	
H414	35.0	3262	38.0	3432	47,100C	
RL-15	31.0	3219	33.5	3430	49,500C	
IMR4350	36.0	3290	38.0	3424	49,100C	
IMR4064	31.0	3221	33.0	3420	50,100C	
H380	33.5	3245	36.0	3418	44,000C	
N140			35.3	3410	53,664Cp	Hdy SP
W760	35.0	3249	38.0	3409	47,000C	
A2700	35.6	3199	37.5	3408	60,900p	Sra SP/2.325"/CCI 200
A4350	36.0	2997	40.0	3406	58,200p	Sra SP/2.325"/CCI 200/(C)
H450	38.5	3229	41.5	3397	48,000C	
A4350	36.0	2988	40.0	3395	53,200p	Hdy HP/2.4"/CCI 200/(C)
IMR4320	31.0	3210	33.0	3393	49,200C	
H4350	36.0	3210	38.0	3391	48,000C	
IMR3031	29.0	3140	31.0	3370	50,200C	
A2015BR	28.8	2959	32.0	3363	60,700p	Sra SP/2.325"/CCI 200
A2230	29.7	2934	33.0	3334	59,200p	Sra SP/2.325"/CCI 200
A2520	30.6	2932	34.0	3332	58,300p	Sra SP/2.325"/CCI 200
RL-19	36.5	3146	38.5	3320	50,000C	
W748	31.0	3166	33.0	3317	50,300C	
A2460	29.7	2912	33.0	3309	57,400p	Sra SP/2.325"/CCI 200
N160			40.1	3260	47,862Cp	Hdy SP
RL-12	29.0	2954	32.5	3240	47,900C	
RL-7	25.0	2988	27.0	3212	47,600C	
A3100	36.0	2648	40.0	3009	39,700p	Sra SP/2.325"/CCI 200/(C)
A3100	36.0	2623	40.0	2981	37,500p	Hdy HP/2.4"/CCI 200/(C)

68-70

Powder	Starting Grs.	MV (fps)	Maximum Grs.	MV (fps)	Press. (CUP/psi)	Comments
RL-15	30.0	3130	32.5	3310	50,400C	
A4350	34.2	2855	38.0	3244	59,500p	Spr S-Sptz/2.325"/CCI 200
RL-19	35.5	3092	37.5	3203	48,500C	
H4831	35.0	2976	38.0	3189	50,300C	(70-gr.)
H1000	36.0	3042	38.0	3187	47,500C	(70-gr.)
IMR4831	35.0	2990	37.0	3170	51,000C	(70-gr.)
N160	36.7	2843	40.7	3157	49,300p	Sra HBBT/2.346"/Rem 9½
A2520	29.3	2767	32.5	3144	61,000p	Spr S-Sptz/2.325"/CCI 200
H4350	34.0	3007	36.0	3129	49,600C	(70-gr.)
A2015BR	27.0	2751	30.0	3126	58,900p	Spr S-Sptz/2.325"/CCI 200
A2700	32.8	2934	34.5	3121	58,900p	Spr S-Sptz/2.325"/CCI 200
RL-12	28.0	2890	31.0	3119	47,600C	
H450	36.0	2952	39.0	3118	48,000C	(70-gr.)
H414	31.0	2860	34.0	3117	49,400C	(70-gr.)
W760	32.0	2910	34.0	3109	49,200C	(70-gr.)
IMR4350	33.0	2964	35.0	3100	50,000C	(70-gr.)
A2230	27.9	2720	31.0	3091	58,400p	Spr S-Sptz/2.325"/CCI 200
IMR4064	29.0	2964	31.0	3090	51,200C	(70-gr.)
IMR4320	29.0	2940	31.0	3080	51,000C	(70-gr.)
A2460	27.9	2708	31.0	3077	57,500p	Spr S-Sptz/2.325"/CCI 200
IMR4895	29.0	2957	31.0	3039	51,800C	(70-gr.)
N140			31.0	2990	53,664Cp	Spr SP
A3100	34.2	2593	38.0	2947	45,700p	Spr S-Sptz/2.325"/CCI 200
N135			27.9	2820	53,664Cp	Spr SP

80

Powder	Starting Grs.	MV (fps)	Maximum Grs.	MV (fps)	Press. (CUP/psi)	Comments
A4350	33.3	2783	37.0	3163	59,900p	Sra HPBT/2.61"/CCI 200
A2700	32.3	2804	34.0	2983	58,600p	Sra HPBT/2.61"/CCI 200

Caution: **Loads exceeding SAAMI OAL Maximum must be verified for bullet-to-rifling clearance and magazine functioning. Where a specific primer or bullet is indicated those components must be used, no substitutions! Where only a maximum load is shown, reduce starting load 10%, unless otherwise specified.**

Key: (C) = compressed charge; C = CUP; p = psi; Plink = Plinker; Bns = Barnes; Hdy = Hornady; Lap = Lapua; Nos = Nosler; Rem = Remington; Sra = Sierra; Spr = Speer; Win = Winchester.

220 Swift

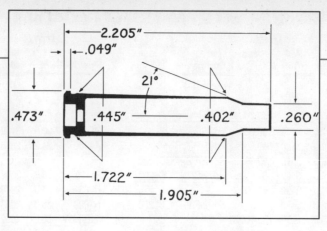

Case: Winchester
Primer: Large Rifle
Barrel: 26″ Accurate
    26″ Hodgdon
    24″ Vihtavuori

Bullet Diameter: 0.224″
Maximum Case Length: 2.205″
Trim to Length: 2.195″
Maximum Cartridge OAL: 2.680″
Minimum Cartridge OAL: 2.650″

The Swift hit the shooting world like a lightning bolt. When it was introduced in 1935, most shooters were still trying hard to get used to the idea of 3000 fps cartridges. Launching a 48-grain bullet at 4140 fps—original rating—the Swift must have seemed almost magical.

With a large capacity and unusually thick-walled case, based on the obsolete 6mm Lee Navy cartridge, the Swift is still, perhaps, the greatest long-range varmint cartridge ever developed as a factory chambering. With a somewhat tapered case and sloping shoulder, the Swift does tend to show considerable case stretching, especially with top loads. It can also burn out a barrel rather quickly, especially if proper care is not taken during shooting (do not get the barrel too hot from too many quick, successive shots) or lack of proper cleaning at reasonable intervals.

These considerations aside, it is still a mystery why Winchester dropped "The Fastest Commercial Loading Ever"

from their line in 1964—that had to have been a very bad decision from the standpoint of marketing and publicity. As proof, their replacement, the 225 Winchester, a fine cartridge in its own right, was a commercial flop. Absence of the Swift from Winchester's line might have spurred Remington to standardize the 22-250 a year later. The 22-250 has since taken over a considerable portion of the Swift's former niche. Further, other manufacturers have continued to offer the Swift as a standard chambering, if only intermittently.

The fact is that for those who want maximum 22 velocity, the Swift is still the best choice of common commercial chamberings in the U.S.

With a 52-grain bullet, seated normally, usable case capacity is about 49.0 grains of water. IMR4064, W760, H414, IMR4831, RL-15, IMR4350, H380, H4895, A2700 and A4350 are all noted performers in the Swift.

220 SWIFT LOADING DATA

Powder	—STARTING— Grs.	MV (fps)	—MAXIMUM— Grs.	MV (fps)	Press. (CUP/psi)	Comments
40						
H414	42.5	3928	46.0	4213	51,600C	
H335	37.0	3923	40.0	4158	53,100C	
RL-15	37.0	3906	40.0	4128	48,500C	
H4895	37.0	3768	40.0	4126	52,000C	
H380	40.5	3867	44.0	4124	50,000C	
W760	43.0	3889	45.0	4119	51,000C	
VarGet			40.5	4113	49,800C	
W748	37.0	3909	39.0	4090	52,000C	
RL-12	35.0	3870	38.0	4029	49,000C	
IMR4320	37.0	3740	39.0	3994	51,000C	
IMR3031	35.0	3707	37.0	3991	51,400C	
IMR4895	36.0	3711	38.0	3969	50,900C	
IMR4064	36.0	3682	38.0	3954	50,400C	
H4350	42.0	3339	45.0	3777	44,800C	
IMR4350	42.0	3380	44.0	3760	44,600C	
H4831	42.0	3269	46.5	3690	40,300C	

Powder	—STARTING— Grs.	MV (fps)	—MAXIMUM— Grs.	MV (fps)	Press. (CUP/psi)	Comments
40 con't						
RL-19	42.0	3411	45.0	3672	43,000C	
IMR4831	43.0	3388	45.0	3612	41,000C	
RL-22	42.0	3379	45.0	3521	41,500C	
45						
H414	41.5	3849	45.0	4100	51,700C	
RL-15	38.0	3874	40.0	4049	50,500C	
H380	40.5	3784	44.0	4041	52,400C	
W760	42.0	3840	44.0	3999	51,400C	
H4895	36.5	3676	39.5	3996	52,100C	
H335	36.5	3815	39.0	3969	51,200C	
IMR3031	35.0	3669	37.0	3937	52,000C	
IMR4895	36.0	3660	38.0	3929	51,900C	
W748	36.0	3791	38.0	3927	51,000C	
RL-12	35.0	3780	38.0	3924	50,000C	

   Never exceed maximum load nor use any load exhibiting signs of excessive pressure. Begin at suggested starting load and work up carefully.

Powder	STARTING Grs.	MV (fps)	MAXIMUM Grs.	MV (fps)	Press. (CUP/psi)	Comments

45 con't

Powder	Grs.	MV (fps)	Grs.	MV (fps)	Press. (CUP/psi)	Comments
IMR4320	36.0	3651	38.0	3892	50,800C	
IMR4064	36.0	3629	38.0	3871	50,500C	
RL-19	42.0	3488	45.0	3687	45,500C	
H4831	42.0	3178	46.5	3681	42,500C	
RL-22	42.0	3422	45.0	3631	42,500C	
IMR4831	43.0	3364	45.0	3620	42,600C	

50

Powder	Grs.	MV (fps)	Grs.	MV (fps)	Press. (CUP/psi)	Comments
A2700	42.8	3793	45.0	4035	62,500p	Spr HP/2.7"/Fed 210
H380	40.0	3668	43.5	3947	53,800C	
A4350	39.6	3467	44.0	3940	56,700p	Spr HP/2.7"/Fed 210/(C)
RL-15	36.0	3709	39.0	3928	49,500C	
N140			38.6	3900	53,664p	Sako FJ 105G
A2495BR	33.8	3424	37.5	3891	58,500p	Spr HP/2.7"/Fed 210
BL-C(2)	35.0	3431	38.0	3888	51,000C	
N550			39.0	3867	58,700p	Hdy SP/Rem 9½
H335	35.0	3520	38.0	3860	52,100C	
H4895	35.0	3460	38.0	3840	51,200C	
N150			39.0	3840	60,700p	Sako SP
H414	40.5	3663	44.0	3826	49,600C	
IMR4895	35.0	3469	37.0	3787	51,000C	
VarGet			36.0	3770	50,200C	
IMR3031	34.0	3449	36.0	3757	51,600C	
IMR4064	35.0	3419	37.0	3740	50,000C	
W748	35.0	3393	37.0	3717	50,400C	
RL-12	34.0	3522	37.0	3717	50,500C	
IMR4320	36.0	3480	38.0	3707	51,400C	
H450	40.0	3197	43.5	3703	50,200C	
W760	40.0	3279	42.0	3670	50,200C	
IMR4350	40.0	3361	42.0	3660	50,600C	
H4831	42.0	3202	46.5	3647	46,300C	
IMR4831	42.0	3319	44.0	3639	44,000C	
H4350	40.0	3349	42.0	3619	50,100C	
A3100	39.6	3158	44.0	3589	45,100p	Spr HP/2.7"/Fed 210/(C)
RL-19	41.0	3349	44.0	3568	44,500C	
RL-22	41.0	3332	44.0	3532	44,000C	

52-53

Powder	Grs.	MV (fps)	Grs.	MV (fps)	Press. (CUP/psi)	Comments
RL-15	35.0	3622	38.0	3814	49,700C	
IMR4895	35.0	3451	37.0	3770	51,600C	
IMR4064	35.0	3429	37.0	3721	50,600C	
RL-12	33.0	3551	36.0	3704	51,200C	
IMR4320	36.0	3466	38.0	3701	51,800C	
IMR3031	33.0	3417	35.0	3682	50,400C	
IMR4350	40.0	3324	42.0	3653	51,000C	
IMR4831	42.0	3260	44.0	3630	44,600C	
RL-19	41.0	3411	44.0	3574	45,000C	
RL-22	41.0	3399	44.0	3520	44,500C	

55

Powder	Grs.	MV (fps)	Grs.	MV (fps)	Press. (CUP/psi)	Comments
A4350	39.6	3428	44.0	3896	59,300p	Nos SBT/2.68"/ Fed 210/(C)
H380	39.0	3580	42.5	3839	53,300C	(52-55-gr.)
H414	40.5	3536	44.0	3833	53,700C	(52-55-gr.)
A2700	41.3	3602	43.5	3832	57,000p	Nos SBT/2.68"/Fed 210
A2495BR	32.4	3364	36.0	3823	63,200p	Nos SBT/2.68"/Fed 210
N160			43.1	3710	44,962p	Norma SP
H4895	34.0	3481	37.0	3698	52,000C	(52-55-gr.)
H335	34.0	3447	36.0	3696	50,400C	(52-55-gr.)
RL-15	34.0	3461	37.0	3690	49,500C	
BL-C(2)	34.0	3426	36.0	3682	49,900C	(52-55-gr.)
IMR4895	34.0	3462	36.0	3670	51,100C	
IMR4320	35.0	3412	37.0	3651	52,000C	
N550			37.0	3650	57,300p	Hdy SP/Rem 9½
VarGet			36.0	3645	51,900C	(52-55-gr.)
IMR4064	34.0	3397	36.0	3634	50,700C	
W748	34.0	3420	36.0	3630	51,600C	
RL-12	32.0	3409	35.0	3629	51,000C	
24N64			40.5	3624	59,950p	Hdy SP
W760	40.0	3497	42.0	3622	51,400C	
H4350	39.0	3225	42.0	3619	50,800C	(52-55-gr.)
H4831	41.5	3194	46.0	3616	46,600C	(52-55-gr.)
IMR4350	39.0	3290	41.0	3604	50,900C	
IMR4831	41.0	3231	43.0	3602	46,100C	
A3100	39.6	3157	44.0	3588	49,000p	Nos SBT/2.68"/ Fed 210/(C)
RL-19	41.0	3414	44.0	3580	46,000C	
N150			37.0	3580	58,600p	Sako SP
IMR3031	33.0	3329	35.0	3540	51,900C	
RL-22	41.0	3340	44.0	3498	45,000C	
N140			37.0	3250	53,664p	Sako SP 110G

▶▶▶▶▶▶▶▶▶▶▶▶▶▶▶▶▶▶▶▶▶▶▶▶▶▶▶

Caution: **Loads exceeding SAAMI OAL Maximum must be verified for bullet-to-rifling clearance and magazine functioning. Where a specific primer or bullet is indicated those components must be used, no substitutions! Where only a maximum load is shown, reduce starting load 10%, unless otherwise specified.**

Key: (C) = compressed charge; C = CUP; p = psi; Plink = Plinker; Bns = Barnes; Hdy = Hornady; Lap = Lapua; Nos = Nosler; Rem = Remington; Sra = Sierra; Spr = Speer; Win = Winchester.

Powder	—STARTING— Grs.	MV (fps)	—MAXIMUM— Grs.	MV (fps)	Press. (CUP/psi)	Comments

60-64

Powder	Grs.	MV (fps)	Grs.	MV (fps)	Press. (CUP/psi)	Comments
A4350	39.6	3362	44.0	3820	63,800p	Hdy HP/2.7"/ Fed 210/(C)
A2700	39.0	3494	41.0	3717	63,400p	Sra SP/2.66"/Fed 210
A4350	37.4	3208	41.5	3646	58,600p	Sra SP/2.66"/Fed 210
A2700	39.9	3391	42.0	3607	59,700p	Hdy HP/2.7"/Fed 210
A2495BR	31.1	3169	34.5	3601	60,000p	Hdy HP/2.7"/Fed 210
H414	38.5	3339	42.0	3595	52,100C	
H4831	41.5	3180	46.0	3586	52,000C	
A3100	39.6	3152	44.0	3582	56,300p	Sra SP/2.66"/Fed 210
H380	38.0	3405	41.0	3580	51,900C	
N160			43.0	3570	60,400p	Hdy HP
24N64			40.5	3530	60,516p	Hdy HP
W760	38.0	3260	40.0	3528	50,800C	
A3100	39.6	3105	44.0	3528	50,900p	Hdy HP/2.7"/ Fed 210/(C)
N560			44.0	3520	55,400p	Hdy HP/Rem 9½
N550			36.0	3500	58,900p	Hdy HP/Rem 9½
H450	39.5	3142	43.0	3510	50,900C	
IMR4831	40.0	3177	42.0	3510	51,900C	
RL-15	32.0	3339	35.0	3490	51,000C	
H4895	32.5	3218	35.5	3484	51,000C	
IMR4895	32.0	3210	34.0	3479	51,200C	
H4350	37.0	3181	39.0	3474	52,000C	
RL-12	31.0	3310	34.0	3470	51,500C	
IMR4350	36.0	3180	38.0	3465	51,800C	
RL-19	40.0	3314	43.0	3462	45,500C	
IMR4064	32.0	3167	34.0	3420	49,600C	
IMR4320	33.0	3222	35.0	3415	51,000C	
VarGet			34.0	3407	49,300C	
RL-22	40.0	3230	43.0	3387	45,400C	
H1000	44.0	3164	45.5	3343	43,600C	
IMR7828	42.0	3182	44.0	3332	46,900C	
H870			49.0	3035	36,000C	

70

Powder	Grs.	MV (fps)	Grs.	MV (fps)	Press. (CUP/psi)	Comments
A4350	37.4	3068	41.5	3486	64,200p	Spr SP/2.66"/Fed 210
RL-19	39.0	3333	42.0	3460	51,000C	
A2700	37.1	3229	39.0	3435	64,000p	Spr SP/2.66"/Fed 210
A3100	39.6	3003	44.0	3412	59,000p	Spr SP/2.66"/Fed 210
RL-22	39.0	3260	42.0	3386	48,500C	
H4831	37.0	2991	42.0	3359	52,600C	
H1000	42.0	3149	44.0	3317	50,200C	
H4350	36.0	3027	38.0	3313	51,200C	
H450	38.0	2981	42.0	3301	50,300C	
IMR7828	39.0	3008	41.0	3284	49,400C	
IMR4350	35.0	2994	37.0	3263	51,000C	
IMR4831	37.0	3019	40.0	3240	51,400C	
H414	34.0	2955	37.0	3148	50,300C	
W760	35.0	3007	37.0	3140	50,400C	

> *Caution:* Loads exceeding SAAMI OAL Maximum must be verified for bullet-to-rifling clearance and magazine functioning. Where a specific primer or bullet is indicated those components must be used, no substitutions! Where only a maximum load is shown, reduce starting load 10%, unless otherwise specified.
>
> *Key:* (C) = compressed charge; C = CUP; p = psi; Plink = Plinker; Bns = Barnes; Hdy = Hornady; Lap = Lapua; Nos = Nosler; Rem = Remington; Sra = Sierra; Spr = Speer; Win = Winchester.

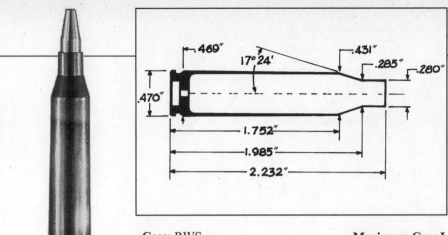

Case: RWS
Primer: Remington 9½
Barrel: 23½" Vihtavuori
Bullet Diameter: 0.224"

Maximum Case Length: 2.232"
Trim to Length: 2.222"
Maximum Cartridge OAL: 2.717"
Minimum Cartridge OAL: Bullet Dependent

Standardized in Europe in 1970 by RWS, this chambering is similar to the 7x57mm simply necked down. However, shoulder placement and angle differ and, what is more important, the case neck is much thicker than normal—most modern cases have a neck-wall thickness of about 0.015"; in this cartridge the neck is a full 0.030". This unusual feature allows rifles so-chambered to be fitted with a cartridge adapter that allows use of 22 WMR ammunition for more mundane uses of the rifle.

RWS designed this cartridge specifically to meet some rather interesting German hunting regulations regarding the range at which game can be taken and the energy the bullet must deliver at that range.

Both case capacity and maximum pressure (European standards) are considerably higher than even the vaunted Swift. Therefore, performance, especially with heavier bullets, can be measurably superior. A rifle chambered for this cartridge can deliver just about all the velocity that is practically available from the 22-caliber bore.

With a 52-grain bullet, seated normally, usable case capacity should be near 55.0 grains of water.

5.6x57mm RWS LOADING DATA

Powder	Grs.	MV (fps)	Grs.	MV (fps)	Press. (CUP/psi)	Comments
50						
N140			39.8	3810	52,200p	Sra SP/2.638"
55						
N140			38.4	3640	50,800p	Sako SP/2.638"

Powder	Grs.	MV (fps)	Grs.	MV (fps)	Press. (CUP/psi)	Comments
74						
N160			40.7	3260	52,200p	RWS FMJ/2.665"

Never exceed maximum load nor use any load exhibiting signs of excessive pressure. Begin at suggested starting load and work up carefully.

117

6mm
PPC

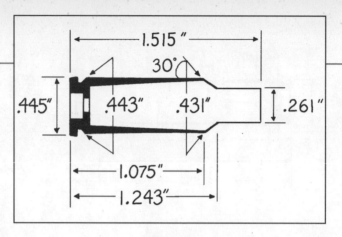

Case: Sako
Primer: Small Rifle
Barrel: 24″ Accurate
       24″ Hodgdon
       23″ Vihtavuori

Bullet Diameter: 0.243″
Maximum Case Length: 1.515″ (Chamber Dependent)
Trim to Length: 1.51″ (Chamber Dependent)
Maximum Cartridge OAL: 2.100″ (Chamber Dependent)
Minimum Cartridge OAL: Bullet Dependent

The history of this chambering begins with the 7.62x39mm case. That cartridge was modified by Russian designers for use in international competition as the 220 Russian. Benchrest shooters, Dr. Lou Palmisano and Ferris Pindell, modified that Russian development into this chambering.

A caution is in order: Since such guns are primarily designed and used in benchrest competition, custom chambers are used. It is entirely possible that one could find a combination of bullet, case and chamber that did not allow sufficient room for the case mouth to expand away from the bullet to properly release it upon firing. Such a situation could result in devastating pressures.

The safest approach is to make a proper chamber cast and measure the barrel's throat. If the necks of your loaded rounds do not measure at least 0.002″ smaller than the chamber throat, you *must* turn the case necks until such

clearance is achieved, see the discussion on outside neck turning in Chapter 2.

Further, this data was developed in a "standard" throated chamber. Use of this data in a tight-chambered gun will necessarily increase pressure somewhat. If you have a tight-chambered gun, reduce starting loads about 5 percent and work up for accuracy, watching carefully for signs of excess pressure.

The 6mm PPC offers startling performance for a cartridge of such limited capacity. Altogether, considering the accuracy available, this cartridge would be an excellent choice for short- to intermediate-range varmint work.

Usable case capacity depends on bullet and case used and on actual chamber dimensions, but is typically about 31.0 grains of water. H322, RL-12 and H335 are noted choices for this number.

6mm PPC LOADING DATA

Powder	STARTING Grs.	MV (fps)	MAXIMUM Grs.	MV (fps)	Press. (CUP/psi)	Comments
60						
H4895	27.0	2913	29.0	3218	48,500C	
H335	26.0	2891	28.0	3201	49,000C	
A2460	27.0	2816	30.0	3200	48,800p	Sra HP/2.05″/Rem 7½
A2230	26.6	2794	29.5	3175	49,500p	Sra HP/2.05″/Rem 7½
A2495BR	25.7	2794	28.5	3175	50,000p	Sra HP/2.05″/Rem 7½/(C)
H322	26.0	3090	27.0	3165	47,000C	
A2015BR	24.5	2783	27.2	3163	49,200p	Sra HP/2.05″/Rem 7½
RL-7	23.0	2885	25.0	3160	50,000C	
IMR3031	24.5	2878	26.5	3150	47,500C	
RL-15	27.0	2849	29.0	3118	46,500C	
RL-12	27.0	2870	29.0	3071	47,000C	
IMR4320	26.0	2862	28.0	3057	48,500C	
IMR4064	27.5	2807	29.0	3049	48,000C	
BL-C(2)	30.0	2959	31.5	3041	46,500C	
W748	30.0	2940	31.5	3029	46,000C	
H4198	21.0	2856	23.0	2973	49,500C	

Powder	STARTING Grs.	MV (fps)	MAXIMUM Grs.	MV (fps)	Press. (CUP/psi)	Comments
68-70						
N133	25.8	2812	28.7	3112	49,313p	Sra HPBTM
H322	25.0	2967	26.5	3068	50,000C	
IMR3031	24.0	2808	26.0	3062	50,500C	
H4895	26.0	2714	28.0	3034	46,500C	
VarGet			29.0	3034	48,000C	
N130	23.5	2743	26.1	3034	49,313p	Sra HPBTM
H335	25.0	2846	27.5	3033	48,500C	
A2495BR	25.7	2658	28.5	3021	48,700p	Hdy SX/2.08″/ Rem 7½/(C)
BL-C(2)	29.0	2812	31.0	3012	47,500C	
W748	29.0	2820	31.0	3008	48,000C	
RL-12	27.0	2784	29.0	3006	48,500C	
RL-15	27.0	2787	29.0	2991	47,000C	
IMR4064	27.0	2807	28.0	2987	48,000C	
A2460	26.6	2623	29.5	2981	46,600p	Hdy SX/2.08″/Rem 7½
RL-7	22.5	2717	24.5	2965	49,500C	

    Never exceed maximum load nor use any load exhibiting signs of excessive pressure. Begin at suggested starting load and work up carefully.

Powder	STARTING Grs.	MV (fps)	MAXIMUM Grs.	MV (fps)	Press. (CUP/psi)	Comments
68-70 con't						
A2015BR	24.3	2602	27.0	2957	46,000p	Hdy SX/2.08"/Rem 7½
N120	21.5	2653	23.9	2956	49,313p	Sra HPBTM
A2230	25.7	2573	28.5	2924	49,000p	Hdy SX/2.08"/Rem 7½
IMR4320	25.5	2725	27.0	2910	47,500C	
H4198	21.0	2745	22.0	2839	50,400C	
75						
H335	24.5	2712	27.0	2990	49,000C	
H4895	25.5	2740	27.5	2981	48,500C	
BL-C(2)	28.5	2788	30.5	2974	47,800C	
H322	24.5	2809	26.0	2974	49,500C	
RL-15	27.0	2764	29.0	2970	47,500C	
W748	28.5	2775	30.0	2952	47,000C	
RL-12	27.0	2751	29.0	2944	48,900C	
IMR3031	23.0	2624	25.0	2930	50,000C	
RL-7	22.0	2686	24.0	2910	49,500C	
VarGet			28.0	2906	47,000C	
IMR4064	26.0	2689	27.0	2890	49,500C	
IMR4320	25.0	2668	26.5	2874	48,000C	
H4198	20.0	2661	21.0	2780	49,000C	
80						
RL-15	26.5	2715	28.5	2940	47,500C	
BL-C(2)	28.0	2748	30.0	2904	47,500C	
H4895	25.0	2641	27.0	2904	47,500C	
W748	28.0	2740	29.5	2884	47,500C	
H322	23.5	2658	25.5	2866	47,500C	
RL-12	26.0	2705	28.0	2866	48,000C	
VarGet			28.0	2843	44,400C	
RL-7	21.0	2639	23.0	2824	49,000C	
H335	24.0	2650	26.0	2822	48,500C	
IMR4064	24.5	2642	26.0	2801	48,000C	
IMR3031	22.5	2605	24.5	2792	47,500C	
IMR4320	24.0	2524	25.5	2771	47,000C	
H4198	19.0	2359	21.0	2641	49,500C	
85						
VarGet			28.0	2848	50,000C	
RL-15	26.0	2660	28.0	2841	48,000C	
BL-C(2)	27.0	2639	29.0	2818	48,100C	
RL-12	25.5	2628	27.5	2811	48,400C	
W748	27.0	2611	29.0	2804	48,500C	
H322	23.0	2571	25.0	2794	49,000C	
H4895	24.0	2540	26.0	2782	48,000C	
IMR4064	24.0	2493	25.5	2764	49,000C	
IMR4320	24.0	2501	25.5	2756	48,500C	
H335	23.5	2560	25.0	2739	47,500C	
IMR3031	22.5	2540	24.0	2714	48,500C	

Powder	STARTING Grs.	MV (fps)	MAXIMUM Grs.	MV (fps)	Press. (CUP/psi)	Comments
90						
RL-15	25.0	2554	27.5	2762	49,500C	
RL-12	25.0	2568	27.0	2742	48,900C	
BL-C(2)	26.5	2580	28.5	2730	47,500C	
W748	26.5	2585	28.5	2729	48,000C	
H4895	23.5	2539	25.5	2719	48,500C	
H322	22.5	2477	24.5	2709	49,100C	
H335	23.0	2511	24.5	2688	48,000C	
IMR3031	22.0	2398	24.0	2684	48,000C	
IMR4064	24.0	2429	25.0	2656	47,500C	
IMR4320	23.5	2440	25.0	2639	48,000C	
RL-19	26.5	2344	28.5	2580	43,000C	
100						
RL-15	24.0	2407	26.0	2611	48,000C	
BL-C(2)	26.0	2405	28.0	2602	48,000C	
H4895	22.0	2390	24.0	2554	50,000C	
W748	25.5	2381	27.5	2551	47,500C	
RL-12	24.0	2347	26.0	2545	48,500C	
H335	22.5	2262	24.0	2529	48,000C	
IMR3031	21.5	2314	23.0	2499	49,500C	
H322	21.5	2340	23.0	2494	49,000C	
IMR4064	23.0	2333	24.0	2488	50,000C	
IMR4320	22.5	2334	23.5	2456	50,500C	
RL-19	26.0	2140	28.0	2255	44,000C	

WARNING: Case necks must be reamed or dangerously high pressures might result.

Caution: Loads exceeding SAAMI OAL Maximum must be verified for bullet-to-rifling clearance and magazine functioning. Where a specific primer or bullet is indicated those components must be used, no substitutions! Where only a maximum load is shown, reduce starting load 10%, unless otherwise specified.

Key: (C) = compressed charge; C = CUP; p = psi; Plink = Plinker; Bns = Barnes; Hdy = Hornady; Lap = Lapua; Nos = Nosler; Rem = Remington; Sra = Sierra; Spr = Speer; Win = Winchester.

6mm

Benchrest Remington (6mm BR)

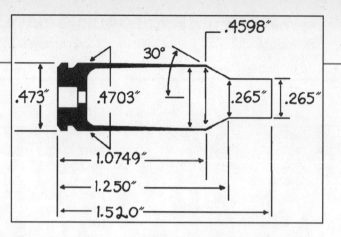

Case: Remington
Primer: Small Rifle
Barrel: 24″ Accurate
          24″ Hodgdon
Bullet Diameter: 0.243″

Maximum Case Length: 1.520″
Trim to Length: 1.515″
Maximum Cartridge OAL: 2.200″
Minimum Cartridge OAL: 2.080″

A standard chambering in the recently discontinued XP-100 handgun, the 6mm BR is based on the more popular 7mm BR. Rifle ballistics are certainly adequate to suggest the 6mm BR as a good choice for intermediate-range varmint use. It could even be used for hunting the smallest species of big game.

Primarily, though, this cartridge has been used in handgun silhouette competition. With limited recoil and superb intrinsic accuracy, this is a good cartridge for that use. For the same reasons, it is also a force in benchrest competition.

Usable case capacity depends on case and chamber, but with lighter bullets, would be about 35.0 grains of water. W748 and H322 are noted choices for accurate loads.

There is a shorter version of the 6mm BR currently gaining favor—ensure you are not loading for the shorter version using this data! Results could be disastrous.

6mm BENCHREST REMINGTON LOADING DATA (6mm BR)

Powder	STARTING Grs.	MV (fps)	MAXIMUM Grs.	MV (fps)	Press. (CUP/psi)	Comments
60						
A2460	31.1	3082	34.5	3502	51,600p	Sra HP/2.125″/Rem 7½
H322	30.0	3281	32.0	3481	49,500C	
A2015BR	27.5	3055	30.5	3472	52,700p	Sra HP/2.125″/Rem 7½
A2520	31.5	3047	35.0	3462	50,500p	Sra HP/2.125″/Rem 7½/(C)
A2230	30.2	3008	33.5	3418	49,400p	Sra HP/2.125″/Rem 7½
H335	30.0	3184	32.0	3411	49,000C	
RL-12	31.5	3098	34.0	3404	47,400C	
A2495BR	29.7	2983	33.0	3390	46,700C	Sra HP/2.125″/Rem 7½/(C)
IMR3031	29.0	3166	31.0	3389	47,800C	
H4895	31.0	3177	33.0	3384	47,000C	
BL-C(2)	34.0	3154	36.0	3375	47,500C	
RL-7	27.0	3203	29.0	3340	47,400C	
IMR4895	30.0	2979	32.0	3297	46,200C	
W748	33.0	3119	35.0	3294	46,500C	
IMR4320	31.0	2955	33.5	3275	48,800C	
IMR4064	30.0	3027	32.0	3238	45,600C	
A2700	33.3	2912	35.0	3098	37,900p	Sra HP/2.125″/Rem 7½/(C)
68-70						
VarGet			34.0	3342	49,400C	
BL-C(2)	33.0	3118	35.0	3289	48,000C	
H335	29.0	3050	31.0	3287	47,000C	
A2520	30.6	2889	34.0	3283	51,900p	Sra HP/2.17″/Rem 7½/(C)
68-70 con't						
A2015BR	27.5	2887	30.5	3281	52,900p	Sra HP/2.17″/Rem 7½
A2460	29.7	2882	33.0	3275	51,600p	Sra HP/2.17″/Rem 7½
A2495BR	28.4	2871	31.5	3262	50,500C	Sra HP/2.17″/Rem 7½/(C)
A2230	29.3	2865	32.5	3256	52,500p	Sra HP/2.17″/Rem 7½
IMR3031	27.0	2906	30.0	3253	49,100C	
RL-12	31.0	3074	33.5	3239	49,100C	
W748	32.0	3080	34.0	3234	47,000C	
H322	28.0	2976	30.0	3200	47,000C	
H4895	29.0	2995	31.0	3188	47,000C	
IMR4895	29.0	3041	31.0	3170	47,700C	
RL-7	26.0	3039	28.5	3170	49,200C	
IMR4320	29.5	2787	32.5	3135	46,700C	
A2700	33.3	2772	35.0	2949	37,900p	Sra HP/2.17″/Rem 7½/(C)

Caution: Loads exceeding SAAMI OAL Maximum must be verified for bullet-to-rifling clearance and magazine functioning. Where a specific primer or bullet is indicated those components must be used, no substitutions! Where only a maximum load is shown, reduce starting load 10%, unless otherwise specified.

Key: (C) = compressed charge; C = CUP; p = psi; Plink = Plinker; Bns = Barnes; Hdy = Hornady; Lap = Lapua; Nos = Nosler; Rem = Remington; Sra = Sierra; Spr = Speer; Win = Winchester.

Never exceed maximum load nor use any load exhibiting signs of excessive pressure. Begin at suggested starting load and work up carefully.

75

Powder	Grs.	MV (fps)	Grs.	MV (fps)	Press. (CUP/psi)	Comments
RL-12	30.5	2994	32.5	3188	48,800C	
IMR3031	26.5	2814	29.5	3139	48,400C	
H4895	28.5	2980	30.5	3129	47,000C	
W748	31.0	2870	33.0	3117	47,500C	
BL-C(2)	31.0	2883	33.0	3113	46,000C	
IMR4895	28.5	2920	30.5	3111	47,900C	
H335	28.0	2928	30.0	3103	47,000C	
H322	26.0	2756	28.0	3096	47,000C	
IMR4320	29.0	2719	32.5	3081	48,600C	
RL-7	25.5	2898	27.5	3064	48,400C	

80

Powder	Grs.	MV (fps)	Grs.	MV (fps)	Press. (CUP/psi)	Comments
VarGet			32.5	3159	50,700C	
A2460	28.8	2749	32.0	3124	51,200p	Spr SP/2.12"/Rem 7½
A2520	29.7	2746	33.0	3121	51,200p	Spr SP/2.12"/Rem 7½
H4895	28.0	2945	30.0	3100	47,000C	
H335	28.0	2957	30.0	3090	48,000C	
RL-12	30.0	2914	32.0	3089	47,400C	
BL-C(2)	31.0	2894	33.0	3089	47,500C	
IMR4064	29.0	2686	31.5	3078	46,200C	
A2495BR	27.0	2706	30.0	3075	53,400p	Spr SP/2.12"/Rem 7½
A2015BR	26.1	2679	29.0	3044	50,200p	Spr SP/2.12"/Rem 7½
A2230	27.9	2673	31.0	3037	49,700p	Spr SP/2.12"/Rem 7½
IMR4895	28.0	2860	30.0	3021	48,800C	
W748	30.0	2888	32.0	3012	48,000C	
H322	26.0	2787	28.0	3005	47,000C	
IMR4320	29.0	2648	32.0	3000	48,600C	
IMR3031	26.0	2680	28.5	2984	46,000C	
RL-7	25.0	2785	27.0	2968	47,700C	
A2700	33.3	2757	35.0	2933	46,700p	Spr SP/2.12"/Rem 7½/(C)

85

Powder	Grs.	MV (fps)	Grs.	MV (fps)	Press. (CUP/psi)	Comments
VarGet			31.0	3007	50,800C	
IMR4064	26.5	2664	29.0	2989	48,600C	
BL-C(2)	29.0	2821	31.0	2947	48,500C	
W748	28.0	2780	30.0	2927	48,000C	
RL-12	27.0	2683	30.0	2922	48,600C	
IMR4320	27.0	2624	30.0	2878	48,000C	
RL-7	23.5	2643	25.0	2827	49,700C	
H335	24.5	2600	26.5	2809	49,000C	
H4895	24.5	2590	26.5	2770	49,500C	
IMR4895	24.0	2592	26.0	2738	47,400C	
H322	22.0	2472	24.0	2632	47,000C	

87

Powder	Grs.	MV (fps)	Grs.	MV (fps)	Press. (CUP/psi)	Comments
A2700	33.3	2747	35.0	2922	53,000p	Hdy HPBT/2.225"/Rem 7½/(C)/*
A2520	27.0	2545	30.0	2892	51,800p	Hdy HPBT/2.225"/Rem 7½/*
A2495BR	25.2	2541	28.0	2888	51,200p	Hdy HPBT/2.225"/Rem 7½/*
A2460	26.6	2539	29.5	2885	50,700p	Hdy HPBT/2.225"/Rem 7½/*
A2230	26.1	2512	29.0	2855	50,500p	Hdy HPBT/2.225"/Rem 7½/*
A2015BR	24.3	2512	27.0	2855	52,000p	Hdy HPBT/2.225"/Rem 7½/*

*Exceeds SAAMI Maximum OAL

90

Powder	Grs.	MV (fps)	Grs.	MV (fps)	Press. (CUP/psi)	Comments
RL-15	28.0	2762	30.0	2943	48,500C	
BL-C(2)	29.0	2738	31.0	2921	48,800C	
W748	28.0	2740	29.0	2877	48,500C	
IMR4064	27.0	2646	29.0	2870	48,000C	
IMR4320	26.0	2673	28.0	2852	49,000C	
IMR4895	25.0	2559	27.0	2767	46,000C	
RL-12	26.5	2564	28.5	2764	48,500C	
H4895	24.5	2560	27.0	2743	48,000C	
H335	24.0	2432	26.0	2688	49,000C	
H322	22.0	2423	24.0	2607	48,000C	

100

Powder	Grs.	MV (fps)	Grs.	MV (fps)	Press. (CUP/psi)	Comments
A2230	25.2	2368	28.0	2691	52,400p	Spr SBT/2.21"/Rem 7½/*
A2520	25.7	2361	28.5	2683	52,000p	Spr SBT/2.21"/Rem 7½/*
A2460	25.2	2357	28.0	2678	50,900p	Spr SBT/2.21"/Rem 7½/*
IMR4064	26.0	2495	28.0	2658	46,500C	
A2700	30.4	2487	32.0	2646	50,100p	Spr SBT/2.21"/Rem 7½/*
A2495BR	23.4	2325	26.0	2642	54,000p	Spr SBT/2.21"/Rem 7½/*
IMR4895	25.0	2475	27.0	2633	49,000C	
A2015BR	22.5	2299	25.0	2612	51,900p	Spr SBT/2.21"/Rem 7½/*
H4895	24.5	2423	27.0	2603	49,000C	
BL-C(2)	27.0	2379	29.0	2599	47,000C	
IMR4320	25.0	2404	27.0	2595	46,500C	
RL-15	25.0	2444	27.0	2581	46,500C	
H335	24.0	2339	26.0	2537	50,000C	
W748	26.5	2311	28.0	2525	46,500C	
H322	22.0	2275	23.5	2519	50,000C	
RL-12	24.5	2332	26.0	2495	47,000C	

*Exceeds SAAMI maximum OAL.

Never exceed maximum load nor use any load exhibiting signs of excessive pressure. Begin at suggested starting load and work up carefully.

243 Winchester

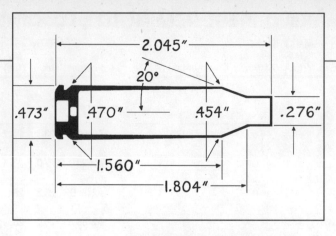

Case: Winchester
Primer: Large Rifle
Barrel: 24″ Accurate
26″ Hodgdon
23″ Vihtavuori

Bullet Diameter: 0.243″
Maximum Case Length: 2.045″
Trim to Length: 2.035″
Maximum Cartridge OAL: 2.710″
Minimum Cartridge OAL: 2.540″

Introduced in 1955, the 243 was created by simply necking down the 308 Winchester and changing the headstamp, with no other changes. This is still a common way of making 243 cases, but it must be noted that with some cases the resulting necks can be too thick and will require reaming or outside turning to allow safe cartridge-neck-to-chamber-throat clearance.

From the outset, Winchester envisioned their new cartridge as a combination varmint and big-game chambering. They chose a rifling rate—1 turn in 10 inches—that would properly stabilize pointed bullets of 100 grains. Original factory loads were with 80-grain bullets, designed for varmint hunting only, and with 100-grain bullets that were very tough—some say too tough for proper performance on deer-sized game.

The 243 produces dramatically less recoil than 30-06-class cartridges, endearing it with recoil-sensitive hunters. When proper bullets are used and shots are well placed, the 243 is fully capable for the purposes Winchester intended.

Usable case capacity with a 100-grain bullet, seated normally, is about 52.8 grains of water. H414, RL-19, A4350, IMR4350, H450 and H1000 are good 243 propellants.

243 WINCHESTER LOADING DATA

Powder	STARTING Grs.	MV (fps)	MAXIMUM Grs.	MV (fps)	Press. (CUP/psi)	Comments
60						
H414	44.0	3350	48.0	3735	47,300C	
IMR4320	41.0	3520	43.0	3711	48,600C	
H335	38.0	3498	41.0	3706	49,400C	
H4895	38.5	3441	42.0	3701	48,200C	
A2230	38.0	3478	40.0	3700	50,800C	Sra HP/2.58″/CCI 200
IMR3031	37.0	3401	39.0	3690	49,600C	
IMR4895	39.0	3449	41.0	3689	48,400C	
A2460	38.0	3466	40.0	3687	50,500C	Sra HP/2.58″/CCI 200
A2015BR	34.2	3244	38.0	3686	50,600C	Sra HP/2.58″/CCI 200
BL-C(2)	38.5	3462	41.5	3677	48,900C	
A2495BR	36.0	3232	40.0	3673	51,500C	Sra HP/2.58″/CCI 200
A2700	41.9	3225	46.5	3665	50,800C	Sra HP/2.58″/CCI 200
W760	46.0	3581	47.0	3659	46,900C	
W748	38.0	3489	40.0	3640	48,000C	
A4350	43.2	3196	48.0	3632	48,300C	Sra HP/2.58″/CCI 200
IMR4064	39.0	3412	41.0	3622	47,200C	
RL-15	40.0	3429	42.5	3602	50,100C	
H380	42.5	3471	44.5	3599	47,000C	
A2520	38.0	3376	40.0	3591	49,900C	Sra HP/2.58″/CCI 200
H4350	44.0	3097	47.0	3520	46,000C	
RL-12	39.0	3370	42.0	3513	48,800C	
60 con't						
H322	34.0	3267	37.0	3513	49,800C	
IMR4350	44.0	3119	46.0	3510	46,400C	
70						
H414	43.5	3187	47.5	3613	49,600C	
VarGet			42.0	3600	50,000C	
W760	45.0	3309	47.0	3581	49,100C	
A4350	43.2	3107	48.0	3531	47,600C	Hdy SX/2.65″/CCI 200/(C)
A2700	40.5	3078	45.0	3498	50,100C	Hdy SX/2.65″/CCI 200
A2495BR	35.1	3070	39.0	3489	49,900C	Hdy SX/2.65″/CCI 200
IMR4320	40.0	3233	42.0	3480	47,900C	
N160	46.1	3004	51.3	3451	50,800p	Hdy SXSP/2.638″/Rem 9½
H335	37.0	3279	40.0	3451	49,000C	
A2460	37.1	3234	39.0	3440	50,400C	Hdy SX/2.65″/CCI 200
BL-C(2)	37.5	3215	41.0	3435	50,200C	
A2230	36.6	3224	38.5	3430	50,200C	Hdy SX/2.65″/CCI 200
H380	41.0	3360	44.0	3422	47,800C	
H4350	44.0	3079	47.0	3421	46,800C	

Never exceed maximum load nor use any load exhibiting signs of excessive pressure. Begin at suggested starting load and work up carefully.

70 con't

Powder	—STARTING— Grs.	MV (fps)	—MAXIMUM— Grs.	MV (fps)	Press. (CUP/psi)	Comments
W748	37.0	3264	39.0	3420	48,400C	
H4895	37.0	3229	40.0	3414	49,100C	
IMR4831	46.0	3111	48.0	3402	44,700C	
IMR4895	38.0	3249	40.0	3400	48,900C	
IMR4350	44.0	3088	46.0	3399	46,600C	
A2015BR	32.9	2988	36.5	3395	46,800C	Hdy SX/2.65"/CCI 200
IMR4064	38.0	3230	40.0	3369	47,200C	
A2520	37.1	3163	39.0	3365	48,200C	Hdy SX/2.65"/CCI 200
H450	46.0	3107	50.0	3324	42,000C	
H322	33.0	3097	36.0	3280	48,000C	
IMR3031	36.0	3136	38.0	3262	48,900C	
A3100	43.2	2830	48.0	3216	42,200C	Hdy SX/2.65"/CCI 200/(C)

75

Powder	—STARTING— Grs.	MV (fps)	—MAXIMUM— Grs.	MV (fps)	Press. (CUP/psi)	Comments
H414	43.0	3235	47.0	3534	49,500C	
RL-19	47.0	3294	49.0	3461	49,500C	
H380	40.0	3299	43.0	3410	48,100C	
H4895	36.0	3180	39.0	3406	50,100C	
W760	43.0	3226	45.0	3392	47,400C	
IMR4895	36.0	3169	39.0	3387	49,900C	
IMR4350	44.0	3127	46.0	3380	48,600C	
VarGet			39.0	3374	49,900C	
RL-15	39.0	3281	41.0	3373	48,000C	
IMR4831	46.0	3119	48.0	3353	45,400C	
RL-22	48.0	3124	50.0	3348	44,000C	
IMR4320	39.0	3107	41.0	3346	48,200C	
N160			45.0	3340	57,000p	Hdy HP
H4350	43.0	2954	47.0	3339	48,200C	
IMR4064	37.0	3113	40.0	3338	49,200C	
H450	45.5	3169	49.5	3335	45,700C	
24N64			42.7	3311	56,121p	Hdy HP
RL-12	38.0	3139	40.0	3276	49,000C	
H335	34.0	3014	37.0	3225	47,800C	
BL-C(2)	34.0	3005	37.0	3210	47,500C	
H322	32.0	2999	35.0	3205	49,800C	
W748	35.0	2992	37.0	3202	47,800C	
IMR3031	34.0	3063	37.0	3180	49,000C	

80

Powder	—STARTING— Grs.	MV (fps)	—MAXIMUM— Grs.	MV (fps)	Press. (CUP/psi)	Comments
H414	42.0	3185	46.0	3453	49,200C	
RL-19	46.0	3198	48.5	3374	48,900C	
W760	43.0	3217	45.0	3368	48,200C	
H380	39.5	3189	43.0	3354	48,200C	
RL-15	38.0	3074	40.0	3326	49,400C	
RL-22	48.0	3100	50.0	3324	46,600C	
H4895	35.0	3170	38.0	3323	48,900C	
A4350	39.6	2918	44.0	3316	47,900C	Spr SP/2.7"/CCI 200
H450	45.0	3143	49.0	3303	45,900C	
H335	35.0	3118	37.0	3298	50,400C	
IMR4895	35.0	3140	38.0	3296	49,000C	
IMR4831	46.0	3130	48.0	3282	46,600C	
H4350	42.0	2910	46.0	3280	48,900C	

80 con't

Powder	—STARTING— Grs.	MV (fps)	—MAXIMUM— Grs.	MV (fps)	Press. (CUP/psi)	Comments
IMR4350	42.0	2990	45.0	3271	48,400C	
A3100	42.3	2878	47.0	3271	49,000C	Spr SP/2.7"/CCI 200/(C)
N160			44.9	3270	56,500p	Hdy SP
WMR			47.5	3250	54,700p	Win PSP
IMR4320	38.0	3080	40.0	3249	48,900C	
BL-C(2)	35.0	3044	38.5	3248	49,200C	
A2700	39.9	3039	42.0	3233	50,400C	Spr SP/2.7"/CCI 200
A2495BR	32.4	2842	36.0	3230	50,900C	Spr SP/2.7"/CCI 200
IMR4064	36.0	3027	39.0	3220	49,400C	
RL-12	37.0	3062	39.0	3204	49,200C	
H4831	44.0	2856	48.0	3156	42,700C	
IMR3031	33.0	2934	36.0	3139	48,900C	
A2015BR	30.2	2746	33.5	3121	48,200C	Spr SP/2.7"/CCI 200
W748	34.0	3039	36.0	3111	50,000C	
H322	31.0	2846	34.0	3042	48,000C	

85

Powder	—STARTING— Grs.	MV (fps)	—MAXIMUM— Grs.	MV (fps)	Press. (CUP/psi)	Comments
RL-19	45.0	3161	47.0	3319	49,100C	
H414	41.5	3040	45.0	3307	49,200C	
RL-22	46.0	3129	48.5	3303	50,000C	
A4350	39.6	2899	44.0	3294	49,800C	Sra HPBT/2.66"/CCI 200
H4350	41.0	2830	45.0	3253	49,200C	
IMR4350	41.0	2860	44.0	3239	49,100C	
H4895	34.0	3079	37.0	3229	49,600C	
IMR4831	45.0	3010	47.0	3222	47,100C	
IMR4895	34.0	3066	37.0	3218	49,500C	
H450	45.0	2912	48.0	3215	47,200C	
W760	42.0	3051	44.0	3210	48,600C	
IMR4320	37.0	2907	39.0	3190	49,400C	
H380	38.0	2977	41.0	3188	49,500C	
RL-15	35.0	2896	38.0	3176	48,500C	
H4831	44.0	2847	48.0	3169	43,300C	
IMR4064	35.0	3009	38.0	3169	49,200C	
BL-C(2)	34.5	3079	36.5	3142	51,200C	
N560	43.2	2890	48.0	3149	50,800p	Hdy HPBT/2.677"/ Rem 9½
A2700	39.0	2952	41.0	3140	49,200C	Sra HPBT/2.66"/CCI 200
A3100	41.4	2756	46.0	3132	46,800C	Sra HPBT/2.66"/CCI 200
H335	34.5	3052	35.5	3110	50,400C	
RL-12	34.5	2947	37.0	3105	50,000C	
W748	33.0	2964	35.0	3088	50,100C	
IMR3031	33.0	2850	35.0	3080	49,000C	

>>>>>>>>>>>>>>>>>>>>>>>>>>>>>>>>

Caution: Loads exceeding SAAMI OAL Maximum must be verified for bullet-to-rifling clearance and magazine functioning. Where a specific primer or bullet is indicated those components must be used, no substitutions! Where only a maximum load is shown, reduce starting load 10%, unless otherwise specified.

Key: (C) = compressed charge; C = CUP; p = psi; Plink = Plinker; Bns = Barnes; Hdy = Hornady; Lap = Lapua; Nos = Nosler; Rem = Remington; Sra = Sierra; Spr = Speer; Win = Winchester.

Never exceed maximum load nor use any load exhibiting signs of excessive pressure. Begin at suggested starting load and work up carefully.

90

Powder	Grs. (Starting)	MV (fps)	Grs. (Max)	MV (fps)	Press. (CUP/psi)	Comments
H414	40.5	2902	44.0	3237	48,300C	
H450	44.0	3028	48.0	3222	45,800C	
W760	41.0	2936	43.0	3189	48,000C	
RL-22	44.0	2969	46.5	3188	50,100C	
H4350	40.0	2789	44.0	3180	50,100C	
RL-19	43.0	2972	45.5	3177	50,000C	
IMR4831	44.0	2954	46.0	3166	48,600C	
N160			45.4	3150	52,214p	Sako SP 112E
IMR4320	35.0	2840	38.0	3137	48,900C	
H4831	44.0	2823	48.0	3122	45,100C	
IMR4350	40.0	2804	43.0	3110	49,600C	
H4895	34.0	2866	37.0	3107	48,200C	
IMR7828	44.0	2930	46.0	3104	46,700C	
H380	38.0	2910	40.0	3073	52,000C	
BL-C(2)	34.0	2927	36.0	3069	50,400C	
IMR4895	33.0	2821	36.0	3059	47,600C	
IMR4064	34.0	2772	37.0	3040	47,900C	
H335	33.0	2890	35.0	3004	49,000C	
RL-15	33.0	2773	36.0	2986	47,500C	
RL-12	32.0	2669	35.0	2871	48,000C	

95

Powder	Grs. (Starting)	MV (fps)	Grs. (Max)	MV (fps)	Press. (CUP/psi)	Comments
A4350	36.0	2680	40.0	3046	50,700C	Nos SP/2.7"/CCI 200
A3100	39.6	2649	44.0	3010	49,300C	Nos SP/2.7"/CCI 200
A2700	37.1	2740	39.0	2915	49,700C	Nos SP/2.7"/CCI 200
A2495BR	29.7	2535	33.0	2881	51,400C	Nos SP/2.7"/CCI 200

100

Powder	Grs. (Starting)	MV (fps)	Grs. (Max)	MV (fps)	Press. (CUP/psi)	Comments
H414	39.5	2862	43.0	3087	51,100C	
RL-22	43.0	2888	45.5	3076	48,500C	
H4831	44.0	2807	46.0	3071	47,400C	
H1000	47.0	2901	48.5	3045	48,900C	
RL-19	42.0	2847	44.5	3034	49,800C	
IMR7828	43.0	2788	46.0	3029	48,000C	
IMR4831	42.0	2824	44.0	3007	50,600C	
H450	43.0	2794	45.0	3004	49,000C	
WMR			44.7	3000	55,500p	Win PSP
H4350	39.0	2664	43.0	2994	51,200C	
W760	40.0	2880	42.0	2991	49,600C	
IMR4320	34.0	2616	37.0	2989	50,500C	
A4350	35.1	2623	39.0	2981	51,800C	Spr SBT/2.7"/CCI 200
N160			41.7	2980	56,800p	Sra SP
A3100	38.7	2610	43.0	2966	51,900C	Spr SBT/2.7"/CCI 200
N560	41.3	2697	45.7	2962	50,800p	Hdy SPBT/2.65"/Rem 9½
IMR4064	34.0	2709	37.0	2940	49,900C	
H380	36.0	2814	38.0	2940	50,500C	
IMR4350	39.0	2690	42.0	2940	50,800C	
H4895	33.5	2734	36.0	2938	47,000C	
IMR4895	33.0	2691	36.0	2934	47,800C	

100 con't

Powder	Grs. (Starting)	MV (fps)	Grs. (Max)	MV (fps)	Press. (CUP/psi)	Comments
24N64			40.0	2927	57,180p	Hdy BTSP
VarGet			35.0	2872	50,900C	
RL-15	32.0	2660	34.5	2793	48,000C	
A2700	34.2	2588	36.0	2753	48,300C	Spr SBT/2.7"/CCI 200
RL-12	31.0	2513	33.5	2735	48,900C	
A2495BR	27.0	2335	30.0	2653	50,300C	Spr SBT/2.7"/CCI 200

105

Powder	Grs. (Starting)	MV (fps)	Grs. (Max)	MV (fps)	Press. (CUP/psi)	Comments
H1000	46.0	2867	48.0	3019	49,200C	
H414	38.5	2761	42.0	3002	50,300C	
RL-22	42.0	2819	45.0	2992	49,100C	
IMR7828	43.0	2770	45.0	2984	49,000C	
IMR4831	41.0	2778	43.0	2979	49,900C	
W760	39.0	2783	41.0	2969	49,400C	
H450	43.0	2790	44.5	2957	49,500C	
RL-19	41.0	2792	44.0	2952	50,000C	
H4831	43.5	2789	45.0	2940	45,900C	
IMR4350	38.0	2619	41.0	2920	49,600C	
H4350	38.0	2631	42.0	2914	50,900C	
IMR4320	33.0	2566	36.0	2898	49,200C	
WMR			43.7	2890	56,500p	Win SP
IMR4895	33.0	2572	36.0	2874	50,100C	
IMR4064	33.0	2517	36.0	2840	48,900C	
H380	35.0	2660	37.0	2839	49,400C	
H4895	33.5	2703	36.0	2830	47,500C	
H335	31.5	2621	33.5	2791	47,400C	
H870			52.0	2788	38,800C	
N560	35.2	2486	38.8	2719	50,800p	Spr Sptz/2.67"/Rem 9½
RL-15	32.0	2565	34.0	2716	48,400C	
RL-12	30.0	2471	33.0	2587	48,900C	

115-117

Powder	Grs. (Starting)	MV (fps)	Grs. (Max)	MV (fps)	Press. (CUP/psi)	Comments
H1000	43.0	2642	45.5	2802	50,400C	
RL-22	40.0	2616	42.5	2767	49,000C	
RL-19	38.0	2545	41.0	2762	49,900C	
H870	45.0	2601	48.0	2755	47,100C	
RL-15	29.0	2363	32.0	2512	47,500C	

Caution: Loads exceeding SAAMI OAL Maximum must be verified for bullet-to-rifling clearance and magazine functioning. Where a specific primer or bullet is indicated those components must be used, no substitutions! Where only a maximum load is shown, reduce starting load 10%, unless otherwise specified.

Key: (C) = compressed charge; C = CUP; p = psi; Plink = Plinker; Bns = Barnes; Hdy = Hornady; Lap = Lapua; Nos = Nosler; Rem = Remington; Sra = Sierra; Spr = Speer; Win = Winchester.

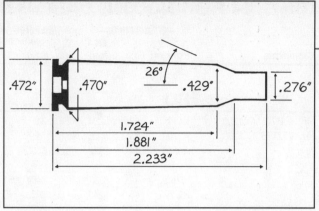

Case: Federal
Primer: Large Rifle
Barrel: 24″ Accurate
      26″ Hodgdon
      22½″ Vihtavuori

Bullet Diameter: 0.243″
Maximum Case Length: 2.233″
Trim to Length: 2.225″
Maximum Cartridge OAL: 2.825″
Minimum Cartridge OAL: 2.730″

Introduced in 1955, at the same time as Winchester's 243, Remington envisioned the 244 as a single-purpose cartridge—rifles and ammunition were intended strictly for long-range varmint hunting, for which it is extremely useful.

To this end, Remington chose a 1-in-12-inch twist for the rifling. In theory, such a slow twist enhances accuracy potential with varmint-weight bullets. Factory loadings offered a choice between 75- and 90-grain bullets. Both were intended to give devastating expansion on varmint-sized animals.

It was immediately apparent that Remington had a major problem. Bluntly, why would anyone buy a single-purpose rifle from Remington when Winchester offered an otherwise similar performing rifle that could launch proper spitzer big-game bullets weighing 100 grains? To Remington's chagrin, most buyers evidently placed much more emphasis on an actual ability to hunt smaller species of big game than they did on a theoretical difference in accuracy potential.

Sales for the 244 rifle were dismal and, in 1963, Remington finally made an effort to correct the problem. Changing the name of the cartridge to 6mm Remington, they also changed the rifling rate to 1-in-9 inches and offered proper 100-grain big game factory loads. The effort was at least partially successful. While the 6mm Remington has never gained a full share of 24 bore sales, it has survived and is finally competing quite well against the 243 Winchester, which cannot equal the performance of a Remington chambering that holds a few percent more powder and works at a somewhat higher pressure.

Remington's decision on a 1-in-9 rifling rate is a mystery. It could be viewed as simple overkill since the 1-in-10 twist will easily do the job for any standard bullet.

We have to note that some 1-in-12 rifles will shoot some 100-grain pointed bullets with *excellent* accuracy, but only when top velocity loads are used. This is especially true in the rare 26-inch-barreled bolt-action rifles. The longer Speer 105-grain spitzer and heavier pointed or semi-pointed bullets simply will not stabilize in standard 244 Remington barrels.

Usable case capacity with a 100-grain bullet, seated normally, is about 53.7 grains of water. H414, IMR4350, IMR4064, IMR4831 and RL-19 are all noted choices in the 244/6mm Remington.

6mm REMINGTON/244 REMINGTON LOADING DATA

Powder	STARTING Grs.	MV (fps)	MAXIMUM Grs.	MV (fps)	Press. (CUP/psi)	Comments
60						
RL-15	42.0	3664	45.0	3802	49,000C	
A2495BR	39.6	3339	44.0	3794	63,300p	Sra HP/2.75″/CCI 200
A2015BR	37.9	3317	42.1	3769	63,200p	Sra HP/2.75″/CCI 200
BL-C(2)	38.5	3405	42.0	3747	49,100C	
A2700	45.5	3295	50.5	3744	60,300p	Sra HP/2.75″/CCI 200
IMR4320	42.0	3535	44.0	3727	50,000C	
VarGet			42.0	3722	50,500C	
H335	38.5	3339	42.0	3694	49,200C	
H4895	38.5	3291	42.0	3674	50,000C	
IMR4064	40.0	3341	43.0	3674	50,200C	
H414	44.0	3432	48.0	3671	49,000C	
W760	46.0	3512	48.0	3662	48,800C	
IMR4895	39.0	3297	42.0	3660	49,800C	
60 con't						
H380	42.5	3452	46.0	3638	49,600C	
RL-12	41.0	3378	44.0	3631	49,500C	
H4350	45.0	3247	48.0	3554	47,900C	
RL-22	49.0	3390	52.0	3545	47,000C	
IMR4350	45.0	3414	47.0	3540	47,200C	
RL-19	48.0	3370	51.0	3527	47,000C	
IMR3031	37.0	3221	40.0	3526	48,000C	
A4350	45.0	3101	50.0	3524	48,300p	Sra HP/2.75″/CCI 200/(C)
H450	47.0	3259	51.0	3519	46,500C	
IMR4831	47.0	3259	49.0	3439	46,900C	
H322	35.0	3183	38.0	3399	48,900C	
H4831	47.0	3228	51.0	3391	45,900C	

➤➤➤➤➤➤➤➤➤➤➤➤➤➤➤➤➤➤➤➤➤➤➤➤➤➤➤

Never exceed maximum load nor use any load exhibiting signs of excessive pressure. Begin at suggested starting load and work up carefully.

70

Powder	STARTING Grs.	MV (fps)	MAXIMUM Grs.	MV (fps)	Press. (CUP/psi)	Comments
A2700	44.1	3145	49.0	3574	62,500p	Hdy SP/2.775"/CCI 200
A2495BR	37.8	3140	42.0	3568	61,800p	Hdy SP/2.775"/CCI 200
VarGet			42.0	3550	50,000C	
H414	43.5	3282	47.5	3549	48,700C	
RL-15	41.0	3313	44.0	3547	48,000C	
H380	40.5	3229	44.0	3544	48,700C	
N160	47.3	3121	52.4	3520	52,200C	Sra HPBT/2.811"/Rem 9½
W760	45.0	3380	47.0	3514	48,600C	
A2015BR	36.7	3081	40.8	3501	61,500p	Hdy SP/2.775"/CCI 200
H335	38.0	3272	42.0	3482	50,700C	
RL-19	47.0	3290	50.0	3447	48,500C	
RL-12	39.0	3211	42.0	3435	47,500C	
RL-22	49.0	3327	52.0	3435	48,000C	
H4350	44.0	3104	47.0	3430	47,000C	
A4350	45.0	3017	50.0	3428	51,900p	Hdy SP/2.775"/CCI 200/(C)
BL-C(2)	38.0	3234	42.0	3419	48,000C	
IMR4350	43.0	3090	46.0	3389	47,400C	
IMR4064	39.0	3177	42.0	3380	50,600C	
H450	47.0	3170	51.0	3368	47,800C	
IMR4320	40.0	3112	43.0	3367	50,700C	
H4831	46.0	3054	50.0	3321	45,400C	
IMR4895	38.0	3092	41.0	3319	48,200C	
IMR4831	47.0	3049	49.0	3318	47,200C	
IMR3031	36.0	3088	39.0	3311	51,000C	
H4895	38.0	3102	41.0	3300	47,600C	
H322	33.0	3079	36.0	3259	48,400C	
A3100	45.9	2805	51.0	3187	41,200p	Hdy SP/2.775"/CCI 200/(C)

75

Powder	STARTING Grs.	MV (fps)	MAXIMUM Grs.	MV (fps)	Press. (CUP/psi)	Comments
BL-C(2)	38.0	3222	42.0	3467	48,400C	
H414	42.5	3218	46.0	3448	48,900C	
H335	38.0	3253	42.0	3448	50,100C	
W760	44.0	3310	46.0	3440	49,000C	
RL-15	41.0	3234	44.0	3435	48,500C	
H380	39.5	3141	43.0	3428	49,200C	
RL-19	47.0	3279	50.0	3415	49,000C	
H4350	44.0	3139	47.0	3410	49,200C	
VarGet			41.0	3395	49,000C	
IMR4350	43.0	3066	46.0	3393	50,800C	
IMR4320	38.0	3082	42.0	3388	51,200C	
RL-22	48.0	3254	51.0	3382	47,500C	
H4831	46.0	3011	50.0	3369	48,700C	
RL-12	39.0	3149	42.0	3366	48,500C	
IMR4064	38.0	3129	41.0	3343	51,200C	
H4895	37.0	3039	40.0	3300	50,600C	
IMR4895	37.0	3047	40.0	3297	51,000C	
H450	44.0	2921	48.0	3281	47,000C	
IMR4831	45.0	3002	47.0	3279	48,800C	
IMR3031	35.0	3041	38.0	3231	50,700C	
H322	33.0	2974	36.0	3151	50,300C	

80

Powder	STARTING Grs.	MV (fps)	MAXIMUM Grs.	MV (fps)	Press. (CUP/psi)	Comments
H414	42.0	3224	46.0	3416	51,200C	
A2700	43.2	3006	48.0	3416	62,900p	Spr SP/2.825"/CCI 200
A4350	44.6	2997	49.5	3406	61,800p	Spr SP/2.825"/CCI 200/(C)
W760	44.0	3289	46.0	3404	51,000C	
RL-22	48.0	3240	51.0	3378	49,000C	
IMR4350	42.0	3091	45.0	3370	50,200C	
RL-15	40.0	3140	43.0	3359	48,500C	
H4831	45.0	2961	49.0	3343	49,600C	
H380	39.0	3142	43.0	3332	49,600C	
H335	36.0	3108	39.0	3331	49,600C	
H4350	42.0	3084	45.0	3320	49,700C	
RL-19	46.0	3188	49.0	3314	48,000C	
H4895	37.0	3035	40.0	3301	50,300C	
IMR4320	38.0	3064	41.0	3297	49,900C	
RL-12	38.0	3111	41.0	3290	49,500C	
A2495BR	36.0	2886	40.0	3280	58,800p	Spr SP/2.825"/CCI 200
IMR4064	37.0	3056	40.0	3279	51,000C	
A2015BR	34.9	2883	38.8	3276	65,000p	Spr SP/2.825"/CCI 200
IMR4831	45.0	3050	47.0	3264	50,900C	
BL-C(2)	35.0	2979	38.0	3255	46,500C	
H450	44.0	2940	48.0	3249	47,200C	
N160	44.1	3032	48.9	3245	52,200p	Hdy FMJ/2.815"/Rem 9½
IMR4895	36.0	3008	39.0	3240	49,100C	
A3100	45.9	2804	51.0	3186	49,400p	Spr SP/2.825"/CCI 200/(C)
IMR3031	34.0	2919	37.0	3104	50,900C	

85

Powder	STARTING Grs.	MV (fps)	MAXIMUM Grs.	MV (fps)	Press. (CUP/psi)	Comments
H414	41.5	3137	45.0	3308	48,600C	
RL-22	47.0	3169	50.0	3307	48,500C	
W760	43.0	3212	45.0	3294	48,800C	
IMR4320	38.0	3052	41.0	3269	50,900C	
H4831	44.0	2883	48.0	3231	50,500C	
H450	44.0	2891	48.0	3229	48,000C	
H4895	36.0	2990	39.0	3229	50,500C	
RL-15	38.0	3104	41.0	3227	49,500C	
RL-19	45.0	3124	48.0	3224	47,500C	
IMR4064	36.0	2994	39.0	3211	50,000C	
IMR4895	36.0	2984	39.0	3209	50,200C	
H380	38.0	2994	41.0	3203	49,200C	
IMR4831	44.0	3004	46.0	3200	50,000C	
IMR4350	41.0	3017	43.0	3174	50,400C	
H335	35.0	2938	38.0	3162	50,100C	
VarGet			38.5	3161	49,800C	
H4350	41.0	2990	43.0	3151	50,100C	
RL-12	35.0	3019	38.0	3140	49,000C	

87

Powder	STARTING Grs.	MV (fps)	MAXIMUM Grs.	MV (fps)	Press. (CUP/psi)	Comments
A4350	43.7	2879	48.5	3272	62,000p	Hdy SP/2.81"/CCI 200
A2700	41.9	2852	46.5	3241	59,800p	Hdy SP/2.81"/CCI 200
A3100	45.9	2825	51.0	3210	56,700p	Hdy SP/2.81"/CCI 200/(C)
N160	44.4	2876	49.1	3141	52,200p	Hdy SP/2.815"/Rem 9½
A2495BR	35.1	2747	39.0	3122	59,000p	Hdy SP/2.81"/CCI 200
A2015BR	34.7	2746	38.5	3120	61,700p	Hdy SP/2.81"/CCI 200

90

Powder	Grs.	MV (fps)	Grs.	MV (fps)	Press. (CUP/psi)	Comments
RL-22	46.0	3100	49.0	3235	48,500C	
H414	40.5	3038	44.0	3224	49,100C	
W760	42.0	3090	44.0	3209	49,000C	
IMR4350	41.0	2964	43.0	3189	51,600C	
IMR4320	37.0	2949	40.0	3168	50,200C	
RL-19	44.0	3044	47.0	3164	48,000C	
H4895	35.0	2881	38.0	3160	49,900C	
IMR4064	36.0	2914	39.0	3159	50,400C	
IMR4895	35.0	2894	38.0	3154	50,000C	
H4350	40.0	2780	43.0	3151	50,100C	
RL-15	37.0	3030	40.0	3150	50,000C	
H450	43.5	2800	47.5	3129	47,000C	
H4831	43.5	2826	47.0	3117	48,200C	
IMR4831	43.0	2904	45.0	3110	49,700C	
IMR7828	44.0	2860	47.0	3074	47,000C	
H380	37.0	2857	40.0	3068	48,700C	
RL-12	34.0	2891	37.0	3048	50,000C	

100

Powder	Grs.	MV (fps)	Grs.	MV (fps)	Press. (CUP/psi)	Comments
RL-22	45.0	2980	48.0	3136	50,000C	
H1000	49.0	2986	51.0	3111	47,500C	
H4831	42.5	2731	46.0	3074	49,600C	
RL-19	43.0	2884	46.0	3064	48,500C	
A2700	41.0	2692	45.5	3059	61,400p	Nos SP/2.825"/CCI 200
H414	39.5	2944	43.0	3054	49,200C	
A4350	41.0	2676	45.6	3041	61,000p	Nos SP/2.825"/CCI 200
IMR7828	44.0	2813	47.0	3039	48,600C	
W760	41.0	2891	43.0	3039	49,000C	
IMR4831	42.0	2848	44.0	3033	50,600C	
IMR4350	39.0	2836	42.0	3023	50,900C	
RL-15	35.0	2866	38.0	3012	50,000C	
IMR4064	34.0	2752	37.0	2984	50,400C	
IMR4320	35.0	2760	38.0	2982	51,000C	
A2015BR	32.9	2548	36.5	2896	63,300p	Nos SP/2.825"/CCI 200
N165	43.4	2745	48.1	2940	52,200p	Hdy SPBT/2.815"/Rem 9½
H4895	33.0	2737	36.0	2888	49,600C	
IMR4895	33.0	2719	36.0	2879	50,000C	
VarGet			36.0	2872	50,700C	
H380	34.0	2628	37.0	2828	47,800C	
RL-12	32.0	2611	35.0	2819	48,500C	
BL-C(2)	30.5	2529	33.0	2791	49,800C	
H335	30.5	2548	33.0	2772	49,600C	

105

Powder	Grs.	MV (fps)	Grs.	MV (fps)	Press. (CUP/psi)	Comments
RL-22	44.0	2939	47.0	3089	50,000C	
H4831	42.5	2707	46.0	3056	50,500C	
H1000	48.0	2871	50.0	2995	48,000C	
RL-19	42.0	2879	45.0	2990	49,500C	
IMR7828	44.0	2878	47.0	2981	49,000C	
H414	39.0	2859	43.0	2976	49,800C	
IMR4831	42.0	2821	44.0	2970	51,100C	
W760	41.0	2886	43.0	2963	49,700C	
RL-15	34.0	2837	37.0	2960	49,500C	
A2700	40.1	2605	44.5	2960	60,900p	Spr SP/2.825"/CCI 200
IMR4350	39.0	2857	41.0	2931	51,200C	
H450	41.5	2662	45.0	2927	46,900C	
IMR4320	34.0	2739	37.0	2918	50,600C	
A4350	39.6	2563	44.0	2912	59,200p	Spr SP/2.825"/CCI 200
H4350	38.0	2684	41.0	2909	49,800C	
N165	42.3	2726	46.5	2888	52,200p	Spr Sptz/2.815"/Rem 9½
IMR4064	33.0	2694	36.0	2860	50,200C	
IMR4895	32.0	2689	35.0	2840	50,100C	
A3100	42.3	2499	47.0	2840	51,400p	Spr SP/2.825"/CCI 200/(C)

107

Powder	Grs.	MV (fps)	Grs.	MV (fps)	Press. (CUP/psi)	Comments
VarGet			35.5	2798	50,600C	

115-117

Powder	Grs.	MV (fps)	Grs.	MV (fps)	Press. (CUP/psi)	Comments
RL-22	42.0	2764	45.0	2901	49,500C	
H1000	46.0	2760	48.0	2898	49,800C	
RL-19	41.0	2741	44.0	2868	50,000C	
A3100	42.3	2503	47.0	2844	60,200p	Bns FP/2.825"/CCI 200/(C)
A4350	39.6	2498	44.0	2839	62,500p	Bns FP/2.825"/CCI 200
H870	46.0	2589	49.0	2724	47,400C	

Caution: **Loads exceeding SAAMI OAL Maximum must be verified for bullet-to-rifling clearance and magazine functioning. Where a specific primer or bullet is indicated those components must be used, no substitutions! Where only a maximum load is shown, reduce starting load 10%, unless otherwise specified.**

Key: (C) = compressed charge; C = CUP; p = psi; Plink = Plinker; Bns = Barnes; Hdy = Hornady; Lap = Lapua; Nos = Nosler; Rem = Remington; Sra = Sierra; Spr = Speer; Win = Winchester.

Never exceed maximum load nor use any load exhibiting signs of excessive pressure. Begin at suggested starting load and work up carefully.

6mm-284

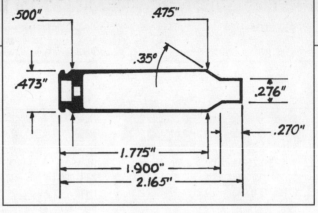

Case: Necked Down
284 Winchester (Winchester)
Primer: Large Rifle
Barrel: 26″ Hodgdon
Bullet Diameter: 0.243″
Maximum Case Length: 2.165″

Trim to Length: 2.155″
Maximum Cartridge OAL: 2.800″
(Chamber Dependent)
Minimum Cartridge OAL:
Bullet Dependent

This is one of the more popular wildcat cartridges based on the rebated-rim, magnum-body-sized 284 Winchester cartridge case. With a usable capacity virtually identical to the longer 6mm-06 and 240-Weatherby Magnum chamberings—about 64.0 grains of water—the 6mm-284 provides maximum performance in a shorter chambering.

Although this cartridge has about 18% greater usable capacity than the 6mm Remington, it can generate only about 50-100 fps more velocity with any given bullet. This fact assumes both are loaded to the same pressure, tested in the same length barrel and loaded with the best available powders.

The claim is that with heavier than standard bullets, the bigger case can offer additional ballistic benefit. This might be one reason such cartridges have continuing appeal to some shooters. More likely, there are those who believe any velocity edge can be turned to useful advantage.

Most rifles chambered for the 243 or 6mm are easily converted to 6mm-284. As with all custom chamberings, chamber and throat dimensions can show unusual variation, compared to SAAMI specification chamberings; use due caution.

This data is also suitable for use in 6mm-06 chambered rifles. H4831, H1000 and H870 are useful powders here.

6mm-284 LOADING DATA

Powder	STARTING Grs.	MV (fps)	MAXIMUM Grs.	MV (fps)	Press. (CUP/psi)	Comments
60						
H4831	54.0	3526	58.0	3807	51,800C	
H414	49.0	3478	51.0	3788	48,500C	
H380	46.0	3427	50.0	3765	51,300C	
H450	54.0	3492	56.0	3702	50,200C	
70						
H450	52.0	3392	56.0	3679	50,700C	
H414	47.0	3521	51.0	3667	51,800C	
H4831	52.0	3551	56.0	3762	51,800C	
H380	42.0	3217	46.0	3402	50,200C	
75						
H4831	52.0	3502	55.0	3691	50,200C	
H450	52.0	3343	55.0	3528	48,500C	
H414	47.0	3492	49.0	3519	48,500C	
H380	42.0	3185	46.0	3375	50,200C	

Powder	STARTING Grs.	MV (fps)	MAXIMUM Grs.	MV (fps)	Press. (CUP/psi)	Comments
80						
H4831	51.0	3397	55.0	3683	51,300C	
H450	51.0	3244	54.0	3494	47,600C	
H414	45.0	3338	48.0	3480	50,700C	
85						
H4831	49.0	3317	53.0	3471	51,800C	
H50	49.0	3214	53.0	3447	51,300C	
H414	44.0	3190	48.0	3394	51,800C	
H870			60.0	3281	40,800C	
90						
H4831	49.0	3281	52.0	3380	50,700C	
H1000	54.0	3178	57.0	3314	47,000C	
H450	49.0	3146	52.0	3268	49,100C	
H870			60.0	3249	41,400C	

Never exceed maximum load nor use any load exhibiting signs of excessive pressure. Begin at suggested starting load and work up carefully.

100

Powder	—STARTING— Grs.	MV (fps)	—MAXIMUM— Grs.	MV (fps)	Press. (CUP/psi)	Comments
H1000	52.0	3092	55.0	3229	48,400C	
H4831	46.0	3011	49.0	3207	49,100C	
H450	47.0	2931	50.0	3202	50,200C	
H870			59.0	3174	42,400C	

105

Powder	—STARTING— Grs.	MV (fps)	—MAXIMUM— Grs.	MV (fps)	Press. (CUP/psi)	Comments
H1000	51.0	3042	54.0	3168	48,000C	
H870			58.0	3147	45,900C	
H4831	45.0	2949	48.0	3130	49,600C	
H450	46.0	2900	50.0	3054	47,000C	

115-117

Powder	—STARTING— Grs.	MV (fps)	—MAXIMUM— Grs.	MV (fps)	Press. (CUP/psi)	Comments
H870	54.0	2788	56.0	2932	47,400C	
H1000	48.0	2719	51.0	2898	49,400C	
H4831	43.0	2622	45.0	2813	48,500C	

Caution: Loads exceeding SAAMI OAL Maximum must be verified for bullet-to-rifling clearance and magazine functioning. Where a specific primer or bullet is indicated those components must be used, no substitutions! Where only a maximum load is shown, reduce starting load 10%, unless otherwise specified.

Key: (C) = compressed charge; C = CUP; p = psi; Plink = Plinker; Bns = Barnes; Hdy = Hornady; Lap = Lapua; Nos = Nosler; Rem = Remington; Sra = Sierra; Spr = Speer; Win = Winchester.

Never exceed maximum load nor use any load exhibiting signs of excessive pressure. Begin at suggested starting load and work up carefully.

240
Weatherby Magnum

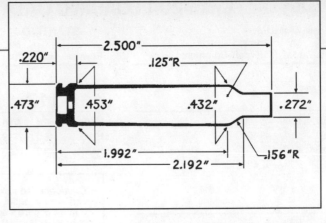

Case: Weatherby
Primer: Large Rifle
Barrel: 26″ Accurate
26″ Hodgdon
Bullet Diameter: 0.243″

Maximum Case Length: 2.500″
Trim to Length: 2.490″
Maximum Cartridge OAL: 3.100″
Minimum Cartridge OAL:
Bullet Dependent

Working at very high pressures and with about 64.0 grains of usable capacity (water), this proprietary belted case offers just about all the performance feasible from the 6mm bore. Since the case features a standard Mauser/'06 family head size, many rifles can easily be rebarreled to this Weatherby hot-rod.

However, anyone considering such a conversion should keep these facts in mind. First, these cases are hard to come by and are expensive. Second, like most Weatherby chamberings, this cartridge works at the outer limits of commonly acceptable pressures—so action and barrel strength are

particularly important. Finally, factory ammunition is designed and loaded around a free-bored barrel—use in a non-free-bored barrel is certain to create unsafe pressures!

Most would agree that anyone who feels the need for a maximum performance 6mm wildcat would be better served with the 6mm-284, 6mm-06 or 6mm-06 Ackley Improved. H450, H4831, H414, A4350 and H380 are good choices. As with all free-bored chamberings, slower powders, that might otherwise seem useful, seldom produce top accuracy.

240 WEATHERBY MAGNUM LOADING DATA

Powder	STARTING Grs.	STARTING MV (fps)	MAXIMUM Grs.	MAXIMUM MV (fps)	MAXIMUM Press. (CUP/psi)	Comments
60						
H414			54.0	3817		
H380			51.0	3775		
H450			58.0	3647		
H4895			47.0	3521		
H4831			57.0	3488		
75						
H414			53.0	3555		
H450			57.0	3542		
H380			49.0	3531		
H4831			56.0	3453		
H4895			46.0	3445		
80						
A3100	50.8	3120	56.5	3570	67,000p	Spr SP/3.1″/CCI 250/(C)
H450			57.0	3536		
H414			52.0	3514		
H4831			56.0	3481		
A4350	45.9	3062	51.0	3480	65,200p	Spr SP/3.1″/CCI 250

Powder	STARTING Grs.	STARTING MV (fps)	MAXIMUM Grs.	MAXIMUM MV (fps)	MAXIMUM Press. (CUP/psi)	Comments
80 con't						
H380			48.0	3451		
H4895			44.0	3359		
H1000	57.0	3082	59.0	3207		
A8700	56.7	2727	63.0	3099	46,100p	Spr SP/3.1″/CCI 250/(C)
85						
H450			56.0	3477		
H4831			56.0	3460		
H414			51.0	3409		
H380			47.0	3344		
H1000	57.0	3043	59.0	3167		

Never exceed maximum load nor use any load exhibiting signs of excessive pressure. Begin at suggested starting load and work up carefully.

Powder	STARTING Grs.	MV (fps)	MAXIMUM Grs.	MV (fps)	Press. (CUP/psi)	Comments
87						
A3100	50.0	3032	55.5	3446	64,900p	Hdy HPBT/3.1"/CCI 250
A4350	45.0	2968	50.0	3373	65,200p	Hdy HPBT/3.1"/CCI 250
A8700	56.7	2717	63.0	3088	49,300p	Hdy HPBT/3.1"/ CCI 250/(C)
90						
H4831			55.0	3394		
H450			55.0	3343		
H414			49.0	3307		
H380			46.0	3287		
H1000	57.0	3037	59.0	3140		
95						
A3100	48.2	2871	53.5	3262	62,300p	Nos Part./3.065"/ CCI 250
A4350	44.1	2852	49.0	3241	65,500p	Nos Part./3.065"/ CCI 250
A8700	55.8	2648	62.0	3009	50,300p	Nos Part./3.065"/ CCI 250/(C)

Powder	STARTING Grs.	MV (fps)	MAXIMUM Grs.	MV (fps)	Press. (CUP/psi)	Comments
100						
H4831			53.0	3202		
H450			53.0	3187		
A3100	46.8	2798	52.0	3179	63,600p	Spr SBT/3.095"/CCI 250
A4350	43.2	2762	48.0	3139	63,600p	Spr SBT/3.095"/CCI 250
H1000	57.0	3018	59.0	3122		
H414			47.0	3080		
A8700	55.8	2680	62.0	3045	56,100p	Spr SBT/3.095"/CCI 250
H380			44.0	3010		
105						
H4831			52.0	3142		
H450			52.0	3107		
H414			46.0	3038		
H380			43.0	2962		
115-117						
H1000	56.0	2971	58.0	3066		
H870			55.0	2880		
H4831			46.0	2779		

Caution: Loads exceeding SAAMI OAL Maximum must be verified for bullet-to-rifling clearance and magazine functioning. Where a specific primer or bullet is indicated those components must be used, no substitutions! Where only a maximum load is shown, reduce starting load 10%, unless otherwise specified.

Key: (C) = compressed charge; C = CUP; p = psi; Plink = Plinker; Bns = Barnes; Hdy = Hornady; Lap = Lapua; Nos = Nosler; Rem = Remington; Sra = Sierra; Spr = Speer; Win = Winchester.

25-20

Winchester
(25-20 WCF)

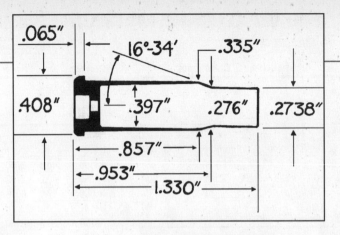

Case: Remington
Primer: Small Rifle
Barrel: 24″ Accurate
      20″ Hodgdon
      22″ Vihtavuori

Bullet Diameter: 0.257″
Maximum Case Length: 1.330″
Trim to Length: 1.325″
Maximum Cartridge OAL: 1.592″
Minimum Cartridge OAL: 1.530″

Designed about 1895 for chambering in John M. Browning's Model 92 Winchester, this diminutive cartridge is simply the 32-20 necked-down. Pressures used in this century-old cartridge reflect its blackpowder heritage and, therefore, performance is limited.

Properly loaded, the 25-20 can, however, substantially surpass the 22 Winchester Rimfire Magnum in effectiveness against small game, predators and vermin. It would seem to be fully capable for use in hunting peccary and, with the proper bullets, it should be adequate against the smallest species of deer at close range. Nevertheless, in spite of orig-

inal claims to the contrary, this is no big game cartridge.

No doubt, the vast majority of all 25-20 ammunition ever fired was shot for the sheer pleasure of plinking with such a mild-mannered chambering. It rolls cans with much more authority than any 22 rimfire....

With cast bullets, the 25-20 can be loaded very economically and will still deliver superior small-game and vermin performance, compared to any 22 rimfire loading.

Usable case capacity with a 60-grain bullet, seated normally, is about 16 grains of water. A1680, A2015BR and H4227 are noted performers in the 25-20.

25-20 WINCHESTER LOADING DATA (25-20 WCF)

Powder	STARTING Grs.	MV (fps)	MAXIMUM Grs.	MV (fps)	Press. (CUP/psi)	Comments
Lead 65 Lyman 257420						
A1680	12.0	1818	13.3	2138	28,000C	1.592″/CCI 400
A2015BR	13.5	1670	15.0	1898	24,600C	1.592″/CCI 400/(C)
XMP5744			11.0	1874		1.592″/CCI 400
No.9	7.2	1606	8.0	1825	26,500C	1.592″/CCI 400
Lead 90						
XMP5744			10.0	1675		CCI 400
60						
A1680	12.6	1979	14.0	2249	25,800C	Hdy FP/1.592″/CCI 400
No.9	7.7	1726	8.5	1961	27,700C	Hdy FP/1.592″/CCI 400
A2015BR	14.4	1721	16.0	1956	25,100C	Hdy FP/1.592″/CCI 400/(C)
XMP5744			11.4	1953		Hdy FP/1.592″/CCI 400
H110			8.5	1827	19,500C	26″ Bbl
70						
N110			10.2	2030	37,710p	Sako SP 111E

Powder	STARTING Grs.	MV (fps)	MAXIMUM Grs.	MV (fps)	Press. (CUP/psi)	Comments
75						
A1680	11.3	1745	12.5	1983	27,600C	Spr FN/1.585″/CCI 400
XMP5744			11.2	1850		Spr FN/1.585″/CCI 400
A2015BR	13.1	1624	14.5	1846	25,700C	Spr FN/1.585″/CCI 400
No.9	7.2	1510	8.0	1716	27,100C	Spr FN/1.585″/CCI 400
86						
H4227	8.0	1412	8.6	1550		
H110			8.0	1444		
HS6			5.5	1362		

***Caution:* Loads exceeding SAAMI OAL Maximum must be verified for bullet-to-rifling clearance and magazine functioning. Where a specific primer or bullet is indicated those components must be used, no substitutions! Where only a maximum load is shown, reduce starting load 10%, unless otherwise specified.**

Key: (C) = compressed charge; C = CUP; p = psi; Plink = Plinker; Bns = Barnes; Hdy = Hornady; Lap = Lapua; Nos = Nosler; Rem = Remington; Sra = Sierra; Spr = Speer; Win = Winchester.

Never exceed maximum load nor use any load exhibiting signs of excessive pressure. Begin at suggested starting load and work up carefully.

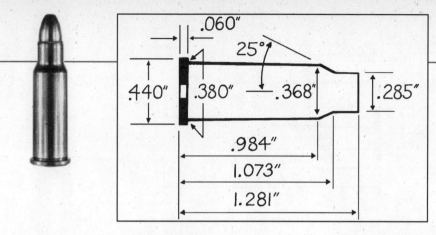

Case: Winchester
Primer: Small Rifle
Barrel: 24″ Accurate
      24″ Hodgdon
Bullet Diameter: 0.257″

Maximum Case Length: 1.281″
Trim to Length: 1.275″
Maximum Cartridge OAL: 1.590″
Minimum Cartridge OAL: 1.540″

This cartridge represents one of those interesting little oddities in the cartridge world. It was introduced in 1960, as a handgun cartridge, but there were no guns then chambered for it! The 256 Winchester Magnum is simply the 357 Magnum necked down, and cases are easily converted.

Ruger soon offered an innovative adaptation of their single-action revolver, called the Hawkeye, chambered for this cartridge. The anticipated Ruger and Smith & Wesson revolver chamberings were never commercially offered because case setback problems could not be solved.

As with any tapered or necked revolver cartridge, the cylinder is easily jammed when the fired case backs out of the chamber and the shoulder is pushed forward—any trace

of lubrication on the case or in the chamber exacerbates this problem.

In a rifle, with moderately high pressure and more capacity than the 25-20, the 256 is a good performer on varmints to, perhaps, 150 yards. Capable of launching a 60 grain bullet at over 2700 fps, 256 Winchester rifle loads offer considerable energy. Nevertheless, this cartridge is relegated to the same category as the 25-20—small game, predator and vermin. However, it should be useful against peccary and the smallest species of deer.

Usable case capacity with a 60-grain bullet, seated normally, is about 18.1 grains of water. H4198 and A1680 are probably the best powder choices.

256 WINCHESTER MAGNUM LOADING DATA

Lead 65 Lyman 257420

Powder	STARTING Grs.	MV (fps)	MAXIMUM Grs.	MV (fps)	Press. (CUP/psi)	Comments
A1680	13.5	2034	15.0	2311	29,300C	1.585″/CCI 250
A2015BR	16.2	1952	18.0	2218	27,000C	1.585″/CCI 250

60

Powder	STARTING Grs.	MV (fps)	MAXIMUM Grs.	MV (fps)	Press. (CUP/psi)	Comments
H4198	17.0	2686	18.0	2794		
A1680	16.2	2423	18.0	2753	40,900C	Hdy FN/1.58″/CCI 250
H110	13.0	2616	14.0	2724		
A2015BR	18.0	2138	20.0	2430	30,600C	Hdy FN/1.58″/CCI 250/(C)

75

Powder	STARTING Grs.	MV (fps)	MAXIMUM Grs.	MV (fps)	Press. (CUP/psi)	Comments
A2015BR	18.0	2133	20.0	2424	36,100C	Spr FN/1.575″/CCI 250/(C)
A1680	14.9	2120	16.5	2409	37,400C	Spr FN/1.575″/CCI 250
H4198	14.0	2019	16.0	2327		

87

Powder	STARTING Grs.	MV (fps)	MAXIMUM Grs.	MV (fps)	Press. (CUP/psi)	Comments
H4198	14.0	2081	15.0	2192		

Never exceed maximum load nor use any load exhibiting signs of excessive pressure. Begin at suggested starting load and work up carefully.

133

Winchester (25-35 WCF)

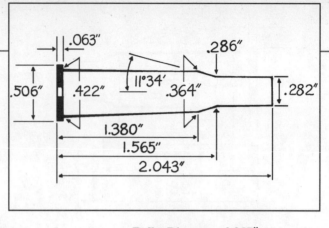

Case: Winchester
Primer: Large Rifle
Barrel: 24″ Accurate
　　　20″ Hodgdon
　　　20″ Vihtavuori

Bullet Diameter: 0.257″
Maximum Case Length: 2.043″
Trim to Length: 2.038″
Maximum Cartridge OAL: 2.550″
Minimum Cartridge OAL: 2.505″

Based on the 30-30 case, this chambering offered very moderate recoil. Original loadings launched a 117-grain bullet at about 2000 fps, compared to the original 30 WCF loading, which launched a 165-grain bullet at about the same velocity.

Today, many might be surprised to learn that in spite of such anemic performance the 25-35 was, for many decades, an extremely popular chambering in lever-action rifles offered by Winchester, Marlin and Savage. Two factors evidently account for this success: Mild recoil and the delivery of sufficient energy to do the job on deer-sized game.

For reasons that are completely obscure to this author, SAAMI pressure specifications for this cartridge are substantially less than those for the 30-30 Winchester. This significantly handicaps 25-35 performance. Nevertheless, properly loaded, the 25-35 is still an effective cartridge, and in sufficiently accurate rifles, lighter bullets can deliver startling varmint performance past 200 yards.

Usable case capacity with a 117-grain bullet, seated normally, is about 33.0 grains of water. A2520, H4895, N140 and H335 are good choices.

25-35 WINCHESTER LOADING DATA (25-35 WCF)

Powder	STARTING Grs.	MV (fps)	MAXIMUM Grs.	MV (fps)	Press. (CUP/psi)	Comments
60						
A2520	28.8	2674	32.0	3039	35,000C	Hdy FN/2.3″/CCI 200/(C)
A2495BR	27.5	2487	30.5	2826	29,800C	Hdy FN/2.3″/CCI 200/(C)
H335	27.0	2469	30.0	2792		
BL-C(2)	27.0	2457	30.0	2786		
H4895	27.0	2479	30.0	2729		
A2700	30.4	2559	32.0	2722	33,800C	Hdy FN/2.3″/CCI 200/(C)
70						
N120			23.5	2950	38,435p	Sako SP 102E
75						
A2520	26.1	2372	29.0	2696	33,400C	Spr FN/2.31″/CCI 200
A2495BR	26.1	2346	29.0	2666	32,900C	Spr FN/2.31″/CCI 200
A2700	30.4	2486	32.0	2645	37,000C	Spr FN/2.31″/CCI 200/(C)
87						
H4895	26.0	2446	29.0	2683		
H335	26.0	2444	29.0	2674		
BL-C(2)	26.0	2432	29.0	2666		

Powder	STARTING Grs.	MV (fps)	MAXIMUM Grs.	MV (fps)	Press. (CUP/psi)	Comments
87 con't						
N120			22.7	2590	39,160p	Lapua SP
93						
N110			15.3	2200	39,160p	Sako SP 107E
100						
H4895	25.0	2167	28.0	2386		
H335	25.0	2144	28.0	2380		
BL-C(2)	25.0	2131	28.0	2364		
H4198	19.0	2006	21.0	2142		
117						
N140			27.2	2360	39,160p	Win SP
A2520	22.5	1952	25.0	2218	33,900C	Hdy FP/2.545″/CCI 200
H4895	24.0	1993	27.0	2207		
H335	24.0	1974	27.0	2199		
BL-C(2)	24.0	1969	27.0	2188		
A4350	27.0	1925	30.0	2187	33,600C	FP/2.545″/CCI 200/(C)
A2495BR	22.5	1919	25.0	2181	32,300C	Hdy FP/2.545″/CCI 200

　　Never exceed maximum load nor use any load exhibiting signs of excessive pressure. Begin at suggested starting load and work up carefully.

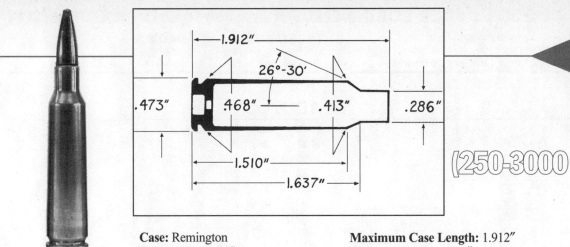

Case: Remington
Primer: Large Rifle
Barrel: 24″ Accurate
26″ Hodgdon
Bullet Diameter: 0.257″

Maximum Case Length: 1.912″
Trim to Length: 1.902″
Maximum Cartridge OAL: 2.515″
Minimum Cartridge OAL: 2.320″

Designed by Charles Newton for Savage and released in 1915, chambered in the Model 99 Savage lever-action rifle, this was the very first commercial chambering to achieve 3000 fps muzzle velocity. Three thousand feet per second might seem rather ho-hum today, but in that era shooters were most familiar with blackpowder cartridges that typically generated 1500 fps!

Evidently Mr. Newton originally designed this cartridge around a 100-grain bullet. Savage, recognizing the sex appeal and marketing advantage of a cartridge that could boast 3000 fps muzzle velocity, adopted the heaviest bullet that could safely achieve that velocity with the powders then available, thus the odd-ball original 87-grain bullet weight. Taking fullest advantage of the fact, Savage then named the cartridge 250-3000 Savage.

Original loads must have been rather hot, considering the powders of the day.

Modern pressure specification is comparatively mild. For this reason, performance is considerably limited. Nevertheless, the 250 Savage gives up surprisingly little to the newer 6mm Remington and 243 Winchester. With lighter bullets, it is fully capable as a varmint chambering, and with heavier bullets, it is still a good choice for recoil-sensitive shooters who want to hunt the smaller species of deer and similar-sized animals.

Usable case capacity with a 100-grain bullet, seated normally, is about 43.2 grains of water. IMR3031, IMR4320, W760, H380, IMR4350 and H414 are all noted performers in Mr. Newton's little wonder.

250 SAVAGE LOADING DATA (250-3000 SAVAGE)

Powder	STARTING Grs.	MV (fps)	MAXIMUM Grs.	MV (fps)	Press. (CUP/psi)	Comments
60						
H4895	37.0	3409	40.0	3667		
H322	33.0	3405	36.0	3647		
BL-C(2)	38.0	3329	40.0	3626		
H335	37.0	3306	39.0	3609		
IMR3031	34.0	3399	36.0	3595		
W748	38.0	3330	40.0	3588		
IMR4895	37.0	3389	39.0	3569		
H414	42.0	3459	44.0	3565		
H380	41.0	3406	43.0	3533		
IMR4064	37.0	3354	39.0	3524		
H4198	30.0	3202	33.0	3515		
RL-7	32.0	3310	34.0	3515		
IMR4320	38.0	3294	40.0	3514		
60 con't						
W760	42.0	3389	44.0	3510		
IMR4198	30.0	3200	32.0	3471		
H4350	39.0	3210	42.0	3394		

Caution: Loads exceeding SAAMI OAL Maximum must be verified for bullet-to-rifling clearance and magazine functioning. Where a specific primer or bullet is indicated those components must be used, no substitutions! Where only a maximum load is shown, reduce starting load 10%, unless otherwise specified.

Key: (C) = compressed charge; C = CUP; p = psi; Plink = Plinker; Bns = Barnes; Hdy = Hornady; Lap = Lapua; Nos = Nosler; Rem = Remington; Sra = Sierra; Spr = Speer; Win = Winchester.

Never exceed maximum load nor use any load exhibiting signs of excessive pressure. Begin at suggested starting load and work up carefully.

75

Powder	STARTING Grs.	MV (fps)	MAXIMUM Grs.	MV (fps)	Press. (CUP/psi)	Comments
H414	42.0	3247	44.0	3460		
W760	41.0	3174	43.0	3394		
H380	40.0	3169	42.0	3393		
H4895	35.0	3212	38.0	3380		
BL-C(2)	36.0	3155	38.0	3299		
W748	36.0	3149	38.0	3281		
H335	35.0	3136	37.0	3258		
IMR4895	34.0	3144	36.0	3231		
H4350	39.0	3080	42.0	3222		
IMR4064	34.0	3123	36.0	3209		
H322	31.0	3031	34.0	3194		
IMR3031	32.0	3081	34.0	3188		
IMR4320	35.0	3111	37.0	3180		
A2460	30.6	2798	34.0	3179	44,300C	Sra HP/2.465"/Rem 9½
RL-7	30.0	2944	32.0	3170		
A2495BR	30.6	2789	34.0	3169	42,600C	Sra HP/2.465"/Rem 9½
H4198	27.0	2872	30.0	3169		
IMR4350	39.0	3101	41.0	3163		
IMR4198	27.0	2874	30.0	3147		
A2520	30.6	2746	34.0	3121	41,300C	Sra HP/2.465"/Rem 9½
A2015BR	28.4	2741	31.5	3115	41,400C	Sra HP/2.465"/Rem 9½
A2230	30.2	2740	33.5	3114	43,800C	Sra HP/2.465"/Rem 9½
A2700	35.6	2859	37.5	3041	43,100C	Sra HP/2.465"/Rem 9½
A4350	36.9	2670	41.0	3034	43,600C	Sra HP/2.465"/Rem 9½/(C)
A3100	36.9	2407	41.0	2735	36,500C	Sra HP/2.465"/Rem 9½/(C)

87-90

Powder	STARTING Grs.	MV (fps)	MAXIMUM Grs.	MV (fps)	Press. (CUP/psi)	Comments
H414	40.0	3138	42.0	3297		
H380	39.0	3114	41.0	3210		
H4895	34.0	3031	37.0	3208		
W760	39.0	3051	41.0	3180		
BL-C(2)	34.0	2956	36.0	3114		
W748	34.0	2960	36.0	3112		
H335	33.0	2918	35.0	3075		
H4350	38.0	2816	41.0	3063		
H322	29.0	2763	32.0	3044		
IMR4895	32.0	2861	34.0	2977		
A2495BR	29.3	2598	32.5	2952	42,500C	Sra HPBT/2.46"/Rem 9½
IMR4320	33.0	2819	35.0	2944		
A4350	36.0	2579	40.0	2931	44,800C	Sra HPBT/2.46"/Rem 9½/(C)
A2015BR	27.5	2578	30.5	2929	41,400C	Sra HPBT/2.46"/Rem 9½
IMR4350	38.0	2830	40.0	2910		
A2230	28.8	2556	32.0	2905	41,000C	Sra HPBT/2.46"/Rem 9½
A2520	29.3	2554	32.5	2902	41,200C	Sra HPBT/2.46"/Rem 9½
A2460	28.8	2549	32.0	2897	41,200C	Sra HPBT/2.46"/Rem 9½
H450	40.0	2704	42.0	2857		
A2700	34.2	2680	36.0	2851	43,800C	Sra HPBT/2.46"/Rem 9½
IMR3031	30.0	2669	32.0	2790		
RL-7	28.0	2640	30.0	2762		
A3100	36.9	2403	41.0	2731	41,900C	Sra HPBT/2.46"/Rem 9½/(C)

100

Powder	STARTING Grs.	MV (fps)	MAXIMUM Grs.	MV (fps)	Press. (CUP/psi)	Comments
H414	38.0	2911	40.0	3102		
H380	36.0	2901	38.0	2998		
H4895	32.0	2686	35.0	2988		
W760	37.0	2754	39.0	2927		
H335	32.0	2804	34.0	2921		
W748	32.0	2742	34.0	2911		
BL-C(2)	32.0	2770	34.0	2900		
H4831	40.0	2717	42.0	2890		
H4350	38.0	2778	40.0	2881		
IMR4320	32.0	2659	34.0	2794		
A2015BR	27.0	2457	30.0	2792	43,100C	Hdy SP/2.5"/Rem 9½
IMR4350	36.0	2630	38.0	2789		
A4350	35.1	2447	39.0	2781	42,500C	Hdy SP/2.5"/Rem 9½
IMR4895	31.0	2621	33.0	2770		
A2495BR	28.8	2435	32.0	2767	43,600C	Hdy SP/2.5"/Rem 9½
A2520	28.8	2429	32.0	2760	42,300C	Hdy SP/2.5"/Rem 9½
IMR3031	29.0	2604	31.0	2740		
H450	38.0	2545	40.0	2727		
A2700	33.3	2549	35.0	2712	42,000C	Hdy SP/2.5"/Rem 9½
IMR4064	31.0	2576	33.0	2710		
H322	26.0	2488	29.0	2709		
RL-7	27.0	2564	29.0	2696		
A2460	27.9	2365	31.0	2687	38,700C	Hdy SP/2.5"/Rem 9½
A3100	36.9	2347	41.0	2667	40,600C	Hdy SP/2.5"/Rem 9½/(C)
A2230	27.0	2343	30.0	2662	40,400C	Hdy SP/2.5"/Rem 9½
IMR4831	36.0	2440	38.0	2590		

117-120

Powder	STARTING Grs.	MV (fps)	MAXIMUM Grs.	MV (fps)	Press. (CUP/psi)	Comments
H4831	40.0	2604	42.0	2789		
H414	35.0	2494	37.0	2719		
H380	33.0	2562	35.0	2718		
W760	35.0	2476	37.0	2688		
H4350	36.0	2545	38.0	2654		
A3100	36.9	2334	41.0	2652	43,700C	Sra SBT/2.515"/Rem 9½/(C)
A4350	33.3	2311	37.0	2626	42,300C	Sra SBT/2.515"/Rem 9½
IMR4895	30.0	2454	32.0	2602		
IMR4320	31.0	2472	33.0	2590		
IMR4064	30.0	2420	32.0	2579		
A2015BR	25.7	2262	28.5	2571	45,000C	Sra SBT/2.515"/Rem 9½
A2495BR	27.0	2259	30.0	2567	45,000C	Sra SBT/2.515"/Rem 9½
IMR4350	34.0	2441	36.0	2561		
A2520	27.0	2225	30.0	2528	44,300C	Sra SBT/2.515"/Rem 9½
IMR4831	35.0	2402	37.0	2525		
H450	37.0	2334	39.5	2516		
A2230	26.1	2208	29.0	2509	43,000C	Sra SBT/2.515"/Rem 9½
A2460	26.6	2198	29.5	2498	40,800C	Sra SBT/2.515"/Rem 9½
A2700	31.4	2340	33.0	2489	41,100C	Sra SBT/2.515"/Rem 9½

125

Powder	STARTING Grs.	MV (fps)	MAXIMUM Grs.	MV (fps)	Press. (CUP/psi)	Comments
H4831	39.0	2530	41.0	2736		
H414	34.0	2458	36.0	2672		
H380	32.0	2482	34.0	2660		
H4350	35.0	2494	37.0	2619		

Never exceed maximum load nor use any load exhibiting signs of excessive pressure. Begin at suggested starting load and work up carefully.

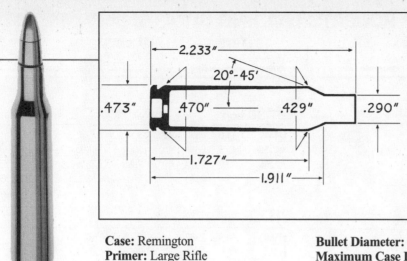

Case: Remington
Primer: Large Rifle
Barrel: 24″ Accurate
26″ Hodgdon
26″ Accurate (+P)
24″ Winchester (+P)

Bullet Diameter: 0.257″
Maximum Case Length: 2.233″
Trim to Length: 2.223″
Maximum Cartridge OAL: 2.775″
Minimum Cartridge OAL: 2.620″

In the first years of the 1930s, Ned Roberts began playing with the idea of necking down the 7x57mm Mauser cartridge to the quarter-bore. In that era, there was still a tremendous inertia toward designing cases with tapered bodies and sloping shoulders. This seems to have been a factor in his work for, besides necking down the case, Roberts reduced the shoulder angle from the 20.75° of the parent cartridge to only 15°.

When Remington commercialized this already popular wildcat chambering in 1934, they fortunately chose to keep the original shoulder angle of the 7x57mm Mauser, a much superior design.

For reasons that this author has never understood, factory 257 Roberts loads were severely handicapped until quite recently. Factory pressure specifications had been set to a very mild level and performance was equally mild. Since

257 Roberts factory cases were always among the most heavily constructed ever made, and the cartridge was never commercially chambered in anything but the strongest of guns, this situation seems doubly odd.

Recently the pressure specification was increased to a more reasonable level and a +P loading was introduced. With +P loads, performance practically duplicates the 6mm Remington, despite working at a considerably lower pressure—the result of a significantly larger bore. For this loading data, see the 257 Roberts +P entry.

Usable case capacity with a 100-grain bullet, seated normally, is about 53.2 grains of water. IMR4064, RL-19, H380, IMR4350, IMR4320, H414, H4350 and W760 are all good choices for loading the Roberts.

257 ROBERTS LOADING DATA

Powder	STARTING Grs.	MV (fps)	MAXIMUM Grs.	MV (fps)	Press. (CUP/psi)	Comments
Lead 100 RCBS						
A8700	47.7	2174	53.0	2471	32,200p	2.66″/CCI 200
60						
H335	44.0	3467	48.0	3885	46,400C	
BL-C(2)	44.0	3469	48.0	3834	45,900C	
H414	49.5	3566	54.0	3818	43,800C	
RL-15	43.0	3616	46.0	3806	46,500C	
H4895	42.0	3376	46.0	3805	45,000C	
IMR4895	42.0	3361	46.0	3774	44,900C	
IMR4064	42.0	3324	46.0	3759	44,700C	
W748	44.0	3454	47.0	3759	44,800C	
H380	45.0	3497	49.0	3752	46,200C	
W760	52.0	3619	53.0	3724	43,200C	
IMR4320	44.0	3397	47.0	3717	46,800C	
IMR3031	39.0	3292	43.0	3690	45,000C	
H4350	48.0	3290	51.0	3612	44,700C	

Powder	STARTING Grs.	MV (fps)	MAXIMUM Grs.	MV (fps)	Press. (CUP/psi)	Comments
60 con't						
IMR4350	47.0	3184	50.0	3555	44,000C	
IMR4831	49.0	3129	52.0	3540	38,600C	
RL-12	40.0	3377	43.0	3496	45,000C	
RL-19	50.0	3184	53.0	3405	41,500C	
H4831	49.0	2847	53.0	3382	33,600C	
RL-22	50.0	3137	53.0	3317	39,300C	

Caution: **Loads exceeding SAAMI OAL Maximum must be verified for bullet-to-rifling clearance and magazine functioning. Where a specific primer or bullet is indicated those components must be used, no substitutions! Where only a maximum load is shown, reduce starting load 10%, unless otherwise specified.**

Key: (C) = compressed charge; C = CUP; p = psi; Plink = Plinker; Bns = Barnes; Hdy = Hornady; Lap = Lapua; Nos = Nosler; Rem = Remington; Sra = Sierra; Spr = Speer; Win = Winchester.

Never exceed maximum load nor use any load exhibiting signs of excessive pressure. Begin at suggested starting load and work up carefully.

137

75

Powder	Grs.	MV (fps)	Grs.	MV (fps)	Press. (CUP/psi)	Comments
	—STARTING—		—MAXIMUM—			
H380	44.0	3258	48.0	3563	45,600C	
H4895	40.5	3201	44.0	3561	47,300C	
H414	48.0	3343	52.0	3555	45,300C	
H335	42.0	3161	46.0	3548	45,000C	
IMR4895	40.0	3184	44.0	3536	46,900C	
BL-C(2)	42.0	3094	46.0	3531	46,700C	
RL-15	41.0	3322	44.0	3480	46,500C	
W748	43.0	3209	45.0	3460	44,200C	
IMR4320	42.0	3147	45.0	3451	44,600C	
W760	49.0	3309	51.0	3444	44,600C	
H4350	47.0	3129	50.0	3422	44,000C	
IMR4064	40.0	3097	44.0	3419	44,300C	
IMR3031	38.0	3074	42.0	3407	46,400C	
IMR4350	46.0	3112	49.0	3344	44,100C	
IMR4831	49.0	3101	52.0	3329	40,200C	
RL-19	49.0	3094	52.0	3314	45,500C	
RL-12	38.0	3188	41.0	3310	46,000C	
H4831	49.0	2886	53.0	3307	37,500C	
A4350	42.3	2866	47.0	3257	43,600p	Sra HP/2.745"/CCI 200
A2700	43.7	3048	46.0	3243	44,800p	Sra HP/2.745"/CCI 200
RL-22	49.0	3039	52.0	3215	43,000C	
A2520	35.6	2789	39.5	3169	42,100p	Sra HP/2.745"/CCI 200
A3100	45.9	2783	51.0	3163	38,100p	Sra HP/2.745"/CCI 200/(C)

85

Powder	Grs.	MV (fps)	Grs.	MV (fps)	Press. (CUP/psi)	Comments
A4350	41.4	2728	46.0	3100	44,500p	Bns-X/2.77"/CCI 200
A2700	40.9	2868	43.0	3051	44,100p	Bns-X/2.77"/CCI 200
A3100	44.1	2667	49.0	3031	39,900p	Bns-X/2.77"/CCI 200
A2520	33.8	2622	37.5	2980	44,000p	Bns-X/2.77"/CCI 200

87-90

Powder	Grs.	MV (fps)	Grs.	MV (fps)	Press. (CUP/psi)	Comments
H4895	38.5	2954	42.0	3372	47,600C	
H414	46.0	3107	50.0	3368	44,400C	
H380	43.0	3083	47.0	3364	45,400C	
RL-15	40.0	3141	43.0	3329	47,000C	
W760	48.0	3151	49.0	3302	43,600C	
H335	39.0	2951	43.0	3300	44,400C	
IMR4895	39.0	2982	41.0	3294	46,200C	
H4831	48.0	2786	52.0	3236	39,500C	
BL-C(2)	40.0	2864	43.5	3231	45,000C	
IMR4320	40.0	2994	43.0	3210	46,000C	
VarGet			40.0	3208	45,300C	
W748	41.0	2944	43.0	3206	44,800C	
RL-19	47.0	3021	50.0	3183	46,000C	
IMR4831	48.0	2990	51.0	3180	43,000C	
IMR4064	40.0	2979	42.0	3170	46,100C	
IMR3031	38.0	2940	40.0	3161	46,600C	
RL-22	48.0	3000	51.0	3145	45,500C	
RL-12	36.0	2941	39.0	3087	45,500C	
IMR4350	44.0	2971	46.0	3066	44,400C	
A3100	45.0	2689	50.0	3056	44,000p	Sra HPBT/2.735"/CCI 200/(C)

87-90 con't

Powder	Grs.	MV (fps)	Grs.	MV (fps)	Press. (CUP/psi)	Comments
H4350	44.0	2890	46.0	3040	43,700C	
A4350	40.5	2641	45.0	3001	42,100p	Sra HPBT/2.735"/CCI 200
A2700	39.9	2810	42.0	2989	42,700p	Sra HPBT/2.735"/CCI 200
A2520	33.3	2593	37.0	2947	43,500p	Sra HPBT/2.735"/CCI 200

100

Powder	Grs.	MV (fps)	Grs.	MV (fps)	Press. (CUP/psi)	Comments
H380	40.5	2868	44.0	3108	46,600C	
H414	43.0	2919	45.0	3098	44,500C	
RL-15	38.0	2894	41.0	3046	46,000C	
H335	36.0	2776	39.0	3042	47,800C	
RL-22	46.0	2887	49.0	3025	47,000C	
IMR4320	36.0	2740	39.0	3012	46,200C	
H4831	45.0	2660	49.0	3010	44,100C	
IMR4831	44.0	2780	47.0	3007	45,400C	
RL-19	45.0	2880	48.0	2997	45,500C	
W760	45.0	2889	46.0	2990	43,400C	
H4895	35.0	2661	38.0	2990	46,100C	
VarGet			38.0	2981	44,900C	
H4350	43.0	2833	45.0	2970	45,400C	
IMR4350	42.0	2850	44.0	2966	45,200C	
BL-C(2)	36.0	2692	39.0	2958	45,400C	
H450	44.0	2702	46.5	2946	41,500C	
W748	36.0	2680	38.0	2898	44,000C	
A4350	40.1	2550	44.5	2898	44,100p	Nos BT/2.785"/CCI 200
A3100	44.1	2520	49.0	2864	39,900p	Nos BT/2.785"/CCI 200/(C)
IMR3031	36.0	2730	38.0	2861	46,200C	
A2700	39.0	2683	41.0	2854	44,000p	Nos BT/2.785"/CCI 200
IMR4064	36.0	2640	39.0	2843	44,900C	
IMR4895	34.0	2652	37.0	2826	45,100C	
A2520	31.5	2416	35.0	2745	43,400p	Nos BT/2.785"/CCI 200
A4350	36.9	2410	41.0	2739	42,700p	Bns-X/2.76"/CCI 200
A3100	41.4	2381	46.0	2706	37,800p	Bns-X/2.76"/CCI 200
A2700	37.1	2522	39.0	2683	42,700p	Bns-X/2.76"/CCI 200
A2520	30.6	2324	34.0	2641	42,700p	Bns-X/2.76"/CCI 200

117-120

Powder	Grs.	MV (fps)	Grs.	MV (fps)	Press. (CUP/psi)	Comments
RL-22	44.0	2689	47.0	2817	46,000C	
RL-15	36.0	2678	39.0	2809	47,500C	
RL-19	43.0	2670	46.0	2804	46,500C	
H4350	41.0	2660	43.0	2777	44,400C	
IMR4350	40.0	2629	42.0	2760	45,000C	
H4831	43.0	2479	46.0	2760	46,000C	
IMR4831	41.0	2549	44.0	2757	44,900C	
H380	37.0	2567	40.0	2754	45,900C	
A3100	43.2	2408	48.0	2736	43,700p	Sra SBT/2.775"/CCI 200/C
H414	39.5	2574	43.0	2720	44,200C	
W760	42.0	2620	43.0	2718	44,400C	
IMR7828	44.0	2560	46.0	2717	44,000C	
IMR4064	34.0	2490	36.0	2709	46,000C	
H4895	33.0	2433	36.0	2702	45,100C	
VarGet			35.0	2701	44,900C	
A4350	38.7	2376	43.0	2700	44,100p	Sra SBT/2.775"/CCI 200

Never exceed maximum load nor use any load exhibiting signs of excessive pressure. Begin at suggested starting load and work up carefully.

117-120 con't

Powder	STARTING Grs.	MV (fps)	MAXIMUM Grs.	MV (fps)	Press. (CUP/psi)	Comments
IMR4320	34.0	2480	37.0	2698	45,900C	
BL-C(2)	33.0	2402	36.0	2673	47,100C	
A2700	37.1	2462	39.0	2619	43,200p	Sra SBT/2.775"/CCI 200
A2520	30.6	2248	34.0	2555	42,700p	Sra SBT/2.775"/CCI 200

125

Powder	STARTING Grs.	MV (fps)	MAXIMUM Grs.	MV (fps)	Press. (CUP/psi)	Comments
RL-22	43.0	2666	46.0	2803	47,000C	
RL-19	42.0	2604	45.0	2748	47,000C	
H414	40.0	2539	42.0	2681	45,800C	
H4350	41.0	2540	43.0	2680	46,600C	
RL-15	34.0	2544	37.0	2680	47,000C	
H4831	43.0	2508	45.0	2677	46,200C	
H380	37.0	2557	39.0	2670	46,700C	
VarGet			33.5	2523	45,500C	

75

Powder	STARTING Grs.	MV (fps)	MAXIMUM Grs.	MV (fps)	Press. (CUP/psi)	Comments
W760			47.8	3420	42,500C	HP
A4350	44.1	2966	49.0	3370	47,200p	Sra HP/2.745"/CCI 200
A2700	44.7	3119	47.0	3318	48,600p	Sra HP/2.745"/CCI 200
A2520	36.9	2912	41.0	3309	48,100p	Sra HP/2.745"/CCI 200

85

Powder	STARTING Grs.	MV (fps)	MAXIMUM Grs.	MV (fps)	Press. (CUP/psi)	Comments
A4350	42.3	2802	47.0	3184	48,900p	Bns-X/2.77"/CCI 200
A2700	42.8	2959	45.0	3148	48,700p	Bns-X/2.77"/CCI 200
A2520	35.1	2709	39.0	3078	48,700p	Bns-X/2.77"/CCI 200

90

Powder	STARTING Grs.	MV (fps)	MAXIMUM Grs.	MV (fps)	Press. (CUP/psi)	Comments
A4350	42.3	2786	47.0	3166	49,900p	Sra HPBT/2.735"/CCI 200
A2700	41.8	2954	44.0	3143	50,300p	Sra HPBT/2.735"/CCI 200
A2520	34.7	2692	38.5	3059	48,200p	Sra HPBT/2.735"/CCI 200
WMR			48.7	2990	45,200p	Win OPE

100

Powder	STARTING Grs.	MV (fps)	MAXIMUM Grs.	MV (fps)	Press. (CUP/psi)	Comments
A4350	41.9	2682	46.5	3048	50,800p	Nos BT/2.785"/CCI 200
A2700	40.9	2761	43.0	2937	49,200p	Nos BT/2.785"/CCI 200
WMR			48.7	2935	48,300p	Win ST
A3100	43.2	2577	48.0	2928	47,800p	Bns-X/2.76"/CCI 200/(C)
A4350	39.6	2570	44.0	2920	50,300p	Bns-X/2.76"/CCI 200
A2520	33.8	2525	37.5	2869	48,700p	Nos BT/2.785"/CCI 200
A2520	33.3	2475	37.0	2813	49,900p	Bns-X/2.76"/CCI 200
A2700	39.0	2640	41.0	2808	47,800p	Bns-X/2.76"/CCI 200

117

Powder	STARTING Grs.	MV (fps)	MAXIMUM Grs.	MV (fps)	Press. (CUP/psi)	Comments
A4350	39.6	2410	44.0	2739	48,400p	Sra SBT/2.775"/CCI 200
A2700	39.0	2532	41.0	2694	48,000p	Sra SBT/2.775"/CCI 200
A2520	32.9	2357	36.5	2678	49,300p	Sra SBT/2.775"/CCI 200

120

Powder	STARTING Grs.	MV (fps)	MAXIMUM Grs.	MV (fps)	Press. (CUP/psi)	Comments
WMR			45.6	2795	55,000p	Win BT

Caution: Loads exceeding SAAMI OAL Maximum must be verified for bullet-to-rifling clearance and magazine functioning. Where a specific primer or bullet is indicated those components must be used, no substitutions! Where only a maximum load is shown, reduce starting load 10%, unless otherwise specified.

Key: (C) = compressed charge; C = CUP; p = psi; Plink = Plinker; Bns = Barnes; Hdy = Hornady; Lap = Lapua; Nos = Nosler; Rem = Remington; Sra = Sierra; Spr = Speer; Win = Winchester.

Never exceed maximum load nor use any load exhibiting signs of excessive pressure. Begin at suggested starting load and work up carefully.

139

257

Roberts
Ackley Improved
(40°)

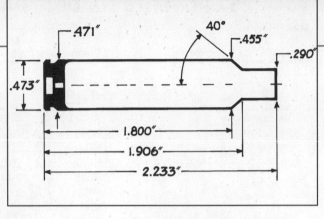

Case: Remington
Primer: Large Rifle
Barrel: 26″ Accurate
Bullet Diameter: 0.257″
Maximum Case Length: 2.233″

Trim to Length: 2.223″
Maximum Cartridge OAL:
 Gun Dependent
Minimum Cartridge OAL:
 Bullet Dependent

There are several versions of this fine cartridge, but this is the most common. It is a splendid example of Dr. Parker Ackley's finest work. By the simple expedient of reducing body taper, moving the shoulder back slightly and increasing the shoulder angle, Ackley was able to significantly increase the capacity of many existing cartridges.

Ackley's designs offered other significant benefits. First, case stretching was greatly reduced because headspace control was increased. Second, factory loads could be safely fired in the improved chamber. Finally, extraction was eased.

The effectiveness of this particular wildcat can best be judged by comparing it to the 1/2-inch longer 25-06. When loaded to equal pressures and chambered in equal-length barrels, the 257 Ackley Improved generates virtually identical velocities.

Current standards would hold that any quarter-bore chambering is best restricted to hunting pronghorn, smaller species of deer and varmints. Nevertheless, loaded with proper bullets, the higher performance 25s are fully capable on big game for those who have the skill and dedication to place their shots properly and avoid shooting at excessive ranges—the same limitations hold for any chambering!

With lighter bullets, this is an explosive performer for truly long-range varminting. Usable case capacity with 100-grain bullet, seated normally, is about 62 grains of water. A4350 and A3100 both provide excellent performance.

257 ROBERTS ACKLEY IMPROVED (40°) LOADING DATA

Powder	Grs.	MV (fps)	Grs.	MV (fps)	Press. (CUP/psi)	Comments
75						
A2700	50.4	3435	53.0	3654	59,100p	Sra HP/2.79″/CCI 200
A4350	49.5	3213	55.0	3651	58,900p	Sra HP/2.79″/CCI 200
A3100	50.4	2966	56.0	3371	45,600p	Sra HP/2.79″/CCI 200
A8700	54.9	2496	61.0	2836	37,000p	Sra HP/2.79″/CCI 200/(C)
85						
A4350	47.7	3056	53.0	3473	61,700p	Bns-X/2.865″/CCI 200
A2700	48.5	3230	51.0	3436	60,500p	Bns-X/2.865″/CCI 200
A3100	50.4	2931	56.0	3331	53,000p	Bns-X/2.865″/CCI 200
A8700	54.9	2435	61.0	2767	40,200p	Bns-X/2.865″/CCI 200/(C)
90						
A4350	47.7	3021	53.0	3433	59,900p	Sra HPBT/2.835″/CCI 200
A3100	50.4	2907	56.0	3303	53,200p	Sra HPBT/2.835″/CCI 200
A2700	46.6	3100	49.0	3298	57,400p	Sra HPBT/2.835″/CCI 200
A8700	54.9	2448	61.0	2782	40,600p	Sra HPBT/2.835″/CCI 200/(C)

Powder	Grs.	MV (fps)	Grs.	MV (fps)	Press. (CUP/psi)	Comments
100						
A4350	46.8	2898	52.0	3293	61,100p	Bns-X/2.885″/CCI 200
A4350	46.4	2886	51.5	3279	61,600p	Nos BT/2.945″/CCI 200
A3100	49.5	2825	55.0	3210	56,600p	Nos BT/2.945″/CCI 200/(C)
A2700	47.5	3008	50.0	3200	59,900p	Bns-X/2.885″/CCI 200
A2700	46.1	2991	48.5	3182	59,600p	Nos BT/2.945″/CCI 200
A3100	49.5	2798	55.0	3179	55,200p	Bns-X/2.885″/CCI 200
A8700	54.9	2380	61.0	2705	39,500p	Nos BT/2.945″/CCI 200/(C)
115						
A3100	48.6	2727	54.0	3099	59,800p	Nos Part./2.945″/CCI 200/(C)
A4350	44.6	2685	49.5	3051	60,200p	Nos Part./2.945″/CCI 200
A2700	44.7	2831	47.0	3012	61,400p	Nos Part./2.945″/CCI 200
120						
A3100	48.6	2689	54.0	3056	60,000p	Spr SBT/2.92″/CCI 200/(C)
A4350	44.6	2660	49.5	3023	61,700p	Spr SBT/2.92″/CCI 200
A2700	44.7	2790	47.0	2968	63,500p	Spr SBT/2.92″/CCI 200

Never exceed maximum load nor use any load exhibiting signs of excessive pressure. Begin at suggested starting load and work up carefully.

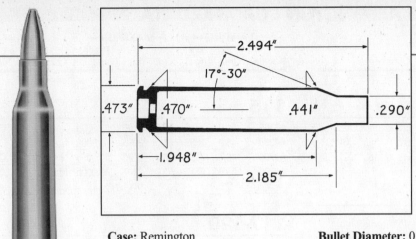

Case: Remington
Primer: Large Rifle
Barrel: 25" Accurate
26" Hodgdon
23" Vihtavuori

Bullet Diameter: 0.257"
Maximum Case Length: 2.494"
Trim to length: 2.484"
Maximum Cartridge OAL: 3.250"
Minimum Cartridge OAL: 3.010"

In 1920, A. O. Neider took the already ubiquitous 30-06 case and necked it down to 25-caliber, making no other changes. Despite the relatively large capacity of the case, performance was never particularly startling simply because the powders then available were not up to the task. With the general availability of slower powders, following WWII, performance finally began to live up to expectations.

In 1969, Remington commercialized this chambering and thus converted it from a wildcat that had always had a limited amount of popularity to a factory hot-rod with a fair share of continuing popularity.

Factory pressure is toward the top end of the normal range and performance is therefore impressive. Nevertheless, this does not seem to this author to be as good a dual-purpose chambering as some might suggest. In the varmint field, the 6mm Remington seems to have a clear edge, since

it provides a flatter trajectory with varmint bullets. In the big game field, the best 25-06 loads take a distant back seat to the 270 in both delivered energy and trajectory.

Nevertheless, the 25-06 is a good compromise for those with sensitive shoulders. It is fully capable, despite what some would proclaim, for use against big game to the size of elk. The key is proper bullet choice and placement. A well placed premium-grade 25-06 bullet will always be more effective than a poorly performing or poorly placed bullet delivering twice the energy.

Usable case capacity with a 100-grain bullet, seated normally, is about 64.0 grains of water. IMR4350, H4831, IMR7828, H1000, A3100, RL-22, H450, H4350, H414, IMR4831, H1000 and A3100 have all been noted as good performers in the 25-06.

25-06 REMINGTON LOADING DATA

Powder	STARTING Grs.	MV (fps)	MAXIMUM Grs.	MV (fps)	Press. (CUP/psi)	Comments
Lead 100						
A8700	48.6	2124	54.0	2414	29,500p	Consistent
75						
A4350	51.3	3247	57.0	3690	60,900p	Sra HP/3.065"/CCI 250
H414	49.5	3537	54.0	3672	48,300C	
W760	52.0	3540	54.0	3656	48,000C	
RL-19	56.0	3233	61.0	3599	48,000C	
H380	47.0	3340	51.0	3573	47,400C	
RL-15	48.0	3351	51.0	3544	47,500C	
A3100	54.0	3108	60.0	3532	52,500p	Sra HP/3.065"/CCI 250/(C)
A2700	47.5	3318	50.0	3530	58,300p	Sra HP/3.065"/CCI 250
RL-22	56.0	3199	61.0	3472	45,400C	
IMR4350	51.0	3251	54.0	3469	50,700C	
IMR4320	46.0	3272	49.0	3452	51,600C	
IMR4895	44.0	3220	47.0	3440	51,900C	

Powder	STARTING Grs.	MV (fps)	MAXIMUM Grs.	MV (fps)	Press. (CUP/psi)	Comments
75 con't						
RL-12	47.0	3317	50.0	3436	48,000C	
H4350	51.0	3209	54.0	3419	48,300C	
IMR4064	44.0	3157	47.0	3419	50,200C	
H1000	59.0	3133	62.0	3359	38,700C	

Caution: Loads exceeding SAAMI OAL Maximum must be verified for bullet-to-rifling clearance and magazine functioning. Where a specific primer or bullet is indicated those components must be used, no substitutions! Where only a maximum load is shown, reduce starting load 10%, unless otherwise specified.

Key: (C) = compressed charge; C = CUP; p = psi; Plink = Plinker; Bns = Barnes; Hdy = Hornady; Lap = Lapua; Nos = Nosler; Rem = Remington; Sra = Sierra; Spr = Speer; Win = Winchester.

Never exceed maximum load nor use any load exhibiting signs of excessive pressure. Begin at suggested starting load and work up carefully.

141

85

Powder	Grs.	MV (fps)	Grs.	MV (fps)	Press. (CUP/psi)	Comments
A3100	54.0	3065	60.0	3483	60,900p	Bns-X/3.165"/CCI 250/(C)
A4350	48.6	3033	54.0	3447	61,800p	Bns-X/3.165"/CCI 250
A2700	49.4	3213	52.0	3418	62,700p	Bns-X/3.165"/CCI 250

86-90

Powder	Grs.	MV (fps)	Grs.	MV (fps)	Press. (CUP/psi)	Comments
H414	47.0	3114	51.0	3470	50,200C	
RL-19	54.0	3148	58.0	3456	49,500C	
W760	49.0	3304	51.0	3441	50,000C	
RL-22	55.0	3209	59.0	3423	49,000C	
IMR4831	53.0	3147	56.0	3414	49,900C	
H380	45.0	3206	49.0	3411	50,000C	
N165	56.0	3013	62.0	3410	53,660p	Spr Sptz SP
IMR7828	55.0	3130	57.0	3404	48,400C	
H4350	50.0	3094	54.0	3393	51,500C	
IMR4320	44.0	3170	47.0	3364	51,400C	
N160			56.3	3360	50,763p	HP Rem
RL-15	45.0	3111	48.0	3343	48,500C	
WMR			58.1	3340	52,700p	Win OPE
H1000	59.0	3098	62.0	3335	46,000C	
IMR4895	42.0	3111	45.0	3332	51,200C	
IMR4350	50.0	3130	53.0	3323	50,900C	
H450	50.5	3042	55.0	3322	47,900C	
IMR4064	43.0	3098	46.0	3319	50,700C	
RL-12	44.0	3171	47.0	3305	49,000C	
N140			47.5	3260	50,763p	HP Rem
H870	60.0	2927	65.0	3230	43,900C	

100

Powder	Grs.	MV (fps)	Grs.	MV (fps)	Press. (CUP/psi)	Comments
A3100	53.1	2944	59.0	3345	59,500p	Nos BT/3.19"/CCI 250/(C)
A4350	48.6	2928	54.0	3327	61,800p	Nos BT/3.19"/CCI 250
H4350	49.0	2904	52.0	3296	51,500C	
H4831	51.0	2797	55.0	3294	49,800C	
WMR			58.1	3280	55,600p	Win ST
IMR4831	51.0	2820	54.0	3272	49,400C	
IMR7828	54.0	2854	56.0	3269	49,000C	
IMR4350	49.0	2932	51.0	3254	51,200C	
H1000	58.0	3023	61.0	3245	50,500C	
A3100	51.3	2853	57.0	3242	62,800p	Bns-X/3.14"/CCI 250/(C)
H870	60.0	2888	65.0	3235	46,800C	
RL-22	52.0	3088	56.0	3218	49,000C	
N165	53.1	2915	58.6	3212	53,660p	Spr BTSP
A4350	46.4	2809	51.5	3192	60,000p	Bns-X/3.14"/CCI 250
RL-19	51.0	3007	55.0	3180	48,500C	
A2700	48.5	2986	51.0	3177	57,400p	Nos BT/3.19"/CCI 250
IMR4320	42.0	2960	45.0	3170	51,800C	
H414	41.5	2760	47.0	3093	50,500C	
A2700	46.6	2899	49.0	3084	59,600p	Bns-X/3.14"/CCI 250
W760	43.0	2878	45.0	3069	50,100C	
A8700	57.6	2549	64.0	2897	50,300p	Bns-X/3.14"/CCI 250
A8700	57.6	2456	64.0	2791	40,200p	Nos BT/3.19"/CCI 250/(C)

115

Powder	Grs.	MV (fps)	Grs.	MV (fps)	Press. (CUP/psi)	Comments
A3100	51.3	2812	57.0	3196	62,800p	Nos Part./3.195"/CCI 250
A4350	45.9	2689	51.0	3056	59,000p	Nos Part./3.195"/CCI 250
A2700	43.7	2750	46.0	2926	62,900p	Nos Part./3.195"/CCI 250
A8700	55.8	2417	62.0	2747	40,000p	Nos Part./3.195"/CCI 250/(C)

117-120

Powder	Grs.	MV (fps)	Grs.	MV (fps)	Press. (CUP/psi)	Comments
A3100	51.3	2750	57.0	3125	63,000p	Sra HPBT/3.12"/CCI 250
H4831	48.0	2760	52.0	3076	49,100C	(117-gr.)
IMR7828	52.0	2898	55.0	3064	51,800C	
WMR			54.3	3055	60,100p	Win BT
A4350	46.8	2682	52.0	3048	62,100p	Sra HPBT/3.12"/CCI 250
H4831	47.0	2726	51.0	3040	49,400C	(120-gr.)
H870	59.0	2752	64.0	3032	44,400C	(117-gr.)
H870	59.0	2794	64.0	3024	48,000C	(120-gr.)
H1000	53.0	2819	57.0	3019	51,500C	(117-gr.)
H1000	53.0	2794	57.0	3007	51,700C	(120-gr.)
IMR4831	47.0	2823	50.0	2994	49,100C	
IMR4350	45.0	2811	48.0	2984	51,800C	
H450	48.0	2694	52.0	2981	48,400C	(117-gr.)
H4350	45.0	2794	48.0	2970	51,500C	(117-gr.)
A2700	46.6	2778	49.0	2955	62,300p	Sra HPBT/3.12"/CCI 250
RL-22	49.0	2784	53.0	2951	48,000C	
RL-19	47.0	2719	51.0	2909	47,500C	
N160			49.2	2890	50,763p	Rem SP
IMR4320	40.0	2649	43.0	2839	51,400C	
N165	46.0	2576	51.5	2833	53,660p	Spr Sptz SP
A8700	55.8	2331	62.0	2649	40,100p	Sra HPBT/3.12"/CCI 250/(C)

125

Powder	Grs.	MV (fps)	Grs.	MV (fps)	Press. (CUP/psi)	Comments
H870	58.0	2737	64.0	3020	50,300C	
H1000	52.0	2612	56.0	2894	50,000C	
RL-22	48.0	2668	52.0	2853	47,500C	
RL-19	46.0	2611	50.0	2833	47,500C	
H4831	45.0	2510	49.0	2770	49,400C	

Caution: Loads exceeding SAAMI OAL Maximum must be verified for bullet-to-rifling clearance and magazine functioning. Where a specific primer or bullet is indicated those components must be used, no substitutions! Where only a maximum load is shown, reduce starting load 10%, unless otherwise specified.

Key: (C) = compressed charge; C = CUP; p = psi; Plink = Plinker; Bns = Barnes; Hdy = Hornady; Lap = Lapua; Nos = Nosler; Rem = Remington; Sra = Sierra; Spr = Speer; Win = Winchester.

Never exceed maximum load nor use any load exhibiting signs of excessive pressure. Begin at suggested starting load and work up carefully.

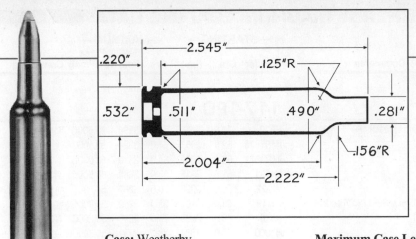

Case: Weatherby
Primer: Large Rifle
Barrel: 26" Accurate
      26" Hodgdon
Bullet Diameter: 0.257"

Maximum Case Length: 2.545"
Trim to Length: 2.535"
Maximum Cartridge OAL: 3.25"
Minimum Cartridge OAL:
      Bullet Dependent

In the late 1940s, Roy Weatherby dropped this bombshell on the shooting world. The 257 Weatherby can be viewed as the original hyper-velocity hunting cartridge. Original loadings, working at very high pressures, launched 100-grain bullets to an advertised 3600 fps!

In an era when most shooters were still trying to reconcile the idea of 3000 fps hunting cartridges, this chambering was viewed as almost magical by many shooters. Roy, himself, used it to cleanly dispatch trophy examples of almost every major species that walks on the face of the earth. His exploits, and those of others, convinced many shooters that there really was something unique about the killing powder of hyper-velocity chamberings.

Nevertheless, by current standards, the 257 Weatherby Magnum is considered by most "experts" to be a marginal cartridge on game the size of elk and inadequate for use against larger species. However, as with all cartridges, this very much depends on two factors, bullet performance and shot placement. With the recent development of truly superior premium-grade big game bullets, the 257 Weatherby can be counted on to deliver even better performance than Mr. Weatherby could ever have imagined.

With a usable capacity of about 85 grains of water, only slower powders can be considered useful. RL-22, IMR4831, H4831, H870, IMR7828 and A8700 have all shown impressive results.

257 WEATHERBY MAGNUM LOADING DATA

Powder	STARTING Grs.	MV (fps)	MAXIMUM Grs.	MV (fps)	Press. (CUP/psi)	Comments
75						
RL-22	72.0	3477	77.0	3880	54,000C	
H4831	67.0	3467	73.0	3849	53,300C	
IMR7828	68.0	3562	73.0	3824	51,400C	
IMR4831	66.0	3581	70.0	3810	52,400C	
RL-19	69.0	3470	74.0	3724	50,000C	
H4350	62.0	3497	65.0	3714	51,900C	
IMR4350	61.0	3490	64.0	3692	51,600C	
H870	75.5	3359	82.0	3658	48,200C	
H1000	76.0	3160	81.0	3368	38,200C	
85						
A4350	61.8	3490	65.0	3713	62,000p	Bns-X/3.150"/Fed 215
A3100	66.5	3435	70.0	3654	61,200p	Bns-X/3.150"/Fed 215
A8700	85.5	3318	90.0	3530	51,500p	Bns-X/3.150"/ Fed 215/(C)

Powder	STARTING Grs.	MV (fps)	MAXIMUM Grs.	MV (fps)	Press. (CUP/psi)	Comments
87-90						
H4831	66.0	3386	72.0	3713	51,900C	
RL-22	69.0	3366	74.0	3684	54,000C	
IMR7828	66.0	3345	71.0	3677	50,900C	
IMR4831	64.0	3366	68.0	3660	51,600C	
H870	75.5	3333	82.0	3640	48,900C	
IMR4350	60.0	3420	63.0	3581	52,000C	
H4350	60.0	3380	63.0	3550	49,800C	
RL-19	67.0	3232	72.0	3549	50,600C	
H1000	75.0	3049	80.0	3308	40,400C	

➤➤➤➤➤➤➤➤➤➤➤➤➤➤➤➤➤➤➤➤➤➤➤➤

100

Powder	STARTING Grs.	MV (fps)	MAXIMUM Grs.	MV (fps)	Press. (CUP/psi)	Comments
A4350	59.4	3301	62.5	3512	61,100C	Hdy SP/3.180"/Fed 215
RL-22	68.0	3291	73.0	3503	52,500C	
RL-19	66.0	3222	71.0	3472	51,600C	
IMR7828	64.0	3241	69.0	3466	51,600C	
H870	73.5	3127	80.0	3463	53,000C	
A3100	65.6	3253	69.0	3461	58,500C	Hdy SP/3.180"/Fed 215
H4831	62.5	3089	68.0	3436	52,300C	
IMR4831	62.0	3212	66.0	3409	52,200C	
A8700	85.5	3173	90.0	3375	58,000C	Hdy SP/3.180"/Fed 215/(C)
IMR4350	58.0	3241	61.0	3364	51,300C	
H1000	75.0	3090	80.0	3351	46,900C	
H4350	59.0	3129	62.0	3319	51,200C	

115

Powder	STARTING Grs.	MV (fps)	MAXIMUM Grs.	MV (fps)	Press. (CUP/psi)	Comments
A8700	81.7	3130	86.0	3330	55,300	Nos SP/3.255"/Fed 215/(C)/*
A3100	63.7	3086	67.0	3283	61,100	Nos SP/3.255"/Fed 215/*
A4350	56.1	3051	59.0	3246	59,600	Nos SP/3.255"/Fed 215/*

*Exceeds recommended OAL maximum.

Caution: **Loads exceeding SAAMI OAL Maximum must be verified for bullet-to-rifling clearance and magazine functioning. Where a specific primer or bullet is indicated those components must be used, no substitutions! Where only a maximum load is shown, reduce starting load 10%, unless otherwise specified.**

Key: (C) = compressed charge; C = CUP; p = psi; Plink = Plinker; Bns = Barnes; Hdy = Hornady; Lap = Lapua; Nos = Nosler; Rem = Remington; Sra = Sierra; Spr = Speer; Win = Winchester.

117-120

Powder	STARTING Grs.	MV (fps)	MAXIMUM Grs.	MV (fps)	Press. (CUP/psi)	Comments
H870	70.0	2955	76.0	3336	53,600C	(117-gr.)
IMR7828	62.0	2951	67.0	3324	52,100C	
IMR4831	60.0	2959	64.0	3310	52,800C	
H4831	61.5	2915	66.0	3282	52,500C	(117-gr.)
RL-22	65.0	3098	70.0	3267	54,000C	
RL-19	63.0	3107	68.0	3259	54,000C	
H870	69.0	2888	76.0	3240	53,200C	(120-gr.)
H1000	73.0	2884	78.0	3231	50,800C	(117-gr.)
H1000	73.0	2884	78.0	3231	50,800C	(120-gr.)
H4831	61.5	3009	65.0	3220	51,500C	(120-gr.)
IMR4350	57.0	2859	60.0	3184	52,000C	
H4350	56.0	2874	60.0	3144	50,600C	(117-gr.)

120

Powder	STARTING Grs.	MV (fps)	MAXIMUM Grs.	MV (fps)	Press. (CUP/psi)	Comments
A8700	80.8	3067	85.0	3263	55,600	Spr SBT/3.215"/Fed 215/(C)
A3100	62.7	3018	66.0	3211	61,100	Spr SBT/3.215"/Fed 215
A4350	56.1	2999	59.0	3190	60,100	Spr SBT/3.215"/Fed 215

125

Powder	STARTING Grs.	MV (fps)	MAXIMUM Grs.	MV (fps)	Press. (CUP/psi)	Comments
H1000	72.0	2841	77.0	3184	53,100C	
RL-22	64.0	2955	69.0	3177	54,000C	
H4831	60.0	2880	64.0	3164	52,000C	
H870	67.0	2740	74.0	3139	52,400C	
RL-19	62.0	2980	67.0	3117	53,400C	

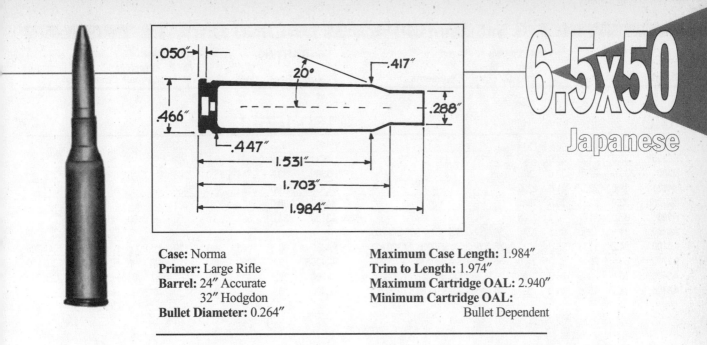

6.5x50
Japanese

Case: Norma
Primer: Large Rifle
Barrel: 24″ Accurate
        32″ Hodgdon
Bullet Diameter: 0.264″

Maximum Case Length: 1.984″
Trim to Length: 1.974″
Maximum Cartridge OAL: 2.940″
Minimum Cartridge OAL:
        Bullet Dependent

This small semi-rimmed cartridge was popularized in the U.S. when large numbers of war souvenirs were returned to this country after WWII. With its limited capacity and mild chamber pressures, ballistics can best be described as anemic. At normal hunting ranges, performance is similar to the 30-30, not much by military standards of the era.

Generally, Arisaka rifles were among the strongest and safest of military shoulder arms ever produced by any nation. However, during the later stages of WWII, some were produced with cast steel components. These rifles were and are absolutely unsafe to fire with any normal load, a fact which Parker Ackley clearly demonstrated. For this reason, we strongly advise that any Arisaka of questionable heritage be carefully checked out by a competent gunsmith before any firing with any ammunition. Somewhere there is that cast-receiver Arisaka that has never been fired—that gun is a bomb just waiting to explode in someone's face!

H380, H335 and H4895 provide good ballistics and accuracy in this little 6.5.

6.5x50mm JAPANESE LOADING DATA

Powder	STARTING Grs.	MV (fps)	MAXIMUM Grs.	MV (fps)	Press. (CUP/psi)	Comments
85						
A2700	34.2	2557	36.0	2720	33,600p	Sra HP/2.625″/CCI 200
A2495BR	32.3	2524	34.0	2685	28,900p	Sra HP/2.625″/CCI 200
A4350	36.0	2347	40.0	2667	31,300p	Sra HP/2.625″/CCI 200/(C)
A3100	36.0	2116	40.0	2405	24,000p	Sra HP/2.625″/CCI 200/(C)
100						
H4895	35.0	2508	37.0	2717		
H380	39.0	2449	42.0	2686		
H335	36.0	2514	38.0	2670		
BL-C(2)	36.0	2502	38.0	2642		
A2495BR	31.4	2470	33.0	2628	34,900p	Hdy SP/2.7″/CCI 200
A4350	35.1	2311	39.0	2626	37,200p	Hdy SP/2.7″/CCI 200/(C)
A2700	33.3	2421	35.0	2576	36,300p	Hdy SP/2.7″/CCI 200
H450	39.0	2339	41.0	2451		
H4831	39.0	2350	41.0	2424		
A3100	36.0	2109	40.0	2397	27,600p	Hdy SP/2.7″/CCI 200/(C)

Powder	STARTING Grs.	MV (fps)	MAXIMUM Grs.	MV (fps)	Press. (CUP/psi)	Comments
120						
H335	35.0	2441	37.0	2597		
H380	38.0	2424	41.0	2595		
BL-C(2)	35.0	2439	37.0	2566		
H4895	33.0	2368	35.0	2505		
H4831	39.0	2300	41.0	2429		
H450	39.0	2290	41.0	2404		
129						
A4350	32.4	2062	36.0	2343	37,800p	Hdy SP/2.77″/CCI 200
A2495BR	28.5	2138	30.0	2274	37,700p	Hdy SP/2.77″/CCI 200
A2700	31.4	2131	33.0	2267	38,100p	Hdy SP/2.77″/CCI 200
A3100	34.2	1953	38.0	2219	31,500p	Hdy SP/2.77″/CCI 200

▶▶▶▶▶▶▶▶▶▶▶▶▶▶▶▶▶▶▶▶▶▶▶▶▶

Never exceed maximum load nor use any load exhibiting signs of excessive pressure. Begin at suggested starting load and work up carefully.

140

Powder	Grs.	MV (fps)	Grs.	MV (fps)	Press. (CUP/psi)	Comments
H335	33.0	2219	35.0	2414		
H4895	32.0	2186	34.0	2407		
H380	36.0	2249	39.0	2396		
H4831	38.0	2222	41.0	2392		
BL-C(2)	33.0	2191	35.0	2388		
H450	37.0	2177	40.0	2360		
A4350	31.5	1980	35.0	2250	36,300p	Sra SBT/2.85"/CCI 200
A3100	34.2	1973	38.0	2242	36,300p	Sra SBT/2.85"/CCI 200/(C)
A2700	30.4	2045	32.0	2176	36,800p	Sra SBT/2.85"/CCI 200
A2495BR	26.6	2035	28.0	2165	35,900p	Sra SBT/2.85"/CCI 200
A8700	38.7	1596	43.0	1814	26,400p	Sra SBT/2.85"/CCI 200/(C)

160-165

Powder	Grs.	MV (fps)	Grs.	MV (fps)	Press. (CUP/psi)	Comments
H450	36.0	2197	38.0	2403		
H4831	36.0	2201	38.0	2393		
H380	33.0	2214	35.0	2366		
BL-C(2)	31.0	2181	33.0	2337		
H4895	30.0	2118	32.0	2334		
A3100	34.2	1897	38.0	2156	36,600p	Hdy RN/2.795"/CCI 200/(C)
A4350	30.6	1865	34.0	2119	35,900p	Hdy RN/2.795"/CCI 200
A2495BR	28.5	1983	30.0	2110	38,700p	Hdy RN/2.795"/CCI 200
A2700	30.4	1938	32.0	2062	37,800p	Hdy RN/2.795"/CCI 200
A8700	38.7	1566	43.0	1779	27,800p	Hdy RN/2.795"/CCI 200/(C)

Caution: Loads exceeding SAAMI OAL Maximum must be verified for bullet-to-rifling clearance and magazine functioning. Where a specific primer or bullet is indicated those components must be used, no substitutions! Where only a maximum load is shown, reduce starting load 10%, unless otherwise specified.

Key: (C) = compressed charge; C = CUP; p = psi; Plink = Plinker; Bns = Barnes; Hdy = Hornady; Lap = Lapua; Nos = Nosler; Rem = Remington; Sra = Sierra; Spr = Speer; Win = Winchester.

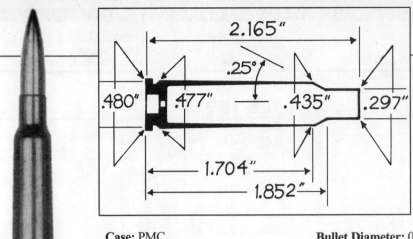

6.5x55
Swedish Mauser

Case: PMC
Primer: Large Rifle
Barrel: 24″ Accurate
28″ Hodgdon
26½″ Vihtavuori

Bullet Diameter: 0.264″
Maximum Case Length: 2.165″
Trim to Length: 2.155″
Maximum Cartridge OAL: 3.149″
Minimum Cartridge OAL: 3.025″

Adopted in 1894, the 6.5mm Swede is one of the original Mauser chamberings and is a unique cartridge case—head diameter is 0.477″ while most Mauser cartridges measure 0.470″, a feature shared with the '06 family of cartridges. For this reason, tempting as it might be, do not form 6.5mm Swedish cartridges from any other case. Resulting cases will chamber, fire and usually extract normally, but the excessive chamber diameter near the case head invites a ruptured case. That is almost certain to eventually happen...with devastating results.

In deference to older guns, featuring weaker designs, maximum chamber pressure is on the mild side and performance is therefore limited. Nevertheless, the 6.5mm Swedish offers surprising ballistics—it can launch a 140-grain bullet at over 2600 fps compared to the 7mm-08 Rem-

ington launching a 140-grain bullet at 2800 fps. With proper hunting spitzers, delivered energy at 200 yards is not much different.

Worldwide, the biggest market for this cartridge has long been as a preferred target chambering for 300 meter target competition in Europe, where it has reigned supreme for generations. A recent influx of surplus rifles and ammunition is driving a resurgence of popularity in the U.S.

This well-balanced and mild-mannered chambering has a lot to offer recoil-sensitive shooters who are looking for a chambering appropriate for smaller species of big game.

Usable case capacity with a 100-grain bullet, seated normally, is about 56.8 grains of water. H380, A3100, IMR4350 and RL-22 are noted performers in this old Mauser-designed chambering.

6.5x55mm SWEDISH MAUSER LOADING DATA

Lead 140 RCBS

Powder	STARTING Grs.	MV (fps)	MAXIMUM Grs.	MV (fps)	Press. (CUP/psi)	Comments
A4350	39.6	2218	44.0	2521	43,500p	3.02″/CCI 200
A2700	39.0	2358	41.0	2509	46,100p	3.02″/CCI 200
A3100	42.3	2179	47.0	2476	40,200p	3.02″/CCI 200/(C)
A2495BR	29.7	2083	33.0	2367	44,800p	3.02″/CCI 200
A2520	30.6	2079	34.0	2362	44,600p	3.02″/CCI 200
A8700	47.7	1932	53.0	2196	32,600p	3.02″/CCI 200/(C)

70-85

Powder	STARTING Grs.	MV (fps)	MAXIMUM Grs.	MV (fps)	Press. (CUP/psi)	Comments
N150	44.8	3153	47.5	3416	46,412p	Norma 70-gr. RN
N140			45.1	3400	44,962p	Norma 77-gr. SP
N133			42.4	3380	44,962p	Norma 77-gr. SP
N135			44.1	3380	44,962p	Norma 77-gr.SP
N140			44.4	3280	44,962p	Norma 80-gr. FMJ
N150	43.9	3002	46.1	3252	46,412p	Sra 85-gr. HP

>>>>>>>>>>>>>>>>>>>>>>>>>>>>>>

Never exceed maximum load nor use any load exhibiting signs of excessive pressure. Begin at suggested starting load and work up carefully.

87-100

Powder	—STARTING— Grs.	MV (fps)	—MAXIMUM— Grs.	MV (fps)	Press. (CUP/psi)	Comments
IMR4831	47.0	3049	50.0	3199		
RL-22	50.0	3044	53.0	3196		
IMR4320	41.0	3051	44.0	3195		
RL-15	41.0	3058	44.0	3181		
RL-19	49.0	3027	52.0	3177		
IMR4064	41.0	3042	44.0	3171		
H414	45.0	2966	47.0	3139		
H4895	39.0	2900	42.0	3098		
A2700	45.6	2907	48.0	3093	50,100p	Hdy SP/2.975"/CCI 200
H380	43.0	2934	45.0	3091		
H335	39.0	2884	42.5	3090		
IMR4350	45.0	2960	48.0	3090		
H450	48.0	2840	51.0	3073		
W760	43.0	2898	46.0	3070		
IMR7828	48.0	2897	51.0	3044		
H4350	46.0	2811	49.0	3033		
N160	46.1	2748	51.0	3024	46,612p	Lapua FMJ 341
BL-C(2)	42.0	2869	44.0	2995		
RL-12	40.0	2866	43.0	2991		
W748	42.0	2860	44.0	2984		
A2520	36.9	2609	41.0	2965	47,900p	Hdy SP/2.975"/CCI 200
N150	38.8	2751	41.9	2931	46,412p	Sra HP
A4350	43.2	2578	48.0	2929	41,900p	Hdy SP/2.975"/CCI 200/(C)
A2495BR	33.3	2550	37.0	2898	50,300p	Hdy SP/2.975"/CCI 200
A3100	44.1	2397	49.0	2724	34,100p	Hdy SP/2.975"/CCI 200/(C)

108

Powder	—STARTING— Grs.	MV (fps)	—MAXIMUM— Grs.	MV (fps)	Press. (CUP/psi)	Comments
N165	48.7	2823	51.2	3000	46,412p	Lapua Scenar GB 404
N160	47.0	2785	49.3	2963	46,412p	Lapua Scenar GB 404
N150	39.5	2724	42.1	2890	46,412p	Lapua Scenar GB 404

120

Powder	—STARTING— Grs.	MV (fps)	—MAXIMUM— Grs.	MV (fps)	Press. (CUP/psi)	Comments
H4350	44.0	2880	47.0	3080		
RL-22	48.0	2898	51.0	3025		
H414	43.0	2894	46.0	3018		
IMR4350	44.0	2807	47.0	3004		
IMR7828	49.0	2845	51.0	2992		
W760	43.0	2888	45.0	2990		
RL-15	39.0	2828	42.0	2952		
H450	48.0	2790	50.0	2946		
H4895	39.0	2792	41.0	2945		
IMR4064	39.0	2792	42.0	2940		
H380	41.0	2804	44.0	2925		
IMR4320	39.0	2781	42.0	2922		
RL-19	46.0	2801	49.0	2915		
IMR4831	46.0	2739	49.0	2898		
H4831	46.0	2714	49.0	2870		
RL-12	38.0	2714	41.0	2805		
H1000	50.0	2649	52.0	2787		
N150	32.7	2427	36.3	2579	46,412p	Sra HP

125-129

Powder	—STARTING— Grs.	MV (fps)	—MAXIMUM— Grs.	MV (fps)	Press. (CUP/psi)	Comments
H4350	43.0	2808	46.0	2944		
RL-22	47.0	2787	50.0	2911		
IMR7828	47.0	2767	50.0	2898		
H450	46.0	2739	49.0	2896		
IMR4350	43.0	2740	46.0	2888		
H414	42.0	2729	45.0	2868		
H4831	45.0	2703	48.0	2863		
IMR4064	37.0	2729	40.0	2861		
IMR4320	37.0	2707	40.0	2849		
RL-19	45.0	2716	48.0	2845		
W760	42.0	2719	44.0	2840		
H4895	37.0	2710	40.0	2834		
H380	40.0	2676	43.0	2824		
IMR4831	45.0	2690	48.0	2820		
RL-15	38.0	2681	41.0	2804		
A4350	41.4	2423	46.0	2753	50,300p	Hdy SP/3.025"/CCI 200
A3100	44.1	2394	49.0	2721	47,500p	Hdy SP/3.025"/CCI 200/(C)
RL-12	37.0	2621	40.0	2708		
H1000	50.0	2611	52.0	2707		
A2700	40.9	2496	43.0	2655	50,300p	Hdy SP/3.025"/CCI 200
A2520	33.8	2251	37.5	2558	49,200p	Hdy SP/3.025"/CCI 200
A2495BR	32.4	2223	36.0	2526	46,100p	Hdy SP/3.025"/CCI 200

139-140

Powder	—STARTING— Grs.	MV (fps)	—MAXIMUM— Grs.	MV (fps)	Press. (CUP/psi)	Comments
RL-22	46.0	2737	49.0	2857		
IMR7828	46.0	2703	49.0	2820		
H450	45.0	2661	48.0	2797		
H414	41.0	2612	44.0	2797		
IMR4831	44.0	2681	47.0	2789		
RL-19	44.0	2677	47.0	2773		
H380	39.0	2597	42.0	2754		
W760	41.0	2619	43.0	2734		
H4831	44.0	2591	47.0	2712		
RL-15	37.0	2639	40.0	2712		
IMR4350	42.0	2534	45.0	2711		
IMR4064	35.0	2533	38.0	2709		
H4350	42.0	2588	45.0	2708		
H4895	35.0	2540	38.0	2701		
H1000	49.0	2579	51.0	2694		
IMR4320	36.0	2554	39.0	2688		
N165	46.0	2529	47.9	2659	46,557p	Norma FMJ
RL-12	36.0	2504	39.0	2643		
A4350	40.5	2314	45.0	2629	48,100p	Spr SP/3.0"/CCI 200
N165	43.6	2447	46.9	2626	46,702p	Sra HP Match
N160	43.3	2461	46.1	2623	46,557p	Norma FMJ
N140			38.7	2580	44,962p	Norma FMJ
A2700	39.9	2416	42.0	2570	50,400p	Spr SP/3.0"/CCI 200
N160	41.6	2406	44.0	2546	46,412p	Sra HP Match
N135			34.7	2530	44,962p	Norma FMJ
A3100	42.3	2221	47.0	2524	41,400p	Spr SP/3.0"/CCI 200/(C)
A2520	33.3	2202	37.0	2502	50,400p	Spr SP/3.0"/CCI 200

Never exceed maximum load nor use any load exhibiting signs of excessive pressure. Begin at suggested starting load and work up carefully.

139-140 con't

Powder	Grs.	MV (fps)	Grs.	MV (fps)	Press. (CUP/psi)	Comments
A2495BR	30.6	2146	34.0	2439	49,500p	Spr SP/3.0"/CCI 200
N150	33.7	2277	36.5	2412	46,412p	Norma FMJ
N150	32.6	2230	34.8	2362	46,412p	Sra HP Match
A8700	47.7	1930	53.0	2193	32,600p	Spr SP/3.0"/ CCI 200/(C)

144

Powder	Grs.	MV (fps)	Grs.	MV (fps)	Press. (CUP/psi)	Comments
N165	42.5	2397	45.4	2543	46,412p	Lapua FMJ BT 8343
N160	41.3	2385	44.1	2522	46,702p	Lapua FMJ BT 8343
N140			34.7	2440	42,061p	Lapua FMJ 343
N150	32.1	2198	34.6	2338	46,412p	Lapua FMJ BT 8343

150

Powder	Grs.	MV (fps)	Grs.	MV (fps)	Press. (CUP/psi)	Comments
RL-22	45.0	2616	48.0	2731		
IMR7828	45.0	2559	48.0	2677		
H414	40.0	2480	43.0	2663		
RL-19	43.0	2534	46.0	2652		
H450	43.0	2490	46.0	2644		
W760	40.0	2488	42.0	2630		
IMR4831	42.0	2524	45.0	2627		
H4831	43.0	2471	46.0	2619		
H4350	41.0	2464	44.0	2618		
H380	39.0	2429	41.0	2614		
IMR4350	40.0	2483	43.0	2590		
H4895	34.0	2414	37.0	2560		
RL-15	36.0	2440	39.0	2559		
IMR4320	34.0	2414	37.0	2541		
IMR4064	33.0	2388	36.0	2529		
H1000	47.0	2404	50.0	2527		
RL-12	35.0	2398	38.0	2494		

156

Powder	Grs.	MV (fps)	Grs.	MV (fps)	Press. (CUP/psi)	Comments
N160			45.2	2660	44,962p	Lapua FMJ R239

160

Powder	Grs.	MV (fps)	Grs.	MV (fps)	Press. (CUP/psi)	Comments
RL-22	44.0	2456	47.0	2605		
RL-19	42.0	2408	45.0	2558		
H450	42.0	2313	45.0	2518		
N160			44.9	2510	44,962p	Hdy RN
H414	39.0	2392	41.0	2506		
IMR4831	40.0	2372	43.0	2505		
IMR7828	43.0	2384	46.0	2500		
H1000	46.0	2344	49.0	2492		
W760	38.0	2341	40.0	2466		
H4831	42.0	2330	45.0	2454		
H4350	40.0	2319	43.0	2450		
IMR4350	38.0	2344	41.0	2449		
RL-15	35.0	2320	38.0	2442		
RL-12	34.0	2260	37.0	2390		
IMR4320	33.0	2240	36.0	2372		
N140			36.9	2350	44,962p	Hdy RN

Caution: Loads exceeding SAAMI OAL Maximum must be verified for bullet-to-rifling clearance and magazine functioning. Where a specific primer or bullet is indicated those components must be used, no substitutions! Where only a maximum load is shown, reduce starting load 10%, unless otherwise specified.

Key: (C) = compressed charge; C = CUP; p = psi; Plink = Plinker; Bns = Barnes; Hdy = Hornady; Lap = Lapua; Nos = Nosler; Rem = Remington; Sra = Sierra; Spr = Speer; Win = Winchester.

6.5mm
Remington
Magnum

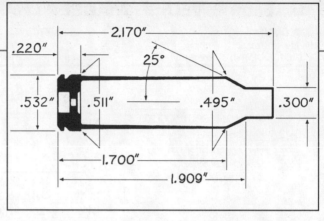

2.170"
.220"
25°
.532" .511" .495" .300"
1.700"
1.909"

Case: Remington
Primer: Large Rifle
Barrel: 24" Accurate
        26" Hodgdon
Bullet Diameter: 0.264"

Maximum Case Length: 2.170"
Trim to Length: 2.160"
Maximum Cartridge OAL: 2.800"
Minimum Cartridge OAL: 2.740"

The 6.5mm Remington Magnum was introduced in 1966 as a new chambering for the innovative Model 600 carbine, which had been offered the previous year chambered for the hard-kicking 350 Remington Magnum. Limited by that carbine's 18½" barrel, 6.5mm Remington Magnum performance was simply not up to the task of competing with existing chamberings such as the 270 Winchester, chambered in 22" barreled rifles. Frankly, there was also an ongoing incomprehensible bias among mainstream gun writers against any chambering designed to work in a shorter-than-standard action and equally against carbine-length long guns.

These prejudices garnered an amazing amount of ink, spilled in all manner of gun publications, to the effect that cartridges such as the 350 Remington Magnum, 6.5mm Remington Magnum and the 284 Winchester, and the guns they were chambered in, were simply useless! Even more amazingly, some of the same writers who made considerable press in the '60s and '70s harping on that exact subject have more recently endorsed the short-action-carbine-chambered 7mm-08 Remington in the most glowing of terms!

The truth is that Remington's 6.5mm Magnum is a serious performer. Offering sufficient capacity for top performance in the 6.5mm bore, it has always been made with very heavy cases and operates at the top end of standard factory pressure levels.

This cartridge was intended to use moderate-weight bullets for hunting medium-sized big game, and for that purpose it is certainly adequate. When loaded to the same pressure with moderate-weight bullets using the best powders available and fired from equal-length barrels, the simple undeniable fact is that the 6.5mm Remington Magnum generates the same velocity as the much longer 264 Winchester Magnum.

Not surprisingly, when handicapped with either a very short barrel or deeply seated heavy bullets, performance suffers.

Usable case capacity with a 120-grain bullet, seated normally, is about 66.0 grains of water. H380, IMR4320, H4350, IMR4350, H414, A4350, H4831 and IMR4831 are noted performers in this short magnum.

6.5mm REMINGTON MAGNUM LOADING DATA

Powder	STARTING Grs.	MV (fps)	MAXIMUM Grs.	MV (fps)	Press. (CUP/psi)	Comments
77						
H414	57.0	3655	62.0	3870	50,500C	
H380	53.5	3588	58.0	3829	49,800C	
H4895	49.0	3500	53.0	3797	51,700C	
H450	58.0	3421	63.0	3731	52,100C	
H4831	56.0	3225	61.0	3567	43,800C	
85-87						
A4350	56.7	3337	63.0	3792	63,900p	Sra HP/2.74"/ Rem 9½M/Case Full
H414	55.0	3451	60.0	3755	51,700C	
H380	52.5	3339	57.0	3681	50,500C	
H4895	47.0	3322	51.0	3613	49,600C	
IMR4831	56.0	3267	60.0	3612	49,400C	

Powder	STARTING Grs.	MV (fps)	MAXIMUM Grs.	MV (fps)	Press. (CUP/psi)	Comments
85-87 con't						
IMR4350	54.0	3240	57.0	3580	51,200C	
A2700	55.1	3358	58.0	3572	55,600p	Sra HP/2.74"/ Rem 9½M
H4831	56.0	3201	61.0	3570	46,700C	
W760	56.0	3469	58.0	3565	51,000C	
H4350	54.0	3220	57.0	3564	50,700C	
IMR4320	46.0	3239	49.0	3552	49,900C	
IMR4064	46.0	3194	49.0	3530	49,400C	
H450	56.0	3244	61.0	3524	51,500C	
IMR4895	45.0	3212	48.0	3523	50,100C	
A3100	57.6	3032	64.0	3446	47,200p	Sra HP/2.74"/ Rem 9½M/(C)

Never exceed maximum load nor use any load exhibiting signs of excessive pressure. Begin at suggested starting load and work up carefully.

100

Powder	Starting Grs.	Starting MV (fps)	Maximum Grs.	Maximum MV (fps)	Maximum Press. (CUP/psi)	Comments
A4350	54.9	3121	61.0	3547	60,700p	Hdy SP/2.8"/ Rem 9½M
H4895	46.0	3186	50.0	3475	52,200C	
H414	51.5	3168	56.0	3466	52,600C	
H380	50.0	3111	54.0	3459	52,800C	
H4831	55.0	3071	60.0	3416	48,100C	
A2700	52.3	3168	55.0	3370	57,900p	Hdy SP/2.8"/ Rem 9½M
W760	53.0	3269	55.0	3360	50,900C	
A3100	56.3	2947	62.5	3349	50,800p	Hdy SP/2.8"/ Rem 9½M/(C)
IMR4350	51.0	3092	55.0	3348	52,000C	
H450	53.5	3010	58.0	3330	50,100C	
H4350	51.0	3071	55.0	3327	51,700C	
IMR4831	53.0	3042	57.0	3294	50,600C	
IMR4320	45.0	3119	48.0	3263	50,800C	
IMR4064	45.0	3097	48.0	3232	51,100C	
IMR4895	44.0	3086	47.0	3221	51,000C	

120

Powder	Starting Grs.	Starting MV (fps)	Maximum Grs.	Maximum MV (fps)	Maximum Press. (CUP/psi)	Comments
H4831	54.0	2985	59.0	3286	51,000C	
H414	47.0	2792	51.0	3099	51,700C	
H450	51.5	2849	56.0	3090	50,200C	
W760	49.0	2898	51.0	3084	51,400C	
H4895	42.5	2872	46.0	3081	50,900C	
H4350	49.0	2780	52.0	3080	51,200C	
H380	45.0	2843	49.0	3059	50,900C	
IMR4831	50.0	2688	54.0	3024	51,200C	
IMR4895	42.0	2729	45.0	3019	51,000C	
IMR4350	48.0	2712	51.0	3009	51,000C	
IMR4064	43.0	2738	46.0	2994	51,900C	
IMR4320	43.0	2732	46.0	2974	52,200C	

129

Powder	Starting Grs.	Starting MV (fps)	Maximum Grs.	Maximum MV (fps)	Maximum Press. (CUP/psi)	Comments
H4831	53.5	2854	58.0	3155	50,800C	
A4350	50.4	2759	56.0	3135	60,400p	Hdy SP/2.8"/ Rem 9½M
A3100	54.0	2737	60.0	3110	56,700p	Hdy SP/2.8"/ Rem 9½M
H450	50.5	2676	55.0	3011	49,800C	
IMR4831	48.0	2704	52.0	3007	51,900C	
A2700	48.9	2826	51.5	3006	59,300p	Hdy SP/2.8"/ Rem 9½M
H4350	47.0	2709	51.0	2994	50,700C	
IMR4350	46.0	2686	50.0	2967	50,500C	
H414	46.0	2673	50.0	2954	51,300C	
W760	48.0	2830	50.0	2950	51,100C	
H380	43.5	2636	47.0	2950	51,300C	
H4895	40.5	2709	44.0	2936	49,900C	
IMR4064	42.0	2694	45.0	2930	50,900C	
IMR4895	41.0	2681	44.0	2911	50,100C	
IMR4320	42.0	2637	45.0	2860	50,000C	

140

Powder	Starting Grs.	Starting MV (fps)	Maximum Grs.	Maximum MV (fps)	Maximum Press. (CUP/psi)	Comments
H4831	49.5	2708	54.0	2943	51,400C	
H450	49.5	2661	54.0	2925	51,700C	
H4350	45.0	2514	49.0	2780	51,200C	
H4895	38.5	2569	42.0	2752	49,200C	
IMR4350	44.0	2501	48.0	2749	51,400C	
IMR4064	39.0	2494	43.0	2744	50,900C	
H414	42.0	2502	46.0	2743	51,100C	
W760	44.0	2681	46.0	2741	51,400C	
IMR4831	47.0	2539	51.0	2740	51,400C	
IMR4895	38.0	2511	42.0	2732	50,000C	
IMR4320	41.0	2480	44.0	2710	50,600C	
H380	40.5	2475	44.0	2666	51,200C	

Caution: Loads exceeding SAAMI OAL Maximum must be verified for bullet-to-rifling clearance and magazine functioning. Where a specific primer or bullet is indicated those components must be used, no substitutions! Where only a maximum load is shown, reduce starting load 10%, unless otherwise specified.

Key: (C) = compressed charge; C = CUP; p = psi; Plink = Plinker; Bns = Barnes; Hdy = Hornady; Lap = Lapua; Nos = Nosler; Rem = Remington; Sra = Sierra; Spr = Speer; Win = Winchester.

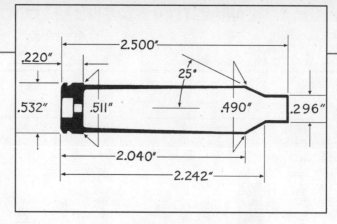

Case: Winchester
Primer: Large Rifle
Barrel: 24″ Accurate
      26″ Hodgdon
      24″ Vihtavuori

Bullet Diameter: 0.264″
Maximum Case Length: 2.500″
Trim to Length: 2.490″
Maximum Cartridge OAL: 3.340″
Minimum Cartridge OAL: 3.160″

Introduced in 1958 by Winchester, the 264 Winchester Magnum was always intended by the factory to offer mainstream competition to Weatherby's 257 Magnum, one of a very short list of ultimate long-range flat-shooting ultra-velocity factory chamberings. To achieve a fair measure of this large capacity cartridge's potential, Winchester designed the initial rifle with a full 26″ barrel. Ultimately, that fact might have been at the heart of the 264's demise from favor and continuing limited success.

The fact is that Winchester was completely correct in their decision to use a 26″ tube. Ballistics are greatly reduced when the barrel is shortened to 24″. Performance in the typical 22″ barrel is inferior to typical 270 Winchester loads! Nevertheless, consumers pressured Winchester with an incessant din of complaints about the unwieldy long barrel. The factory's response was predictable, if nonsensical. They changed the barrel length on 264 Winchester Magnum chambered rifles to 24″, and later a 22″ version was offered.

Soon enough two other problems became apparent. First, shooters who little understood the importance of letting the barrel cool properly between shots soon learned about limited barrel life. This might have been the first commercial chambering commonly available at an affordable price that could be ruined by the expeditious firing of only a few box-es of ammunition! The folks in Hornady's ballistics lab proved that fact. They completely ruined four barrels working up data for a whopping thirty-two bullet and powder combinations! Rest assured, they fired no more shots than were absolutely necessary to generate that short list of data.

Second in the 264's fall from grace was the appearance of affordable chronographs. Those who bothered to check soon learned, to their chagrin, that in spite of their best efforts their powder-and-barrel-burning little monster could seldom be coaxed into delivering ballistics anywhere near what the factory claimed. This was true even for those who owned 26″ barreled guns. Those with 22″ barreled guns found they were lucky to duplicate what they could easily accomplish with the 270 Winchester.

In spite of these problems, when equipped with a 26″ barrel, and when loaded, fired and cleaned carefully, the 264 can deliver good performance. For those who want to shoot heavier than standard bullets, it offers a good basis. Nevertheless, it is hard to see any measure whereby it can compete with the 7mm Remington Magnum.

Usable case capacity with a 120-grain bullet, seated normally, is about 81.7 grains of water. H4831, IMR4350, IMR4831, H870, H1000 and IMR7828 are noted performers in the 264 Win. Mag.

264 WINCHESTER MAGNUM LOADING DATA

Powder	STARTING Grs.	MV (fps)	MAXIMUM Grs.	MV (fps)	Press. (CUP/psi)	Comments
77						
H4831	67.0	3410	73.0	3899	52,600C	
H414	57.0	3431	62.0	3780	50,000C	
H380	55.0	3347	59.0	3779	50,200C	
H4895	50.5	3249	55.0	3712	52,700C	
H870			80.0	3568	43,900C	
85-87						
IMR7828	66.0	3519	70.0	3844	49,400C	
H450	66.5	3401	72.0	3834	51,000C	

Powder	STARTING Grs.	MV (fps)	MAXIMUM Grs.	MV (fps)	Press. (CUP/psi)	Comments
85-87 con't						
H4831	67.0	3404	73.0	3812	54,100C	
N160			67.1	3770	56,565p	Sra HP
IMR4831	61.0	3464	64.0	3762	51,100C	
H4350	59.0	3396	61.0	3669	52,400C	
H414	57.0	3310	62.0	3633	52,200C	
IMR4320	53.0	3310	56.0	3629	51,900C	
H4895	50.5	3264	55.0	3625	52,900C	
W760	60.0	3429	62.0	3619	52,000C	
H380	54.5	3295	58.0	3612	50,600C	
IMR4350	58.0	3380	60.0	3612	51,400C	

85-87 con't

Powder	—STARTING— Grs.	MV (fps)	—MAXIMUM— Grs.	MV (fps)	Press. (CUP/psi)	Comments
H870			80.0	3557	46,800C	
N140			57.4	3540	56,565p	Sra HP
H1000	74.0	3270	78.0	3480	48,000C	

100

Powder	Grs.	MV (fps)	Grs.	MV (fps)	Press. (CUP/psi)	Comments
H4831	65.5	3239	71.0	3680	53,900C	
H450	64.5	3192	70.0	3642	51,200C	
IMR7828	63.0	3277	67.0	3612	51,200C	
H4350	56.0	3294	59.0	3570	52,600C	
A4350	60.3	3102	67.0	3523	62,900C	Sra SP/3.22"/CCI 250
IMR4350	55.0	3180	58.0	3507	51,900C	
A3100	64.8	3054	72.0	3471	61,900C	Sra SP/3.22"/CCI 250
H1000	72.0	3164	77.0	3428	47,500C	
IMR4831	59.0	3240	62.0	3410	52,100C	
H4895	49.0	3070	53.0	3405	54,200C	
H414	54.0	3202	59.0	3389	52,600C	
H380	51.5	3039	56.0	3374	51,000C	
W760	57.0	3239	59.0	3373	52,400C	
IMR4320	51.0	3101	54.0	3367	53,000C	
H870			78.0	3325	44,800C	
A8700	74.7	2732	83.0	3105	40,800p	Sra SP/3.22"/CCI 250/(C)

120

Powder	Grs.	MV (fps)	Grs.	MV (fps)	Press. (CUP/psi)	Comments
H450	61.5	3015	66.5	3391	52,100C	
H870			76.0	3389	53,300C	
H4831	60.0	3023	65.0	3369	52,100C	
IMR7828	61.0	3027	65.0	3224	52,000C	
H4350	54.0	3029	57.0	3190	52,900C	
H1000	67.0	3059	72.0	3185	49,000C	
IMR4831	56.0	3009	59.0	3180	52,400C	
IMR4350	53.0	3036	56.0	3177	52,600C	

125

Powder	Grs.	MV (fps)	Grs.	MV (fps)	Press. (CUP/psi)	Comments
A8700	69.3	2765	77.0	3142	64,000p	Nos Part./3.265"/CCI 250
A3100	52.2	2534	58.0	2880	61,300p	Nos Part./3.265"/CCI 250
A4350	48.6	2502	54.0	2843	60,800p	Nos Part./3.265"/CCI 250

129

Powder	Grs.	MV (fps)	Grs.	MV (fps)	Press. (CUP/psi)	Comments
H4831	62.0	2905	65.0	3206	50,600C	
IMR7828	60.0	2944	64.0	3194	50,900C	
H1000	67.0	3027	71.0	3187	50,400C	
H4350	53.0	3081	56.0	3177	51,800C	
H870			76.0	3170	49,100C	
IMR4350	52.0	2991	55.0	3142	51,600C	
IMR4831	55.0	2909	58.0	3111	51,800C	

140

Powder	—STARTING— Grs.	MV (fps)	—MAXIMUM— Grs.	MV (fps)	Press. (CUP/psi)	Comments
H870			73.0	3163	54,200C	
H450	58.0	2792	63.0	3119	51,600C	
H4831	56.0	2794	61.0	3065	52,000C	
N140			47.8	3020	56,565p	Hdy SP
H1000	63.0	2843	68.0	3019	51,500C	
IMR7828	59.0	2762	63.0	2994	51,000C	
N160			57.1	2990	56,565p	Sako SP 115E
H4350	50.0	2766	53.0	2965	53,400C	
IMR4831	52.0	2718	55.0	2923	52,200C	
IMR4350	50.0	2781	52.0	2909	52,400C	
A8700	64.8	2559	72.0	2908	62,700p	Nos Part./3.265"/CCI 250
A4350	47.7	2414	53.0	2743	64,000p	Nos Part./3.265"/CCI 250
A3100	50.4	2402	56.0	2729	61,600p	Nos Part./3.265"/CCI 250

150

Powder	Grs.	MV (fps)	Grs.	MV (fps)	Press. (CUP/psi)	Comments
H1000	62.0	2790	66.0	2922	50,500C	

160

Powder	Grs.	MV (fps)	Grs.	MV (fps)	Press. (CUP/psi)	Comments
IMR7828	56.0	2630	60.0	2889	52,200C	
H4831	52.5	2571	57.0	2886	52,400C	
H870			68.0	2868	51,300C	
H1000	61.0	2538	65.0	2860	49,900C	
IMR4350	48.0	2588	50.0	2696	52,200C	
IMR4831	50.0	2464	53.0	2690	51,400C	
N160			56.3	2690	56,565p	Norma FMJ
H4350	47.0	2555	50.0	2686	51,200C	

165

Powder	Grs.	MV (fps)	Grs.	MV (fps)	Press. (CUP/psi)	Comments
H1000	60.0	2611	63.0	2844	52,500C	
H4831	51.0	2575	55.0	2830	51,400C	
H870	63.0	2630	66.0	2809	51,000C	
H4350	46.0	2489	48.0	2626	50,900C	

> *Caution:* Loads exceeding SAAMI OAL Maximum must be verified for bullet-to-rifling clearance and magazine functioning. Where a specific primer or bullet is indicated those components must be used, no substitutions! Where only a maximum load is shown, reduce starting load 10%, unless otherwise specified.
>
> *Key:* (C) = compressed charge; C = CUP; p = psi; Plink = Plinker; Bns = Barnes; Hdy = Hornady; Lap = Lapua; Nos = Nosler; Rem = Remington; Sra = Sierra; Spr = Speer; Win = Winchester.

Never exceed maximum load nor use any load exhibiting signs of excessive pressure. Begin at suggested starting load and work up carefully.

270
Winchester

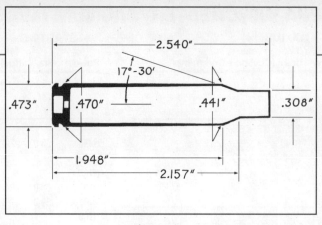

Case: Remington
Primer: Large Rifle
Barrel: 24″ Accurate
      26″ Hodgdon
      24½″ Vihtavuori

Bullet Diameter: 0.277″
Maximum Case Length: 2.540″
Trim to Length: 2.530″
Maximum Cartridge OAL: 3.340″
Minimum Cartridge OAL: 3.065″

Introduced in 1925, the 270 is nothing more and nothing less than the standard 30-06 necked down, although the neck is slightly longer—this is of no consequence and 270 cases are readily formed by necking down '06 cases.

Jack O'Connor was a genuine champion of the 270 Winchester and cleanly dispatched all manner of big game with the standard 130-grain loading. Nevertheless, the author's experience has been that, with conventional bullets, performance is generally improved with 140- or 150-grain bullets. These shoot essentially as flat and tend to do less unnecessary damage on smaller species while delivering better penetration on elk. As with any cartridge, shot placement and

bullet performance are important, but the 270 has all the performance necessary to get the job done cleanly.

As an added bonus, the 270 is about the biggest cartridge that can truly double as a varmint chambering. The various 90- to 110-grain bullets loaded to top velocities offer true varmint performance. The aerodynamically superior 100- and 110-grain offerings deliver superior wind-bucking capabilities with flat-enough trajectories for long-range use.

Usable case capacity with a 130-grain bullet, seated normally, is about 65.4 grains of water. IMR4350, IMR4831, H4831, RL-22, H4350, RL-19, H414, W760, H380 and IMR4064 are noted for accuracy and consistency in the 270.

270 WINCHESTER LOADING DATA

Powder	STARTING Grs.	MV (fps)	MAXIMUM Grs.	MV (fps)	Press. (CUP/psi)	Comments
Lead 150 RCBS						
A8700	54.0	2089	60.0	2374	42,200C	3.25″/Rem 9½
90						
H414	55.0	3323	60.0	3618	49,900C	
VarGet			55.0	3596	51,400C	
H4895	50.5	3348	54.5	3594	49,300C	
H335	47.0	3320	51.0	3564	51,400C	
H380	51.5	3355	56.0	3558	51,300C	
W760	57.0	3401	59.0	3549	49,200C	
IMR4320	51.0	3334	54.0	3535	52,600C	
IMR4895	51.0	3351	54.0	3517	51,000C	
BL-C(2)	46.0	3267	50.0	3502	50,800C	
IMR4350	57.0	3364	60.0	3484	49,400C	
A4350	54.9	3066	61.0	3484	49,900C	Sra HP/3.09″/Rem 9½/(C)
IMR4064	51.0	3292	54.0	3480	50,400C	
H4350	57.0	3352	60.0	3466	48,200C	
RL-15	50.0	3277	54.0	3462	47,000C	
A2700	54.2	3245	57.0	3452	52,000C	Sra HP/3.09″/Rem 9½
H450	61.0	3256	66.0	3448	49,600C	

Powder	STARTING Grs.	MV (fps)	MAXIMUM Grs.	MV (fps)	Press. (CUP/psi)	Comments
90 con't						
IMR4831	58.0	3209	61.0	3429	47,700C	
RL-12	49.0	3198	52.0	3410	49,900C	
RL-22	60.0	3128	64.0	3353	43,500C	
RL-19	60.0	3144	64.0	3337	44,000C	
H4831	59.0	3036	64.0	3317	42,000C	
A3100	54.9	2752	61.0	3127	44,100C	Sra HP/3.09″/Rem 9½/(C)

> *Caution:* Loads exceeding SAAMI OAL Maximum must be verified for bullet-to-rifling clearance and magazine functioning. Where a specific primer or bullet is indicated those components must be used, no substitutions! Where only a maximum load is shown, reduce starting load 10%, unless otherwise specified.
>
> *Key:* (C) = compressed charge; C = CUP; p = psi; Plink = Plinker; Bns = Barnes; Hdy = Hornady; Lap = Lapua; Nos = Nosler; Rem = Remington; Sra = Sierra; Spr = Speer; Win = Winchester.

100

Powder	Grs.	MV (fps)	Grs.	MV (fps)	Press. (CUP/psi)	Comments
H4895	48.0	3133	52.0	3426	49,400C	
H414	52.5	3048	57.0	3397	48,100C	
VarGet			52.0	3397	50,200C	
RL-22	61.0	3149	64.0	3394	47,500C	
IMR4320	49.0	3139	52.0	3394	53,000C	
H380	49.5	3207	54.0	3387	51,100C	
W760	55.0	3229	57.0	3381	48,400C	
H4350	57.0	3124	60.0	3372	53,900C	
IMR4895	48.0	3107	51.0	3371	51,400C	
A4350	54.0	2953	60.0	3356	48,700C	Hdy SP/3.175"/Rem 9½/(C)
IMR4064	49.0	3123	52.0	3354	51,600C	
RL-19	60.0	3150	63.0	3342	48,000C	
BL-C(2)	45.0	3121	49.0	3340	51,000C	
A2700	53.2	3140	56.0	3340	52,000C	Hdy SP/3.175"/Rem 9½
RL-15	49.0	3229	53.0	3335	48,500C	
H335	44.0	3064	48.0	3326	50,100C	
RL-12	48.0	3133	51.0	3320	50,200C	
H450	58.0	3193	63.0	3314	49,900C	
IMR4350	57.0	3111	59.0	3307	53,200C	
IMR4831	58.0	3161	61.0	3299	50,900C	
N165	58.2	3023	64.8	3297	49,310p	Spr Sptz SP
H4831	57.0	2988	62.0	3159	42,600C	
WMR			59.5	3120	45,500p	Win SP
A3100	54.9	2728	61.0	3100	44,200C	Hdy SP/3.175"/Rem 9½/(C)
N140			49.4	3050	52,214p	Rem SP

110

Powder	Grs.	MV (fps)	Grs.	MV (fps)	Press. (CUP/psi)	Comments
H414	52.5	3015	57.0	3323	49,500C	
H450	58.0	3054	63.0	3317	50,800C	
A4350	53.0	2900	59.0	3300	52,000C	Sra SP/3.24"/Rem 9½
RL-22	60.0	3127	63.0	3279	47,500C	
W760	54.0	3127	56.0	3268	50,000C	
RL-19	58.0	3087	61.0	3246	49,000C	
H4350	54.0	3102	57.0	3243	52,100C	
A2700	52.3	3038	55.0	3232	52,000C	Sra SP/3.24"/Rem 9½
IMR4831	57.0	3079	60.0	3219	52,100C	
H380	48.0	3072	52.0	3211	49,400C	
IMR4350	53.0	3090	56.0	3210	52,900C	
H4831	57.0	2958	62.0	3201	48,100C	
H4895	45.5	2927	49.0	3196	49,600C	
RL-15	48.0	3020	52.0	3188	47,500C	

110 con't

Powder	Grs.	MV (fps)	Grs.	MV (fps)	Press. (CUP/psi)	Comments
RL-12	46.0	3009	49.0	3177	51,000C	
VarGet			48.0	3149	48,800C	
IMR4320	47.0	2997	50.0	3149	52,600C	
IMR4895	45.0	2971	48.0	3131	50,700C	
A3100	54.9	2753	61.0	3128	47,200C	Sra SP/3.24"/Rem 9½/(C)
BL-C(2)	43.0	2910	46.0	3111	49,000C	
IMR4064	46.0	2960	49.0	3102	50,400C	
H335	41.5	2885	45.0	3093	48,700C	
H1000	62.0	2805	64.0	2913	36,000C	

130

Powder	Grs.	MV (fps)	Grs.	MV (fps)	Press. (CUP/psi)	Comments
H450	55.0	2766	60.0	3150	48,700C	
IMR7828	55.0	2899	59.0	3141	51,000C	
RL-22	58.0	2904	61.0	3133	51,000C	
H4831	55.0	2789	60.0	3113	48,500C	
IMR4831	55.0	2940	58.0	3112	53,100C	
H4350	52.0	2797	55.0	3109	52,400C	
H414	49.5	2941	54.0	3100	50,300C	
W760	52.0	3006	54.0	3091	50,600C	
IMR4350	51.0	2811	54.0	3090	52,600C	
A4350	52.2	2702	58.0	3070	52,000C	Bns-X/3.33"/Rem 9½/(C)
A3100	54.9	2697	61.0	3065	51,500C	Nos BT/3.33"/Rem 9½/(C)
H380	47.5	2866	52.0	3054	50,800C	
N560	54.9	2808	59.7	3034	52,200p	Rem PSPCL/3.228"/Rem 9½
N160			54.8	3030	52,214p	Sako FMJ 1148
RL-19	55.0	2860	58.0	3029	48,000C	
A4350	49.5	2660	55.0	3020	52,000C	Nos BT/3.33"/Rem 9½
WMR			58.9	3000	53,500p	Win SP
N165	53.8	2761	59.3	2975	52,210p	Spr BT SP
A3100	54.9	2616	61.0	2973	48,500C	Bns-X/3.33"/Rem 9½/(C)
H4895	42.5	2777	46.0	2970	50,100C	
A2700	49.4	2777	52.0	2954	52,000C	Nos BT/3.33"/Rem 9½
IMR4064	43.0	2741	46.0	2951	52,400C	
A2700	50.4	2765	53.0	2941	51,700C	Bns-X/3.33"/Rem 9½
VarGet			46.0	2931	49,600C	
H1000	62.0	2788	64.0	2929	43,600C	
IMR4895	42.0	2710	45.0	2920	52,400C	
IMR4320	43.0	2721	46.0	2912	53,200C	
RL-15	46.0	2747	50.0	2894	49,400C	
N140			45.5	2850	52,214p	Sako FMJ 1148
RL-12	43.0	2693	46.0	2844	50,900C	
H870			65.0	2840	43,900C	

>>>>>>>>>>>>>>>>>>>>>>>>>>>>>

Never exceed maximum load nor use any load exhibiting signs of excessive pressure. Begin at suggested starting load and work up carefully.

155

140

Powder	STARTING Grs.	MV (fps)	MAXIMUM Grs.	MV (fps)	Press. (CUP/psi)	Comments
H4831	53.0	2849	58.0	3051	50,800C	
RL-22	56.0	2832	59.0	3020	50,000C	
A4350	50.4	2629	56.0	2988	52,000C	Hdy SBT/3.33"/Rem 9½/(C)
A3100	54.0	2607	60.0	2962	49,300C	Hdy SBT/3.33"/Rem 9½/(C)
RL-19	54.0	2741	57.0	2962	51,000C	
H450	54.0	2790	58.0	2960	50,100C	
N165			58.4	2960	56,800p	BTSP
IMR4831	53.0	2770	56.0	2949	53,200C	
IMR7828	54.0	2755	57.0	2930	49,900C	
WMR			57.6	2930	57,800p	Win SP
H414	47.0	2747	52.0	2927	50,800C	
H4350	49.0	2711	53.0	2924	51,900C	
W760	50.0	2808	52.0	2920	51,100C	
H380	46.0	2739	50.0	2909	51,400C	
A2700	49.4	2719	52.0	2893	51,600C	Hdy SBT/3.33"/Rem 9½
IMR4350	49.0	2740	52.0	2869	52,000C	
RL-15	45.0	2680	49.0	2834	48,500C	
H4895	41.0	2660	44.0	2814	51,800C	
H1000	61.0	2714	63.0	2807	44,200C	
H870			64.0	2792	43,400C	
RL-12	42.0	2694	45.0	2780	50,500C	
IMR4320	41.0	2569	44.0	2730	53,400C	
A8700	57.6	2159	64.0	2453	43,700C	Hdy SBT/3.33"/Rem 9½/(C)

150

Powder	STARTING Grs.	MV (fps)	MAXIMUM Grs.	MV (fps)	Press. (CUP/psi)	Comments
H4831	54.5	2810	58.0	3015	52,600C	
IMR7828	54.0	2744	56.0	2929	51,100C	
IMR4831	52.0	2732	55.0	2910	53,800C	
A3100	52.2	2547	58.0	2894	52,000C	Sra SBT/3.3"/Rem 9½/(C)
A4350	47.0	2515	53.0	2880	52,000C	Sra SBT/3.3"/Rem 9½
H380	46.0	2690	50.0	2878	52,600C	
H450	53.5	2690	57.5	2876	50,200C	
H4350	48.0	2575	52.0	2870	51,400C	
RL-22	54.0	2743	57.0	2869	50,000C	
RL-19	52.0	2714	55.0	2852	51,500C	
WMR			57.5	2850	58,200p	Win SP
N560	50.9	2634	55.5	2808	52,200p	Rem PSPCL/3.228"/Rem 9½
H414	46.0	2624	50.0	2800	50,800C	
IMR4350	48.0	2618	51.0	2799	53,100C	
W760	48.0	2670	50.0	2788	50,400C	
H1000	61.0	2666	63.0	2783	45,800C	
H870			63.0	2769	43,200C	
A2700	47.5	2574	50.0	2738	52,000C	Sra SBT/3.3"/Rem 9½
RL-15	44.0	2611	48.0	2727	50,000C	
N160			51.1	2710	52,214p	Hdy SP
H4895	40.0	2567	43.0	2704	52,300C	
N165	47.9	2461	53.2	2650	52,210p	Spr Sptz SP
VarGet			43.0	2648	50,300C	
A8700	56.7	2228	63.0	2532	47,200C	Sra SBT/3.3"/Rem 9½/(C)

155

Powder	STARTING Grs.	MV (fps)	MAXIMUM Grs.	MV (fps)	Press. (CUP/psi)	Comments
N160			52.0	2760	52,214p	Sako SP 1118

160

Powder	STARTING Grs.	MV (fps)	MAXIMUM Grs.	MV (fps)	Press. (CUP/psi)	Comments
H4831	53.0	2729	57.0	2912	50,800C	
H450	53.0	2640	57.0	2866	50,600C	
IMR7828	53.0	2686	55.0	2809	51,500C	
IMR4831	51.0	2649	54.0	2797	53,200C	
H414	45.0	2552	48.0	2777	50,400C	
RL-22	52.0	2545	56.0	2777	51,000C	
W760	45.0	2560	48.0	2775	50,600C	
A3100	52.2	2442	58.0	2775	52,000C	Nos S-Sptz/3.335"/Rem 9½/(C)
RL-19	50.0	2504	54.0	2767	51,500C	
IMR4350	47.0	2586	50.0	2727	52,900C	
H1000	59.0	2561	62.0	2709	47,400C	
A4350	47.2	2375	52.5	2705	52,000C	Nos S-Sptz/3.335"/Rem 9½
H4350	46.0	2461	50.0	2696	51,000C	
H870			62.0	2660	42,800C	
H380	44.0	2600	47.0	2646	51,200C	
N165	47.8	2452	53.1	2634	52,210p	Nos Part.
A2700	47.5	2470	50.0	2630	52,000C	Nos S-Sptz/3.335"/Rem 9½
RL-15	42.0	2360	46.0	2592	49,500C	
A8700	57.6	2138	64.0	2429	44,900C	Nos S-Sptz/3.335"/Rem 9½/(C)

180

Powder	STARTING Grs.	MV (fps)	MAXIMUM Grs.	MV (fps)	Press. (CUP/psi)	Comments
H1000	57.0	2460	60.0	2614	50,300C	
H4831	51.0	2434	54.0	2581	52,000C	
RL-22	49.0	2411	53.0	2557	49,000C	
H870	60.0	2449	62.0	2543	45,000C	
RL-19	47.0	2379	51.0	2541	49,500C	
H4350	46.0	2269	48.0	2387	50,100C	

Caution: Loads exceeding SAAMI OAL Maximum must be verified for bullet-to-rifling clearance and magazine functioning. Where a specific primer or bullet is indicated those components must be used, no substitutions! Where only a maximum load is shown, reduce starting load 10%, unless otherwise specified.

Key: (C) = compressed charge; C = CUP; p = psi; Plink = Plinker; Bns = Barnes; Hdy = Hornady; Lap = Lapua; Nos = Nosler; Rem = Remington; Sra = Sierra; Spr = Speer; Win = Winchester.

Never exceed maximum load nor use any load exhibiting signs of excessive pressure. Begin at suggested starting load and work up carefully.

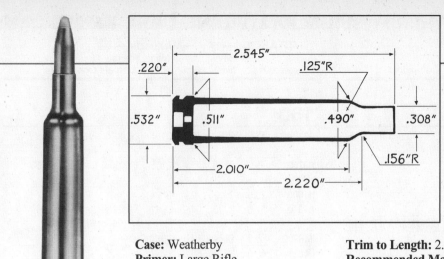

Case: Weatherby
Primer: Large Rifle
Barrel: 26″ Accurate
　　　　26″ Hodgdon
Bullet Diameter: 0.277″
Maximum Case Length: 2.545″

Trim to Length: 2.535″
Recommended Maximum OAL: 3.25″
Maximum Cartridge OAL: 3.25″
Minimum Cartridge OAL:
　　　　Bullet Dependent

This was the first of the now-famous "Weatherby Magnum" cartridges. Introduced in 1943, it is based on the 300 H&H Magnum case. The parent case was shortened to about the same length as the 30-06, and overall cartridge length is also similar. With little body taper and a sharp shoulder, the 270 Weatherby has about 80 grains of usable capacity (grains of water) compared to about 65.0 grains for the standard 270. Further, factory 270 Weatherby ammunition produces some of the highest chamber pressures of any commercial loading today.

Primarily because of the higher pressures used, the 270

Weatherby can drive any given bullet about 200 fps faster than the standard 270, given equal-length barrels. With proper bullets, 270 Weatherby Magnum performance is practically indistinguishable from the 7mm Remington Magnum.

As with all such high-performance chamberings, barrels shorter than 26″ are a poor choice since ballistics soon drop to the level of more mundane chamberings. H4831, IMR7828 and H4831 are noted 270 Weatherby choices. As with any free-bored chambering, the slowest usable powders seldom deliver good accuracy.

▐ 270 WEATHERBY MAGNUM LOADING DATA ▐

Powder	STARTING Grs.	MV (fps)	MAXIMUM Grs.	MV (fps)	Press. (CUP/psi)	Comments
90						
H450	74.0	3481	79.0	3799		
H4895	63.0	3388	67.0	3647		
H4831	72.0	3386	78.0	3631		
H4350	66.0	3317	70.0	3631		
H414	65.0	3304	68.0	3592		
H1000	78.0	3183	81.0	3269		
100						
H450	74.0	3398	78.0	3685		
H4831	74.0	3482	77.0	3666		
H4895	63.0	3377	66.0	3597		
IMR7828	74.0	3464	76.0	3590		
IMR4831	68.0	3381	71.0	3540		
H4350	65.0	3282	69.0	3509		
IMR4350	65.0	3347	68.0	3471		
W760	66.0	3239	68.0	3451		
H414	65.0	3231	68.0	3450		
H1000	77.0	3062	81.0	3287		

Powder	STARTING Grs.	MV (fps)	MAXIMUM Grs.	MV (fps)	Press. (CUP/psi)	Comments
110						
H450	73.0	3380	76.0	3541		
IMR7828	72.0	3412	75.0	3539		
A4350	62.1	3105	69.0	3528	65,900p	Hdy HP/3.285″/ Fed 215
H4831	73.0	3397	76.0	3482		
H4350	64.0	3214	68.0	3477		
IMR4831	66.0	3329	69.0	3471		
IMR4350	64.0	3228	67.0	3441		
A3100	67.5	2980	75.0	3386	69,000p	Hdy HP/3.285″/ Fed 215
H414	63.0	3187	66.0	3334		
W760	64.0	3219	66.0	3327		
H1000	76.0	3045	81.0	3242		
A8700	80.1	2831	89.0	3217	47,900p	Hdy HP/3.285″/ Fed 215/(C)
H870			81.0	3200		

▶▶▶▶▶▶▶▶▶▶▶▶▶▶▶▶▶▶▶▶▶▶▶▶▶▶▶

Never exceed maximum load nor use any load exhibiting signs of excessive pressure. Begin at suggested starting load and work up carefully.

Powder	STARTING Grs.	MV (fps)	MAXIMUM Grs.	MV (fps)	Press. (CUP/psi)	Comments
130						
A3100	65.3	2937	72.5	3338	67,000p	Bns-X/3.295"/Fed 215
IMR7828	68.0	3119	71.0	3277		
H4350	62.0	3110	66.0	3262		
H1000	76.0	2941	81.0	3259		
IMR4350	62.0	3130	65.0	3250		
IMR4831	64.0	3106	67.0	3244		
A4350	59.4	2840	66.0	3227	62,900p	Bns-X/3.295"/Fed 215
H870			80.0	3214		
H4831	67.0	3087	70.0	3205		
A8700	79.2	2806	88.0	3189	55,000p	Bns-X/3.295"/Fed 215/(C)
H450	66.0	3041	69.0	3144		
140						
A3100	63.5	2853	70.5	3242	68,100p	Nos BT/3.295"/Fed 215
IMR7828	66.0	3004	70.0	3206		
IMR4831	62.0	2947	65.0	3194		
IMR4350	61.0	2969	64.0	3175		
H1000	75.0	2849	80.0	3145		
H4350	60.0	2926	64.0	3140		
A4350	57.6	2761	64.0	3137	65,300p	Nos BT/3.295"/Fed 215
A8700	79.2	2759	88.0	3135	54,500p	Nos BT/3.295"/Fed 215/(C)
H4831	65.0	2904	68.0	3112		
H450	65.0	2880	68.0	3066		
H870			79.0	2890		

Powder	STARTING Grs.	MV (fps)	MAXIMUM Grs.	MV (fps)	Press. (CUP/psi)	Comments
150						
A3100	63.0	2782	70.0	3161	68,800p	Sra SBT/3.295"/Fed 215
A8700	79.2	2776	88.0	3155	57,700p	Sra SBT/3.295"/Fed 215/(C)
H1000	75.0	2902	79.0	3132		
A4350	57.6	2720	64.0	3091	68,000p	Sra SBT/3.295"/Fed 215
IMR7828	65.0	2862	69.0	3077		
H4831	65.0	2872	68.0	3057		
H4350	60.0	2846	63.0	2986		
IMR4350	59.0	2797	62.0	2974		
H870	79.0	2943				
IMR4831	61.0	2810	64.0	2920		
H450	65.0	2827	68.0	2902		
160						
H1000	74.0	2872	78.0	3051		
IMR7828	62.0	2767	66.0	2914		
H4831	62.0	2674	65.0	2901		
H870	78.0	2899				
H450	62.0	2666	65.0	2870		
IMR4831	59.0	2641	62.0	2844		
IMR4350	57.0	2630	60.0	2740		
H4350	58.0	2666	61.0	2738		
180						
H1000	71.0	2678	75.0	2852		
H870	72.0	2673	76.0	2808		
H4831	60.0	2558	63.0	2669		

Caution: Loads exceeding SAAMI OAL Maximum must be verified for bullet-to-rifling clearance and magazine functioning. Where a specific primer or bullet is indicated those components must be used, no substitutions! Where only a maximum load is shown, reduce starting load 10%, unless otherwise specified.

Key: (C) = compressed charge; C = CUP; p = psi; Plink = Plinker; Bns = Barnes; Hdy = Hornady; Lap = Lapua; Nos = Nosler; Rem = Remington; Sra = Sierra; Spr = Speer; Win = Winchester.

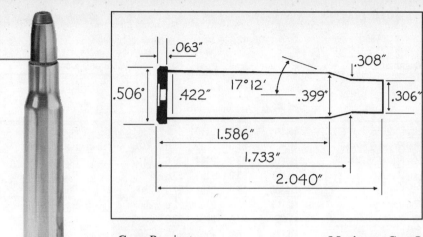

Case: Remington
Primer: Large Rife
Barrel: 24″ Accurate/24″ Hodgdon
Bullet Diameter: 0.284″

Maximum Case Length: 2.040″
Trim to Length: 2.035″
Maximum Cartridge OAL: 2.55″
Minimum Cartridge OAL: 2.48″

Ken Waters, well-known ballistics expert, designed this cartridge specifically to flatten the trajectory available from typical lever-action rifles without appreciably increasing recoil levels. His original version was tinkered with by Federal before standardization. U.S. Repeating Arms Company offered the Angle-Eject version of the Model 94 in this new standardized chambering in 1983.

It is genuinely unfortunate that Federal did not adopt a small primer pocket as standard for this case. That decision would have allowed safe use of bullets with a much smaller meplat (the flat point of such bullets) and therefore with notably superior external ballistics.

Cases are easily formed from standard 30-30 cases.

SAAMI pressure standards for the 7-30 Waters are about 5 percent higher than for the 30-30, and performance is just a bit better. The 7-30 will launch a 140-grain bullet as much as 150 fps faster than the 30-30 will launch a 150-grain bullet and can therefore deliver considerably more energy with a flatter trajectory inside the useful range of about 250 yards.

Rifles with tubular magazines require use of flatpoint bullets. The specter of a chain-reaction firing of cartridges in the magazine is best left to the imagination.

Case capacity with a 139-grain bullet, seated normally, is about 40.0 grains of water. W748, IMR3031, H414, H335, A2460 and H4895 are noted performers in Water's little 7-30.

7-30 WATERS LOADING DATA

Powder	STARTING Grs.	MV (fps)	MAXIMUM Grs.	MV (fps)	Press. (CUP/psi)	Comments
120						
H414	40.0	2620	42.0	2757		Flat Point
H380	39.0	2605	41.0	2735		Flat Point
A2520	33.3	2406	37.0	2734	39,400C	Nos FN/BT/2.53″/Rem 9½
H4895	31.0	2537	34.0	2733		Flat Point
H4350	39.0	2601	41.0	2724		Flat Point
BL-C(2)	35.0	2501	37.0	2701		Flat Point
A2495BR	33.3	2372	37.0	2696	35,100C	Nos FN/BT/2.53″/Rem 9½
H322	29.0	2558	32.0	2687		Flat Point
A2015BR	29.7	2365	33.0	2687	37,600C	Nos FN/BT/2.53″/Rem 9½
H335	32.0	2469	34.0	2683		Flat Point
A2230	30.6	2328	34.0	2646	38,800C	Nos FN/BT/2.53″/Rem 9½

Powder	STARTING Grs.	MV (fps)	MAXIMUM Grs.	MV (fps)	Press. (CUP/psi)	Comments
120 con't						
A2460	30.6	2300	34.0	2614	35,800C	Nos FN/BT/2.53″/Rem 9½
H4831	39.0	2411	41.0	2561		Flat Point
A2700	35.6	2240	39.5	2546	36,300C	Nos FN/BT/2.53″/Rem 9½

▶▶▶▶▶▶▶▶▶▶▶▶▶▶▶▶▶▶▶▶▶▶▶▶▶▶

139

Powder	Grs.	MV (fps)	Grs.	MV (fps)	Press. (CUP/psi)	Comments
A2460	31.1	2242	34.5	2548	39,300C	Hdy FN/2.665"/Rem 9½
A2230	30.6	2237	34.0	2542	40,000C	Hdy FN/2.665"/Rem 9½
A2495BR	32.0	2210	35.5	2511	38,100C	Hdy FN/2.665"/Rem 9½
A2520	31.1	2175	34.5	2472	36,000C	Hdy FN/2.665"/Rem 9½
H4895	29.0	2310	31.0	2458		Flat Point
IMR4831	36.0	2302	38.0	2447		Flat Point
RL-15	31.0	2288	33.0	2447		Flat Point
H414	36.0	2239	38.0	2442		Flat Point
IMR4320	29.0	2300	31.0	2440		Flat Point
W760	36.0	2229	38.0	2437		Flat Point
RL-22	40.0	2308	42.0	2431		Flat Point
H335	30.0	2280	32.0	2430		Flat Point
IMR4064	30.0	2232	32.0	2423		Flat Point
A2700	34.2	2131	38.0	2422	38,200C	Hdy FN/2.665"/Rem 9½
H4350	36.0	2262	38.0	2418		Flat Point
IMR4895	29.0	2240	31.0	2410		Flat Point
A2015BR	27.9	2115	31.0	2403	38,900C	Hdy FN/2.665"/Rem 9½
H380	34.0	2188	36.0	2396		Flat Point
RL-12	31.0	2197	33.0	2396		Flat Point
H4831	37.0	2240	39.0	2384		Flat Point
BL-C(2)	33.0	2221	35.0	2373		Flat Point
IMR4350	35.0	2210	37.0	2367		Flat Point
H322	27.0	2209	29.0	2342		Flat Point
W748	32.0	2199	34.0	2342		Flat Point
RL-19	38.0	2243	40.0	2333		Flat Point
IMR3031	27.0	2227	29.0	2304		Flat Point

154

Powder	Grs.	MV (fps)	Grs.	MV (fps)	Press. (CUP/psi)	Comments
H414	35.0	2170	37.0	2347		Round Nose
BL-C(2)	31.0	2129	33.0	2320		Round Nose
H380	33.0	2144	35.0	2310		Round Nose
W760	35.0	2157	37.0	2310		Round Nose
H4350	35.0	2151	37.0	2308		Round Nose
RL-15	30.0	2156	32.0	2307		Round Nose
H335	27.0	2134	29.0	2300		Round Nose
RL-22	38.0	2141	40.0	2287		Round Nose
IMR4350	34.0	2112	36.0	2269		Round Nose
W748	30.0	2104	32.0	2259		Round Nose
RL-19	37.0	2157	39.0	2255		Round Nose
H4895	28.0	2098	30.0	2253		Round Nose
IMR4831	34.0	2137	36.0	2242		Round Nose
IMR4320	27.0	2005	29.0	2189		Round Nose
RL-12	29.0	2009	31.0	2169		Round Nose
H4831	35.0	2037	37.0	2161		Round Nose
IMR4895	27.0	1954	29.0	2147		Round Nose
IMR4064	28.0	1996	30.0	2134		Round Nose

Caution: Loads exceeding SAAMI OAL Maximum must be verified for bullet-to-rifling clearance and magazine functioning. Where a specific primer or bullet is indicated those components must be used, no substitutions! Where only a maximum load is shown, reduce starting load 10%, unless otherwise specified.

Key: (C) = compressed charge; C = CUP; p = psi; Plinker; Bns = Barnes; Hdy = Hornady; Lap = Lapua; Nos = Nosler; Rem = Remington; Sra = Sierra; Spr = Speer; Win = Winchester.

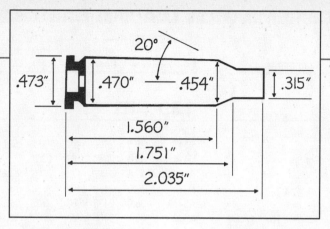

Case: Remington
Primer: Large Rifle
Barrel: 24″ Accurate
  18½″ Hodgdon
  24″ Vihtavuori

Bullet Diameter: 0.284″
Maximum Case Length: 2.035″
Trim to Length: 2.025″
Maximum Cartridge OAL: 2.800″
Minimum Cartridge OAL: 2.530″

This was originally a wildcat chambering developed for Metallic Silhouette Shooting Competition. With the proper bullet the 7mm-08 can deliver sufficient momentum to topple the Metallic Ram target at 500 meters and without producing as much recoil as similarly performing 308 loads. The 7mm-08 was created by the simple expedient of necking down the standard 308 Winchester to 7mm. Excepting the headstamp, there are no other differences in the two cases, and 7mm-08 cases can easily be formed from 308 cases.

In 1980, Remington offered the 7mm-08 as a factory chambering, complete with factory ammunition featuring an unusually aerodynamic 140-grain bullet—compared to typical factory loads of the day. The cartridge was given rave reviews by the gun press, but has since lost ground and holds on only because it can provide reasonable ballistic performance with moderate recoil in lighter short-barreled guns.

(The 284 Winchester, which has the same rim size and is the same overall length, can deliver considerably more velocity, if loaded to the same pressure.... Interestingly, some of the same gun writers who so loudly lauded the 7mm-08 in the early 1980s had demonized the 284 Winchester as less than useless in the mid-1960s.)

The 7mm-08 is an excellent choice for those who are recoil sensitive or who want a very light rifle for hunting smaller species of big game. Loaded with the proper bullet and with careful shot placement, the 7mm-08 would certainly be capable as an elk cartridge.

Case capacity with a 145-grain bullet, seated normally, is about 51.2 grains of water. W760, H414, H380, W748, IMR4064, IMR4320, H4895, H335, A3100 and IMR4895 have all been noted as good 7-08 performers.

7mm-08 REMINGTON LOADING DATA

Powder	STARTING Grs.	MV (fps)	MAXIMUM Grs.	MV (fps)	Press. (CUP/psi)	Comments
100						
N540	45.1	2969	49.2	3301	50,500p	Hdy HP/2.717″/Rem 9½
N150	44.4	2918	49.4	3222	50,500p	Hdy HP/2.717″/Rem 9½
A2460	38.7	2790	43.0	3171	49,500C	Sra HP/2.665″/CCI 200
A2520	40.1	2782	44.5	3161	48,400C	Sra HP/2.665″/CCI 200
A2230	38.3	2780	42.5	3159	49,800C	Sra HP/2.665″/CCI 200
A2015BR	36.5	2749	40.5	3124	48,500C	Sra HP/2.665″/CCI 200
A2495BR	38.3	2739	42.5	3113	48,500C	Sra HP/2.665″/CCI 200
RL-12	42.0	2878	45.0	3108		
RL-15	43.0	2864	46.0	3095		
A2700	45.6	2859	48.0	3041	50,700C	Sra HP/2.665″/CCI 200
H414	48.0	2881	50.0	3040		
W760	48.0	2877	50.0	3027		
H4895	42.0	2879	44.0	3021		
H380	46.0	2810	48.0	2997		
IMR4064	42.0	2834	44.0	2994		
IMR4320	42.0	2821	44.0	2977		
BL-C(2)	43.0	2880	45.0	2967		

Powder	STARTING Grs.	MV (fps)	MAXIMUM Grs.	MV (fps)	Press. (CUP/psi)	Comments
100 con't						
W748	43.0	2878	45.0	2962		
IMR4895	41.0	2786	43.0	2960		
H335	42.0	2887	44.0	2954		
A4350	42.8	2531	47.5	2876	44,200C	Sra HP/2.665″/CCI 200/(C)
H450	50.0	2684	52.0	2826		
H4350	48.0	2637	50.0	2814		
IMR4350	47.0	2616	49.0	2801		
IMR3031	36.0	2689	38.0	2790		
IMR4831	47.0	2519	49.0	2714		
H4831	49.0	2574	50.0	2669		
RL-19	47.0	2413	50.0	2654		
RL-22	48.0	2396	51.0	2614		
A3100	42.8	2248	47.5	2555	40,600C	Sra HP/2.665″/CCI 200/(C)

>>>>>>>>>>>>>>>>>>>>>>>>>>>>>>>>>

Never exceed maximum load nor use any load exhibiting signs of excessive pressure. Begin at suggested starting load and work up carefully.

115-120

Powder	Grs.	MV (fps)	Grs.	MV (fps)	Press. (CUP/psi)	Comments
VarGet			46.0	3138	49,200C	26" Bbl
H4895	41.0	2808	43.0	2973		
N150	42.2	2684	46.9	2967	50,500p	Sra Sptz
H414	48.0	2824	50.0	2959		
N140	41.4	2548	45.4	2941	50,500p	Sra Sptz
IMR4895	40.0	2764	42.0	2933		
A2495BR	36.0	2577	40.0	2928	49,000C	Nos SP/2.765"/CCI 200
A2460	36.6	2571	40.7	2922	48,800C	Nos SP/2.765"/CCI 200
H335	42.0	2855	44.0	2917		
W760	47.0	2743	49.0	2898		
N135	38.7	2519	42.7	2893	50,500p	Sra Sptz
BL-C(2)	42.0	2799	44.0	2891		
A2230	36.3	2541	40.3	2887	48,900C	Nos SP/2.765"/CCI 200
A2015BR	34.4	2541	38.2	2887	49,000C	Nos SP/2.765"/CCI 200
W748	42.0	2781	44.0	2882		
RL-15	41.0	2671	44.0	2881		
H380	45.0	2728	47.0	2880		
A2520	37.3	2529	41.4	2874	47,700C	Nos SP/2.765"/CCI 200
A2700	44.2	2699	46.5	2871	49,200C	Nos SP/2.765"/CCI 200
IMR4064	41.0	2694	43.0	2857		
IMR4320	41.0	2707	43.0	2848		
RL-12	40.0	2680	43.0	2812		
A4350	42.8	2459	47.5	2794	45,500C	Nos SP/2.765"/CCI 200/(C)
H450	50.0	2616	52.0	2792		
IMR4350	47.0	2575	49.0	2789		
H4350	47.0	2537	49.0	2760		
IMR4831	47.0	2540	49.0	2751		

125-130

Powder	Grs.	MV (fps)	Grs.	MV (fps)	Press. (CUP/psi)	Comments
H414	47.0	2737	49.0	2886		
RL-15	41.0	2660	44.0	2860		
H335	41.0	2728	43.0	2843		
A4350	42.8	2497	47.5	2838	48,600C	Spr SP/2.77"/CCI 200/(C)
A2460	35.8	2482	39.8	2821	52,000C	Spr SP/2.77"/CCI 200
IMR4064	40.0	2669	42.0	2820		
W760	46.0	2686	48.0	2812		
IMR4320	40.0	2634	42.0	2808		
A2230	35.4	2468	39.3	2804	51,800C	Spr SP/2.77"/CCI 200
H380	45.0	2655	47.0	2795		
A2015BR	33.8	2457	37.6	2792	52,000C	Spr SP/2.77"/CCI 200
IMR4350	46.0	2598	48.0	2788		
H450	49.0	2492	52.0	2781		
A2495BR	35.1	2446	39.0	2779	49,800C	Spr SP/2.77"/CCI 200
A2700	42.8	2612	45.0	2779	50,500C	Spr SP/2.77"/CCI 200
H4895	40.0	2631	42.0	2774		
H4350	47.0	2612	49.0	2769		
RL-12	40.0	2579	43.0	2763		
IMR4895	39.0	2594	41.0	2760		
BL-C(2)	41.0	2669	43.0	2755		
A2520	35.6	2423	39.6	2753	51,400C	Spr SP/2.77"/CCI 200
W748	41.0	2645	43.0	2750		
RL-22	48.0	2502	51.0	2626		
RL-19	47.0	2412	50.0	2617		

139-140

Powder	Grs.	MV (fps)	Grs.	MV (fps)	Press. (CUP/psi)	Comments
VarGet			44.0	2947	50,400C	26" Bbl
N140	38.5	2607	42.7	2857	50,500p	Nos BT
H414	45.0	2646	48.0	2807		
A4350	42.8	2467	47.5	2803	49,800C	Sra SBT/2.8"/CCI 200
H380	43.0	2490	46.0	2770		
A2460	36.0	2436	40.0	2768	51,900C	Sra SBT/2.8"/CCI 200
N550	39.7	2465	45.4	2767	50,500p	Nos B-Tip/Rem 9½
H335	39.0	2570	41.0	2736		
H450	49.0	2530	52.0	2729		
BL-C(2)	40.0	2554	42.0	2715		
A2230	35.1	2386	39.0	2711	49,600C	Sra SBT/2.8"/CCI 200
IMR4064	39.0	2567	41.0	2710		
IMR4320	38.0	2553	40.0	2707		
H4895	39.0	2594	41.0	2705		
A2495BR	34.7	2379	38.5	2703	49,200C	Sra SBT/2.8"/CCI 200
A2700	42.3	2538	44.5	2700	49,500C	Sra SBT/2.8"/CCI 200
A2520	35.6	2376	39.5	2700	50,800C	Sra SBT/2.8"/CCI 200
A2015BR	33.3	2375	37.0	2699	49,300C	Sra SBT/2.8"/CCI 200
IMR4831	45.0	2559	47.0	2691		
H4350	46.0	2580	48.0	2690		
IMR4350	45.0	2574	47.0	2679		
IMR4895	38.0	2509	40.0	2674		
H4831	49.0	2558	50.0	2672		

139-145

Powder	Grs.	MV (fps)	Grs.	MV (fps)	Press. (CUP/psi)	Comments
RL-15	39.0	2488	42.0	2714		
RL-12	38.0	2439	41.0	2666		
RL-19	47.0	2450	50.0	2658		
RL-22	48.0	2414	51.0	2644		

145-150

Powder	Grs.	MV (fps)	Grs.	MV (fps)	Press. (CUP/psi)	Comments
H414	44.0	2672	46.0	2787		
W760	44.0	2680	46.0	2782		
H4350	45.0	2561	47.0	2752		
A4350	41.9	2403	46.5	2731	51,100C	Sra SBT/2.8"/CCI 200
H335	37.0	2490	39.0	2707		
H380	42.0	2520	44.0	2704		
H450	48.0	2530	50.0	2699		
H4831	47.0	2501	49.0	2686		
H4895	37.0	2443	39.0	2680		
IMR4350	43.0	2494	45.0	2680		
IMR4064	37.0	2470	39.0	2666		
BL-C(2)	38.0	2474	40.0	2660		
W748	38.0	2460	40.0	2651		
IMR4320	37.0	2447	39.0	2640		
A2700	41.3	2477	43.5	2635	51,900C	Sra SBT/2.8"/CCI 200
IMR4831	44.0	2480	46.0	2634		
IMR4895	36.0	2449	38.0	2631		
A2460	34.5	2310	38.3	2625	50,200C	Sra SBT/2.8"/CCI 200
A2230	34.2	2306	38.0	2620	51,000C	Sra SBT/2.8"/CCI 200
A2520	35.1	2299	39.0	2612	51,600C	Sra SBT/2.8"/CCI 200
A2495BR	33.6	2293	37.3	2606	50,300C	Sra SBT/2.8"/CCI 200

Never exceed maximum load nor use any load exhibiting signs of excessive pressure. Begin at suggested starting load and work up carefully.

7mm-08 REMINGTON LOADING DATA

Powder	—STARTING— Grs.	MV (fps)	—MAXIMUM— Grs.	MV (fps)	Press. (CUP/psi)	Comments

154-162

Powder	Grs.	MV (fps)	Grs.	MV (fps)	Press. (CUP/psi)	Comments
N160	45.8	2421	50.2	2667	50,500p	Sra SBT;
VarGet			40.0	2650	49,700C	
A4350	41.4	2314	46.0	2630	49,400C	Nos Part./2.8"/CCI 200/(C)
H4350	43.0	2464	45.0	2575		
H450	47.0	2451	49.0	2565		
IMR4350	42.0	2377	44.0	2555		
IMR4831	43.0	2380	45.0	2540		
H414	43.0	2447	45.0	2534		
W760	43.0	2431	45.0	2530		
IMR4320	37.0	2388	39.0	2521		
IMR7828	45.0	2364	48.0	2511		
H4831	46.0	2409	48.0	2506		
RL-15	37.0	2321	40.0	2503		
H380	41.0	2390	43.0	2486		
RL-19	45.0	2306	48.0	2486		
RL-22	46.0	2288	49.0	2484		
H4895	36.0	2380	38.0	2476		
N140	38.5	2263	40.3	2472	50,500p	Sra Sptz
BL-C(2)	37.0	2413	39.0	2470		
IMR4895	35.0	2329	37.0	2470		
A2700	39.9	2311	42.0	2458	45,600C	Nos Part./2.8"/CCI 200
A2520	34.2	2160	38.0	2455	48,500C	Nos Part./2.8"/CCI 200
A3100	42.3	2158	47.0	2452	43,400C	Nos Part./2.8"/CCI 200/(C)
A2460	33.3	2158	37.0	2452	48,500C	Nos Part./2.8"/CCI 200
A2495BR	32.4	2156	36.0	2450	49,900C	Nos Part./2.8"/CCI 200
N150	36.8	2268	40.7	2449	50,500p	Sra Sptz
W748	37.0	2394	39.0	2448		
H335	36.0	2392	38.0	2443		
IMR4064	36.0	2303	38.0	2441		

168

Powder	Grs.	MV (fps)	Grs.	MV (fps)	Press. (CUP/psi)	Comments
A4350	41.4	2284	46.0	2596	50,400C	Sra HPBT/2.8"/CCI 200
RL-22	45.0	2343	48.0	2528		
RL-19	44.0	2349	47.0	2507		
A2495BR	34.2	2202	38.0	2502	52,000C	Sra HPBT/2.8"/CCI 200
H414	41.0	2389	43.0	2486		
W760	41.0	2394	43.0	2475		
IMR7828	44.0	2340	47.0	2463		
RL-15	35.0	2260	38.0	2460		
H4350	41.0	2354	43.0	2459		
A2460	33.3	2159	37.0	2453	50,100C	Sra HPBT/2.8"/CCI 200
IMR4831	41.0	2361	43.0	2448		
H450	45.0	2316	47.0	2446		
H4831	45.0	2319	47.0	2420		
IMR4350	40.0	2344	42.0	2419		
A2015BR	31.5	2127	35.0	2417	49,300C	Sra HPBT/2.8"/CCI 200
IMR4064	35.0	2283	37.0	2415		
A2230	33.3	2123	37.0	2413	49,500C	Sra HPBT/2.8"/CCI 200
IMR4320	36.0	2312	38.0	2404		
A2520	33.3	2116	37.0	2404	49,400C	Sra HPBT/2.8"/CCI 200
H380	39.0	2301	41.0	2396		
A3100	42.3	2102	47.0	2389	42,600C	Sra HPBT/2.8"/CCI 200/(C)
H4895	35.0	2295	36.0	2365		

175

Powder	Grs.	MV (fps)	Grs.	MV (fps)	Press. (CUP/psi)	Comments
A4350	41.0	2201	45.5	2501	49,400C	Rem PSPCL/2.795"/CCI 200
VarGet			38.0	2420	50,700C	
A2700	39.9	2244	42.0	2387	47,400C	Rem PSPCL/2.795"/CCI 200
RL-19	43.0	2156	46.0	2374		
A2230	33.3	2088	37.0	2373	49,600C	Rem PSPCL/2.795"/CCI 200
A2460	33.3	2082	37.0	2366	49,800C	Rem PSPCL/2.795"/CCI 200
A2520	34.2	2080	38.0	2364	51,200C	Rem PSPCL/2.795"/CCI 200
A2495BR	34.2	2072	38.0	2354	47,900C	Rem PSPCL/2.795"/CCI 200
A8700	42.3	2070	47.0	2352	42,600C	Rem PSPCL/2.795"/CCI 200/(C)
RL-22	44.0	2201	47.0	2343		
A2015BR	31.5	2038	35.0	2316	47,700C	Rem PSPCL/2.795"/CCI 200
N160	39.4	2099	43.1	2298	50,500p	Spr Mag-Tip/2.795"/Rem 9½
IMR4350	39.0	2181	41.0	2260		
H414	39.0	2078	41.0	2259		
H4831	43.0	2147	45.0	2249		
H4350	39.0	2152	41.0	2249		
RL-15	33.0	2052	36.0	2249		
H450	43.0	2179	45.0	2239		
IMR7828	41.0	2078	45.0	2239		
IMR4831	40.0	2094	42.0	2237		
IMR4320	34.0	2100	36.0	2232		
W760	39.0	2103	41.0	2232		
RL-12	32.0	2008	35.0	2225		
H4895	33.0	2083	35.0	2219		
H380	37.0	2100	39.0	2214		
N140	32.8	2017	36.2	2195	50,500p	Spr Mag-Tip
IMR4895	32.0	2079	34.0	2190		
N150	32.0	1953	35.2	2123	50,500p	Spr Mag-Tip

195

Powder	Grs.	MV (fps)	Grs.	MV (fps)	Press. (CUP/psi)	Comments
RL-22	41.0	2043	44.0	2239		
RL-19	40.0	2014	43.0	2225		
H4350	36.0	2054	38.0	2169		
H414	36.0	2042	38.0	2157		

Caution: Loads exceeding SAAMI OAL Maximum must be verified for bullet-to-rifling clearance and magazine functioning. Where a specific primer or bullet is indicated those components must be used, no substitutions! Where only a maximum load is shown, reduce starting load 10%, unless otherwise specified.

Key: (C) = compressed charge; C = CUP; p = psi; Plink = Plinker; Bns = Barnes; Hdy = Hornady; Lap = Lapua; Nos = Nosler; Rem = Remington; Sra = Sierra; Spr = Speer; Win = Winchester.

Never exceed maximum load nor use any load exhibiting signs of excessive pressure. Begin at suggested starting load and work up carefully.

7mm
Mauser
(7x57 Mauser)

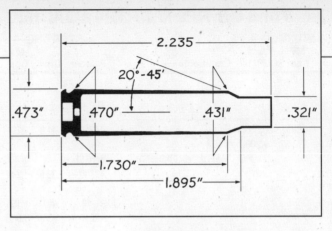

Case: Winchester
Primer: Large Rifle
Barrel: 24″ Accurate
24″ Hodgdon
22″ Vihtavuori

Bullet Diameter: 0.284″
Maximum Case Length: 2.235″
Trim to Length: 2.225″
Maximum Cartridge OAL: 3.065″
Minimum Cartridge OAL: 2.940″

This military chambering was developed in 1892 for the Mauser rifle. These soon became the combination of choice in Spain and much of South America. As Theodore Roosevelt and the Rough Riders soon learned the hard way at San Juan Hill in Cuba, the 7x57mm Mauser and the turnbolt rifle it was chambered in far outclassed blackpowder-era chamberings and rifles.

So influential was the Mauser that within a few years the U.S. had adopted the 1903 Springfield chambered for the 30-03, the forerunner to the 30-06, as the standard-issue military shoulder weapon. The Springfield rifle and its new chambering so copied Mr. Mauser's work that the courts

awarded Mauser a royalty for every Springfield rifle built!

In deference to century-old rifles that might still be in use, the pressure limit for the 7x57 is considerably lower than that of the 270 Winchester or the 280 Remington. Further, the 7mm Mauser has somewhat less case capacity than these 30-06 based chamberings. Nevertheless, when loaded to its modern pressure limit it is still an impressive performer and is a capable big game cartridge.

Case capacity with a 145-grain bullet, seated normally, is about 56.8 grains of water. IMR4350, IMR4064, IMR4320, H414, IMR4831, H414, H4350, H380 and W760 are all good choices in the 7mm Mauser.

7mm MAUSER LOADING DATA (7x57mm MAUSER)

Powder	Grs.	MV (fps)	Grs.	MV (fps)	Press. (CUP/psi)	Comments
79						
N110			27.8	2950	49,313p	Sako FMJ 1088
100						
RL-15	47.0	3079	49.0	3294	44,000C	
H414	53.0	3188	55.0	3256	46,900C	
W760	53.0	3138	55.0	3211	47,000C	
H380	51.0	3062	53.0	3209	45,000C	
IMR4064	46.0	2989	49.0	3204	48,500C	
BL-C(2)	46.0	2877	48.5	3202	46,400C	
RL-12	45.0	2948	47.0	3190	44,800C	
W748	46.0	3054	48.0	3189	46,600C	
IMR4320	46.0	3033	49.0	3177	46,200C	
H4895	44.0	3041	46.0	3149	46,400C	
IMR4350	51.0	2830	54.0	3091	41,400C	
IMR4831	51.0	2779	54.0	3084	40,400C	
H4350	51.0	2760	54.0	2967	36,500C	
H450	52.0	2660	55.0	2940	34,400C	
RL-19	52.0	2841	54.0	2915	37,100C	
H4831	51.0	2688	54.0	2886	33,600C	

Powder	Grs.	MV (fps)	Grs.	MV (fps)	Press. (CUP/psi)	Comments
100 con't						
RL-22	52.0	2654	54.0	2817	32,700C	
IMR7828	52.0	2664	54.0	2741	31,800C	
115-120						
IMR4831	51.0	2764	54.0	3052	45,000C	
N140			47.4	3050	49,313p	Hdy SP
IMR4064	44.0	2864	47.0	3036	48,500C	
H414	51.0	2937	53.0	3025	47,400C	
W760	51.0	2930	53.0	3012	47,600C	
H380	47.0	2901	50.0	3006	48,000C	
IMR4350	50.0	2780	53.0	3002	46,400C	
BL-C(2)	45.0	2829	47.0	3002	47,400C	
IMR4320	44.0	2842	47.0	2990	48,000C	
W748	45.0	2831	47.0	2990	48,000C	
VarGet			44.5	2979	46,300C	
H4350	50.0	2729	53.0	2952	43,400C	
A2700	47.5	2749	50.0	2924	44,800C	Spr SP/2.9″/CCI 200
RL-19	51.0	2788	54.0	2923	40,900C	
A2495BR	39.6	2569	44.0	2919	42,300C	Spr SP/2.9″/CCI 200

Never exceed maximum load nor use any load exhibiting signs of excessive pressure. Begin at suggested starting load and work up carefully.

115-120 con't

Powder	STARTING Grs.	MV (fps)	MAXIMUM Grs.	MV (fps)	Press. (CUP/psi)	Comments
H450	52.0	2738	55.0	2919	42,900C	
RL-15	43.0	2859	46.0	2900	48,000C	
A4350	45.9	2541	51.0	2887	40,400C	Spr SP/2.9"/ CCI 200/(C)
N150			46.6	2880	47,900p	Sra Sptz
RL-12	41.0	2731	43.0	2877	48,400C	
N140			46.1	2873	47,900p	Sra Sptz
H4895	41.0	2680	43.0	2870	46,900C	
RL-22	52.0	2670	54.0	2849	38,200C	
H4831	51.0	2711	54.0	2844	43,100C	
N135			43.4	2826	47,900p	Sra Sptz
IMR7828	52.0	2654	54.0	2770	38,700C	
A3100	45.9	2263	51.0	2572	34,000p	Spr SP/2.9"/ CCI 200/(C)

125-130

Powder	STARTING Grs.	MV (fps)	MAXIMUM Grs.	MV (fps)	Press. (CUP/psi)	Comments
IMR4831	50.0	2710	53.0	2961	47,500C	
W760	50.0	2794	52.0	2951	48,500C	
H414	50.0	2809	52.0	2949	48,400C	
IMR4350	49.0	2654	52.0	2940	47,000C	
H380	46.0	2690	49.0	2887	48,000C	
H4350	50.0	2640	53.0	2886	46,200C	
H450	52.0	2720	55.0	2869	47,000C	
BL-C(2)	43.0	2719	45.0	2839	48,500C	
IMR4320	43.0	2660	46.0	2833	46,600C	
W748	43.0	2714	45.0	2830	48,400C	
IMR4064	43.0	2619	46.0	2826	46,400C	
RL-19	50.0	2664	53.0	2814	42,500C	
RL-15	41.0	2629	44.0	2799	44,000C	
H4831	50.0	2646	53.0	2763	44,000C	
IMR7828	52.0	2640	54.0	2762	42,600C	
RL-22	51.0	2549	53.0	2760	41,500C	
H4895	39.0	2549	42.0	2749	48,500C	
RL-12	39.0	2545	42.0	2736	45,000C	

139-140

Powder	STARTING Grs.	MV (fps)	MAXIMUM Grs.	MV (fps)	Press. (CUP/psi)	Comments
A4350	45.9	2496	51.0	2836	43,900C	Sra SBT/3.025"/ CCI 200/(C)
IMR4831	49.0	2639	51.0	2822	47,900C	
IMR4350	48.0	2629	50.0	2814	47,500C	
H4350	49.0	2598	52.0	2807	48,000C	
H414	46.0	2698	48.0	2805	48,800C	
H450	51.0	2629	54.0	2794	47,400C	
W760	46.0	2704	48.0	2792	48,500C	
IMR4320	42.0	2584	45.0	2775	47,500C	
RL-19	49.0	2631	52.0	2774	44,000C	
IMR4064	41.0	2538	44.0	2764	48,000C	
H4831	50.0	2617	53.0	2757	48,500C	
IMR7828	52.0	2622	54.0	2754	46,400C	

139-140 con't

Powder	STARTING Grs.	MV (fps)	MAXIMUM Grs.	MV (fps)	Press. (CUP/psi)	Comments
A2495BR	37.8	2416	42.0	2745	43,400C	Sra SBT/3.025"/ CCI 200
H380	44.0	2611	47.0	2743	48,400C	
A2700	45.1	2577	47.5	2742	42,800C	Sra SBT/3.025"/ CCI 200
RL-15	40.0	2594	43.0	2724	45,500C	
RL-22	50.0	2529	52.0	2707	42,500C	
H4895	38.0	2512	41.0	2693	48,400C	
RL-12	38.0	2544	41.0	2679	45,000C	
VarGet			40.5	2678	44,900C	
BL-C(2)	40.0	2520	42.0	2646	48,000C	
W748	40.0	2491	42.0	2630	47,700C	
N150			43.6	2599	47,900p	Nos BT
N140			42.5	2568	47,900p	Nos BT
A3100	45.9	2254	51.0	2561	34,200C	Sra SBT/3.025"/ CCI 200/(C)

145-150

Powder	STARTING Grs.	MV (fps)	MAXIMUM Grs.	MV (fps)	Press. (CUP/psi)	Comments
H4350	48.0	2534	51.0	2748	47,600C	
H450	50.0	2544	53.0	2736	48,000C	
H414	45.0	2559	47.0	2724	47,000C	
A4350	44.1	2395	49.0	2722	44,000C	Nos BT/3.06"/ CCI 200/(C)
IMR7828	52.0	2607	54.0	2717	47,200C	
IMR4320	41.0	2529	44.0	2711	48,000C	
IMR4831	46.0	2554	50.0	2710	47,100C	
W760	45.0	2548	47.0	2709	47,400C	
IMR4064	40.0	2517	43.0	2696	47,400C	
H380	43.0	2539	46.0	2694	48,500C	
IMR4350	46.0	2560	49.0	2689	47,700C	
RL-19	48.0	2414	51.0	2674	44,500C	
RL-22	50.0	2519	52.0	2673	43,600C	
RL-15	39.0	2411	42.0	2670	45,500C	
H4831	49.0	2549	52.0	2662	47,400C	
RL-12	37.0	2404	39.0	2637	46,000C	
A2700	43.7	2468	46.0	2626	43,200C	Nos BT/3.06"/ CCI 200
A3100	45.9	2271	51.0	2581	38,200C	Nos BT/3.06"/ CCI 200/(C)
A2495BR	36.0	2269	40.0	2578	44,400C	Nos BT/3.06"/CCI 200

▶▶▶▶▶▶▶▶▶▶▶▶▶▶▶▶▶▶▶▶▶▶▶▶▶▶▶▶▶

Caution: Loads exceeding SAAMI OAL Maximum must be verified for bullet-to-rifling clearance and magazine functioning. Where a specific primer or bullet is indicated those components must be used, no substitutions! Where only a maximum load is shown, reduce starting load 10%, unless otherwise specified.

Key: (C) = compressed charge; C = CUP; p = psi; Plink = Plinker; Bns = Barnes; Hdy = Hornady; Lap = Lapua; Nos = Nosler; Rem = Remington; Sra = Sierra; Spr = Speer; Win = Winchester.

154-162

Powder	Grs. (start)	MV (fps) start	Grs. (max)	MV (fps) max	Press. (CUP/psi)	Comments
N160			48.6	2710	49,313p	Sako SP 1108
IMR4831	44.0	2479	47.0	2665	48,100C	
RL-22	49.0	2512	51.0	2662	47,000C	
IMR7828	49.0	2529	52.0	2652	48,000C	
RL-19	46.0	2488	49.0	2634	46,000C	
A4350	43.2	2308	48.0	2623	45,100C	Spr SP/3.02"/CCI 200
H4831	47.0	2370	50.0	2597	47,100C	
W760	43.0	2479	45.0	2596	48,500C	
H414	43.0	2482	45.0	2594	48,500C	
H4350	46.0	2443	49.0	2592	48,500C	
H450	49.0	2423	51.0	2588	46,800C	
A3100	45.9	2238	51.0	2543	39,000C	Spr SP/3.02"/ CCI 200/(C)
IMR4350	43.0	2390	46.0	2540	47,500C	
N160			49.4	2539	47,900p	Sra SBT
IMR4320	39.0	2381	42.0	2539	48,500C	
IMR4064	38.0	2340	41.0	2523	47,500C	
RL-15	38.0	2362	41.0	2505	44,000C	
H380	41.0	2311	43.0	2497	48,200C	
RL-12	34.0	2318	36.0	2474	45,000C	
VarGet			38.0	2444	45,400C	
A2495BR	34.2	2130	38.0	2420	46,000C	Spr SP/3.02"/CCI 200
N150			41.4	2414	47,900p	Sra SBT
A2700	40.9	2255	43.0	2399	39,700C	Spr SP/3.02"/CCI 200

168-170

Powder	Grs. (start)	MV (fps) start	Grs. (max)	MV (fps) max	Press. (CUP/psi)	Comments
IMR7828	48.0	2410	51.0	2639	48,500C	
IMR4831	43.0	2342	46.0	2599	47,000C	
RL-22	47.0	2439	49.0	2566	46,500C	
H4831	46.0	2334	49.0	2563	48,900C	
H4350	45.0	2366	48.0	2540	48,500C	
RL-19	45.0	2404	48.0	2536	46,500C	
H1000	52.0	2398	55.0	2534	43,100C	
IMR4350	42.0	2316	45.0	2533	48,000C	
H450	47.0	2342	50.0	2518	47,700C	
H414	42.0	2363	44.0	2496	47,400C	
N160			45.5	2490	49,313p	Sako SP 1168
W760	42.0	2360	44.0	2484	47,200C	
RL-15	37.0	2330	40.0	2472	45,500C	
IMR4320	38.0	2326	40.0	2444	48,500C	
IMR4064	37.0	2290	39.0	2388	47,000C	

175

Powder	Grs. (start)	MV (fps) start	Grs. (max)	MV (fps) max	Press. (CUP/psi)	Comments
N160			47.5	2530	49,313p	Hdy SP
A4350	42.3	2206	47.0	2507	45,000C	Hdy SP/3.04"/CCI 200
IMR7828	47.0	2354	50.0	2507	47,500C	
RL-22	46.0	2342	48.0	2503	46,000C	
IMR4831	43.0	2261	46.0	2477	46,600C	
RL-19	44.0	2282	47.0	2463	46,000C	
H450	46.0	2249	49.0	2457	47,400C	
H4350	47.0	2300	49.0	2449	48,400C	
H4831	45.0	2266	48.0	2443	47,000C	
A3100	45.0	2149	50.0	2442	38,400C	Hdy SP/3.04"/ CCI 200/(C)
IMR4350	42.0	2266	45.0	2429	47,500C	
H1000	50.0	2309	53.0	2419	41,400C	
A2700	40.9	2257	43.0	2401	44,500C	Hdy SP/3.04"/ CCI 200
H414	42.0	2306	44.0	2400	48,400C	
W760	41.0	2240	43.0	2370	48,000C	
N165			49.5	2357	47,900p	Spr Magnum-Tip
RL-15	35.0	2110	38.0	2325	44,500C	
N160			45.9	2319	47,900p	Spr Magnum-Tip
A2495BR	34.2	2026	38.0	2302	45,400C	Hdy SP/3.04"/CCI 200
VarGet			35.0	2205	45,200C	

195

Powder	Grs. (start)	MV (fps) start	Grs. (max)	MV (fps) max	Press. (CUP/psi)	Comments
RL-22	44.0	2148	47.0	2353	46,000C	
IMR7828	45.0	2180	48.0	2339	48,200C	
RL-19	42.0	2114	45.0	2336	46,500C	
IMR4831	40.0	2129	43.0	2335	48,500C	
H1000	47.0	2192	50.0	2331	45,300C	
H450	44.0	2150	47.0	2294	48,200C	
H4831	43.0	2166	46.0	2289	48,500C	
H4350	42.0	2188	44.0	2288	48,500C	
IMR4350	39.0	2070	42.0	2287	48,000C	

Caution: Loads exceeding SAAMI OAL Maximum must be verified for bullet-to-rifling clearance and magazine functioning. Where a specific primer or bullet is indicated those components must be used, no substitutions! Where only a maximum load is shown, reduce starting load 10%, unless otherwise specified.

Key: (C) = compressed charge; C = CUP; p = psi; Plink = Plinker; Bns = Barnes; Hdy = Hornady; Lap = Lapua; Nos = Nosler; Rem = Remington; Sra = Sierra; Spr = Speer; Win = Winchester.

Never exceed maximum load nor use any load exhibiting signs of excessive pressure. Begin at suggested starting load and work up carefully.

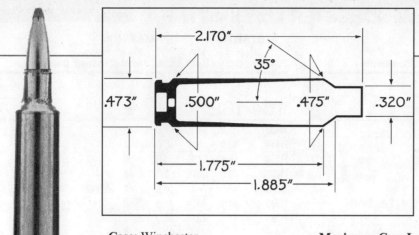

Case: Winchester
Primer: Large Rifle
Barrel: 24″ Accurate
       22″ Hodgdon
Bullet Diameter: 0.284″

Maximum Case Length: 2.170″
Trim to Length: 2.160″
Maximum Cartridge OAL: 2.800″
Minimum Cartridge OAL: 2.765″

In 1963, along with a rash of other economizing schemes, Winchester introduced a pair of interesting new rifles that were hoped capable of capturing existing markets and creating new ones, while, at the same time, bringing much needed profit to Winchester's gun line.

The Model 88 lever-action featured a rotary-bolt-action articulated by a finger-lever. The Model 100 used the same basic action, but was a gas-operated semi-automatic. These guns were capable of fine accuracy and were chambered in 308 Winchester, 243 Winchester (both were already popular cartridges) and the then-new 284 Winchester.

Winchester engineers designed the rebated-rim 284 Winchester to work on the same bolt-face as the 308 Winchester, but to have sufficient capacity to duplicate 270 Winchester ballistics in a 2.8″ cartridge. In that endeavor they completely succeeded. Original factory loads featured 125- or 150-grain bullets and advertised ballistics were quite similar to the 130- and 150-grain 270 Winchester loads of the time.

In spite of its handy modern design, gun writers soon

came to the collective conclusion that the 284 Winchester was completely worthless. One writer went so far as to state that 175-grain bullets had to be seated so deeply that performance was vastly inferior to that provided by the 270 Winchester loaded with 150-grain bullets...therefore, the 284 Winchester just could not measure up! (That line of "reasoning" still baffles me after nearly twenty years of occasional pondering....)

Regardless of that resounding negative din, the 284 Winchester is a fine cartridge, and with proper loadings it is every bit the equal of the 270 Winchester or 280 Remington. It is a natural for chambering in lightweight rifles and has formed the basis for a myriad of more-or-less useful wildcats from 22-caliber through 375-caliber.

Interestingly, general case shape is very reminiscent of Ackley's improved cartridges.

Case capacity with a 145-grain bullet, seated normally, is about 61.3 grains of water. H4831, H450, H4350 and H414 are noted performers in the 284 Winchester.

284 WINCHESTER LOADING DATA

100

Powder	STARTING Grs.	MV (fps)	MAXIMUM Grs.	MV (fps)	Press. (CUP/psi)	Comments
A4350	50.9	2794	56.5	3175	53,800p	Hdy HP/2.8″/Win WLR
H4350	55.0	3044	57.0	3169		
H4895	45.0	3006	48.0	3156		
H414	54.0	2981	56.0	3110		
H4831	56.0	2924	59.0	3090		
H450	57.0	2969	59.0	3074		
H335	45.0	2980	47.0	3074		
H380	50.0	2937	52.0	3070		
BL-C(2)	45.0	2971	47.0	3060		
A2700	48.0	2865	50.5	3048	50,800p	Hdy HP/2.8″/Win WLR
A3100	53.1	2618	59.0	2975	45,700p	Hdy HP/2.8″/Win WLR/(C)

115-120

Powder	STARTING Grs.	MV (fps)	MAXIMUM Grs.	MV (fps)	Press. (CUP/psi)	Comments
H4895	43.0	2776	47.0	3104		
H4350	53.0	2838	56.0	3090		
H4831	54.0	2703	59.0	3036		
H380	47.0	2762	51.0	3023		
A4350	49.1	2612	54.5	2968	54,300p	Spr SP/2.8″/Win WLR
A3100	53.1	2587	59.0	2940	54,000p	Spr SP/2.8″/Win WLR/(C)
BL-C(2)	44.0	2640	48.0	2934		
H335	43.0	2574	47.0	2922		
A2700	46.1	2640	48.5	2808	51,200p	Spr SP/2.8″/Win WLR

>>>>>>>>>>>>>>>>>>>>>>>>>

Never exceed maximum load nor use any load exhibiting signs of excessive pressure. Begin at suggested starting load and work up carefully.

167

125-130

Powder	STARTING Grs.	MV (fps)	MAXIMUM Grs.	MV (fps)	Press. (CUP/psi)	Comments
H4350	52.0	2779	55.0	3030		
H4831	53.0	2609	58.0	3013		
BL-C(2)	45.0	2793	49.0	3013	45,800C	26" Test Barrel
H414	50.5	2704	55.0	2976		
H380	45.0	2675	49.0	2971		
H450	52.5	2634	57.0	2913	46,200C	26" Test Barrel
H4895	42.5	2640	46.0	2894		
H335	43.0	2625	47.0	2875		

139-140

Powder	STARTING Grs.	MV (fps)	MAXIMUM Grs.	MV (fps)	Press. (CUP/psi)	Comments
H4350	51.0	2732	54.0	2957		
H4831	53.0	2613	58.0	2954		
BL-C(2)	44.0	2610	48.0	2914	47,400C	26" Test Barrel
H450	52.5	2686	57.0	2894	47,400C	26" Test Barrel
H335	42.0	2561	46.0	2869		
H380	44.0	2571	48.0	2856		
H4895	41.5	2545	45.0	2847		
A4350	48.6	2504	54.0	2845	54,200p	Hdy SP/2.8"/Win WLR
A3100	53.1	2495	59.0	2835	53,000p	Hdy SP/2.8"/Win WLR/(C)
A2700	44.7	2471	47.0	2629	50,000p	Hdy SP/2.8"/Win WLR

145-150

Powder	STARTING Grs.	MV (fps)	MAXIMUM Grs.	MV (fps)	Press. (CUP/psi)	Comments
H4831	53.0	2577	57.0	2893		
H4350	50.0	2690	53.0	2869		
H414	49.0	2664	53.0	2833		
A4350	46.8	2432	52.0	2764	53,400p	Sra SBT/2.8"/Win WLR
A3100	51.3	2424	57.0	2754	52,400p	Sra SBT/2.8"/Win WLR/(C)
A2700	42.8	2382	45.0	2534	50,300p	Sra SBT/2.8"/Win WLR

154-162

Powder	STARTING Grs.	MV (fps)	MAXIMUM Grs.	MV (fps)	Press. (CUP/psi)	Comments
H4831	51.5	2436	57.0	2803		
H414	46.0	2517	50.0	2794		
H450	51.5	2485	56.0	2793	45,400C	26" Test Barrel
H4350	49.0	2619	52.0	2754		
BL-C(2)	43.0	2446	46.5	2754	47,000C	26" Test Barrel
H335	41.0	2374	44.0	2686		
H380	41.5	2316	46.0	2675		
H4895	38.5	2378	42.0	2641		
H870	63.0	2560				

168

Powder	STARTING Grs.	MV (fps)	MAXIMUM Grs.	MV (fps)	Press. (CUP/psi)	Comments
H4350	48.0	2590	51.0	2692		
H4831	50.0	2496	54.0	2690		
H414	43.0	2371	47.0	2543		

175

Powder	STARTING Grs.	MV (fps)	MAXIMUM Grs.	MV (fps)	Press. (CUP/psi)	Comments
H450	50.5	2467	54.5	2679	46,800C	26" Test Barrel
H4831	49.5	2352	54.0	2630		
H4350	47.0	2474	50.0	2597		
H380	40.5	2272	45.0	2549		
H870	63.0	2528				
H4895	37.0	2320	40.0	2520		
H414	43.0	2325	47.0	2506		
BL-C(2)	36.0	2237	39.0	2457	47,400C	26" Test Barrel
H335	35.0	2186	38.0	2409		

195

Powder	STARTING Grs.	MV (fps)	MAXIMUM Grs.	MV (fps)	Press. (CUP/psi)	Comments
H4831	47.0	2282	50.0	2414		
H4350	43.0	2233	46.0	2380		
H414	43.0	2244	45.0	2330		
H870	59.0	2240	61.0	2320		

Caution: Loads exceeding SAAMI OAL Maximum must be verified for bullet-to-rifling clearance and magazine functioning. Where a specific primer or bullet is indicated those components must be used, no substitutions! Where only a maximum load is shown, reduce starting load 10%, unless otherwise specified.

Key: (C) = compressed charge; C = CUP; p = psi; Plink = Plinker; Bns = Barnes; Hdy = Hornady; Lap = Lapua; Nos = Nosler; Rem = Remington; Sra = Sierra; Spr = Speer; Win = Winchester.

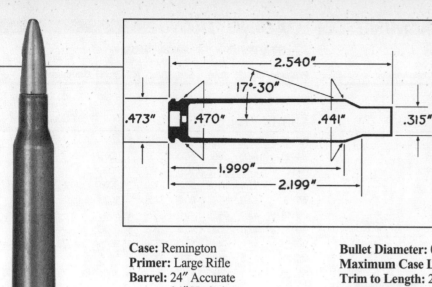

Case: Remington
Primer: Large Rifle
Barrel: 24″ Accurate
24″ Hodgdon
24″ Winchester

Bullet Diameter: 0.284″
Maximum Case Length: 2.540″
Trim to Length: 2.530″
Maximum Cartridge OAL: 3.330″
Minimum Cartridge OAL: 3.150″

Introduced in 1957, Remington's 280 was intended to directly compete with Winchester's highly successful 270. Similar to the wildcat 7mm-06, but with the shoulder pushed forward, the 280 Remington was originally handicapped by the adoption of a lower pressure standard than that for the 270 Winchester, and performance suffered greatly.

Finally, after decades in the ballistic doldrums, Remington upped the ante, increasing the pressure standard to within about 8 percent of that for Winchester's 270. With a slightly larger bullet and a few grains additional usable capacity, the 280 Remington could finally live up to its designer's expectations. Modern factory loads are ballistically indistinguishable from the best 270 Winchester factory loads.

As a big game chambering, the 280 Remington does have a slight theoretical edge since substantially heavier bullets are available, compared to the 270 Winchester. For practical purposes this is of little consequence, and there is genuinely precious little to separate these fine performers.

One interesting fact cannot be ignored. When fired from equal-length barrels, 280 Remington and 7mm Remington Magnum loads are typically no more than 150 fps apart with any given bullet. Factory ballistics are often even closer.

Remington 280 cases cannot safely be formed by the simple expedient of necking down 30-06 Springfield cases. The minuscule shoulder created is insufficient to hold the headspace, and case separations are likely. The results could be devastating. Because of the similarity in appearance, it is an easy matter to accidentally chamber a 270 round in a 280 rifle. Again, a devastating head separation could result. The only foolproof course of action is to use only 280 head-stamped cases for 280 Remington loads—this is no problem since Winchester, Federal and Remington all offer 280 ammunition, and Winchester and Remington offer component cases.

Case capacity with a 145-grain bullet, seated normally, is about 67.7 grains of water. H4831, IMR4350, H4895, RL-19, IMR7828, H4350, H414, IMR4831, W760 and IMR4831 are all good choices for loading the 280.

280 REMINGTON LOADING DATA

Powder	STARTING Grs.	MV (fps)	MAXIMUM Grs.	MV (fps)	Press. (CUP/psi)	Comments
100						
RL-15	52.0	3273	55.0	3489	50,500C	
H4895	48.0	3193	51.0	3389	50,500C	
BL-C(2)	51.0	3208	54.0	3371	50,000C	
H4350	57.0	3140	61.0	3369	49,000C	
IMR4320	49.0	3144	52.0	3351	50,500C	
IMR4064	50.0	3148	52.0	3347	48,500C	
IMR4831	57.0	3168	60.0	3336	50,000C	
IMR4895	48.0	3151	51.0	3328	50,500C	
H414	53.0	3195	56.0	3325	50,500C	
H4831	59.0	3161	62.0	3321	50,500C	
A4350	53.1	2918	59.0	3316	55,800p	Sra HP/3.15″/Rem 9½/(C)
IMR4350	56.0	3140	59.0	3301	50,500C	
W760	52.0	3149	55.0	3289	50,000C	
H380	52.0	3140	55.0	3267	49,000C	

Powder	STARTING Grs.	MV (fps)	MAXIMUM Grs.	MV (fps)	Press. (CUP/psi)	Comments
100 con't						
RL-19	59.0	3173	62.0	3255	50,000C	
A2700	53.2	3057	56.0	3252	53,100p	Sra HP/3.15″/Rem 9½
H450	58.0	3111	61.0	3218	47,000C	
RL-22	59.0	3022	62.0	3194	48,500C	
A3100	54.0	2665	60.0	3028	44,900p	Sra HP/3.15″/Rem 9½/(C)

➤➤➤➤➤➤➤➤➤➤➤➤➤➤➤➤➤➤➤➤➤➤➤➤➤➤

Never exceed maximum load nor use any load exhibiting signs of excessive pressure. Begin at suggested starting load and work up carefully.

115-120

Powder	STARTING Grs.	MV (fps)	MAXIMUM Grs.	MV (fps)	Press. (CUP/psi)	Comments
IMR4831	55.0	2962	58.0	3186	51,000C	
IMR4064	47.0	2980	50.0	3180	49,500C	
RL-15	49.0	3004	51.0	3177	49,500C	
H4350	54.0	2973	58.0	3157	50,000C	
H414	51.0	2965	55.0	3155	51,000C	
W760	50.0	2924	54.0	3139	50,500C	
RL-22	59.0	2966	62.0	3138	50,500C	
IMR4895	46.0	2920	49.0	3136	50,500C	
H4831	57.0	3023	60.0	3129	50,000C	
RL-19	57.0	2938	60.0	3122	50,000C	
A4350	51.3	2739	57.0	3112	57,700p	Spr SP/3.2"/Rem 9½
H380	49.0	2909	53.0	3109	49,000C	
IMR4350	53.0	2949	56.0	3108	50,000C	
H450	56.0	2958	60.0	3090	47,000C	
H4895	44.0	2895	47.0	3071	49,500C	
IMR4320	45.0	2868	48.0	3027	50,000C	
A3100	57.0	2844	60.0	3025	53,300p	Spr SP/3.2"/Rem 9½/(C)
A2700	49.9	2821	52.5	3001	57,000p	Spr SP/3.2"/Rem 9½
BL-C(2)	42.0	2754	46.0	2966	50,000C	
H1000	60.0	2749	63.0	2894	46,500C	
H870	63.0	2690	65.0	2744	46,000C	

125-130

Powder	STARTING Grs.	MV (fps)	MAXIMUM Grs.	MV (fps)	Press. (CUP/psi)	Comments
IMR4831	54.0	2871	57.0	3088	51,800C	
H4831	56.0	2957	59.0	3066	51,000C	
RL-15	48.0	2810	51.0	3062	49,500C	
H450	55.0	2910	59.0	3046	49,000C	
H4350	52.0	2780	56.0	3026	49,000C	
IMR4350	53.0	2833	56.0	3017	48,000C	
RL-22	58.0	2889	61.0	3015	49,500C	
RL-19	56.0	2842	59.0	3010	49,000C	
H4895	44.0	2740	48.0	2993	50,500C	
IMR4895	45.0	2879	48.0	2989	50,000C	
H1000	60.0	2788	63.0	2982	48,400C	
H414	49.0	2857	52.0	2979	50,000C	
VarGet			46.5	2977	49,400C	
IMR4064	46.0	2780	49.0	2974	48,500C	
IMR4320	45.0	2824	48.0	2973	51,000C	
H380	48.0	2751	51.0	2965	50,000C	
W760	48.0	2818	51.0	2928	49,000C	
H870	63.0	2678	65.0	2709	47,000C	

139-140

Powder	STARTING Grs.	MV (fps)	MAXIMUM Grs.	MV (fps)	Press. (CUP/psi)	Comments
IMR4831	52.0	2778	55.0	3009	51,000C	
H4831	54.0	2808	57.0	2976	51,000C	
RL-15	47.0	2790	50.0	2962	48,500C	
H450	54.0	2756	57.0	2949	50,000C	
IMR4350	51.0	2760	54.0	2949	50,500C	
RL-19	55.0	2759	58.0	2949	50,500C	
H4350	51.0	2763	54.0	2938	49,000C	
RL-22	56.0	2742	59.0	2914	49,500C	
H1000	59.0	2698	62.0	2890	49,000C	

139-140 con't

Powder	STARTING Grs.	MV (fps)	MAXIMUM Grs.	MV (fps)	Press. (CUP/psi)	Comments
IMR4064	44.0	2664	47.0	2880	50,500C	
H4895	42.0	2666	46.0	2861	50,000C	
H414	47.0	2713	50.0	2842	49,000C	
A3100	51.3	2498	57.0	2839	56,800p	Bns-X/3.31"/Rem 9½/(C)
W760	47.0	2707	50.0	2838	49,500C	
IMR4895	43.0	2658	46.0	2829	48,500C	
IMR4320	42.0	2639	45.0	2808	51,000C	
A4350	45.9	2443	51.0	2776	55,900p	Bns-X/3.31"/Rem 9½
H870	62.0	2659	65.0	2720	48,000C	
A2700	46.1	2547	48.5	2710	55,300p	Bns-X/3.31"/Rem 9½

145-150

Powder	STARTING Grs.	MV (fps)	MAXIMUM Grs.	MV (fps)	Press. (CUP/psi)	Comments
A3100	53.1	2580	59.0	2932	59,000p	Spr HPBT/3.25"/Rem 9½/(C)
WMR			60.4	2930	53,500p	Win SP
H4831	52.0	2639	55.0	2871	50,500C	
IMR4831	50.0	2688	53.0	2867	51,000C	
A4350	47.7	2519	53.0	2862	59,800p	Spr HPBT/3.25"/Rem 9½
H4350	50.0	2661	53.0	2852	50,000C	
IMR4350	49.0	2646	52.0	2849	51,000C	
H450	51.0	2644	54.0	2829	50,000C	
H414	48.0	2626	51.0	2783	50,000C	
IMR4064	43.0	2611	46.0	2757	50,000C	
VarGet			44.0	2753	50,400C	
IMR4895	42.0	2560	45.0	2744	48,000C	
H4895	41.0	2602	44.0	2743	50,500C	
IMR4320	41.0	2488	44.0	2743	50,500C	
H1000	58.0	2598	61.0	2729	49,500C	
W760	46.0	2590	49.0	2713	49,000C	
A2700	45.6	2546	48.0	2709	57,000p	Spr HPBT/3.25"/Rem 9½
H870	57.0	2440	61.0	2568	46,500C	

154

Powder	STARTING Grs.	MV (fps)	MAXIMUM Grs.	MV (fps)	Press. (CUP/psi)	Comments
A4350	48.6	2486	54.0	2825	59,600p	Hdy SP/3.33"/Rem 9½
RL-19	52.0	2624	55.0	2804	47,500C	
RL-22	53.0	2629	56.0	2795	48,500C	
A3100	52.2	2457	58.0	2792	54,500p	Hdy SP/3.33"/Rem 9½
IMR4831	50.0	2555	53.0	2769	48,500C	
IMR4350	48.0	2566	51.0	2752	49,000C	
H4831	52.0	2617	54.0	2749	49,500C	
H4350	50.0	2603	53.0	2740	50,000C	
IMR7828	54.0	2606	57.0	2738	49,500C	
RL-15	42.0	2512	46.0	2724	49,000C	
H450	52.0	2615	54.0	2720	49,000C	
A2700	46.6	2555	49.0	2718	60,000p	Hdy SP/3.33"/Rem 9½
H414	47.0	2590	50.0	2706	49,000C	
W760	45.0	2577	48.0	2634	48,500C	
VarGet			43.0	2618	49,200C	
H1000	58.0	2506	60.0	2590	47,000C	
H870	57.0	2376	61.0	2543	46,000C	

Never exceed maximum load nor use any load exhibiting signs of excessive pressure. Begin at suggested starting load and work up carefully.

160

Powder	STARTING Grs.	MV (fps)	MAXIMUM Grs.	MV (fps)	Press. (CUP/psi)	Comments
WMR			57.8	2795	56,800p	Win ST
A3100	51.8	2442	57.5	2775	56,100p	Nos Part./3.3"/ Rem 9½
A4350	46.8	2413	52.0	2742	58,200p	Nos Part./3.3"/ Rem 9½
A2700	46.1	2503	48.5	2663	60,000p	Nos Part./3.3"/ Rem 9½

168

Powder	STARTING Grs.	MV (fps)	MAXIMUM Grs.	MV (fps)	Press. (CUP/psi)	Comments
IMR4831	49.0	2604	52.0	2761	51,000C	
IMR7828	53.0	2577	56.0	2759	50,500C	
RL-19	52.0	2571	55.0	2757	50,000C	
RL-22	53.0	2580	56.0	2724	49,500C	
A3100	51.3	2396	57.0	2723	56,300C	Sra HPBT/3.3"/ Rem 9½
IMR4350	47.0	2508	50.0	2711	50,000C	
H450	50.0	2534	53.0	2688	51,000C	
H1000	57.0	2525	60.0	2681	51,000C	
H4350	49.0	2553	51.0	2680	50,000C	
A4350	46.4	2350	51.5	2670	57,400C	Sra HPBT/3.3"/ Rem 9½
H4831	50.0	2536	53.0	2669	49,000C	
H870	57.0	2415	61.0	2588	46,500C	
A2700	45.6	2422	48.0	2577	55,100p	Sra HPBT/3.3"/ Rem 9½
W760	44.0	2433	47.0	2544	50,500C	

175

Powder	STARTING Grs.	MV (fps)	MAXIMUM Grs.	MV (fps)	Press. (CUP/psi)	Comments
A3100	51.3	2359	57.0	2681	58,900p	Hdy SP/3.3"/Rem 9½
IMR7828	52.0	2513	55.0	2642	50,000C	
RL-22	51.0	2410	54.0	2639	48,000C	
RL-19	50.0	2437	53.0	2620	50,000C	
IMR4831	47.0	2387	50.0	2610	49,000C	
IMR4350	46.0	2370	49.0	2585	50,000C	
A4350	46.4	2273	51.5	2583	55,300p	Hdy SP/3.3"/Rem 9½
H4831	48.0	2411	51.0	2581	51,000C	
H1000	55.0	2388	58.0	2543	47,500C	
H450	48.0	2390	51.0	2540	51,000C	
H870	57.0	2403	61.0	2538	48,000C	
H4350	46.0	2373	49.0	2529	49,000C	
W760	42.0	2240	45.0	2441	51,000C	
A2700	43.7	2282	46.0	2428	53,400p	Hdy SP/3.3"/Rem 9½

195

Powder	STARTING Grs.	MV (fps)	MAXIMUM Grs.	MV (fps)	Press. (CUP/psi)	Comments
RL-22	49.0	2244	52.0	2528	48,500C	
RL-19	48.0	2230	51.0	2509	49,500C	
IMR7828	51.0	2370	54.0	2503	48,000C	
H1000	54.0	2373	57.0	2448	50,000C	
IMR4831	46.0	2319	49.0	2442	50,000C	
H870	55.0	2233	58.0	2419	46,500C	
H4831	46.0	2287	49.0	2402	51,000C	
H4350	45.0	2281	47.0	2390	51,000C	
H450	46.0	2279	48.0	2382	50,500C	
IMR4350	43.0	2192	47.0	2370	48,500C	

Caution: **Loads exceeding SAAMI OAL Maximum must be verified for bullet-to-rifling clearance and magazine functioning. Where a specific primer or bullet is indicated those components must be used, no substitutions! Where only a maximum load is shown, reduce starting load 10%, unless otherwise specified.**

Key: (C) = compressed charge; C = CUP; p = psi; Plink = Plinker; Bns = Barnes; Hdy = Hornady; Lap = Lapua; Nos = Nosler; Rem = Remington; Sra = Sierra; Spr = Speer; Win = Winchester.

Never exceed maximum load nor use any load exhibiting signs of excessive pressure. Begin at suggested starting load and work up carefully.

171

7mm Remington Magnum

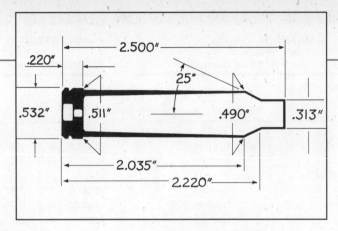

Case: Remington
Primer: Large Rifle
Barrel: 24″ Accurate
      24″ Hodgdon
      24″ Vihtavuori

Bullet Diameter: 0.284″
Maximum Case Length: 2.500″
Trim to Length: 2.490″
Maximum Cartridge OAL: 3.290″
Minimum Cartridge OAL: 3.150″

Along with the long-awaited improved version of their bolt-action rifle, Remington introduced the 7mm Remington Magnum in 1962. There is no way anyone could have anticipated the success this high-performance chambering would achieve within a few short years thereafter. The Model 700 rifle is still with us and is likely to remain essentially unchanged for some time to come, but it is unlikely that it will outlast what is now commonly referred to as simply the "7mm."

Ballistically, the 7mm Remington Magnum offers slightly more delivered energy than the 30-06 with similar recoil while providing a somewhat flatter trajectory than the 270 Winchester can achieve. With modern slow-burning powders, this Magnum can drive the heaviest 7mm bullets surprisingly fast while maintaining truly moderate pressures.

Consider the 195-grain Barnes original-style spitzer bullet. Accurate 8700 can launch this bullet just as fast as any

powder can launch any 180-grain 30-06 bullet yet generate considerably *less* maximum chamber pressure!

The 7mm Rem. Mag. offers considerable performance with recoil most shooters can handle and with acceptable barrel life. Those attributes likely explain, in no small measure, this chambering's continued market success. Within a few short years of its introduction, the 7mm Remington Magnum became one of the most successful big game chamberings ever offered. There is no evidence suggesting that trend might abate anytime soon.

Case capacity with a 145-grain bullet, seated normally, is about 81.3 grains of water. Until recently there has been a paucity of truly great powder choices for use in this and similar chamberings. Today, we have a wide selection: H4831, IMR7828, RL-22, IMR4831, IMR4350, RL-19, H1000, H4350, A4350, A3100 and A8700 have all been noted as good performers.

7mm REMINGTON MAGNUM LOADING DATA

Powder	STARTING Grs.	MV (fps)	MAXIMUM Grs.	MV (fps)	Press. (CUP/psi)	Comments
79						
N160			76.4	3710	55,114p	Sako FMJ 1088
100						
RL-19	71.0	3455	74.0	3683	51,000C	
RL-22	73.0	3440	76.0	3633	50,000C	
H4831	70.0	3481	74.0	3610	54,000C	
IMR7828	70.0	3310	75.0	3589	51,600C	
N160	68.5	3269	75.0	3570	52,200p	Hdy HP/3.189″/Rem 9½
H450	70.0	3431	72.0	3544	53,800C	
H414	60.0	3404	63.0	3530	52,900C	
W760	60.0	3388	63.0	3512	52,000C	
H4350	61.0	3388	64.0	3460	52,000C	
IMR4350	61.0	3398	63.0	3449	52,000C	
IMR4831	67.0	3220	69.5	3386	52,000C	
IMR4320	53.0	3098	56.0	3329	51,800C	

Powder	STARTING Grs.	MV (fps)	MAXIMUM Grs.	MV (fps)	Press. (CUP/psi)	Comments
115-120						
H4831	67.0	3309	73.0	3536	54,300C	
IMR7828	68.0	3241	73.0	3490	52,000C	
H414	57.0	3157	62.0	3462	54,900C	
RL-22	70.0	3329	73.0	3460	51,500C	
H450	65.0	3165	71.0	3394	55,100C	
A3100	65.3	2964	72.5	3368	58,800p	Spr HP/3.28″/CCI 200
RL-19	67.0	3241	70.0	3360	49,000C	
A4350	60.3	2944	67.0	3345	60,300p	Spr HP/3.28″/CCI 200
IMR4831	66.0	3171	69.0	3339	51,900C	
W760	59.0	3271	60.0	3325	52,000C	
A3100	64.2	2926	71.3	3325	59,900p	Spr SP/3.26″/CCI 200
N165	69.2	2984	76.3	3298	52,200p	Sra S/3.268″/Rem 9½
N160	65.1	3006	71.5	3295	52,200p	Sra S/3.268″/Rem 9½
IMR4350	59.0	3087	62.0	3257	52,000C	
A2700	59.4	3047	62.5	3241	58,700p	Spr HP/3.28″/CCI 200
H4350	58.0	3069	62.0	3234	51,000C	

Never exceed maximum load nor use any load exhibiting signs of excessive pressure. Begin at suggested starting load and work up carefully.

Powder	—STARTING— Grs.	MV (fps)	—MAXIMUM— Grs.	MV (fps)	Press. (CUP/psi)	Comments
115-120 con't						
A4350	56.7	2829	63.0	3215	57,800p	Spr SP/3.26"/CCI 200
A2700	58.4	2984	61.5	3174	58,700p	Spr SP/3.26"/CCI 200
A8700	71.1	2624	79.0	2982	46,000p	Spr SP/3.26"/CCI 200
A8700	71.1	2563	79.0	2913	39,100p	Spr HP/3.28"/CCI 200
125-130						
H4831	65.5	3188	71.0	3437	55,300C	
IMR7828	67.0	3164	72.0	3349	52,000C	
RL-22	69.0	3144	72.0	3268	50,500C	
RL-19	66.0	3152	69.0	3267	51,000C	
H1000	74.0	3105	78.0	3250	48,000C	
IMR4831	63.0	3125	66.0	3248	51,600C	
H450	62.0	2990	67.0	3214	55,300C	
H4350	57.0	2980	61.0	3194	51,700C	
IMR4350	58.0	3004	60.0	3161	52,000C	
A3100	61.0	2776	67.8	3155	59,000p	Spr SP/3.245"/CCI 200
A4350	55.8	2735	62.0	3108	58,400p	Spr SP/3.245"/CCI 200
W760	55.0	2994	56.5	3103	52,000C	
A8700	71.1	2658	79.0	3020	45,900p	Spr SP/3.245"/CCI 200
A2700	57.0	2817	60.0	2997	57,200p	Spr SP/3.245"/CCI 200
139-140						
IMR7828	66.0	3128	70.0	3232	51,900C	
RL-22	67.0	3087	70.0	3208	51,500C	
RL-19	64.0	3069	67.0	3203	51,000C	
H1000	73.0	3040	76.0	3166	52,000C	
H870			79.0	3153	46,800C	
H4831	64.0	2984	67.0	3114	51,600C	
IMR4831	61.0	2964	64.0	3100	52,000C	
A3100	61.2	2721	68.0	3092	58,200p	Sra SBT/3.27"/CCI 200
N165			64.5	3070	59,600p	Hdy BTSP
H450	61.0	2866	66.0	3049	55,300C	
A4350	54.9	2665	61.0	3028	54,900p	Sra SBT/3.27"/CCI 200
A2700	56.5	2815	59.5	2995	55,200p	Sra SBT/3.27"/CCI 200
H4350	56.0	2724	60.0	2930	51,900C	
IMR4350	56.0	2749	59.0	2910	51,400C	
A8700	72.0	2444	80.0	2777	41,500p	Sra SBT/3.27"/CCI 200
145-150						
H1000	72.0	2971	76.0	3159	52,000C	
N160			68.5	3130	52,939p	Norma SP
RL-19	63.0	2880	66.0	3102	51,000C	
RL-22	65.0	2898	68.0	3094	50,000C	
IMR7828	65.0	2849	69.0	3088	52,000C	
H870			79.0	3080	51,700C	

Powder	—STARTING— Grs.	MV (fps)	—MAXIMUM— Grs.	MV (fps)	Press. (CUP/psi)	Comments
145-150 con't						
N560	58.6	1788	65.2	3054	52,200p	Spr SPBT/3.268"/ Rem 9½
A3100	59.4	2643	66.0	3003	60,200p	Sra BT/3.28"/CCI 200
N140			58.2	3000	53,664p	Norma SP
H4831	61.0	2874	65.0	2997	53,400C	
A4350	54.9	2612	61.0	2968	61,000p	Sra BT/3.28"/CCI 200
H450	59.0	2837	64.0	2964	55,100C	
A8700	71.1	2597	79.0	2951	50,900p	Sra BT/3.28"/CCI 200/(C)
IMR4831	60.0	2780	63.0	2942	52,000C	
A2700	54.6	2726	57.5	2900	59,600p	Sra BT/3.28"/CCI 200
IMR4350	55.0	2690	58.0	2851	51,700C	
H4350	55.0	2666	59.0	2841	51,200C	
N170			60.3	2713	44,961p	Spr BTSP
154-162						
H870			79.0	3099	49,700C	
N160			67.1	3080	53,664p	Hdy SP
N160			65.1	3050	55,114p	RWS SP
H1000	71.0	2983	72.5	3038	52,000C	
H4831	61.0	2872	66.0	3028	50,600C	
RL-22	63.0	2872	66.0	3009	51,000C	
IMR7828	64.0	2860	68.0	3009	51,100C	
H450	59.0	2781	64.0	2997	50,000C	
IMR4831	59.0	2837	62.0	2981	51,900C	
RL-19	61.0	2840	64.0	2935	50,500C	
A8700	71.1	2581	79.0	2933	53,800p	Nos SP/3.28"/ CCI 200/(C)
A3100	57.2	2512	63.5	2855	59,000p	Nos SP/3.28"/CCI 200
N560	53.0	2605	58.8	2821	52,200p	Spr GS/3.268"/Rem 9½
A2700	54.6	2614	57.5	2781	58,500p	Nos SP/3.28"/CCI 200
A4350	51.3	2436	57.0	2768	58,300p	Nos SP/3.28"/CCI 200
H4350	54.0	2612	58.0	2727	51,000C	
IMR4350	54.0	2646	57.0	2719	50,900C	
N170			55.7	2605	44,961p	Sra Sptz BT

▶▶▶▶▶▶▶▶▶▶▶▶▶▶▶▶▶▶▶▶▶▶▶▶▶▶▶▶

Caution: Loads exceeding SAAMI OAL Maximum must be verified for bullet-to-rifling clearance and magazine functioning. Where a specific primer or bullet is indicated those components must be used, no substitutions! Where only a maximum load is shown, reduce starting load 10%, unless otherwise specified.

Key: (C) = compressed charge; C = CUP; p = psi; Plinker = Plinker; Bns = Barnes; Hdy = Hornady; Lap = Lapua; Nos = Nosler; Rem = Remington; Sra = Sierra; Spr = Speer; Win = Winchester.

Powder	STARTING Grs.	MV (fps)	MAXIMUM Grs.	MV (fps)	Press. (CUP/psi)	Comments

168-170

Powder	Grs.	MV (fps)	Grs.	MV (fps)	Press. (CUP/psi)	Comments
N160			63.1	3070	55,114p	Sako SP 116B
H1000	69.0	2896	72.0	3015	52,000C	
IMR7828	63.0	2821	67.0	2974	51,900C	
H870			77.0	2963	49,300C	
RL-22	62.0	2839	65.0	2942	51,500C	
H4831	58.0	2780	63.0	2927	52,600C	
RL-19	60.0	2808	63.0	2896	50,000C	
IMR4831	58.0	2799	60.5	2891	52,000C	
A8700	70.2	2520	78.0	2864	50,700C	Sra HPBT/3.28"/ CCI 200/(C)
A4350	52.2	2448	58.0	2782	61,000p	Sra HPBT/3.28"/CCI 200
A3100	55.8	2442	62.0	2775	57,900p	Sra HPBT/3.28"/CCI 200
H450	57.0	2598	62.0	2762	51,600C	
A2700	53.2	2550	56.0	2713	58,400p	Sra HPBT/3.28"/CCI 200
H4350	53.0	2509	57.0	2672	51,400C	
IMR4350	53.0	2530	56.0	2666	51,000C	

175

Powder	Grs.	MV (fps)	Grs.	MV (fps)	Press. (CUP/psi)	Comments
H1000	69.0	2812	72.0	2949	55,000C	
H870			77.0	2918	48,600C	
IMR7828	62.0	2666	66.0	2902	52,000C	
H4831	58.0	2732	63.0	2869	53,800C	
RL-22	60.0	2711	63.0	2834	50,500C	
N160			60.2	2810	55,114p	Spr SP
IMR4831	57.0	2634	60.0	2787	51,600C	
RL-19	58.0	2670	61.0	2786	50,000C	
A8700	67.5	2424	75.0	2754	51,800p	Nos SP/3.275"/ CCI 200/(C)
H450	57.0	2527	62.0	2719	52,200C	
A3100	54.5	2376	60.5	2700	59,700p	Nos SP/3.275"/ CCI 200
A4350	50.4	2335	56.0	2653	58,700p	Nos SP/3.275"/ CCI 200
H4350	51.0	2454	55.0	2617	50,900C	
A2700	50.4	2426	53.0	2581	59,800p	Nos SP/3.275"/ CCI 200
IMR4350	52.0	2471	54.0	2580	51,000C	

195

Powder	Grs.	MV (fps)	Grs.	MV (fps)	Press. (CUP/psi)	Comments
H1000	64.0	2592	67.5	2737	52,000C	
H870	67.0	2509	72.0	2719	53,100C	
A8700	69.3	2383	77.0	2708	51,600p	Bns SP/3.275"/ CCI 200/(C)
RL-22	57.0	2571	60.0	2680	51,000C	
RL-19	55.0	2529	58.0	2642	50,500C	
A3100	52.7	2233	58.5	2538	59,800p	Bns SP/3.275"/ CCI 200
A4350	47.3	2147	52.6	2440	56,500p	Bns SP/3.275"/ CCI 200
A2700	48.5	2263	51.0	2407	58,400p	Bns SP/3.275"/ CCI 200

Caution: Loads exceeding SAAMI OAL Maximum must be verified for bullet-to-rifling clearance and magazine functioning. Where a specific primer or bullet is indicated those components must be used, no substitutions! Where only a maximum load is shown, reduce starting load 10%, unless otherwise specified.

Key: (C) = compressed charge; C = CUP; p = psi; Plink = Plinker; Bns = Barnes; Hdy = Hornady; Lap = Lapua; Nos = Nosler; Rem = Remington; Sra = Sierra; Spr = Speer; Win = Winchester.

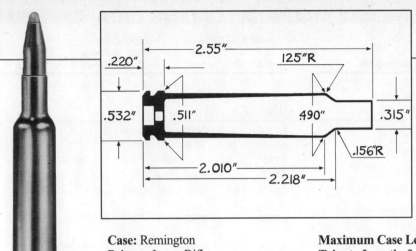

Case: Remington
Primer: Large Rifle
Barrel: 26″ Accurate
     24″ Hodgdon
Bullet Diameter: 0.284″

Maximum Case Length: 2.55″
Trim to Length: 2.54″
Maximum Cartridge OAL: 3.36″
Minimum Cartridge OAL: 3.10″

The 7mm Weatherby Magnum differs from its parent cartridge, the 270 Weatherby, in only two ways. First, it is necked up to accept a 0.007″ larger diameter bullet. Second, it is normally loaded to about .1-inch longer overall length. As a result, when loaded to equal pressures, it can deliver slightly more muzzle energy.

The 7mm Weatherby Magnum was recently standardized as a SAAMI chambering, and SAAMI pressures are somewhat less than typical 270 Weatherby loads, so any ballistic difference largely disappears.

The 7mm Weatherby was introduced in 1944 specifically to compete with other short magnum 7mm chamberings that were then the wildcatting rage. Capacity and performance are practically identical to the 7mm Remington Magnum.

Some have postulated that the ballistic advantage the 7mm Weatherby Magnum has over the 7mm Remington Magnum proves that Weatherby's free-bore theory is valid. However, if one compares equal-length barrels, with the same bullet, loaded to the same pressure, with the best powder used in each chambering, the only difference found is in the name applied. Further, it must be stated that the most accurate handloads always have the bullets seated to within a few thousandths of an inch of the rifling, something impossible in a free-bored barrel.

H4831, IMR7828, IMR4831, A8700, H4350 and H1000 are good choices for the 7mm Weatherby Magnum. As with all free-bored chamberings, the slowest usable powders seldom deliver acceptable accuracy and ballistic uniformity.

7mm WEATHERBY MAGNUM LOADING DATA

Powder	STARTING Grs.	MV (fps)	MAXIMUM Grs.	MV (fps)	Press. (CUP/psi)	Comments
100						
H4831	75.0	3340	78.0	3529		
H4350	68.0	3234	72.0	3477		
H1000	77.0	3266	80.0	3414		
H414	65.0	3160	68.0	3303		
H870			82.0	3151		
115-120						
IMR7828	74.0	3284	78.0	3511		
A4350	63.9	3066	71.0	3484	63,300p	Spr SP/3.285″/Rem 9½M
A3100	68.4	3060	76.0	3477	59,100p	Spr SP/3.285″/ Rem 9½M/(C)
H4831	74.0	3281	77.0	3475		
IMR4350	68.0	3297	71.0	3470		
A3100	68.4	3054	76.0	3470	62,200p	Bns-X/3.31″/ Rem 9½M/(C)
H450	74.0	3289	77.0	3461		
IMR4831	71.0	3344	74.0	3459		

Powder	STARTING Grs.	MV (fps)	MAXIMUM Grs.	MV (fps)	Press. (CUP/psi)	Comments
115-120 con't						
H4350	67.0	3183	71.0	3434		
A4350	62.1	3010	69.0	3420	62,800p	Bns-X/3.31″/Rem 9½M
H1000	77.0	3239	80.0	3369		
H414	64.0	3067	67.0	3225		
H870			82.0	3085		
A8700	77.4	2704	86.0	3073	42,100p	Spr SP/3.285″/ Rem 9½M/(C)
A8700	76.5	2686	85.0	3052	43,800p	Bns-X/3.31″/Rem 9½M/(C)

➤➤➤➤➤➤➤➤➤➤➤➤➤➤➤➤➤➤➤➤➤➤➤➤➤

Caution: Loads exceeding SAAMI OAL Maximum must be verified for bullet-to-rifling clearance and magazine functioning. Where a specific primer or bullet is indicated those components must be used, no substitutions! Where only a maximum load is shown, reduce starting load 10%, unless otherwise specified.

Key: (C) = compressed charge; C = CUP; p = psi; Plink = Plinker; Bns = Barnes; Hdy = Hornady; Lap = Lapua; Nos = Nosler; Rem = Remington; Sra = Sierra; Spr = Speer; Win = Winchester.

Never exceed maximum load nor use any load exhibiting signs of excessive pressure. Begin at suggested starting load and work up carefully.

Powder	—STARTING— Grs.	MV (fps)	—MAXIMUM— Grs.	MV (fps)	Press. (CUP/psi)	Comments
125-130						
IMR7828	71.0	3162	75.0	3341		
IMR4831	69.0	3190	72.0	3319		
IMR4350	67.0	3111	70.0	3310		
H4350	66.0	3029	70.0	3292		
H4831	70.0	3097	73.0	3263		
H870			82.0	3230		
H450	70.0	3066	73.0	3202		
H1000	76.0	3019	79.0	3194		
139-140						
A3100	66.6	2915	74.0	3313	62,000p	Hdy BTSP/3.34"/Rem 9½M
A4350	62.1	2898	69.0	3293	62,400p	Hdy BTSP/3.34"/Rem 9½M
IMR7828	70.0	3040	74.0	3238		
H4831	70.0	3107	73.0	3232		
H4350	65.0	2984	69.0	3222		
H450	70.0	3096	73.0	3217		
A3100	64.8	2828	72.0	3214	60,900p	Bns-X/3.345"/Rem 9½M
H1000	76.0	3090	78.0	3190		
IMR4831	67.0	3087	70.0	3188		
IMR4350	65.0	3024	68.0	3179		
A4350	59.4	2782	66.0	3161	62,800p	Bns-X/3.345"/Rem 9½M
N170			77.0	3142	56,499p	Hdy BTSP
H870			81.0	3037		
A8700	73.8	2578	82.0	2929	41,200p	Hdy BTSP/3.34"/ Rem 9½M/(C)
A8700	73.8	2571	82.0	2922	44,300p	Bns-X/3.345"/ Rem 9½M/(C)
145-150						
IMR7828	68.0	3009	73.0	3222		
H4831	68.0	3072	71.0	3207		
A3100	64.8	2815	72.0	3199	63,200p	Nos BT/3.35"/Rem 9½M
H1000	75.0	3041	77.0	3180		
H4350	64.0	2941	68.0	3159		
IMR4831	66.0	3012	69.0	3144		
IMR4350	64.0	2979	67.0	3129		
H450	67.0	2929	70.0	3092		
A4350	58.5	2719	65.0	3090	62,700p	Nos BT/3.35"/Rem 9½M
H870			81.0	3008		
A8700	73.8	2554	82.0	2902	43,200p	Nos BT/3.35"/ Rem 9½M/(C)
154-162						
H450	70.0	3014	73.0	3171		
H4831	69.0	2964	72.0	3119		
A3100	63.5	2733	70.5	3106	61,400p	Nos Part./3.355"/ Rem 9½M
H1000	75.0	2969	77.0	3082		
A3100	63.9	2688	71.0	3055	63,000p	Bns-X/3.34"/Rem 9½M
IMR7828	67.0	2864	72.0	3039		
A4350	58.5	2674	65.0	3039	63,100p	Nos Part./3.355"/Rem 9½M

Powder	—STARTING— Grs.	MV (fps)	—MAXIMUM— Grs.	MV (fps)	Press. (CUP/psi)	Comments
154-162 con't						
H4350	61.0	2830	65.0	3013		
IMR4831	64.0	2898	67.0	3007		
N170			74.0	3002	58,978p	Hdy SP
A4350	57.6	2602	64.0	2957	62,300p	Bns-X/3.34"/Rem 9½M
IMR4350	62.0	2840	64.0	2955		
H870			80.0	2952		
A8700	72.9	2545	81.0	2892	45,000p	Nos Part./3.355"/ Rem 9½M/(C)
A8700	72.9	2450	81.0	2784	43,200p	Bns-X/3.34"/ Rem 9½M/(C)
168						
H1000	75.0	2998	77.0	3169		
H450	69.0	3002	72.0	3150		
H4831	69.0	3019	72.0	3143		
H870			80.0	3030		
IMR7828	67.0	2833	72.0	2988		
IMR4831	63.0	2811	66.0	2937		
H4350	60.0	2772	64.0	2932		
IMR4350	60.0	2771	63.0	2921		
175						
A3100	62.1	2619	69.0	2976	63,700p	Nos Part./3.36"/Rem 9½M
H1000	72.0	2788	75.0	2946		
H870			79.0	2929		
H450	67.0	2802	70.0	2925		
H4831	67.0	2794	70.0	2904		
IMR7828	66.0	2744	71.0	2900		
A4350	56.7	2547	63.0	2894	61,200p	Nos Part./3.36"/Rem 9½M
IMR4831	62.0	2702	65.0	2840		
H4350	59.0	2664	63.0	2801		
IMR4350	59.0	2679	62.0	2788		
A8700	72.0	2442	80.0	2775	42,700p	Nos Part./3.36"/ Rem 9½M/(C)
N170			68.0	2755	57,415p	Hdy SP
195						
H1000	68.0	2650	70.0	2804		
H870	70.0	2551	75.0	2770		
H4831	62.0	2498	66.0	2710		

Caution: **Loads exceeding SAAMI OAL Maximum must be verified for bullet-to-rifling clearance and magazine functioning. Where a specific primer or bullet is indicated those components must be used, no substitutions! Where only a maximum load is shown, reduce starting load 10%, unless otherwise specified.**

Key: (C) = compressed charge; C = CUP; p = psi; Plink = Plinker; Bns = Barnes; Hdy = Hornady; Lap = Lapua; Nos = Nosler; Rem = Remington; Sra = Sierra; Spr = Speer; Win = Winchester.

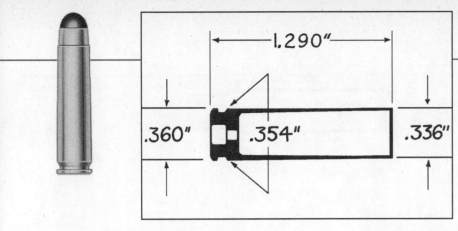

Case: Remington
Primer: Small Rifle
Barrel: 20″ Accurate
  18″ Hodgdon
  18″ Vihtavuori

Bullet Diameter: 0.308″
Maximum Case Length: 1.290″
Trim to Length: 1.286″
Maximum Cartridge OAL: 1.680″
Minimum Cartridge OAL: 1.625″

If ever a cartridge was maligned just because it existed, this is a good candidate. The 30 Carbine was designed as a military expedient, intended for use in a lightweight carbine to replace the 45 ACP Colt 1911A1 that the average soldier seemed uninterested in learning how to shoot properly.

The 30 Carbine is loosely based on the old Winchester 32 Self-Loading. That cartridge was described by the late Frank Barnes, long-time author of *Cartridges Of The World,* as: "...the number one candidate for the title of the world's most useless centerfire rifle cartridge." With such a heritage, can it be any wonder the 30 Carbine is looked on with general disdain.

Had the Army chosen to adopt the 30 Carbine as a full-pressure chambering, rather than relegating it to 30-30 class pressures, things might be different. With limited capacity and pressure, the 30 Carbine offers ballistics that are of limited value apart from varmint hunting. Most 30 M1 Carbines have poor triggers and sights, further limiting their utility.

However, the 30 Carbine is a rare breed—a semi-automatic chambering that thrives on cast bullet loads and can, therefore, be shot very inexpensively. Case capacity with a 110-grain bullet, seated normally, is about 15.5 grains of water. H4227, IMR4227, N110, H110, W296 and No. 9 are all good choices.

30 CARBINE LOADING DATA

Powder	—STARTING— Grs.	MV (fps)	—MAXIMUM— Grs.	MV (fps)	Press. (CUP/psi)	Comments
Lead 125 Lyman 311410						
No.9	9.9	1557	11.0	1769	36,400C	1.705″/CCI 400
A1680	13.5	1545	15.0	1756	33,600C	1.705″/CCI 400
XMP5744			13.5	1711	39,000C	1.705″/CCI 400
77						
H110			17.0	2382		
85						
H110			16.0	2356		
93						
H110			15.5	2221		
100						
N110	13.2	1952	14.5	2121	39,160p	Spr Plink
No.9	12.0	1773	13.3	2015	39,000C	Spr Plink/1.675″/CCI 400
H110			14.5	2013		

Powder	—STARTING— Grs.	MV (fps)	—MAXIMUM— Grs.	MV (fps)	Press. (CUP/psi)	Comments
100 con't						
IMR4227	14.5	1831	15.5	1957		
W296	14.0	1819	15.0	1940		
H4227			14.5	1897		
W680	14.5	1774	15.5	1871		
XMP5744			15.0	1846	35,300C	Spr Plink/1.675″/CCI 400
Her2400	11.0	1684	12.5	1841		
Blue Dot	8.5	1669	9.5	1806		
110						
H4227			14.5	1935		
N110	11.9	1752	13.3	1908	39,160p	Spr RN
H110			14.0	1906	32,400C	26″ Test Barrel
No.9	11.3	1666	12.6	1893	39,800C	Spr FMJ/1.67″/CCI 400
W296	13.0	1791	14.5	1877		
W680	14.0	1707	15.0	1828		
IMR4227	13.5	1724	14.5	1811		
XMP5744			14.5	1787	35,500C	Spr FMJ/1.67″/CCI 400
A1680	14.4	1553	16.0	1765	26,800C	Spr FMJ/1.67″/CCI 400/(C)
Her2400	10.0	1514	12.0	1735		
Blue Dot	8.0	1621	9.0	1716		

Never exceed maximum load nor use any load exhibiting signs of excessive pressure. Begin at suggested starting load and work up carefully.

30-30 Winchester

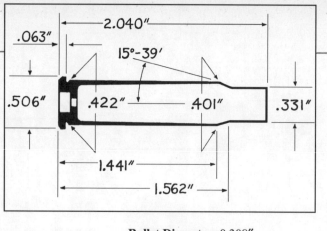

Case: Federal
Primer: Large Rifle
Barrel: 20″ Accurate
24″ Hodgdon
20″ Vihtavuori

Bullet Diameter: 0.308″
Maximum Case Length: 2.040″
Trim to Length: 2.035″
Maximum Cartridge OAL: 2.550″
Minimum Cartridge OAL: 2.450″

John M. Browning designed what became the Model 94 Winchester, selling the patent rights to Winchester in that year. He envisioned that his new gun would chamber intermediate blackpowder cartridges, specifically the 38-55 WCF (originally the 38-55 Ballard) and a tapered version of that case, the 32-40 WCF.

Winchester, recognizing the extraordinary safety of Browning's Model 94, began designing a new series of 38-55 WCF-based cartridges loaded, via smokeless powder, to about twice the pressure of blackpowder counterparts. The series included the 25-35 WCF, 30-30 (advertised as the 30 Winchester but headstamped 30 WCF, the 30-30 name derived from the charge weight of a then-available smokeless powder), 32 Winchester Special and a special high-velocity loading of the 38-55 WCF.

Introduced in 1895 with this new gun, the 30 WCF became the first U.S. small-bore smokeless commercial chambering. Despite rather anemic ballistics by today's standards—a 165-grain bullet at about 2000 fps—the 30-30 was so far ahead of blackpowder loads of the day that it was revolutionary.

Loading pressures for this popular cartridge have remained remarkably stable over the intervening century since its introduction. For this reason, significant improvements in powder allow equally significant improvements in 30-30 ballistics.

Bullets in the 125-130-grain range offer startling performance when used on smaller species of deer and various vermin and predators. The 150-grain bullets have a lot to offer for use against mule deer-sized game. For those who must hunt elk-sized game with the 30-30, we can only recommend use of premium-grade bullets such as Nosler's 170-grain or Barnes' 150-grain X.

When loading Speer's 110-grain Varminter bullet, ensure that your rifle's throat is long enough to prevent the chambered bullet from impinging upon the rifling! This condition, common in new rifles, increases chamber pressure dramatically.

Case capacity with a 170-grain bullet, seated normally, is about 37.8 grains of water. Never use pointed bullets in any tubular magazine rifle. XMP5744 (lead bullets), A2015BR, H322, IMR4064, H414, W760 and many others work well in the 30-30.

30-30 WINCHESTER LOADING DATA

Lead 152 Lyman 311466

Powder	STARTING Grs.	MV (fps)	MAXIMUM Grs.	MV (fps)	Press. (CUP/psi)	Comments
XMP5744			22.5	2112	39,100p	2.45″/CCI 200
A2700	32.3	1933	34.0	2056	28,100p	2.45″/CCI 200
A2495BR	25.7	1803	28.5	2049	28,400p	2.45″/CCI 200
A2520	24.8	1764	27.5	2004	25,700p	2.45″/CCI 200
A2460	24.3	1755	27.0	1994	26,400p	2.45″/CCI 200
A2015BR	23.0	1749	25.5	1987	27,700p	2.45″/CCI 200
A2230	23.4	1736	26.0	1973	27,800p	2.45″/CCI 200

Lead 173 Lyman 31141

Powder	STARTING Grs.	MV (fps)	MAXIMUM Grs.	MV (fps)	Press. (CUP/psi)	Comments
A2520	25.7	1807	28.5	2053	29,300p	2.55″/CCI 200
XMP5744			22.0	2035	38,000p	2.55″/CCI 200
A2460	24.8	1775	27.5	2017	28,300p	2.55″/CCI 200
A2495BR	24.8	1771	27.5	2013	35,100p	2.55″/CCI 200

Lead 173 Lyman 31141 con't

Powder	STARTING Grs.	MV (fps)	MAXIMUM Grs.	MV (fps)	Press. (CUP/psi)	Comments
A2700	31.4	1879	33.0	1999	32,800p	2.55″/CCI 200
A2015BR	23.4	1749	26.0	1988	29,000p	2.55″/CCI 200
A2230	23.4	1720	26.0	1954	27,400p	2.55″/CCI 200

Caution: Loads exceeding SAAMI OAL Maximum must be verified for bullet-to-rifling clearance and magazine functioning. Where a specific primer or bullet is indicated those components must be used, no substitutions! Where only a maximum load is shown, reduce starting load 10%, unless otherwise specified.

Key: (C) = compressed charge; C = CUP; p = psi; Plink = Plinker; Bns = Barnes; Hdy = Hornady; Lap = Lapua; Nos = Nosler; Rem = Remington; Sra = Sierra; Spr = Speer; Win = Winchester.

100

Powder	STARTING Grs.	MV (fps)	MAXIMUM Grs.	MV (fps)	Press. (CUP/psi)	Comments
A2015BR	33.8	2534	37.5	2879	39,900p	Spr Plink/2.345"/CCI 200
A2230	35.1	2514	39.0	2857	39,500p	Spr Plink/2.345"/CCI 200
H4198	31.0	2602	33.0	2837	32,400C	
A2460	35.1	2478	39.0	2816	37,200p	Spr Plink/2.345"/CCI 200
IMR4198	30.0	2566	32.0	2788	31,800C	
RL-7	32.0	2570	34.0	2759	38,400C	
A2495BR	33.3	2359	37.0	2681	34,800p	Spr Plink/2.345"/CCI 200
A2520	34.2	2358	38.0	2680	30,600p	Spr Plink/2.345"/CCI 200
RL-12	34.0	2440	37.0	2655	33,400C	
H4895	34.0	2439	37.0	2652	30,000C	
H335	35.0	2502	38.0	2644	31,800C	
IMR4320	35.0	2510	37.0	2642	29,800C	
IMR4064	35.0	2521	37.0	2638	29,400C	
H322	33.0	2494	35.0	2633	30,000C	
IMR3031	32.0	2494	34.0	2619	29,900C	
W748	36.0	2519	38.0	2597	31,000C	
A2700	38.0	2417	40.0	2571	30,700p	Spr Plink/2.345"/CCI 200/(C)
IMR4895	34.0	2430	36.0	2539	29,400C	
H4227	15.0	1908	18.0	2077	26,300C	
IMR4227	15.0	1889	18.0	2071	26,200C	

110

Powder	STARTING Grs.	MV (fps)	MAXIMUM Grs.	MV (fps)	Press. (CUP/psi)	Comments
A2015BR	32.0	2398	35.5	2725	40,900p	Hdy RN/2.44"/CCI 200
A2495BR	33.3	2375	37.0	2699	41,000p	Hdy RN/2.44"/CCI 200
A2460	33.3	2369	37.0	2692	37,400p	Hdy RN/2.44"/CCI 200
A2520	34.2	2366	38.0	2689	35,700p	Hdy RN/2.44"/CCI 200
A2230	32.4	2340	36.0	2659	37,000p	Hdy RN/2.44"/CCI 200

125-130

Powder	STARTING Grs.	MV (fps)	MAXIMUM Grs.	MV (fps)	Press. (CUP/psi)	Comments
H322	35.0	2484	37.0	2663	37,600C	
H335	36.0	2369	38.0	2643	35,400C	
H4895	35.0	2393	37.0	2618	36,000C	
BL-C(2)	36.0	2343	38.0	2606	34,800C	
RL-7	28.0	2449	30.0	2595	34,000C	
W748	36.0	2340	38.0	2589	34,600C	
H4198	29.0	2427	31.0	2589	37,600C	
RL-12	33.0	2380	36.0	2509	37,500C	
IMR3031	33.0	2251	35.0	2484	37,100C	
IMR4895	34.0	2280	36.0	2474	35,500C	
N133	29.5	2238	32.8	2467	39,200p	Spr FSP/2.547"/Rem 9½
H380	37.0	2219	39.0	2464	33,000C	
IMR4064	35.0	2244	37.0	2460	35,400C	
N135	31.1	2242	34.6	2455	39,200p	Spr FSP/2.547"/Rem 9½
IMR4320	34.0	2306	36.0	2432	37,200C	
IMR4198	27.0	2218	29.0	2421	35,100C	
N130	27.3	2198	30.5	2420	39,200p	Spr FSP/2.547"/Rem 9½
H4227	20.0	1939	22.0	2167	38,200C	
IMR4227	20.0	1918	22.0	2143	37,600C	
H450	38.0	1973	40.0	2089	24,800C	
IMR4350	36.0	1971	38.0	2089	32,000C	
IMR4831	36.0	1954	38.0	2069	28,700C	
H4350	35.0	1935	38.0	2054	31,000C	

150

Powder	STARTING Grs.	MV (fps)	MAXIMUM Grs.	MV (fps)	Press. (CUP/psi)	Comments
H4895	32.0	2242	34.0	2409	40,900C	
H335	32.0	2249	35.0	2406	38,700C	
IMR4320	33.0	2230	35.0	2391	39,200C	
BL-C(2)	32.0	2214	35.0	2384	37,600C	
IMR4895	32.0	2240	34.0	2380	39,900C	
W748	33.0	2249	35.0	2379	37,600C	
IMR4064	33.0	2210	35.0	2379	39,000C	
H322	31.0	2194	33.0	2366	39,300C	
IMR3031	31.0	2184	33.0	2364	38,600C	
H414	37.0	2164	39.0	2327	38,200C	
A2520	30.2	2046	33.5	2325	38,800p	Spr FN/2.54"/CCI 200
H4198	26.0	2207	28.0	2317	40,900C	
RL-12	30.0	2184	33.0	2306	38,000C	
W760	37.0	2144	39.0	2297	37,900C	
IMR4198	26.0	2191	28.0	2292	39,900C	
A2460	29.3	2015	32.5	2290	40,200p	Spr FN/2.54"/CCI 200
A2230	28.5	2000	31.7	2273	41,300p	Spr FN/2.54"/CCI 200
A2700	35.2	2129	37.0	2265	39,300p	Spr FN/2.54"/CCI 200
N140	31.5	2011	34.7	2240	39,200p	Spr FSP/2.539"/Rem 9½
A2495BR	27.5	1960	30.5	2227	40,600p	Spr FN/2.54"/CCI 200
RL-7	26.0	2031	28.0	2210	34,900C	
N135	29.4	2000	32.4	2193	39,200p	Spr FSP/2.539"/Rem 9½
A2015BR	26.1	1929	29.0	2192	38,400p	Spr FN/2.54"/CCI 200
N133	25.7	1935	28.6	2115	39,200p	Spr FSP/2.539"/Rem 9½
N130	24.7	1911	27.5	2103	39,200p	Spr FSP/2.539"/Rem 9½
IMR4350	36.0	1914	38.0	2069	36,100C	

170

Powder	STARTING Grs.	MV (fps)	MAXIMUM Grs.	MV (fps)	Press. (CUP/psi)	Comments
H414	35.0	1926	37.0	2259	37,400C	
W760	35.0	1909	37.0	2254	37,700C	
H335	31.0	2090	33.0	2220	41,500C	
H4895	30.0	1919	32.0	2212	40,900C	
H380	34.0	2016	36.0	2182	37,600C	
BL-C(2)	31.0	1940	33.0	2174	38,200C	
W748	31.0	1949	33.0	2160	38,000C	
A2520	28.4	1874	31.5	2129	38,400p	Nos FN/2.545"/CCI 200
A2230	27.0	1869	30.0	2124	42,000p	Nos FN/2.545"/CCI 200
A2460	27.2	1864	30.2	2118	39,900p	Nos FN/2.545"/CCI 200
RL-12	28.0	1971	31.0	2111	37,700C	
H322	28.0	1966	30.0	2096	40,900C	
A2495BR	26.6	1844	29.5	2095	40,200p	Nos FN/2.545"/CCI 200
IMR4895	29.0	1847	31.0	2049	39,100C	
IMR4320	31.0	1914	33.0	2041	37,400C	
A2015BR	24.3	1793	27.0	2038	38,600p	Nos FN/2.545"/CCI 200
IMR4064	30.0	1838	32.0	2037	38,200C	
H4350	35.0	1837	38.0	2030	37,100C	
H4198	24.0	1899	26.0	2027	39,300C	
N140	28.2	1803	31.7	2025	39,200p	Spr FSP/2.539"/Rem 9½
N140			31.5	2020	39,160p	Sako SP 128A
N135	27.0	1825	30.1	2015	39,200p	Spr FSP/2.539"/Rem 9½
IMR4198	24.0	1880	26.0	2008	39,000C	
H450	35.0	1841	38.0	2003	33,000C	
IMR4350	35.0	1860	37.0	2001	36,800C	

Never exceed maximum load nor use any load exhibiting signs of excessive pressure. Begin at suggested starting load and work up carefully.

30 Remington

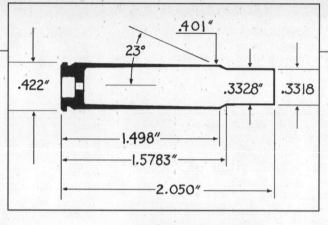

Case: Remington
Primer: Large Rifle
Barrel: 20″ Accurate
24″ Hodgdon
20″ Vihtavuori

Bullet Diameter: 0.308″
Maximum Case Length: 2.050″
Trim to Length: 2.045″
Maximum Cartridge OAL: 2.525″
Minimum Cartridge OAL: 2.465″

Introduced in 1906, this cartridge is nothing more than a rimless version of the 30-30 Winchester with essentially identical case capacity. Rifles chambered for the 30 Remington are generally considered to be a bit stronger than typical 30-30-chambered guns.

Unlike most 30-30-chambered rifles, with tubular magazines, Remington's Model 8 and Model 81 autoloaders can safely use pointed bullets, allowing loads to carry a bit more energy to their extreme useful range.

Nevertheless, for incomprehensible reasons, the 30 Remington has always been factory loaded with blunt bullets and slightly lower pressures than the 30-30. For Remington rifles in good condition, the following loads are perfectly acceptable. Unfortunately, we do not have access to pressure data generated with spitzer bullets and, therefore, cannot recommend any such loads.

Case capacity with a 170-grain bullet, seated normally, is about 37.4 grains of water.

30 REMINGTON LOADING DATA

Lead 152 Lyman 311466

Powder	—STARTING— Grs.	MV (fps)	—MAXIMUM— Grs.	MV (fps)	Press. (CUP/psi)	Comments
XMP5744			22.5	2112	39,100p	2.45″/CCI 200
A2700	32.3	1933	34.0	2056	28,100p	2.45″/CCI 200
A2495BR	25.7	1803	28.5	2049	28,400p	2.45″/CCI 200
A2520	24.8	1764	27.5	2004	25,700p	2.45″/CCI 200
A2460	24.3	1755	27.0	1994	26,400p	2.45″/CCI 200
A2015BR	23.0	1749	25.5	1987	27,700p	2.45″/CCI 200
A2230	23.4	1736	26.0	1973	27,800p	2.45″/CCI 200

Lead 173 Lyman 31141

Powder	—STARTING— Grs.	MV (fps)	—MAXIMUM— Grs.	MV (fps)	Press. (CUP/psi)	Comments
A2520	25.7	1807	28.5	2053	29,300p	2.55″/CCI 200
XMP5744			22.0	2035	38,000p	2.55″/CCI 200
A2460	24.8	1775	27.5	2017	28,300p	2.55″/CCI 200
A2495BR	24.8	1771	27.5	2013	35,100p	2.55″/CCI 200
A2700	31.4	1879	33.0	1999	32,800p	2.55″/CCI 200
A2015BR	23.4	1749	26.0	1988	29,000p	2.55″/CCI 200
A2230	23.4	1720	26.0	1954	27,400p	2.55″/CCI 200

100

Powder	—STARTING— Grs.	MV (fps)	—MAXIMUM— Grs.	MV (fps)	Press. (CUP/psi)	Comments
A2015BR	33.8	2534	37.5	2879	39,900p	Spr Plink/2.345″/CCI 200
A2230	35.1	2514	39.0	2857	39,500p	Spr Plink/2.345″/CCI 200
H4198	31.0	2602	33.0	2837	32,400C	

100 con't

Powder	—STARTING— Grs.	MV (fps)	—MAXIMUM— Grs.	MV (fps)	Press. (CUP/psi)	Comments
A2460	35.1	2478	39.0	2816	37,200p	Spr Plink/2.345″/CCI 200
IMR4198	30.0	2566	32.0	2788	31,800C	
RL-7	32.0	2570	34.0	2759	38,400C	
A2495BR	33.3	2359	37.0	2681	34,800p	Spr Plink/2.345″/CCI 200
A2520	34.2	2358	38.0	2680	30,600p	Spr Plink/2.345″/CCI 200
RL-12	34.0	2440	37.0	2655	33,400C	
H4895	34.0	2439	37.0	2652	30,000C	
H335	35.0	2502	38.0	2644	31,800C	
IMR4320	35.0	2510	37.0	2642	29,800C	
IMR4064	35.0	2521	37.0	2638	29,400C	
H322	33.0	2494	35.0	2633	30,000C	
IMR3031	32.0	2494	34.0	2619	29,900C	
W748	36.0	2519	38.0	2597	31,000C	
A2700	38.0	2417	40.0	2571	30,700p	Spr Plink/2.345″/CCI 200/(C)
IMR4895	34.0	2430	36.0	2539	29,400C	
H4227	15.0	1908	18.0	2077	26,300C	
IMR4227	15.0	1889	18.0	2071	26,200C	
SR4759	15.0	1834	18.0	2034	30,900C	

110

Powder	—STARTING— Grs.	MV (fps)	—MAXIMUM— Grs.	MV (fps)	Press. (CUP/psi)	Comments
A2015BR	32.0	2398	35.5	2725	40,900p	Hdy RN/2.44″/CCI 200
A2495BR	33.3	2375	37.0	2699	41,000p	Hdy RN/2.44″/CCI 200

Never exceed maximum load nor use any load exhibiting signs of excessive pressure. Begin at suggested starting load and work up carefully.

Powder	STARTING Grs.	MV (fps)	MAXIMUM Grs.	MV (fps)	Press. (CUP/psi)	Comments

110 con't

Powder	Grs.	MV (fps)	Grs.	MV (fps)	Press. (CUP/psi)	Comments
A2460	33.3	2369	37.0	2692	37,400p	Hdy RN/2.44"/CCI 200
A2520	34.2	2366	38.0	2689	35,700p	Hdy RN/2.44"/CCI 200
A2230	32.4	2340	36.0	2659	37,000p	Hdy RN/2.44"/CCI 200
A2700	38.0	2391	40.0	2544	33,300p	Hdy RN/2.44"/CCI 200/(C)

125-130

Powder	Grs.	MV (fps)	Grs.	MV (fps)	Press. (CUP/psi)	Comments
H322	35.0	2484	37.0	2663	37,600C	
H335	36.0	2369	38.0	2643	35,400C	
H4895	35.0	2393	37.0	2618	36,000C	
BL-C(2)	36.0	2343	38.0	2606	34,800C	
RL-7	28.0	2449	30.0	2595	34,000C	
W748	36.0	2340	38.0	2589	34,600C	
H4198	29.0	2427	31.0	2589	37,600C	
RL-12	33.0	2380	36.0	2509	37,500C	
IMR3031	33.0	2251	35.0	2484	37,100C	
IMR4895	34.0	2280	36.0	2474	35,500C	
N133	29.5	2238	32.8	2467	39,200p	Spr FSP/2.547"/Rem 9½
H380	37.0	2219	39.0	2464	33,000C	
IMR4064	35.0	2244	37.0	2460	35,400C	
N135	31.1	2242	34.6	2455	39,200p	Spr FSP/2.547"/Rem 9½
IMR4320	34.0	2306	36.0	2432	37,200C	
IMR4198	27.0	2218	29.0	2421	35,100C	
N130	27.3	2198	30.5	2420	39,200p	Spr FSP/2.547"/Rem 9½
H4227	20.0	1939	22.0	2167	38,200C	
IMR4227	20.0	1918	22.0	2143	37,600C	
H450	38.0	1973	40.0	2089	24,800C	
IMR4350	36.0	1971	38.0	2089	32,000C	
IMR4831	36.0	1954	38.0	2069	28,700C	
H4350	35.0	1935	38.0	2054	31,000C	
H4831	35.0	1936	38.0	2031	30,600C	

150

Powder	Grs.	MV (fps)	Grs.	MV (fps)	Press. (CUP/psi)	Comments
H4895	32.0	2242	34.0	2409	40,900C	
H335	32.0	2249	35.0	2406	38,700C	
IMR4320	33.0	2230	35.0	2391	39,200C	
BL-C(2)	32.0	2214	35.0	2384	37,600C	
IMR4895	32.0	2240	34.0	2380	39,900C	
W748	33.0	2249	35.0	2379	37,600C	
IMR4064	33.0	2210	35.0	2379	39,000C	
H322	31.0	2194	33.0	2366	39,300C	
IMR3031	31.0	2184	33.0	2364	38,600C	
H414	37.0	2164	39.0	2327	38,200C	
A2520	30.2	2046	33.5	2325	38,800p	Spr FN/2.54"/CCI 200
H4198	26.0	2207	28.0	2317	40,900C	
RL-12	30.0	2184	33.0	2306	38,000C	
W760	37.0	2144	39.0	2297	37,900C	
IMR4198	26.0	2191	28.0	2292	39,900C	
A2460	29.3	2015	32.5	2290	40,200p	Spr FN/2.54"/CCI 200
A2230	28.5	2000	31.7	2273	41,300p	Spr FN/2.54"/CCI 200
A2700	35.2	2129	37.0	2265	39,300p	Spr FN/2.54"/CCI 200
N140	31.5	2011	34.7	2240	39,200p	Spr FSP/2.539"/Rem 9½

150 con't

Powder	Grs.	MV (fps)	Grs.	MV (fps)	Press. (CUP/psi)	Comments
A2495BR	27.5	1960	30.5	2227	40,600p	Spr FN/2.54"/CCI 200
RL-7	26.0	2031	28.0	2210	34,900C	
N135	29.4	2000	32.4	2193	39,200p	Spr FSP/2.539"/Rem 9½
A2015BR	26.1	1929	29.0	2192	38,400p	Spr FN/2.54"/CCI 200
N133	25.7	1935	28.6	2115	39,200p	Spr FSP/2.539"/Rem 9½
N130	24.7	1911	27.5	2103	39,200p	Spr FSP/2.539"/Rem 9½
IMR4350	36.0	1914	38.0	2069	36,100C	
H4350	35.0	1904	38.0	2041	35,600C	
IMR4831	36.0	1898	38.0	2034	33,000C	
H4831	35.0	1801	38.0	1965	31,200C	
H4227	17.0	1695	19.0	1881	38,700C	
IMR4227	17.0	1683	19.0	1874	38,900C	

170

Powder	Grs.	MV (fps)	Grs.	MV (fps)	Press. (CUP/psi)	Comments
H414	35.0	1926	37.0	2259	37,400C	
W760	35.0	1909	37.0	2254	37,700C	
H335	31.0	2090	33.0	2220	41,500C	
H4895	30.0	1919	32.0	2212	40,900C	
H380	34.0	2016	36.0	2182	37,600C	
BL-C(2)	31.0	1940	33.0	2174	38,200C	
W748	31.0	1949	33.0	2160	38,000C	
A2520	28.4	1874	31.5	2129	38,400p	Nos FN/2.545"/CCI 200
A2230	27.0	1869	30.0	2124	42,000p	Nos FN/2.545"/CCI 200
A2460	27.2	1864	30.2	2118	39,900p	Nos FN/2.545"/CCI 200
RL-12	28.0	1971	31.0	2111	37,700C	
H322	28.0	1966	30.0	2096	40,900C	
A2495BR	26.6	1844	29.5	2095	40,200p	Nos FN/2.545"/CCI 200
IMR4895	29.0	1847	31.0	2049	39,100C	
IMR4320	31.0	1914	33.0	2041	37,400C	
A2015BR	24.3	1793	27.0	2038	38,600p	Nos FN/2.545"/CCI 200
IMR4064	30.0	1838	32.0	2037	38,200C	
H4350	35.0	1837	38.0	2030	37,100C	
H4198	24.0	1899	26.0	2027	39,300C	
N140	28.2	1803	31.7	2025	39,200p	Spr FSP/2.539"/Rem 9½
N140			31.5	2020	39,160p	Sako SP 128A
N135	27.0	1825	30.1	2015	39,200p	Spr FSP/2.539"/Rem 9½
IMR4198	24.0	1880	26.0	2008	39,000C	
H450	35.0	1841	38.0	2003	33,000C	
IMR4350	35.0	1860	37.0	2001	36,800C	
H4831	35.0	1822	38.0	1991	34,800C	
IMR3031	28.0	1858	30.0	1987	38,000C	
IMR4831	35.0	1800	37.0	1956	34,900C	
RL-7	23.0	1839	25.0	1952	36,900C	

Caution: Loads exceeding SAAMI OAL Maximum must be verified for bullet-to-rifling clearance and magazine functioning. Where a specific primer or bullet is indicated those components must be used, no substitutions! Where only a maximum load is shown, reduce starting load 10%, unless otherwise specified.

Key: (C) = compressed charge; C = CUP; p = psi; Plink = Plinker; Bns = Barnes; Hdy = Hornady; Lap = Lapua; Nos = Nosler; Rem = Remington; Sra = Sierra; Spr = Speer; Win = Winchester.

Never exceed maximum load nor use any load exhibiting signs of excessive pressure. Begin at suggested starting load and work up carefully.

30-40 Krag

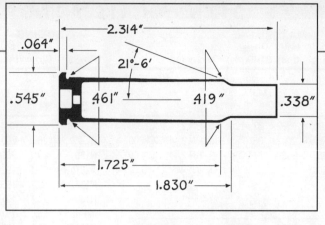

Case: Remington
Primer: Large Rifle
Barrel: 24″ Accurate/24″ Hodgdon
Bullet Diameter: 0.308″

Maximum Case Length: 2.314″
Trim to Length: 2.304″
Maximum Cartridge OAL: 3.089″
Minimum Cartridge OAL: 2.965″

Adopted by the U.S. government as the 30 U.S. Army, this cartridge was a modification of older blackpowder chamberings, but was designed from the outset as a smokeless loading. As with most military chamberings, it soon achieved commercial standardization and widespread popularity.

Just like the rimmed case design, the original 220-grain round-nosed bullet reflected U.S. military prejudice and inertia. While the rest of the modernizing world was perfecting rimless military cartridges firing moderate-weight spitzer bullets at high velocity, the U.S. decided to replace the 45-70 with a more modern chambering and ended up adopting what was an already thoroughly obsolete loading by European standards.

Amazingly, ten years later, when the 30-03 (forerunner to the 30-06) was introduced in response to a perceived need for more power and better magazine feeding characteristics,

the Army adopted a circa-1870s round-nose bullet!

In deference to limited safety features and strength of the original Krag rifle (the 1895 Winchester lever action, commonly chambered in 30-40 Krag, is considerably stronger), factory loads have grown more circumspect in recent decades. It is almost certain the original military loading generated considerably higher pressures than any modern 30-40 Krag factory load. To achieve the ballistics reported with the powders then available, original loads must have been stressing the weak Krag design rather harshly.

Properly loaded with modern bullets the 30-40 Krag is fully capable for use against big game to the size of elk.

Case capacity with a 150-grain bullet, seated normally, is about 53.8 grains of water. H322, H414, W760, A4350, IMR4064 and A3100 are good 30-40 powders.

30-40 KRAG LOADING DATA

Lead 165 Lyman FNGC

Powder	Grs.	MV (fps)	Grs.	MV (fps)	Press. (CUP/psi)	Comments
XMP5744			28.0	2198	38,400C	

Lead 180 Lyman 311467

Powder	Grs.	MV (fps)	Grs.	MV (fps)	Press. (CUP/psi)	Comments
A4350	39.6	2014	44.0	2289	34,500C	2.9″/CCI 200
A3100	43.2	1971	48.0	2240	35,700C	2.9″/CCI 200

Lead 210 Lyman RNGC

Powder	Grs.	MV (fps)	Grs.	MV (fps)	Press. (CUP/psi)	Comments
XMP5744			25.0	1870	36,800C	

100

Powder	Grs.	MV (fps)	Grs.	MV (fps)	Press. (CUP/psi)	Comments
H322	39.0	2542	43.0	2898		
IMR4320	45.0	2754	47.0	2898		
BL-C(2)	42.0	2677	44.0	2894		
H4198	30.0	2604	34.0	2886		
W748	42.0	2664	44.0	2884		
H335	42.0	2669	44.0	2881		

100 con't

Powder	Grs.	MV (fps)	Grs.	MV (fps)	Press. (CUP/psi)	Comments
IMR4198	31.0	2657	34.0	2870		
IMR3031	41.0	2653	43.0	2839		
H4895	42.0	2707	44.0	2835		
IMR4064	44.0	2709	46.0	2824		
IMR4895	42.0	2676	44.0	2819		

110

Powder	Grs.	MV (fps)	Grs.	MV (fps)	Press. (CUP/psi)	Comments
H322	39.0	2497	43.0	2841		
H4198	30.0	2417	34.0	2807		
IMR4198	31.0	2477	34.0	2794		
H414	46.0	2552	50.0	2773		
IMR3031	41.0	2625	43.0	2761		
W760	48.0	2642	50.0	2760		
IMR4320	44.0	2590	46.0	2709		
IMR4064	43.0	2550	45.0	2657		
IMR4895	41.0	2524	43.0	2640		
IMR4350	49.0	2393	51.0	2520		
H4350	48.0	2300	51.0	2492		

Never exceed maximum load nor use any load exhibiting signs of excessive pressure. Begin at suggested starting load and work up carefully.

125-130

Powder	Starting Grs.	MV (fps)	Max Grs.	MV (fps)	Press. (CUP/psi)	Comments
H414	45.0	2507	49.0	2746		(130-gr.)
W760	47.0	2614	49.0	2724		
H335	40.0	2514	42.0	2717		(130-gr.)
W748	40.0	2469	42.0	2713		
H322	38.0	2458	42.0	2698		(130-gr.)
H4198	29.0	2224	33.0	2565		(130-gr.)
IMR4198	29.0	2219	33.0	2544		
IMR4064	42.0	2390	44.0	2537		
H4350	48.0	2330	51.0	2535		(130-gr.)
IMR3031	40.0	2379	42.0	2524		
IMR4320	43.0	2391	45.0	2510		

150

Powder	Starting Grs.	MV (fps)	Max Grs.	MV (fps)	Press. (CUP/psi)	Comments
H4895	38.5	2410	42.0	2575		
A4350	44.1	2258	49.0	2566	36,800C	Hdy SP/3.045"/CCI 200/(C)
IMR4895	40.0	2374	42.0	2559		
W760	45.0	2445	47.0	2539		
H414	45.0	2403	47.0	2531		
IMR4064	40.0	2340	42.0	2527		
H322	36.0	2369	40.0	2518		
H335	35.0	2349	37.0	2508		
BL-C(2)	35.0	2351	37.0	2491		
H380	40.5	2311	44.0	2489		
IMR4320	41.0	2324	43.0	2481		
W748	35.0	2363	37.0	2480		
IMR3031	39.0	2333	41.0	2460		
IMR4831	47.0	2290	49.0	2410		
IMR4350	47.0	2294	49.0	2398		
H4350	46.0	2198	49.0	2388		

165

Powder	Starting Grs.	MV (fps)	Max Grs.	MV (fps)	Press. (CUP/psi)	Comments
A4350	42.8	2190	47.5	2489	36,100C	Sra SBT/3.085"/CCI 200
H322	35.0	2228	39.0	2402		
W760	43.0	2292	45.0	2370		
H335	35.0	2242	36.0	2364		
A3100	45.0	2079	50.0	2363	35,300C	Sra SBT/3.085"/CCI 200/(C)
W748	34.0	2210	36.0	2357		
IMR4895	38.0	2191	40.0	2310		
IMR4831	46.0	2166	48.0	2309		
IMR4320	38.0	2178	40.0	2294		
IMR4350	46.0	2149	48.0	2281		
IMR3031	36.0	2144	38.0	2270		

180

Powder	Starting Grs.	MV (fps)	Max Grs.	MV (fps)	Press. (CUP/psi)	Comments
A4350	41.4	2077	46.0	2360	37,200C	Sra SP/3.09"/CCI 200
A3100	45.0	2049	50.0	2328	36,700C	Sra SP/3.09"/CCI 200/(C)
IMR4320	37.0	2133	39.0	2297		
H414	39.5	2125	43.0	2276		
W760	41.0	2209	43.0	2271		
H4895	35.0	2171	38.0	2265		
H322	33.0	2111	37.0	2250		
IMR4895	36.0	2182	38.0	2249		
IMR4064	36.0	2139	38.0	2190		
IMR4831	45.0	2069	47.0	2184		
H380	37.0	2057	40.0	2182		
H4831	44.0	1967	48.0	2176		
IMR4350	44.0	2002	46.0	2163		

190

Powder	Starting Grs.	MV (fps)	Max Grs.	MV (fps)	Press. (CUP/psi)	Comments
W760	40.0	2147	42.0	2204		
IMR4064	35.0	2004	37.0	2144		
IMR4895	34.0	1988	36.0	2140		
IMR3031	33.0	1969	35.0	2130		
IMR4320	35.0	1994	37.0	2129		
IMR4831	44.0	2009	46.0	2119		
IMR4350	43.0	1974	45.0	2104		
W748	31.0	1987	33.0	2080		

200

Powder	Starting Grs.	MV (fps)	Max Grs.	MV (fps)	Press. (CUP/psi)	Comments
H414	37.0	2013	40.0	2151		
W760	38.0	2069	40.0	2140		
W748	31.0	1914	33.0	2109		
H335	30.0	1894	33.0	2106		
H322	32.0	1915	35.0	2075		
H4350	42.0	1929	44.0	2018		
IMR4320	34.0	1894	36.0	2012		
IMR4831	43.0	1889	45.0	1998		
IMR4350	41.0	1860	43.0	1977		
IMR4895	33.0	1839	35.0	1944		
IMR4064	34.0	1820	36.0	1938		
IMR3031	32.0	1780	34.0	1919		

220-225

Powder	Starting Grs.	MV (fps)	Max Grs.	MV (fps)	Press. (CUP/psi)	Comments
A3100	43.2	1908	48.0	2168	39,400C	Sra FP/3.005"/CCI 200
A4350	38.7	1852	43.0	2104	38,200C	Sra FP/3.005"/CCI 200
H335	30.0	1836	33.0	1974		
W760	37.0	1863	39.0	1969		(220-gr.)
H322	30.0	1852	43.0	1969		
IMR4831	41.0	1850	43.0	1964		(220-gr.)
H4350	40.0	1874	42.0	1947		
W748	30.0	1828	32.0	1940		(220-gr.)
IMR4350	39.0	1833	41.0	1931		(220-gr.)
IMR4320	32.0	1791	34.0	1909		(220-gr.)
IMR4064	32.0	1766	34.0	1899		(220-gr.)
IMR4895	31.0	1757	33.0	1881		(220-gr.)

Caution: Loads exceeding SAAMI OAL Maximum must be verified for bullet-to-rifling clearance and magazine functioning. Where a specific primer or bullet is indicated those components must be used, no substitutions! Where only a maximum load is shown, reduce starting load 10%, unless otherwise specified.

Key: (C) = compressed charge; C = CUP; p = psi; Plink = Plinker; Bns = Barnes; Hdy = Hornady; Lap = Lapua; Nos = Nosler; Rem = Remington; Sra = Sierra; Spr = Speer; Win = Winchester.

Never exceed maximum load nor use any load exhibiting signs of excessive pressure. Begin at suggested starting load and work up carefully.

307 Winchester

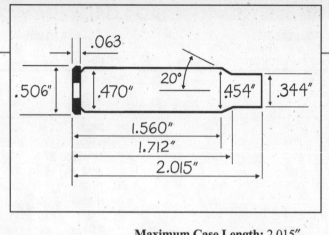

Case: IMI
Primer: Large Rifle
Barrel: 24″ Accurate/20″ Hodgdon
Bullet Diameter: 0.308″

Maximum Case Length: 2.015″
Trim to Length: 2.010″
Maximum Cartridge OAL: 2.560″
Minimum Cartridge OAL: 2.530″

The 307 Winchester is simply the 308 Winchester fitted with a 30-30 size rim. This design can be described as semi-rimmed since, unlike true rimmed cartridges, the extractor groove *is* necessary to achieve proper purchase for the extractor. Excepting the rim, case dimensions are identical to the 308.

This cartridge was designed to allow use of a high-pressure case with increased capacity in the Model 94 Winchester rifle without significant modifications to the action. Necessarily loaded with flat-nosed bullets and to a shorter length than the 308 Winchester, the 307 Winchester cannot match 308 ballistics, but it does provide a significant ballistic advantage over the 30-30 Winchester.

Nevertheless, this chambering is a perfect example of inertia in motion. Shooters had been begging Winchester for such a chambering since the end of WWII, if not before that. Myriad gunsmiths had converted thousands of 30-30 Winchester rifles to Mr. Ackley's improved version of the 30-30 Winchester—a simple rechambering job that achieved a sig-

nificant ballistic improvement, while allowing use of factory 30-30 ammunition in a pinch.

Finally, in 1982, Winchester got around to answering their mail.... Trouble was, the mail was, by then, decades old and no one really cared any more. Partly in response to having long been denied chamberings of superior performance in lever-action rifles, those who had patiently awaited the development of a cartridge like the 307 Winchester had, by 1982, long-since abandoned the lever action.

Nevertheless, where the 30-30 Winchester can only be considered a marginal elk rifle, the 307 Winchester is fully up to the task, within the range constraints imposed by the blunt bullets it must bear.

Case capacity with a 170-grain bullet, seated normally, is about 49.2 grains of water. W748, IMR4064 and H335 are among the best choices for the 307 Winchester.

Never use pointed bullets in any tubular magazine rifle.

307 WINCHESTER LOADING DATA

110

Powder	STARTING Grs.	MV (fps)	MAXIMUM Grs.	MV (fps)	Press. (CUP/psi)	Comments
H322	41.0	2814	44.0	3000		Round Nose
BL-C(2)	47.0	2839	49.0	2950		Round Nose
IMR4064	45.0	2741	48.0	2940		Round Nose
H380	50.0	2747	52.0	2939		Round Nose
H4895	42.0	2724	45.0	2930		Round Nose
W748	47.0	2892	49.0	2923		Round Nose
IMR4895	42.0	2700	45.0	2906		Round Nose
H335	45.0	2769	47.0	2899		Round Nose
IMR3031	41.0	2690	44.0	2898		Round Nose
H414	51.0	2688	53.0	2828		Round Nose
IMR4320	45.0	2689	48.0	2811		Round Nose
W760	51.0	2676	53.0	2809		Round Nose
H4350	47.0	2320	50.0	2589		Round Nose
H4831	48.0	2340	50.0	2451		Round Nose
IMR4350	45.0	2269	47.0	2441		Round Nose
IMR4831	45.0	2166	47.0	2320		Round Nose

125-130

Powder	STARTING Grs.	MV (fps)	MAXIMUM Grs.	MV (fps)	Press. (CUP/psi)	Comments
H4895	40.0	2540	43.0	2762		Flat Nose
IMR4895	40.0	2533	43.0	2751		Flat Nose
IMR4064	42.0	2544	45.0	2749		Flat Nose
W748	44.0	2494	47.0	2740		Flat Nose
BL-C(2)	44.0	2510	47.0	2732		Flat Nose
IMR3031	41.0	2559	43.0	2697		Flat Nose
H335	42.0	2439	45.0	2695		Flat Nose
H322	39.0	2481	42.0	2669		Flat Nose
H414	48.0	2489	50.0	2665		Flat Nose
W760	48.0	2477	50.0	2661		Flat Nose
H380	47.0	2424	49.0	2639		Flat Nose
IMR4320	42.0	2466	45.0	2639		Flat Nose
H4350	47.0	2380	50.0	2522		Flat Nose
H4831	48.0	2269	50.0	2400		Flat Nose
IMR4350	45.0	2274	47.0	2363		Flat Nose
IMR4831	45.0	2121	47.0	2288		Flat Nose

Never exceed maximum load nor use any load exhibiting signs of excessive pressure. Begin at suggested starting load and work up carefully.

150

Powder	—STARTING— Grs.	MV (fps)	—MAXIMUM— Grs.	MV (fps)	Press. (CUP/psi)	Comments
A2520	39.6	2370	44.0	2693	45,500C	Spr FN/2.53"/CCI 200
A2495BR	39.2	2335	43.5	2653	44,400C	Spr FN/2.53"/CCI 200
A2015BR	35.1	2319	39.0	2635	45,300C	Spr FN/2.53"/CCI 200
IMR4895	39.0	2393	42.0	2611		Flat Nose
IMR4064	41.0	2414	44.0	2607		Flat Nose
H4895	39.0	2402	42.0	2604		Flat Nose
A2460	37.4	2285	41.5	2597	43,600C	Spr FN/2.53"/CCI 200
IMR4320	41.0	2388	44.0	2595		Flat Nose
BL-C(2)	43.0	2390	46.0	2593		Flat Nose
A2230	36.5	2281	40.5	2592	45,400C	Spr FN/2.53"/CCI 200
H335	41.0	2377	44.0	2590		Flat Nose
W748	43.0	2381	46.0	2589		Flat Nose
H414	47.0	2347	49.0	2562		Flat Nose
W760	47.0	2339	49.0	2559		Flat Nose
IMR3031	38.0	2338	41.0	2549		Flat Nose
H380	46.0	2329	48.0	2543		Flat Nose
H322	38.0	2319	41.0	2513		Flat Nose
H4350	46.0	2292	48.0	2453		Flat Nose
IMR4350	45.0	2237	47.0	2423		Flat Nose
H4831	47.0	2154	49.0	2349		Flat Nose
IMR4831	45.0	2114	47.0	2282		Flat Nose

165-170

Powder	—STARTING— Grs.	MV (fps)	—MAXIMUM— Grs.	MV (fps)	Press. (CUP/psi)	Comments
A2520	38.3	2262	42.5	2570	49,300C	Spr FN/2.53"/CCI 200
BL-C(2)	41.0	2351	44.0	2535		Round & Flat Noses
W748	41.0	2350	44.0	2535		Round & Flat Noses
IMR4064	39.0	2329	42.0	2526		Round & Flat Noses
A2495BR	37.4	2213	41.5	2515	50,100C	Spr FN/2.53"/CCI 200
H414	45.0	2333	47.0	2513		Round & Flat Noses
IMR4320	39.0	2303	42.0	2505		Round & Flat Noses
W760	45.0	2341	47.0	2499		Round & Flat Noses
A2015BR	34.2	2193	38.0	2492	48,900C	Spr FN/2.53"/CCI 200
H4895	37.0	2314	40.0	2474		Round & Flat Noses
IMR4895	37.0	2292	40.0	2461		Round & Flat Noses
A2460	36.5	2163	40.5	2458	48,100C	Spr FN/2.53"/CCI 200
IMR3031	36.0	2272	39.0	2449		Round & Flat Noses
H335	38.0	2282	41.0	2432		Round & Flat Noses
H380	44.0	2279	46.0	2429		Round & Flat Noses
A2230	35.1	2129	39.0	2419	47,000C	Spr FN/2.53"/CCI 200
H322	35.0	2234	38.0	2418		Round & Flat Noses
IMR4350	45.0	2225	47.0	2410		Round & Flat Noses
H4350	45.0	2210	47.0	2380		Round & Flat Noses
IMR4831	45.0	2221	47.0	2319		Round & Flat Noses
H4831	45.0	2161	47.0	2290		Round & Flat Noses

180

Powder	—STARTING— Grs.	MV (fps)	—MAXIMUM— Grs.	MV (fps)	Press. (CUP/psi)	Comments
IMR4895	38.0	2318	40.0	2479		Round Nose
BL-C(2)	40.0	2290	43.0	2474		Round Nose
IMR4064	39.0	2340	41.0	2472		Round Nose
H414	44.0	2323	46.0	2470		Round Nose
IMR4320	39.0	2333	41.0	2464		Round Nose
W760	44.0	2309	46.0	2462		Round Nose
W748	40.0	2287	43.0	2442		Round Nose
H335	37.0	2231	40.0	2417		Round Nose
H4350	45.0	2290	47.0	2416		Round Nose
IMR3031	35.0	2217	38.0	2410		Round Nose
H4895	36.0	2227	39.0	2373		Round Nose
IMR4350	44.0	2228	46.0	2371		Round Nose
H322	34.0	2169	37.0	2359		Round Nose
IMR4831	44.0	2171	46.0	2320		Round Nose
H4831	45.0	2140	47.0	2289		Round Nose

200

Powder	—STARTING— Grs.	MV (fps)	—MAXIMUM— Grs.	MV (fps)	Press. (CUP/psi)	Comments
W760	43.0	2121	45.0	2374		Round Nose
H414	43.0	2111	45.0	2367		Round Nose
H380	42.0	2083	44.0	2344		Round Nose
IMR4350	43.0	2118	46.0	2336		Round Nose
IMR4320	37.0	2139	39.0	2322		Round Nose
H4895	35.0	2151	38.0	2309		Round Nose
H4350	43.0	2098	46.0	2306		Round Nose
IMR4895	35.0	2144	38.0	2302		Round Nose
IMR4831	44.0	2069	46.0	2280		Round Nose
BL-C(2)	37.0	2070	40.0	2248		Round Nose
IMR4064	37.0	2131	39.0	2240		Round Nose
H335	35.0	2048	38.0	2215		Round Nose
H4831	43.0	2007	46.0	2207		Round Nose

Caution: **Loads exceeding SAAMI OAL Maximum must be verified for bullet-to-rifling clearance and magazine functioning. Where a specific primer or bullet is indicated those components must be used, no substitutions! Where only a maximum load is shown, reduce starting load 10%, unless otherwise specified.**

Key: (C) = compressed charge; C = CUP; p = psi; Plink = Plinker; Bns = Barnes; Hdy = Hornady; Lap = Lapua; Nos = Nosler; Rem = Remington; Sra = Sierra; Spr = Speer; Win = Winchester.

Never exceed maximum load nor use any load exhibiting signs of excessive pressure. Begin at suggested starting load and work up carefully.

185

300

Savage

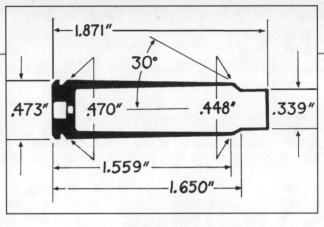

Case: Federal
Primer: Large Rifle
Barrel: 24″ Accurate
      22″ Hodgdon
Bullet Diameter: 0.308″

Maximum Case Length: 1.871″
Trim to Length: 1.865″
Maximum Cartridge OAL: 2.600″
Minimum Cartridge OAL: 2.495″

Introduced in the popular Model 99 lever-action rifle in 1920, the 300 Savage was designed to duplicate the performance of the original 30-06 Springfield military loading. The 300 Savage achieved that goal, launching 150-grain bullets at 2700 fps—original military 30-06 ballistics. Considering its significant reduction in usable capacity, compared to the 30-06, such a result might seem surprising, but in that era improvements in smokeless powders were rapid and significant.

Today's 300 Savage factory ammunition, and handloads, are restricted to somewhat less maximum pressure than the original loadings, and where 30-06 ballistics have improved markedly, the 300 Savage is still restricted to about its original performance. This is, nevertheless, sufficient to place it very close to 308 Winchester performance.

While this would not be this author's choice for use against the largest of bear, properly loaded and handled, the 300 Savage is capable for use against any species in North America. Until the advent of the 308 Winchester, it was alone in the high-performance short-action 30-caliber field and gained a considerable following for that reason. The 300 Savage is still a good cartridge and is loaded by a surprising number of Model 99 owners who prove every hunting season what it can do.

Case capacity with a 150-grain bullet, seated normally, is about 49.1 grains of water. H4198, A2520 and H4895 are good choices for the 300 Savage.

300 SAVAGE LOADING DATA

Powder	—STARTING— Grs.	MV (fps)	—MAXIMUM— Grs.	MV (fps)	Press. (CUP/psi)	Comments
100						
H4198	34.0	2914	37.0	3103		
H4895	41.0	2819	43.0	3002		
BL-C(2)	41.0	2755	43.0	2959		
H335	41.0	2741	43.0	2952		
110						
H4198	34.0	2742	37.0	2978		
H335	39.0	2639	43.0	2947		
H4895	39.5	2669	43.0	2944		
BL-C(2)	39.5	2652	43.0	2940		
130						
H4198	33.0	2624	36.0	2837		
H4895	39.5	2424	43.0	2698		
BL-C(2)	38.0	2503	41.0	2634		
H335	38.0	2494	41.0	2631		

Powder	—STARTING— Grs.	MV (fps)	—MAXIMUM— Grs.	MV (fps)	Press. (CUP/psi)	Comments
150						
A2520	38.3	2433	42.5	2765	43,400C	PMC FMJ/2.6″/Rem 9½
A2015BR	34.7	2413	38.5	2742	43,600C	PMC FMJ/2.6″/Rem 9½
A2495BR	37.8	2405	42.0	2733	40,000C	PMC FMJ/2.6″/Rem 9½(C)
A2460	36.0	2378	40.0	2702	43,200C	PMC FMJ/2.6″/Rem 9½
A2230	35.3	2345	39.2	2665	43,500C	PMC FMJ/2.6″/Rem 9½
BL-C(2)	36.0	2321	39.0	2574	48,700C	26″ Test Barrel
A2700	41.8	2408	44.0	2562	42,900C	PMC FMJ/2.6″/Rem 9½
H335	36.0	2303	39.0	2545		
A4350	39.6	2128	44.0	2418	35,100C	PMC FMJ/2.6″/Rem 9½(C)
H4895	37.0	2187	40.0	2408		

> *Caution:* Loads exceeding SAAMI OAL Maximum must be verified for bullet-to-rifling clearance and magazine functioning. Where a specific primer or bullet is indicated those components must be used, no substitutions! Where only a maximum load is shown, reduce starting load 10%, unless otherwise specified.
>
> *Key:* (C) = compressed charge; C = CUP; p = psi; Plink = Plinker; Bns = Barnes; Hdy = Hornady; Lap = Lapua; Nos = Nosler; Rem = Remington; Sra = Sierra; Spr = Speer; Win = Winchester.

Powder	—STARTING— Grs.	MV (fps)	—MAXIMUM— Grs.	MV (fps)	Press. (CUP/psi)	Comments
165						
A2495BR	36.9	2355	41.0	2676	44,000C	Rem PSPCL/2.58"/ Rem 9½
A2520	37.8	2331	42.0	2649	43,800C	Rem PSPCL/2.58"/ Rem 9½
A2230	35.6	2282	39.5	2593	45,000C	Rem PSPCL/2.58"/ Rem 9½
A2460	36.0	2280	40.0	2591	44,200C	Rem PSPCL/2.58"/ Rem 9½
A2015BR	33.8	2261	37.5	2569	41,900C	Rem PSPCL/2.58"/ Rem 9½
A2700	41.3	2269	43.5	2414	43,600C	Rem PSPCL/2.58"/ Rem 9½
A4350	39.6	2069	44.0	2351	36,400C	Rem PSPCL/2.58"/ Rem 9½
H4895	35.0	2164	38.0	2341		

Powder	—STARTING— Grs.	MV (fps)	—MAXIMUM— Grs.	MV (fps)	Press. (CUP/psi)	Comments
180						
A2520	35.1	2203	39.0	2503	45,000C	Sra SBT/2.59"/Rem 9½
A2495BR	35.1	2194	39.0	2493	41,600C	Sra SBT/2.59"/Rem 9½
A2015BR	32.4	2172	36.0	2468	44,400C	Sra SBT/2.59"/Rem 9½
A2460	33.8	2137	37.5	2428	40,800C	Sra SBT/2.59"/Rem 9½
A2230	33.3	2134	37.0	2425	43,700C	Sra SBT/2.59"/Rem 9½
A2700	39.4	2203	41.5	2344	44,100C	Sra SBT/2.59"/Rem 9½
A4350	38.7	2047	43.0	2326	39,800C	Sra SBT/2.59"/Rem 9½
H4895	34.0	1981	37.0	2130		
H335	32.0	1974	35.0	2074		
BL-C(2)	32.0	1987	35.0	2069		
200						
H4895	32.0	1973	35.0	2089		
H335	31.0	1934	34.0	2047		

Never exceed maximum load nor use any load exhibiting signs of excessive pressure. Begin at suggested starting load and work up carefully.

308

Winchester
(7.62 NATO)

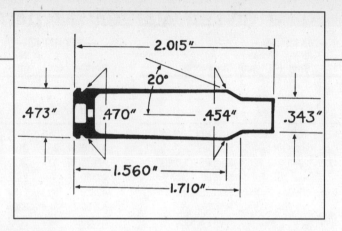

Cases: Remington (p.188)
Winchester (p.192)
GI (p.192)
Primer: Large Rifle (Rem. case)
Winchester 120 (Win.
& GI cases)
Barrel: 24″ Accurate (Rem. case)
24″ Vihtavuori (Rem. case)

26″ Hodgdon (Rem. case)
24″ Hodgdon (Win. & GI cases)
Bullet Diameter: 0.308″
Maximum Case Length: 2.015″
Trim to Length: 2.005″
Maximum Cartridge OAL: 2.819″
Minimum Cartridge OAL: 2.499″

Commercialized in 1952, the 308 Winchester originated as a military cartridge, known as the T-65 or 7.62x51mm NATO. Improvements in smokeless powder had made it possible to duplicate 30-06 military specification load performance in a much smaller package without the use of pressures that were notably higher than those of the original 30-06 military loading. The military did not perceive the need for more power than military specification 30-06 loads provided.

By shortening the case almost 0.5″ and the loaded round a full 0.5″, the designers created a lighter, more compact cartridge that was cheaper to produce, easier to transport, easier to handle and—as a bonus—more accurate than the military loading of the 30-06.

By 1954, the commercialized 308 Winchester had already achieved a lofty position as the premier 30-caliber target chambering. It is not likely to fall from that position any time soon.

With sufficient ballistics to "Do anything the '06 can do,"

the 308 Winchester has a loyal following among hunters who do not see the need for shots at distances exceeding a few hundred yards.

Military cases are ubiquitous. These cases can be used, but since they are markedly heavier than typical commercial cases, charges must be reduced to maintain safe pressures. Accurate Arms recommends a full 12 percent reduction in charge weight. We suggest measuring your military cases for capacity, then compare that to commercial Remington cases and adjust your charges accordingly—if the military case holds 5 percent less water, reduce the charge 5 percent, etc.

In commercial cases, capacity with a 150-grain bullet, seated normally, is about 52.9 grains of water. In typical military cases, capacity with a 150-grain bullet, seated normally, is about 52.0 grains of water. W748, H380, IMR4064, RL-12, BL-C(2), A2460, H335 and IMR4895 are noted choices for accuracy and performance in the 308 Winchester.

308 WINCHESTER LOADING DATA (Rem. cases)

Powder	STARTING Grs.	MV (fps)	MAXIMUM Grs.	MV (fps)	Press. (CUP/psi)	Comments
Lead 152 Lyman RNGC						
XMP5744			27.0	2230	38,500C	CCI 200
Lead 165 RCBS SIL						
XMP5744			27.0	2165	37,200C	CCI 200
73						
N130			48.5	3794	50,800p	Lapua HP
N120			43.7	3717	50,800p	Lapua HP

Powder	STARTING Grs.	MV (fps)	MAXIMUM Grs.	MV (fps)	Press. (CUP/psi)	Comments
73 con't						
N133			49.8	3613	40,600p	Lapua HP
N110			33.9	3487	50,800p	Lapua HP
93						
N133			46.3	3250	46,412p	Sako FMJ 110A
N120			39.4	3250	51,488p	Sako FMJ 110A
N135			47.1	3120	43,511p	Sako FMJ 110A
N110			30.9	2970	52,214p	Sako FMJ 110A

100

Powder	STARTING Grs.	MV (fps)	MAXIMUM Grs.	MV (fps)	Press. (CUP/psi)	Comments
N130	41.0	3087	43.3	3241	50,763p	Spr RN
RL-15	48.0	3174	51.0	3226	49,000C	
RL-12	47.0	2988	50.0	3190	49,500C	
RL-7	40.0	2898	42.0	3110	47,000C	
H4198	35.0	2952	38.0	3097	42,000C	
H380	47.0	2680	50.0	2928		
BL-C(2)	42.0	2664	45.0	2839		
H4895	33.0	2146	45.0	2833		
H322	39.0	2708	41.0	2831	34,000C	
H4227	14.0	1439	16.0	1606		

105

Powder	STARTING Grs.	MV (fps)	MAXIMUM Grs.	MV (fps)	Press. (CUP/psi)	Comments
N133			48.4	3293	50,800p	Lapua MP
N135	46.1	3084	48.8	3238	50,763p	Lapua G450
N130			44.3	3230	50,800p	Lapua HP
N133	43.4	3068	45.7	3205	50,763p	Lapua G450
N120	38.3	3100	39.0	3150	50,763p	Lapua G450
N120			40.0	3127	50,800p	Lapua HP
N110			31.0	2872	50,800p	Lapua HP

110

Powder	STARTING Grs.	MV (fps)	MAXIMUM Grs.	MV (fps)	Press. (CUP/psi)	Comments
H335	45.0	3145	49.0	3320	49,600C	
H4895	45.0	2920	49.0	3239	49,500C	
H322	43.0	2965	46.0	3229	50,700C	
N135			48.6	3220	47,862p	Sako HP
N135			48.6	3220	49,313p	Sra RN
IMR4895	47.0	2999	49.0	3211	49,200C	
N133			47.6	3210	50,800p	Sako HP
A2460	43.7	2810	48.5	3193	49,300C	Sra HP/2.595"/CCI 200
A2015BR	40.5	2806	45.0	3189	48,100C	Sra HP/2.595"/CCI 200
BL-C(2)	48.0	3004	52.0	3181	49,800C	
N133			46.3	3180	52,214p	Sra SP
W748	50.0	3096	52.0	3177	49,900C	
A2230	42.8	2790	47.5	3171	49,300C	Sra HP/2.595"/CCI 200
H4198	37.0	2999	40.0	3168	49,600C	
H380	49.0	2966	53.0	3145	46,800C	
N130			44.1	3145	50,800p	Sako HP
IMR3031	45.0	2969	47.0	3124	48,900C	
N120			40.1	3120	52,214p	Sra RN
IMR4064	47.0	2861	49.0	3080	47,600C	
N130	40.5	2928	42.5	3074	50,763p	Spr HP
N120			40.0	3069	50,800p	Sako HP
A2495BR	42.3	2659	47.0	3022	42,000C	Sra HP/2.595"/CCI 200/(C)
A2520	42.8	2658	47.5	3020	41,500C	Sra HP/2.595"/CCI 200/(C)
IMR4320	47.0	2834	49.0	3010	47,400C	
IMR4198	36.0	2844	38.0	3009	49,600C	
VarGet			47.0	3002	38,500C	

125-130

Powder	STARTING Grs.	MV (fps)	MAXIMUM Grs.	MV (fps)	Press. (CUP/psi)	Comments
N140			48.6	3150	50,763p	Sako SP
BL-C(2)	46.0	2786	51.0	3109	51,300C	
RL-15	46.0	2984	49.0	3097	48,500C	
H4895	43.0	2748	47.0	3075	51,300C	
N140			49.9	3070	50,800p	Nos BT
H335	43.0	2777	47.0	3064	49,400C	
W748	48.0	2917	50.0	3057	50,200C	
N135			47.2	3050	52,214p	Sako FMJ 120A
N135			47.2	3048	50,800p	Nos BT
N133			44.9	3028	50,800p	Nos BT
N140			48.6	3020	50,763p	Hdy SP
N133			44.6	3020	52,214p	Sako FMJ 120A
N135			46.8	3020	52,214p	Hdy SP
N140			47.8	3020	52,214p	Lapua HP
A2015BR	39.2	2656	43.5	3018	49,700C	Nos BT/2.78"/CCI 200
A2230	42.3	2655	47.0	3017	49,800C	Nos BT/2.78"/CCI 200
A2460	42.3	2652	47.0	3014	48,600C	Nos BT/2.78"/CCI 200
RL-12	45.0	2891	48.0	3004	49,000C	
N135			45.5	3000	52,214p	Lapua HP
RL-7	39.0	2869	41.0	2994	47,100C	
H380	48.0	2825	52.0	2986	49,200C	
N130			41.7	2977	50,800p	Nos BT
A2520	42.8	2600	47.5	2955	45,100C	Nos BT/2.78"/CCI 200/(C)
VarGet			47.0	2954	41,000C	
H322	41.0	2725	44.0	2945	51,200C	
H4198	36.0	2774	39.0	2936	50,200C	
A2495BR	42.3	2579	47.0	2931	45,200C	Nos BT/2.78"/CCI 200/(C)
IMR4064	45.0	2781	47.0	2929	50,200C	
IMR3031	43.0	2794	45.0	2919	50,900C	
H414	48.0	2674	52.0	2914	48,300C	
IMR4895	44.0	2770	46.0	2911	50,900C	
N133			43.5	2900	52,214p	Hdy SP
W760	50.0	2770	52.0	2890	48,000C	
IMR4320	45.0	2651	47.0	2888	50,100C	
N130	37.5	2674	40.6	2832	50,763p	Spr HP
IMR4198	35.0	2690	37.0	2814	51,000C	

➤➤➤➤➤➤➤➤➤➤➤➤➤➤➤➤➤➤➤➤➤➤➤➤

Caution: Loads exceeding SAAMI OAL Maximum must be verified for bullet-to-rifling clearance and magazine functioning. Where a specific primer or bullet is indicated those components must be used, no substitutions! Where only a maximum load is shown, reduce starting load 10%, unless otherwise specified.

Key: (C) = compressed charge; C = CUP; p = psi; Plink = Plinker; Bns = Barnes; Hdy = Hornady; Lap = Lapua; Nos = Nosler; Rem = Remington; Sra = Sierra; Spr = Speer; Win = Winchester.

Never exceed maximum load nor use any load exhibiting signs of excessive pressure. Begin at suggested starting load and work up carefully.

189

150

Powder	Grs.	MV (fps)	Grs.	MV (fps)	Press. (CUP/psi)	Comments
RL-15	44.0	2742	47.0	2919	50,000C	
H380	47.0	2681	51.0	2876	51,500C	
N140			46.8	2870	52,214p	Lapua 8334 147-gr.
N140			46.3	2840	52,214p	Hdy RN
BL-C(2)	45.5	2706	49.5	2835	50,400C	
H4895	40.5	2559	44.0	2830	49,000C	
VarGet			47.0	2829	50,200C	
N135			44.9	2820	52,214p	Lapua 8334 147-gr.
H335	42.0	2602	45.0	2818	49,400C	
N140			46.8	2814	50,800p	Sra SBT
N135			44.8	2810	52,214p	Spr RN
A2520	41.9	2472	46.5	2809	48,700C	Hdy SP/2.745"/CCI 200/(C)
A2495BR	41.4	2469	46.0	2806	47,900C	Hdy SP/2.745"/CCI 200/(C)
IMR4895	42.0	2618	44.0	2794	51,500C	
N150			48.2	2790	47,900C	Sra SBT
W748	47.0	2709	49.0	2788	50,100C	
IMR4064	43.0	2591	45.0	2786	51,100C	
N135			44.3	2776	50,800C	Sra SBT
A2460	40.5	2433	45.0	2765	48,500C	Hdy SP/2.745"/CCI 200
A2015BR	37.4	2432	41.5	2764	49,700C	Hdy SP/2.745"/CCI 200
H414	47.0	2554	51.0	2760	48,000C	
RL-12	42.0	2639	45.0	2760	49,000C	
W760	49.0	2719	51.0	2751	48,200C	
RL-7	37.0	2647	39.0	2744	47,200C	
N133			42.0	2730	50,800p	Sra SBT
A2230	39.2	2387	43.5	2712	48,400C	Hdy SP/2.745"/CCI 200
IMR3031	41.0	2524	43.0	2706	50,900C	
IMR4320	43.0	2544	45.0	2690	50,600C	
H322	38.0	2495	41.0	2667	48,400C	
RL-19	50.0	2535	52.0	2624	43,500C	

155-156

Powder	Grs.	MV (fps)	Grs.	MV (fps)	Press. (CUP/psi)	Comments
N150			48.3	2771	50,800C	Sako SPBT
N140			44.0	2770	52,214p	Sako SP 122A
N135			43.4	2740	52,214p	Sako SP 122A
N140			45.4	2695	50,800p	Sako SPBT
N135			43.1	2668	50,800p	Sako SPBT

165-168

Powder	Grs.	MV (fps)	Grs.	MV (fps)	Press. (CUP/psi)	Comments
RL-15	42.0	2594	45.0	2763	49,500C	
VarGet			46.0	2731	50,600C	(168-172-gr. Match)
A2520	40.5	2387	45.0	2712	50,200C	Sra HPBT/2.8"/CCI 200
H380	45.0	2534	48.0	2704	50,300C	(165-gr.)
BL-C(2)	42.0	2517	46.0	2703	49,900C	(165-gr.)
W748	44.0	2566	46.0	2696	49,700C	(165-gr.)
N150			46.3	2681	50,800p	Spr BTSP
H4895	38.5	2394	42.0	2679	49,200C	(165-gr.)
RL-7	35.0	2529	37.0	2671	48,400C	
RL-12	40.0	2488	43.0	2666	48,500C	
H335	38.0	2398	42.0	2666	49,100C	(165-gr.)
N140			44.9	2666	50,800p	Spr BTSP
N150			46.1	2657	50,800p	Lapua Scenar

165-168 con't

Powder	Grs.	MV (fps)	Grs.	MV (fps)	Press. (CUP/psi)	Comments
A2495BR	40.1	2336	44.5	2654	47,900C	Sra HPBT/2.8"/CCI 200/(C)
H414	45.0	2450	49.0	2645	49,900C	(165-gr.)
A2015BR	36.0	2325	40.0	2642	50,500C	Sra HPBT/2.8"/CCI 200
N140	42.1	2520	44.0	2641	50,763p	Lapua Scenar GB 422
W760	47.0	2551	49.0	2640	50,000C	(165-gr.)
IMR4895	40.0	2514	42.0	2637	49,900C	(165-gr.)
IMR4064	41.0	2460	43.0	2630	49,600C	(165-gr.)
N135			42.7	2627	50,800C	Spr BTSP
A2230	37.8	2297	42.0	2610	49,500C	Sra HPBT/2.8"/CCI 200
N140			42.0	2610	52,214p	Lapua FMJ S283
N140			44.0	2604	50,800p	Lapua Scenar
A2460	38.3	2289	42.5	2601	48,600C	Sra HPBT/2.8"/CCI 200
N150	42.6	2461	44.6	2598	50,763p	Lapua Scenar GB 422
N133			40.7	2583	50,800p	Spr BTSP
IMR4320	42.0	2491	44.0	2582	50,400C	(165-gr.)
IMR3031	39.0	2404	41.0	2549	50,400C	(165-gr.)
RL-19	47.0	2404	50.0	2548	49,000C	
H322	36.0	2320	39.0	2534	47,400C	(165-gr.)
A2700	42.3	2194	47.0	2493	48,800C	Sra HPBT/2.8"/CCI 200/(C)
N130	33.0	2251	36.0	2401	50,763p	Spr RSP
H450	46.0	2184	50.0	2350	40,100C	(165-gr.)

170

Powder	Grs.	MV (fps)	Grs.	MV (fps)	Press. (CUP/psi)	Comments
N150			45.9	2647	50,800p	Lapua FMJBT
N140			44.1	2614	50,800p	Lapua FMJBT
N140			42.9	2610	52,214p	Lapua FMJ D46
N135			41.6	2572	50,800p	Lapua FMJBT

180

Powder	Grs.	MV (fps)	Grs.	MV (fps)	Press. (CUP/psi)	Comments
VarGet			45.0	2661	49,600C	
H380	43.0	2403	47.0	2624	50,200C	
N150			44.4	2620	52,214p	Sako RN 226A
A2520	40.1	2302	44.5	2616	49,200C	Nos BT/2.8"/CCI 200
RL-15	40.0	2398	43.0	2610	48,000C	
A2495BR	38.7	2281	43.0	2592	50,800C	Nos BT/2.8"/CCI 200
N140			40.9	2590	52,214p	Sako RN 226A
BL-C(2)	41.5	2453	45.0	2559	51,900C	
H4895	37.0	2307	40.0	2540	48,900C	
IMR4895	38.0	2343	40.0	2529	49,200C	
W760	45.0	2431	47.0	2524	48,900C	
H414	45.0	2301	47.0	2523	48,700C	
H335	37.0	2323	40.0	2520	49,900C	
N150			44.5	2514	50,800p	Hdy SP

Caution: **Loads exceeding SAAMI OAL Maximum must be verified for bullet-to-rifling clearance and magazine functioning. Where a specific primer or bullet is indicated those components must be used, no substitutions! Where only a maximum load is shown, reduce starting load 10%, unless otherwise specified.**

Key: (C) = compressed charge; C = CUP; p = psi; Plink = Plinker; Bns = Barnes; Hdy = Hornady; Lap = Lapua; Nos = Nosler; Rem = Remington; Sra = Sierra; Spr = Speer; Win = Winchester.

180 con't

Powder	Grs.	MV (fps)	Grs.	MV (fps)	Press. (CUP/psi)	Comments
RL-7	33.0	2388	35.0	2511	48,600C	
RL-12	38.0	2358	41.0	2492	47,500C	
IMR4064	40.0	2334	42.0	2488	51,200C	
W748	42.0	2371	44.0	2480	50,200C	
N140			42.8	2477	50,800p	Hdy SP
A2460	37.4	2177	41.5	2474	49,500C	Nos BT/2.8"/CCI 200
A2700	42.3	2174	47.0	2470	40,000C	Nos BT/2.8"/CCI 200/(C)
IMR4320	40.0	2303	42.0	2469	50,600C	
RL-19	46.0	2303	49.0	2449	48,500C	
A2230	36.0	2146	40.0	2439	48,800C	Nos BT/2.8"/CCI 200
N135			40.4	2430	50,800p	Hdy SP
IMR3031	37.0	2291	39.0	2410	50,400C	
H322	34.0	2153	37.0	2388	46,900C	

185-186

Powder	Grs.	MV (fps)	Grs.	MV (fps)	Press. (CUP/psi)	Comments
N150			44.8	2530	52,214p	Lapua SP E375
N140	40.0	2372	42.1	2507	50,763p	Lapua Scenar G8432
N140			43.2	2490	52,214p	Lapua SP E375
N150	41.0	2362	42.7	2480	50,763p	Lapua Scenar GB 432
N140			42.2	2474	50,800p	Lapua FMJBT
N150			43.5	2460	50,800p	Lapua Scenar
N140	39.4	2290	42.1	2454	50,763C	Lapua Mira EB 423
N140	39.4	2297	41.8	2428	50,763p	Lapua Mega 415
N135			39.9	2425	50,800p	Lapua FMJBT
N150	40.4	2297	42.0	2411	50,763p	Lapua Mira EB 423
N150	40.1	2280	42.1	2395	50,763p	Lapua Mega 415
N160			47.1	2380	52,214p	Lapua FMJ D46

190

Powder	Grs.	MV (fps)	Grs.	MV (fps)	Press. (CUP/psi)	Comments
RL-15	39.0	2330	42.0	2515	47,500C	
W760	44.0	2359	46.0	2492	49,100C	
RL-12	38.0	2313	41.0	2460	49,000C	
W748	40.0	2329	42.0	2437	49,200C	
IMR4064	39.0	2280	41.0	2429	51,000C	
A2520	37.4	2128	41.5	2418	47,100C	Sra HPBT/2.8"/CCI 200
IMR4320	39.0	2284	41.0	2410	50,900C	
RL-19	45.0	2180	48.0	2399	47,000C	
A2495BR	36.0	2108	40.0	2395	45,300C	Sra HPBT/2.8"/CCI 200
IMR4350	44.0	2200	46.0	2391	44,900C	
IMR4895	37.0	2271	39.0	2388	49,000C	
A2460	35.1	2083	39.0	2367	46,400C	Sra HPBT/2.8"/CCI 200
A2700	40.5	2035	45.0	2312	46,000C	Sra HPBT/2.8"/CCI 200

200

Powder	Grs.	MV (fps)	Grs.	MV (fps)	Press. (CUP/psi)	Comments
H380	41.5	2229	45.0	2468	50,800C	
N140			40.0	2440	52,214p	Sako RN 227A
H4895	36.0	2115	39.0	2398	48,700C	
H414	41.5	2182	45.0	2392	46,200C	
H335	36.0	2265	38.0	2387	48,400C	
RL-15	38.0	2220	41.0	2384	49,000C	
W760	43.0	2244	45.0	2381	47,000C	

200 con't

Powder	Grs.	MV (fps)	Grs.	MV (fps)	Press. (CUP/psi)	Comments
H4350	43.0	2180	46.0	2375	44,300C	
BL-C(2)	37.5	2197	40.0	2356	48,000C	
W748	38.0	2212	40.0	2349	47,800C	
IMR4350	43.0	2157	45.0	2337	45,900C	
A2520	36.3	2041	40.3	2319	45,500C	Nos Part./2.8"/CCI 200
IMR4895	36.0	2165	38.0	2318	50,600C	
RL-12	36.0	2153	39.0	2303	48,500C	
IMR4320	37.0	2177	39.0	2294	50,200C	
A2495BR	34.7	2012	38.5	2286	47,100C	Nos Part./2.8"/CCI 200
A2230	34.2	2004	38.0	2277	46,500C	Nos Part./2.8"/CCI 200
IMR4064	37.0	2199	39.0	2263	50,400C	
RL-19	44.0	2114	47.0	2262	46,500C	
A2460	34.2	1990	38.0	2261	43,900C	Nos Part./2.8"/CCI 200
N150			40.4	2259	50,800p	Spr SP
N140			39.9	2256	50,800p	Spr SP
IMR4831	44.0	2149	46.0	2245	46,200C	
IMR3031	35.0	2110	37.0	2230	50,500C	
A2700	39.6	1962	44.0	2229	46,600C	Nos Part./2.8"/CCI 200

220-225

Powder	Grs.	MV (fps)	Grs.	MV (fps)	Press. (CUP/psi)	Comments
H4350	43.0	2142	46.0	2369	45,900C	
W760	42.0	2177	44.0	2295	46,900C	(220-gr.)
H414	40.5	2110	44.0	2289	46,200C	
H4831	43.0	1983	47.0	2286	45,700C	
H380	39.5	2118	43.0	2286	47,300C	
BL-C(2)	35.0	2080	38.0	2240	50,200C	
RL-15	36.0	2119	39.0	2236	48,500C	
W748	36.0	2111	38.0	2232	49,900C	(220-gr.)
IMR4350	42.0	2094	44.0	2229	46,600C	(220-gr.)
A2495BR	34.7	1959	38.5	2226	47,300C	Sra HPBT/2.8"/CCI 200
H4895	34.0	2014	37.0	2224	48,400C	
H335	34.0	2047	36.0	2216	49,100C	
H450	44.0	1961	48.0	2203	42,400C	
RL-19	42.0	2090	45.0	2181	47,000C	
IMR4831	43.0	2009	45.0	2176	46,900C	(220-gr.)
A2460	33.3	1911	37.0	2172	46,200C	Sra HPBT/2.8"/CCI 200
IMR4895	34.0	2007	36.0	2164	48,800C	(220-gr.)
A2700	37.8	1900	42.0	2159	48,300C	Sra HPBT/2.8"/CCI 200
A2520	34.2	1896	38.0	2154	44,900C	Sra HPBT/2.8"/CCI 200
IMR4064	35.0	2036	37.0	2154	50,100C	(220-gr.)
RL-12	34.0	1989	37.0	2149	49,000C	
IMR4320	35.0	2040	37.0	2141	49,900C	(220-gr.)
A2230	32.4	1883	36.0	2140	45,300C	Sra HPBT/2.8"/CCI 200

250

Powder	Grs.	MV (fps)	Grs.	MV (fps)	Press. (CUP/psi)	Comments
H414	41.0	2009	43.0	2142	49,000C	
RL-19	40.0	2009	43.0	2131	48,000C	
RL-15	34.0	1969	37.0	2105	48,500C	
H4831	43.0	1990	45.0	2099	47,000C	
H380	40.0	2025	41.0	2088	50,200C	
H4350	41.0	1988	43.0	2083	47,100C	

➤➤➤➤➤➤➤➤➤➤➤➤➤➤➤➤➤➤➤➤➤➤➤➤➤

Never exceed maximum load nor use any load exhibiting signs of excessive pressure. Begin at suggested starting load and work up carefully.

308 WINCHESTER/7.62 NATO MATCH LOADING DATA (Win. Cases)

150

Powder	STARTING Grs.	MV (fps)	MAXIMUM Grs.	MV (fps)	Press. (CUP/psi)	Comments
BL-C(2)	47.0	2769	49.0	2878	48,000C	BT
H4895	41.0	2694	43.0	2822	50,200C	BT
H335	43.0	2619	45.0	2806	47,500C	BT
H322	40.0	2606	42.0	2727	49,000C	BT

168-172

Powder	Grs.	MV (fps)	Grs.	MV (fps)	Press. (CUP/psi)	Comments
H380	46.0	2515	48.0	2634	46,500C	BT
BL-C(2)	44.0	2492	46.0	2614	46,500C	BT
H335	40.0	2429	42.0	2548	47,000C	BT
H4895	38.0	2403	40.0	2525	47,000C	BT
H322	37.0	2399	39.0	2506	47,200C	BT

180

Powder	Grs.	MV (fps)	Grs.	MV (fps)	Press. (CUP/psi)	Comments
BL-C(2)	42.0	2439	44.0	2544	49,000C	BT
H414	44.0	2349	46.0	2488	47,600C	BT
H335	38.0	2340	40.0	2469	48,400C	BT
H380	43.0	2311	45.0	2448	47,000C	BT
H4350	45.0	2310	47.0	2437	46,500C	BT
H4895	37.0	2330	39.0	2434	47,000C	BT
H322	36.0	2221	38.0	2379	46,500C	BT

190

Powder	Grs.	MV (fps)	Grs.	MV (fps)	Press. (CUP/psi)	Comments
H380	43.0	2347	45.0	2510	50,100C	BT
BL-C(2)	40.0	2344	42.0	2474	50,200C	BT
H414	44.0	2269	46.0	2440	48,000C	BT
H4350	44.0	2206	46.0	2427	47,000C	BT
H335	36.0	2204	38.0	2419	49,400C	BT

200

Powder	Grs.	MV (fps)	Grs.	MV (fps)	Press. (CUP/psi)	Comments
H414	43.0	2240	45.0	2391	47,000C	BT
H380	42.0	2252	44.0	2380	47,400C	BT
BL-C(2)	40.0	2210	42.0	2361	47,100C	BT
H4350	44.0	2212	46.0	2354	48,000C	BT
H335	37.0	2221	39.0	2346	47,000C	BT
H4831	44.0	2194	47.0	2306	45,000C	BT

220

Powder	Grs.	MV (fps)	Grs.	MV (fps)	Press. (CUP/psi)	Comments
H4350	43.0	2139	45.0	2297	50,000C	BT
H414	42.0	2144	44.0	2292	47,000C	BT
H4831	44.0	2090	47.0	2266	47,000C	BT
H380	41.0	2104	43.0	2239	47,200C	BT
H335	35.0	2099	37.0	2229	47,900C	BT
BL-C(2)	38.0	2111	40.0	2224	47,400C	BT

308 WINCHESTER/7.62 NATO MATCH LOADING DATA (GI Cases)

150

Powder	STARTING Grs.	MV (fps)	MAXIMUM Grs.	MV (fps)	Press. (CUP/psi)	Comments
H4895	40.0	2567	42.0	2735	48,400C	BT
H335	42.0	2589	44.0	2728	47,000C	BT
BL-C(2)	45.0	2581	47.0	2719	47,200C	BT
H322	38.0	2516	41.0	2692	48,500C	BT

168-172

Powder	Grs.	MV (fps)	Grs.	MV (fps)	Press. (CUP/psi)	Comments
BL-C(2)	41.0	2360	43.0	2565	47,600C	BT
H335	38.0	2399	40.0	2558	47,500C	BT
H4895	37.0	2388	39.0	2508	48,200C	BT
H380	43.0	2340	45.0	2459	46,900C	BT
H322	36.0	2330	38.0	2442	46,900C	BT

180

Powder	Grs.	MV (fps)	Grs.	MV (fps)	Press. (CUP/psi)	Comments
H414	44.0	2388	46.0	2469	48,000C	BT
BL-C(2)	40.0	2311	42.0	2434	47,200C	BT
H4895	36.0	2304	38.0	2432	48,400C	BT
H335	37.0	2282	39.0	2414	47,100C	BT
H380	42.0	2294	44.0	2395	47,000C	BT
H4350	44.0	2259	46.0	2343	46,000C	BT

190

Powder	Grs.	MV (fps)	Grs.	MV (fps)	Press. (CUP/psi)	Comments
H414	43.5	2264	45.5	2368	47,400C	BT
BL-C(2)	39.0	2199	41.0	2349	47,000C	BT
H380	42.0	2230	44.0	2314	47,200C	BT
H4350	44.0	2227	46.0	2311	46,600C	BT
H335	35.5	2141	37.5	2310	46,900C	BT
H4895	35.5	2139	37.5	2292	47,800C	BT

200

Powder	Grs.	MV (fps)	Grs.	MV (fps)	Press. (CUP/psi)	Comments
H414	43.0	2231	45.0	2344	48,000C	BT
H380	41.5	2181	43.5	2303	46,900C	BT
H4895	34.5	2152	36.5	2272	47,900C	BT
H4350	43.5	2201	45.5	2270	46,900C	BT
BL-C(2)	37.0	2100	39.0	2264	46,900C	BT

220

Powder	Grs.	MV (fps)	Grs.	MV (fps)	Press. (CUP/psi)	Comments
H414	41.0	2119	43.0	2255	48,500C	BT
H4350	42.0	2156	43.0	2207	46,000C	BT
H380	40.0	2047	42.0	2191	47,100C	BT
H4895	33.5	2041	35.5	2130	47,000C	BT
BL-C(2)	35.5	2017	37.5	2127	47,200C	BT

Never exceed maximum load nor use any load exhibiting signs of excessive pressure. Begin at suggested starting load and work up carefully.

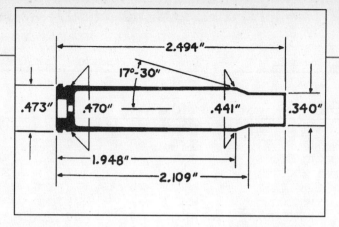

Case: IMI
Primer: Large Rifle
Barrel: 24″ Accurate
26″ Hodgdon
24″ Vihtavuori

Bullet Diameter: 0.308″
Maximum Case Length: 2.494″
Trim to Length: 2.484″
Maximum Cartridge OAL: 3.340″
Minimum Cartridge OAL: 2.940″

The 30-03 Springfield was co-introduced with the 1903 Springfield rifle in that year. That chambering featured a 220-grain round-nosed bullet at a surprising 2300 fps. Considering the powders then available, pressures must have been extremely high. Upon standardization, the military brass, about a generation late, finally realized that no modern military rifle cartridge had any business featuring a round-nosed bullet!

In 1906, a redesigned version of the same basic cartridge was standardized with a slightly shorter case neck and a 150-grain spitzer FMJ bullet at 2700 fps. Because the new bullet was so much shorter on the bearing surface, the case was redesigned with a shorter neck. Barrels of existing issue 1903 Springfield rifles were turned back two threads and their chambers recut to proper 30-06 dimensions.

With good case capacity, high loading pressures and per-

haps the widest selection of applicable components available to any cartridge, the 30-06 is a handloading natural. For the same reasons, and because it can deliver significant energy with a usefully flat trajectory, the 30-06 is the most popular hunting cartridge in the U.S. and perhaps the world.

As with all original military chamberings, use of military cases is common. While safe in theory, handloaders must consider the reduction in usable case capacity associated with military cases, reduce charges accordingly—often 5 to 10 percent.

Case capacity with a 150-grain bullet, seated normally, is about 67.6 grains of water. A2495BR, VarGet, H414, RL-22, H4831 and IMR4350 are good choices for the 30-06.

(These loads are also suitable for the 30-284 wildcat, but always start low and use caution because wildcat chamber dimensions might vary more than in commercial chambers.)

30-06 SPRINGFIELD LOADING DATA

Lead 152 Lyman 311466

Powder	—STARTING— Grs.	MV (fps)	—MAXIMUM— Grs.	MV (fps)	Press. (CUP/psi)	Comments
A2015BR	36.0	2308	40.0	2623	48,300p	3.035″/CCI 250
A2460	36.9	2286	41.0	2598	50,100p	3.035″/CCI 250
A2230	36.9	2276	41.0	2586	46,600p	3.035″/CCI 250
A2520	37.8	2272	42.0	2582	44,300p	3.035″/CCI 250
A2700	41.4	2200	46.0	2500	42,500p	3.035″/CCI 250
XMP5744			33.5	2451	47,100p	3.035″/CCI 200
A2495BR	37.8	2143	42.0	2435	31,800p	3.035″/CCI 250
A4350	45.9	2138	51.0	2430	34,100p	3.035″/CCI 250

Lead 180 Lyman 31141

Powder	—STARTING— Grs.	MV (fps)	—MAXIMUM— Grs.	MV (fps)	Press. (CUP/psi)	Comments
A2015BR	36.0	2174	40.0	2470	49,600p	3.015″/CCI 250
A2495BR	37.8	2156	42.0	2450	42,300p	3.015″/CCI 250
A4350	45.9	2134	51.0	2425	37,200p	3.015″/CCI 250
A2230	36.9	2131	41.0	2422	45,600p	3.015″/CCI 250
A2520	37.8	2123	42.0	2412	43,400p	3.015″/CCI 250
A2460	36.9	2117	41.0	2406	42,800p	3.015″/CCI 250
A2700	41.4	2078	46.0	2361	38,900p	3.015″/CCI 250
XMP5744			32.0	2337	41,100p	3.015″/CCI 200
A3100	47.7	2041	53.0	2319	31,300p	3.015″/CCI 250
A8700	54.0	1759	60.0	1999	26,600p	3.015″/CCI 250/(C)

Caution: Loads exceeding SAAMI OAL Maximum must be verified for bullet-to-rifling clearance and magazine functioning. Where a specific primer or bullet is indicated those components must be used, no substitutions! Where only a maximum load is shown, reduce starting load 10%, unless otherwise specified.

Key: (C) = compressed charge; C = CUP; p = psi; Plink = Plinker; Bns = Barnes; Hdy = Hornady; Lap = Lapua; Nos = Nosler; Rem = Remington; Sra = Sierra; Spr = Speer; Win = Winchester.

Never exceed maximum load nor use any load exhibiting signs of excessive pressure. Begin at suggested starting load and work up carefully.

193

Powder	—STARTING— Grs.	MV (fps)	—MAXIMUM— Grs.	MV (fps)	Press. (CUP/psi)	Comments
Lead 210 Lyman 311284						
A4350	45.9	2093	51.0	2378	43,600p	3.195"/CCI 250
A3100	47.7	2028	53.0	2304	40,000p	3.195"/CCI 250
A2495BR	36.0	1965	40.0	2233	44,500p	3.195"/CCI 250
A2520	36.0	1964	40.0	2232	46,600p	3.195"/CCI 250
A2700	39.6	1932	44.0	2196	42,000p	3.195"/CCI 250
A2460	34.7	1928	38.5	2191	46,300p	3.195"/CCI 250
A2015BR	32.4	1925	36.0	2188	49,600p	3.195"/CCI 250
A2230	34.2	1924	38.0	2186	45,400p	3.195"/CCI 250
100						
A2495BR	52.2	3135	58.0	3563	60,000p	Spr Plink/2.6"/CCI 200
A2015BR	49.5	3119	55.0	3544	58,300p	Spr Plink/2.6"/CCI 200
A2230	51.3	3058	57.0	3475	54,900p	Spr Plink/2.6"/CCI 200
A2460	51.8	3045	57.5	3460	57,800p	Spr Plink/2.6"/CCI 200
A2520	54.0	3024	60.0	3436	60,000p	Spr Plink/2.6"/CCI 200
H380	53.0	2947	55.0	3163		
H4198	36.0	2892	40.0	3131		
H4895	45.0	2625	50.0	3043		
BL-C(2)	45.0	2646	50.0	3041		
H414	56.0	2898	58.0	3021		
H322	40.0	2496	44.0	2781		
105						
N140	55.9	3232	58.2	3379	49,313p	Lapua G450
N140			59.1	3362	49,300p	Lapua HP
N135	53.7	3215	55.5	3337	49,313p	Lapua G450
N135			55.1	3314	49,300p	Lapua HP
N133			51.3	3241	49,300p	Lapua HP
110						
A2495BR	52.2	3032	58.0	3446	59,600p	Hdy RN/2.9"/CCI 200
A2520	54.0	3024	60.0	3436	60,000p	Hdy RN/2.9"/CCI 200
VarGet			59.0	3432	49,500C	
A2460	52.7	3010	58.5	3421	57,000p	Hdy RN/2.9"/CCI 200
H335	48.0	3108	53.0	3416	49,600C	
A2230	51.3	2979	57.0	3385	55,700p	Hdy RN/2.9"/CCI 200
A2015BR	48.2	2969	53.5	3374	56,400p	Hdy RN/2.9"/CCI 200
N140			57.9	3350	50,763p	Sako HP 136A
BL-C(2)	52.0	3066	56.0	3349	49,000C	
H4895	49.5	2969	54.0	3343	47,600C	
N140			56.9	3330	50,763p	Sra HP
H380	53.5	3130	58.0	3311	48,700C	
N135			54.3	3310	50,763p	Sako HP 136A
N135			54.0	3300	50,763p	Sra HP
H414	56.0	3029	61.0	3299	46,400C	
N150			60.8	3288	49,300p	Hdy RN
W748	52.0	3181	54.0	3280	47,900C	
N133			52.0	3280	50,763p	Sako HP 136A
A2700	55.8	2886	62.0	3280	53,400p	Hdy RN/2.9"/CCI 200
IMR4064	54.0	3107	57.0	3277	49,500C	
IMR4895	51.0	3064	54.0	3269	49,900C	

Powder	—STARTING— Grs.	MV (fps)	—MAXIMUM— Grs.	MV (fps)	Press. (CUP/psi)	Comments
110 con't						
IMR3031	50.0	3090	53.0	3266	49,100C	
RL-15	55.0	3080	58.0	3257	42,800C	
W760	58.0	3119	60.0	3239	45,600C	
N133			53.7	3224	49,300p	Hdy RN
IMR4320	54.0	3034	57.0	3210	49,000C	
N140			57.8	3205	49,300p	Hdy RN
H322	46.0	2908	50.0	3204	51,200C	
RL-12	48.0	3044	52.0	3197	49,200C	
N135			53.5	3164	49,300p	Hdy RN
H450	61.0	2931	66.0	3016	43,600C	
IMR4350	54.0	2640	59.0	2952	37,100C	
H4350	55.0	2680	59.0	2942	37,000C	
125-130						
VarGet			57.2	3267	49,500C	
A2495BR	48.6	2834	54.0	3220	56,700p	Sra SP/3.15"/CCI 200
RL-15	54.0	2994	57.0	3208	47,000C	
A2700	55.8	2812	62.0	3195	56,300p	Sra SP/3.15"/CCI 200
A2015BR	46.8	2806	52.0	3189	56,200p	Sra SP/3.15"/CCI 200
H335	49.0	2794	53.0	3187	49,000C	(130-gr.)
H414	55.0	2868	60.0	3176	48,200C	(130-gr.)
H4895	48.5	2823	53.0	3176	49,800C	(130-gr.)
A2230	48.0	2791	53.3	3172	58,200p	Sra SP/3.15"/CCI 200
A2495BR	47.7	2790	53.0	3170	59,800p	Hdy SP/3.15"/CCI 200
N150			58.7	3169	49,300p	Nos BT
H380	51.5	2860	56.0	3151	49,500C	(130-gr.)
N140			56.1	3142	49,300p	Nos BT
A2015BR	46.4	2763	51.5	3140	55,300p	Hdy SP/3.15"/CCI 200
W760	57.0	2940	59.0	3129	48,000C	
A2520	48.6	2751	54.0	3126	55,800p	Sra SP/3.15"/CCI 200
A2700	54.9	2750	61.0	3125	55,500p	Hdy SP/3.15"/CCI 200
A2460	48.2	2750	53.5	3125	56,300p	Sra SP/3.15"/CCI 200
N140			51.9	3120	49,313p	Sako SP 129A
IMR4064	51.0	2840	54.0	3111	50,000C	
A2230	47.4	2738	52.7	3111	57,700p	Hdy SP/3.15"/CCI 200
A2520	48.6	2732	54.0	3104	57,900p	Hdy SP/3.15"/CCI 200
IMR4895	49.0	2808	52.0	3094	49,800C	
A2460	48.0	2723	53.3	3094	57,900p	Hdy SP/3.15"/CCI 200
N135			51.2	3080	50,763p	Sako FMJ 120A
N140			52.8	3080	50,763p	Lapua HP G402
N140			54.6	3080	50,763p	Hdy SP
N135			52.4	3067	50,800p	Nos BT
BL-C(2)	51.0	2883	55.0	3064	45,600C	(130-gr.)
N135			50.0	3050	50,763p	Hdy SP
W748	51.0	2838	53.0	3044	45,200C	
IMR3031	48.0	2808	51.0	3039	49,800C	
RL-12	46.0	2878	50.0	3029	48,800C	
IMR4320	51.0	2811	54.0	3009	50,100C	
IMR4350	54.0	2644	59.0	2964	44,900C	
H4350	55.0	2717	59.0	2934	44,400C	(130-gr.)
H322	44.0	2711	48.0	2933	50,700C	(130-gr.)
H450	59.0	2688	64.0	2906	44,300C	(130-gr.)
A4350	54.0	2545	60.0	2892	39,400p	Sra SP/3.15"/CCI 200/(C)

150

Powder	STARTING Grs.	MV (fps)	MAXIMUM Grs.	MV (fps)	Press. (CUP/psi)	Comments
H414	53.5	2797	58.0	3043	48,700C	
RL-15	50.0	2829	53.0	2989	47,500C	
VarGet			51.5	2980	49,600C	
N140			51.7	2950	50,763p	Lapua 8334 147-gr. bullet
W760	55.0	2810	57.0	2940	48,900C	
H4895	45.0	2676	49.0	2932	51,000C	
A2700	53.1	2580	59.0	2932	54,900p	Sra SP/3.25"/CCI 200
H4350	55.0	2747	59.0	2926	47,200C	
H380	49.5	2734	54.0	2921	50,500C	
A2495BR	46.4	2558	51.5	2907	58,300p	Sra SP/3.25"/CCI 200
IMR4350	54.0	2660	59.0	2904	47,400C	
N140			50.9	2900	50,763p	RWS FMJ
A2700	51.3	2544	57.0	2891	57,900p	Bns-X/3.285"/CCI 200
N135			48.6	2890	50,763p	Lapua 8334 147-gr. bullet
RL-19	60.0	2776	62.0	2887	44,000C	
A2015BR	43.2	2535	48.0	2881	58,400p	Sra SP/3.25"/CCI 200
N150			55.3	2877	49,300p	Lapua Lock Base
A2520	46.1	2526	51.2	2870	58,200p	Sra SP/3.25"/CCI 200
24N64			56.0	2865	51,466p	Hdy BTSP
A2230	44.5	2521	49.4	2865	57,900p	Sra SP/3.25"/CCI 200
A2460	44.6	2519	49.5	2862	58,500p	Sra SP/3.25"/CCI 200
N140			53.2	2861	49,300p	Lapua Lock Base
A4350	51.3	2516	57.0	2859	54,100p	Bns-X/3.285"/CCI 200/(C)
BL-C(2)	47.0	2693	51.0	2857	49,200C	
IMR4895	45.0	2629	49.0	2852	50,000C	
N135			48.5	2850	50,763p	Rem SP
H335	46.0	2710	50.0	2839	48,400C	
IMR3031	44.0	2631	48.0	2838	49,900C	
W748	48.0	2703	50.0	2830	49,100C	
H450	58.0	2620	63.5	2825	48,000C	
IMR4064	46.0	2609	50.0	2824	49,200C	
A2495BR	42.8	2480	47.5	2818	59,400p	Bns-X/3.285"/CCI 200
A2520	45.0	2479	50.0	2817	57,800p	Bns-X/3.285"/CCI 200
A4350	53.1	2477	59.0	2815	50,300C	Sra SP/3.25"/CCI 200
N160			59.9	2810	50,763p	Hdy SP
A2015BR	40.5	2468	45.0	2805	58,400p	Bns-X/3.285"/CCI 200
A2460	43.7	2462	48.5	2798	57,100p	Bns-X/3.285"/CCI 200
A2230	43.7	2460	48.5	2796	56,400p	Bns-X/3.285"/CCI 200
N135			49.9	2790	49,300p	Lapua Lock Base
RL-12	44.0	2630	48.0	2784	49,400C	
IMR4320	46.0	2610	50.0	2778	49,100C	
H322	42.0	2521	46.0	2720	50,700C	
A3100	53.1	2353	59.0	2674	46,900p	Bns-X/3.285"/CCI 200/(C)
A3100	53.1	2297	59.0	2610	41,000p	Sra SP/3.25"/CCI 200

155-156

Powder	STARTING Grs.	MV (fps)	MAXIMUM Grs.	MV (fps)	Press. (CUP/psi)	Comments
N140			48.1	2900	50,763p	Sako SP 122A
N150			54.5	2831	49,300p	Sako SPBT
N140			52.7	2818	49,300p	Sako SPBT
N160			59.3	2810	50,763p	Sako SP 122A
N135			50.8	2793	49,300p	Sako SPBT
N135			45.5	2720	50,763p	Sako SP 122A

165-168

Powder	STARTING Grs.	MV (fps)	MAXIMUM Grs.	MV (fps)	Press. (CUP/psi)	Comments
H414	51.5	2695	56.0	2899	48,700C	
VarGet			50.5	2873	49,700C	
W760	53.0	2707	55.0	2829	48,200C	
IMR4350	54.0	2634	57.0	2828	48,900C	
A4350	53.1	2486	59.0	2825	56,200p	Sra HPBT/3.295"/CCI 200
H4350	54.0	2618	57.0	2818	48,600C	
H4895	44.0	2569	48.0	2813	50,600C	
RL-19	59.0	2707	61.0	2812	46,500C	
N160			58.8	2810	50,763p	Hdy FMJ
24N64			55.2	2794	57,980p	Hdy SP
H380	48.0	2583	52.0	2792	49,600C	
IMR4831	57.0	2679	59.0	2780	45,400C	
H4831	56.0	2481	61.0	2770	44,700C	
N160			58.6	2770	50,038p	Hdy SP
24N64			54.7	2766	56,506p	Hdy BTSP
RL-22	61.0	2696	63.0	2764	44,400C	
A4350	51.3	2428	57.0	2759	56,300p	Bns-X/3.245"/CCI 200/(C)
IMR4320	46.0	2595	49.0	2739	49,100C	
H335	43.0	2540	47.0	2738	48,900C	
RL-15	48.0	2584	51.0	2737	49,600C	
IMR4895	44.0	2551	47.0	2734	50,200C	
A2700	48.6	2404	54.0	2732	57,700p	Sra HPBT/3.295"/CCI 200
IMR4064	46.0	2582	49.0	2720	49,100C	
A2015BR	41.0	2385	45.5	2710	59,000p	Sra HPBT/3.295"/CCI 200
A2495BR	42.3	2382	47.0	2707	57,300p	Sra HPBT/3.295"/CCI 200
A2700	48.6	2382	54.0	2707	58,500p	Bns-X/3.245"/CCI 200
BL-C(2)	45.0	2534	49.0	2698	48,700C	
N150			52.1	2694	49,300p	Lapua Scenar
N140			47.8	2690	50,763p	Hdy FMJ
A2520	42.8	2359	47.5	2681	58,000p	Sra HPBT/3.295"/CCI 200
IMR3031	42.0	2519	45.0	2680	49,900C	
A2520	42.8	2347	47.5	2667	60,000p	Bns-X/3.245"/CCI 200
N140			50.2	2664	49,300p	Lapua Scenar
A2230	41.4	2343	46.0	2663	58,800p	Sra HPBT/3.295"/CCI 200
A2460	42.0	2340	46.7	2659	58,800p	Sra HPBT/3.295"/CCI 200
A2495BR	41.0	2328	45.5	2645	58,500p	Bns-X/3.245"/CCI 200
H450	55.0	2480	60.0	2643	43,700C	
W748	46.0	2538	48.0	2642	49,500C	
N150			50.6	2625	49,313p	Lapua Scenar GB 422
A2015BR	38.7	2304	43.0	2618	58,600p	Bns-X/3.245"/CCI 200
A3100	53.1	2300	59.0	2614	48,800p	Sra HPBT/3.295"/CCI 200/(C)
RL-12	41.0	2449	45.0	2610	48,800C	
A2460	40.5	2272	45.0	2582	60,000p	Bns-X/3.245"/CCI 200

▶▶▶▶▶▶▶▶▶▶▶▶▶▶▶▶▶▶▶▶▶▶▶▶▶▶

Caution: Loads exceeding SAAMI OAL Maximum must be verified for bullet-to-rifling clearance and magazine functioning. Where a specific primer or bullet is indicated those components must be used, no substitutions! Where only a maximum load is shown, reduce starting load 10%, unless otherwise specified.

Key: (C) = compressed charge; C = CUP; p = psi; Plink = Plinker; Bns = Barnes; Hdy = Hornady; Lap = Lapua; Nos = Nosler; Rem = Remington; Sra = Sierra; Spr = Speer; Win = Winchester.

Never exceed maximum load nor use any load exhibiting signs of excessive pressure. Begin at suggested starting load and work up carefully.

180

Powder	—STARTING— Grs.	MV (fps)	—MAXIMUM— Grs.	MV (fps)	Press. (CUP/psi)	Comments
IMR4350	53.0	2591	56.0	2787	49,900C	
RL-22	58.0	2640	61.0	2773	47,000C	
H4831	55.0	2459	60.0	2737	46,600C	
H4350	53.0	2481	56.0	2733	48,800C	
RL-19	56.0	2611	59.0	2720	46,500C	
A4350	51.3	2389	57.0	2715	56,400p	Sra HPBT/3.295"/ CCI 200/(C)
N160			57.1	2710	50,763p	Sako SP 226A
H380	47.0	2472	51.0	2702	49,600C	
H414	49.5	2481	54.0	2700	47,600C	
VarGet			49.0	2700	49,800C	
IMR4831	57.0	2511	59.0	2694	47,100C	
A4350	50.0	2357	55.5	2678	60,000p	Bns-X/3.32"/CCI 200
RL-15	47.0	2550	50.0	2665	46,500C	
24N64			52.7	2650	55,492p	Hdy BTSP
A2700	48.6	2329	54.0	2647	58,800p	Bns-X/3.32"/CCI 200
IMR4064	45.0	2459	48.0	2646	49,600C	
A2700	49.5	2328	55.0	2646	56,000p	Sra HPBT/3.295"/CCI 200
W760	51.0	2504	53.0	2630	47,200C	
N140			46.3	2620	50,763p	Sako SP 226A
A3100	53.1	2298	59.0	2611	53,300p	Sra HPBT/3.295"/ CCI 200/(C)
H450	54.0	2374	59.0	2604	48,200C	
N160			57.6	2603	49,300p	Spr Sptz
H4895	40.5	2298	44.0	2600	50,000C	
A2495BR	41.0	2284	45.5	2595	59,500p	Sra HPBT/3.295"/CCI 200
A3100	53.1	2281	59.0	2592	52,400p	Bns-X/3.32"/CCI 200/(C)
A2015BR	40.1	2277	44.5	2588	59,300p	Sra HPBT/3.295"/CCI 200
A2520	42.1	2275	46.8	2585	57,000p	Sra HPBT/3.295"/CCI 200
IMR4320	45.0	2420	48.0	2580	49,400C	
IMR4895	41.0	2313	44.0	2577	50,200C	
A2230	39.6	2260	44.0	2568	60,000p	Sra HPBT/3.295"/CCI 200
H1000	61.0	2440	64.0	2564	38,200C	
A2460	41.2	2255	45.8	2563	55,800p	Sra HPBT/3.295"/CCI 200
A2520	41.4	2251	46.0	2558	58,900p	Bns-X/3.32"/CCI 200
BL-C(2)	43.5	2380p	47.5	2550	49,200C	
A2495BR	40.5	2238	45.0	2543	59,300p	Bns-X/3.32"/CCI 200
H335	41.0	2350	45.0	2530	48,400C	
A2460	40.1	2218	44.5	2521	59,000p	Bns-X/3.32"/CCI 200
W748	44.0	2402	46.0	2510	48,500C	
RL-12	38.0	2210	43.0	2479	47,000C	
A2230	39.2	2179	43.5	2476	57,900p	Bns-X/3.32"/CCI 200
A2015BR	36.9	2176	41.0	2473	58,100p	Bns-X/3.32"/CCI 200
H870			64.0	2424	36,600C	
H322	38.0	2178	42.0	2399	48,400C	

185-186

Powder	—STARTING— Grs.	MV (fps)	—MAXIMUM— Grs.	MV (fps)	Press. (CUP/psi)	Comments
N160			58.6	2710	50,763p	Lapua SP E375
N150			50.2	2670	50,763p	Lapua SP E375
N160			56.5	2670	50,763p	Lapua FMJ D46
N160			59.2	2637	49,300p	Lapua Mira
N165			58.6	2620	44,962p	Lapua SP E375
N140			47.1	2620	50,763p	Lapua SP E375

185-186 con't

Powder	—STARTING— Grs.	MV (fps)	—MAXIMUM— Grs.	MV (fps)	Press. (CUP/psi)	Comments
N150	48.0	2444	49.8	2543	49,313p	Lapua Scenar G8432
N150	46.6	2395	48.9	2503	49,313p	Lapua Mira EB 423
N150			48.9	2485	49,300p	Lapua Mira
N150	44.3	2335	46.1	2475	49,313p	Lapua Mega 415
N140			47.1	2460	49,300p	Lapua Mira

190

Powder	—STARTING— Grs.	MV (fps)	—MAXIMUM— Grs.	MV (fps)	Press. (CUP/psi)	Comments
RL-22	57.0	2692	60.0	2714	48,000C	
H4831	55.0	2425	59.0	2710	48,200C	
IMR4831	56.0	2543	58.0	2703	48,800C	
RL-19	54.0	2549	57.0	2687	47,000C	
IMR4350	52.0	2461	55.0	2682	49,600C	
H4350	53.0	2530	55.0	2680	49,400C	
A4350	50.0	2343	55.5	2663	60,000p	Sra HPBT/3.325"/ CCI 200/(C)
RL-15	45.0	2494	48.0	2602	48,500C	
IMR4064	44.0	2339	47.0	2592	49,900C	
H414	50.0	2438	53.0	2589	47,800C	
H380	46.0	2411	49.0	2577	49,900C	
A3100	53.1	2265	59.0	2574	53,200p	Sra HPBT/3.325"/ CCI 200/(C)
H450	54.0	2294	57.0	2560	47,600C	
IMR4320	44.0	2414	47.0	2540	50,000C	
A2460	41.0	2233	45.5	2537	58,400p	Sra HPBT/3.325"/CCI 200
IMR4895	40.0	2380	43.0	2524	50,000C	
A2700	46.8	2217	52.0	2519	53,700p	Sra HPBT/3.325"/CCI 200
A2520	41.0	2212	45.5	2514	58,400p	Sra HPBT/3.325"/CCI 200
A2495BR	39.6	2193	44.0	2492	59,100p	Sra HPBT/3.325"/CCI 200
A2015BR	38.7	2193	43.0	2492	60,000p	Sra HPBT/3.325"/CCI 200
H4895	40.0	2253	43.0	2488	50,000C	
W760	50.0	2396	52.0	2480	46,600C	
A2230	39.6	2180	44.0	2477	56,600p	Sra HPBT/3.325"/CCI 200
H1000	60.0	2330	63.0	2465	37,600C	
BL-C(2)	43.0	2321	46.0	2443	48,400C	
H335	39.0	2209	42.0	2430	48,600C	
H870			64.0	2419	39,600C	
A8700	55.8	1912	62.0	2173	31,400p	Sra HPBT/3.325"/ CCI 200/(C)

200

Powder	—STARTING— Grs.	MV (fps)	—MAXIMUM— Grs.	MV (fps)	Press. (CUP/psi)	Comments
H4831	54.5	2378	59.0	2690	49,000C	
IMR4831	55.0	2509	57.0	2639	49,400C	
H4350	52.0	2420	55.0	2635	50,000C	
IMR4350	52.0	2449	54.0	2631	50,400C	
RL-22			58.0	2620	48,000C	
RL-19	53.0	2480	56.0	2589	48,500C	
A4350	49.5	2261	55.0	2569	58,800p	Nos Part/3.295"/CCI 200/(C)
A3100	53.1	2254	59.0	2561	58,900p	Nos Part/3.295"/CCI 200/(C)
H380	44.5	2300	48.0	2533	50,300C	
N160			57.6	2510	49,300p	Nos (Part)
N160			53.2	2490	50,763p	Lapua SP E401
H414	48.0	2374	52.0	2483	46,400C	

Never exceed maximum load nor use any load exhibiting signs of excessive pressure. Begin at suggested starting load and work up carefully.

200 con't

Powder	—STARTING— Grs.	MV (fps)	—MAXIMUM— Grs.	MV (fps)	Press. (CUP/psi)	Comments
IMR4064	43.0	2244	46.0	2477	49,900C	
H1000	59.0	2321	62.0	2468	39,800C	
H450	51.5	2232	56.0	2455	46,800C	
IMR4320	43.0	2237	46.0	2451	49,000C	
A2700	46.4	2148	51.5	2441	53,900C	Nos Part./3.295″/CCI 200
WMR			55.7	2435	48,200C	Win SP
A2520	40.5	2140	45.0	2432	58,900C	Nos Part./3.295″/CCI 200
H4895	39.5	2192	43.0	2431	50,900C	
IMR4895	40.0	2210	43.0	2430	50,200C	
W760	49.0	2351	51.0	2429	46,800C	
A2460	40.1	2138	44.5	2429	58,500C	Nos Part./3.295″/CCI 200
IMR7828	55.0	2311	57.0	2404	44,600C	
H870			64.0	2401	41,200C	
A2230	39.2	2100	43.5	2386	57,300C	Nos Part./3.295″/CCI 200
A2495BR	38.7	2094	43.0	2379	59,900C	Nos Part./3.295″/CCI 200
N150			47.5	2374	49,300C	Nos (Part)
A2015BR	37.8	2062	42.0	2343	54,800C	Nos Part./3.295″/CCI 200
A8700	55.8	1925	62.0	2187	34,800C	Nos Part./3.295″/CCI 200/(C)

220-225

Powder	—STARTING— Grs.	MV (fps)	—MAXIMUM— Grs.	MV (fps)	Press. (CUP/psi)	Comments
H4831	53.0	2227	57.0	2526	50,800C	
IMR4831	54.0	2439	56.0	2478	49,600C	
A3100	53.1	2174	59.0	2470	59,900C	Sra FP/3.2″/CCI 200/(C)
RL-22	53.0	2331	56.0	2469	48,500C	
A4350	49.5	2171	55.0	2467	59,400C	Sra FP/3.2″/CCI 200
H4350	50.0	2290	53.0	2464	48,800C	
IMR4350	50.0	2340	52.0	2454	49,400C	
N165			56.3	2440	50,763p	Sako SP 228A
H450	52.5	2266	57.0	2423	49,800C	
N160			52.6	2410	50,763p	Sako SP 228A
H1000	58.0	2307	61.0	2407	42,000C	
H414	46.0	2258	50.0	2399	48,500C	
W760	48.0	2281	50.0	2387	48,400C	(220-gr.)
VarGet			45.0	2382	49,400C	
IMR7828	54.0	2240	56.0	2380	46,000C	
WMR			55.7	2380	51,100p	Win SP
RL-19	51.0	2266	54.0	2379	47,500C	

220-225 con't

Powder	—STARTING— Grs.	MV (fps)	—MAXIMUM— Grs.	MV (fps)	Press. (CUP/psi)	Comments
N160			56.0	2368	49,300p	Hdy RN
H870			63.0	2348	42,300C	
A2700	44.6	2048	49.5	2327	58,200p	Sra RN/3.2″/CCI 200
IMR4064	42.0	2169	45.0	2309	49,900C	
IMR4320	41.0	2180	44.0	2290	49,500C	
A2520	39.6	2013	44.0	2288	59,000p	Sra RN/3.2″/CCI 200
RL-15	42.0	2156	45.0	2279	47,000C	
A2460	38.7	1996	43.0	2268	58,600p	Sra RN/3.2″/CCI 200
IMR4895	38.0	2110	41.0	2254	50,100C	
A2015BR	37.8	1983	42.0	2253	59,500p	Sra RN/3.2″/CCI 200
A2230	38.3	1978	42.5	2248	58,400p	Sra RN/3.2″/CCI 200
A2495BR	38.3	1955	42.5	2222	56,900p	Sra RN/3.2″/CCI 200
A8700	55.8	1908	62.0	2168	38,700p	Sra RN/3.2″/CCI 200/(C)

250

Powder	—STARTING— Grs.	MV (fps)	—MAXIMUM— Grs.	MV (fps)	Press. (CUP/psi)	Comments
IMR7828	53.0	2120	55.0	2279	46,400C	
IMR4831	49.0	2100	52.0	2272	50,000C	
H1000	55.0	2095	58.0	2234	42,000C	
RL-19	49.0	2101	52.0	2229	49,000C	
RL-22	51.0	2096	54.0	2216	48,500C	
W760	46.0	2101	48.0	2185	48,500C	
H4831	52.0	2086	54.0	2180	48,000C	
H4350	48.0	2049	50.0	2131	46,500C	
H870	59.0	2004	61.0	2117	44,700C	
IMR4350	47.0	1982	50.0	2110	47,100C	
RL-15	40.0	2007	43.0	2102	48,000C	

Caution: Loads exceeding SAAMI OAL Maximum must be verified for bullet-to-rifling clearance and magazine functioning. Where a specific primer or bullet is indicated those components must be used, no substitutions! Where only a maximum load is shown, reduce starting load 10%, unless otherwise specified.

Key: (C) = compressed charge; C = CUP; p = psi; Plink = Plinker; Bns = Barnes; Hdy = Hornady; Lap = Lapua; Nos = Nosler; Rem = Remington; Sra = Sierra; Spr = Speer; Win = Winchester.

Never exceed maximum load nor use any load exhibiting signs of excessive pressure. Begin at suggested starting load and work up carefully.

300

Holland & Holland Magnum

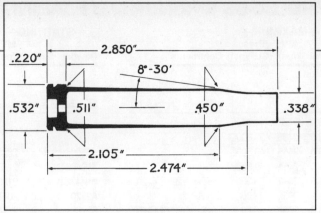

Case: Winchester
Primer: Large Rifle
Barrel: 26″ Accurate
    24″ Hodgdon
    24″ Vihtavuori

Bullet Diameter: 0.308″
Maximum Case Length: 2.850″
Trim to Length: 2.840″
Maximum Cartridge OAL: 3.600″
Minimum Cartridge OAL: 3.420″

Having carried several monikers during its long and distinguished career, the "Super 30" was the basis for an entire industry and many a fortune. Ammunition for the 300 H&H was offered by the Western Cartridge Company from the very year of its introduction (1925), but no so-chambered rifles were commercially manufactured in the U.S. until 1937 when Winchester finally offered it in their famous Model 70—until then getting a U.S.-made Super 30 was strictly a custom proposition.

With a larger body diameter, compared to the 30-06, and common availability, the 300 H&H case formed the basis for a plethora of wildcat chamberings between the date of its introduction and the early 1960s. Popular myth has it that the belt somehow added strength to the case. Nothing could be further from the truth. In reality, the belt is nothing more than a thick rim with a groove cut in it. This design facilitat-

ed simple and proper extraction in the H&H double rifles for which this cartridge was designed. It adds nothing whatsoever to the strength of the case. A persisting myth to the contrary merely signifies a general lack of understanding regarding what makes a case head strong.

The 300 H&H holds vastly more powder than the 30-06 and, when loaded to similar pressures, generates considerably more velocity with any given bullet. Further, standard loading pressures are among the highest used in any standard chambering and, therefore, performance is still very impressive. The H&H falls only a scant 100 fps short of the 300 Weatherby Magnum with top loads in both chamberings.

Case capacity with a 150-grain bullet, seated normally, is about 82.2 grains of water. H4831, H414, A4350 and H4350 are good performers in the 300 H&H.

300 HOLLAND & HOLLAND MAGNUM LOADING DATA

Powder	STARTING Grs.	MV (fps)	MAXIMUM Grs.	MV (fps)	Press. (CUP/psi)	Comments
110						
H4831	76.5	3325	83.0	3611		
H4350	69.0	3329	73.0	3550		
H414	64.5	3280	70.0	3534		
H450	69.0	3258	75.0	3458	46,500C	26″ Test Barrel
125-130						
N160			77.2	3610	53,684p	Sako FJ 120A
A2700	68.9	3294	72.5	3504	53,700C	Nos BT/3.585″/CCI 250
A4350	70.2	3066	78.0	3484	48,300C	Nos BT/3.585″/CCI 250/(C)
H4350	68.0	3142	72.0	3394		(125-gr.)
H4831	75.0	3186	81.0	3362		(125-gr.)
H450	70.5	2992	76.5	3336	46,100C	(125-gr.)/26″ Test Barrel
H414	62.0	3153	67.0	3301		(125-gr.)
A3100	70.2	2814	78.0	3198	43,200C	Nos BT/3.585″/CCI 250/(C)

Powder	STARTING Grs.	MV (fps)	MAXIMUM Grs.	MV (fps)	Press. (CUP/psi)	Comments
150						
H4831	72.0	3096	78.0	3313		
A4350	67.5	2915	75.0	3313	51,400C	Hdy SP/3.555″/CCI 250
H414	60.0	2985	65.0	3247		
H4350	67.0	2998	71.0	3202		
A2700	66.0	3002	69.5	3194	51,200C	Hdy SP/3.555″/CCI 250
N160			75.6	3180	56,565p	Spr SP
A3100	70.2	2778	78.0	3157	45,700C	Hdy SP/3.555″/CCI 250/(C)
H450	67.0	2886	72.0	3110	45,400C	26″ Test Barrel
155						
N160			72.8	3070	56,565p	Sako SP 122A

Never exceed maximum load nor use any load exhibiting signs of excessive pressure. Begin at suggested starting load and work up carefully.

165

Powder	—STARTING— Grs.	MV (fps)	—MAXIMUM— Grs.	MV (fps)	Press. (CUP/psi)	Comments
H4350	66.0	3018	69.0	3164		
A4350	64.8	2762	72.0	3139	54,000C	Bns-X/3.6″/CCI 250
A3100	70.2	2743	78.0	3117	49,600C	Bns-X/3.6″/CCI 250/(C)
H450	68.0	2867	73.0	3113	50,500C	26″ Test Barrel
H4831	71.0	2849	77.0	3099		
A2700	64.6	2869	68.0	3052	53,000C	Bns-X/3.6″/CCI 250
H414	59.0	2899	63.0	3046		
N160			70.7	2970	56,565p	Spr SP

180

Powder	Grs.	MV (fps)	Grs.	MV (fps)	Press. (CUP/psi)	Comments
A3100	70.2	2705	78.0	3074	53,600C	Sra SP/3.6″/CCI 250/(C)
A4350	63.5	2639	70.5	2999	51,700C	Sra SP/3.6″/CCI 250
N160			68.2	2920	56,565p	Sako SP 226A
A2700	61.8	2729	65.0	2903	51,400C	Sra SP/3.6″/CCI 250
A8700	76.5	2292	85.0	2604	43,000C	Sra SP/3.6″/CCI 250/(C)

200

Powder	Grs.	MV (fps)	Grs.	MV (fps)	Press. (CUP/psi)	Comments
H4831	67.0	2737	72.0	2932		
A3100	65.7	2563	73.0	2912	52,900C	Sra HPBT/3.665″/CCI 250
H4350	62.0	2747	66.0	2909		
A4350	58.5	2479	65.0	2817	51,000C	Sra HPBT/3.665″/CCI 250
H870			83.0	2779		
A2700	58.0	2575	61.0	2739	54,000C	Sra HPBT/3.665″/CCI 250
A8700	76.5	2348	85.0	2668	47,400C	Sra HPBT/3.665″/CCI 250/(C)
H414	52.0	2423	56.0	2649		

220-225

Powder	—STARTING— Grs.	MV (fps)	—MAXIMUM— Grs.	MV (fps)	Press. (CUP/psi)	Comments
A3100	65.7	2451	73.0	2785	53,400C	Hdy RN/3.59″/CCI 250/(C)
H4350	60.0	2595	64.0	2717		
H4831	65.0	2555	70.0	2714		
H870			82.0	2706		
A4350	58.5	2355	65.0	2676	50,900C	Hdy RN/3.59″/CCI 250
N160			65.4	2590	56,565p	Hdy RN
A2700	57.5	2433	60.5	2588	52,000C	Hdy RN/3.59″/CCI 250
A8700	76.5	2262	85.0	2571	44,600C	Hdy RN/3.59″/CCI 250/(C)

250

Powder	Grs.	MV (fps)	Grs.	MV (fps)	Press. (CUP/psi)	Comments
H870	75.0	2456	79.0	2616		
H4831	63.0	2372	67.0	2563		
H4350	59.0	2344	62.0	2493		

> *Caution:* Loads exceeding SAAMI OAL Maximum must be verified for bullet-to-rifling clearance and magazine functioning. Where a specific primer or bullet is indicated those components must be used, no substitutions! Where only a maximum load is shown, reduce starting load 10%, unless otherwise specified.
>
> *Key:* (C) = compressed charge; C = CUP; p = psi; Plink = Plinker; Bns = Barnes; Hdy = Hornady; Lap = Lapua; Nos = Nosler; Rem = Remington; Sra = Sierra; Spr = Speer; Win = Winchester.

Never exceed maximum load nor use any load exhibiting signs of excessive pressure. Begin at suggested starting load and work up carefully.

199

300

Winchester Magnum

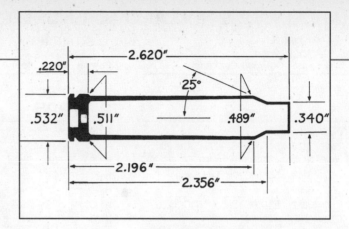

Case: Remington
Primer: Large Rifle
Barrel: 24" Accurate
26" Hodgdon
24" Vihtavuori

Bullet Diameter: 0.308"
Maximum Case Length: 2.620"
Trim to Length: 2.610"
Maximum Cartridge OAL: 3.340"
Minimum Cartridge OAL: 3.280"

When Norma beat Winchester to the 30-caliber magnum punch, with the introduction of the 308 Norma Magnum in 1960, Winchester set out to develop a standard-length magnum chambering that could offer a performance advantage over Norma's version. No mean task.

Instead of designing a larger diameter beltless case—too bad—Winchester adopted a longer version of the same basic belted case with a shorter case neck and seated the bullets rather deep for a similar overall length. Winchester's design succeeded in achieving a surprising increase in usable capacity, almost 10 percent, but there really is not much difference in performance—partly because the 300 Winchester Magnum is generally loaded to slightly less pressure.

This cartridge can launch moderate-weight bullets at sufficient velocity to make it a premier choice for use on smaller species at longer range. With the heaviest standard bullets, it still offers a reasonably flat trajectory and can deliver sufficient energy to longer ranges for use against elk-sized game. It also enjoys considerable popularity in the various long-range target shooting games.

Case capacity with a 150-grain bullet, seated normally, is about 86.8 grains of water. H4831, IMR7828, IMR4350, RL-22, H380, RL-19, H870 and H1000 are all noted performers in the 300 Winchester Magnum.

300 WINCHESTER MAGNUM LOADING DATA

Powder	STARTING Grs.	MV (fps)	MAXIMUM Grs.	MV (fps)	Press. (CUP/psi)	Comments
110						
VarGet			72.5	3660	51,700C	
H450	77.5	3327	84.0	3659	51,200C	
A2700	74.6	3437	78.5	3656	64,000p	Sra HP/3.17"/CCI 200
H380	66.0	3458	72.0	3638	47,400C	
H4831	77.5	3308	84.0	3621	47,400C	
H4350	76.0	3380	79.0	3610	51,700C	
IMR4350	76.0	3391	79.0	3609	52,000C	
IMR4831	78.0	3241	83.0	3603	48,500C	
H414	70.0	3284	76.0	3597	49,800C	
W760	72.0	3394	76.0	3594	50,400C	
IMR7828	79.0	3344	83.0	3582	46,000C	
IMR4320	69.0	3459	72.0	3562	51,000C	
A4350	71.6	3116	79.5	3541	55,600p	Sra HP/3.17"/CCI 200
BL-C(2)	56.0	3268	61.0	3531	51,400C	
A2520	60.3	3091	67.0	3512	58,400p	Sra HP/3.17"/CCI 200
H4895	62.0	3210	68.0	3494	49,800C	
N160	76.5	3145	83.3	3489	47,900p	Hdy SP/3.268"/Rem 9½
IMR4895	65.0	3390	68.0	3477	50,200C	
IMR4064	67.0	3364	70.0	3469	49,900C	
RL-19	78.0	3284	82.0	3459	46,000C	
110 con't						
RL-22	80.0	3278	84.0	3448	45,000C	
A3100	73.8	3009	82.0	3419	51,900p	Sra HP/3.17"/CCI 200/(C)
H1000	81.0	3044	85.0	3211	33,600C	
125-130						
IMR7828	78.0	3244	82.0	3479	49,900C	
A2700	70.8	3269	74.5	3478	63,100p	Sra SP/3.25"/CCI 200
A4350	70.7	3047	78.5	3462	58,200p	Sra SP/3.25"/CCI 200
IMR4831	76.0	3230	80.0	3457	50,100C	
RL-22	79.0	3254	83.0	3439	48,500C	
IMR4350	73.0	3249	77.0	3431	52,600C	
H450	73.5	3086	80.0	3426	47,600C	
RL-19	76.0	3221	80.0	3420	48,500C	
N160			78.7	3410	56,565p	Sako FMJ 120A
H414	68.0	3193	74.0	3409	49,300C	
H380	64.5	3168	71.0	3403	51,600C	
W760	70.0	3231	74.0	3398	49,800C	
VarGet			68.5	3398	52,100C	
H4350	74.0	3271	76.0	3390	52,200C	

Never exceed maximum load nor use any load exhibiting signs of excessive pressure. Begin at suggested starting load and work up carefully.

Powder	STARTING Grs.	MV (fps)	MAXIMUM Grs.	MV (fps)	Press. (CUP/psi)	Comments

125-130 con't

Powder	Grs.	MV (fps)	Grs.	MV (fps)	Press. (CUP/psi)	Comments
A2700	69.8	3183	73.5	3386	63,200p	Hdy SP/3.3"/CCI 200
A3100	73.8	2973	82.0	3378	59,500C	Hdy SP/3.3"/CCI 200/(C)
A4350	69.3	2973	77.0	3378	60,000C	Hdy SP/3.3"/CCI 200
A3100	73.8	2968	82.0	3373	57,500C	Sra SP/3.25"/CCI 200/(C)
IMR4320	64.0	3209	67.0	3371	51,900C	
H4831	76.5	3062	81.0	3347	52,200C	
A2520	58.5	2942	65.0	3343	61,000p	Sra SP/3.25"/CCI 200
IMR4064	62.0	3104	66.0	3318	50,700C	
H4895	60.5	2974	66.0	3309	52,100C	
IMR4895	61.0	3007	65.0	3289	51,600C	
A2520	56.7	2849	63.0	3237	58,800C	Hdy SP/3.3"/CCI 200
H1000	81.0	3029	85.0	3228	39,300C	

150

Powder	Grs.	MV (fps)	Grs.	MV (fps)	Press. (CUP/psi)	Comments
N160			75.3	3310	56,565p	Spr RN
RL-22	77.0	3189	81.0	3305	52,000C	
H380	64.5	2979	71.0	3303	54,500C	
IMR7828	77.0	3139	81.0	3285	53,100C	
N160			75.6	3280	56,565p	Norma FMJ 147-gr. bullet
RL-19	73.0	3124	77.0	3259	51,500C	
H4895	60.5	2952	66.0	3259	55,000C	
H450	72.0	2953	78.0	3253	51,800C	
H4831	76.5	3056	80.0	3252	53,400C	
IMR4350	71.0	3084	74.0	3249	53,000C	
H4350	71.0	3060	74.0	3244	53,000C	
H1000	81.0	3064	85.0	3240	45,300C	
IMR4831	73.0	3020	77.0	3214	51,600C	
W760	68.0	3044	71.0	3209	50,100C	
H414	65.0	2961	71.0	3202	49,800C	
A2700	66.0	2986	69.5	3177	62,300p	Sra SP/3.338"/CCI 200
VarGet			65.0	3155	52,300C	
A4350	65.7	2767	73.0	3144	59,400C	Sra SP/3.338"/CCI 200
A3100	68.4	2735	76.0	3108	58,900C	Sra SP/3.338"/CCI 200
H870	82.0	2872	87.0	3050	48,200C	
N165			79.0	2990	54,600C	Hdy SP

155

Powder	Grs.	MV (fps)	Grs.	MV (fps)	Press. (CUP/psi)	Comments
N160			74.8	3260	56,565p	Sako SP 122A

165-168

Powder	Grs.	MV (fps)	Grs.	MV (fps)	Press. (CUP/psi)	Comments
RL-22	75.0	3118	79.0	3240	51,500C	
H1000	79.0	3031	84.0	3207	51,400C	(165-gr.)
RL-19	72.0	3074	76.0	3196	51,000C	
IMR4350	69.0	2944	73.0	3192	52,100C	(165-gr.)
H4350	70.0	3040	73.0	3188	52,700C	(165-gr.)
IMR7828	76.0	2990	80.0	3187	51,000C	(165-gr.)

165-168 con't

Powder	Grs.	MV (fps)	Grs.	MV (fps)	Press. (CUP/psi)	Comments
H4831	75.5	3010	78.0	3180	53,300C	(165-gr.)
H450	71.0	3024	76.0	3169	53,000C	(165-gr.)
N160			74.1	3150	55,114p	Spr SP
IMR4831	71.0	2979	75.0	3149	51,400C	(165-gr.)
N165			78.0	3080	55,800p	BTSP
A4350	64.8	2693	72.0	3060	63,200p	Sra HPBT/3.475"/CCI 200
H414	64.0	2934	68.0	3036	48,400C	(165-gr.)
W760	65.0	2974	68.0	3030	48,900C	(165-gr.)
WMR			76.0	3010	53,800p	Win SP
H870	82.0	2860	87.0	2971	51,200C	(165-gr.)
A2700	63.7	2781	67.0	2959	61,900p	Sra HPBT/3.475"/CCI 200
A3100	66.2	2592	73.5	2945	57,200p	Sra HPBT/3.475"/CCI 200

180

Powder	Grs.	MV (fps)	Grs.	MV (fps)	Press. (CUP/psi)	Comments
RL-22	73.0	3030	77.0	3142	51,000C	
H1000	78.0	2945	83.0	3121	50,900C	
H4831	73.5	2902	76.0	3088	52,900C	
IMR7828	74.0	2884	78.0	3083	52,200C	
RL-19	70.0	2961	74.0	3080	49,500C	
H4350	68.0	2914	71.0	3079	53,700C	
IMR4350	67.0	2829	70.0	3077	53,600C	
H450	69.0	2873	75.0	3064	52,200C	
IMR4831	69.0	2754	73.0	3016	52,400C	
N160			73.0	2990	55,114p	Nos SP
H870	81.0	2841	86.0	2982	53,000C	
N165			75.5	2980	60,000p	SPBT
WMR			74.0	2960	60,300p	Win SP
H414	63.0	2767	67.0	2928	54,000C	
W760	64.0	2811	67.0	2920	54,000C	
A3100	64.8	2551	72.0	2899	58,300p	Sra SBT/3.45"/CCI 200
N165	70.8	2626	77.6	2898	52,200p	Nos Part./3.339"/ Rem 9½
A4350	62.1	2547	69.0	2894	62,200p	Sra SBT/3.45"/CCI 200
A2700	62.7	2706	66.0	2879	62,800p	Sra SBT/3.45"/CCI 200
A8700	77.4	2475	86.0	2813	45,100p	Sra SBT/3.45"/CCI 200/(C)
N170			76.0	2811	54,305p	Hdy BTSP

185

Powder	Grs.	MV (fps)	Grs.	MV (fps)	Press. (CUP/psi)	Comments
N160			72.5	2920	56,565p	Lapua FMJ D46

▶▶▶▶▶▶▶▶▶▶▶▶▶▶▶▶▶▶▶▶▶▶▶▶▶

Caution: Loads exceeding SAAMI OAL Maximum must be verified for bullet-to-rifling clearance and magazine functioning. Where a specific primer or bullet is indicated those components must be used, no substitutions! Where only a maximum load is shown, reduce starting load 10%, unless otherwise specified.

Key: (C) = compressed charge; C = CUP; p = psi; Plink = Plinker; Bns = Barnes; Hdy = Hornady; Lap = Lapua; Nos = Nosler; Rem = Remington; Sra = Sierra; Spr = Speer; Win = Winchester.

Never exceed maximum load nor use any load exhibiting signs of excessive pressure. Begin at suggested starting load and work up carefully.

190

Powder	STARTING Grs.	STARTING MV (fps)	MAXIMUM Grs.	MAXIMUM MV (fps)	Press. (CUP/psi)	Comments
H1000	77.0	2921	82.0	3101	53,500C	
IMR7828	73.0	2812	76.0	3022	51,700C	
RL-22	71.0	2903	75.0	3016	52,000C	
RL-19	67.0	2860	71.0	2979	50,500C	
H450	70.0	2774	73.0	2950	53,000C	
H4831	70.0	2829	74.0	2937	54,400C	
H870	80.0	2788	85.0	2924	52,400C	
WMR			74.0	2920	59,500p	Win SPBT
H4350	66.0	2752	69.0	2914	53,700C	
IMR4831	67.0	2717	71.0	2909	52,200C	
IMR4350	65.0	2730	68.0	2900	53,200C	
N165			73.4	2890	59,500p	Hdy BTSP
A4350	61.2	2518	68.0	2861	63,300p	Sra HPBT/3.45"/CCI 200
A8700	77.4	2475	86.0	2813	49,300p	Sra HPBT/3.45"/CCI 200/(C)
A3100	63.0	2467	70.0	2803	59,500p	Sra HPBT/3.45"/CCI 200
A2700	60.3	2611	63.5	2778	60,600p	Sra HPBT/3.45"/CCI 200
N170			74.0	2742	64,228p	Hdy BTSP

200

Powder	STARTING Grs.	STARTING MV (fps)	MAXIMUM Grs.	MAXIMUM MV (fps)	Press. (CUP/psi)	Comments
H1000	75.0	2806	80.0	2984	53,100C	
IMR7828	72.0	2867	74.0	2980	52,200C	
RL-22	69.0	2811	73.0	2940	51,500C	
H870	79.0	2691	84.0	2897	52,100C	
H450	66.0	2594	72.0	2895	51,900C	
N160			72.2	2890	56,565p	Nos SP
RL-19	66.0	2749	70.0	2863	50,500C	
IMR4831	66.0	2624	70.0	2821	53,100C	
H4831	70.0	2675	73.0	2814	54,000C	
H4350	65.0	2660	68.0	2807	53,600C	
IMR4350	63.0	2580	67.0	2771	52,900C	
N165	68.1	2524	75.0	2754	52,200p	Sra HPBT/3.339"/Rem 9½
WMR			69.0	2750	59,000p	Win SP
A8700	77.4	2417	86.0	2747	53,800p	Sra HPBT/3.34"/CCI 200/(C)
A3100	62.1	2379	69.0	2703	58,100p	Sra HPBT/3.34"/CCI 200
A2700	58.9	2535	62.0	2697	61,800p	Sra HPBT/3.34"/CCI 200
A4350	57.6	2372	64.0	2696	61,700p	Sra HPBT/3.34"/CCI 200

220-225

Powder	STARTING Grs.	STARTING MV (fps)	MAXIMUM Grs.	MAXIMUM MV (fps)	Press. (CUP/psi)	Comments
H1000	72.0	2693	77.0	2881	54,500C	
IMR7828	70.0	2711	72.0	2794	51,000C	
H870	78.0	2620	83.0	2777	51,600C	
RL-22	67.0	2644	71.0	2755	52,000C	
A8700	77.4	2371	86.0	2694	53,300p	Sra RN/3.3"/CCI 200/(C)
H4350	63.0	2531	66.0	2694	54,000C	
H4831	66.0	2456	72.0	2693	52,600C	
RL-19	63.0	2583	67.0	2690	50,000C	
N160			71.0	2690	55,114p	Hdy SP
IMR4831	64.0	2541	68.0	2689	52,400C	
WMR			68.2	2665	59,800p	Win SP
IMR4350	61.0	2510	65.0	2660	52,700C	
A4350	58.5	2288	65.0	2600	61,600p	Sra RN/3.3"/CCI 200
A3100	60.3	2253	67.0	2560	59,800p	Sra RN/3.3"/CCI 200
N170			70.0	2543	56,573p	Hdy RN

250

Powder	STARTING Grs.	STARTING MV (fps)	MAXIMUM Grs.	MAXIMUM MV (fps)	Press. (CUP/psi)	Comments
H1000	68.0	2505	73.0	2670	53,500C	
H870	78.0	2489	81.0	2656	52,600C	
IMR7828	67.0	2449	71.0	2628	51,200C	
H4831	66.0	2443	69.0	2569	51,700C	
IMR4831	61.0	2360	65.0	2549	54,000C	
RL-22	62.0	2371	66.0	2508	51,000C	
RL-19	60.0	2343	64.0	2496	51,500C	
H4350	61.0	2321	64.0	2460	50,800C	
IMR4350	58.0	2294	62.0	2460	59,300C	

Caution: Loads exceeding SAAMI OAL Maximum must be verified for bullet-to-rifling clearance and magazine functioning. Where a specific primer or bullet is indicated those components must be used, no substitutions! Where only a maximum load is shown, reduce starting load 10%, unless otherwise specified.

Key: (C) = compressed charge; C = CUP; p = psi; Plink = Plinker; Bns = Barnes; Hdy = Hornady; Lap = Lapua; Nos = Nosler; Rem = Remington; Sra = Sierra; Spr = Speer; Win = Winchester.

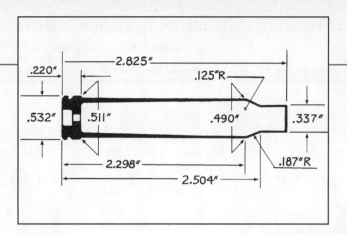

Case: Remington
Primer: Large Rifle
Barrel: 26″ Accurate
26″ Hodgdon
26″ Vihtavuori

Bullet Diameter: 0.308″
Maximum Case length: 2.825″
Trim to Length: 2.815″
Maximum Cartridge OAL: 3.590″
Minimum Cartridge OAL: 3.390″

Introduced in 1944, this cartridge was originally developed by the simple expedient of fireforming the 300 H&H Magnum to reduce body taper, move the shoulder forward and increase the shoulder angle. Capacity was increased about 20 percent and folks expected a similar increase in performance....

But ballistics do not work that way, at least not when the original design is already of reasonably high capacity. Without increasing pressures, the Weatherby version can only offer about a 100 fps (3 percent) increase in velocity, compared to the more mundane 300 H&H.

Nevertheless, 100 fps is 100 fps, and many believe any ballistic improvement is worth whatever cost. For this reason, the 300 Weatherby has garnered a considerable following.

This is most recognized as a big game chambering, espe-cially adept at delivering large doses of lead poisoning to distant targets. However, there are those who custom-chamber for this basic cartridge, eliminating the free bore and tightening throat dimension, for long-range target work. If you have one of these custom rifles, beware that significant charge reductions will be necessary to maintain safe pressure levels. Such guns are loaded with accuracy rather than velocity as the primary concern, but pressure must still be monitored. Never fire any factory load in such a chamber!

Case capacity with a 150-grain bullet, seated normally, is about 98.8 grains of water (Weatherby cases). H4831, IMR4350, H4831, H450, IMR4831, IMR7828, RL-22 and A3100 are all good choices in the 300 Weatherby Magnum. As with all free-bored chamberings, the slowest useable powders seldom generate good ballistic uniformity or accuracy.

▌ 300 WEATHERBY MAGNUM LOADING DATA ▌

Powder	STARTING Grs.	MV (fps)	MAXIMUM Grs.	MV (fps)	Press. (CUP/psi)	Comments
110						
H4895	70.0	3506	76.0	3829	54,500C	
H414	75.5	3593	82.0	3787	51,800C	
H4350	81.0	3540	85.0	3779	52,800C	
H450	83.0	3562	90.0	3753	50,800C	
H380	71.5	3592	78.0	3752	51,200C	
H4831	85.0	3429	92.0	3720	48,200C	
IMR4350	79.0	3479	83.0	3697	51,100C	
IMR4831	80.0	3424	84.0	3676	51,000C	
IMR4064	72.0	3444	75.0	3674	52,200C	
IMR4895	70.0	3480	73.0	3660	52,000C	
IMR7828	88.0	3390	92.0	3640	48,700C	
RL-19	85.0	3444	90.0	3611	48,800C	
IMR4320	71.0	3349	74.0	3609	50,900C	
125-130						
A4350	74.7	3205	83.0	3642	63,000p	Nos BT/3.56″/Fed 215
125-130 con't						
N160	80.3	3179	88.8	3612	53,700p	Nos B-Tip/3.543″/Rem 9½
H4831	84.0	3332	89.0	3590	52,400C	
IMR7828	85.0	3311	90.0	3588	48,900C	
RL-19	85.0	3438	88.0	3549	50,300C	
H4350	78.0	3394	81.0	3545	53,100C	
H450	80.0	3237	87.0	3536	52,400C	
IMR4350	77.0	3344	80.0	3529	52,700C	
H414	73.0	3244	79.0	3509	52,800C	
H380	69.0	3355	75.0	3501	53,300C	
IMR4831	78.0	3212	82.0	3494	51,400C	
H4895	65.5	3277	71.0	3478	54,500C	
IMR4320	69.0	3269	72.0	3419	51,400C	
A3100	76.5	2985	85.0	3392	45,500p	Nos BT/3.56″/Fed 215/(C)
H1000	90.0	2980	94.0	3277	43,600C	
A8700	83.7	2600	93.0	2954	33,700p	Nos BT/3.56″/Fed 215/(C)

▶▶▶▶▶▶▶▶▶▶▶▶▶▶▶▶▶▶▶▶▶▶▶▶▶▶

Never exceed maximum load nor use any load exhibiting signs of excessive pressure. Begin at suggested maximum load and work up carefully.

150

Powder	STARTING Grs.	MV (fps)	MAXIMUM Grs.	MV (fps)	Press. (CUP/psi)	Comments
RL-22	81.0	3306	86.0	3447	54,500C	
RL-19	79.0	3246	84.0	3439	52,700C	
IMR7828	84.0	3161	89.0	3377	50,800C	
H4831	81.0	3177	86.0	3369	51,900C	
H4350	76.0	3256	79.0	3369	53,700C	
H450	77.5	3128	84.0	3350	52,600C	
A4350	71.1	2933	79.0	3333	63,300p	PSPCL/3.535"/Fed 215
H4895	63.5	3122	69.0	3325	54,200C	
IMR4831	77.0	3078	81.0	3324	50,900C	
H380	66.0	3028	72.0	3323	54,700C	
A3100	76.5	2915	85.0	3313	57,800p	PSPCL/3.535"/Fed 215/(C)
IMR4350	75.0	3147	78.0	3304	52,900C	
N165	82.0	2967	90.8	3300	53,700p	Nos B-Tip/3.547"/Rem 9½
H1000	90.0	3081	94.0	3279	48,900C	
H414	68.0	3039	74.0	3262	53,300C	

165-168

Powder	STARTING Grs.	MV (fps)	MAXIMUM Grs.	MV (fps)	Press. (CUP/psi)	Comments
H4831	79.0	3079	84.0	3339	52,800C	
IMR7828	82.0	3094	87.0	3272	51,500C	(165-gr.)
RL-22	79.0	3076	83.0	3267	53,500C	(165-gr.)
RL-19	77.0	3055	82.0	3259	52,200C	(165-gr.)
A3100	76.5	2845	85.0	3233	63,700p	Bns-X/3.555"/Fed 215/(C)
A3100	76.5	2838	85.0	3225	60,400p	PSPCL/3.56"/Fed 215/(C)
H1000	88.0	3043	93.0	3224	52,100C	
N165	80.9	2823	89.6	3216	53,700p	Spr SPBT/3.555"/Rem 9½
IMR4831	76.0	2990	80.0	3184	52,400C	(165-gr.)
H450	74.5	2992	81.0	3171	53,600C	
A4350	68.9	2790	76.5	3171	62,900p	Bns-X/3.555"/Fed 215
A4350	69.3	2784	77.0	3164	61,200p	PSPCL/3.560"/Fed 215
H4350	73.0	3030	76.0	3161	52,700C	
IMR4350	72.0	3009	75.0	3151	53,100C	(165-gr.)
H4895	60.5	2892	66.0	3110	53,400C	
H380	63.5	2915	68.0	3066	53,700C	
H414	64.5	2782	70.0	3038	53,400C	

180

Powder	STARTING Grs.	MV (fps)	MAXIMUM Grs.	MV (fps)	Press. (CUP/psi)	Comments
IMR7828	80.0	2970	85.0	3200	53,100C	
RL-22	78.0	3055	82.0	3169	54,400C	
H1000	86.0	3005	91.0	3152	52,000C	
A3100	74.7	2765	83.0	3142	64,800p	Bns-X/3.56"/Fed 215/(C)
A3100	73.8	2761	82.0	3137	64,300p	Nos BT/3.56"/Fed 215/(C)
H4831	74.5	2901	81.0	3127	55,100C	
N165	78.6	2756	86.7	3079	53,700p	Hdy SP/3.555"/Rem 9½
RL-19	74.0	2898	79.0	3075	50,900C	
A4350	67.1	2692	74.5	3059	63,100p	Nos BT/3.56"/Fed 215
IMR4350	71.0	2900	74.0	3040	52,900C	
IMR4831	74.0	2893	78.0	3014	52,200C	
A4350	66.2	2643	73.5	3003	61,800p	Bns-X/3.56"/Fed 215
H450	70.0	2714	76.0	2988	54,300C	
N170			84.0	2985	54,147p	Hdy BTSP
H870			92.0	2949	47,100C	
H380	59.0	2818	64.0	2900	54,300C	

190

Powder	STARTING Grs.	MV (fps)	MAXIMUM Grs.	MV (fps)	Press. (CUP/psi)	Comments
IMR7828	77.0	2875	81.0	3119	52,600C	
RL-22	75.0	2864	80.0	3060	51,200C	
H1000	81.0	2848	86.0	3052	53,100C	
H870			92.0	3040	49,400C	
RL-19	72.0	2771	77.0	2990	50,400C	
N170			84.0	2961	56,279p	Hdy BTSP
H4831	74.0	2792	78.0	2924	52,900C	
IMR4831	71.0	2651	75.0	2880	52,400C	
H450	72.0	2711	74.0	2860	51,200C	
IMR4350	68.0	2644	72.0	2859	53,400C	
H4350	69.0	2699	72.0	2841	53,400C	

200

Powder	STARTING Grs.	MV (fps)	MAXIMUM Grs.	MV (fps)	Press. (CUP/psi)	Comments
H870			92.0	3094	50,300C	
RL-22	73.0	2814	78.0	2989	53,500C	
A3100	72.0	2629	80.0	2987	63,800p	Nos Part/3.555"/Fed 215/(C)
RL-19	70.0	2825	75.0	2972	54,000C	
N165	74.8	2642	83.1	2949	53,700p	Sra HPBT/3.555"/Rem 9½
A4350	65.7	2589	73.0	2942	65,000p	Nos Part/3.555"/Fed 215
H1000	75.0	2728	81.0	2897	54,000C	
H4831	72.0	2758	75.0	2880	51,800C	
A8700	83.7	2453	93.0	2787	47,500p	Nos Part/3.555"/Fed 215/(C)
IMR4350	67.0	2590	70.0	2774	55,000C	
H4350	68.0	2598	71.0	2770	55,000C	
IMR4831	70.0	2554	74.0	2766	53,900C	
H450	64.5	2512	70.0	2744	52,900C	

220-225

Powder	STARTING Grs.	MV (fps)	MAXIMUM Grs.	MV (fps)	Press. (CUP/psi)	Comments
H870			92.0	3008	52,600C	
A3100	69.3	2473	77.0	2810	63,900p	Sra FP/3.53"/Fed 215
RL-22	70.0	2543	75.0	2785	55,000C	
N170			82.0	2779	59,119p	Hdy RN
A8700	83.7	2430	93.0	2761	64,700p	Sra FP/3.53"/Fed 215/(C)
H1000	74.0	2561	80.0	2717	52,600C	
H4350	65.0	2560	68.0	2711	54,300C	
RL-19	66.0	2572	71.0	2709	53,100C	
H4831	70.0	2586	74.0	2707	52,000C	
A4350	62.1	2379	69.0	2703	62,500p	Sra FP/3.53"/Fed 215
IMR4831	67.0	2530	71.0	2688	53,600C	
IMR4350	64.0	2520	67.0	2656	54,000C	

250

Powder	STARTING Grs.	MV (fps)	MAXIMUM Grs.	MV (fps)	Press. (CUP/psi)	Comments
H870	84.0	2562	88.0	2704	52,600C	
RL-22	67.0	2480	72.0	2633	54,500C	
H1000	71.0	2426	77.0	2571	54,000C	
IMR7828	68.0	2380	73.0	2556	51,200C	
RL-19	62.0	2378	67.0	2516	52,000C	
H4831	67.0	2331	71.0	2507	52,200C	

Never exceed maximum load nor use any load exhibiting signs of excessive pressure. Begin at suggested starting load and work up carefully.

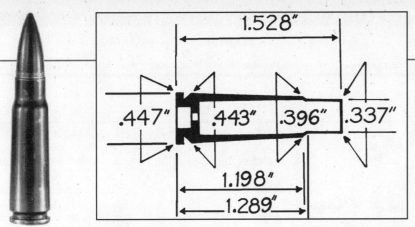

7.62x39
(7.62x39 Russian)

Case: IMI
Primer: Large Rifle
Barrel: 20″ Accurate
    24″ Hodgdon
    16½″ Vihtavuori

Bullet Diameter: 0.311″
Maximum Case Length: 1.528″
Trim to Length: 1.523″
Maximum Cartridge OAL: 2.200″
Minimum Cartridge OAL: 2.170″

When the Soviets encountered the 7.92 Kurz (what we would call a short 8mm carbine cartridge), they were evidently impressed and embarked on rapid development of their own similar chambering. This program culminated in the M43, which we now know as the 7.62x39.

This thoroughly modern high-pressure cartridge comes close to duplicating 30-30 performance in a much smaller package. Since rifles so chambered can use spitzer bullets, it can deliver 30-30 energy levels at ranges beyond 100 yards. This would suggest it as a splendid choice for shorter range hunting on smaller species of deer and similar animals. However, because of limitations in usable bullet weight, this cannot be a good choice for any larger species and use on black bear seems questionable.

Proper bullet diameter is closer to 0.311″ than to 0.308″. Nevertheless, useful loads can often be concocted using standard 0.308″ bullets. Some early domestic commercial chamberings featured standard 0.308″ bores, and one should slug the barrel before assuming 0.311″ bullets will work properly. Generally, throat diameter in such chambers will accommodate larger bullets without creating an unsafe condition, but accuracy can be dismal. If in doubt, make a proper chamber cast and ensure your loads have sufficient case-neck-to-throat clearance (minimum of 0.002″) to allow the case to properly release the bullet. If this is not the situation use only 0.308″ bullets.

This case is the basis for the current crop of the world's most accurate benchrest cartridges. Despite its small size, this is a high-pressure cartridge and appropriate care should be exercised in all loading.

Case capacity with a 130-grain bullet, seated normally, is about 31.4 grains of water. RL-7, H335 A1680, H322 and N120 work well in this chambering.

7.62x39mm LOADING DATA (7.62x39mm RUSSIAN)

Powder	STARTING Grs.	MV (fps)	MAXIMUM Grs.	MV (fps)	Press. (CUP/psi)	Comments
100						
A1680	25.7	2325	28.5	2642	47,100C	Spr .308″ RN/1.95″/ Rem 9½
XMP5744			23.0	2374		Spr .308″ RN/1.95″/ Rem 9½
A2015BR	25.7	1994	28.5	2266	39,400C	Spr .308″ RN/1.95″/ Rem 9½/(C)
100 con't						
A2230	26.6	1959	29.5	2226	42,400C	Spr .308″ RN/1.95″/ Rem 9½/(C)
A2460	26.6	1922	29.5	2184	42,600C	Spr .308″ RN/1.95″/ Rem 9½/(C)

> **Caution:** Loads exceeding SAAMI OAL Maximum must be verified for bullet-to-rifling clearance and magazine functioning. Where a specific primer or bullet is indicated those components must be used, no substitutions! Where only a maximum load is shown, reduce starting load 10%, unless otherwise specified.
>
> **Key:** (C) = compressed charge; C = CUP; p = psi; Plink = Plinker; Bns = Barnes; Hdy = Hornady; Lap = Lapua; Nos = Nosler; Rem = Remington; Sra = Sierra; Spr = Speer; Win = Winchester.

Never exceed maximum load nor use any load exhibiting signs of excessive pressure. Begin at suggested starting load and work up carefully.

205

Powder	—STARTING— Grs.	MV (fps)	—MAXIMUM— Grs.	MV (fps)	Press. (CUP/psi)	Comments
110						
W680	25.5	2390	26.5	2559	42,500C	
A1680	24.8	2241	27.5	2547	48,300C	Sra .308" HP/2.115"/ Rem 9½
RL-7	25.0	2327	26.0	2440	31,000C	
IMR4198	24.0	2204	26.0	2364	44,400C	
XMP5744			22.5	2294	48,900C	Sra .308" HP/Rem 9½
IMR4227	18.0	2098	20.0	2275	45,000C	
A2015BR	25.7	1998	28.5	2271	41,500C	Sra .308" HP/2.115"/ Rem 9½/(C)
IMR3031	26.0	2070	27.5	2260	34,400C	
Her2400	17.5	2143	18.5	2249	43,400C	
A2230	26.6	1958	29.5	2225	46,000C	Sra .308" HP/2.115"/ Rem 9½/(C)
A2460	26.6	1931	29.5	2194	45,400C	Sra .308" HP/2.115"/ Rem 9½/(C)
122-125						
N120	23.2	2258	26.5	2500	53,952p	Hdy FMJ
W680	23.0	2321	25.0	2480	44,000C	
N120			26.7	2460	46,412p	Sako FMJ 127A
H335	30.0	2219	31.5	2408	40,900C	
H4198	24.5	2190	26.5	2378	40,400C	
A1680	23.0	2084	25.5	2368	48,500C	Spr .311" SP/2.195"/ Rem 9½
N120			26.7	2360	43,511p	Sako SP 134A
IMR4198	23.0	2110	25.0	2351	46,000C	
BL-C(2)	30.0	2155	31.5	2349	38,800C	
N130			26.4	2330	43,200p	Win FMJ/SP
H322	28.0	2210	29.0	2323	35,400C	
RL-7	24.5	2180	25.5	2314	36,000C	
A2015BR	25.7	2032	28.5	2309	47,700C	Spr .311" SP/2.195"/ Rem 9½/(C)
IMR3031	25.0	2144	27.0	2257	37,100C	
H4895	28.0	2171	29.0	2249	33,600C	
XMP5744			22.0	2245	48,100C	Hdy SP (123-gr.)/ 2.18"/Rem 9½/(C)
A2230	26.6	1943	29.5	2208	49,800C	Spr .311" SP/2.195"/ Rem 9½/(C)
A2460	26.6	1915	29.5	2176	46,600C	Spr .311" SP/2.195"/ Rem 9½/(C)
IMR4227	17.5	1982	19.5	2149	44,500C	
XMP5744			21.5	2145		Spr .311" SP/2.195"/ Rem 9½
Her2400	16.5	2007	17.5	2119	43,000C	

Powder	—STARTING— Grs.	MV (fps)	—MAXIMUM— Grs.	MV (fps)	Press. (CUP/psi)	Comments
130						
A1680	22.5	2020	25.0	2296	47,900C	Hdy .308" SSP/2.18"/ Rem 9½
A2015BR	25.2	1947	28.0	2213	45,300C	Hdy .308" SSP/2.18"/ Rem 9½/(C)
A2460	26.1	1866	29.0	2120	47,000C	Hdy .308" SSP/2.18"/ Rem 9½/(C)
A2230	25.2	1843	28.0	2094	47,000C	Hdy .308" SSP/2.18"/ Rem 9½/(C)
XMP5744			20.5	2051	45,500C	Hdy .308" SSP/2.18"/ Rem 9½/(C)
150						
W680	21.0	2089	23.0	2240	43,500C	
H322	27.0	2084	28.5	2192	40,400C	
H4895	27.0	2080	28.0	2154	39,300C	
H335	27.0	2055	29.0	2132	42,500C	
H4198	22.5	1947	24.5	2122	39,800C	
RL-7	23.0	2003	24.0	2110	40,400C	
IMR4198	21.0	1940	23.0	2109	46,100C	
IMR3031	24.0	1871	26.0	2101	38,800C	
BL-C(2)	27.0	1904	29.5	2090	40,400C	
A2015BR	23.4	1823	26.0	2072	46,500C	Sra .311" SP/2.18"/ Rem 9½/(C)
A1680	20.3	1808	22.5	2055	49,000C	Sra .311" SP/2.18"/ Rem 9½
Her2400	15.0	1891	16.0	1989	42,400C	
A2230	24.3	1739	27.0	1976	49,500C	Sra .311" SP/2.18"/ Rem 9½/(C)
A2460	24.3	1721	27.0	1956	47,600C	Sra .311" SP/2.18"/ Rem 9½
IMR4227	16.5	1749	18.5	1912	47,000C	
XMP5744			19.5	1900	46,400C	Sra .311" SP/2.18"/ Rem 9½/(C)

Caution: **Loads exceeding SAAMI OAL Maximum must be verified for bullet-to-rifling clearance and magazine functioning. Where a specific primer or bullet is indicated those components must be used, no substitutions! Where only a maximum load is shown, reduce starting load 10%, unless otherwise specified.**

Key: (C) = compressed charge; C = CUP; p = psi; Plink = Plinker; Bns = Barnes; Hdy = Hornady; Lap = Lapua; Nos = Nosler; Rem = Remington; Sra = Sierra; Spr = Speer; Win = Winchester.

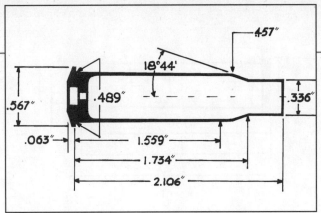

7.62x54R
(7.62x53R)

Case: Norma
Primer: Large Rifle
Barrel: 24″ Accurate
    26″ Vihtavuori
Bullet Diameter: 0.308″-0.311″
(Slug your rifle's barrel to determine correct bullet size to use.)

Maximum Case Length: 2.106″
Trim to Length: 2.090″
Maximum Recommended OAL: 2.990″
Maximum Cartridge OAL: 2.990″
Minimum Cartridge OAL:
    Bullet Dependent

Developed for the Czar's army, this chambering was introduced in 1891 along with a round-nose loading. Belatedly, in 1909, a 150-grain spitzer loading was standardized. Like many near-standard 30-caliber chamberings, bore dimensions have never been solidly established worldwide. It is not uncommon to find bores of 0.308″ diameter, but 0.311″ is the correct size, and larger, circa WWII, bores are common.

Useful loads using standard 0.308″ bullets are generally reasonably accurate in almost any barrel. This is because the grooves are usually deeper than standard. Generally, throat diameter in the tighter bores will accommodate 0.311″ bullets without creating an unsafe condition. Nevertheless, before loading 0.311″ bullets, slug your rifle's bore to

ensure the grooves are 0.310″ to 0.311″ in diameter. If not, we can only recommend loads with 0.308″ bullets.

Case capacity is similar to the 308 Winchester, but pressures reflect the era of the chambering's birth. Performance is just about midway between the 30-40 Krag and the 303 British. The Czar's chambering is more than up to the task of hunting almost any species of big game. More surprisingly, Soviet marksmen set many world records for long-range marksmanship with this round, and until quite recently it was a force in such competition worldwide.

This is the basis for an entire genre of Soviet and Scandinavian wildcat chamberings. A4350 is a noted performer in this rimmed case.

7.62x54Rmm LOADING DATA (7.62x53Rmm)

Powder	Grs.	MV (fps)	Grs.	MV (fps)	Press. (CUP/psi)	Comments
Lead 180 Lyman 311467						
A4350	45.0	2146	50.0	2439	40,400p	2.83″/CCI 250
A3100	47.7	2062	53.0	2343	37,100p	2.83″/CCI 250/(C)
A8700	49.5	1601	55.0	1819	26,100p	2.83″/CCI 250/(C)
150						
A4350	48.6	2352	54.0	2673	44,100p	Sra SP/2.85″/CCI 250/(C)
A3100	49.5	2169	55.0	2465	36,000p	Sra SP/2.85″/CCI 250/(C)
A8700	52.2	1670	58.0	1898	24,700p	Sra SP/2.85″/CCI 250/(C)
170						
N140			46.0	2670	49,313p	Lapua FMJ D46

Powder	Grs.	MV (fps)	Grs.	MV (fps)	Press. (CUP/psi)	Comments
180						
N140			44.8	2610	49,313p	Sako SP 226A
A4350	45.9	2197	51.0	2497	43,000p	Sra SP/2.9″/CCI 250
A3100	49.5	2162	55.0	2457	42,600p	Sra SP/2.9″/CCI 250/(C)
A8700	51.3	1596	57.0	1814	25,300p	Sra SP/2.9″/CCI 250/(C)
185						
N140			44.9	2560	49,313p	Lapua FMJ D46
200						
N160			50.9	2460	47,862p	Lapua FMJ D166
N140			44.0	2440	49,313p	Sako SP 227A

303 British

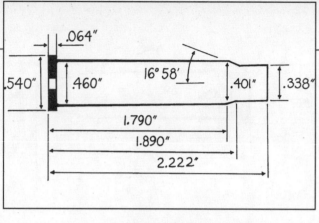

Case: Remington
Primer: Large Rifle
Barrel: 24″ Accurate
24″ Hodgdon
24″ Vihtavuori

Bullet Diameter: 0.311″
Maximum Case Length: 2.222″
Trim to Length: 2.212″
Maximum Cartridge OAL: 3.075″
Minimum Cartridge OAL: 2.915″

Originally a blackpowder chambering featuring a 215-grain round-nose bullet with a compressed charge of the powder of the day, the 303 British was adopted in 1888 for the British Empire worldwide. Almost immediately, 1892, a cordite (a type of smokeless powder based on nitro-glycerin) loading was adopted and ballistics were improved by about 200 fps though at a lower chamber pressure! In 1910, a spitzer flat-base 174-grain loading was standardized and velocity was increased significantly.

Rifles for the 303 British have long been made in the U.S. with the 1895 Winchester being a prime example. This became the standard shoulder gun of the Canadian Mounted Police, where it accorded a splendid record of performance under adverse conditions.

With pressure standards in the moderate range and suffi-cient usable capacity, the 303 British comes quite close to 308 Winchester performance—some European factory loads achieve performance indistinguishable from any 308 Winchester factory load. Obviously, with the proper bullet, the 303 British is a capable hunting chambering for any but the largest species worldwide. Limited velocity suggests trajectory-induced range limitations, but this is certainly a 300-yard hunting chambering.

The author cannot suggest any good explanation for the striking similarity of 30-40 Krag and 303 British cases. This appears to have been a coincidence. Nevertheless, dimensional differences are practically nonexistent.

Case capacity with a 150-grain bullet, seated normally, is about 50.6 grains of water. H335, A2015BR, BL-C(2), A2520 and H414 are good 303 performers.

303 BRITISH LOADING DATA

Powder	STARTING Grs.	MV (fps)	MAXIMUM Grs.	MV (fps)	Press. (CUP/psi)	Comments

Lead 180 Lyman 311467 (Sized/0.312″)

Powder	Grs.	MV (fps)	Grs.	MV (fps)	Press. (CUP/psi)	Comments
A2495BR	39.6	2226	44.0	2529	39,500C	2.93″/CCI 250
A2460	36.0	2182	40.0	2480	40,600C	2.93″/CCI 250
A2015BR	34.2	2167	38.0	2462	41,400C	2.93″/CCI 250
A2230	35.1	2164	39.0	2459	42,500C	2.93″/CCI 250
A2520	36.0	2154	40.0	2448	40,300C	2.93″/CCI 250
A2700	37.8	2035	42.0	2312	41,400C	2.93″/CCI 250
A4350	41.4	2026	46.0	2302	36,000C	2.93″/CCI 250/(C)
XMP5744			28.0	2159	40,700C	2.93″/CCI 250
A3100	41.4	1815	46.0	2063	28,700C	2.93″/CCI 250/(C)
A8700	43.2	1434	48.0	1630	26,500C	2.93″/CCI 250/(C)

100

Powder	Grs.	MV (fps)	Grs.	MV (fps)	Press. (CUP/psi)	Comments
H4198	32.0	2561	36.0	2917		(0.308″ Dia.)
H380	46.0	2596	48.0	2759		(0.308″ Dia.)
H4895	42.0	2503	45.0	2750		(0.308″ Dia.)

100 con't

Powder	Grs.	MV (fps)	Grs.	MV (fps)	Press. (CUP/psi)	Comments
BL-C(2)	44.0	2539	46.0	2705		(0.308″ Dia.)
H335	43.0	2512	45.0	2680		(0.308″ Dia.)
H4227	15.0	1424	17.0	1666		(0.308″ Dia.)

125-130

Powder	Grs.	MV (fps)	Grs.	MV (fps)	Press. (CUP/psi)	Comments
A2015BR	41.4	2706	46.0	3075	44,200C	Spr SP/2.87″/CCI 250
A2520	42.8	2657	47.5	3019	44,800C	Spr SP/2.87″/CCI 250
A2460	41.4	2622	46.0	2979	42,500C	Spr SP/2.87″/CCI 250
A2230	39.6	2561	44.0	2910	42,600C	Spr SP/2.87″/CCI 250
H335	45.0	2714	49.0	2890		(130-gr.)
A2495BR	43.2	2541	48.0	2887	35,900C	Spr SP/2.87″/CCI 250/(C)
BL-C(2)	46.0	2651	50.0	2886	37,300C	26″ Bbl (130-gr.)
A2700	45.0	2419	50.0	2749	43,400C	Spr SP/2.87″/CCI 250
XMP5744			32.5	2660	45,000C	Spr SP/2.87″/CCI 250
H4895	39.5	2484	43.0	2650		(130-gr.)

Never exceed maximum load nor use any load exhibiting signs of excessive pressure. Begin at suggested starting load and work up carefully.

Powder	Grs.	MV (fps)	Grs.	MV (fps)	Press. (CUP/psi)	Comments
125-130 con't						
H414	45.0	2431	49.0	2617		(130-gr.)
H4350	45.0	2272	48.0	2430		(130-gr.)
150						
BL-C(2)	45.0	2604	49.0	2783	45,900C	26" Bbl
A2520	41.4	2437	46.0	2769	45,000C	Hdy SP/3.01"/CCI 250
H335	44.0	2574	48.0	2729		
A2460	39.6	2401	44.0	2728	42,900C	Hdy SP/3.01"/CCI 250
A2495BR	41.4	2400	46.0	2727	42,500C	Hdy SP/3.01"/CCI 250/(C)
A2015BR	36.9	2388	41.0	2714	42,300C	Hdy SP/3.01"/CCI 250
A2230	38.7	2380	43.0	2704	43,600C	Hdy SP/3.01"/CCI 250
A2700	43.2	2254	48.0	2561	43,200C	Hdy SP/3.01"/CCI 250/(C)
H4350	45.0	2321	48.0	2501		
H414	44.0	2320	48.0	2482		
H4895	38.5	2288	42.0	2479		
H380	40.5	2287	44.0	2443		
XMP5744			31.0	2413	45,000C	Hdy SP/3.01"/CCI 250
A4350	41.4	1984	46.0	2254	30,100C	Hdy SP/3.01"/CCI 250/(C)

Caution: Loads exceeding SAAMI OAL Maximum must be verified for bullet-to-rifling clearance and magazine functioning. Where a specific primer or bullet is indicated those components must be used, no substitutions! Where only a maximum load is shown, reduce starting load 10%, unless otherwise specified.

Key: (C) = compressed charge; C = CUP; p = psi; Plink = Plinker; Bns = Barnes; Hdy = Hornady; Lap = Lapua; Nos = Nosler; Rem = Remington; Sra = Sierra; Spr = Speer; Win = Winchester.

Powder	Grs.	MV (fps)	Grs.	MV (fps)	Press. (CUP/psi)	Comments
180						
A2520	39.6	2260	44.0	2568	45,000C	Sra SP/3.0"/CCI 250
N140			41.7	2540	46,412p	Sako SP 131A
A2495BR	39.6	2181	44.0	2478	42,700C	Sra SP/3.0"/CCI 250
A2230	36.0	2175	40.0	2472	43,800C	Sra SP/3.0"/CCI 250
A2460	36.5	2149	40.5	2442	41,500C	Sra SP/3.0"/CCI 250
A2700	41.4	2137	46.0	2428	44,100C	Sra SP/3.0"/CCI 250
A2015BR	34.2	2130	38.0	2420	42,300C	Sra SP/3.0"/CCI 250
H4350	43.0	2209	46.0	2333		
H335	38.0	2189	41.0	2323		
H4895	37.0	2121	40.0	2295		
H450	46.0	2145	50.0	2281		
A4350	41.4	2006	46.0	2280	35,800C	Sra SP/3.0"/CCI 250/(C)
H380	38.5	2133	42.0	2276		
H4831	43.0	2027	47.0	2238		
XMP5744			29.0	2189	44,900C	Sra SP/3.0"/CCI 250
A3100	41.4	1797	46.0	2042	30,800C	Sra SP/3.0"/CCI 250/(C)
215						
H414	39.5	2048	43.0	2114		
H4350	40.0	1920	43.0	2090		
H335	36.0	1907	39.0	2047		
H4831	42.0	1800	45.0	2001		

Never exceed maximum load nor use any load exhibiting signs of excessive pressure. Begin at suggested starting load and work up carefully.

7.65x53
Belgian Mauser

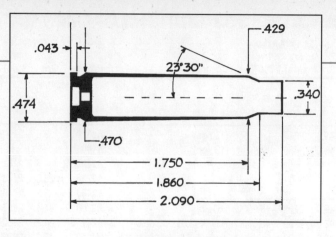

Case: Norma
Primer: Remington 9½
Barrel: 24″ Accurate
29″ Hodgdon
Bullet Diameter: 0.311-0.313″

Maximum Case Length: 2.090″
Trim to Length: 2.080″
Maximum Cartridge OAL: 2.970″
Minimum Cartridge OAL:
Bullet Dependent

Commonly known as the 7.65mm Belgian Mauser, this circa 1889 design was adopted by a host of South American countries in the first few years after its introduction. Widely chambered, it was also loaded commercially in this country until about 1938.

Considering the age of the earliest rifles so chambered, current factory loads offer a surprising level of performance because of equally surprising pressure levels. Excepting a slight increase in loaded round length, this cartridge is so similar in appearance to the 308 Winchester as to be easily

confused. It has a slightly longer body, with a slightly shorter neck with a bit more body taper. Nevertheless with the same weight bullet, seated normally, capacity is considerably greater than the 308 Winchester—primarily due to a longer overall length.

The result is that, even though it works at a lower pressure, the 7.65x53mm very nearly duplicates 308 Winchester performance. This is certainly a capable hunting cartridge for any application where the 308 Winchester is appropriate.

7.65x53mm BELGIUM MAUSER LOADING DATA

Powder	—STARTING— Grs.	MV (fps)	—MAXIMUM— Grs.	MV (fps)	Press. (CUP/psi)	Comments
Lead 152 Lyman 311466						
A2700	39.6	2119	44.0	2408	35,000p	2.73″
A2495BR	37.8	2030	42.0	2307	25,700p	2.73″
A4350	42.3	1950	47.0	2216	23,500p	2.73″
A3100	43.2	1786	48.0	2029	18,200p	2.73″
A8700	47.3	1537	52.5	1747	17,100p	2.73″
150						
A2495BR	42.8	2436	47.5	2768	48,800p	Hdy SP/2.85″/(C)
A2520	41.9	2431	46.5	2763	50,300p	Hdy SP/2.85″
A2230	40.5	2411	45.0	2740	48,200p	Hdy SP/2.85″
A2460	40.5	2377	45.0	2701	48,600p	Hdy SP/2.85″
A2700	46.4	2373	51.5	2697	46,400p	Hdy SP/2.85″/(C)
A2015BR	37.4	2367	41.5	2690	47,900p	Hdy SP/2.85″
BL-C(2)	39.5	2378	43.0	2650		
H414	45.0	2491	49.0	2648		
H335	39.0	2353	43.0	2639		
A4350	43.2	2047	48.0	2326	30,600p	Hdy SP/2.85″/(C)

Powder	—STARTING— Grs.	MV (fps)	—MAXIMUM— Grs.	MV (fps)	Press. (CUP/psi)	Comments
175						
H4831			53.0	2456		
H4350	43.0	2266	47.0	2454		
H414	43.0	2332	47.0	2452		
H380	41.5	2232	45.0	2447		
180						
A2520	40.5	2262	45.0	2570	51,100p	Sra SP/2.85″
A2495BR	41.4	2237	46.0	2542	47,500p	Sra SP/2.85″/(C)
A2460	38.7	2217	43.0	2519	49,700p	Sra SP/2.85″
A2230	38.3	2203	42.5	2503	49,300p	Sra SP/2.85″
A2015BR	36.0	2172	40.0	2468	48,700p	Sra SP/2.85″
A2700	43.2	2167	48.0	2463	45,100p	Sra SP/2.85″/(C)

Caution: Loads exceeding SAAMI OAL Maximum must be verified for bullet-to-rifling clearance and magazine functioning. Where a specific primer or bullet is indicated those components must be used, no substitutions! Where only a maximum load is shown, reduce starting load 10%, unless otherwise specified.

Key: (C) = compressed charge; C = CUP; p = psi; Plink = Plinker; Bns = Barnes; Hdy = Hornady; Lap = Lapua; Nos = Nosler; Rem = Remington; Sra = Sierra; Spr = Speer; Win = Winchester.

Never exceed maximum load nor use any load exhibiting signs of excessive pressure. Begin at suggested starting load and work up carefully.

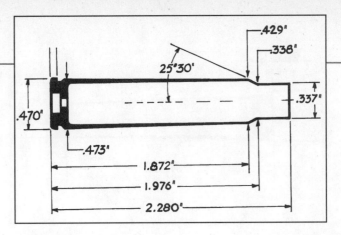

7.7x58
Japanese
(Arisaka)

Case: Norma
Primer: Large Rifle
Barrel: 24″ Accurate/26″ Hodgdon
Bullet Diameter: 0.311″
Maximum Case Length: 2.280″

Trim to Length: 2.270″
Maximum Cartridge OAL
(Recommended): 3.130″
Minimum Cartridge OAL:
Bullet Dependent

In response to concerns over the limited performance offered by the 6.5 Arisaka, the 7.7 was adopted as Japan's standard military shoulder arm in 1939. However, before all of the 6.5-chambered guns could be replaced, Japan embroiled itself in war. Thereafter, with increasing war-time demands, the replacement program was suspended. No doubt the problems associated with supplying ammunition in two calibers complicated Japan's efforts of conquest.

An interesting rumor of WWII was that Japan designed the 7.7x58mm rifle expressly so that 30-06 ammunition could be used in it; conversely, 7.7x58mm ammunition could not be used in 30-06-chambered rifles! Of course, this is nonsense. It would be impossible to chamber any standard 30-06 load in any standard 7.7x58mm chamber. However, the converse could possi-

bly be accomplished with potentially devastating consequences, the result of a combination of an oversize bullet and an extreme headspace condition. However, most 7.7x58mm ammunition will not freely chamber in any standard 30-06 chamber because the 7.7x58mm case head is slightly larger in diameter.

Evidently, the Japanese military establishment was extremely cautious because, despite the very high level of strength and quality of 7.7x58mm-chambered Japanese military rifles and the thoroughly modern design of the gun and ammunition, pressures were held to very modest levels. Therefore, performance is limited to about that of the 303 British, despite considerable usable capacity.

Usable case capacity is somewhat less than the 30-06. H414, H335 and H4895 are noted performers in the 7.7x58mm.

◼ 7.7x58mm JAPANESE (ARISAKA) LOADING DATA ◼

Powder	—STARTING— Grs.	MV (fps)	—MAXIMUM— Grs.	MV (fps)	Press. (CUP/psi)	Comments
150						
A2700	48.5	2602	51.0	2768	46,400p	Hdy SP/3.175″/ CCI 200
A4350	46.8	2346	52.0	2666	39,500p	Hdy SP/3.175″/ CCI 200/(C)
H4895	41.0	2337	44.0	2529		
H4350	48.0	2330	51.0	2514		
H335	41.0	2309	44.0	2499		
BL-C(2)	41.0	2289	44.0	2487		
H380	44.0	2169	47.0	2461		
H4831	50.0	2180	55.0	2445		
H414	45.0	2155	48.0	2424		
A3100	46.8	2132	52.0	2423	31,000p	Hdy SP/3.175″/ CCI 200/(C)
H450	51.0	2210	55.0	2420		

Powder	—STARTING— Grs.	MV (fps)	—MAXIMUM— Grs.	MV (fps)	Press. (CUP/psi)	Comments
180						
A4350	46.8	2240	52.0	2545	42,300p	Sra SP/3.15″/ CCI 200/(C)
A2700	44.2	2318	46.5	2466	45,700p	Sra SP/3.15″/CCI 200
H4350	44.0	2090	47.0	2309		
A3100	46.8	2024	52.0	2300	31,900p	Sra SP/3.15″/ CCI 200/(C)
H380	42.0	2090	45.0	2257		
H450	47.0	2049	50.0	2247		
H414	43.0	2070	46.0	2234		
H4831	46.0	2011	50.0	2233		
H4895	37.0	2060	40.0	2230		
H335	37.0	2077	40.0	2202		
BL-C(2)	37.0	2054	40.0	2191		

Never exceed maximum load nor use any load exhibiting signs of excessive pressure. Begin at suggested starting load and work up carefully.

211

32-20

Winchester
(32-20 WCF)

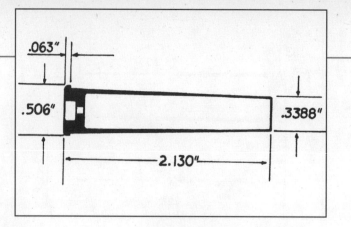

.063″
.506″
.3388″
2.130″

Case: Remington
Primer: CCI 400
Barrel: 22″ Accurate
Bullet Diameter: 0.312″-0.313″

Maximum Length: 1.315″
Trim to Length: 1.310″
Maximum Cartridge OAL: 1.592″
Minimum Cartridge OAL: 1.540″

Introduced in 1882, chambered in the Model 73 Winchester rifle and carbine, the 32-20 gained considerable popularity and was also chambered in the Colt Single Action Army revolver. Launching a 100-grain lead bullet at about 1200 fps, recoil is minuscule but this cartridge is a superior small game load.

Perhaps amazingly, the 32-20 is still chambered in a Marlin lever action plus several types of handguns and factory ammunition is available. The latter is no small testimony to the one-time popularity of this cartridge; the number of Colt revolvers so fitted was enormous.

These loads are intended only for use in the Model 92 Winchester and other more modern guns safe for use with smokeless powder loads.

With an 86-grain bullet, seated normally, usable capacity is about 17.1 grains of water. A1680 is a good choice for high-pressure loads in the 32-20, while XMP5744 is ideal for low-pressure, blackpowder-equivalent loads.

32-20 WINCHESTER LOADING DATA (32-20 WCF)

Powder	STARTING Grs.	MV (fps)	MAXIMUM Grs.	MV (fps)	Press. (CUP/psi)	Comments
Lead 100 Lyman 313631						
A2015BR	16.2	1575	17.0	1676	22,200C	1.585″/CCI 400/(C)
A1680	13.3	1545	14.0	1644	21,400C	1.585″/CCI 400
No.9	8.1	1454	8.5	1547	21,700C	1.585″/CCI 400
No.7	6.7	1357	7.0	1444	21,600C	1.585″/CCI 400
No.5	5.7	1350	6.0	1436	23,300C	1.585″/CCI 400
XMP5744			9.3	1236		*
90						
A1680	15.7	1794	16.5	1909	21,700C	Sra JHC/1.565″/CCI 400
A2015BR	17.1	1645	18.0	1750	20,000C	Sra JHC/1.565″/CCI 400/(C)
No.9	8.7	1568	9.2	1668	22,000C	Sra JHC/1.565″/CCI 400
No.7	7.4	1497	7.8	1593	22,000C	Sra JHC/1.565″/CCI 400
No.5	5.9	1383	6.2	1471	21,100C	Sra JHC/1.565″/CCI 400
XMP5744			9.7	1253		Sra JHC/1.565″/CCI 400/*

Powder	STARTING Grs.	MV (fps)	MAXIMUM Grs.	MV (fps)	Press. (CUP/psi)	Comments
100						
A1680	14.7	1738	15.5	1849	23,600C	Hdy XTP/1.565″/CCI 400
A2015BR	16.6	1653	17.5	1758	22,000C	Hdy XTP/1.565″/CCI 400/(C)
No.9	8.4	1485	8.8	1580	22,800C	Hdy XTP/1.565″/CCI 400
No.7	7.0	1400	7.4	1489	22,700C	Hdy XTP/1.565″/CCI 400
No.5	5.7	1332	6.0	1417	23,800C	Hdy XTP/1.565″/CCI 400
XMP5744			9.5	1207		*

* Safe for use in Model 1873 Winchester rifles in sound condition.

Caution: Loads exceeding SAAMI OAL Maximum must be verified for bullet-to-rifling clearance and magazine functioning. Where a specific primer or bullet is indicated those components must be used, no substitutions! Where only a maximum load is shown, reduce starting load 10%, unless otherwise specified.

Key: (C) = compressed charge; C = CUP; p = psi; Plink = Plinker; Bns = Barnes; Hdy = Hornady; Lap = Lapua; Nos = Nosler; Rem = Remington; Sra = Sierra; Spr = Speer; Win = Winchester.

Never exceed maximum load nor use any load exhibiting signs of excessive pressure. Begin at suggested starting load and work up carefully.

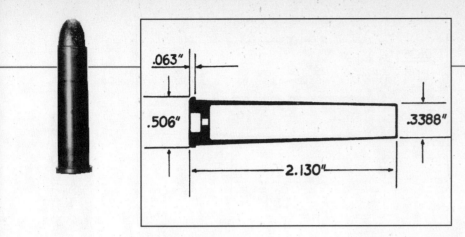

32-40 Winchester (32-40 WCF)

Case: Remington
Primer: Large Rifle
Barrel: 24″ Accurate/23″ Hodgdon
Bullet Diameter: 0.321″

Maximum Case Length: 2.130″
Trim to Length: 2.125″
Maximum Cartridge OAL: 2.50″
Minimum Cartridge OAL: 2.46″

Introduced in 1884, the original factory loading featured a 165-grain bullet over 40 grains of blackpowder. Performance was then considered adequate for smaller species of deer and similar game, but range was seriously limited as a result of the limited velocity achieved. For many years, Winchester offered a high-velocity smokeless loading, but even that fell well short of modern 30-30 performance—not surprising considering the many old blackpowder guns in existence and the limited strength of domestic iron alloys of the 1880s.

More recently, Winchester has offered commemorative Model 94s chambered for this antique round, and with the best of modern powders, the co-produced modern ammunition can achieve performance quite similar to the 30-30. While likely completely safe, we would recommend against firing any smokeless load in any gun from the 1880s.

H4198 and IMR4198 are good choices for 32-40 loads.

32-40 WINCHESTER LOADING DATA (32-40 WCF)

Powder	STARTING Grs.	MV (fps)	MAXIMUM Grs.	MV (fps)	Press. (CUP/psi)	Comments
Lead Penny's 170						
A2495BR	27.5	1810	30.5	2057	26,200C	2.410″/Rem 9½/(C)
A2015BR	23.4	1787	26.0	2031	28,600C	2.410″/Rem 9½
A2520	26.1	1774	29.0	2016	29,300C	2.410″/Rem 9½
A2460	24.8	1738	27.5	1975	28,800C	2.410″/Rem 9½
A2230	24.3	1712	27.0	1946	27,300C	2.410″/Rem 9½
XMP5744			20.0	1802	28,800C	Rem 9½
170						
A2495BR	28.4	1825	31.5	2074	27,100C	Hdy FP/2.575″/Rem 9½/(C)
A2015BR	24.3	1810	27.0	2057	29,300C	Hdy FP/2.575″/Rem 9½
A2520	27.0	1783	30.0	2026	27,800C	Hdy FP/2.575″/Rem 9½
A2460	25.7	1734	28.5	1971	28,300C	Hdy FP/2.575″/Rem 9½
A2230	24.8	1716	27.5	1950	29,400C	Hdy FP/2.575″/Rem 9½
H335	19.0	1640	23.0	1891		
H4895	16.0	1409	22.0	1864		
H322	15.0	1411	21.0	1837		

Powder	STARTING Grs.	MV (fps)	MAXIMUM Grs.	MV (fps)	Press. (CUP/psi)	Comments
170 con't						
IMR4895	17.0	1519	21.0	1821		
BL-C(2)	20.0	1622	25.0	1806		
W748	21.0	1654	25.0	1792		
IMR3031	16.0	1304	20.0	1777		
XMP5744			20.0	1777	29,400C	Hdy FN/Rem 9½
RL-15	20.0	1554	23.0	1776		
RL-12	19.0	1471	22.0	1774		
H4198	14.0	1339	19.0	1760		
RL-7	15.0	1454	18.0	1699		
IMR4198	13.0	1267	18.0	1688		
W680	14.0	1484	17.0	1670		
H110	11.0	1344	14.0	1594		
W296	11.0	1339	14.0	1592		
H4227	11.0	1163	14.0	1511		
IMR4227	11.0	1154	14.0	1498		
Her2400	10.0	1219	12.0	1475		
SR4759	10.0	1232	13.0	1431		

Never exceed maximum load nor use any load exhibiting signs of excessive pressure. Begin at suggested starting load and work up carefully.

213

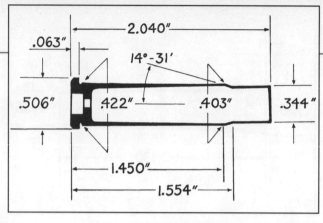

Case: Winchester
Primer: Large Rifle
Barrel: 20″ Hodgdon
      24″ Winchester
Bullet Diameter: 0.321″

Maximum Case Length: 2.040″
Trim to Length: 2.035″
Maximum Cartridge OAL: 2.565″
Minimum Cartridge OAL:
          Bullet Dependent

To quote Winchester's 1916 catalogue, "...a smokeless powder cartridge of larger caliber than the 30-30 and yet not so powerful as the 30 Army...a 170-grain bullet...2112 foot seconds..." Since contemporary 170-grain 30-30 loads generated only 2008 fps, it would seem Winchester had met the demand for a somewhat more powerful chambering. With more bore area and significantly more usable powder capacity, the 32 Special, if loaded to equal pressure, can generate greater than 10 percent more muzzle energy than the 30-30—the actual theoretical advantage approaches a full 14 percent!

One of the most preposterous stories in all the annals of self-contained cartridges revolves around the 32 Winchester Special. Rather than reiterate that late-night fireside yarn, we can simply state the following: Winchester did not design this chambering to offer shooters a modern chambering that could be handloaded with blackpowder more easily than the 30-30. They simply took an existing standard bore, from the 32-40, built the gun of nickel steel, chambered the barrel to a dead ringer for a necked-up 30-30 and loaded the ammunition with smokeless powder to offer increased performance over the 30-30. All anyone who wanted to shoot blackpowder had to do was acquire an ever so similar 32-40-chambered Model 94 for about half the cost of the nick-

el-steel 32 Special-chambered version—nickel-steel was expensive in that day.

There seems to have been an inordinate amount of bore and bullet diameter variation in the 32 Winchester Special, and this, no doubt, contributed to the failure of this chambering to establish any permanent market. The story goes that "shot-out" 32 Special barrels lose all semblance of accuracy while similarly "shot-out" 30-30 barrels retain adequate hunting accuracy. Again, this is nonsense. Properly cleaned and with a bullet of proper diameter, just like any other gun, the 32 Special shoots with reasonable accuracy. However, it is not uncommon for factory ammunition to be loaded with 0.318″ bullets, which will never shoot properly from standard 0.321″ bores. However, some rifles do have 0.318″ bores and, in those, standard 0.321″ loads do not shoot all that great!

Paradoxically, factory loads have long been held to a somewhat lower pressure than 30-30 loads, and performance is, therefore, quite similar although the edge still goes to the 32 Special.

Case capacity with a 170-grain bullet, seated normally, is about 39.2 grains of water. The 32 Special is one of those oddball chamberings that manages to fit a gap in available powder burning rates. However, W748 and H4198 are good choices.

32 WINCHESTER SPECIAL LOADING DATA

	—STARTING—			—MAXIMUM—		
Powder	Grs.	MV (fps)	Grs.	MV (fps)	Press. (CUP/psi)	Comments
170						
W748			36.2	2240	32,500C	
H4198	24.0	1944	27.0	2168		
BL-C(2)	30.0	1872	32.0	1964		
H335	30.0	1866	32.0	1960		
H4895	31.0	1881	33.0	1941		

Caution: Loads exceeding SAAMI OAL Maximum must be verified for bullet-to-rifling clearance and magazine functioning. Where a specific primer or bullet is indicated those components must be used, no substitutions! Where only a maximum load is shown, reduce starting load 10%, unless otherwise specified.

Key: (C) = compressed charge; C = CUP; p = psi; Plink = Plinker; Bns = Barnes; Hdy = Hornady; Lap = Lapua; Nos = Nosler; Rem = Remington; Sra = Sierra; Spr = Speer; Win = Winchester.

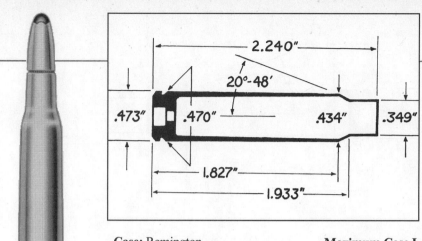

Case: Remington
Primer: Large Rifle
Barrel: 24″ Accurate
      23″ Hodgdon
Bullet Diameter: 0.323″

Maximum Case Length: 2.240″
Trim to Length: 2.230″
Maximum Cartridge OAL: 3.230″
Minimum Cartridge OAL: 2.815″

Co-introduced, as the original chambering for the 1888 Mauser rifle, the 8mm Mauser and that rifle were perhaps the tidewater design pair, heralding an entire generation of modern turnbolt actions and the rimless cartridges they chambered. The original loading used a typical round-nose bullet of 226 grains at about 2100 fps. This level of performance was unheard of in that era and reflected the use of superior nickel alloy steel that Germany then had a monopoly on. With stronger guns available, Mauser could safely load to higher pressures using smokeless powders.

In 1905, bore diameter was changed from 0.318″ to 0.323″ (by the simple expedient of deepening the grooves of existing barrels, deemed necessary to increase accurate barrel life) when a 154-grain spitzer bullet at an equally surprising 2880 fps was standardized. Without going into details, this change was the basis for an ongoing confusion in nomenclature.

Safety issues exist because, while all military rifles were rebarreled to the 0.323″ size, many civilian rifles chambered for both the 7.92x57mm and 7.92x57Rmm (a rimmed version of the same cartridge) were also in use. These generally were not rebarreled. Therefore, the "8mm" has always been loaded with two basic bullet sizes in Europe.

U.S. companies have chosen a different path. Domestic loads are held to such a low pressure that, should someone chamber and fire one of these 0.323″ bulleted rounds in an antique 0.318″ bored rifle, dangerous pressures would not be generated.

This load data reflects that concern. If your rifle has a 0.318″ bore, these loads should be safe. Nevertheless, we recommend using only the minimum (starting) listed loads in such a rifle. These loads are for use only in .323″ barrels.

Case capacity with a 150-grain bullet, seated normally, is about 60 grains of water. A4350 and A3100 are good choices here.

8mm MAUSER LOADING DATA (8x57mm MAUSER)

Powder	—STARTING— Grs.	MV (fps)	—MAXIMUM— Grs.	MV (fps)	Press. (CUP/psi)	Comments
Lead 170 RCBS						
A4350	42.3	1983	47.0	2253	31,700p	2.71″/CCI 250
A3100	47.7	1940	53.0	2205	29,700p	2.71″/CCI 250/(C)
A8700	49.1	1581	54.5	1797	24,100p	2.71″/CCI 250/(C)
125						
H450	52.0	2327	56.0	2509		
H4350	50.0	2217	54.0	2480		
A4350	47.7	2128	53.0	2418	25,200p	Hdy SP/2.89″/CCI 250/(C)
A3100	47.7	1923	53.0	2185	20,400p	Hdy SP/2.89″/CCI 250/(C)
150						
BL-C(2)	42.5	2433	46.0	2553	33,500C	26″ Bbl
A4350	45.0	2107	50.0	2394	32,500p	Hdy SP/2.95″/CCI 250/(C)
H450	49.0	2162	53.0	2285	35,900C	26″ Bbl
A3100	47.7	1961	53.0	2228	27,100p	Hdy SP/2.95″/CCI 250/(C)

Powder	—STARTING— Grs.	MV (fps)	—MAXIMUM— Grs.	MV (fps)	Press. (CUP/psi)	Comments
170						
A4350	43.2	1991	48.0	2262	33,600p	Hdy RN/2.84″/CCI 250
A3100	47.7	1919	53.0	2181	30,400p	Hdy RN/2.84″/CCI 250/(C)
H450	46.0	1966	49.0	2138	36,500C	26″ Bbl
A8700	49.1	1523	54.5	1731	25,400p	Hdy RN/2.84″/CCI 250/(C)
200						
A4350	39.6	1794	44.0	2039	31,200p	Spr SP/2.97″/CCI 250
A3100	44.1	1742	49.0	1980	28,100p	Spr SP/2.97″/CCI 250/(C)
A8700	49.1	1489	54.5	1692	26,600p	Spr SP/2.97″/CCI 250/(C)
220						
A3100	44.3	1712	49.2	1946	30,900p	Hdy SP/2.99″/CCI 250/(C)
A4350	37.8	1677	42.0	1906	30,800p	Hdy SP/2.99″/CCI 250
A8700	46.4	1331	51.5	1512	23,200p	Hdy SP/2.99″/CCI 250/(C)

WARNING: Rifles with 0.318″ bores must use 0.318″ diameter bullets. Mauser Model 1888, before 1905, and some sporters have 0.318″ bores.

Never exceed maximum load nor use any load exhibiting signs of excessive pressure. Begin at suggested starting load and work up carefully.

8x57JS
Mauser

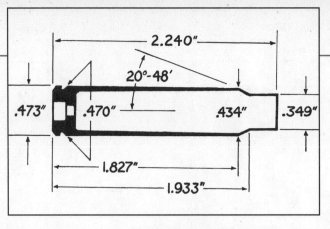

Case: Remington
Primer: Large Rifle
Barrel: 24" Accurate
    23" Hodgdon
    24" Vihtavuori

Bullet Diameter: 0.323"
Maximum Case Length: 2.240"
Trim to Length: 2.230"
Maximum Cartridge OAL: 3.230"
Minimum Cartridge OAL: 2.815"

The load data presented here are for rifles known to have 0.323" bores, and then only in such rifles known to be in good condition.

Released in 1905, the 8x57mmJS Mauser replaced the 1888 version by increasing bullet diameter from 0.318" to 0.323" and using a 154-grain spitzer bullet rather than the original 226-grain round-nose. With a muzzle velocity of 2880 fps, this loading offered a significant edge over the upcoming standard military 30-06 load with its 150-grain bullet at only 2700 fps—in spite of the 30-06's significantly greater usable capacity. The difference amounted to a 16.8 percent increase in muzzle energy in favor of the 8mm! The

standard '06 Ball load was by no measure superior. (It should be noted that these ballistics also reflect a 4-inch longer standard barrel in the 8mm.)

Loads at these pressure levels are patently unsafe for use in any 0.318" bored rifle. These loads duplicate typical European factory-load performance and demonstrate that the 8mm Mauser is still the ballistic equivalent of the 30-06.

If you are unsure of your rifle's bore, have it properly slugged. If it has a 0.318" bore, do not use any of these loads.

Case capacity with a 150-grain bullet, seated normally, is about 60 grains of water. A2520 is a particularly good choice for top 8mmJS loads.

8x57mmJS MAUSER LOADING DATA

Powder	STARTING Grs.	MV (fps)	MAXIMUM Grs.	MV (fps)	Press. (CUP/psi)	Comments
125-127						
A2460	50.0	2845	55.5	3233	56,600p	Hdy SP/2.88"/CCI 200
A2230	49.5	2842	55.0	3230	56,300p	Hdy SP/2.88"/CCI 200
N135			54.8	3200	49,313p	Hdy SP
A2520	50.4	2803	56.0	3185	51,100p	Hdy SP/2.88"/ CCI 200/(C)
N135			54.8	3180	49,313p	Sako FMJ 102F
N140			55.1	3070	44,962p	Sako FMJ 102F
H4198	39.0	2943	42.0	3054		
H380	50.5	2708	55.0	2909		
H414	53.5	2644	58.0	2893		
H335	47.0	2637	51.0	2891		
H322	43.0	2550	47.0	2840		
H4895	47.0	2565	51.0	2796		
BL-C(2)	46.0	2614	50.0	2789		

Powder	STARTING Grs.	MV (fps)	MAXIMUM Grs.	MV (fps)	Press. (CUP/psi)	Comments
150						
A2520	47.3	2600	52.5	2955	55,800p	Hdy SP/2.94"/CCI 200
A2230	45.5	2558	50.5	2907	54,800p	Hdy SP/2.94"/CCI 200
A2460	45.9	2557	51.0	2906	53,700p	Hdy SP/2.94"/CCI 200
A2015BR	42.3	2507	47.0	2849	52,000p	Hdy SP/2.94"/CCI 200
H4198	38.0	2688	41.0	2848		
H380	49.5	2562	54.0	2778		
H414	51.5	2546	56.0	2773		
H4895	46.0	2524	50.0	2747		
H335	45.0	2507	49.0	2744		
H322	42.0	2490	46.0	2726		

   Never exceed maximum load nor use any load exhibiting signs of excessive pressure. Begin at suggested starting load and work up carefully.

Powder	STARTING Grs.	MV (fps)	MAXIMUM Grs.	MV (fps)	Press. (CUP/psi)	Comments
170						
A2520	45.0	2439	50.0	2752	57,500p	Hdy RN/2.855"/CCI 200
A2230	44.1	2414	49.0	2743	56,600p	Hdy RN/2.855"/CCI 200
A2460	44.1	2401	49.0	2728	55,600p	Hdy RN/2.855"/CCI 200
A2015BR	41.0	2382	45.5	2707	55,400p	Hdy RN/2.855"/CCI 200
H414	49.0	2446	53.0	2586		
H322	40.0	2327	44.0	2555		
H380	45.0	2387	49.0	2509		
H4350	50.0	2339	54.0	2507		
H4895	42.5	2380	46.0	2501		
H335	42.5	2370	46.0	2470		
BL-C(2)	41.5	2287	45.0	2421		
H4831	53.0	2207	57.0	2418		
175						
N140			49.7	2670	49,313p	Sra SP
N135			46.6	2580	49,313p	Sra SP

Powder	STARTING Grs.	MV (fps)	MAXIMUM Grs.	MV (fps)	Press. (CUP/psi)	Comments
200						
N140			46.3	2530	49,313p	Sako SP 201F
220						
A2700	50.4	2295	53.0	2442	57,600p	Hdy SP/2.99"/CCI 200/(C)
A2520	40.5	2069	45.0	2351	55,600p	Hdy SP/2.99"/CCI 200
A2460	39.2	2064	43.5	2345	57,800p	Hdy SP/2.99"/CCI 200
A2015BR	36.9	2036	41.0	2314	56,100p	Hdy SP/2.99"/CCI 200
A2230	37.8	2020	42.0	2296	58,200p	Hdy SP/2.99"/CCI 200
A4350	45.9	2001	51.0	2274	42,400p	Hdy SP/2.99"/CCI 200/(C)
225						
H4831	53.0	2116	57.0	2346		
H414	46.0	2208	50.0	2342		
H380	42.5	2109	46.0	2285		
H4350	44.0	2084	46.0	2221		

Caution: **Loads exceeding SAAMI OAL Maximum must be verified for bullet-to-rifling clearance and magazine functioning. Where a specific primer or bullet is indicated those components must be used, no substitutions! Where only a maximum load is shown, reduce starting load 10%, unless otherwise specified.**

Key: (C) = compressed charge; C = CUP; p = psi; Plink = Plinker; Bns = Barnes; Hdy = Hornady; Lap = Lapua; Nos = Nosler; Rem = Remington; Sra = Sierra; Spr = Speer; Win = Winchester.

8mm-06

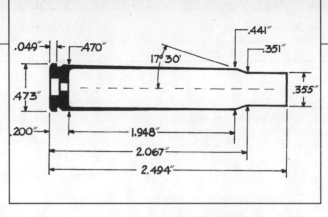

Case: IMI
Primer: CCI 200
Barrel: 24″ Accurate
Bullet Diameter: 0.323″
Maximum Case Length: 2.494″

Trim to Length: 2.484″
**Maximum Cartridge OAL
 (Recommended):** 3.340″
**Minimum Cartridge OAL
 (Recommended):** 2.940″

Thousands of 8mm Mauser rifles were brought back to the U.S. by returning GIs at the end of WWII. Evidently, it was deemed easier to pay a gunsmith to rechamber those fine rifles to accept a necked-up version of the standard 30-06 than to simply shorten the ubiquitous 30-06 case to 8mm Mauser dimensions. Perhaps there was also a certain prejudice involved.

With a substantial increase in bore area over the 30-06, the 8mm-06 wildcat, loaded to equal pressures, would offer

a substantial increase in performance. However, most 8mm-06 data is limited to somewhat less pressure than typical 30-06 data and, therefore, ballistics are quite similar.

With high-performance bullets, the 8mm-06 has become an even better hunting cartridge, and there is precious little to separate its performance from that of the 30-06—no faint praise.

Case capacity with a 150-grain bullet, seated normally, is about 69 grains of water.

8mm-06 LOADING DATA

Powder	STARTING Grs.	MV (fps)	MAXIMUM Grs.	MV (fps)	Press. (CUP/psi)	Comments
125						
A2460	54.0	3008	60.0	3418	58,100p	Hdy SP/3.2″
A2520	53.6	2966	59.5	3370	57,600p	Hdy SP/3.2″
A2230	52.2	2952	58.0	3354	55,600p	Hdy SP/3.2″
A2015BR	49.5	2939	55.0	3340	53,300p	Hdy SP/3.2″
A2495BR	50.9	2913	56.5	3310	56,100p	Hdy SP/3.2″
A2700	59.9	3019	63.0	3212	55,400p	Hdy SP/3.2″/(C)
150						
A2520	50.4	2730	56.0	3102	57,600p	Hdy SP/3.2″
A2495BR	48.6	2702	54.0	3071	57,600p	Hdy SP/3.2″
A2460	49.5	2698	55.0	3066	56,400p	Hdy SP/3.2″
A2700	58.0	2839	61.0	3020	52,300p	Hdy SP/3.2″/(C)
A2230	47.7	2652	53.0	3014	55,900p	Hdy SP/3.2″
A2015BR	45.0	2617	50.0	2974	52,200p	Hdy SP/3.2″
A4350	53.1	2481	59.0	2819	39,700p	Hdy SP/3.2″/(C)
170						
A2700	55.1	2698	58.0	2870	54,900p	Hdy RN/3.055″
A2015BR	43.2	2505	48.0	2847	59,300p	Hdy RN/3.055″
A2495BR	46.4	2500	51.5	2841	57,500p	Hdy RN/3.055″
A2520	46.8	2487	52.0	2826	58,400p	Hdy RN/3.055″
A2460	45.9	2484	51.0	2823	58,900p	Hdy RN/3.055″

Powder	STARTING Grs.	MV (fps)	MAXIMUM Grs.	MV (fps)	Press. (CUP/psi)	Comments
170 con't						
A4350	54.0	2482	60.0	2820	51,400p	Hdy RN/3.055″/(C)
A2230	45.0	2475	50.0	2812	58,700p	Hdy RN/3.055″
200						
A4350	49.5	2300	55.0	2614	57,400p	Spr SP/3.22″/(C)
A2700	50.4	2402	53.0	2555	55,300p	Spr SP/3.22″
A2015BR	38.7	2174	43.0	2470	54,600p	Spr SP/3.22″
A2520	41.0	2159	45.5	2453	54,000p	Spr SP/3.22″
A3100	51.3	2158	57.0	2452	45,400p	Spr SP/3.22″/(C)
A2230	39.6	2157	44.0	2451	51,500p	Spr SP/3.22″
A2495BR	38.3	2152	42.5	2445	55,300p	Spr SP/3.22″
A2460	39.6	2151	44.0	2444	54,200p	Spr SP/3.22″
220						
A4350	50.0	2238	55.5	2543	58,600p	Hdy SP/3.3″
A2700	52.3	2387	55.0	2539	56,900p	Hdy SP/3.3″
A3100	51.3	2122	57.0	2411	47,200p	Hdy SP/3.3″/(C)
A2015BR	37.8	2104	42.0	2391	58,200p	Hdy SP/3.3″
A2460	39.2	2099	43.5	2385	58,800p	Hdy SP/3.3″
A2230	38.3	2067	42.5	2349	57,900p	Hdy SP/3.3″
A2520	39.6	2052	44.0	2332	57,900p	Hdy SP/3.3″
A2495BR	37.8	2050	42.0	2329	57,100p	Hdy SP/3.3″

Never exceed maximum load nor use any load exhibiting signs of excessive pressure. Begin at suggested starting load and work up carefully.

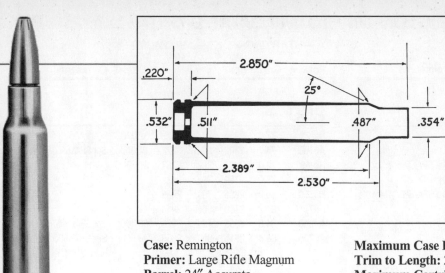

Case: Remington
Primer: Large Rifle Magnum
Barrel: 24″ Accurate
24″ Hodgdon
Bullet Diameter: 0.322-0.323″

Maximum Case Length: 2.850″
Trim to Length: 2.840″
Maximum Cartridge OAL: 3.600″
Minimum Cartridge OAL: 3.450″

Introduced in 1978, this is a full-length belted magnum case with minimal body taper, a short neck and a sharp shoulder. The case body is very similar to thc 340 Wcather-by Magnum, as is capacity.

With lighter bullets, this chambering can produce a slightly flatter trajectory and deliver as much energy to long-range targets as the best 300 Magnum. With heavier bullets, it can just about duplicate 338 Winchester Magnum perfor-mance. Nevertheless, the 8mm Remington Magnum was an almost instant commercial failure.

In fairness, limited bullet selection shares a measure of

blame. With a wider selection of bullet designs available in both 30- and 33-caliber, those magnum chamberings could do things the 8mm could not.

In any case, Remington's big 8mm seems to have filled a niche that did not matter to U.S. shooters because sales were dismal. It was quietly dropped as a standard chambering, and although still loaded, ammunition is difficult to find.

Case capacity with a 150-grain bullet, seated normally, is about 93.9 grains of water. RL-22, IMR4350 and A3100 are noted performers in the 8mm Rem. Mag.

8mm REMINGTON MAGNUM LOADING DATA

Powder	—STARTING— Grs.	MV (fps)	—MAXIMUM— Grs.	MV (fps)	Press. (CUP/psi)	Comments
125						
IMR4064	71.0	3309	75.0	3530		
IMR4320	71.0	3298	75.0	3519		
IMR4350	79.0	3281	83.0	3494		
H4350	79.0	3271	83.0	3488		
H4895	69.0	3400	71.0	3463		
IMR4895	69.0	3367	71.0	3461		
IMR4831	83.0	3261	87.0	3454		
H380	73.0	3304	76.0	3392		
150						
A3100	80.1	3026	89.0	3439	58,400p	Hdy SP/3.565″/Rem 9½
A4350	73.8	3013	82.0	3424	60,100p	Hdy SP/3.565″/Rem 9½
H414	77.0	3225	79.0	3320		
IMR4350	75.0	3069	79.0	3291		
H4831	83.0	3194	85.0	3290		
H4350	76.0	3122	79.0	3272		
H450	82.0	3171	85.0	3270		
IMR4831	79.0	3017	83.0	3244		
IMR4064	68.0	3074	71.0	3242		
IMR4320	69.0	3074	72.0	3198		

Powder	—STARTING— Grs.	MV (fps)	—MAXIMUM— Grs.	MV (fps)	Press. (CUP/psi)	Comments
150 con't						
H380	71.0	3098	73.0	3185		
H4895	64.0	3037	67.0	3172		
IMR4895	64.0	3011	67.0	3168		
H870	90.0	2965	93.0	3029		
A8700	88.2	2655	98.0	3017	44,700p	Hdy SP/3.565″/Rem 9½/(C)

Caution: **Loads exceeding SAAMI OAL Maximum must be verified for bullet-to-rifling clearance and magazine func-tioning. Where a specific primer or bullet is indicated those components must be used, no substitutions! Where only a maximum load is shown, reduce starting load 10%, unless otherwise specified.**

Key: (C) = compressed charge; C = CUP; p = psi; Plink = Plink-er; Bns = Barnes; Hdy = Hornady; Lap = Lapua; Nos = Nosler; Rem = Remington; Sra = Sierra; Spr = Speer; Win = Winchester.

170-175

Powder	STARTING Grs.	MV (fps)	MAXIMUM Grs.	MV (fps)	Press. (CUP/psi)	Comments
RL-22	83.0	3206	87.0	3329	51,500C	
RL-19	78.0	3180	83.0	3294	51,000C	
A3100	78.8	2865	87.5	3256	60,900p	Sra SP/3.565"/ Rem 9½/(C)
A4350	71.1	2833	79.0	3219	59,400p	Sra SP/3.565"/Rem 9½
H4831	80.0	3054	82.0	3144		
IMR4831	76.0	2959	80.0	3137		
H4350	73.0	2923	77.0	3128		
H450	80.0	3043	82.0	3103		
IMR4350	72.0	2898	76.0	3088		
H414	72.0	2962	75.0	3076		
IMR4320	66.0	2881	69.0	3011		
H870	89.0	2881	92.0	2967		
A8700	87.3	2475	97.0	2813	40,000p	Sra SP/3.565"/ Rem 9½/(C)

180-185

Powder	STARTING Grs.	MV (fps)	MAXIMUM Grs.	MV (fps)	Press. (CUP/psi)	Comments
RL-22	80.0	3077	84.0	3192	51,000C	
RL-19	76.0	3049	80.0	3180	52,000C	
IMR4350	70.0	2831	75.0	3057		
H4831	77.0	2865	80.0	3024		
IMR4831	74.0	2844	78.0	3020		
H4350	71.0	2852	75.0	3007		
H450	77.0	2931	79.0	2987		
H870	85.0	2795	91.0	2939		

200

Powder	STARTING Grs.	MV (fps)	MAXIMUM Grs.	MV (fps)	Press. (CUP/psi)	Comments
RL-22	77.0	2954	81.0	3079	52,000C	
A3100	74.7	2703	83.0	3072	62,300p	Spr SP/3.595"/Rem 9½
RL-19	74.0	2907	78.0	3057	51,500C	
H4831	75.0	2799	79.0	2932		
H4350	69.0	2736	73.0	2919		
H870	87.0	2780	90.0	2914		
A4350	64.8	2533	72.0	2878	59,400p	Spr SP/3.595"/Rem 9½
A8700	86.4	2516	96.0	2859	48,600p	Spr SP/3.595"/ Rem 9½/(C)

220-225

Powder	STARTING Grs.	MV (fps)	MAXIMUM Grs.	MV (fps)	Press. (CUP/psi)	Comments
RL-22	73.0	2720	77.0	2888	51,000C	
A3100	72.5	2538	80.5	2884	61,600p	Hdy SP/3.595"/Rem 9½
H4831	74.0	2747	78.0	2871		
RL-19	71.0	2718	75.0	2871	51,500C	
H870	87.0	2730	90.0	2856		
IMR4831	72.0	2691	76.0	2852		
IMR4350	67.0	2629	71.0	2831		
H450	74.0	2754	76.0	2822		
A8700	84.6	2423	94.0	2753	48,500p	Hdy SP/3.595"/ Rem 9½/(C)
A4350	63.5	2416	70.5	2745	58,500p	Hdy SP/3.595"/Rem 9½

250

Powder	STARTING Grs.	MV (fps)	MAXIMUM Grs.	MV (fps)	Press. (CUP/psi)	Comments
H4831	72.0	2669	76.0	2776		
H870	84.0	2651	86.0	2764		
RL-22	70.0	2560	74.0	2694	50,800C	
RL-19	67.0	2521	71.0	2639	51,000C	

Caution: Loads exceeding SAAMI OAL Maximum must be verified for bullet-to-rifling clearance and magazine functioning. Where a specific primer or bullet is indicated those components must be used, no substitutions! Where only a maximum load is shown, reduce starting load 10%, unless otherwise specified.

Key: (C) = compressed charge; C = CUP; p = psi; Plink = Plinker; Bns = Barnes; Hdy = Hornady; Lap = Lapua; Nos = Nosler; Rem = Remington; Sra = Sierra; Spr = Speer; Win = Winchester.

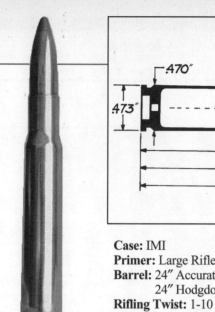

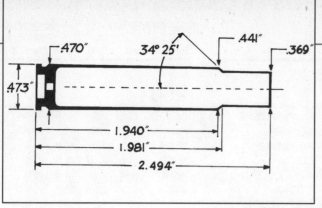

338-06

Case: IMI
Primer: Large Rifle
Barrel: 24" Accurate
24" Hodgdon
Rifling Twist: 1-10
Bullet Diameter: 0.338"

Maximum Case Length: 2.494"
Trim to Length: 2.484"
Maximum Cartridge OAL
(Recommended): 3.340"
Minimum Cartridge OAL
(Recommended): Bullet Dependent

This popular wildcat is formed by necking up the 30-06 to accept 0.338" bullets. Since there is a good selection of such bullets, those who feel they need a bit more bullet than the 30-06 can deliver have found this a good alternative. Had it not been for Remington's standardization of the 35 Whelen in 1988, this might have already become a standard factory offering.

With 20 percent more bore area and considerably more usable capacity, the 338-06 can launch equal-weight bullets considerably faster than the 30-06. Its main claim to fame, however, is an ability to launch 10 percent heavier bullets at the same velocity as the 30-06. For example, it can safely launch a 200-grain bullet faster than the 30-06 can launch a 180-grain bullet. Further, it can launch heavier bullets than any available in the 30-06 while still maintaining useful velocities.

The popular improved version features considerably more usable capacity and comes surprisingly close to 338 Winchester Magnum performance. Unfortunately, we do not have any pressure data for that version.

A3100, IMR4320, W760, H414 and IMR4350 are good 338-06 choices.

338-06 LOADING DATA

Lead 200 Lyman 338320

Powder	STARTING Grs.	MV (fps)	MAXIMUM Grs.	MV (fps)	Press. (CUP/psi)	Comments
A2520	41.4	2208	46.0	2509	41,700p	3.08"/CCI 200
A2460	40.5	2198	45.0	2498	40,300p	3.08"/CCI 200
A4350	48.6	2195	54.0	2494	39,800p	3.08"/CCI 200/ 100% Density
A2230	39.6	2188	44.0	2486	49,600p	3.08"/CCI 200
A2495BR	38.7	2184	43.0	2482	39,400p	3.08"/CCI 200
A2015BR	37.8	2180	42.0	2477	38,400p	3.08"/CCI 200
A2700	48.5	2321	51.0	2469	38,900p	3.08"/CCI 200
A3100	52.2	2128	58.0	2418	36,400p	3.08"/CCI 200/(C)
A8700	58.5	1833	65.0	2083	30,300p	3.08"/CCI 200/(C)

200

Powder	STARTING Grs.	MV (fps)	MAXIMUM Grs.	MV (fps)	Press. (CUP/psi)	Comments
IMR4320	53.0	2588	57.0	2827		
IMR4350	57.0	2522	63.0	2817		
H414	57.0	2525	63.0	2802		
IMR4831	59.0	2495	65.0	2775		
A2495BR	45.0	2394	50.0	2720	58,900p	Nos BT/3.335"/ CCI 200
H4350	59.0	2449	65.0	2710		

200 con't

Powder	STARTING Grs.	MV (fps)	MAXIMUM Grs.	MV (fps)	Press. (CUP/psi)	Comments
A4350	54.9	2380	61.0	2704	51,100p	Nos BT/3.335"/ CCI 200/(C)
A2700	57.0	2542	60.0	2704	55,600p	Nos BT/3.335"/ CCI 200/(C)
W760	57.0	2533	61.0	2693		
A2460	45.0	2368	50.0	2691	56,800p	Nos BT/3.335"/ CCI 200
A2520	45.9	2367	51.0	2690	58,800p	Nos BT/3.335"/ CCI 200
A2230	44.6	2350	49.5	2670	57,700p	Nos BT/3.335"/ CCI 200
A2015BR	41.9	2336	46.5	2654	57,100p	Nos BT/3.335"/ CCI 200
A3100	55.8	2216	62.0	2518	42,100p	Nos BT/3.335"/ CCI 200/(C)

>>>>>>>>>>>>>>>>>>>>>>>>>>>>>

Never exceed maximum load nor use any load exhibiting signs of excessive pressure. Begin at suggested starting load and work up carefully.

221

210

Powder	Grs.	MV (fps)	Grs.	MV (fps)	Press. (CUP/psi)	Comments
A4350	54.0	2372	60.0	2695	57,600p	Nos Part./3.265"/ CCI 200/(C)
A2700	56.1	2510	59.0	2670	58,600p	Nos Part./3.265"/ CCI 200
A2520	44.6	2283	49.5	2594	58,300p	Nos Part./3.265"/ CCI 200
A2495BR	42.3	2267	47.0	2576	59,200p	Nos Part./3.265"/ CCI 200
A2460	43.2	2242	48.0	2548	55,700p	Nos Part./3.265"/ CCI 200
A2230	42.8	2242	47.5	2548	56,900p	Nos Part./3.265"/ CCI 200
A3100	55.8	2222	62.0	2525	46,400p	Nos Part./3.265"/ CCI 200/(C)
A2015BR	40.5	2217	45.0	2519	56,300p	Nos Part./3.265"/ CCI 200

210-225

Powder	Grs.	MV (fps)	Grs.	MV (fps)	Press. (CUP/psi)	Comments
IMR4350	56.0	2541	62.0	2829		210-gr. Bullets
H414	56.0	2603	62.0	2807		210-gr. Bullets
H4350	56.0	2546	62.0	2744		
IMR4350	55.0	2464	61.0	2710		
IMR4320	50.0	2459	54.0	2681		
A4350	54.0	2306	60.0	2620	55,900p	Hdy SP/3.315"/ CCI 200/(C)
A2700	55.1	2404	58.0	2557	55,800p	Hdy SP/3.315"/ CCI 200/100% Density
A2700	54.2	2396	57.0	2549	57,400p	Bns-X/3.315"/CCI 200
A4350	52.2	2226	58.0	2530	53,500p	Bns-X/3.315"/ CCI 200/(C)
A2520	44.1	2211	49.0	2512	58,000p	Hdy SP/3.315"/ CCI 200
A2495BR	42.3	2203	47.0	2503	56,700p	Hdy SP/3.315"/ CCI 200
A2015BR	41.0	2190	45.5	2489	56,600p	Hdy SP/3.315"/ CCI 200
A2460	42.3	2189	47.0	2488	54,800p	Hdy SP/3.315"/ CCI 200
A2230	42.3	2166	47.0	2461	55,600p	Hdy SP/3.315"/ CCI 200
A2520	42.8	2162	47.5	2457	57,300p	Bns-X/3.315"/CCI 200
A2460	41.0	2117	45.5	2406	57,800p	Bns-X/3.315"/CCI 200
A2015BR	38.7	2113	43.0	2401	57,100p	Bns-X/3.315"/CCI 200
A3100	54.0	2103	60.0	2390	42,000p	Hdy SP/3.315"/ CCI 200/(C)
A2230	40.5	2079	45.0	2363	56,000p	Bns-X/3.315"/CCI 200
A3100	52.2	2010	58.0	2284	39,400p	Bns-X/3.315"/ CCI 200/(C)
A2495BR	39.6	1991	44.0	2262	59,600p	Bns-X/3.315"/CCI 200

250

Powder	Grs.	MV (fps)	Grs.	MV (fps)	Press. (CUP/psi)	Comments
IMR4350	53.0	2272	59.0	2610		
H414	54.0	2295	60.0	2583		
H4350	54.0	2277	60.0	2569		
W760	54.0	2307	60.0	2569		
IMR4831	55.0	2263	61.0	2541		
A4350	52.2	2214	58.0	2516	52,400p	Sra SBT/3.315"/ CCI 200/(C)
A2700	52.3	2269	55.0	2414	55,700p	Sra SBT/3.315"/ CCI 200/(C)
H4831	55.0	2216	61.0	2408		
A2520	41.4	2030	46.0	2307	59,000p	Sra SBT/3.315"/ CCI 200
A3100	52.2	2028	58.0	2304	43,700p	Sra SBT/3.315"/ CCI 200/(C)
IMR7828	55.0	2019	61.0	2278		
A2015BR	38.3	2000	42.5	2273	58,100p	Sra SBT/3.315"/ CCI 200
A2495BR	38.7	1999	43.0	2272	55,500p	Sra SBT/3.315"/ CCI 200
A2230	39.6	1996	44.0	2268	58,700p	Sra SBT/3.315"/ CCI 200
A2460	39.2	1969	43.5	2238	56,200p	Sra SBT/3.315"/ CCI 200

275

Powder	Grs.	MV (fps)	Grs.	MV (fps)	Press. (CUP/psi)	Comments
H4831	53.0	2069	59.0	2348		
IMR4831	52.0	2098	56.0	2328		
IMR7828	54.0	2039	58.0	2231		
H450	54.0	1981	58.0	2184		

Caution: Loads exceeding SAAMI OAL Maximum must be verified for bullet-to-rifling clearance and magazine functioning. Where a specific primer or bullet is indicated those components must be used, no substitutions! Where only a maximum load is shown, reduce starting load 10%, unless otherwise specified.

Key: (C) = compressed charge; C = CUP; p = psi; Plink = Plinker; Bns = Barnes; Hdy = Hornady; Lap = Lapua; Nos = Nosler; Rem = Remington; Sra = Sierra; Spr = Speer; Win = Winchester.

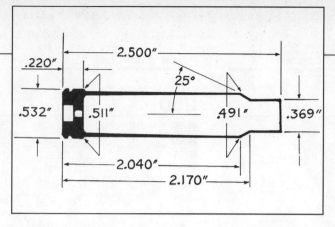

Case: Federal
Primer: Large Rifle
Barrel: 24″ Accurate/24″ Hodgdon
24″ Vihtavuori/24″ Winchester

Bullet Diameter: 0.338″
Maximum Case Length: 2.500″
Trim to Length: 2.490″
Maximum Cartridge OAL: 3.340″
Minimum Cartridge OAL: 3.280″

In 1958, Winchester became the first U.S. manufacturer to offer a 33-caliber chambering since their introduction of the 33 Winchester in 1902. In the '50s and '60s, Elmer Keith and others had played with a variety of 33-caliber chamberings based on the 30-06 case and the belted magnum, although those all used 0.333″ bullets.

For whatever reason, when Winchester standardized their own belted magnum, they settled on a 0.338″ bullet diameter. The designed case length of 2.50″ allowed the round to be chambered in standard-length actions. Originally offered with 200-, 250- and 300-grain loadings, the 338 was, and is, a genuinely wonderful cartridge. Where the 30-06 can

launch a 150-grain bullet at about 2950 fps, the 338 can launch a 200-grain bullet at the same velocity.

The 338 delivers heavy bullets to distant targets with a trajectory not far behind the various 300 Magnums. The most efficient bullets typically deliver more energy to hunted targets at 500 yards than the 30-30 Winchester generates at the muzzle.

For those who feel the 30-06 Springfield just does not quite deliver the requisite performance, the 338 Winchester Magnum is, perhaps, the next logical step up.

Case capacity with a 225-grain bullet, seated normally, is about 78.3 grains of water. H4350, RL-22, WMR, N165, W760 and RL-19 are noted 338 Win. Mag. performers.

338 WINCHESTER MAGNUM LOADING DATA

Powder	STARTING Grs.	MV (fps)	MAXIMUM Grs.	MV (fps)	Press. (CUP/psi)	Comments
Lead 200						
A4350	56.7	2264	63.0	2573	36,400p	3.2″/CCI 250
A8700	72.5	2219	80.5	2522	35,800p	3.2″/CCI 250/(C)
A3100	58.5	2195	65.0	2494	36,900p	3.2″/CCI 250
175						
H4350	74.0	2974	77.0	3187	53,000C	
H4895	63.0	2944	67.0	3166	53,000C	
H414	70.0	2947	73.0	3139	53,000C	
H4831	78.0	2986	81.0	3092	53,000C	
H450	77.0	2919	80.0	3039	50,500C	
H380	69.0	2880	72.0	2985	52,500C	
200						
H4350	72.0	2917	77.0	3054	53,000C	
IMR4350	70.0	2790	75.0	3024	53,500C	
IMR4831	68.0	2746	73.0	3015	52,500C	
H4895	62.0	2787	67.0	3011	53,000C	
RL-22	75.0	2813	80.0	2994	48,000C	
200 con't						
RL-19	72.0	2787	77.0	2985	48,500C	
N160	72.8	2631	80.8	2969	52,200p	Hdy SP/3.346″/Rem 9½
H414	67.0	2781	72.0	2968	52,000C	
RL-15	60.0	2799	65.0	2955	51,000C	
W760	66.0	2747	71.0	2951	52,500C	
N165			82.6	2950	55,114p	Sako SP 108F
A4350	65.7	2596	73.0	2950	62,200p	Hdy SP/3.335″/CCI 250
H4831	73.0	2743	78.0	2949	52,500C	
H450	74.0	2812	79.0	2942	47,500C	
IMR7828	73.0	2678	78.0	2925	50,500C	
N160			75.6	2920	55,114p	Sako SP 108F
A2700	67.0	2724	70.5	2898	61,200p	Hdy SP/3.335″/CCI 250
IMR4320	59.0	2701	64.0	2891	51,500C	
H380	66.0	2715	71.0	2877	52,000C	
A2520	56.3	2502	62.5	2843	58,600p	Hdy SP/3.335″/CCI 250
A3100	68.4	2493	76.0	2833	55,200p	Hdy SP/3.335″/CCI 250/(C)
A2495BR	51.3	2470	57.0	2807	62,200p	Hdy SP/3.335″/CCI 250
WMR			71.7	2660	43,400p	Win SP

▶▶▶▶▶▶▶▶▶▶▶▶▶▶▶▶▶▶▶▶▶▶▶▶▶▶

Never exceed maximum load nor use any load exhibiting signs of excessive pressure. Begin at suggested starting load and work up carefully.

210

Powder	Grs.	MV (fps)	Grs.	MV (fps)	Press. (CUP/psi)	Comments
RL-22	72.0	2796	77.0	2960	52,500C	
IMR4831	67.0	2732	72.0	2943	52,500C	
H414	65.0	2753	70.0	2928	52,500C	
H4350	67.0	2688	73.0	2920	53,500C	
RL-19	70.0	2755	75.0	2917	53,000C	
H450	71.0	2733	76.0	2914	49,000C	
IMR4350	67.0	2691	72.0	2910	53,000C	
W760	64.0	2710	69.0	2898	52,000C	
RL-15	58.0	2702	63.0	2857	53,000C	
H4831	70.0	2682	75.0	2853	50,500C	
IMR7828	72.0	2685	77.0	2852	50,000C	
H4895	57.0	2664	62.0	2828	53,000C	
IMR4320	57.0	2611	62.0	2819	52,000C	

220

Powder	Grs.	MV (fps)	Grs.	MV (fps)	Press. (CUP/psi)	Comments
WMR			72.2	2640	41,800p	Win SP

225

Powder	Grs.	MV (fps)	Grs.	MV (fps)	Press. (CUP/psi)	Comments
N165			80.2	2820	55,114p	Hdy SP
A4350	63.5	2464	70.5	2800	63,000p	Hdy SP/3.34"/CCI 250
RL-22	71.0	2617	76.0	2799	49,500C	
IMR4350	66.0	2548	71.0	2795	51,500C	
H4350	66.0	2587	72.0	2794	50,500C	
H414	63.0	2630	68.0	2787	51,500C	
H4831	70.0	2566	75.0	2785	52,000C	
N160	69.5	2509	77.4	2783	52,200p	Hdy SP/3.307"/Rem 9½
IMR4831	66.0	2575	71.0	2774	50,000C	
H450	70.0	2642	75.0	2765	49,500C	
W760	62.0	2588	67.0	2764	52,500C	
N160			70.2	2760	55,114p	Hdy SP
IMR7828	71.0	2545	76.0	2741	48,500C	
RL-15	56.0	2505	61.0	2722	50,500C	
IMR4320	56.0	2430	61.0	2714	50,500C	
H4895	56.0	2489	61.0	2710	51,000C	
RL-19	68.0	2575	73.0	2709	49,000C	
A2700	62.7	2541	66.0	2703	61,900p	Hdy SP/3.34"/CCI 250
A3100	65.7	2360	73.0	2682	55,900p	Hdy SP/3.34"/CCI 250/(C)
H380	61.0	2498	66.0	2657	52,500C	

230

Powder	Grs.	MV (fps)	Grs.	MV (fps)	Press. (CUP/psi)	Comments
WMR			66.8	2450	44,900p	Win FS

Caution: Loads exceeding SAAMI OAL Maximum must be verified for bullet-to-rifling clearance and magazine functioning. Where a specific primer or bullet is indicated those components must be used, no substitutions! Where only a maximum load is shown, reduce starting load 10%, unless otherwise specified.

Key: (C) = compressed charge; C = CUP; p = psi; Plink = Plinker; Bns = Barnes; Hdy = Hornady; Lap = Lapua; Nos = Nosler; Rem = Remington; Sra = Sierra; Spr = Speer; Win = Winchester.

250

Powder	Grs.	MV (fps)	Grs.	MV (fps)	Press. (CUP/psi)	Comments
W760	61.0	2520	66.0	2739	52,500C	
RL-22	69.0	2534	74.0	2733	50,000C	
N165			77.9	2720	55,114p	Hdy RN
N165			74.8	2710	55,114p	Sako SP 211F
H4350	66.0	2511	71.0	2709	53,000C	
H450	70.0	2603	75.0	2708	51,500C	
IMR4350	65.0	2498	70.0	2707	51,500C	
IMR7828	71.0	2500	76.0	2703	50,000C	
IMR4831	65.0	2464	70.0	2696	50,500C	
H414	62.0	2493	67.0	2683	53,000C	
H4831	69.0	2498	74.0	2679	53,000C	
RL-19	66.0	2492	71.0	2678	48,500C	
N160			67.9	2670	55,114p	Sako SP 211F
A3100	63.9	2294	71.0	2607	59,100p	Sra SBT/3.34"/CCI 250
H1000	76.0	2431	81.0	2606	48,500C	
N165	69.4	2357	77.2	2604	52,210p	Spr AGS
RL-15	55.0	2436	60.0	2590	50,500C	
A4350	58.5	2276	65.0	2586	60,700p	Sra SBT/3.34"/CCI 250
WMR			72.0	2550	51,600p	Win SP
A2700	59.9	2394	63.0	2547	62,800p	Sra SBT/3.34"/CCI 250

275

Powder	Grs.	MV (fps)	Grs.	MV (fps)	Press. (CUP/psi)	Comments
RL-22	67.0	2447	72.0	2617	52,000C	
RL-19	65.0	2403	70.0	2598	50,000C	
IMR4831	62.0	2341	67.0	2587	52,500C	
H1000	74.0	2423	79.0	2577	52,500C	
IMR7828	67.0	2382	72.0	2560	51,500C	
IMR4350	61.0	2359	66.0	2555	52,500C	
H450	64.0	2356	68.0	2529	52,500C	
N165	67.1	2265	74.4	2488	52,210p	Spr S-Sptz
H414	56.0	2281	62.0	2485	52,500C	
H4350	60.0	2320	65.0	2461	51,500C	
A4350	57.6	2164	64.0	2459	63,200p	Spr SSP/3.33"/CCI 250
H4831	61.0	2269	67.0	2454	51,500C	
A2700	60.3	2304	63.5	2451	62,900p	Spr SSP/3.33"/CCI 250
W760	56.0	2270	61.0	2445	51,500C	
A3100	61.2	2140	68.0	2432	60,000p	Spr SSP/3.33"/CCI 250
N160			65.1	2430	55,114p	Spr SP
H870	74.0	2261	79.0	2416	43,000C	
WMR			67.1	2390	50,800p	Win SP
RL-15	51.0	2214	56.0	2383	50,000C	

300

Powder	Grs.	MV (fps)	Grs.	MV (fps)	Press. (CUP/psi)	Comments
RL-22	63.0	2289	68.0	2481	52,000C	
RL-19	62.0	2321	67.0	2475	51,500C	
H450	63.0	2318	67.0	2447	51,500C	
IMR4831	58.0	2224	63.0	2411	52,000C	
H1000	71.0	2281	76.0	2403	49,500C	
IMR4350	57.0	2234	62.0	2402	52,500C	
IMR7828	62.0	2214	67.0	2392	50,500C	
H4831	61.0	2223	65.0	2366	49,500C	
H870	72.0	2104	77.0	2308	42,500C	

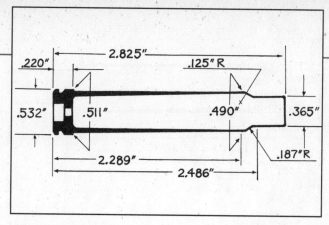

Case: Weatherby
Primer: Large Rifle
Barrel: 26″ Accurate
       26″ Hodgdon
Bullet Diameter: 0.338″

Maximum Case Length: 2.825″
Trim to Length: 2.815″
Maximum Cartridge OAL: 3.563″
Minimum Cartridge OAL:
       Bullet Dependent

In 1962, four years after Winchester's introduction of their 338 Winchester Magnum, Roy Weatherby necked up the existing 300 Weatherby Magnum—with no other changes—to create this more powerful cartridge. Yet, the extreme softness of factory 340 Weatherby cases generally has made it impossible for handloaders to significantly exceed 338 performance, in spite of a considerable increase in capacity and a higher nominal working pressure.

Much better cases can easily be formed from 8mm Remington Magnum or 375 H&H cases, but capacity will be about 5 percent less and top loads will have to be reduced a similar amount to maintain safe pressures. When Weatherby cases are reloaded more than a few times at factory pressures levels, the primer pockets open until they will no longer properly hold a primer!

With top loads in the stronger cases, the 340 can generate truly impressive performance. With hunting-weight bullets, this chambering will shoot just as flat as any commercial 300 Magnum and can deliver considerably more energy to distant targets.

Case capacity with a 225-grain bullet, seated normally, is about 95.4 grains of water. Case capacity of a converted Winchester 375 H&H case, with a 225-grain bullet, seated normally, is about 91.0 grains of water.

340 WEATHERBY MAGNUM LOADING DATA

Powder	Grs.	MV (fps)	Grs.	MV (fps)	Press. (CUP/psi)	Comments
200						
A4350	74.7	2777	83.0	3156	64,100p	Nos BT/3.6″/Fed 215
A3100	81.0	2746	90.0	3121	54,300p	Nos BT/3.6″/Fed 215/(C)
H4831	85.0	2837	90.0	3040		
H450	84.0	2842	89.0	3031		
H4350	77.0	2777	80.0	2994		
A2700	73.2	2811	77.0	2990	57,100p	Nos BT/3.6″/Fed 215
225						
A3100	81.0	2607	90.0	2963	59,800p	Bns-X/3.6″/Fed 215/(C)
A4350	72.9	2564	81.0	2914	61,900p	Bns-X/3.6″/Fed 215
H4831	81.0	2620	86.0	2889		
H4350	75.0	2707	78.0	2866		
H450	81.0	2609	86.0	2848		
A2700	70.3	2619	74.0	2786	60,700p	Bns-X/3.6″/Fed 215
250						
A3100	79.7	2534	88.5	2879	63,500p	Hdy SP/3.6″/Fed 215
H4831	78.0	2587	83.0	2784		

Powder	Grs.	MV (fps)	Grs.	MV (fps)	Press. (CUP/psi)	Comments
250 con't						
A4350	71.1	2446	79.0	2780	61,800p	Hdy SP/3.6″/Fed 215
H450	78.0	2539	83.0	2747		
H4350	73.0	2570	76.0	2724		
A2700	71.3	2555	75.0	2718	63,400p	Hdy SP/3.6″/Fed 215
H870			92.0	2524		
275						
A3100	77.4	2387	86.0	2713	63,500p	Spr SSP/3.6″/Fed 215
A4350	68.4	2286	76.0	2598	59,600p	Spr SSP/3.6″/Fed 215
H870			90.0	2594		
H4350	71.0	2460	74.0	2575		
H4831	75.0	2377	80.0	2569		
H450	75.0	2349	80.0	2537		
A2700	66.5	2335	70.0	2484	61,700p	Spr SSP/3.6″/Fed 215
300						
H870			88.0	2474		
H4350	66.0	2210	70.0	2419		

Never exceed maximum load nor use any load exhibiting signs of excessive pressure. Begin at suggested starting load and work up carefully.

338-378

Keith-Thompson Magnum

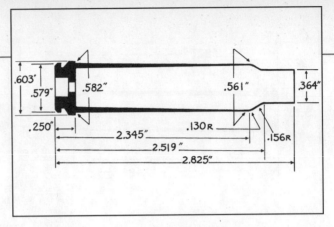

Case: Weatherby (Converted 378 Weatherby Magnum)
Primer: Large Rifle
Barrel: 26″ Hodgdon
Bullet Diameter: 0.338″
Maximum Case Length: 2.825″

Trim to Length: 2.815″
Maximum Cartridge OAL: 3.645″
    (Custom Chamber Dependent)
Minimum Cartridge OAL:
    Bullet Dependent

Invented to fulfill Elmer Keith's desire for a truly long-range powerhouse chambering, specifically for elk hunting, the 338-378 has ample case capacity to launch heavy bullets at high velocity. With a wide selection of excellent big game bullets available, this is a splendid choice for the person not afraid to carry a 10-pound, or heavier, rifle into the hills.

Those demanding a flat trajectory and the delivery of substantial energy at long range will find no better cartridge. At typical elk-hunting elevations, Sierra's 250 SBT easily delivers more energy to targets 600 yards distant than the 30-06 generates at the muzzle!

Cases are formed by running 378 Weatherby cases through the full-length 338-378 KT sizing die. Unfortunately, for those interested in taking the fullest advantage of what this chambering has to offer, there is a genuine pauci-ty of pressure-tested load data. Several powders—H1000, IMR7828, N165, N170, H870 and A8700—promise significant improvements in 338-378 ballistics. The best combinations could safely add 100-200 fps! Hopefully such data will soon be available.

Considering the velocities possible with the 338-378, premium-grade bullets are a particularly good idea. Lighter 338-caliber bullets are designed for use at considerably lower velocity than the cartridge is capable of.

This data was generated in a free-bored barrel. These loads should not be used in any rifle that is not free-bored. Pressure differences are unpredictable so no non-free-bored loads can be suggested. Further, chambering variations are often greater in custom wildcats, compared to commercialized chamberings—pay particular attention to pressure signs.

338-378 KEITH-THOMPSON MAGNUM LOADING DATA

Powder	—STARTING— Grs.	MV (fps)	—MAXIMUM— Grs.	MV (fps)	Press. (CUP/psi)	Comments
250						
H4831	90.0	2746	98.0	3009	54,500C	
275						
H4831	88.0	2629	95.0	2859	53,800C	

Powder	—STARTING— Grs.	MV (fps)	—MAXIMUM— Grs.	MV (fps)	Press. (CUP/psi)	Comments
300						
H4831	84.0	2488	90.0	2731	53,500C	

Caution: Loads exceeding SAAMI OAL Maximum must be verified for bullet-to-rifling clearance and magazine functioning. Where a specific primer or bullet is indicated those components must be used, no substitutions! Where only a maximum load is shown, reduce starting load 10%, unless otherwise specified.

Key: (C) = compressed charge; C = CUP; p = psi; Plink = Plinker; Bns = Barnes; Hdy = Hornady; Lap = Lapua; Nos = Nosler; Rem = Remington; Sra = Sierra; Spr = Speer; Win = Winchester.

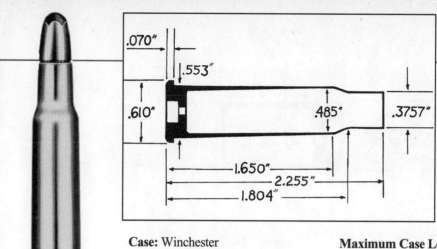

Case: Winchester
Primer: Large Rifle
Barrel: 24″ Accurate
24″ Hodgdon
Bullet Diameter: 0.348″

Maximum Case Length: 2.255″
Trim to Length: 2.250″
Maximum Cartridge OAL: 2.795″
Minimum Cartridge OAL: 2.770″

Introduced in 1936, the 348 must be viewed as the last gasp for rimmed cartridges designed for lever actions. The cartridge was based on the 50-110 Winchester case, necked down. The Model 71, for which the 348 was designed, is nothing more than a modernized version of John M. Browning's Model of 1886. Fifty years after the M86's introduction, Winchester could find nothing of any significance to improve upon. They settled on making a few minor changes and used the best steels available in 1936.

The Model 71 was, and is, a wonderful rifle. The action is slicker working than seems possible, and this rifle is so strong, durable and reliable that many in Alaska still use it as *the* rifle of choice where conditions are rugged and the hunted tend to bite back in a permanent way. In a land where bolt-action belted magnums often fill used guns racks, the Model 71 is

almost never seen for sale at any price!

As a testament to the gun's strength, thousands of these rifles have been converted to a 45-caliber version of this cartridge. Normal handloads in that chambering come very close to duplicating 458 Winchester Magnum performance. Several of those rifles are known to have been fired thousands of times with such loads.

With the necessary blunt bullets and moderate velocity of factory ammunition, which is loaded to truly anemic pressures, the 348 is limited by trajectory to about 200 yards of usable range. This is, nevertheless, a good performer and can deliver plenty of energy for hunting elk-sized game.

Case capacity with a 200-grain bullet, seated normally, is about 66.7 grains of water. Here case-filling slow powders like H4831, A4350 and A3100 work well.

348 WINCHESTER LOADING DATA

Powder	STARTING Grs.	MV (fps)	MAXIMUM Grs.	MV (fps)	Press. (CUP/psi)	Comments
Lead 250 Lyman 350457						
A4350	49.5	1947	55.0	2212	23,700p	2.8″/CCI 200
A3100	54.0	1874	60.0	2130	20,000p	2.8″/CCI 200
180						
BL-C(2)			44.5	2381	31,900C	26″ Bbl
H450			56.5	2338	32,600C	26″ Bbl
200						
A4350	55.8	2223	62.0	2526	24,600p	Hdy FN/2.81″/CCI 200
A2700	53.2	2332	56.0	2481	26,700p	Hdy FN/2.81″/CCI 200
A3100	61.2	2178	68.0	2475	26,700p	Hdy FN/2.81″/CCI 200
200						
H4831	65.0	2316	68.0	2510		26″ Bbl
H450			62.0	2319	32,800C	26″ Bbl

Powder	STARTING Grs.	MV (fps)	MAXIMUM Grs.	MV (fps)	Press. (CUP/psi)	Comments
220						
H4831			65.0	2472		
A4350	53.1	2114	59.0	2402	24,900p	Spr FP/2.75″/CCI 200
A3100	57.6	2095	64.0	2381	25,400p	Spr FP/2.75″/CCI 200
A2700	50.4	2175	53.0	2314	25,800p	Spr FP/2.75″/CCI 200
H450			57.0	2214	33,500C	26″ Bbl
250						
A3100	55.8	2021	62.0	2297	27,100p	Bns FP/2.8″/CCI 200
A4350	49.5	1974	55.0	2243	26,300p	Bns FP/2.8″/CCI 200
A2700	47.5	2018	50.0	2147	26,300p	Bns FP/2.8″/CCI 200
H4895	44.0	1925	47.0	2066		

Never exceed maximum load nor use any load exhibiting signs of excessive pressure. Begin at suggested starting load and work up carefully.

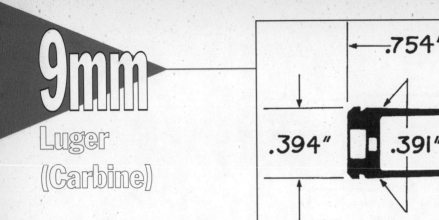

9mm Luger (Carbine)

Case: Federal
Primer: Winchester WSP
Barrel: 18" Accurate
Bullet Diameter: 0.355"

Maximum Case Length: 0.754"
Trim to Length: 0.749"
Maximum Cartridge OAL: 1.169"
Minimum Cartridge OAL: 1.095"

Carbines chambered for this pistol cartridge do not demonstrate any particularly significant increase in performance compared to typical pistols. Limited case capacity, requiring the use of very small charges of fast-burning powder, is to blame. For this reason, and because of limited accuracy, such guns are of only two possible values.

First, they are used in informal target shooting. Military surplus 9mm Luger ammunition is often available at prices that the handloader cannot match, even with home-cast bullets. Ammunition cost is no small factor in the popularity of any chambering. Many of those who like to shoot something a bit more powerful than a rimfire and shoot it cheap-

ly find 9mm Luger-chambered guns irresistible for this reason alone.

Second, these carbines are effective home-defense guns. With energy levels not too far behind actual 357 Magnum revolver performance, the 9mm Luger carbine is a serious performer. The availability of inexpensive practice ammo and a marvelous selection of high-performance factory ammunition and bullets combine to suggest this as a good choice for the purpose.

Case capacity with a 100-grain bullet, seated normally, is about 11.4 grains of water. No. 7 was specifically designed for the 9mm Luger, and its performance is most impressive.

9mm LUGER LOADING DATA (Carbine Specific Loads)

Powder	STARTING Grs.	MV (fps)	MAXIMUM Grs.	MV (fps)	Press. (CUP/psi)	Comments
90						
No.7	8.6	1377	9.5	1565	31,200C	PMC JHP/1.095"
No.5	6.8	1343	7.5	1526	33,000C	PMC JHP/1.095"
No.2	4.8	1331	5.3	1512	33,000C	PMC JHP/1.095"
95						
No.7	8.2	1308	9.1	1486	29,100C	IMI FMJ/1.08"
No.5	6.5	1294	7.2	1470	30,700C	IMI FMJ/1.08"
No.2	4.8	1241	5.3	1410	33,000C	IMI FMJ/1.08"
100						
No.7	8.1	1301	9.0	1478	29,800C	Hdy FMJ/1.095"
No.5	6.3	1289	7.0	1465	29,800C	Hdy FMJ/1.095"
No.2	4.9	1245	5.4	1415	33,000C	Hdy FMJ/1.095"
115						
No.7	7.9	1263	8.8	1435	29,700C	Hdy FMJ/1.095"
No.5	6.3	1261	7.0	1433	31,400C	Hdy FMJ/1.095"
No.2	4.0	1199	4.4	1362	29,900C	Hdy FMJ/1.095"
124						
No.7	7.7	1223	8.5	1390	29,800C	Hdy RN/1.095"
No.5	5.9	1166	6.5	1325	33,000C	Hdy RN/1.095"
No.2	3.7	1103	4.1	1253	29,500C	Hdy RN/1.095"
130						
No.7	7.3	1158	8.1	1316	31,500C	PMC FMJ/1.095"
No.5	5.4	1078	6.0	1225	33,000C	PMC FMJ/1.095"
No.2	4.2	1016	4.7	1155	30,900C	PMC FMJ/1.095"
135						
No.7	6.8	1099	7.5	1249	31,000C	Elite FMJ/1.095"
No.5	5.5	1081	6.1	1228	33,000C	Elite FMJ/1.095"
No.2	4.0	971	4.4	1103	27,500C	Elite FMJ/1.095"
147						
No.7	6.5	1025	7.2	1165	31,900C	Spr TMJ/1.095"
No.5	4.8	964	5.3	1095	30,900C	Spr TMJ/1.095"
No.2	3.6	889	4.0	1010	29,200C	Spr TMJ/1.095"

Never exceed maximum load nor use any load exhibiting signs of excessive pressure. Begin at suggested starting load and work up carefully.

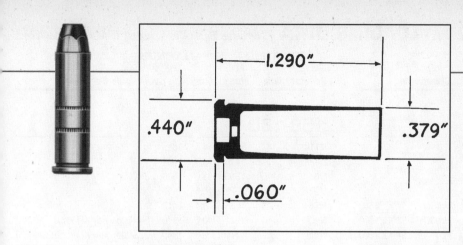

Case: Frontier
Primer: Small Pistol Magnum
Barrel: 20″ Accurate
   20″ Hodgdon
Bullet Diameter: 0.358″

Maximum Case Length: 1.290″
Trim to Length: 1.285″
Maximum Cartridge OAL: 1.590″
Minimum Cartridge OAL: 1.540″

In 1873, Winchester introduced a rifle, the Model 73, chambered for the 44-40 cartridge. Almost immediately, Colt chambered their single-action revolver for the same cartridge. Other Model 73 chamberings followed, each soon adapted to the Colt. That began a tradition which continues to this day. For whatever reason, there seems to be an ongoing fascination with cartridges that can be chambered in both a handgun and a shoulder gun.

Custom-chambered 357 Magnum rifles have been around almost from the day the 357 was released in 1935. Marlin and others have offered the chambering commercially in later years. Performance is considerably better than in a revolver. With reasonable case capacity, the slower powders can generate considerable benefit past 12″ of bar-

rel, and the lack of a vent in the barrel—where the cylinder and barrel do not quite meet—adds more velocity still.

Loaded to top velocity with heavier bullets, the 357 Magnum in a carbine is a capable hunting choice for the smallest species of deer and similar game and for hunting varmints and smaller predators. It is also, obviously, a good choice for a home-defense gun.

Case capacity with a 158-grain bullet, seated normally, is about 17.8 grains of water. H110, No.9 and H4227 are all good choices for loading 357 Magnum-chambered carbines. For target loads, at reduced velocity, use faster powders.

Never use hard round-nose or pointed bullets in any tubular magazine rifle.

357 MAGNUM LOADING DATA (Carbine Specific Loads)

Powder	—STARTING— Grs.	MV (fps)	—MAXIMUM— Grs.	MV (fps)	Press. (CUP/psi)	Comments
Lead 150						
No.9	11.9	1470	13.2	1670	34,100p	1.595″/CCI 500
No.7	9.5	1324	10.6	1505	34,500p	1.595″/CCI 500
No.5	7.6	1283	8.4	1458	34,300p	1.595″/CCI 500
No.2	5.4	1170	6.0	1329	26,800p	1.595″/CCI 500
Lead 158						
No.9	11.0	1359	12.2	1544	32,400p	1.58″/CCI 500
No.7	9.5	1307	10.5	1485	34,400p	1.58″/CCI 500
No.5	7.4	1256	8.2	1427	33,800p	1.58″/CCI 500
No.2	5.2	1112	5.8	1264	26,200p	1.58″/CCI 500
110						
H4227	18.0	1909	19.5	2114		
HS7	12.0	1804	13.0	1949		
HS6	9.0	1619	10.6	1827		
No.7	11.7	1566	13.0	1780	34,100p	Spr JHP/1.575″/CCI 500

Powder	—STARTING— Grs.	MV (fps)	—MAXIMUM— Grs.	MV (fps)	Press. (CUP/psi)	Comments
110 con't						
No.5	9.7	1551	10.8	1763	34,500p	Spr JHP/1.575″/CCI 500
No.2	7.9	1514	8.8	1721	34,400p	Spr JHP/1.575″/CCI 500
HP38	6.2	1417	8.2	1683		
Trap100	6.2	1410	8.2	1672		

▶▶▶▶▶▶▶▶▶▶▶▶▶▶▶▶▶▶▶▶▶▶▶▶▶▶▶▶▶

Caution: Loads exceeding SAAMI OAL Maximum must be verified for bullet-to-rifling clearance and magazine functioning. Where a specific primer or bullet is indicated those components must be used, no substitutions! Where only a maximum load is shown, reduce starting load 10%, unless otherwise specified.

Key: (C) = compressed charge; C = CUP; p = psi; Plink = Plinker; Bns = Barnes; Hdy = Hornady; Lap = Lapua; Nos = Nosler; Rem = Remington; Sra = Sierra; Spr = Speer; Win = Winchester.

125

Powder	STARTING Grs.	MV (fps)	MAXIMUM Grs.	MV (fps)	Press. (CUP/psi)	Comments
H110	18.5	1969	19.0	2050		
H4227	16.0	1768	18.0	1858		
HS7	11.5	1663	12.5	1823		
HS6	8.5	1500	10.0	1714		
No.5	9.1	1443	10.1	1640	35,000p	Hdy XTP/1.57″/CCI 500
No.7	10.8	1416	12.0	1609	33,400p	Hdy XTP/1.57″/CCI 500
No.2	7.4	1391	8.2	1581	34,400p	Hdy XTP/1.57″/CCI 500
HP38	5.4	1274	7.4	1569		
Trap100	5.4	1266	7.4	1554		

140

Powder	STARTING Grs.	MV (fps)	MAXIMUM Grs.	MV (fps)	Press. (CUP/psi)	Comments
H110	16.5	1789	17.0	1853		
No.9	13.0	1518	14.4	1725	33,600p	Spr JHP/1.58″/CCI 500
H4227	15.0	1568	16.0	1674		
HS6	8.2	1403	9.6	1614		
HS7	10.0	1442	11.0	1571		
No.7	10.4	1360	11.6	1545	33,600p	Spr JHP/1.58″/CCI 500
No.5	8.7	1338	9.7	1520	34,900p	Spr JHP/1.58″/CCI 500
No.2	7.0	1289	7.8	1465	34,400p	Spr JHP/1.58″/CCI 500
HP38	4.8	1020	6.8	1381		
Trap100	4.8	1011	6.8	1374		

146-150

Powder	STARTING Grs.	MV (fps)	MAXIMUM Grs.	MV (fps)	Press. (CUP/psi)	Comments
H110	15.0	1659	15.5	1734		
H4227	13.5	1429	15.5	1651		
No.9	12.5	1426	13.9	1620	33,400p	Nos JHP/1.59″/CCI 500
HS7	9.5	1394	10.5	1526		
HS6	7.6	1347	9.0	1505		
No.7	10.0	1261	11.1	1433	33,300p	Nos JHP/1.59″/CCI 500
No.5	8.3	1255	9.2	1426	34,000p	Nos JHP/1.59″/CCI 500
No.2	6.8	1246	7.5	1416	34,200p	Nos JHP/1.59″/CCI 500
HP38	4.3	949	6.3	1345		
Trap100	4.3	936	6.3	1320		

158-160

Powder	STARTING Grs.	MV (fps)	MAXIMUM Grs.	MV (fps)	Press. (CUP/psi)	Comments
H110	14.0	1593	14.5	1645		
H4227	13.0	1410	15.0	1604		
No.9	11.7	1390	13.0	1580	34,000p	Hdy XTP/1.58″/CCI 500
HS7	9.0	1328	10.0	1466		
HS6	7.0	1236	8.4	1412		
No.7	9.5	1211	10.5	1376	34,100p	Hdy XTP/1.58″/CCI 500
No.5	7.7	1179	8.6	1340	32,900p	Hdy XTP/1.58″/CCI 500
No.2	6.2	1117	6.9	1269	33,500p	Hdy XTP/1.58″/CCI 500
HP38	3.6	839	5.6	1208		
Trap100	3.6	824	5.6	1200		

170

Powder	STARTING Grs.	MV (fps)	MAXIMUM Grs.	MV (fps)	Press. (CUP/psi)	Comments
H110	13.5	1487	14.0	1578		
H4227	12.0	1350	14.0	1515		
HS7	8.0	1162	9.0	1316		
HS6	6.6	1142	8.0	1302		
HP38	4.0	867	5.0	1096		
Trap100	4.0	826	5.0	1027		

180

Powder	STARTING Grs.	MV (fps)	MAXIMUM Grs.	MV (fps)	Press. (CUP/psi)	Comments
No.9	10.5	1260	11.7	1432	35,000p	Hdy XTP/1.575″/CCI 500
No.5	7.2	1105	8.0	1256	35,000p	Hdy XTP/1.575″/CCI 500
No.7	8.5	1103	9.4	1253	34,900p	Hdy XTP/1.575″/CCI 500

Caution: Loads exceeding SAAMI OAL Maximum must be verified for bullet-to-rifling clearance and magazine functioning. Where a specific primer or bullet is indicated those components must be used, no substitutions! Where only a maximum load is shown, reduce starting load 10%, unless otherwise specified.

Key: (C) = compressed charge; C = CUP; p = psi; Plink = Plinker; Bns = Barnes; Hdy = Hornady; Lap = Lapua; Nos = Nosler; Rem = Remington; Sra = Sierra; Spr = Speer; Win = Winchester.

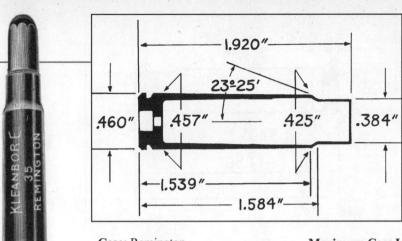

Case: Remington
Primer: Large Rifle
Barrel: 24″ Accurate/20″ Hodgdon
Bullet Diameter: 0.358″

Maximum Case Length: 1.920″
Trim to Length: 1.915″
Maximum Cartridge OAL: 2.525″
Minimum Cartridge OAL: 2.460″

Originally introduced by Remington in 1906, the 35 Remington was chambered in their Model 8 semi-automatic rifle along with a host of other cartridges designed to compete with Winchester's Model 94 chamberings. This cartridge developed a strong following—which cannot be said of the other Remington rimless cartridges or the rifles Remington once so chambered. Marlin has long chambered their Model 336 for the 35 Remington, and this cartridge is also becoming a popular choice for chambering in various handguns.

Pressures have always been low in the 35 Remington, and factory loads seem to skirt maximum pressure specifications with an unusually wide margin. For this reason, in spite having substantially more usable case capacity and increased bore area, 35 Remington ballistics are practically indistinguishable from 30-30 Winchester ballistics. Nevertheless, with a much larger and heavier bullet, the 35 Remington is generally considered to be a better killer on deer and black bear.

Case capacity with a 200-grain bullet, seated normally, is about 44.0 grains of water. RL-7, H335 and BL-C(2) are on the short list of good performers in the 35 Remington.

35 REMINGTON LOADING DATA

Lead 200

Powder	Grs.	MV (fps)	Grs.	MV (fps)	Press. (CUP/psi)	Comments
A2520	34.2	1834	38.0	2084	30,900p	2.41″/CCI 200
A2495BR	36.0	1769	40.0	2010	24,000p	2.41″/CCI 200/(C)
A2460	30.6	1726	34.0	1961	30,300p	2.41″/CCI 200

180

Powder	Grs.	MV (fps)	Grs.	MV (fps)	Press. (CUP/psi)	Comments
BL-C(2)	38.5	1972	42.0	2290		
H335	38.0	1940	42.0	2286		
W748	40.0	2069	42.0	2242		
H4198	32.0	2017	35.0	2202		
A2520	35.1	1867	39.0	2122	27,100p	Spr FN/2.465″/CCI 200
A2495BR	36.9	1866	41.0	2121	30,000p	Spr FN/2.465″/CCI 200/(C)
IMR4064	37.0	1971	40.0	2119		
H414	42.5	1903	46.0	2106		
A2015BR	32.4	1847	36.0	2099	27,800p	Spr FN/2.465″/CCI 200
A2460	33.3	1838	37.0	2089	28,300p	Spr FN/2.465″/CCI 200
H380	40.5	1877	44.0	2075		
IMR4320	37.0	1884	40.0	2070		
A2230	32.9	1814	36.5	2061	28,900p	Spr FN/2.465″/CCI 200
IMR3031	34.0	1849	37.0	2020		
RL-7	28.0	1818	31.0	1992		

200

Powder	Grs.	MV (fps)	Grs.	MV (fps)	Press. (CUP/psi)	Comments
A2520	35.1	1822	39.0	2071	27,800p	Sra FP/2.47″/CCI 200
H4895	36.0	1881	39.0	2069		
H335	35.0	1779	39.0	2057		
A2015BR	31.5	1806	35.0	2052	31,000p	Sra FP/2.47″/CCI 200
A2460	33.3	1785	37.0	2028	27,200p	Sra FP/2.47″/CCI 200
W748	37.0	1869	39.0	2027		
A2495BR	36.0	1784	40.0	2027	25,500p	Sra FP/2.47″/CCI 200/(C)
W760	44.0	1888	45.0	2012		
IMR4064	36.0	1841	39.0	1997		
A2230	31.5	1744	35.0	1982	30,900p	Sra FP/2.47″/CCI 200
IMR4320	36.0	1827	39.0	1966		
IMR3031	32.0	1750	35.0	1941		
H4198	26.0	1675	29.0	1914		
RL-7	26.0	1742	29.0	1899		

220

Powder	Grs.	MV (fps)	Grs.	MV (fps)	Press. (CUP/psi)	Comments
H335	33.0	1749	36.0	1910		
BL-C(2)	33.0	1759	36.0	1908		
H380	36.0	1795	39.0	1878		
H414	38.0	1789	41.0	1862		
H4895	32.0	1624	35.0	1747		
H4198	22.0	1342	25.0	1558		

356
Winchester

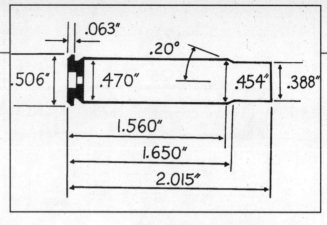

Case dimensions: .063″, .20°, .506″, .470″, .454″, .388″, 1.560″, 1.650″, 2.015″

Case: Winchester
Primer: Large Rifle
Barrel: 24″ Accurate
      20″ Hodgdon
Bullet Diameter: 0.358″

Maximum Case Length: 2.015″
Trim to Length: 2.010″
Maximum Cartridge OAL: 2.560″
Minimum Cartridge OAL: 2.530″

Co-introduced in 1980 with the "Angle-Eject" version of the Model 94 Winchester—which allows proper mounting of a scope sight—this cartridge is simply the 358 Winchester with an added rim that fits the standard 30-30 bolt-face. Since the extractor groove is still necessary to facilitate proper functioning of the extractor, this case is best described as semi-rimmed.

Performance is quite impressive. When loaded to top pressures, the 356 Winchester easily launches a 220-grain flat-nose bullet just as fast as the 30-06 can launch a 220-grain round-nose bullet. Impressive performance for the Model 94. However, the market just does not seem to exist. First, recoil in such a light rifle can only be described as bru-

tal. Second, few elk hunters are interested in a cartridge and gun that limits them to 200-yard shots. Third, there really is not any call for more power than the 30-30 can deliver for hunting smaller species at such short ranges.

Nevertheless, the 356 could have a niche—if only a small one. In a handy carbine, this chambering is a ballistic dead ringer for the 348 Winchester. It should make an excellent choice for a camp gun in the wilds of Alaska.

Case capacity with a 250-grain bullet, seated normally, is about 44.9 grains of water. H335, H4895, IMR4064 and W748 are all good choices for loading the 356 Winchester.

Never use hard round-nose or pointed bullets in any tubular magazine rifle.

356 WINCHESTER LOADING DATA

180

Powder	STARTING Grs.	MV (fps)	MAXIMUM Grs.	MV (fps)	Press. (CUP/psi)	Comments
A2015BR	40.5	2379	45.0	2703	46,300C	Spr FN/2.545″/ Win WLR
H4198	40.0	2441	43.0	2600		
A2520	44.1	2267	49.0	2576	41,800C	Spr FN/2.545″/ Win WLR/(C)
IMR4198	39.0	2396	42.0	2559		
H322	44.0	2360	47.0	2552		
A2460	41.4	2244	46.0	2550	44,400C	Spr FN/2.545″/ Win WLR
H4895	46.0	2360	49.0	2535		
IMR4895	46.0	2354	49.0	2515		
A2230	40.5	2207	45.0	2508	45,500C	Spr FN/2.545″/ Win WLR

180 con't

Powder	STARTING Grs.	MV (fps)	MAXIMUM Grs.	MV (fps)	Press. (CUP/psi)	Comments
RL-7	40.0	2371	43.0	2498		
IMR3031	44.0	2349	47.0	2484		
A2495BR	43.2	2177	48.0	2474	37,600C	Spr FN/2.545″/ Win WLR/(C)
W748	50.0	2349	52.0	2466		
IMR4064	46.0	2280	49.0	2464		
H335	49.0	2311	51.0	2449		
IMR4320	47.0	2310	49.0	2449		
BL-C(2)	50.0	2353	52.0	2431		
A2700	46.6	2161	49.0	2299	40,600C	Spr FN/2.545″/ Win WLR/(C)
H4227	24.0	1878	30.0	2238		
IMR4227	23.0	1837	29.0	2201		

Never exceed maximum load nor use any load exhibiting signs of excessive pressure. Begin at suggested starting load and work up carefully.

200

Powder	Grs.	MV (fps)	Grs.	MV (fps)	Press. (CUP/psi)	Comments
H4198	37.0	2201	40.0	2383		
IMR4198	37.0	2194	40.0	2374		
RL-7	38.0	2147	41.0	2344		
H322	41.0	2199	44.0	2340		
H4895	43.0	2170	46.0	2338		
IMR4895	43.0	2184	46.0	2330		
IMR4064	45.0	2158	48.0	2319		
IMR3031	41.0	2180	44.0	2303		
IMR4320	45.0	2138	48.0	2284		
H335	48.0	2189	49.0	2269		
W748	48.0	2166	50.0	2257		
BL-C(2)	49.0	2162	50.0	2243		

220

Powder	Grs.	MV (fps)	Grs.	MV (fps)	Press. (CUP/psi)	Comments
A2520	41.9	2116	46.5	2404	45,400C	Spr FN/2.555"/ Win WLR/(C)
A2015BR	35.1	2037	39.0	2315	44,200C	Spr FN/2.555"/ Win WLR
A2495BR	40.5	2015	45.0	2290	39,100C	Spr FN/2.555"/ Win WLR/(C)
A2460	36.9	1992	41.0	2264	45,300C	Spr FN/2.555"/ Win WLR
A2230	36.0	1961	40.0	2228	46,600C	Spr FN/2.555"/ Win WLR
A2700	45.6	2029	48.0	2158	44,800C	Spr FN/2.555"/ Win WLR/(C)

250

Powder	Grs.	MV (fps)	Grs.	MV (fps)	Press. (CUP/psi)	Comments
BL-C(2)	46.0	2010	48.0	2163		
W748	46.0	2006	48.0	2160		
H335	44.0	1988	46.0	2151		
IMR4064	41.0	1952	44.0	2141		
H4198	34.0	1879	37.0	2133		
H4895	40.0	1919	43.0	2128		
IMR4320	41.0	1929	44.0	2126		
H322	38.0	1866	41.0	2106		
IMR3031	38.0	1845	41.0	2100		
RL-7	33.0	1888	36.0	2089		
IMR4895	39.0	1914	42.0	2088		
IMR4198	32.0	1822	35.0	2009		

Caution: Loads exceeding SAAMI OAL Maximum must be verified for bullet-to-rifling clearance and magazine functioning. Where a specific primer or bullet is indicated those components must be used, no substitutions! Where only a maximum load is shown, reduce starting load 10%, unless otherwise specified.

Key: (C) = compressed charge; C = CUP; p = psi; Plink = Plinker; Bns = Barnes; Hdy = Hornady; Lap = Lapua; Nos = Nosler; Rem = Remington; Sra = Sierra; Spr = Speer; Win = Winchester.

358
Winchester

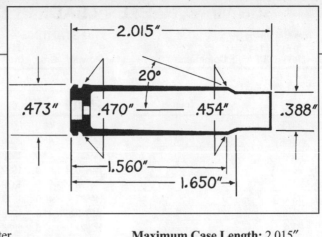

Case: Winchester
Primer: Large Rifle
Barrel: 24″ Accurate/26″ Hodgdon
Bullet Diameter: 0.358″

Maximum Case Length: 2.015″
Trim to Length: 2.005″
Maximum Cartridge OAL: 2.780″
Minimum Cartridge OAL: 2.730″

Co-introduced in 1955, the Model 88 Winchester lever-action rifle and the 358 Winchester cartridge were intended as a more modern and profitable replacement for the Model 71 rifle and the 348 Winchester cartridge. Performance was identical, while the clip feed certainly would have seemed to have been a preferable design over the 71's tubular magazine. Nevertheless, the Model 88 and the 358 Winchester never garnered much consumer support. One reason for this might have been a little design flaw in the Model 88. I watched one fire while being carried, slung over the shoulder, with the safety on and nothing touching the trigger. I

know of two other 88s that did the same thing.

The 358 was also chambered in the Model 70 and in Savage's Model 99, among others.

With pressures near the top end of the normal range, the 358 can generate spectacular performance and is fully capable for use against any species in North America and most critters anywhere in the world. In spite of this, it has languished and is no long commercially chambered.

Case capacity with a 250-grain bullet, seated normally, is about 47.4 grains of water. A2520 and H4198 are good 358 Win. choices.

358 WINCHESTER LOADING DATA

Lead 205 Lyman 358315

Powder	STARTING Grs.	MV (fps)	MAXIMUM Grs.	MV (fps)	Press. (CUP/psi)	Comments
A2495BR	38.7	2177	43.0	2474	44,800C	2.595″/Win WLR
A2015BR	36.9	2174	41.0	2470	41,600C	2.595″/Win WLR
A2520	40.5	2167	45.0	2462	41,200C	2.595″/Win WLR
A2460	38.7	2132	43.0	2423	42,700C	2.595″/Win WLR

180

Powder	STARTING Grs.	MV (fps)	MAXIMUM Grs.	MV (fps)	Press. (CUP/psi)	Comments
H4198	40.0	2525	43.0	2711		

200

Powder	STARTING Grs.	MV (fps)	MAXIMUM Grs.	MV (fps)	Press. (CUP/psi)	Comments
A2520	44.6	2260	49.5	2568	48,900C	Hdy SP/2.64″/Win WLR/(C)
H4198	38.0	2359	41.0	2532		
A2015BR	37.8	2218	42.0	2520	49,400C	Hdy SP/2.64″/Win WLR
A2460	41.4	2206	46.0	2507	51,400C	Hdy SP/2.64″/Win WLR
A2230	39.6	2160	44.0	2454	51,400C	Hdy SP/2.64″/Win WLR

220

Powder	STARTING Grs.	MV (fps)	MAXIMUM Grs.	MV (fps)	Press. (CUP/psi)	Comments
H4148	38.0	2287	41.0	2502		
H335	46.0	2281	48.0	2464		
BL-C(2)	46.0	2294	48.0	2461	52,000C	26″ Test Barrel

225

Powder	STARTING Grs.	MV (fps)	MAXIMUM Grs.	MV (fps)	Press. (CUP/psi)	Comments
A2520	43.2	2167	48.0	2462	49,000C	Sra SBT/2.74″/Win WLR/(C)
A2495BR	41.4	2116	46.0	2405	47,800C	Sra SBT/2.74″/Win WLR/(C)
A2015BR	36.9	2109	41.0	2397	49,300C	Sra SBT/2.74″/Win WLR
A2460	39.6	2090	44.0	2375	51,000C	Sra SBT/2.74″/Win WLR
A2230	38.7	2062	43.0	2343	50,800C	Sra SBT/2.74″/Win WLR
A2700	47.5	2111	50.0	2246	47,600C	Sra SBT/2.74″/Win WLR/(C)

250

Powder	STARTING Grs.	MV (fps)	MAXIMUM Grs.	MV (fps)	Press. (CUP/psi)	Comments
A2520	45.6	2247	48.0	2390	49,700C	Hdy RN/2.745″/Win WLR/(C)
BL-C(2)	45.0	2219	48.0	2374	52,200C	26″ Test Barrel
H4198	36.0	2198	39.0	2312		
A2460	39.6	2033	44.0	2310	52,000C	Hdy RN/2.745″/Win WLR
A2495BR	41.4	2027	46.0	2303	43,400C	Hdy RN/2.745″/Win WLR/(C)
H335	44.0	2197	46.0	2299		
A2015BR	36.0	2013	40.0	2288	49,600C	Hdy RN/2.745″/Win WLR
A2230	38.7	1998	43.0	2271	52,000C	Hdy RN/2.745″/Win WLR
A2700	47.5	2081	50.0	2214	49,800C	Hdy RN/2.745″/Win WLR/(C)

275

Powder	STARTING Grs.	MV (fps)	MAXIMUM Grs.	MV (fps)	Press. (CUP/psi)	Comments
H4198	34.0	1918	37.0	2079		

Never exceed maximum load nor use any load exhibiting signs of excessive pressure. Begin at suggested starting load and work up carefully.

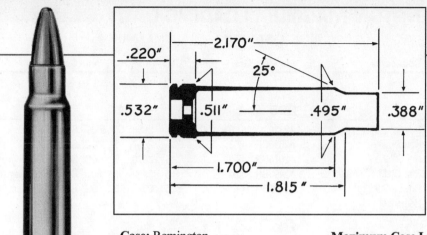

Case: Remington
Primer: Large Rifle
Barrel: 20″ Accurate/26″ Hodgdon
Bullet Diameter: 0.358″

Maximum Case Length: 2.170″
Trim to Length: 2.16″
Maximum Cartridge OAL: 2.80″
Minimum Cartridge OAL: 2.73″

Introduced in 1965 and chambered in the innovative Model 600 Carbine, the 350 Remington Magnum offers 35 Whelen performance in a ½-inch shorter cartridge and with a much shorter barrel. In that carbine's 18½″ barrel, performance was somewhat limited. On the other hand, in that very light gun, recoil did not seem quite so limited!

At that time, there developed an incomprehensible bias in the mainstream gun press against any chambering designed to work through a shorter-than-standard action. An equal prejudice developed against carbine-length long guns. Evidently, the shooting public was just simply not ready for such a light and handy combination—or at least the gun press seemed to think so.

Equipped with a 20″ barrel, the 350 Magnum can launch a 200-grain bullet at over 3000 fps. Obviously, this chambering is capable for use against larger North American big game even to longer ranges. Nevertheless, the chambering seems destined to achieve obsolescence in the not too distant future. However, with the increasing popularity of short, light and otherwise handy carbines, and increasing acceptance of muzzlebrakes, it seems there may yet develop a market for this little powerhouse.

Usable case capacity with a 200-grain bullet, seated normally, is about 66 grains of water. IMR4064, IMR4320, H4895, H335 and A2460 all do well in this chambering.

350 REMINGTON MAGNUM LOADING DATA

Lead 204 Lyman 358315

Powder	STARTING Grs.	MV (fps)	MAXIMUM Grs.	MV (fps)	Press. (CUP/psi)	Comments
A2015BR	47.7	2389	53.0	2715	47,300C	2.7″/Rem 9½M
A2230	48.6	2353	54.0	2674	42,200C	2.7″/Rem 9½M
A2520	49.5	2348	55.0	2668	43,600C	2.7″/Rem 9½M
A2460	48.6	2312	54.0	2627	39,000C	2.7″/Rem 9½M
A2495BR	49.1	2311	54.5	2626	41,400C	2.7″/Rem 9½M

180

Powder	STARTING Grs.	MV (fps)	MAXIMUM Grs.	MV (fps)	Press. (CUP/psi)	Comments
H4895	56.0	2696	61.0	3015	52,300C	
H335	57.0	2769	62.0	3006	50,600C	
BL-C(2)	57.0	2776	62.0	2992	50,300C	
IMR4064	58.0	2725	62.0	2919	51,000C	
IMR4895	58.0	2710	61.0	2909	51,200C	
IMR3031	56.0	2690	59.0	2901	51,400C	
H322	53.0	2688	58.0	2894	50,300C	
IMR4320	58.0	2660	61.0	2814	50,100C	
H4198	48.0	2622	51.0	2808	48,000C	
H4831			62.0	2254	21,000C	

Caution: Loads exceeding SAAMI OAL Maximum must be verified for bullet-to-rifling clearance and magazine functioning. Where a specific primer or bullet is indicated those components must be used, no substitutions! Where only a maximum load is shown, reduce starting load 10%, unless otherwise specified.

Key: (C) = compressed charge; C = CUP; p = psi; Plink = Plinker; Bns = Barnes; Hdy = Hornady; Lap = Lapua; Nos = Nosler; Rem = Remington; Sra = Sierra; Spr = Speer; Win = Winchester.

>>>>>>>>>>>>>>>>>>>>>>>>>>>>>>>>

Never exceed maximum load nor use any load exhibiting signs of excessive pressure. Begin at suggested starting load and work up carefully.

200

Powder	—STARTING— Grs.	MV (fps)	—MAXIMUM— Grs.	MV (fps)	Press. (CUP/psi)	Comments
A2520	54.0	2647	60.0	3008	51,800C	Hdy SP/2.8"/ Rem 9½M
A2230	53.1	2504	59.0	2846	51,300C	Hdy SP/2.8"/ Rem 9½M
A2460	53.6	2499	59.5	2840	50,700C	Hdy SP/2.8"/ Rem 9½M
H4895	54.5	2625	59.0	2822	52,100C	
IMR4895	56.0	2669	59.0	2818	51,800C	
BL-C(2)	55.0	2639	60.0	2808	50,100C	
IMR4064	57.0	2680	60.0	2797	51,200C	
H335	55.0	2634	58.0	2794	50,000C	
A2015BR	48.6	2445	54.0	2778	50,700C	Hdy SP/2.8"/ Rem 9½M
A2495BR	53.1	2441	59.0	2774	51,700C	Hdy SP/2.8"/ Rem 9½M
IMR4320	57.0	2624	60.0	2771	50,200C	
H380	59.0	2556	64.0	2753	45,900C	
IMR3031	52.0	2513	55.0	2688	51,000C	
H322	50.0	2427	55.0	2684	49,300C	
H4198	45.0	2382	48.0	2512	44,100C	
H4831			61.0	2144	24,000C	

220

Powder	Grs.	MV (fps)	Grs.	MV (fps)	Press. (CUP/psi)	Comments
H4895	51.5	2434	56.0	2651	51,200C	
BL-C(2)	51.5	2480	56.0	2640	51,000C	
H335	51.0	2451	54.0	2640	51,600C	
IMR4895	53.0	2479	56.0	2627	51,400C	
IMR4064	54.0	2466	57.0	2619	50,700C	
H380	56.0	2388	61.0	2569	47,300C	
IMR4320	55.0	2418	58.0	2539	50,800C	
IMR3031	49.0	2377	52.0	2474	50,100C	
H322	48.0	2293	52.0	2473	49,300C	
H4198	43.0	2304	46.0	2423	48,500C	
H4831			60.0	2141	30,000C	

225

Powder	Grs.	MV (fps)	Grs.	MV (fps)	Press. (CUP/psi)	Comments
A2230	51.3	2409	57.0	2738	52,600C	Nos SP/2.8"/Rem 9½M
A2460	51.8	2407	57.5	2735	53,000C	Nos SP/2.8"/Rem 9½M
A2230	51.3	2392	57.0	2718	52,400C	Sra SBT/2.8"/Rem 9½M
A2460	51.8	2384	57.5	2709	52,500C	Sra SBT/2.8"/Rem 9½M
A2520	51.8	2374	57.5	2698	52,500C	Nos SP/2.8"/Rem 9½M

225 con't

Powder	Grs.	MV (fps)	Grs.	MV (fps)	Press. (CUP/psi)	Comments
A2520	51.8	2367	57.5	2690	52,500C	Sra SBT/2.8"/Rem 9½M
A2015BR	47.3	2338	52.5	2657	52,600C	Sra SBT/2.8"/Rem 9½M
A2015BR	47.3	2306	52.5	2620	53,000C	Nos SP/2.8"/Rem 9½M
A2495BR	50.0	2270	55.5	2580	49,600C	Sra SBT/2.8"/Rem 9½M
A2495BR	49.1	2269	54.5	2578	52,400C	Nos SP/2.8"/Rem 9½M

250

Powder	Grs.	MV (fps)	Grs.	MV (fps)	Press. (CUP/psi)	Comments
A2460	50.4	2267	56.0	2576	53,000C	Nos SP/2.8"/Rem 9½M
A2230	48.6	2217	54.0	2519	49,600C	Nos SP/2.8"/Rem 9½M
A2520	50.9	2213	56.5	2515	53,000C	Nos SP/2.8"/Rem 9½M
A2015BR	45.9	2200	51.0	2500	52,600C	Nos SP/2.8"/Rem 9½M
H4895	49.5	2225	54.0	2497	53,200C	
BL-C(2)	48.5	2214	53.0	2464	52,100C	
H335	48.0	2190	51.0	2457	51,800C	
A2495BR	48.6	2141	54.0	2433	53,000C	Nos SP/2.8"/Rem 9½M
H380	54.0	2206	59.0	2410	47,300C	
IMR4320	52.0	2248	55.0	2410	50,400C	
IMR4895	50.0	2229	54.0	2364	52,000C	
IMR4064	51.0	2166	55.0	2342	49,400C	
H322	45.0	2092	49.0	2333	51,600C	
IMR3031	48.0	2180	51.0	2319	50,000C	
H4198	39.0	2069	42.0	2190	45,900C	
H4831			59.0	2125	32,400C	

275

Powder	Grs.	MV (fps)	Grs.	MV (fps)	Press. (CUP/psi)	Comments
H380	54.0	2196	59.0	2350	48,200C	
BL-C(2)	48.0	2143	52.0	2311	49,600C	
H335	48.0	2141	50.0	2303	48,200C	
H4895	48.0	2111	52.0	2269	47,600C	
H4831			59.0	2100	34,800C	
H322	43.0	1908	47.0	2079	50,300C	

300

Powder	Grs.	MV (fps)	Grs.	MV (fps)	Press. (CUP/psi)	Comments
H335	49.0	2069	50.0	2171	50,000C	
BL-C(2)	50.0	2055	51.0	2142	49,700C	
IMR4064	48.0	2010	51.0	2140	51,200C	
IMR4320	49.0	2006	51.0	2132	51,900C	
H4895	48.0	2043	50.0	2131	49,900C	
IMR4895	47.0	1994	50.0	2129	50,600C	

Caution: **Loads exceeding SAAMI OAL Maximum must be verified for bullet-to-rifling clearance and magazine functioning. Where a specific primer or bullet is indicated those components must be used, no substitutions! Where only a maximum load is shown, reduce starting load 10%, unless otherwise specified.**

Key: (C) = compressed charge; C = CUP; p = psi; Plink = Plinker; Bns = Barnes; Hdy = Hornady; Lap = Lapua; Nos = Nosler; Rem = Remington; Sra = Sierra; Spr = Speer; Win = Winchester.

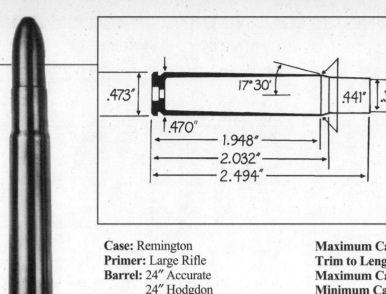

Case: Remington
Primer: Large Rifle
Barrel: 24″ Accurate
      24″ Hodgdon
Bullet Diameter: 0.358″

Maximum Case Length: 2.494″
Trim to Length: 2.484″
Maximum Cartridge OAL: 3.34″
Minimum Cartridge OAL: 2.97″

For decades, the man whose name designates this cartridge was not properly honored with having designed it. For reasons of historical confusion, it was believed that James Howe developed the cartridge and merely named it in honor of Col. Whelen. Recent literary research proves that Whelen was solely responsible for the design, circa 1922—nothing more complicated than necking up the standard 30-06 to 35-caliber with no other changes—and that Mr. Howe merely built the first rifles so chambered.

In 1988, Remington commercialized this chambering. Most knowledgeable shooters would agree that it is a shame Remington chose not to standardize Mr. Ackley's vastly superior improved version instead. That version features a significant increase in usable case capacity, controls headspace three times as well and would have eliminated concerns about loads developed for custom-chambered rifles being used in possibly tighter and likely shorter-throated commercial guns—thereby possibly creating dangerous pressures.

However, the 35 Whelen in standard form is what we have, and it is a fine cartridge. Interestingly, the standardized Whelen is rated at a higher working pressure than the 30-06. When loaded to top pressures, it can easily launch 225-grain bullets as fast as the 30-06 can launch 180-grain bullets. Bullets of 250 grains can come very near to duplicating 180-grain 30-06 velocities. Obviously, the Whelen is a good choice for use on the biggest and most dangerous of animals in North America and for most species worldwide.

Usable case capacity with a 250-grain bullet, seated normally, is about 63.6 grains of water. IMR4064, BL-C(2), RL-15, H380 and IMR4320 are noted performers in the Whelen.

35 WHELEN LOADING DATA

Lead 205 Lyman 358315

Powder	—STARTING— Grs.	MV (fps)	—MAXIMUM— Grs.	MV (fps)	Press. (CUP/psi)	Comments
A2520	48.6	2410	54.0	2739	50,000p	3.045″/CCI 200
A2495BR	46.8	2388	52.0	2714	48,700p	3.045″/CCI 200
A2015BR	45.0	2387	50.0	2713	49,400p	3.045″/CCI 200
A2230	46.8	2378	52.0	2702	53,700p	3.045″/CCI 200
A2700	57.0	2521	60.0	2682	48,000p	3.045″/Rem 9½
A2460	46.8	2358	52.0	2679	48,400p	3.045″/CCI 200
A4350	54.0	2220	60.0	2523	38,300p	3.045″/CCI 200/(C)
XMP5744			38.0	2452	45,100p	3.045″/CCI 200
A3100	54.0	1996	60.0	2268	28,900p	3.045″/CCI 200/(C)
A8700	58.5	1648	65.0	1873	26,600p	3.045″/CCI 200/(C)

Lead 250 RCBS Silhouette

Powder	—STARTING— Grs.	MV (fps)	—MAXIMUM— Grs.	MV (fps)	Press. (CUP/psi)	Comments
A2495BR	50.0	2190	55.5	2489	50,100p	3.25″/CCI 200
A2520	45.0	2088	50.0	2373	53,000p	3.25″/CCI 200
A4350	54.0	2084	60.0	2368	44,800p	3.25″/CCI 200/(C)
A2460	42.3	2029	47.0	2306	48,200p	3.25″/CCI 200
A2230	41.4	2028	46.0	2305	50,900p	3.25″/CCI 200
A2015BR	40.5	2020	45.0	2296	48,900p	3.25″/CCI 200
A2700	49.4	2069	52.0	2201	43,100p	3.25″/Rem 9½
XMP5744			36.0	2173	47,700p	3.25″/CCI-200
A3100	54.0	1894	60.0	2152	31,900p	3.25″/CCI 200/(C)
A8700	58.5	1573	65.0	1788	28,300p	3.25″/CCI 200/(C)

Never exceed maximum load nor use any load exhibiting signs of excessive pressure. Begin at suggested starting load and work up carefully.

Lead 280 Lyman 358009

Powder	—STARTING— Grs.	MV (fps)	—MAXIMUM— Grs.	MV (fps)	Press. (CUP/psi)	Comments
A4350	49.5	1939	55.0	2203	41,600p	3.05"/CCI 200
A2495BR	43.2	1925	48.0	2188	38,500p	3.05"/CCI 200
A2520	40.5	1909	45.0	2169	46,000p	3.05"/CCI 200
A2460	38.3	1863	42.5	2117	44,400p	3.05"/CCI 200
A2015BR	36.9	1857	41.0	2110	46,100p	3.05"/CCI 200
A2230	37.8	1846	42.0	2098	42,700p	3.05"/CCI 200
A2700	45.6	1966	48.0	2091	42,400p	3.05"/Rem 9½
A3100	51.3	1824	57.0	2073	34,300p	3.05"/CCI 200
XMP5744			34.0	2015	43,900p	3.05"/CCI 200
A8700	54.0	1463	60.0	1663	28,700p	3.05"/CCI 200

180

Powder	—STARTING— Grs.	MV (fps)	—MAXIMUM— Grs.	MV (fps)	Press. (CUP/psi)	Comments
A2015BR	50.9	2607	56.5	2963	51,900p	Spr FN/3.035"/CCI 200
A2495BR	53.6	2585	59.5	2937	51,800p	Spr FN/3.035"/CCI 200
A2520	54.5	2564	60.5	2914	48,500p	Spr FN/3.035"/CCI 200
H335	56.0	2741	60.0	2870	50,000C	
A2460	53.1	2518	59.0	2861	45,000p	Spr FN/3.035"/CCI 200
BL-C(2)	62.0	2644	65.0	2860	48,500C	
W748	61.0	2610	64.0	2829	48,000C	
H322	55.0	2707	58.0	2829	48,500C	
A2230	51.3	2482	57.0	2820	44,600p	Spr FN/3.035"/CCI 200
RL-15	58.0	2684	62.0	2803	46,500C	
H4895	56.0	2649	60.0	2798	46,800C	
A2700	62.7	2609	66.0	2776	43,400p	Spr FN/3.035"/Rem 9½/(C)
IMR3031	54.0	2611	58.0	2760	47,500C	
RL-12	60.0	2580	62.0	2746	46,000C	
RL-7	49.0	2606	52.0	2743	49,000C	
IMR4064	56.0	2591	60.0	2742	47,000C	
IMR4895	55.0	2619	59.0	2739	49,000C	
IMR4320	56.0	2577	60.0	2727	49,500C	
A4350	58.5	2252	65.0	2559	31,200p	Spr FN/3.035"/CCI 200/(C)
A3100	58.5	2006	65.0	2279	24,400p	Spr FN/3.035"/CCI 200/(C)

200

Powder	—STARTING— Grs.	MV (fps)	—MAXIMUM— Grs.	MV (fps)	Press. (CUP/psi)	Comments
BL-C(2)	60.0	2636	63.0	2807	49,000C	
A2015BR	48.6	2462	54.0	2798	52,400p	Hdy SP/3.14"/CCI 200
A2495BR	51.3	2458	57.0	2793	50,200p	Hdy SP/3.14"/CCI 200
W748	59.0	2566	62.0	2774	49,500C	
A2520	52.7	2424	58.5	2755	47,900p	Hdy SP/3.14"/CCI 200
RL-15	57.0	2589	61.0	2752	48,500C	
A2460	50.4	2420	56.0	2750	48,300p	Bns-X/3.225"/CCI 200
A2700	61.8	2579	65.0	2744	48,500p	Hdy SP/3.14"/Rem 9½/(C)
A2460	51.3	2401	57.0	2728	49,800p	Hdy SP/3.14"/CCI 200
IMR4064	53.0	2566	57.0	2713	47,500C	
A2230	49.5	2379	55.0	2703	50,700p	Hdy SP/3.14"/CCI 200
A2230	49.1	2378	54.5	2702	46,500p	Bns-X/3.225"/CCI 200
A2520	50.9	2374	56.5	2698	46,200p	Bns-X/3.225"/CCI 200
H322	52.0	2540	56.0	2691	48,500C	
H4895	54.0	2544	57.0	2689	49,000C	
H335	52.0	2588	55.0	2684	50,000C	
A2015BR	45.9	2359	51.0	2681	46,900p	Bns-X/3.225"/CCI 200
IMR3031	51.0	2539	55.0	2681	50,000C	

200 con't

Powder	—STARTING— Grs.	MV (fps)	—MAXIMUM— Grs.	MV (fps)	Press. (CUP/psi)	Comments
IMR4895	52.0	2510	56.0	2659	49,000C	
RL-12	58.0	2499	61.0	2652	48,000C	
IMR4320	54.0	2509	58.0	2652	50,000C	
A2495BR	49.1	2316	54.5	2632	46,600p	Bns-X/3.225"/CCI 200
H380	59.0	2511	61.0	2602	45,000C	
RL-7	46.0	2437	49.0	2584	50,000C	
A2700	57.5	2422	60.5	2577	42,300p	Bns-X/3.225"/Rem 9½/(C)
W760	61.0	2398	65.0	2544	44,000C	
A4350	53.1	2074	59.0	2357	29,500p	Hdy SP/3.14"/CCI 200/(C)
A4350	54.0	2033	60.0	2310	29,800p	Bns-X/3.225"/CCI 200/(C)
A3100	54.0	1881	60.0	2138	24,100p	Hdy SP/3.14"/CCI 200/(C)
A3100	54.0	1797	60.0	2042	24,500p	Bns-X/3.225"/CCI 200/(C)

220

Powder	—STARTING— Grs.	MV (fps)	—MAXIMUM— Grs.	MV (fps)	Press. (CUP/psi)	Comments
BL-C(2)	58.0	2492	61.0	2636	49,000C	
RL-15	55.0	2477	59.0	2622	48,000C	
W748	57.0	2494	60.0	2598	48,500C	
H4895	51.0	2461	55.0	2588	50,100C	
RL-12	56.0	2398	59.0	2587	48,500C	
H322	50.0	2392	54.0	2566	49,500C	
IMR3031	49.0	2404	53.0	2549	49,500C	
IMR4895	50.0	2379	54.0	2542	49,000C	
IMR4064	52.0	2430	55.0	2539	47,500C	
IMR4320	52.0	2421	56.0	2534	49,500C	
H335	50.0	2429	53.0	2519	49,500C	
H380	58.0	2384	60.0	2490	44,800C	
W760	60.0	2340	63.0	2424	45,600C	
RL-7	44.0	2227	47.0	2410	48,500C	

225

Powder	—STARTING— Grs.	MV (fps)	—MAXIMUM— Grs.	MV (fps)	Press. (CUP/psi)	Comments
A2460	48.6	2299	54.0	2613	51,900p	Sra SBT/3.28"/CCI 200
A2460	48.6	2292	54.0	2604	52,200p	Nos Part./3.215"/CCI 200
A2700	59.4	2447	62.5	2603	49,800p	Nos Part./3.215"/Rem 9½/(C)
A2520	49.5	2291	55.0	2603	52,300p	Nos Part./3.215"/CCI 200
A2700	58.4	2445	61.5	2601	51,200p	Sra SBT/3.28"/Rem 9½
A2520	49.5	2287	55.0	2599	51,100p	Sra SBT/3.28"/CCI 200
A2230	47.7	2278	53.0	2589	52,400p	Nos Part./3.215"/CCI 200
A2015BR	44.1	2271	49.0	2581	51,700p	Nos Part./3.215"/CCI 200
A2230	47.3	2264	52.5	2573	49,200p	Sra SBT/3.28"/CCI 200
A2495BR	45.9	2264	51.0	2573	52,200p	Nos Part./3.215"/CCI 200
A2460	46.8	2261	52.0	2569	50,400p	Bns-X/3.22"/CCI 200
A2230	46.8	2251	52.0	2558	51,300p	Bns-X/3.22"/CCI 200
A2015BR	44.1	2248	49.0	2554	51,200p	Sra SBT/3.28"/CCI 200
A2520	48.2	2226	53.5	2529	48,900p	Bns-X/3.22"/CCI 200
A2495BR	44.6	2207	49.5	2508	51,300p	Sra SBT/3.28"/CCI 200
A2015BR	43.2	2198	48.0	2498	50,600p	Bns-X/3.22"/CCI 200
A2495BR	47.7	2174	53.0	2470	48,800p	Bns-X/3.22"/CCI 200
A2700	56.1	2305	59.0	2452	43,700p	Bns-X/3.22"/Rem 9½/(C)
A4350	54.0	2153	60.0	2447	39,200p	Nos Part./3.215"/CCI 200/(C)

Never exceed maximum load nor use any load exhibiting signs of excessive pressure. Begin at suggested starting load and work up carefully.

Powder	—STARTING— Grs.	MV (fps)	—MAXIMUM— Grs.	MV (fps)	Press. (CUP/psi)	Comments
225 con't						
A4350	53.1	2121	59.0	2410	38,100p	Sra SBT/3.28"/CCI 200/(C)
A4350	53.1	2027	59.0	2303	35,100p	Bns-X/3.22"/CCI 200/(C)
A3100	54.0	1946	60.0	2211	31,500p	Nos Part./3.215"/CCI 200/(C)
A3100	54.0	1905	60.0	2165	28,800p	Sra SBT/3.28"/CCI 200/(C)
A3100	53.1	1807	59.0	2053	27,500p	Bns-X/3.22"/CCI 200/(C)
250						
A2495BR	47.7	2220	53.0	2523	54,000p	Hdy RN/3.25"/CCI 200
BL-C(2)	56.0	2382	59.0	2503	48,900C	
A2015BR	46.8	2200	52.0	2500	54,000p	Hdy RN/3.25"/CCI 200
W748	55.0	2370	58.0	2486	49,000C	
RL-15	53.0	2333	57.0	2480	48,000C	
H4895	49.0	2330	53.0	2455	50,000C	
A2520	45.9	2146	51.0	2439	53,300p	Nos Part./3.255"/CCI 200
IMR4064	50.0	2214	54.0	2434	47,500C	
A2495BR	45.5	2142	50.5	2434	53,100p	Spr SP/3.245"/CCI 200
A2460	46.4	2140	51.5	2432	52,800p	Spr SP/3.245"/CCI 200
A2700	57.0	2285	60.0	2431	50,100p	Spr SP/3.245"/Rem 9½/(C)
A2700	55.1	2284	58.0	2430	49,100p	Nos Part./3.255"/Rem 9½/(C)
A2230	45.9	2138	51.0	2429	51,700p	Spr SP/3.245"/CCI 200
A2520	48.3	2131	53.7	2422	50,600p	Hdy RN/3.25"/CCI 200
H380	57.0	2304	59.0	2416	44,500C	
A2495BR	44.1	2126	49.0	2416	54,500p	Nos Part./3.255"/CCI 200
A2700	56.1	2268	59.0	2413	48,500p	Hdy RN/3.25"/Rem 9½
A2460	44.1	2123	49.0	2412	52,500p	Bns-X/3.22"/CCI 200
A2520	46.8	2122	52.0	2411	51,500p	Spr SP/3.245"/CCI 200
A2015BR	42.8	2122	47.5	2411	52,200p	Spr SP/3.245"/CCI 200
A2460	46.8	2119	52.0	2408	47,500p	Hdy RN/3.25"/CCI 200
A2230	44.1	2116	49.0	2405	52,800p	Bns-X/3.22"/CCI 200
H335	49.0	2288	52.0	2404	50,000C	
RL-12	53.0	2229	56.0	2403	47,000C	
A2460	44.1	2111	49.0	2399	53,000p	Nos Part./3.255"/CCI 200
H322	48.0	2249	52.0	2398	48,500C	
A2520	45.9	2109	51.0	2397	51,500p	Bns-X/3.22"/CCI 200
A2700	55.1	2252	58.0	2396	49,400p	Bns-X/3.22"/Rem 9½/(C)
A2230	45.9	2108	51.0	2395	48,300p	Hdy RN/3.25"/CCI 200
W760	56.0	2269	60.0	2394	45,000C	
IMR4320	50.0	2249	54.0	2394	49,500C	
A2015BR	42.8	2106	47.5	2393	51,200p	Bns-X/3.22"/CCI 200
A4350	54.0	2098	60.0	2384	43,100p	Spr SP/3.245"/CCI 200/(C)
IMR4895	48.0	2244	52.0	2383	50,000C	
A2230	43.7	2092	48.5	2377	52,100p	Nos Part./3.255"/CCI 200
A2495BR	47.3	2084	52.5	2368	53,500p	Bns-X/3.22"/CCI 200
IMR3031	47.0	2240	51.0	2364	48,000C	
A4350	52.2	2079	58.0	2363	41,100p	Nos Part./3.255"/CCI 200/(C)
A2015BR	40.5	2062	45.0	2343	50,800p	Nos Part./3.255"/CCI 200
RL-7	42.0	2141	45.0	2264	49,500C	
A4350	52.2	1951	58.0	2217	33,500p	Hdy RN/3.25"/CCI 200/(C)

Powder	—STARTING— Grs.	MV (fps)	—MAXIMUM— Grs.	MV (fps)	Press. (CUP/psi)	Comments
250 con't						
A4350	52.2	1945	58.0	2210	34,700p	Bns-X/3.22"/CCI 200/(C)
A3100	54.0	1880	60.0	2136	31,600p	Spr SP/3.245"/CCI 200/(C)
A3100	52.2	1858	58.0	2111	30,100p	Nos Part./3.255"/CCI 200/(C)
A3100	53.1	1769	59.0	2010	26,100p	Hdy RN/3.25"/CCI 200/(C)
A3100	52.2	1701	58.0	1933	26,200p	Bns-X/3.22"/CCI 200/(C)
275						
RL-15	51.0	2234	55.0	2392	47,500C	
BL-C(2)	54.0	2301	57.0	2390	49,500C	
W748	53.0	2280	56.0	2344	49,000C	
H380	56.0	2231	58.0	2336	44,700C	
H4895	48.0	2214	51.0	2313	48,500C	
IMR4064	48.0	2130	52.0	2296	47,500C	
H335	48.0	2181	51.0	2292	48,000C	
IMR4895	46.0	2111	50.0	2292	49,500C	
W760	56.0	2210	59.0	2290	45,500C	
RL-12	52.0	2151	55.0	2277	47,000C	
IMR3031	45.0	2131	49.0	2261	48,000C	
IMR4320	48.0	2144	52.0	2250	48,500C	
H322	45.0	2114	49.0	2241	47,500C	
RL-7	41.0	2084	44.0	2184	49,000C	
300						
RL-15	48.0	2088	52.0	2264	49,500C	
BL-C(2)	50.0	2149	54.0	2260	49,000C	
W748	49.0	2132	53.0	2251	49,500C	
H380	54.0	2090	56.0	2206	46,000C	
W760	54.0	2060	57.0	2194	45,900C	
RL-12	49.0	2019	52.0	2185	48,000C	
IMR4064	45.0	1967	49.0	2144	49,000C	
H4895	44.0	1940	48.0	2134	48,000C	
IMR4895	43.0	1919	47.0	2127	50,000C	
RL-7	40.0	2014	43.0	2124	50,000C	
H322	43.0	1931	47.0	2105	49,000C	
IMR4320	44.0	1951	48.0	2102	49,500C	
H335	45.0	1989	47.0	2099	49,500C	

Caution: **Loads exceeding SAAMI OAL Maximum must be verified for bullet-to-rifling clearance and magazine functioning. Where a specific primer or bullet is indicated those components must be used, no substitutions! Where only a maximum load is shown, reduce starting load 10%, unless otherwise specified.**

Key: (C) = compressed charge; C = CUP; p = psi; Plink = Plinker; Bns = Barnes; Hdy = Hornady; Lap = Lapua; Nos = Nosler; Rem = Remington; Sra = Sierra; Spr = Speer; Win = Winchester.

Never exceed maximum load nor use any load exhibiting signs of excessive pressure. Begin at suggested starting load and work up carefully.

239

9.3x64

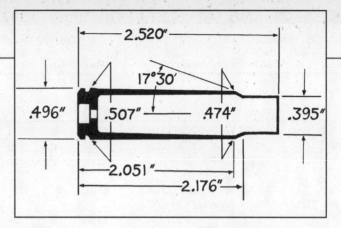

Case: RWS
Primer: Rem 9½
Barrel: 25½" Vihtavuori
Bullet Diameter: 0.366"
Maximum Case Length: 2.520"

Trim to Length: 2.512"
Maximum Cartridge OAL: 3.370"
Minimum Cartridge OAL:
               Load Dependent

Released in 1930, this cartridge says magnum any way you look at it. Capable of generating well over 4000 foot pounds of muzzle energy when equipped with the proper bullet, this is a serious contender for use on any species anywhere in the world—although some African nations prohibit any sub-40-caliber chambering for use against dangerous game.

The case is a rebated-rim type and shares no dimensions with any popular cartridge. Nevertheless, conversion of any standard Mauser-type action with a standard bolt face could be quite easily accomplished.

9.3x64mm LOADING DATA

Powder	STARTING Grs.	MV (fps)	MAXIMUM Grs.	MV (fps)	Press. (CUP/psi)	Comments
258						
N140			67.9	2670	53,700p	RWS HMK/3.366"
285						
N140			67.0	2530	53,700p	RWS TMR/3.326"

Powder	STARTING Grs.	MV (fps)	MAXIMUM Grs.	MV (fps)	Press. (CUP/psi)	Comments
293						
N160			75.9	2550	53,700p	RWS TUG/3.366"

Caution: **Loads exceeding SAAMI OAL Maximum must be verified for bullet-to-rifling clearance and magazine functioning. Where a specific primer or bullet is indicated those components must be used, no substitutions! Where only a maximum load is shown, reduce starting load 10%, unless otherwise specified.**

Key: (C) = compressed charge; C = CUP; p = psi; Plink = Plinker; Bns = Barnes; Hdy = Hornady; Lap = Lapua; Nos = Nosler; Rem = Remington; Sra = Sierra; Spr = Speer; Win = Winchester.

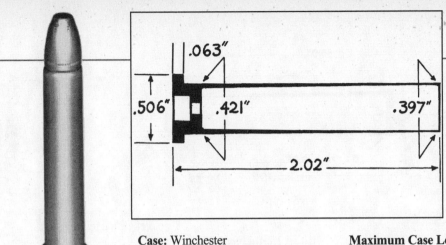

Case: Winchester
Primer: Large Rifle
Barrel: 24″ Accurate/20″ Hodgdon
Bullet Diameter: 0.375″

Maximum Case Length: 2.02″
Trim to Length: 2.015″
Maximum Cartridge OAL: 2.560″
Minimum Cartridge OAL: 2.530″

Co-introduced in 1978 with the Winchester Model 94 Big Bore lever-action carbine, this is simply a modernized version of the circa 1880s 38-55 Winchester. Pressure is near the top, by modern standards, and firing one of these cartridges in an older 38-55 rifle could be disastrous.

Performance is impressive. If loaded to anything approaching the pressure limit, this diminutive cartridge can easily generate more muzzle energy than the 30-06. Recoil in the light carbine can be described as rather harsh.

Most data is limited to more moderate levels, severely restricting the evident ballistic potential of this chambering. The reason for such a course eludes this author. Nevertheless, with top listed loads it is certainly capable for use against elk to moderate ranges.

Usable case capacity with a 220-grain bullet, seated normally, is about 40.5 grains of water.

Never use hard round-nose or pointed bullets in any tubular magazine rifle.

375 WINCHESTER LOADING DATA

Powder	—STARTING— Grs.	MV (fps)	—MAXIMUM— Grs.	MV (fps)	Press. (CUP/psi)	Comments
Lead 250 RCBS						
A2015BR	28.8	1674	32.0	1902	40,700C	2.4″/Rem 9½/(C)
A1680	25.2	1624	28.0	1845	33,600C	2.4″/Rem 9½
200						
A1680	36.0	2211	40.0	2512	41,500C	Sra FN/2.525″/Rem 9½
A2015BR	36.0	1981	40.0	2251	35,800C	Sra FN/2.525″/Rem 9½/(C)
H4198	30.0	1894	33.0	2137		
RL-7	35.0	1934	37.0	2094		
IMR4198	30.0	1909	32.0	2090		
H4895	39.0	1893	41.0	2044		
IMR3031	38.0	1879	40.0	2041		
IMR4895	39.0	1895	41.0	2037		
H322	38.0	1896	40.0	2033		
H335	41.0	1846	43.0	2027		
BL-C(2)	42.0	1825	44.0	2018		
W748	42.0	1809	44.0	2004		
IMR4064	39.0	1838	41.0	1980		
220						
A1680	34.2	2087	38.0	2372	44,800C	Hdy FN/2.535″/Rem 9½
A2015BR	36.0	1947	40.0	2213	39,500C	Hdy FN/2.535″/Rem 9½/(C)
H4198	29.0	1830	31.0	1988		

Powder	—STARTING— Grs.	MV (fps)	—MAXIMUM— Grs.	MV (fps)	Press. (CUP/psi)	Comments
220 con't						
IMR4198	29.0	1839	31.0	1980		
RL-7	33.0	1830	35.0	1979		
IMR3031	36.0	1842	38.0	1964		
H322	36.0	1837	38.0	1955		
W748	40.0	1777	42.0	1929		
H4895	37.0	1804	39.0	1924		
BL-C(2)	40.0	1787	42.0	1919		
IMR4895	37.0	1794	39.0	1913		
H335	39.0	1774	41.0	1907		
IMR4064	37.0	1740	39.0	1888		
250-255						
H322	34.0	1729	36.0	1858		
IMR3031	34.0	1737	36.0	1854		
IMR4895	35.0	1699	37.0	1849		
H4198	28.0	1737	30.0	1848		
H4895	35.0	1713	37.0	1845		
RL-7	31.0	1700	33.0	1844		250-gr. bullets
H335	38.0	1706	40.0	1839		
W748	38.0	1690	40.0	1821		250-gr. bullets
BL-C(2)	38.0	1693	40.0	1820		
IMR4198	27.0	1698	29.0	1814		
IMR4064	36.0	1684	38.0	1810		

Never exceed maximum load nor use any load exhibiting signs of excessive pressure. Begin at suggested starting load and work up carefully.

375

Holland & Holland Magnum (375 H&H)

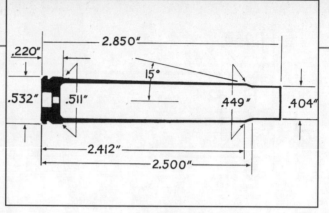

Case: Winchester
Primer: Large Rifle
Barrel: 25" Accurate
      26" Hodgdon
      24" Vihtavuori

Bullet Diameter: 0.375"
Maximum Case Length: 2.850"
Trim to Length: 2.84"
Maximum Cartridge OAL: 3.60"
Minimum Cartridge OAL: 3.54"

Dating to 1912, this is one of the original "Belted Magnum" cartridges. Developed by the firm of Holland & Holland for chambering in their breech-break double rifles, the 375 H&H Magnum was envisioned as a dangerous game chambering. This cartridge is fully capable for use against any species in the world. Some argue that it is minimal for use against the big-five in Africa, but it has been used extensively for that purpose, and with the proper bullets and shot placement has accounted for itself quite adequately.

The 375 H&H has always been loaded to top pressures and has adequate case capacity to take advantage of some of the slower burning powders so it can generate considerable energy. Typical loads are not far behind the 458 Winchester Magnum in actual muzzle energy. Once the range gets out past about 50 yards, the 375 generally delivers more energy then the 458 Winchester Magnum.

The data listed here reflect the prudence of loading any chambering that might be used in blistering heat against dangerous game to somewhat reduced pressures. This practice limits the possibility that an overheated round fired from an overheated gun might stick in the chamber—such a result could leave an unfortunate shooter at the mercy of a wounded animal, certain varieties of which are known to take a serious disliking to anyone who shoots at them. Should your plans include the hunting of dangerous game with the 375 H&H (or any high-pressure chambering), consider using loads restricted to about 55,000 psi/50,000 CUP.

While this cartridge is a bit much for hunting most North American species—except in the case of Elmer Keith, who honestly considered it just a little on the light side for elk hunting—it has a loyal following here. The best of the current superior modern bullets only serve to extend the 375 H&H Magnum's performance. Barnes' 250-grain X would seem a good choice for those anticipating longer shots.

Usable case capacity with a 235-grain bullet, seated normally, is about 86.5 grains of water. IMR4350, IMR4064, W760, H4895, A4350 and A2700 are all noted for good performance in this old powerhouse.

375 HOLLAND & HOLLAND MAGNUM LOADING DATA (375 H&H)

Powder	STARTING Grs.	MV (fps)	MAXIMUM Grs.	MV (fps)	Press. (CUP/psi)	Comments
235						
A2495BR	66.6	2560	74.0	2909	57,000p	Spr SSP/3.45"/ Rem 9½M
N160			86.7	2900	55,114p	Spr SP
N140			76.4	2890	55,114p	Spr SP
VarGet			73.0	2881	49,800C	
A2700	76.0	2706	80.0	2879	56,600p	Spr SSP/3.45"/ Rem 9½M/100% Density
A2520	63.9	2530	71.0	2875	57,000p	Spr SSP/3.45"/ Rem 9½M
A4350	77.4	2495	86.0	2835	46,700p	Spr SSP/3.45"/ Rem 9½M/(C)
IMR4831	81.0	2669	84.0	2770		

Powder	STARTING Grs.	MV (fps)	MAXIMUM Grs.	MV (fps)	Press. (CUP/psi)	Comments
235 con't						
IMR4350	79.0	2590	82.0	2729		
H4350	79.0	2590	82.0	2716		
IMR4064	70.0	2549	73.0	2715		
H414	80.0	2519	83.0	2711		
IMR4320	69.0	2544	72.0	2711		
H450	85.0	2591	87.0	2675		
H4831	83.0	2544	86.0	2669		
W760	81.0	2519	83.0	2662		
H4895	69.0	2520	73.0	2650		
IMR4895	69.0	2519	72.0	2639		
A3100	77.4	2259	86.0	2567	33,300p	Spr SSP/3.45"/ Rem 9½M/(C)

Never exceed maximum load nor use any load exhibiting signs of excessive pressure. Begin at suggested starting load and work up carefully.

250

Powder	—STARTING— Grs.	MV (fps)	—MAXIMUM— Grs.	MV (fps)	Press. (CUP/psi)	Comments
A2700	76.0	2644	80.0	2813	59,800p	Sra SBT/3.585"/ Rem 9½M
A4350	75.6	2431	84.0	2763	48,900p	Sra SBT/3.585"/ Rem 9½M/(C)
H4350	75.0	2588	79.0	2759		
H414	78.0	2550	81.0	2742		
A2495BR	60.8	2409	67.5	2738	60,000p	Sra SBT/3.585"/ Rem 9½M
A2700	75.1	2539	79.0	2701	54,100p	Bns-X/3.55"/ Rem 9½M/(C)
H4831	82.0	2580	85.0	2656		
A4350	74.3	2332	82.5	2650	45,500p	Bns-X/3.55"/ Rem 9½M/(C)
H450	82.0	2569	84.0	2649		
H4895	68.0	2560	70.0	2649		
A3100	77.4	2233	86.0	2537	36,800p	Sra SBT/3.585"/ Rem 9½M/(C)
A2495BR	54.0	2193	60.0	2492	54,200p	Bns-X/3.55"/ Rem 9½M
A3100	75.6	2113	84.0	2401	32,800p	Bns-X/3.55"/ Rem 9½M/(C)

270

Powder	—STARTING— Grs.	MV (fps)	—MAXIMUM— Grs.	MV (fps)	Press. (CUP/psi)	Comments
N160			84.1	2790	55,114p	Hdy RN
N140			73.3	2760	55,114p	Hdy RN
A4350	75.6	2386	84.0	2711	50,300p	Hdy SP/3.605"/ Rem 9½M
IMR4350	75.0	2595	78.0	2709		
H4350	74.0	2563	78.0	2704		
VarGet			71.0	2701	49,600C	
H414	78.0	2514	81.0	2700		
A2700	76.0	2530	80.0	2691	55,800p	Hdy SP/3.57"/ Rem 9½M/(C)
IMR4831	80.0	2537	83.0	2684		
A2495BR	63.5	2346	70.5	2666	59,000p	Hdy SP/3.57"/ Rem 9½M
H450	83.0	2579	85.0	2627		
IMR4064	65.0	2480	68.0	2611		
H4831	82.0	2510	85.0	2609		
H4895	67.0	2498	69.0	2609		
IMR4320	64.0	2482	67.0	2600		
IMR4895	63.0	2474	66.0	2597		
W760	80.0	2482	82.0	2580		
A3100	77.4	2217	86.0	2519	38,700p	Hdy SP/3.615"/ Rem 9½M/(C)

300

Powder	—STARTING— Grs.	MV (fps)	—MAXIMUM— Grs.	MV (fps)	Press. (CUP/psi)	Comments
N160			81.8	2560	55,114p	Hdy RN
IMR4831	77.0	2420	80.0	2555		
A2700	71.3	2397	75.0	2550	56,600p	Sra SBT/3.585"/ Rem 9½M/***
A4350	71.1	2241	79.0	2547	51,500p	Sra SBT/3.585"/ Rem 9½M/(C)
H4350	73.0	2417	77.0	2545		
H4831	80.0	2397	84.0	2539		
VarGet			67.0	2536	49,600C	
IMR4350	73.0	2429	76.0	2530		
N140			69.6	2530	55,114p	Hdy RN
H450	81.0	2440	84.0	2516		
H414	74.0	2444	76.0	2513		
A2700	71.3	2327	75.0	2476	59,500p	Spr AGS/3.48"/ Rem 9½M
A3100	74.7	2159	83.0	2453	43,200p	Sra SBT/3.585"/ Rem 9½M/(C)
W760	75.0	2354	77.0	2449		
A2495BR	56.3	2148	62.5	2441	58,600p	Sra SBT/3.585"/ Rem 9½M
H4895	65.0	2339	67.0	2440		
A4350	71.1	2128	79.0	2418	46,800p	Spr AGS/3.48"/ Rem 9½M/***
A2495BR	56.3	2110	62.5	2398	61,200p	Spr AGS/3.48"/ Rem 9½M
IMR4320	62.0	2282	65.0	2390		
A3100	74.7	2028	83.0	2305	40,000p	Spr AGS/3.48"/ Rem 9½M/(C)

350

Powder	—STARTING— Grs.	MV (fps)	—MAXIMUM— Grs.	MV (fps)	Press. (CUP/psi)	Comments
H414	68.0	2280	71.0	2461		
H4831	72.0	2288	76.0	2452		
H4350	68.0	2261	72.0	2432		
H380	63.0	2238	67.0	2414		
A4350	67.5	2072	75.0	2355	54,800p	Bns RN/3.56"/ Rem 9½M
A2700	63.7	2123	67.0	2259	56,600p	Bns RN/3.56"/ Rem 9½M
A3100	65.7	1853	73.0	2106	36,600p	Bns RN/3.56"/ Rem 9½M/(C)/***
A2495BR	49.5	1851	55.0	2103	56,100p	Bns RN/3.56"/ Rem 9½M

*** Extremely uniform pressure and velocity.

> *Caution:* **Loads exceeding SAAMI OAL Maximum must be verified for bullet-to-rifling clearance and magazine functioning. Where a specific primer or bullet is indicated those components must be used, no substitutions! Where only a maximum load is shown, reduce starting load 10%, unless otherwise specified.**
>
> *Key:* (C) = compressed charge; C = CUP; p = psi; Plink = Plinker; Bns = Barnes; Hdy = Hornady; Lap = Lapua; Nos = Nosler; Rem = Remington; Sra = Sierra; Spr = Speer; Win = Winchester.

Never exceed maximum load nor use any load exhibiting signs of excessive pressure. Begin at suggested starting load and work up carefully.

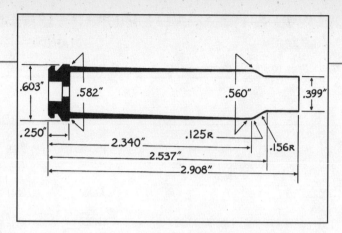

378 Weatherby Magnum

Case: Weatherby
Primer: Large Rifle
Barrel: 26″ Accurate
26″ Hodgdon
Bullet Diameter: 0.375″

Maximum Case Length: 2.908″
Trim to Length: 2.898″
Maximum Cartridge OAL: 3.690″
Minimum Cartridge OAL:
Bullet Dependent

Based on a belted version of the 416 Rigby case—a Weatherby innovation of considerable marketing value—the 378 Weatherby is a massive cartridge capable of generating massive energy while shooting as flat as the best 270 Winchester or 7mm Remington Magnum load. Introduced in 1953, this number replaced the never particularly popular 375 Weatherby, which was based on the much smaller 375 H&H case.

The 378 Weatherby is a high-pressure chambering, like all Weatherby numbers, and easily surpasses the energy developed by almost any of the big British Nitro cartridges. Typical loads far surpass the 458 Winchester Magnum in delivered energy.

The data listed here reflect the prudence of loading any chambering that might be used in blistering heat against dangerous game to somewhat reduced pressures. This practice limits the possibility that an overheated round fired from an overheated gun might stick in the chamber—such a result could leave an unfortunate shooter at the mercy of a wounded animal, certain varieties of which are known to take a serious disliking to anyone who shoots at them. Should your plans include the hunting of dangerous game with the 378 Weatherby (or any high-pressure chambering), consider using loads restricted to no more than 55,000 psi/50,000 CUP.

This cartridge is certainly sufficient for any North American species—even Elmer Keith considered it plenty for elk. The best of the current superior modern bullets only serve to extend 378 Weatherby Magnum performance. Barnes' 250-grain X would seem a good choice for those anticipating longer shots.

Usable case capacity with typical bullets, seated normally, is well over 120 grains of water. H4831, A4350 and A3100 are good powder choices. As with all free-bored designs, the slowest usable powders seldom deliver consistent velocity or commendable accuracy.

378 WEATHERBY MAGNUM LOADING DATA

Powder	STARTING Grs.	MV (fps)	MAXIMUM Grs.	MV (fps)	Press. (CUP/psi)	Comments
235						
H4350	102.0	3003	109.0	3224		
H4831	107.0	2972	117.0	3202		
H450	107.0	2925	117.0	3147		
250						
A4350	94.5	2762	105.0	3139	57,200p	Bns-X/3.665″/Fed 215
A3100	101.7	2711	113.0	3081	57,600p	Bns-X/3.665″/Fed 215
A8700	123.3	2516	137.0	2859	48,300p	Bns-X/3.665″/Fed 215/(C)
270						
H4831	105.0	2724	115.0	3102		
H4350	99.0	2779	105.0	3091		
H450	105.0	2739	115.0	3081		
A4350	93.6	2700	104.0	3068	59,200p	Spr SBT/3.685″/Fed 215
A3100	100.8	2687	112.0	3053	59,200p	Spr SBT/3.685″/Fed 215

Powder	STARTING Grs.	MV (fps)	MAXIMUM Grs.	MV (fps)	Press. (CUP/psi)	Comments
270 con't						
A8700	121.5	2495	135.0	2835	43,600p	Spr SBT/3.685″/Fed 215/(C)
300						
H4350	95.0	2795	100.0	2940		
H4831	102.0	2624	112.0	2926		
H450	102.0	2587	112.0	2902		
A4350	90.9	2508	101.0	2850	57,300p	Spr AGS/3.53″/Fed 215
A3100	98.0	2492	109.0	2832	55,500p	Spr AGS/3.53″/Fed 215
A8700	117.0	2385	130.0	2710	47,900p	Spr AGS/3.53″/Fed 215
H870			120.0	2620		
350						
H4831	96.0	2612	102.0	2779		
H4350	93.0	2584	98.0	2767		
H870			110.0	2480		

Never exceed maximum load nor use any load exhibiting signs of excessive pressure. Begin at suggested starting load and work up carefully.

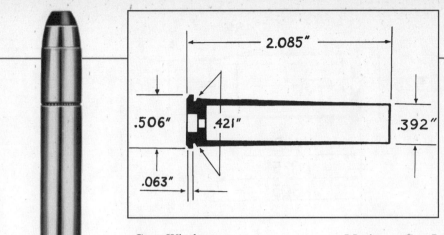

38-55 Winchester (38-55 WCF)

Case: Winchester
Primer: Large Rifle
Barrel: 24″ Accurate
      26″ Hodgdon
Bullet Diameter: 0.378″

Maximum Case Length: 2.085″
Trim to Length: 2.080″
Maximum Cartridge OAL: 2.510″
Minimum Cartridge OAL: 2.470″

The 38-55 was originally introduced in 1884 for the Ballard rifle. Proper bullet diameter is 0.378″ and barrels are often somewhat larger. This fact explains why this blackpowder number is listed after the more modern 375-caliber powerhouses, which use 0.375″ bullets. The 38-55 case is the grandfather of an entire host of cartridges from the 30-30 on down.

Winchester once offered a high-velocity smokeless load launching a 255-grain bullet at about 1600 fps, but that is long-since gone. Current factory loadings very nearly duplicate the original blackpowder load, generating about 1320 fps with the standard 255-grain bullet.

With modern powders, it is no trick to launch a 220-grain bullet to over 2000 fps while staying well under the top pressure specifications of the chambering. With such loads, the 38-55 is fully capable for use against deer-sized species at ranges under about 200 yards, delivering considerably more punch than the 30-30 can. However, no such load should ever be used in any gun designed for use with blackpowder.

Usable case capacity with a 220-grain bullet, seated normally, is about 40.2 grains of water. H322, H4895 and H335 make up the short list of noted good performers in the 38-55.

Never use hard round-nose or pointed bullets in any tubular magazine rifle.

38-55 WINCHESTER LOADING DATA (38-55 WCF)

Powder	Grs.	MV (fps)	Grs.	MV (fps)	Press. (CUP/psi)	Comments
Lead 240						
A2495BR	34.2	1778	38.0	2020	25,200C	2.51″/CCI 200/(C)
A2015BR	28.4	1710	31.5	1943	28,000C	2.51″/CCI 200
XMP5744			22.0	1601		2.51″/CCI 200
200						
A2015BR	32.4	1876	36.0	2132	27,900C	Sra FN/2.59″/CCI 200
A2495BR	36.0	1793	40.0	2037	22,800C	Sra FN/2.59″/CCI 200/(C)
XMP5744			25.5	1853		Sra FN/CCI 200
220						
A2495BR	34.2	1800	38.0	2045	25,700C	Hdy FN/2.58″/CCI 200/(C)
A2015BR	28.8	1660	32.0	1886	25,200C	Hdy FN/2.58″/CCI 200
XMP5744			23.5	1648		Hdy FN/CCI 200

Powder	Grs.	MV (fps)	Grs.	MV (fps)	Press. (CUP/psi)	Comments
255						
H4895	30.0	1519	35.0	1729		JSP
H335	35.0	1564	37.0	1679		JSP
BL-C(2)	36.0	1551	38.0	1666		JSP
H322	29.0	1479	33.0	1640		JSP
H4198	20.0	1256	24.0	1415		JSP

Caution: **Loads exceeding SAAMI OAL Maximum must be verified for bullet-to-rifling clearance and magazine functioning. Where a specific primer or bullet is indicated those components must be used, no substitutions! Where only a maximum load is shown, reduce starting load 10%, unless otherwise specified.**

Key: (C) = compressed charge; C = CUP; p = psi; Plink = Plinker; Bns = Barnes; Hdy = Hornady; Lap = Lapua; Nos = Nosler; Rem = Remington; Sra = Sierra; Spr = Speer; Win = Winchester.

Never exceed maximum load nor use any load exhibiting signs of excessive pressure. Begin at suggested starting load and work up carefully.

245

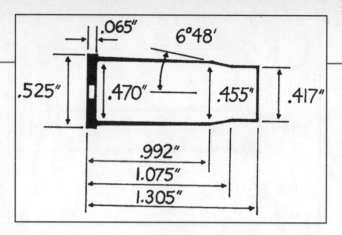

38-40 Winchester (38-40 WCF)

Case: Winchester
Primer: Larger Pistol
Barrel: 24″ Accurate (1873 Win.)
Bullet Diameter: 0.401″

Maximum Case Length: 1.305″
(Very rare)
Trim to Length: 1.295″ (Rare)
Maximum Cartridge OAL: 1.593″
Minimum Cartridge OAL: 1.560″

Introduced by Winchester in 1874 and chambered in the Model 1873 lever-action rifle and carbine, the 38-40 is very likely the first of a long pedigree of factory wildcat centerfire cartridges. This number was created by necking down the 44-40 to accept 40-caliber bullets.

Interestingly, it seems at least possible that this cartridge was named in the following manner: 38, for the original charge of blackpowder, 40 for the bullet diameter. The facts? The original blackpowder charge was 38 grains, not 40 as is often reported, and designed bullet diameter is 0.401″. Also note, cases are typically short.

Just as with all other Model '73 chamberings, Colt picked up this cartridge for chambering in their Single Action Army revolver. Other manufacturers chambered it in their revolvers and shoulder guns. Various proprietary loads were also developed, but all were interchangeable in chambering.

Although the 38-40 is denigrated by many today, it has to

be noted that original 38-40 loads fired in a revolver were ballistically indistinguishable from the 180-grain loading in the 40 S&W! Fired from a rifle, the cartridge was certainly capable for use against the smallest species of big game, and this was certainly a formidable self-defense chambering.

Winchester once offered a high-velocity loading for the 38-40. With a 180-grain bullet at about 1775 fps muzzle velocity, that load was certainly adequate for hunting the smaller species of big game.

With unusually thin case walls, the 38-40 is a genuine challenge to the handloader. The listed loads do work, but they leave a huge amount of unburned powder behind. Faster powders have been tested by the author, but those are extremely sensitive to powder position. Powders in the middle of the usable burning range produce both problems!

Usable case capacity with a 180-grain bullet, seated normally, is about 32.9 grains of water.

38-40 WINCHESTER LOADING DATA (38-40 WCF)

Powder	STARTING Grs.	MV (fps)	MAXIMUM Grs.	MV (fps)	Press. (CUP/psi)	Comments
Lead 185 FP-BB						
A1680	21.2	1337	23.5	1519	14,000C	1.58″/Win WLP
A2015BR	22.5	1133	25.0	1287	13,800C	1.58″/Win WLP/(C)
150						
A1680	24.8	1481	27.5	1683	13,200C	Sra HP/1.575″/Win WLP
A2015BR	27.0	1269	30.0	1442	13,900C	Sra HP/1.575″/Win WLP

Powder	STARTING Grs.	MV (fps)	MAXIMUM Grs.	MV (fps)	Press. (CUP/psi)	Comments
180						
A1680	23.0	1268	25.5	1441	14,000C	Spr HP/1.585″/Win WLP
A2015BR	24.3	1175	27.0	1335	14,000C	Spr HP/1.585″/Win WLP

Caution: Loads exceeding SAAMI OAL Maximum must be verified for bullet-to-rifling clearance and magazine functioning. Where a specific primer or bullet is indicated those components must be used, no substitutions! Where only a maximum load is shown, reduce starting load 10%, unless otherwise specified.

Key: (C) = compressed charge; C = CUP; p = psi; Plink = Plinker; Bns = Barnes; Hdy = Hornady; Lap = Lapua; Nos = Nosler; Rem = Remington; Sra = Sierra; Spr = Speer; Win = Winchester.

Never exceed maximum load nor use any load exhibiting signs of excessive pressure. Begin at suggested starting load and work up carefully.

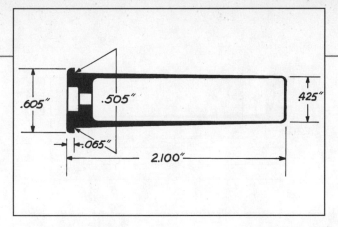

Case: Winchester (Converted 45-70 cases will work, though usually a bit short.)
Primer: Large Rifle
Barrel: 36″ Accurate (C. Sharps)
Bullet Diameter: 0.400″

Maximum Case Length: 2.100″
Trim to Length: 2.095″
Maximum Cartridge OAL: 2.47″
Minimum Cartridge OAL: Bullet Dependent

Introduced in 1887 for chambering in the John Browning-designed Winchester Model 1886 lever-action rifle, this cartridge is a straight-taper version of the 45-70. Cases can easily be formed by running 45-70 brass into a 40-65 sizing die.

These loads were developed by Accurate Arms, and the pressure limit was established by first firing 65 grains of FFg blackpowder behind a 300-grain bullet. That seems a reasonable method, but it must still be noted that some of the oldest guns, especially any in poor condition, are probably best left as wall hangers. These should not be fired with any load.

Comparing original loads in the 45-70 and 40-65, the former launched a 405-grain bullet at practically the same velocity as the latter launched a 260-grain bullet. Obviously, the 45-70 could deliver much more punch. Just as obviously, the 40-65 generated much less recoil—less than one-half.

The 40-65 has grown in popularity in modern times for chambering in replica guns used in blackpowder accuracy competitions. With reduced recoil, it has a lot to offer over numbers launching heavier bullets and can still deliver sufficient momentum to topple the metallic targets of silhouette competition.

Usable case capacity with a 300-grain bullet, seated normally, is about 55 grains of water.

These loads are for use only in guns known to be safe for use with smokeless powder.

40-65 WINCHESTER LOADING DATA (40-65 WCF)

Powder	STARTING Grs.	MV (fps)	MAXIMUM Grs.	MV (fps)	Press. (CUP/psi)	Comments
Lead 260						
XMP5744			26.0	1651		Win WLR
Lead 300 CSA						
A2495BR	38.7	1649	43.0	1874	18,800p	2.66″/Win WLR
XMP5744			24.0	1521		2.26″/Win WLR
XMP5744			24.0	1515		2.26″/Win WLR
A8700	54.0	1255	60.0	1426	21,900p	2.66″/Win WLR/(C)

Powder	STARTING Grs.	MV (fps)	MAXIMUM Grs.	MV (fps)	Press. (CUP/psi)	Comments
Cast Lead 350						
A2495BR	36.0	1556	40.0	1768	20,800p	CSA/2.66″/Win WLR
XMP5744			23.0	1436		CSA/2.66″/Win WLR
A8700	48.6	1104	54.0	1255	19,700p	CSA/2.66″/Win WLR/(C)
Cast Lead 400						
A2495BR	33.3	1437	37.0	1633	19,600p	CSA/2.83″/Win WLR
XMP5744			23.0	1364		CSA/2.83″/Win WLR
A8700	46.8	1041	52.0	1183	16,800p	CSA/2.83″/Win WLR/(C)

NOTE: CSA bullets are designed for single shot rifles. All loads listed exceed recommended maximum OAL designated for use in lever-action rifles.

Never exceed maximum load nor use any load exhibiting signs of excessive pressure. Begin at suggested starting load and work up carefully.

416

Remington Magnum

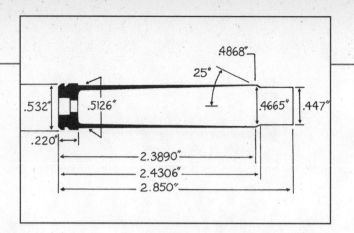

Case: Remington
Primer: Large Rifle
Barrel: 24″ Accurate/24″ Hodgdon
Bullet Diameter: 0.416″

Maximum Case Length: 2.850″
Trim to Length: 2.845″
Maximum Cartridge OAL: 3.600″
Minimum Cartridge OAL: 3.350″

Two factors can explain Remington's introduction of this 41-caliber powerhouse chambering in 1990. First, there was, and is, a huge resurgence of interest in the 416 Rigby—a proven African performer. Second, Remington's 8mm Magnum—which uses the same basic case—was withering on the vine. Nobody seemed interested in rifles chambered in that caliber.

By necking up the 8mm Remington Magnum case and loading to modern turnbolt rifle pressures, Remington created a much smaller cartridge that could duplicate the ballistics of Mr. Rigby's chambering. This cartridge could also be chambered in any long-action magnum rifle with no alterations to the magazine or bolt-face—the Rigby requires a longer, wider magazine and a larger bolt face.

Performance is certainly impressive. With loads backed down about 10 percent from the pressure limit—a prudent practice for any chambering that might be used in blistering heat against critters that tend to try to bite back—the 350-grain Barnes-X can be driven to about 2600 fps and the Hornady 400-grain can exceed 2400 fps.

Compared to 458 Winchester Magnum performance, the 416 Remington Magnum has a clear advantage in trajectory and impact velocity while delivering somewhat more energy. Those who feel bullet diameter and mass are more important would probably choose the 458. Nevertheless, this 416 is fully capable against the world's most dangerous game.

NOTE: Some of these loads exceed SAAMI maximum OAL; nevertheless, they will fit the magazine in Remington's Model 700 rifle.

416 REMINGTON MAGNUM LOADING DATA

Powder	STARTING Grs.	MV (fps)	MAXIMUM Grs.	MV (fps)	Press. (CUP/psi)	Comments
Lead 350 FNGC						
XMP5744			55.0	2206		Rem 9½M
300						
RL-15	88.0	2852	93.0	2961	53,000C	
H4895	81.0	2783	86.0	2930	53,000C	
RL-12	89.0	2748	94.0	2895	52,500C	
BL-C(2)	91.0	2770	95.0	2850	49,000C	
IMR4064	83.0	2707	88.0	2829	49,500C	
H380	95.0	2742	100.0	2820	51,500C	
IMR4320	80.0	2671	85.0	2816	53,000C	
W748	85.0	2660	90.0	2804	49,500C	
H335	82.0	2638	87.0	2767	49,000C	
350						
BL-C(2)	86.0	2536	91.0	2684	51,000C	
RL-15	79.0	2541	84.0	2679	52,000C	
IMR4064	80.0	2563	85.0	2663	51,500C	
A2230	71.1	2328	79.0	2645	53,000C	Bns-X/3.68″/Rem 9½M

Powder	STARTING Grs.	MV (fps)	MAXIMUM Grs.	MV (fps)	Press. (CUP/psi)	Comments
350 con't						
H4895	76.0	2526	81.0	2640	53,500C	
W748	80.0	2469	85.0	2636	50,500C	
A2015BR	67.5	2304	75.0	2618	51,400C	Bns-X/3.68″/Rem 9½M
A2460	71.1	2298	79.0	2611	51,000C	Bns-X/3.68″/Rem 9½M
H380	89.0	2540	94.0	2610	53,000C	
400						
A4350	78.3	2155	87.0	2449	43,900C	Hdy RN/3.58″/Rem 9½M(C)
A2495BR	72.0	2154	80.0	2448	50,000C	Hdy RN/3.58″/Rem 9½M
A2700	80.8	2295	85.0	2442	49,800C	Hdy RN/3.58″/Rem 9½M
RL-15	75.0	2332	80.0	2441	52,500C	
H4350	85.0	2311	90.0	2437	48,500C	
IMR4064	75.0	2321	80.0	2435	51,500C	
H414	80.0	2286	85.0	2429	52,000C	
W760	79.0	2266	84.0	2404	52,500C	
A2015BR	63.0	2104	70.0	2391	52,200C	Hdy RN/3.58″/Rem 9½M
A2520	67.5	2099	75.0	2385	51,900C	Hdy RN/3.58″/Rem 9½M
A2460	66.6	2097	74.0	2383	50,300C	Hdy RN/3.58″/Rem 9½M
A2230	65.7	2094	73.0	2380	49,900C	Hdy RN/3.58″/Rem 9½M

Never exceed maximum load nor use any load exhibiting signs of excessive pressure. Begin at suggested starting load and work up carefully.

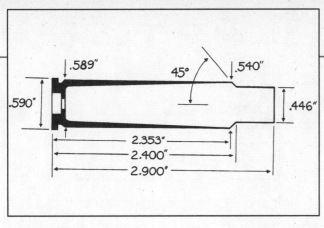

Case: Federal
Primer: Large Rifle
Barrel: 26″ Accurate
      24″ Hodgdon
Bullet Diameter: 0.416″

Maximum Case Length: 2.900″
Trim to Length: 2.895″
Maximum Cartridge OAL: 3.720″
Minimum Cartridge OAL: 3.630″

In 1911, Mr. John Rigby offered this proprietary chambering in his custom magnum-action Mauser. This cartridge features a very progressive design, especially for the era, with the sharpest shoulder of any chambering ever commercialized—45°! Usable capacity exceeds 120 grains of water.

No doubt with an eye to the conditions typically encountered in African hunting, Rigby wisely designed sufficient case capacity to achieve the desired ballistics without using particularly high pressures—chamber pressure differs little from standard 30-30 loads. How he might have guessed at the appropriate muzzle velocity and bullet mass are open questions. Nevertheless, it cannot be denied that his choices

were very prescient. Most experienced African hunting guides agree that the 416 Rigby is among the best of all chamberings for hunting the world's largest and most dangerous game.

Top 400-grain loads listed here very nearly duplicate the original loading. The 350-grain Barnes-X adds a new dimension to the Rigby. This superior bullet can shoot flat enough for longer shots and still deliver huge doses of energy, while providing superior penetration and wound generating expansion.

IMR4831, IMR7828 and H4831 are good choices in the Rigby.

416 RIGBY LOADING DATA

Powder	STARTING Grs.	MV (fps)	MAXIMUM Grs.	MV (fps)	Press. (CUP/psi)	Comments
Lead 350 FNGC						
XMP5744			55.0	2173		Fed 215
350						
A3100	91.8	2218	102.0	2521	42,800p	Bns-X/3.75″/Fed 215
H4350	98.0	2412	102.0	2518		
A8700	112.5	2013	125.0	2287	38,800p	Bns-X/3.75″/Fed 215/(C)
400						
H4831	100.0	2311	106.0	2422		
IMR7828	102.0	2294	107.0	2422		
RL-22	100.0	2340	104.0	2417		
RL-19	92.0	2302	96.0	2417		
H4350	96.0	2292	100.0	2414		
IMR4831	93.0	2319	97.0	2411		
H1000	106.0	2331	110.0	2409		
IMR4350	92.0	2328	96.0	2405		
H450	100.0	2366	103.0	2404		
A8700	114.8	2097	127.5	2383	42,400p	Hdy RN/3.61″/Fed 215/(C)

Powder	STARTING Grs.	MV (fps)	MAXIMUM Grs.	MV (fps)	Press. (CUP/psi)	Comments
400 con't						
A3100	90.0	2057	100.0	2337	43,200p	Spr AGS/3.635″/Fed 215
A3100	86.4	2052	96.0	2332	43,700p	Hdy RN/3.61″/Fed 215
A3100	88.2	2042	98.0	2320	43,000p	Spr Solid/3.615″/Fed 215
A8700	114.8	2028	127.5	2305	40,400p	Spr Solid/3.615″/Fed 215/(C)
A8700	108.0	1882	120.0	2139	38,900p	Spr AGS/3.635″/Fed 215/(C)

Caution: **Loads exceeding SAAMI OAL Maximum must be verified for bullet-to-rifling clearance and magazine functioning. Where a specific primer or bullet is indicated those components must be used, no substitutions! Where only a maximum load is shown, reduce starting load 10%, unless otherwise specified.**

Key: (C) = compressed charge; C = CUP; p = psi; Plink = Plinker; Bns = Barnes; Hdy = Hornady; Lap = Lapua; Nos = Nosler; Rem = Remington; Sra = Sierra; Spr = Speer; Win = Winchester.

Never exceed maximum load nor use any load exhibiting signs of excessive pressure. Begin at suggested starting load and work up carefully.

416
Weatherby Magnum

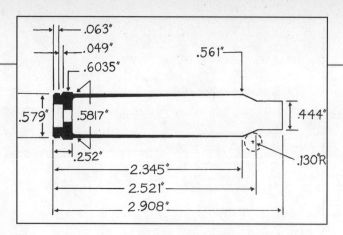

Case: Weatherby
Primer: Federal 215
Barrel: 26″ Accurate
       24″ Hodgdon
Bullet Diameter: 0.416″

Maximum Case Length: 2.908″
Trim to Length: 2.903″
Maximum Cartridge OAL: 3.750″
Minimum Cartridge OAL:
       Bullet Dependent

When Remington announced their 416 Magnum, it was inevitable that Weatherby would follow suit with their own more powerful 41-caliber chambering. Their choice for the parent case was equally predictable. By the simple expedient of necking the 378 Weatherby case to the proper size, they created a cartridge capable of pushing the same bullets as Remington's new magnum about 10 percent faster—generating about 20-percent more muzzle energy as a result.

For those who can handle the recoil, the 416 Weatherby Magnum offers a first-class dangerous-game chambering that has one other benefit—it can launch the 350-grain Barnes-X fast enough to produce a long-range trajectory that the 270 Win-chester cannot equal! In the process it can deliver more energy to 600 yards, at sea level, than the 30-06 produces at the muzzle!

Assembled with bullets that are up to the task, the 416 Weatherby Magnum would seem to be a serious contender for an all-around dangerous—and plains—game chambering for African hunting. Nevertheless, nothing comes free, and recoil is sufficient to suggest that the standard Weatherby muzzlebrake is a very good idea indeed.

IMR4831, IMR7828, RL-19, H4831, H4350 and RL-22 are all good choices. As with all free-bored chamberings, the slowest usable powders are seldom good choices for accuracy or consistency.

416 WEATHERBY MAGNUM LOADING DATA

Powder	STARTING Grs.	MV (fps)	MAXIMUM Grs.	MV (fps)	Press. (CUP/psi)	Comments
300						
RL-19	118.0	2942	124.0	3077		
IMR4350	110.0	2922	116.0	3061		
RL-22	121.0	2855	127.0	3057		
IMR4831	115.0	2972	120.0	3054		
H414	110.0	2911	115.0	3052		
H4350	117.0	2917	122.0	3051		
350						
RL-22	120.0	2849	125.0	2933		
IMR4350	109.0	2793	114.0	2917		
IMR4831	113.0	2789	118.0	2912		
H4350	112.0	2728	118.0	2891		
RL-19	114.0	2729	119.0	2862		
A4350	98.1	2484	109.0	2823	59,300p	Bns-X/3.785″/Fed 215
A3100	100.8	2316	112.0	2632	47,900p	Bns-X/3.785″/ Fed 215/(C)

Powder	STARTING Grs.	MV (fps)	MAXIMUM Grs.	MV (fps)	Press. (CUP/psi)	Comments
400						
RL-19	112.0	2653	115.0	2737		
RL-22	111.0	2603	116.0	2729		
IMR7828	115.0	2587	120.0	2721		
H450	116.0	2565	124.0	2711		
H4831	118.0	2625	120.0	2703		
H4350	105.0	2564	110.0	2687		
IMR4831	105.0	2533	110.0	2681		
A4350	95.4	2297	106.0	2610	58,300p	Hdy RN/3.64″/Fed 215
A3100	100.8	2261	112.0	2569	52,900p	Hdy RN/3.64″/ Fed 215/(C)
H1000	116.0	2348	120.0	2419		

Caution: Loads exceeding SAAMI OAL Maximum must be verified for bullet-to-rifling clearance and magazine functioning. Where a specific primer or bullet is indicated those components must be used, no substitutions! Where only a maximum load is shown, reduce starting load 10%, unless otherwise specified.

Key: (C) = compressed charge; C = CUP; p = psi; Plink = Plinker; Bns = Barnes; Hdy = Hornady; Lap = Lapua; Nos = Nosler; Rem = Remington; Sra = Sierra; Spr = Speer; Win = Winchester.

Never exceed maximum load nor use any load exhibiting signs of excessive pressure. Begin at suggested starting load and work up carefully.

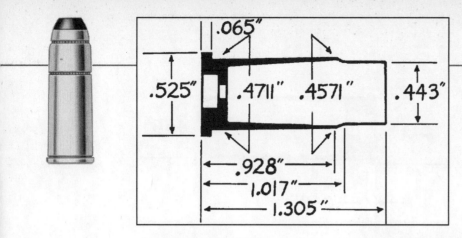

Case: Remington
Primer: Large Pistol
Barrel: 20″ Accurate
  (Winchester Model 92)
Bullet Diameter: 0.427″

Maximum Case Length: 1.305″ (Very rare)
Trim to Length: 1.300″ (Rare)
Maximum Cartridge OAL: 1.592″
Minimum Cartridge OAL: 1.540″

Co-introduced in 1873 with Winchester's wildly successful lever-action rifle, this chambering has persisted and is still chambered in both revolvers and shoulder guns. Colt's adoption for chambering in their Single Action Army revolver probably was more responsible for the cartridge's survival than any other factor.

Typical of chamberings of the era, the cartridge is not a true 44-caliber, but, like the more modern 44 S&W Special and 44 Magnum, is a 42-caliber. Somehow 42 just does not roll off the tongue, and it is not surprising that something a bit more sexy was chosen to name the chambering. However, it is also possible, nay likely, that such early chamberings were named for another dimension—the diameter of the case neck!

To understand this, it is necessary to discuss cartridge conversions of cap-and-ball revolvers. That process centered on the simple expedient of boring holes completely through the chambers and facing off the back of the cylinder so that self-contained metallic cartridges could be used in those revolvers. It is easy to note that most such conversions used cylinder holes that were bigger than bore diameter. This accommodated the case walls so a bore-diameter bullet could be inserted into the case. For example, the original "38-caliber" conversion cartridges were actually adapted to 36-caliber guns.

Performance of the 44-40 in a rifle was never startling, but it was more than sufficient for self-defense. The original load launched a 200-grain bullet at over 1200 fps and was certainly adequate for hunting the smallest species. It could be used on smaller deer at close range with careful shot placement. At one time, Winchester offered a high-velocity load launching a 200-grain bullet at close to 1600 fps from a rifle, certainly an adequate deer load.

Usable case capacity with a 200-grain bullet, seated normally, is about 32.0 grains of water. No. 5 and No. 7 are noted 44-40 performers. Also note, cases are typically short.

Use all loads as listed, do not reduce.

44-40 WINCHESTER LOADING DATA (44-40 WCF)

Powder	STARTING Grs.	MV (fps)	MAXIMUM Grs.	MV (fps)	Press. (CUP/psi)	Comments
Lead 200 Lyman 42798						
No.7			11.2	1000	11,300C	1.575″/CCI 300
No.5			9.2	980	11,900C	1.575″/CCI 300
Nitro100			5.3	925	12,800C	1.575″/CCI 300
No.2			6.3	884	12,800C	1.575″/CCI 300
Lead 215 Lyman 429434						
No.9			13.0	1073	12,200C	1.56″/CCI 300
No.5			8.8	950	12,800C	1.56″/CCI 300
No.7			10.5	917	11,600C	1.56″/CCI 300
Nitro100			5.1	860	13,000C	1.56″/CCI 300
No.2			5.5	778	11,300C	1.56″/CCI 300

Powder	STARTING Grs.	MV (fps)	MAXIMUM Grs.	MV (fps)	Press. (CUP/psi)	Comments
180						
No.7			12.9	1053	13,000C	Hdy JHP/1.51″/CCI 300
No.5			10.5	990	11,700C	Hdy JHP/1.51″/CCI 300
Nitro100			6.0	860	12,600C	Hdy JHP/1.51″/CCI 300
No.2			6.7	819	11,800C	Hdy JHP/1.51″/CCI 300
200						
H4227			18.0	1552		Win Model '92 only/JSP
HS6			9.0	1292		JSP
HP38			6.5	1140		JSP
No.5			9.8	1008	13,000C	Nos JHP/1.6″/CCI 300
No.7			11.8	995	13,000C	Nos JHP/1.6″/CCI 300
Nitro100			5.5	828	12,500C	Nos JHP/1.6″/CCI 300
No.2			6.0	761	11,600C	Nos JHP/1.6″/CCI 300

Never exceed maximum load nor use any load exhibiting signs of excessive pressure. Begin at suggested starting load and work up carefully.

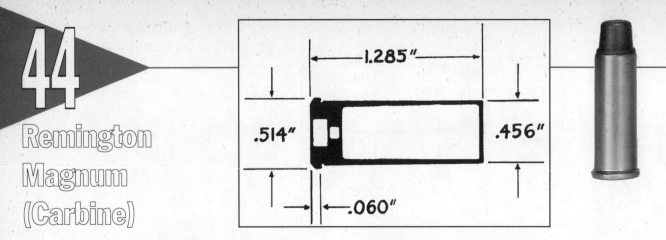

Case: Winchester
Primer: Large Rifle
Barrel: 20″ Accurate
    20″ Hodgdon
Bullet Diameter: 0.429″

Maximum Case Length: 1.285″
Trim to Length: 1.280″
Maximum Cartridge OAL: 1.610″
Minimum Cartridge OAL: 1.535″

Developed through the efforts of independent handgunners—Elmer Keith and others—this revolver chambering is a natural for use in short, handy carbines. Several manufacturers have offered guns chambered for the 44 Magnum, and it continues to garner a level of popularity.

Properly loaded, the 44 Magnum carbine is fully capable for hunting of any species up to the size of elk—many elk and even larger game have been taken with the 44 Magnum revolver, but most would agree the combination is marginal and requires the utmost in skill.

The best hunting combinations depend entirely on the game at hand. For smaller species of deer, the lighter modern expanding bullets can deliver instantaneous kills when placed through the lungs on broadside shots and will do the same thing on elk, if the shot is properly placed. However, if heavy bone might be struck, 300-grain bullets are a much better choice.

Usable case capacity with a 240-grain bullet, seated normally, is about 25.2 grains of water.

W296, H110 and No. 9 are excellent choices for 44 Magnum carbine loads.

44 REMINGTON MAGNUM LOADING DATA (Carbine Specific Loads)

Powder	STARTING Grs.	MV (fps)	MAXIMUM Grs.	MV (fps)	Press. (CUP/psi)	Comments
180						
H110			28.0	2108		*
W296	27.0	1994	28.0	2098		
No.7	18.5	1705	20.5	1938	40,000C	Hdy JHP/1.56″/CCI 300
H4227			27.0	1864		
Her2400	22.5	1690	23.5	1854		
IMR4227	24.0	1684	26.0	1830		
SR4759	22.5	1697	23.5	1819		
No.5	14.8	1596	16.4	1814	38,100C	Hdy JHP/1.56″/CCI 300
200						
No.7	16.8	1755	18.7	1994	37,500C	Nos JHP/1.595″/CCI 300
W296	25.0	1880	26.0	1951		
H110			26.0	1944		*
No.9	22.5	1667	25.0	1894	37,800C	Nos JHP/1.595″/CCI 300
Her2400	20.5	1640	21.5	1809		
H4227			25.0	1756		
IMR4227	23.0	1629	25.0	1755		
SR4759	20.5	1577	22.5	1732		
No.5	14.2	1504	15.8	1709	40,000C	Nos JHP/1.595″/CCI 300
No.2	9.9	1364	11.0	1550	39,500C	Nos JHP/1.595″/CCI 300

Powder	STARTING Grs.	MV (fps)	MAXIMUM Grs.	MV (fps)	Press. (CUP/psi)	Comments
215						
H110			25.0	1826		*
H4227			25.0	1698		Ruger 18″ barrel
225						
H110			24.5	1915		*
W296	23.5	1847	24.5	1910		
Her2400	19.5	1614	20.5	1791		
H4227			24.5	1717		
IMR4227	22.0	1549	24.0	1711		
SR4759	19.5	1504	21.5	1654		
240						
H110			24.0	1886		*
W296	23.0	1814	24.0	1871		
IMR4227	21.5	1528	23.5	1689		
Her2400	18.5	1594	19.5	1680		
H4227			24.0	1670		
SR4759	19.0	1484	21.0	1634		
No.9	19.1	1420	21.3	1625	40,000C	

Never exceed maximum load nor use any load exhibiting signs of excessive pressure. Begin at suggested starting load and work up carefully.

Powder	STARTING Grs.	MV (fps)	MAXIMUM Grs.	MV (fps)	Press. (CUP/psi)	Comments
240 con't						
No.7	15.6	1366	17.3	1552	40,000C	
No.5	13.0	1307	14.4	1485	39,800C	
No.2	9.0	1135	10.0	1290	38,600C	
250						
No.9	18.9	1353	21.0	1538	39,200C	Sra FPJ/1.6"/CCI 300
No.7	15.3	1298	17.0	1475	37,700C	Sra FPJ/1.6"/CCI 300
No.5	13.1	1223	14.5	1390	39,700C	Sra FPJ/1.6"/CCI 300
No.2	9.5	1091	10.5	1240	38,400C	Sra FPJ/1.6"/CCI 300
255						
H110			24.0	1775		*
H4227			23.0	1566		Ruger 18" barrel

Powder	STARTING Grs.	MV (fps)	MAXIMUM Grs.	MV (fps)	Press. (CUP/psi)	Comments
265						
H110			21.0	1522		*
Her2400	17.5	1438	18.5	1520		
H4227			21.0	1360		
300						
No.9	17.1	1309	19.0	1488	40,000C	Sra JSP/1.735"/CCI 300
H110	18.0	1280	20.0	1452		*
No.7	14.6	1236	16.2	1404	40,000C	Sra JSP/1.735"/CCI 300
H4227	17.0	1188	20.0	1389		
No.5	12.6	1206	14.0	1370	40,000C	Sra JSP/1.735"/CCI 300
No.2	8.7	1056	9.7	1200	38,700C	Sra JSP/1.735"/CCI 300

* Do not reduce H110 loads more than 3%.

Caution: **Loads exceeding SAAMI OAL Maximum must be verified for bullet-to-rifling clearance and magazine functioning. Where a specific primer or bullet is indicated those components must be used, no substitutions! Where only a maximum load is shown, reduce starting load 10%, unless otherwise specified.**

Key: (C) = compressed charge; C = CUP; p = psi; Plink = Plinker; Bns = Barnes; Hdy = Hornady; Lap = Lapua; Nos = Nosler; Rem = Remington; Sra = Sierra; Spr = Speer; Win = Winchester.

444

Marlin

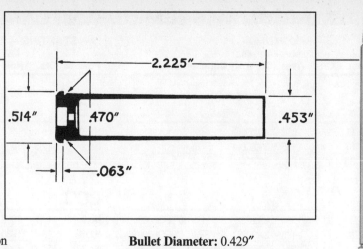

2.225″

.514″ .470″ .453″

.063″

Case: Remington
Primer: Large Rifle
Barrel: 24″ Accurate
       24″ Hodgdon
       22″ Vihtavuori

Bullet Diameter: 0.429″
Maximum Case Length: 2.225″
Trim to Length: 2.220″
Maximum Cartridge OAL: 2.570″
Minimum Cartridge OAL: 2.500″

Marlin co-introduced this lever-action powerhouse in 1964 with a special version of their famous lever-action rifle. Billed as the only big-bore lever-action chambering offered in decades, the 444 Marlin was loaded to comparatively high pressures and delivered impressive performance. Despite a certain mystic to the contrary, the 444 Marlin is nothing more sophisticated than a semi-rimmed version of the 30-06 case, shortened and with a slight taper.

The 444 is currently loaded to somewhat reduced pressures, but it can still easily exceed the muzzle energy of the 30-06 and, therefore, can still deliver a massive punch at short ranges. The original factory load launched a 240-grain bullet

at 2400 fps. Remington once offered a superior 265-grain loading, but that has been dropped. The best hunting combination for all-around use is probably based on Hornady's excellent 265-grain bullet. For use against the lightest species of big game at closer ranges, the 200-grain Hornady XTP launched at over 2700 fps presents an interesting option.

The introduction of Marlin's new Model 1895, chambered in 45-70, has likely done more to limit the 444's success than any other factor.

Usable case capacity with a 240-grain bullet, seated normally, is about 51.2 grains of water. H335, IMR3031, W748, RL-7 and H322 are good performers.

444 MARLIN LOADING DATA

Powder	STARTING Grs.	STARTING MV (fps)	MAXIMUM Grs.	MAXIMUM MV (fps)	Press. (CUP/psi)	Comments
Lead 200 FNGC						
XMP5744			38.0	2175		Rem 9½
Lead 240 Lyman SWC						
XMP5744			36.0	2001		Rem 9½
200						
N120			55.4	2754	43,500p	Hdy HP-XTP
A1680	54.2	2566	57.0	2730	41,300C	Hdy XTP/2.52″/ Rem 9½
A2015BR	57.0	2409	60.0	2563	42,700C	Hdy XTP/2.52″/ Rem 9½/(C)
N110			45.0	2531	43,500p	Hdy HP-XTP
A2460	58.9	2338	62.0	2487	42,800C	Hdy XTP/2.52″/ Rem 9½/(C)
A2230	58.0	2326	61.0	2474	42,700C	Hdy XTP/2.52″/ Rem 9½/(C)
XMP5744			40.0	2247		Hdy XTP/Rem 9½

Powder	STARTING Grs.	STARTING MV (fps)	MAXIMUM Grs.	MAXIMUM MV (fps)	Press. (CUP/psi)	Comments
225						
H4198	47.0	2297	50.0	2480	37,800C	
RL-7	49.0	2239	51.0	2369	36,400C	
IMR4198	45.0	2179	48.0	2361	39,900C	
BL-C(2)	59.0	2190	61.0	2358	33,600C	
H335	59.0	2231	61.0	2340	33,000C	
W748	59.0	2209	61.0	2330	33,700C	
H322	53.0	2269	55.0	2325	34,000C	
H4895	54.0	2172	56.0	2301	33,000C	
IMR3031	53.0	2137	55.0	2244	35,000C	
IMR4895	54.0	2119	56.0	2239	34,400C	
RL-12	54.0	2106	56.0	2221	32,800C	
IMR4320	54.0	2084	56.0	2210	32,900C	
IMR4064	54.0	1981	56.0	2166	31,400C	
H4227	30.0	1914	33.0	2099	33,300C	

Never exceed maximum load nor use any load exhibiting signs of excessive pressure. Begin at suggested starting load and work up carefully.

240

Powder	Starting Grs.	Starting MV (fps)	Max Grs.	Max MV (fps)	Press. (CUP/psi)	Comments
N130			54.4	2468	43,500p	Hdy JTC-SIL
N120			50.3	2455	43,500p	Hdy JTC-SIL
H4148	46.0	2259	49.0	2407	38,400C	
A2015BR	52.3	2217	55.0	2359	43,000C	Sra HP/2.52"/Rem 9½/(C)
A2230	54.2	2181	57.0	2320	44,000C	Sra HP/2.52"/Rem 9½
IMR4198	44.0	2121	47.0	2310	40,900C	
H335	58.0	2162	60.0	2309	31,400C	
BL-C(2)	58.0	2145	60.0	2302	31,000C	
W748	58.0	2184	60.0	2290	31,400C	
RL-7	48.0	2170	50.0	2290	37,900C	
A2460	54.2	2138	57.0	2274	42,700C	Sra HP/2.52"/Rem 9½
H4895	53.0	2194	56.0	2265	33,800C	
H322	53.0	2183	55.0	2249	34,600C	
IMR4895	54.0	1979	56.0	2164	34,700C	
IMR3031	52.0	2009	54.0	2157	35,100C	
RL-12	54.0	1977	56.0	2144	34,000C	
IMR4320	54.0	1947	56.0	2131	36,900C	
IMR4064	54.0	1924	56.0	2111	33,000C	
H4227	29.0	1862	32.0	2061	35,400C	
XMP5744			37.0	2019		Sra JHC/Rem 9½

250

Powder	Starting Grs.	Starting MV (fps)	Max Grs.	Max MV (fps)	Press. (CUP/psi)	Comments
H4198	44.0	2147	47.0	2322	38,900C	
BL-C(2)	57.0	2094	59.0	2292	31,400C	
H335	57.0	2120	59.0	2290	33,300C	
H4895	53.0	2101	55.0	2221	32,000C	
H322	52.0	2140	54.0	2211	34,400C	

265

Powder	Starting Grs.	Starting MV (fps)	Max Grs.	Max MV (fps)	Press. (CUP/psi)	Comments
N120			48.1	2320	43,500p	Hdy FP
N130			51.3	2320	43,500p	Hdy FP
H322	52.0	2170	54.0	2248	35,300C	
H4198	43.0	2078	46.0	2242	37,200C	
A2015BR	49.4	2088	52.0	2221	41,500C	Hdy SP/2.57"/Rem 9½
A2460	53.2	2084	56.0	2217	43,700C	Hdy SP/2.57"/Rem 9½/(C)
A2230	52.3	2074	55.0	2206	44,000C	Hdy SP/2.57"/Rem 9½
IMR4198	41.0	2031	44.0	2190	37,100C	
IMR3031	49.0	2004	52.0	2166	35,200C	
A2520	52.3	2036	55.0	2166	39,300C	Hdy SP/2.57"/Rem 9½/(C)
RL-7	43.0	1994	46.0	2149	37,700C	
IMR4064	51.0	1927	54.0	2129	36,600C	
IMR4320	51.0	1909	54.0	2111	37,000C	
RL-12	51.0	1914	54.0	2106	36,400C	
W748	54.0	2011	56.0	2104	33,900C	
IMR4895	50.0	1866	53.0	2069	37,700C	
XMP5744			35.0	1873		Hdy FP/Rem 9½

300

Powder	Starting Grs.	Starting MV (fps)	Max Grs.	Max MV (fps)	Press. (CUP/psi)	Comments
H322	49.0	1918	52.0	2089	34,200C	
H4895	51.0	1921	53.0	2039	31,800C	
H335	55.0	1861	57.0	1952	39,600C	
H4198	39.0	1804	41.0	1938	39,900C	
BL-C(2)	56.0	1796	58.0	1904	31,000C	

Caution: Loads exceeding SAAMI OAL Maximum must be verified for bullet-to-rifling clearance and magazine functioning. Where a specific primer or bullet is indicated those components must be used, no substitutions! Where only a maximum load is shown, reduce starting load 10%, unless otherwise specified.

Key: (C) = compressed charge; C = CUP; p = psi; Plink = Plinker; Bns = Barnes; Hdy = Hornady; Lap = Lapua; Nos = Nosler; Rem = Remington; Sra = Sierra; Spr = Speer; Win = Winchester.

Never exceed maximum load nor use any load exhibiting signs of excessive pressure. Begin at suggested starting load and work up carefully.

45
Automatic (Carbine)

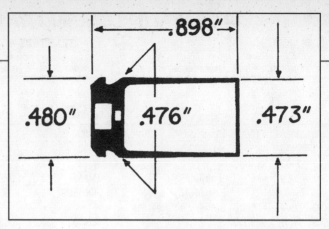

Case: Remington
Primer: Large Pistol
Barrel: 16 1/2"
Bullet Diameter: 0.451"-0.452"

Maximum Case Length: 0.898"
Trim to Length: 0.893"
Maximum Cartridge OAL: 1.275"
Minimum Cartridge OAL: 1.190"

Developed to meet a purpose—the delivery of a bullet of a specified size, weight and shape at a specified velocity—the 45 Automatic has been with us since it was adopted in 1911 as the official cartridge for service sidearms in the U.S. military. It was a common chambering in submachine guns for military, police and civilian(!) markets and, inevitably, was eventually chambered in a carbine by Marlin.

Because of limited powder space, carbine performance is not all that much better than that delivered in the 1911. The

45 Automatic cannot be considered a big game cartridge, and it certainly lacks the velocity necessary to suggest much value in varmint hunting except at the shortest ranges. Nevertheless, this is certainly a serious self-defense combination, just as it is in a handgun.

Usable case capacity with a 230-grain bullet, seated normally, is about 17.6 grains of water. No. 5 and No. 7 are good choices for carbine loads.

45 AUTOMATIC LOADING DATA (Carbine Specific Loads)

Powder	—STARTING— Grs.	MV (fps)	—MAXIMUM— Grs.	MV (fps)	Press. (CUP/psi)	Comments
185						
No.7	11.7	1134	13.0	1289	18,000p	Hdy XTP/1.210"/Rem 2 1/2
No.5	9.2	1125	10.2	1278	19,900p	Hdy XTP/1.210"/Rem 2 1/2
No.2	6.8	1096	7.5	1245	20,400p	Hdy XTP/1.210"/Rem 2 1/2
Nitro100	5.9	1025	6.6	1165	19,800p	Hdy XTP/1.210"/Rem 2 1/2
200						
No.5	8.7	1052	9.7	1195	20,600p	Hdy XTP/1.225"/Rem 2 1/2
No.7	10.8	1043	12.0	1185	19,200p	Hdy XTP/1.225"/Rem 2 1/2
No.2	5.9	943	6.5	1072	19,700p	Hdy XTP/1.225"/Rem 2 1/2
Nitro100	5.4	914	6.0	1039	17,500p	Hdy XTP/1.225"/Rem 2 1/2

Powder	—STARTING— Grs.	MV (fps)	—MAXIMUM— Grs.	MV (fps)	Press. (CUP/psi)	Comments
230						
No.7	9.9	920	11.0	1045	17,800p	Sra FMJ/1.250"/Rem 2 1/2
No.5	7.8	920	8.7	1045	19,300p	Sra FMJ/1.250"/Rem 2 1/2
Nitro100	5.0	822	5.6	934	19,100p	Sra FMJ/1.250"/Rem 2 1/2
No.2	5.5	821	6.1	933	19,200p	Sra FMJ/1.250"/Rem 2 1/2

Caution: **Loads exceeding SAAMI OAL Maximum must be verified for bullet-to-rifling clearance and magazine functioning. Where a specific primer or bullet is indicated those components must be used, no substitutions! Where only a maximum load is shown, reduce starting load 10%, unless otherwise specified.**

Key: (C) = compressed charge; C = CUP; p = psi; Plink = Plinker; Bns = Barnes; Hdy = Hornady; Lap = Lapua; Nos = Nosler; Rem = Remington; Sra = Sierra; Spr = Speer; Win = Winchester.

Never exceed maximum load nor use any load exhibiting signs of excessive pressure. Begin at suggested starting load and work up carefully.

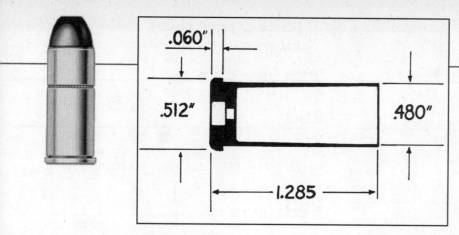

Case: Winchester
Primer: CCI 300
Barrel: 16½" Accurate
Bullet Diameter: 0.451"-0.452"

Maximum Case Length: 1.285" (Rare)
Trim to Length: 1.280"
Maximum Cartridge OAL: 1.600"
Minimum Cartridge OAL: 1.550"

Co-introduced in 1873 with the Colt Single Action Army revolver, this—along with the 45-70—is one of the most successful chamberings dating from the first years of self-contained centerfire cartridges. Others have survived, but excepting the 45-70, none are nearly so popular.

(Since there was never any other 45 Colt chambering, and since, obviously, there is no 45 Short Colt chambering, the moniker 45 Long Colt is senseless and has no *logical* historical basis. Nevertheless, none other than Colt at one time marketed ammunition under that very name! The confusion arises from the existence of the similar but shorter 45 Smith & Wesson cartridge that could also be used in some standard 45 Colt chambers.)

The 45 Colt is a natural for chambering in carbines. *These loads are not safe for use in Colt or similar revolvers or reproduction revolvers.* They are specifically intended for use only in carbines, however they were developed as safe for T/C Contender and Ruger handguns. Such loads are handy for those who want to carry one load for both their Ruger revolver and Marlin or Winchester carbine.

Even with these higher-than-standard-pressure loads, performance is quite a bit behind the 44 Magnum. Nevertheless, these loads offer adequate performance for hunting smaller species of big game and are certainly formidable self-defense combinations.

Usable case capacity with a 250-grain bullet, seated normally, is about 29.8 grains of water. No.7 and No.9 are good carbine 45 Colt choices.

45 COLT LOADING DATA (Carbine Specific Loads)

Powder	STARTING Grs.	MV (fps)	MAXIMUM Grs.	MV (fps)	Press. (CUP/psi)	Comments
Lead 215						
No.5	12.2	1189	13.6	1351	20,800C	1.55"
No.7	14.9	1181	16.6	1342	20,900C	1.55"
Nitro100	8.1	1125	9.0	1278	20,700C	1.55"
Lead 225						
No.5	12.2	1186	13.6	1348	21,400C	1.575"
No.7	14.8	1173	16.4	1333	21,000C	1.575"
Nitro100	7.9	1121	8.8	1274	20,800C	1.575"
Lead 230						
No.5	12.2	1171	13.5	1331	20,900C	1.60"
No.7	14.6	1148	16.2	1304	20,600C	1.60"
Nitro100	7.7	1062	8.6	1207	20,300C	1.60"

Powder	STARTING Grs.	MV (fps)	MAXIMUM Grs.	MV (fps)	Press. (CUP/psi)	Comments
Lead 240						
No.7	14.1	1163	15.7	1322	20,600C	1.57"
No.5	11.1	1121	12.3	1274	20,000C	1.57"
Nitro100	7.6	1084	8.4	1232	20,300C	1.57"
Lead 255 Lyman 452424						
No.9	15.8	1101	17.6	1251	20,100C	1.60"
No.7	13.6	1093	15.1	1242	19,700C	1.60"
No.5	10.6	1037	11.8	1178	18,200C	1.60"
Nitro100	7.3	1035	8.1	1176	20,200C	1.60"
Lead 280						
No.9	15.8	1198	17.5	1361	19,300C	1.65"
No.7	12.6	1128	14.0	1282	19,000C	1.65"
No.5	9.9	971	11.0	1103	18,300C	1.65"
Nitro100	6.9	951	7.7	1081	19,100C	1.65"

▶▶▶▶▶▶▶▶▶▶▶▶▶▶▶▶▶▶▶▶▶▶▶▶▶▶

Never exceed maximum load nor use any load exhibiting signs of excessive pressure. Begin at suggested starting load and work up carefully.

Powder	STARTING Grs.	MV (fps)	MAXIMUM Grs.	MV (fps)	Press. (CUP/psi)	Comments
Lead 300						
No.7	11.7	1005	13.0	1142	19,200C	1.585"
No.9	13.5	1001	15.0	1138	17,600C	1.585"
200						
No.5	13.1	1234	14.6	1402	20,000C	Sra FPJ/1.585"
Nitro100	8.3	1136	9.2	1291	19,300C	Sra FPJ/1.585"
No.7	14.8	1083	16.4	1231	15,300C	Sra FPJ/1.585"
230						
No.5	11.7	1117	13.0	1269	18,600C	Hdy RNFMJ/1.60"
No.7	13.9	1076	15.4	1223	18,500C	Hdy RNFMJ/1.60"
Nitro100	7.8	1067	8.7	1213	19,600C	Hdy RNFMJ/1.60"
240						
No.7	14.0	1081	15.5	1228	20,400C	Sra JHC/1.59"
No.5	11.7	1067	13.0	1212	18,300C	Sra JHC/1.59"
Nitro100	7.7	1030	8.5	1170	20,100C	Sra JHC/1.59"

Powder	STARTING Grs.	MV (fps)	MAXIMUM Grs.	MV (fps)	Press. (CUP/psi)	Comments
250						
No.7	13.7	1058	15.2	1202	19,600C	Nos JHP/1.585"
No.5	10.9	983	12.1	1117	18,100C	Nos JHP/1.585"
Nitro100	7.5	967	8.3	1099	19,300C	Nos JHP/1.585"
260						
No.7	13.5	1046	15.0	1189	19,400C	Spr JHP/1.585"
No.5	10.7	1000	11.9	1136	19,300C	Spr JHP/1.585"
Nitro100	7.3	950	8.1	1080	19,700C	Spr JHP/1.585"
300						
No.9	13.5	956	15.0	1086	19,500C	Hdy XTP/1.58"
No.9	13.5	906	15.0	1030	19,200C	Spr SP/1.585"
No.7	11.7	906	13.0	1030	20,200C	Hdy XTP/1.58"
No.7	11.7	900	13.0	1023	20,300C	Spr SP/1.585"

Caution: **Loads exceeding SAAMI OAL Maximum must be verified for bullet-to-rifling clearance and magazine functioning. Where a specific primer or bullet is indicated those components must be used, no substitutions! Where only a maximum load is shown, reduce starting load 10%, unless otherwise specified.**

Key: (C) = compressed charge; C = CUP; p = psi; Plink = Plinker; Bns = Barnes; Hdy = Hornady; Lap = Lapua; Nos = Nosler; Rem = Remington; Sra = Sierra; Spr = Speer; Win = Winchester.

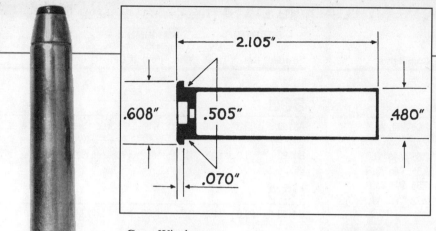

Case: Winchester
Primer: Large Rifle
Barrel: 24″ Accurate
32″ Hodgdon
22″ Vihtavuori

Bullet Diameter: 0.457″-0.458″
Maximum Case Length: 2.105″
Trim to Length: 2.100″
Maximum Cartridge OAL: 2.550″
Minimum Cartridge OAL: 2.490″

The 45-70 started a trend that continues to this day. When the U.S. military adopts a small-arm chambering, they simultaneously ensure instant and long-standing success for that number in the civilian market.

Adopted in 1873 for chambering in the Model 1873 Trapdoor Springfield Rifle, the 45-70 is as popular today as it ever was! In recent years, it has been chambered in bolt-action custom rifles, single shot falling-block commercial actions, the Marlin lever-action and several runs of Model 86 Winchester reproductions.

Performance of modern factory smokeless loads reflects the continued use of original Trapdoor rifles and carbines—testimony to the ruggedness and quality of those archaic guns.

The current pressure limit for the 45-70 ensures that any specification load will be safe to fire in any sound gun ever commercially chambered for the 45-70. Nevertheless, it is unwise to fire any jacketed load from an original Trapdoor rifle because the soft steel of the barrel will suffer rapid wear. For original Trapdoors, the best practice is to use only cast lead bullets and to keep pressures below about 20,000 psi.

Usable case capacity with a 300-grain bullet, seated normally, is about 62.7 grains of water.

H4198, A2495BR and XMP5744 are noted for good 45-70 performance.

The loads are intended for blackpowder guns that are safe with smokeless propellant loads.

45-70 GOVERNMENT LOADING DATA (Trapdoor Springfield)

Lead 330

Powder	Grs.	MV (fps)	Grs.	MV (fps)	Press. (CUP/psi)	Comments
A2495BR	53.1	1738	59.0	1975	19,200p	2.52″/Win WLR/(C)
A4350	53.1	1384	59.0	1573	17,900p	2.52″/Win WLR
A3100	54.0	1255	60.0	1426	15,100p	2.52″/Win WLR
A8700	54.0	1059	60.0	1203	10,400p	2.52″/Win WLR

Lead 340 Lyman 457122HP

Powder	Grs.	MV (fps)	Grs.	MV (fps)	Press. (CUP/psi)	Comments
A2495BR	51.3	1628	57.0	1850	18,000p	2.52″/Win WLR
A4350	53.1	1384	59.0	1573	17,900p	2.52″/Win WLR/(C)
XMP5744			30.0	1494		2.52″/Win WLR
A3100	54.0	1255	60.0	1426	15,100p	2.52″/Win WLR/(C)
A8700	54.0	1059	60.0	1203	10,400p	2.52″/Win WLR/(C)

Lead 378 Lyman 457483

Powder	Grs.	MV (fps)	Grs.	MV (fps)	Press. (CUP/psi)	Comments
A2495BR	45.0	1479	50.0	1681	14,500p	2.565″/Win WLR
A3100	54.0	1307	60.0	1485	19,800p	2.565″/Win WLR/(C)
A4350	48.6	1259	54.0	1431	15,400p	2.565″/Win WLR
XMP5744			28.5	1418		2.565″/Win WLR

Lead 378 Lyman 457483 con't

Powder	Grs.	MV (fps)	Grs.	MV (fps)	Press. (CUP/psi)	Comments
A3100	50.4	1159	56.0	1317	13,900p	2.565″/Win WLR
A8700	54.0	1015	60.0	1153	8,300p	2.565″/Win WLR
A8700	54.0	903	60.0	1026	8,300p	2.565″/Win WLR/(C)

Lead 405

Powder	Grs.	MV (fps)	Grs.	MV (fps)	Press. (CUP/psi)	Comments
A4350	50.4	1297	56.0	1474	16,200p	2.55″/Win WLR/(C)
A3100	54.0	1251	60.0	1422	18,200p	2.55″/Win WLR/(C)
XMP5744			28.5	1375		2.55″/Win WLR
A8700	54.0	1025	60.0	1165	11,700p	2.55″/Win WLR/(C)

Lead 420 Lyman 457193

Powder	Grs.	MV (fps)	Grs.	MV (fps)	Press. (CUP/psi)	Comments
A2495BR	45.0	1457	50.0	1656	17,700p	2.60″/Win WLR
A4350	50.4	1297	56.0	1474	16,200p	2.60″/Win WLR/(C)
A3100	54.0	1251	60.0	1422	18,200p	2.60″/Win WLR/(C)
A8700	54.0	1025	60.0	1165	11,700p	2.60″/Win WLR/(C)

Never exceed maximum load nor use any load exhibiting signs of excessive pressure. Begin at suggested starting load and work up carefully.

Lead 475 Lyman 457406

Powder	—STARTING— Grs.	MV (fps)	—MAXIMUM— Grs.	MV (fps)	Press. (CUP/psi)	Comments
A2495BR	40.5	1377	45.0	1565	16,000p	2.68"/Win WLR
XMP5744	27.0	1253	28.5	1375		2.725"/Win WLR
A4350	40.5	1107	45.0	1258	16,100p	2.68"/Win WLR
A3100	44.1	1074	49.0	1221	16,300p	2.68"/Win WLR
A8700	54.0	915	60.0	1040	15,900p	2.68"/Win WLR
A8700	54.0	915	60.0	1040	15,900p	2.725"/Win WLR/(C)

Lead 500 SAECO 22

Powder	Grs.	MV (fps)	Grs.	MV (fps)	Press. (CUP/psi)	Comments
A2495BR	39.6	1348	44.0	1532	18,400p	2.635"/Win WLR
XMP5744			26.0	1217		2.795"/Win WLR
A4350	37.8	1034	42.0	1175	16,300p	2.635"/Win WLR/(C)
A3100	40.5	1001	45.0	1138	16,500p	2.635"/Win WLR/(C)
A8700	54.0	880	60.0	1000	15,800p	2.795"/Win WLR/(C)
A8700	49.5	842	55.0	957	9,800p	2.635"/Win WLR/(C)

Lead 530 Lyman 457124

Powder	Grs.	MV (fps)	Grs.	MV (fps)	Press. (CUP/psi)	Comments
A2495BR	41.4	1237	46.0	1406	11,600p	2.83"/Win WLR
A3100	49.5	1196	55.0	1359	16,900p	2.83"/Win WLR
A4350	43.2	1167	48.0	1326	16,600p	2.83"/Win WLR
XMP5744			28.5	1280		2.83"/Win WLR
A8700	58.5	932	65.0	1059	15,800p	2.83"/Win WLR

300

Powder	—STARTING— Grs.	MV (fps)	—MAXIMUM— Grs.	MV (fps)	Press. (CUP/psi)	Comments
A3100	63.0	1500	70.0	1705	18,300p	Sra HP/2.55"/ Win WLR/(C)
H4198	31.0	1426	33.0	1542		32" barrel

350

Powder	Grs.	MV (fps)	Grs.	MV (fps)	Press. (CUP/psi)	Comments
H4198	28.0	1159	32.0	1387		32" barrel

400-405

Powder	Grs.	MV (fps)	Grs.	MV (fps)	Press. (CUP/psi)	Comments
BL-C(2)			35.0	1354	16,400C	
H4198	28.0	1124	30.0	1204		32" barrel
A8700	54.0	873	60.0	992	14,300p	Spr FN/2.56"/ Win WLR/(C)

500

Powder	Grs.	MV (fps)	Grs.	MV (fps)	Press. (CUP/psi)	Comments
BL-C(2)			35.0	1191	17,600C	
H4198	25.0	1003	28.0	1082		32" barrel
A8700	54.0	909	60.0	1033	10,000p	Hdy RNSP/2.825"/ Win WLR/(C)

Caution: Loads exceeding SAAMI OAL Maximum must be verified for bullet-to-rifling clearance and magazine functioning. Where a specific primer or bullet is indicated those components must be used, no substitutions! Where only a maximum load is shown, reduce starting load 10%, unless otherwise specified.

Key: (C) = compressed charge; C = CUP; p = psi; Plink = Plinker; Bns = Barnes; Hdy = Hornady; Lap = Lapua; Nos = Nosler; Rem = Remington; Sra = Sierra; Spr = Speer; Win = Winchester.

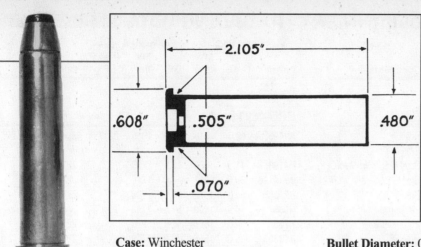

Case: Winchester
Primer: Large Rifle
Barrel: 24″ Accurate
       22″ Hodgdon
       22″ Vihtavuori

Bullet Diameter: 0.457″-0.458″
Maximum Case Length: 2.105″
Trim to Length: 2.100″
Maximum Cartridge OAL
         (SAAMI): 2.550″
Minimum Cartridge OAL: 2.530″

While there is no such official designation or commercial loading, we have separated these loads from the lower-pressure loads for good reason. Even the oldest lever-action rifles, if in good repair, are perfectly safe for use with any load within the current SAAMI pressure limit for the 45-70. Even with jacketed bullets, these loads will not cause undue wear in the bores of these "newer" rifles. However, older rifles, Trapdoor Springfields and other single shot designs, should not be used with any such load or with any jacketed bullet load. In those guns, the bores are so soft that jacketed bullets will cause very rapid wear.

While the new Model 1895 Marlin and the reproduction Model 1886 Winchester guns are certainly capable of safely handling loads considerably exceeding any listed here, we were unable to attain pressure data for such loads, and lack-

ing any such basis, we have regrettably felt compelled to omit such loads. For those wanting to achieve top performance from such a rifle, we recommend the data offered in the most recent Speer, Hornady or Hodgdon manuals. Here, the 45-70 is not far behind the 458 Winchester Magnum for use against any but the biggest of critters.

Usable case capacity with a 300-grain bullet, seated normally, is about 62.7 grains of water. IMR4198, H322 and RL-7 are good choices for accuracy.

Many of these loads greatly exceed SAAMI maximum OAL. Such loads are intended for use in the 1886 Winchester and single shot rifles only. Other loads that slightly exceed SAAMI maximum OAL are intended for use in Marlin's New Model 1895. Ensure functionality before finalizing OAL.

45-70 GOVERNMENT +P LOADING DATA

Powder	STARTING Grs.	MV (fps)	MAXIMUM Grs.	MV (fps)	Press. (CUP/psi)	Comments
Lead 330						
A2015BR	45.0	1697	50.0	1928	23,200p	2.52″/Win WLR
A2700	52.2	1627	58.0	1849	26,100p	2.52″/Win WLR
Lead 378 Lyman 457483						
A2495BR	49.5	1703	55.0	1935	23,800p	2.565″/Win WLR
A2015BR	44.1	1602	49.0	1821	23,400p	2.565″/Win WLR
A2700	51.3	1525	57.0	1733	25,600p	2.565″/Win WLR
A4350	54.0	1427	60.0	1622	21,500p	2.565″/Win WLR/(C)
Lead 405						
A2495BR	48.6	1585	54.0	1801	22,200p	2.55″/Win WLR/(C)
A2015BR	48.6	1465	54.0	1665	26,800p	2.55″/Win WLR
A2700	48.6	1465	54.0	1665	26,800p	2.55″/Win WLR

Powder	STARTING Grs.	MV (fps)	MAXIMUM Grs.	MV (fps)	Press. (CUP/psi)	Comments
Lead 475 Lyman 457406						
A2495BR	45.0	1538	50.0	1748	24,300p	2.725″/Win WLR/(C)
A2015BR	39.6	1461	44.0	1660	26,300p	2.725″/Win WLR
A4350	52.2	1425	58.0	1619	26,300p	2.725″/Win WLR/(C)
A3100	54.0	1331	60.0	1513	25,700p	2.725″/Win WLR/(C)
A2700	44.1	1309	49.0	1488	26,900p	2.725″/Win WLR
Lead 500 SAECO 22						
A2495BR	44.1	1470	49.0	1670	24,400p	2.55″/Win WLR/(C)
A4350	52.2	1392	58.0	1582	24,200p	2.795″/Win WLR/(C)
A2015BR	37.8	1379	42.0	1567	25,900p	2.55″/Win WLR
A3100	54.0	1314	60.0	1493	25,000p	2.795″/Win WLR/(C)
A2700	42.3	1244	47.0	1414	25,900p	2.55″/Win WLR

▶▶▶▶▶▶▶▶▶▶▶▶▶▶▶▶▶▶▶▶▶▶▶▶▶▶

Never exceed maximum load nor use any load exhibiting signs of excessive pressure. Begin at suggested starting load and work up carefully.

300

Powder	Grs. (Start)	MV (fps) Start	Grs. (Max)	MV (fps) Max	Press. (CUP/psi)	Comments
N133	58.7	2048	63.2	2242	27,557p	Hdy HP
N133	57.6	2057	60.0	2187	28,137p	Sra HP FN
A2495BR	59.4	1914	66.0	2175	22,100p	Sra HP/2.55"/Win WLR/(C)
A2015BR	53.1	1904	59.0	2164	25,100p	Sra HP/2.55"/Win WLR
N135	58.6	1982	61.7	2134	28,137p	Sra HP FN
H4198	48.0	1956	52.0	2123		22" barrel
VarGet			62.0	2090	24,700C	26" test barrel
N130	48.8	1947	52.1	2090	28,137p	Hdy HP
RL-7	45.0	1819	50.0	2069		22" barrel
IMR4198	45.0	1798	50.0	2054		22" barrel
N120	38.9	1732	46.5	2047	28,137p	Sra HP FN
N120	40.6	1864	45.0	2029	28,137p	Hdy HP
H322	54.0	1694	60.0	1965		22" barrel
H4227	38.0	1773	40.0	1942		22" barrel
A2700	58.5	1706	65.0	1939	25,200p	Sra HP/2.55"/Win WLR/(C)
IMR3031	51.0	1664	56.0	1929		22" barrel
IMR4227	36.0	1722	39.0	1919		22" barrel
A4350	63.0	1597	70.0	1815	20,100p	Sra HP/2.55"/Win WLR/(C)
SR4759	32.0	1559	35.0	1737		22" barrel
Her2400	28.0	1588	30.0	1647		22" barrel

350

Powder	Grs. (Start)	MV (fps) Start	Grs. (Max)	MV (fps) Max	Press. (CUP/psi)	Comments
A2520	54.0	1836	60.0	2086	28,000p	Hdy RN/2.55"/Win WLR
A2495BR	54.9	1810	61.0	2057	27,100p	Hdy RN/2.55"/Win WLR/(C)
VarGet			61.0	2027	27,300C	26" test barrel
A2460	53.1	1748	59.0	1986	26,200p	Hdy RN/2.55"/Win WLR
A2015BR	47.7	1700	53.0	1932	25,400p	Hdy RN/2.55"/Win WLR
IMR4895	54.0	1743	57.0	1900		22" barrel
H4895	56.0	1710	60.0	1894		22" barrel
IMR4198	42.0	1688	47.0	1889		22" barrel
IMR3031	50.0	1660	55.0	1874		22" barrel
A2230	48.6	1648	54.0	1873	26,200p	Hdy RN/2.55"/Win WLR
IMR4320	56.0	1760	58.0	1866		22" barrel
H322	54.0	1672	58.0	1858		22" barrel
IMR4064	56.0	1739	58.0	1856		22" barrel
RL-7	43.0	1678	48.0	1851		22" barrel
H4198	42.0	1693	46.0	1841		22" barrel
H4227	35.0	1622	37.0	1800		22" barrel
A2700	54.9	1579	61.0	1794	26,900p	Hdy RN/2.55"/Win WLR
A4350	58.5	1527	65.0	1735	22,700C	Hdy RN/2.55"/Win WLR/(C)
IMR4227	31.0	1504	34.0	1658		22" barrel
A3100	58.5	1399	65.0	1590	21,600p	Hdy RN/2.55"/Win WLR/(C)
Her2400	27.0	1503	29.0	1579		22" barrel

385-400

Powder	Grs. (Start)	MV (fps) Start	Grs. (Max)	MV (fps) Max	Press. (CUP/psi)	Comments
A2460	51.3	1695	57.0	1926	28,000p	Spr FN/2.56"/Win WLR
N133	46.6	1695	51.4	1854	28,137p	Spr SP
H322	50.0	1750	54.0	1852		22" barrel
H4895	52.0	1678	56.0	1850		22" barrel
A2520	48.6	1626	54.0	1848	23,800p	Spr FN/2.56"/Win WLR
VarGet			55.0	1845	25,000C	26" test barrel (405-gr. only)

385-400 con't

Powder	Grs. (Start)	MV (fps) Start	Grs. (Max)	MV (fps) Max	Press. (CUP/psi)	Comments
A2495BR	49.5	1616	55.0	1836	23,800p	Spr Light FN/2.56"/Win WLR/(C)
H4198	41.0	1680	44.0	1788		22" barrel
IMR4198	39.0	1611	44.0	1788		22" barrel
BL-C(2)	54.0	1652	58.0	1786		22" barrel
N135	46.6	1609	51.6	1783	28,137p	Spr SP
H335	54.0	1666	58.0	1780		22" barrel
IMR3031	48.0	1558	53.0	1779		22" barrel
A2015BR	44.1	1550	49.0	1761	24,000p	Spr FN/2.56"/Win WLR
IMR4320	52.0	1671	55.0	1749		22" barrel
IMR4895	50.0	1644	53.0	1742		22" barrel
A2230	44.1	1532	49.0	1741	23,100p	Spr FN/2.56"/Win WLR
IMR4064	52.0	1651	55.0	1730		22" barrel
H4227	34.0	1595	36.0	1631		22" barrel
H4895	40.0	1312	50.0	1622		405-gr. JSP suitable for 1886 Win.
A2700	49.5	1415	55.0	1608	25,900p	Spr FN/2.56"/Win WLR
N120	31.7	1455	35.8	1604	28,137p	Spr SP
RL-7	37.0	1469	40.0	1598		22" barrel
A4350	54.0	1382	60.0	1570	21,300p	Spr FN/2.56"/Win WLR/(C)
A3100	54.0	1278	60.0	1452	20,100p	Spr FN/2.56"/Win WLR/(C)

500

Powder	Grs. (Start)	MV (fps) Start	Grs. (Max)	MV (fps) Max	Press. (CUP/psi)	Comments
H4895	48.0	1471	52.0	1679		22" barrel
H322	46.0	1504	50.0	1667		22" barrel
IMR4320	48.0	1444	51.0	1640		22" barrel
IMR3031	44.0	1454	48.0	1639		22" barrel
H335	49.0	1451	53.0	1638		22" barrel
BL-C(2)	49.0	1448	53.0	1623		22" barrel
IMR4895	47.0	1438	50.0	1611		22" barrel
IMR4064	48.0	1429	51.0	1610		22" barrel
VarGet			50.0	1603	28,000C	26" test barrel
A4350	52.2	1410	58.0	1602	25,300p	Hdy RNSP/2.825"/Win WLR/(C)
IMR4198	37.0	1408	41.0	1588		22" barrel
H4198	39.0	1431	41.0	1549		22" barrel
A2495BR	41.4	1353	46.0	1538	26,400p	Hdy RNSP/2.58"/Win WLR
A2460	39.6	1328	44.0	1509	25,400p	Hdy RNSP/2.58"/Win WLR
H4227	32.0	1405	34.0	1468		22" barrel
A2230	37.8	1287	42.0	1462	26,000p	Hdy RNSP/2.58"/Win WLR
A3100	54.0	1268	60.0	1441	26,400p	Hdy RNSP/2.825"/Win WLR
A2520	39.6	1262	44.0	1434	28,000p	Hdy RNSP/2.58"/Win WLR
A2015BR	36.0	1251	40.0	1422	23,800p	Hdy RNSP/2.58"/Win WLR
RL-7	35.0	1300	38.0	1411		22" barrel
H4831			60.0	1383		Hdy RN suitable for 1886 Win.
A2700	41.4	1168	46.0	1327	23,600p	Hdy RNSP/2.58"/Win WLR

Never exceed maximum load nor use any load exhibiting signs of excessive pressure. Begin at suggested starting load and work up carefully.

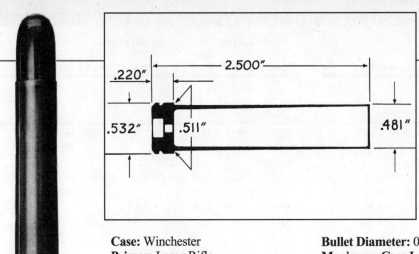

Case: Winchester
Primer: Large Rifle
Barrel: 26″ Accurate
    22″ Hodgdon
    25″ Vihtavuori

Bullet Diameter: 0.457″-0.458″
Maximum Case Length: 2.500″
Trim to Length: 2.495″
Maximum Cartridge OAL: 3.340″
Minimum Cartridge OAL: 3.300″

Co-introduced in 1956 for a special "African" version of the famous Model 70 Winchester, there is nothing particularly unique about the 458 Winchester Magnum. Slightly taper a standard belted magnum casing to properly hold a 0.458″ bullet and trim it to 2.5″ for a loaded round length of 3.34″, the same as any "short-magnum" chambering, and load it to moderately high pressures. You will have a chambering that can do almost anything any of the much bigger British Nitro Express chamberings can do. Besides impressive ballistics, this is a natural for chambering in standard-length bolt-action rifles and allows three rounds to fit in the magazine.

Original loads were rated with a 500-grain solid or a 510 softpoint at about 2200 fps. Soon thereafter, Winchester reduced performance and the rating slightly, likely in response to concerns about pressure excursions associated

with use in extreme heat. Current factory loads produce about 2050 fps in 22″ barreled guns. The handloads listed here reflect the same prudence of limited pressure, well below the SAAMI pressure limit, while still generating sufficient energy for the task intended.

Those who can tolerate the substantial recoil to do a bit of bench-testing often report extraordinary accuracy from this and similar big-bore chamberings. Unlike some smaller-bored similar-purpose chamberings, the 458 Winchester Magnum cannot be considered as a good choice where ranges might be a bit longer—velocity potential and ballistic coefficient of the bullets are both too limited.

Usable case capacity with a 500-grain bullet, seated normally, is about 74.7 grains of water. H335, H4895, IMR-3031, RL-7 and H4198 are all good choices in the 458.

458 WINCHESTER MAGNUM LOADING DATA

Lead 375 RNGC

Powder	—STARTING— Grs.	MV (fps)	—MAXIMUM— Grs.	MV (fps)	Press. (CUP/psi)	Comments
XMP5744			52.0	2240		Rem 9½M

Lead 400 FN

Powder	—STARTING— Grs.	MV (fps)	—MAXIMUM— Grs.	MV (fps)	Press. (CUP/psi)	Comments
XMP5744			51.0	2170		Rem 9½M

Lead 455 RNGC

Powder	—STARTING— Grs.	MV (fps)	—MAXIMUM— Grs.	MV (fps)	Press. (CUP/psi)	Comments
XMP5744			49.0	2022		Rem 9½M

Lead 475 Lyman 457406

Powder	—STARTING— Grs.	MV (fps)	—MAXIMUM— Grs.	MV (fps)	Press. (CUP/psi)	Comments
A2230	54.0	1763	60.0	2003	32,700C	3.085″/Rem 9½M
A2460	54.9	1753	61.0	1992	30,800C	3.085″/Rem 9½M
A2015BR	49.5	1660	55.0	1886	28,200C	3.085″/Rem 9½M

Lead 500 RN

Powder	—STARTING— Grs.	MV (fps)	—MAXIMUM— Grs.	MV (fps)	Press. (CUP/psi)	Comments
XMP5744			47.0	1901		Rem 9½M

▶▶▶▶▶▶▶▶▶▶▶▶▶▶▶▶▶▶▶▶▶▶▶▶▶▶▶▶▶

Caution: Loads exceeding SAAMI OAL Maximum must be verified for bullet-to-rifling clearance and magazine functioning. Where a specific primer or bullet is indicated those components must be used, no substitutions! Where only a maximum load is shown, reduce starting load 10%, unless otherwise specified.

Key: (C) = compressed charge; C = CUP; p = psi; Plink = Plinker; Bns = Barnes; Hdy = Hornady; Lap = Lapua; Nos = Nosler; Rem = Remington; Sra = Sierra; Spr = Speer; Win = Winchester.

300

Powder	Grs.	MV (fps)	Grs.	MV (fps)	Press. (CUP/psi)	Comments
A2015BR	68.4	2293	76.0	2606	35,500C	Hdy HP/2.94"/ Rem 9½M/(C)
N120	64.7	2427	70.0	2599	52,214p	Sra HP
A2230	70.2	2248	78.0	2554	33,500C	Hdy HP/2.94"/ Rem 9½M/(C)
A2460	70.2	2205	78.0	2506	30,800C	Hdy HP/2.94"/ Rem 9½M/(C)
H4198	59.0	2197	63.0	2410		

350

Powder	Grs.	MV (fps)	Grs.	MV (fps)	Press. (CUP/psi)	Comments
A2015BR	67.5	2250	75.0	2557	44,600C	Hdy RN/2.965"/ Rem 9½M/(C)
N130	69.0	2373	73.7	2518	52,214p	Spr SP
A2230	70.2	2211	78.0	2512	45,100C	Hdy RN/2.965"/ Rem 9½M/(C)
A2460	70.2	2189	78.0	2487	42,300C	Hdy RN/2.965"/ Rem 9½M/(C)
H4198	64.0	2321	68.0	2469		
N120	63.5	2288	69.1	2462	52,214p	Spr SP
W748	77.0	2290	81.0	2419		
RL-7	66.0	2352	69.0	2410		
IMR4198	63.0	2252	67.0	2374		
IMR3031	71.0	2244	74.0	2349		
IMR4895	74.0	2230	77.0	2311		
RL-12	74.0	2212	77.0	2294		
VarGet			74.0	2233	30,600C	

400

Powder	Grs.	MV (fps)	Grs.	MV (fps)	Press. (CUP/psi)	Comments
A2015BR	68.4	2172	76.0	2468	48,800C	Spr FN/3.14"/ Rem 9½M/(C)
A2230	72.0	2162	80.0	2457	45,500C	Spr FN/3.14"/ Rem 9½M/(C)
A2460	72.0	2158	80.0	2452	44,700C	Spr FN/3.14"/ Rem 9½M/(C)
W748	75.0	2240	78.0	2353		
IMR4895	72.0	2171	75.0	2266		
H4198	62.0	2088	66.0	2242		405-gr. bullet
IMR4198	61.0	2151	64.0	2229		
VarGet			75.0	2229	32,000C	405-gr. bullet
RL-7	64.0	2122	67.0	2222		
IMR3031	67.0	2040	71.0	2202		
RL-12	71.0	2090	74.0	2199		

500

Powder	Grs.	MV (fps)	Grs.	MV (fps)	Press. (CUP/psi)	Comments
A2460	66.6	1929	74.0	2192	44,800C	Hdy RN/3.305"/ Rem 9½M/(C)
IMR4895	69.0	1993	72.0	2170		
A2230	64.8	1900	72.0	2159	45,600C	Hdy RN/3.305"/ Rem 9½M
H4895	70.0	2048	74.0	2156		
A2015BR	61.2	1891	68.0	2149	49,200C	Hdy RN/3.305"/ Rem 9½M
W748	73.0	2036	76.0	2132		
H335	72.0	1979	75.0	2129		
BL-C(2)	75.0	2001	77.0	2117	43,800C	26" test barrel
IMR3031	65.0	1937	68.0	2111		
N140	70.1	1983	74.5	2100	52,214p	Hdy RN
H4198	60.0	1943	64.0	2072		
VarGet			71.0	2064	41,600C	
N135	65.5	1930	70.4	2060	52,214p	Hdy RN
N135	67.5	1920	72.5	2053	52,214p	Spr AGS
RL-12	68.0	1944	71.0	2040		
RL-7	61.0	1931	64.0	2014		
IMR4198	58.0	1887	61.0	1998		

600

Powder	Grs.	MV (fps)	Grs.	MV (fps)	Press. (CUP/psi)	Comments
H335	66.0	1794	68.0	1939		
BL-C(2)	68.0	1831	70.0	1924		
H4895	64.0	1773	67.0	1920		
VarGet			65.0	1852	44,600C	26" test barrel

Caution: **Loads exceeding SAAMI OAL Maximum must be verified for bullet-to-rifling clearance and magazine functioning. Where a specific primer or bullet is indicated those components must be used, no substitutions! Where only a maximum load is shown, reduce starting load 10%, unless otherwise specified.**

Key: (C) = compressed charge; C = CUP; p = psi; Plink = Plinker; Bns = Barnes; Hdy = Hornady; Lap = Lapua; Nos = Nosler; Rem = Remington; Sra = Sierra; Spr = Speer; Win = Winchester.

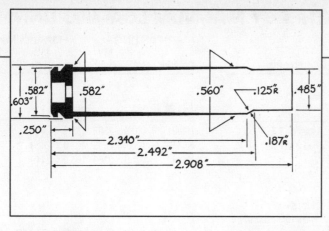

Case: Weatherby
Primer: Large Rifle
Barrel: 26″ Accurate
       26″ Hodgdon
Bullet Diameter: 0.457″–0.458″

Maximum Case Length: 2.908″
Trim to Length: 2.903″
Maximum Cartridge OAL: 3.750″
Minimum Cartridge OAL: 3.335″

It took four years for Roy Weatherby to answer Winchester's introduction of the 458 Win. Mag., but answer it did. In 1960 he introduced as a standard chambering what was, for quite a few years, the world's most powerful commercial sporting cartridge, the 460 Weatherby Magnum.

This chambering was created by the simple expedient of necking the 378 Weatherby Magnum—itself simply a belted and necked-down version of the 416 Rigby loaded to higher pressures—to 45-caliber. With close to twice the case capacity and higher working pressures than the 458 Winchester Magnum, performance is, predictably, just a tad better!

Where typical 458 loads launch 500-grain bullets at about 2050 fps and generate about 4700 foot pounds of muzzle energy, the 460 easily achieves 2500 fps and gener-

ates over 6900 foot pounds of muzzle energy. Original advertised ballistics for both chamberings were somewhat higher, but these numbers represent more prudent loads for use in hot climes where ease of gun functioning to facilitate possible follow-up shots is a critical concern.

The 460 Weatherby generates sufficient velocity with lighter bullets to be useful for shots to longer ranges on plains species of almost any size.

Weatherby rifles are factory equipped with muzzle-brakes, so recoil is not as harsh as it might be. H380, IMR4350, H4350, H414, W760 and A8700 are noted for good performance here. As with all free-bored chamberings, the slowest usable powders seldom generate consistent velocity and accuracy.

460 WEATHERBY MAGNUM LOADING DATA

350

Powder	STARTING Grs.	STARTING MV (fps)	MAXIMUM Grs.	MAXIMUM MV (fps)	MAXIMUM Press. (CUP/psi)	Comments
A2520	106.4	2779	112.0	2956	62,300p	Hdy RN/3.345″/Fed 215
A2700	115.9	2673	122.0	2844	53,000p	Hdy RN/3.345″/Fed 215/(C)
A4350	118.8	2657	125.0	2827	49,100p	Hdy RN/3.345″/Fed 215/(C)
IMR4064	105.0	2631	110.0	2812		
H380	104.0	2583	114.0	2808		
H414	110.0	2442	120.0	2791		
IMR3031	97.0	2616	102.0	2791		
IMR4320	105.0	2649	110.0	2784		
W760	116.0	2707	120.0	2782		
IMR4895	103.0	2599	108.0	2769		
H4895	100.0	2514	110.0	2760		
W748	106.0	2662	110.0	2743		
IMR4350	115.0	2609	120.0	2740		
H4350	115.0	2595	120.0	2737		
H450	118.0	2523	128.0	2688		
IMR4831	116.0	2505	124.0	2679		
H4831	118.0	2481	128.0	2678		

400

Powder	STARTING Grs.	STARTING MV (fps)	MAXIMUM Grs.	MAXIMUM MV (fps)	MAXIMUM Press. (CUP/psi)	Comments
IMR4350	113.0	2490	118.0	2684		
IMR4320	103.0	2494	108.0	2656		
IMR4895	101.0	2481	106.0	2640		
H414	107.0	2494	117.0	2640		Also 405-gr. bullets
W748	102.0	2484	107.0	2639		
W760	114.0	2551	118.0	2632		
IMR3031	95.0	2473	100.0	2619		
IMR4064	102.0	2459	107.0	2610		
H4350	112.0	2431	118.0	2610		Also 405-gr. bullets
H380	100.0	2448	110.0	2593		Also 405-gr. bullets
H4895	97.0	2404	107.0	2589		Also 405-gr. bullets
H4831	117.0	2434	127.0	2565		Also 405-gr. bullets
IMR4831	114.0	2379	122.0	2540		

▶▶▶▶▶▶▶▶▶▶▶▶▶▶▶▶▶▶▶▶▶▶▶▶▶▶▶

Never exceed maximum load nor use any load exhibiting signs of excessive pressure. Begin at suggested starting load and work up carefully.

500

Powder	—STARTING— Grs.	MV (fps)	—MAXIMUM— Grs.	MV (fps)	Press. (CUP/psi)	Comments
A4350	114.0	2454	120.0	2611	62,400p	Hdy RN/3.71"/ Fed 215/(C)
H450	118.0	2396	128.0	2578		
W760	109.0	2458	114.0	2544		
IMR4350	107.0	2358	114.0	2539		
A2700	108.3	2383	114.0	2535	64,700p	Hdy RN/3.71"/ Fed 215/Case Full
H414	106.0	2369	116.0	2530		
IMR4895	99.0	2374	104.0	2512		
IMR4064	99.0	2361	104.0	2509		
H4350	108.0	2371	115.0	2508		
A3100	120.7	2355	127.0	2505	56,700p	Hdy RN/3.71"/ Fed 215/(C)
IMR4320	100.0	2369	105.0	2490		
IMR4831	111.0	2309	119.0	2479		
W748	99.0	2385	104.0	2462		
IMR3031	90.0	2290	95.0	2434		
A8700	128.3	1894	135.0	2015	34,600p	Hdy RN/3.71"/ Fed 215/(C)

600

Powder	—STARTING— Grs.	MV (fps)	—MAXIMUM— Grs.	MV (fps)	Press. (CUP/psi)	Comments
H4831	110.0	2302	115.0	2457		
H4350	98.0	2292	104.0	2439		
H414	102.0	2369	105.0	2419		

Caution: **Loads exceeding SAAMI OAL Maximum must be verified for bullet-to-rifling clearance and magazine functioning. Where a specific primer or bullet is indicated those components must be used, no substitutions! Where only a maximum load is shown, reduce starting load 10%, unless otherwise specified.**

Key: (C) = compressed charge; C = CUP; p = psi; Plink = Plinker; Bns = Barnes; Hdy = Hornady; Lap = Lapua; Nos = Nosler; Rem = Remington; Sra = Sierra; Spr = Speer; Win = Winchester.

Never exceed maximum load nor use any load exhibiting signs of excessive pressure. Begin at suggested starting load and work up carefully.

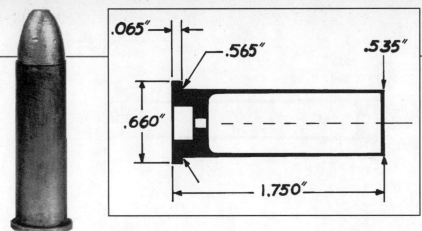

Case: Dixie
Primer: Federal 215
Barrel: 28″ Accurate (C. Sharps)
Bullet Diameter: 0.515″
Maximum Case Length: 1.750″

Trim to Length: 1.745″
Maximum Cartridge OAL: 2.250″
Minimum Cartridge OAL:
   Bullet Dependent

One of the earliest successful self-contained centerfire chamberings, the 50-70 Government was adopted in 1866 for use in converted muskets, the 50-70 Springfield. These were the forerunner to the 45-70 Springfield rifles and carbines.

This cartridge was commonly chambered in the middle to late 1800s, but performance was not at all impressive. The 45-70 seems to have been recognized as a better all-around performer very early on.

While reasonably effective as a hunting cartridge and widely used against the great bison of the American plains, this was not so impressive as a military long-arm chambering.

Accurate Arms developed this data. They determined a reasonable pressure limit by firing a 65-grain load of FFg behind a 550-grain bullet to mimic the original load. That test load generated a surprising 22,500 psi.

Nevertheless, we suggest only the lightest loads listed for use in the oldest guns, which should never be fired with any jacketed bullet since that practice will erode the bore quite rapidly. Truth is, it would be prudent to relegate any such antique to wall-hanger status.

Of the listed powders, only XMP5744 seemed to offer consistent velocity.

These loads are for use only in guns known to be safe for use with smokeless powder.

50-70 GOVERNMENT LOADING DATA

	—STARTING—		—MAXIMUM—			
Powder	Grs.	MV (fps)	Grs.	MV (fps)	Press. (CUP/psi)	Comments

Lead 425 Lyman 515141

Powder	Grs.	MV (fps)	Grs.	MV (fps)	Press. (CUP/psi)	Comments
A2015BR	36.0	1274	40.0	1448	16,800p	2.83″
A2495BR	45.9	1272	51.0	1445	9,500p	2.83″/(C)
XMP5744	27.0	1249	30.0	1419	18,200p	2.83″
A1680	27.0	1189	30.0	1351	14,200p	2.83″
A4350	46.8	1085	52.0	1233	15,700p	2.83″/(C)

Lead 550 RCBS

Powder	Grs.	MV (fps)	Grs.	MV (fps)	Press. (CUP/psi)	Comments
A2495BR	37.8	1210	42.0	1375	17,000p	2.20″
A1680	25.2	1139	28.0	1294	16,400p	2.20″
A2015BR	30.6	1101	34.0	1251	18,300p	2.20″
XMP5744	22.5	1063	25.0	1208	18,600p	2.20″
A4350	43.2	1041	48.0	1183	18,200p	2.20″/(C)

400

Powder	Grs.	MV (fps)	Grs.	MV (fps)	Press. (CUP/psi)	Comments
A2015BR	49.5	1627	55.0	1844	19,400p	Bns SP/2.315″

50-90
Sharps

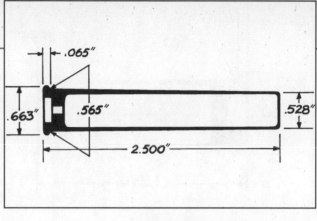

Case: Eldorado
Primer: Federal 215
Barrel: 30″ Accurate (C. Sharps)
Bullet Diameter: .512″

Maximum Case Length: 2.500″
Trim to Length: 2.495″
Maximum Cartridge OAL: 3.200″
Minimum Cartridge OAL:
Bullet Dependent

Introduced in 1875, this, the "Big Fifty," was intended for one purpose only—buffalo hunting. It was soon recognized as the premier choice for that pursuit. Various loadings used as much as 110 grains of blackpowder, and bullets to 550 grains of weight were commonly used for long-range performance.

As a matter of interest, this is the cartridge Billy Dixon used at the battle of Adobe Wells. With a 550-grain bullet in front of a heavy charge of FFg, he made one of the longest documented shots of the era, and thereby stopped an attack by marauding Comanche warriors.

Accurate Arms developed the data listed here. They deter-mined reasonable working pressures by loading 90 grains of FFg behind a 440-grain bullet, similar to an original loading, and measuring the resulting pressure. This generated only 20,000 psi—likely because of the relatively light bullet.

Only the lightest loads listed should be used in antique guns and then only in those in good condition. Such guns deserve a due measure of respect.

XMP5744 is a consistent performer in this, the most popular of the buffalo gun chamberings.

These loads are for use only in guns known to be safe for use with smokeless powder.

50-90 SHARPS LOADING DATA

Powder	STARTING Grs.	MV (fps)	MAXIMUM Grs.	MV (fps)	Press. (CUP/psi)	Comments
Lead 365						
A4350	73.8	1596	82.0	1814	16,600p	2.87″
XMP5744			43.0	1795		
A3100	76.5	1496	85.0	1700	15,800p	2.87″/(C)
XMP5744	33.3	1454	37.0	1652	16,000p	2.87″
A8700	81.0	1365	90.0	1551	14,700p	2.87″/(C)
Lead 440 Lyman 515141						
A4350	72.0	1539	80.0	1749	19,500p	3.00″
A3100	76.5	1492	85.0	1695	18,300p	3.00″/(C)
XMP5744			38.0	1557		
XMP5744	29.7	1248	33.0	1418	14,100p	3.00″
A8700	76.5	1242	85.0	1411	15,300p	3.00″/(C)

Powder	STARTING Grs.	MV (fps)	MAXIMUM Grs.	MV (fps)	Press. (CUP/psi)	Comments
Lead 550 RCBS						
A4350	58.5	1274	65.0	1448	17,000p	2.925″
XMP5744			35.0	1411		
A3100	62.1	1220	69.0	1386	16,300p	2.925″
XMP5744	27.0	1122	30.0	1275	15,600p	2.925″
A8700	64.8	1035	72.0	1176	16,700p	2.925″
400						
A4350	75.6	1571	84.0	1785	16,800p	Bns SP/3.00″
A3100	76.5	1382	85.0	1571	13,100p	Bns SP /3.00″/(C)
A8700	81.0	1276	90.0	1450	14,800p	Bns SP /3.00″/(C)

Caution: Loads exceeding SAAMI OAL Maximum must be verified for bullet-to-rifling clearance and magazine functioning. Where a specific primer or bullet is indicated those components must be used, no substitutions! Where only a maximum load is shown, reduce starting load 10%, unless otherwise specified.

Key: (C) = compressed charge; C = CUP; p = psi; Plink = Plinker; Bns = Barnes; Hdy = Hornady; Lap = Lapua; Nos = Nosler; Rem = Remington; Sra = Sierra; Spr = Speer; Win = Winchester.

Never exceed maximum load nor use any load exhibiting signs of excessive pressure. Begin at suggested starting load and work up carefully.

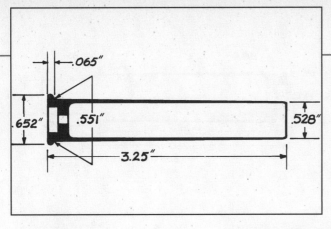

Case: Eldorado
Primer: Federal 215
Barrel: 30″ Accurate (C. Sharps)
Bullet Diameter: .512″
Maximum Case Length: 3.25″

Trim to Length: 3.245″
Maximum Cartridge OAL: 3.95″
Minimum Cartridge OAL:
    Bullet Dependent

Contrary to modern perception, this is not the "Big Fifty" of buffalo era lore. By the time the 50-140 was standardized and offered by Sharps in 1880, the big herds were already vanishing. No doubt this chambering was used to kill a fair measure of bison, but it was the 50-90 that garnered the moniker, "Big Fifty." That shorter cartridge was responsible for a huge percentage of the tens of millions of kills.

Original loads varied, but a typical long-range load featured a 700-grain bullet launched by a full 140 grains of FFg at about 1355 fps. It can be taken as a matter of fact that such a load fired from a typical Sharps rifle in the prone position generated brutal recoil.

To develop this data, for use only in modern replica guns, Accurate Arms fired a test load with a 550-grain bullet ahead of 140 grains of FFg. Pressure was 28,000 psi.

Even restrained by such a modest pressure limit, this huge case can easily launch a 550-grain bullet as fast as the 458 Winchester Magnum can launch a 500-grain bullet!

XMP5744 has been noted to provide very consistent velocities in this, the biggest of the buffalo chamberings.

These loads are for use only in guns known to be safe for use with smokeless powder.

50-140 SHARPS LOADING DATA

Lead 440 Lyman 515141

Powder	STARTING Grs.	MV (fps)	MAXIMUM Grs.	MV (fps)	Press. (CUP/psi)	Comments
A4350	103.5	1972	115.0	2241	25,000p	3.785″/100% density
A3100	108.0	1891	120.0	2149	24,200p	3.785″
A8700	115.0	1745	135.0	1983	25,400p	3.785″/(C)
XMP5744	43.0	1600	55.0	1978	24,500p	3.785″

Lead 550 RCBS

Powder	STARTING Grs.	MV (fps)	MAXIMUM Grs.	MV (fps)	Press. (CUP/psi)	Comments
A4350	94.5	1922	105.0	2184	27,500p	3.735″
A3100	99.0	1889	110.0	2033	26,300p	3.735″
A8700	100.0	1653	120.0	1806	25,100p	3.735″/(C)
XMP5744	40.0	1466	50.0	1736	24,800p	3.735″

Lead 700

Powder	STARTING Grs.	MV (fps)	MAXIMUM Grs.	MV (fps)	Press. (CUP/psi)	Comments
XMP5744			48.0	1529		Fed 215

Never exceed maximum load nor use any load exhibiting signs of excessive pressure. Begin at suggested starting load and work up carefully.

269

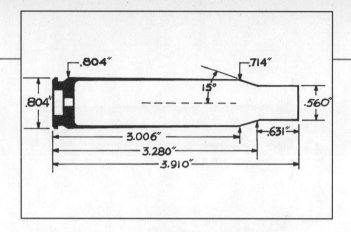

Case: IMI
Primer: BMG (IMI 50/CCI 35)
Barrel: 44″ Accurate
45″ Hodgdon
45″ Vihtavuori

Bullet Diameter: 0.511″
Maximum Case Length: 3.910″
Trim to Length: 3.900″
Maximum Cartridge OAL: 5.545″
Minimum Cartridge OAL: 5.400″

A decade ago one might have gotten an argument whether this can be considered a legitimate sporting chambering or not. Growing popularity suggests it was already then a legitimate sporting chambering, and it is today, only more so.

Introduced in 1921 as the chambering for John M. Browning's famous heavy machinegun, the 50 BMG cartridge easily generates twice the muzzle energy of the vaunted 460 Weatherby Magnum. Even with the necessary muzzlebrakes with which 50 BMG-chambered shoulder guns are always fitted, gun weight has to be kept in the 30-pound range to keep recoil below the level of "actually dangerous to shoot." (A quote from an expert who witnessed a 20-pound rifle being shot—one time.)

The only significant current sporting use for this chambering is long-range accuracy shooting—and we do mean long range, with some competitions exceeding one mile. The 1000-yard 50-caliber record, as of this writing, is a five-shot group of just over 3 inches on centers. Obviously, such a chambering has serious potential for those who can locate stationary game targets at extended known ranges under windless conditions. Under those constraints, it would be no trick for a marksman to deliver a bullet carrying several tons

of energy to the vitals of such a target at ranges exceeding one mile—in fact this has been done. So much for those expressing grave concerns about the "sportsmanship" of taking game at extended ranges!

Handloading for the 50 BMG requires a plethora of specialized tools and equipment. In no way can it be said that this is just like loading for any other chambering, only bigger. Expect to spend several thousand dollars just to get the proper equipment. Further, our best suggestion, based on expert opinion, is that no one lacking a serious background in handloading should even consider the task.

In recent decades, the military has considered dropping the 50 BMG in favor of more modern, and generally bigger, chamberings. However, ammunition developments, including saboted loads generating 4500 fps muzzle velocities with devastating armor-penetration capabilities, and this chambering's outstanding performance in the recent Gulf War would seem to cement its continued existence as a stable part of NATO's arsenal.

Usable case capacity with standard bullets, seated normally, is about 200 grains of water. All the listed powders provide good performance.

50 BROWNING MACHINE GUN LOADING DATA (50 BMG)

	—STARTING—		—MAXIMUM—			
Powder	Grs.	MV (fps)	Grs.	MV (fps)	Press. (CUP/psi)	Comments
642						
A8700	205.0	2610	228.0	2930		CCI 35
647						
H870	210.0	2789	225.0	2980		
24N41			240.6	2960	47,100p	
H5010	205.0	2710	220.0	2924		

	—STARTING—		—MAXIMUM—			
Powder	Grs.	MV (fps)	Grs.	MV (fps)	Press. (CUP/psi)	Comments
750						
A8700	195.0	2322	218.0	2700		CCI 35

Caution: Loads exceeding SAAMI OAL Maximum must be verified for bullet-to-rifling clearance and magazine functioning. Where a specific primer or bullet is indicated those components must be used, no substitutions! Where only a maximum load is shown, reduce starting load 10%, unless otherwise specified.

Key: (C) = compressed charge; C = CUP; p = psi; Plink = Plinker; Bns = Barnes; Hdy = Hornady; Lap = Lapua; Nos = Nosler; Rem = Remington; Sra = Sierra; Spr = Speer; Win = Winchester.

Introduction To Pistol Data

IN THIS SECTION, we list the largest selection of data compiled and published into one source for 31 popular pistol and revolver cartridges. Where a particular chambering is especially popular in the T/C Contender, we have included it in this section because these cartridges have become "standards" in handgun use. We have omitted several reasonably common chamberings because of the obvious constraints of space and the lack of pressure-tested data precluded their inclusion.

Many listed loads do not include pressure data. In those instances, we had comparative pressure data, thereby gaining a measure of security in the reasonableness of these loads. We would have preferred to use only pressure-tested data. However, this compromise allowed us to provide significant data for these popular chamberings.

Test barrel length is given for each cartridge under "Barrel" in the cartridge-specific information. Generally, if the test barrels were similar in length and type, we have melded the data for any given bullet-weight range. Where barrel lengths or type were significantly different, we have listed the bullet-weight ranges separately and indicated the barrel type or length in the bullet-weight heading.

Non-vented test barrels generate substantially more velocity than revolvers. The difference is about 150-300 fps. The only common exception is Freedom Arms' revolvers, where the barrel-to-cylinder gap is so small that velocity loss is often 50 fps, or less.

Revolver velocity loss varies with bore size. Smaller bored guns lose more velocity because, on average, the vent is a greater percentage of the bore area. Again, the variation in handgun velocity is so great that it is useless to try to guess what any given gun might do. If you must know what your gun and load actually do, with an accuracy better than ±100 fps, you will have to use a chronograph!

Despite the popularity of long-barreled revolvers, the ballistic advantage is not particularly significant compared to 6″ barreled guns. Rest assured, the average 10″ barreled 44 Magnum revolver will not generate significantly more velocity than the average 7¹/₂″ barreled 44 Magnum, given the same load. Often there is very little or no velocity difference. Just as often, a shorter barreled revolver that is otherwise similar will generate more velocity with any given load.

Caution: The maximum charge for your firearms will depend, in part, on the specific components you use, and your specific assembly methods and equipment, as well as your specific firearm.

In that neither the publisher nor the author has any control over the manufacture, assembly, and storage of components, or the method of assembling a handload, the condition of the firearm in which it is used, or the degree of knowledge of the handloader, we cannot assume any responsibility, either expressed or implied, for the use of this data. While this data was safe in the original test firearm, it could prove otherwise in your gun with your components. Use of this data is entirely at the risk of the handloader.

No warranty or guarantee is expressed or implied. The publisher and author assume no responsibility for any use of this data. It is offered solely as a comparison to other such data.

PISTOL CARTRIDGE DATA

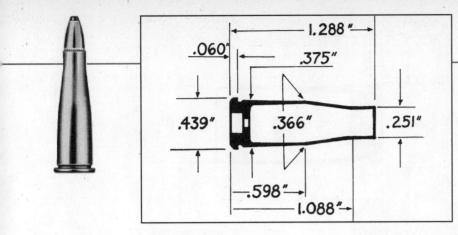

Case: Federal
Primer: Small Pistol
Barrel: 8³/₈″ Hodgdon (S&W)
Bullet Diameter: 0.2225″

Maximum Case Length: 1.288″
Trim to Length: 1.283″
Maximum Cartridge OAL: 1.659″
Minimum Cartridge OAL: 1.610″

A similar wildcat 22-caliber revolver chambering introduced by Jim Harvey in the 1950s gained such popularity that Remington and Smith & Wesson were compelled to introduce a factory 22 centerfire revolver cartridge and gun combination in 1961. By necking down the 357 Magnum case and adopting a two-position firing pin to revolvers so chambered, Remington and Smith & Wesson created a versatile interchangeable-cylinder revolver. The centerfire chambering offered substantial performance for small game and varmint hunting, and the rimfire cylinder offered economical ammunition for plinking or other informal target practice.

The 22 Jet case design is very poor. Evidently, the engineers did not understand what they were about. The problem with any bottlenecked cartridge in any revolver is that such cases tend to back out from the chamber when fired. Obviously, as the case backs out of the cylinder, the shoulder is pushed forward. This tends to lock the cylinder in place, preventing rotation and further shots. Contamination of the case or chamber with any lubricant exacerbates the problem.

To minimize this effect, the best course is to use a straight case body with a sharp shoulder. Remington designed a sharply tapered case body with a gently sloping shoulder! To minimize and hopefully prevent gun-locking tie-ups, keep chambers and cases completely free of any form of lubrication.

The only common jacketed bullet that properly fits the Jet's bore is Hornady's 0.222″ Jet. With a 45-grain bullet, seated normally, usable case capacity is about 16.2 grains of water.

22 REMINGTON JET MAGNUM LOADING DATA

Powder	STARTING Grs.	MV (fps)	MAXIMUM Grs.	MV (fps)	Press. (CUP/psi)	Comments
40						
H110	10.0	1892	11.0	2019		
HS6	6.5	1769	7.5	1883		

Caution: Loads exceeding SAAMI OAL Maximum must be verified for bullet-to-rifling clearance and magazine functioning. Where a specific primer or bullet is indicated those components must be used, no substitutions! Where only a maximum load is shown, reduce starting load 10%, unless otherwise specified.

Key: (C) = compressed charge; C = CUP; p = psi; Plink = Plinker; Bns = Barnes; Hdy = Hornady; Lap = Lapua; Nos = Nosler; Rem = Remington; Sra = Sierra; Spr = Speer; Win = Winchester.

Never exceed maximum load nor use any load exhibiting signs of excessive pressure. Begin at suggested starting load and work up carefully.

273

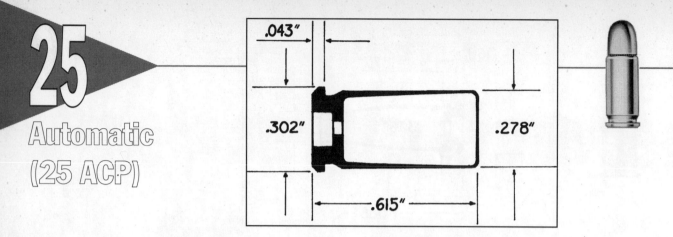

25 Automatic (25 ACP)

Case: Hornady
Primer: Small Pistol
Barrel: 2″ Accurate (Raven)
2³/₈″ Hodgdon
2″ Vihtavuori

Bullet Diameter: 0.251″
Maximum Case Length: 0.615″
Trim to Length: 0.610″
Maximum Cartridge OAL: 0.91″
Minimum Cartridge OAL: 0.86″

Introduced in 1908 for Browning's diminutive 25 Pocket Automatic, this little number has since been widely chambered in compact semi-automatic handguns from diverse manufacturers. This is the smallest of Browning's cartridges. While most guns chambered for the 25 Auto can be described as "inexpensive," there are a few truly high-quality 25 Automatic-chambered guns available

In direct contradiction to what is often claimed, by those who have evidently never fired these guns, some of the inexpensive models and many of the best 25s are capable of unexpected accuracy. These would certainly be useful for taking small game at short range. Using an improvised rest, the author once fired a 25-yard ten-shot group from a Beretta Model 20 that was well under 3″.

Performance of the 25 Auto is often compared to the 22 LR. Pocket pistol ballistics are quite similar, but the 25 does offer one undeniable advantage—dependability. The heavier and shorter cases are less prone to damage; the FMJ bullets tend to feed more reliably; and the centerfire construction evidently offers more dependable ignition. In a life-or-death situation, the 25 Auto is almost certainly a better choice.

While the 25 Auto delivers limited energy, it is no toy. As an esteemed colleague once suggested, "Aimed bullets from any gun beat thrown rocks." Perhaps this explains why the 25 Auto is still popular as a last-ditch backup gun for police use.

With a 50-grain bullet, seated normally, usable case capacity is about 4.4 grains of water.

25 AUTOMATIC LOADING DATA (25 ACP)

Powder	—STARTING—Grs.	MV (fps)	—MAXIMUM—Grs.	MV (fps)	Press. (CUP/psi)	Comments
35						
N330			2.1	1024	22,500p	Hdy XTP/0.855″
N310			1.3	921	21,800p	Hdy XTP/0.855″

Powder	—STARTING—Grs.	MV (fps)	—MAXIMUM—Grs.	MV (fps)	Press. (CUP/psi)	Comments
50						
HP38	1.2	761	1.4	848		
Trap100	1.4	729	1.6	825		
N310			1.1	804	18,800p	Sako FMJ/0.91″
No.2	1.4	660	1.6	717	13,900C	Hdy FMJ/0.9″/Win WSP

Caution: Loads exceeding SAAMI OAL Maximum must be verified for bullet-to-rifling clearance and magazine functioning. Where a specific primer or bullet is indicated those components must be used, no substitutions! Where only a maximum load is shown, reduce starting load 10%, unless otherwise specified.

Key: (C) = compressed charge; C = CUP; p = psi; Plink = Plinker; Bns = Barnes; Hdy = Hornady; Lap = Lapua; Nos = Nosler; Rem = Remington; Sra = Sierra; Spr = Speer; Win = Winchester.

Never exceed maximum load nor use any load exhibiting signs of excessive pressure. Begin at suggested starting load and work up carefully.

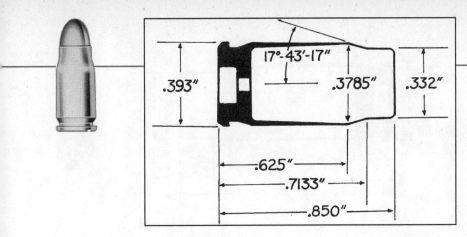

Case: Fiocchi
Primer: Small Pistol
Barrel: 6″ Accurate
4″ Hodgdon
8″ Vihtavuori

Bullet Diameter: 0.309″-0.310″
Maximum Case Length: 0.850″
Trim to Length: 0.840″
Maximum Cartridge OAL: 1.175″
Minimum Cartridge OAL: 1.130″

Introduced in 1900, this was the original chambering for the now-famous Luger semi-automatic pistol that later popularized a different Luger cartridge, the 9mm. This bottlenecked case is longer than the later 9mm Luger, but overall cartridge length is quite similar.

Performance is not up to what is now commonly considered as minimum for effective self-defense use. However, in its day this was a revolutionary chambering. It is still a formidable round offering effective small game performance. With such light bullets, recoil is minimal while muzzle energy easily surpasses anything the 38 Special can safely produce in typical revolvers.

This cartridge is still produced domestically, ample evidence of continued popularity.

30 LUGER LOADING DATA (7.65mm)

Powder	STARTING Grs.	MV (fps)	MAXIMUM Grs.	MV (fps)	Press. (CUP/psi)	Comments
86						
No.7	6.8	1247	7.6	1417	26,800C	Hdy RN/1.175″/ CCI 500
No.5	5.6	1240	6.2	1409	28,000C	Hdy RN/1.175″/ CCI 500
No.2	4.1	1158	4.5	1316	27,900C	Hdy RN/1.175″/ CCI 500
93						
Unique	4.3	1002	4.8	1123		
Red Dot	3.8	1029	4.2	1121		
Bullseye	3.4	977	3.9	1097		
IMR700-X	3.4	1016	3.9	1094		
W231	3.5	1009	4.1	1080		
HP38	3.4	960	3.9	1070		
Trap100	3.3	955	3.8	1050		
93						
No.7	6.5	1177	7.2	1338	26,400C	Hdy RN/1.17″/CCI 500
No.5	5.2	1145	5.8	1301	26,300C	Hdy RN/1.17″/CCI 500
N340			5.4	1280	37,700p	Sako FMJ/1.169″
No.2	4.1	1106	4.5	1257	28,000C	Hdy RN/1.17″/CCI 500

Powder	STARTING Grs.	MV (fps)	MAXIMUM Grs.	MV (fps)	Press. (CUP/psi)	Comments
100						
No.7	6.2	1139	6.9	1294	26,200C	Spr Plink/1.18″/ CCI 500/*
No.5	5.0	1126	5.5	1280	26,700C	Spr Plink/1.18″/ CCI 500/*
No.2	3.9	1085	4.3	1233	26,600C	Spr Plink/1.18″/ CCI 500/*

* Exceeds SAAMI maximum OAL.

Caution: **Loads exceeding SAAMI OAL Maximum must be verified for bullet-to-rifling clearance and magazine functioning. Where a specific primer or bullet is indicated those components must be used, no substitutions! Where only a maximum load is shown, reduce starting load 10%, unless otherwise specified.**

Key: (C) = compressed charge; C = CUP; p = psi; Plink = Plinker; Bns = Barnes; Hdy = Hornady; Lap = Lapua; Nos = Nosler; Rem = Remington; Sra = Sierra; Spr = Speer; Win = Winchester.

Never exceed maximum load nor use any load exhibiting signs of excessive pressure. Begin at suggested starting load and work up carefully.

275

30

Mauser

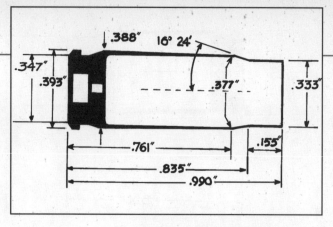

Case: Fiocchi
Primer: CCI 500
Barrel: 9″ Accurate
Bullet Diameter: 0.309″-0.310″

Maximum Case Length: 0.990″
Trim to Length: 0.980″
Maximum Cartridge OAL: 1.381″
Minimum Cartridge OAL: NA

Very similar to the 30 Luger in performance, this cartridge was chambered in the very first commercially successful semi-automatic pistol in 1893. That gun was designed in the U.S. by Hugo Borchardt. Performance of current factory loads and SAAMI specification handloads is somewhat limited in deference to the many circa 1890s pistols still in use.

The most notable chambering was in the Mauser military pistol that was adapted to full-automatic fire and a detachable stock. Performance was never particularly impressive, but this chambering easily generates more muzzle energy than any SAAMI-specification 38 Special revolver loading.

The 30 Mauser offers plenty of performance for small game and varmint hunting to ranges of about 100 yards. This loading data can also be used in the Russian 7.62mm Tokarev, which is an essentially identical cartridge.

30 MAUSER LOADING DATA

Powder	—STARTING— Grs.	MV (fps)	—MAXIMUM— Grs.	MV (fps)	Press. (CUP/psi)	Comments
86						
No.7	6.9	1250	7.7	1421	24,400C	Hdy RN/1.325″
No.5	5.7	1219	6.3	1385	24,600C	Hdy RN/1.325″
No.2	4.2	1170	4.7	1330	25,100C	Hdy RN/1.325″
93						
No.7	6.8	1199	7.5	1363	24,800C	Hdy RN/1.325″
No.5	5.6	1182	6.2	1343	25,400C	Hdy RN/1.325″
No.2	4.2	1113	4.7	1265	25,000C	Hdy RN/1.325″

Powder	—STARTING— Grs.	MV (fps)	—MAXIMUM— Grs.	MV (fps)	Press. (CUP/psi)	Comments
100						
No.7	6.5	1146	7.2	1302	24,300C	Spr Plink/1.325″
No.5	5.2	1116	5.8	1268	24,700C	Spr Plink/1.325″
No.2	4.0	1056	4.4	1200	25,100C	Spr Plink/1.325″

Caution: Loads exceeding SAAMI OAL Maximum must be verified for bullet-to-rifling clearance and magazine functioning. Where a specific primer or bullet is indicated those components must be used, no substitutions! Where only a maximum load is shown, reduce starting load 10%, unless otherwise specified.

Key: (C) = compressed charge; C = CUP; p = psi; Plinker; Bns = Barnes; Hdy = Hornady; Lap = Lapua; Nos = Nosler; Rem = Remington; Sra = Sierra; Spr = Speer; Win = Winchester.

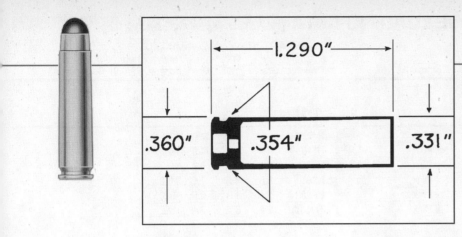

Case: Remington
Primer: Small Rifle
Barrel: 10″ Accurate (T/C)
      7½″ Hodgdon (Ruger)
Bullet Diameter: 0.308″

Maximum Case Length: 1.290″
Trim to Length: 1.285″
Maximum Cartridge OAL: 1.680″
Minimum Cartridge OAL: 1.625″

If there was ever a cartridge that was maligned just because it existed, this is a good candidate. The 30 Carbine was designed as a military expedient, intended for use in a lightweight carbine to replace the 45 Automatic-chambered 1911A1 Colt pistol, which the average soldier seemed uninterested in learning how to shoot properly—even if his life might depend upon it!

The 30 Carbine delivers impressive handgun performance. Recoil is in an entirely different class from the 357 Magnum and similar cartridges. Equally, because of high muzzle pressures and small bore size, muzzleblast is particularly sharp. Hearing protection is probably even more important than with some larger-bored guns.

This chambering is proving useful in Hunter Metallic Silhouette competition and is certainly a 125-yard varmint option. The 30 Carbine also performs admirably with heavier cast bullets, which offer economical shooting. In the T/C Contender, it can generate surprising energy.

Case capacity with a 110-grain bullet, seated normally, is about 15.5 grains of water. H110 and No.9 are good choices for the 30 Carbine.

30 CARBINE LOADING DATA (Handgun Specific Loads)

Powder	STARTING Grs.	MV (fps)	MAXIMUM Grs.	MV (fps)	Press. (CUP/psi)	Comments
Lead 115 GC						
H110			13.0	1580		
H4227			13.0	1563		
HS7	6.2	1007	8.2	1221		
HS6	5.5	848	7.5	1189		
Trap100	2.8	768	3.3	880		
HP38	2.8	764	3.3	850		
Lead 125 Lyman 311410 RN (Revolver)						
No.9	9.9	1448	11.0	1645	38,400C	1.705″/CCI 400/*
A1680	13.5	1282	15.0	1457	33,600C	1.705″/CCI 400/*
Lead 130 GC						
H110			11.5	1401		
H4227			11.5	1372		
HS7	6.0	969	7.0	1194		
HS6	5.0	889	6.5	1113		
77						
H4227			16.0	1808		
H110			17.0	1764		
HS7	7.2	1198	9.2	1516		
HS6	6.2	1066	8.2	1371		
Trap100	3.2	889	4.4	1076		
HP38	3.3	857	4.4	1029		
93						
H110			15.5	1729		
H4227			15.0	1651		
HS7	7.0	1141	9.0	1434		
HS6	6.0	947	8.0	1275		
Trap100	3.0	827	4.2	1047		
HP38	3.0	816	4.2	998		

▶▶▶▶▶▶▶▶▶▶▶▶▶▶▶▶▶▶▶▶▶▶▶▶▶

Never exceed maximum load nor use any load exhibiting signs of excessive pressure. Begin at suggested starting load and work up carefully.

277

100

Powder	STARTING Grs.	MV (fps)	MAXIMUM Grs.	MV (fps)	Press. (CUP/psi)	Comments
H110			14.5	1608		Spr Plink
H4227			14.5	1583		Spr Plink
HS7	6.5	1049	8.5	1298		Spr Plink
HS6	5.7	907	7.7	1230		Spr Plink
Trap100	2.9	825	3.7	1014		Spr Plink
HP38	2.9	790	3.7	934		Spr Plink

100 (Revolver)

Powder	STARTING Grs.	MV (fps)	MAXIMUM Grs.	MV (fps)	Press. (CUP/psi)	Comments
No.9	12.0	1646	13.3	1871	39,000C	Spr Plink/1.675"/ CCI 400
A1680	15.3	1357	17.0	1542	24,200C	Spr Plink/1.675"/ CCI 400/(C)

110

Powder	STARTING Grs.	MV (fps)	MAXIMUM Grs.	MV (fps)	Press. (CUP/psi)	Comments
H4227			14.0	1533		
H110			14.0	1502		
HS7	6.2	966	8.2	1192		
HS6	5.5	839	7.5	1162		
HP38	2.9	801	3.5	896		
Trap100	2.8	802	3.4	882		

110 (Revolver)

Powder	STARTING Grs.	MV (fps)	MAXIMUM Grs.	MV (fps)	Press. (CUP/psi)	Comments
No.9	11.3	1514	12.6	1721	39,800C	Spr FMJ/1.67"/ CCI 400
A1680	14.4	1287	16.0	1462	26,800C	Spr FMJ/1.67"/ CCI 400/(C)

Never exceed maximum load nor use any load exhibiting signs of excessive pressure. Begin at suggested starting load and work up carefully.

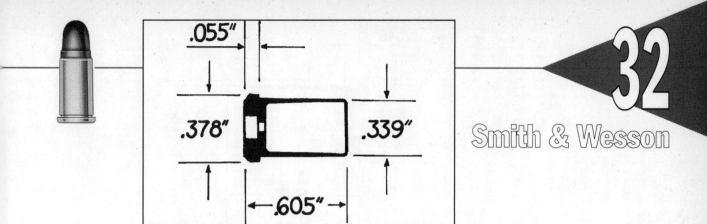

Case: Winchester
Primer: Small Pistol
Barrel: 3″ Hodgdon
Bullet Diameter: 0.312″-0.314″

Maximum Case Length: 0.605″
Trim to Length: 0.600″
Maximum Cartridge OAL: 0.930″
Minimum Cartridge OAL: 0.880″

This 1878 vintage chambering lingers on, despite puny performance and a total lack of recent chamberings. This is ample evidence of the huge popularity this blackpowder-era round once enjoyed. The loads listed here are intended only for use in revolvers known to be in good condition and safe for use with smokeless-powder loads. If in doubt, the best course is to retire such a gun as an antique wall-hanger.

Despite limited performance, the smallest revolvers so chambered are a good choice as a backup gun for police work. Their rounded profile is much easier to hide than that of similar-sized pistols.

With an 86-grain bullet, seated normally, usable capacity is about 6.2 grains of water.

32 SMITH & WESSON LOADING DATA

Powder	STARTING Grs.	MV (fps)	MAXIMUM Grs.	MV (fps)	Press. (CUP/psi)	Comments
Lead 85						
HP38	1.1	610	1.4	680		
Bullseye	1.2	590	1.4	680		
IMR700-X	1.2	600	1.5	676		
W231	1.1	598	1.4	670		
Trap100	1.0	570	1.3	665		

Caution: Loads exceeding SAAMI OAL Maximum must be verified for bullet-to-rifling clearance and magazine functioning. Where a specific primer or bullet is indicated those components must be used, no substitutions! Where only a maximum load is shown, reduce starting load 10%, unless otherwise specified.

Key: (C) = compressed charge; C = CUP; p = psi; Plink = Plinker; Bns = Barnes; Hdy = Hornady; Lap = Lapua; Nos = Nosler; Rem = Remington; Sra = Sierra; Spr = Speer; Win = Winchester.

Never exceed maximum load nor use any load exhibiting signs of excessive pressure. Begin at suggested starting load and work up carefully.

279

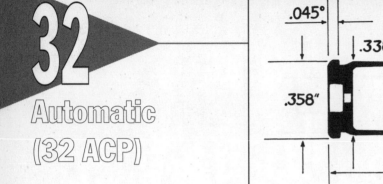

32
Automatic
(32 ACP)

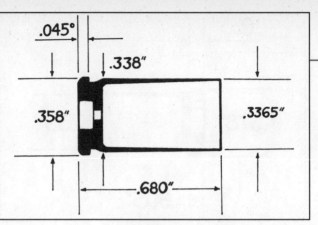

Case: Hornady
Primer: Small Pistol
Barrel: 4″ Accurate
  3³/₄″ Hodgdon (Savage)
  3½″ Vihtavuori

Bullet Diameter: 0.312″
Maximum Case Length: 0.680″
Trim to Length: 0.675″
Maximum Cartridge OAL: 0.984″
Minimum Cartridge OAL: 0.940″

Introduced in 1900 as a pistol chambering, the 32 Automatic is also known as the 7.65mm Browning, European testimony to the gun's designer. Pressure is similar to the 38 Special, but capacity is limited and performance can only be regarded as minuscule.

Since similar-sized pistols are easily chambered for the considerably more powerful 380 Automatic, the 32 has lost a great measure of popularity to the latter round.

With a 71-grain bullet, seated normally, usable case capacity is about 7.0 grains of water.

32 AUTOMATIC LOADING DATA (32 ACP)

Powder	STARTING Grs.	MV (fps)	MAXIMUM Grs.	MV (fps)	Press. (CUP/psi)	Comments
Lead 84 RCBS-32ACP (RN)						
No.2	1.6	679	1.8	772	19,000p	0.95″/CCI 500
No.5	2.0	671	2.2	762	19,800p	0.95″/CCI 500
71						
N310			2.2	1001	26,100p	Sako FMJ/0.984″
Trap100	2.1	829	2.3	877		
HP38	2.2	821	2.5	860		
W231	2.1	802	2.4	844		
IMR700-X	1.9	790	2.2	835		
Bullseye	2.0	788	2.2	830		
Red Dot	2.1	766	2.3	828		
Unique	2.2	784	2.5	822		
Green Dot	2.2	779	2.4	814		
No.5	2.9	619	3.2	703	19,700p	Sra FMJ/0.955″/CCI 500
No.2	2.0	572	2.2	650	19,300p	Sra FMJ/0.955″/CCI 500

Powder	STARTING Grs.	MV (fps)	MAXIMUM Grs.	MV (fps)	Press. (CUP/psi)	Comments
85						
No.5	2.2	615	2.4	699	19,100p	Hdy XTP/0.94″/CCI 500
No.2	1.6	612	1.8	695	18,800p	Hdy XTP/0.94″/CCI 500

Caution: Loads exceeding SAAMI OAL Maximum must be verified for bullet-to-rifling clearance and magazine functioning. Where a specific primer or bullet is indicated those components must be used, no substitutions! Where only a maximum load is shown, reduce starting load 10%, unless otherwise specified.

Key: (C) = compressed charge; C = CUP; p = psi; Plink = Plinker; Bns = Barnes; Hdy = Hornady; Lap = Lapua; Nos = Nosler; Rem = Remington; Sra = Sierra; Spr = Speer; Win = Winchester.

Never exceed maximum load nor use any load exhibiting signs of excessive pressure. Begin at suggested starting load and work up carefully.

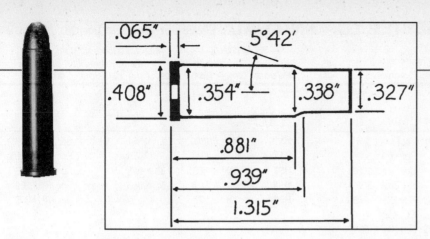

Case: Remington
Primer: Small Rifle
Barrel: 6½″ Accurate (Ruger)
       7½″ Hodgdon (Ruger)
Bullet Diameter: 0.308″-0.312″

Maximum Case Length: 1.315″
Trim to Length: 1.310″
Maximum Cartridge OAL: 1.592″
Minimum Cartridge OAL: 1.540″

Introduced in 1882 and chambered in the Model 73 Winchester rifle and carbine, the 32-20 gained considerable popularity and was soon chambered in Colt's Single Action Army revolver. Launching a 100-grain lead bullet at about 1000 fps from the Colt, recoil is minuscule. This is a superior small game chambering for traditional revolvers. The number of 32-20 Colt revolvers produced was enormous.

Top loads in the Ruger offer performance that somewhat surpasses the much more recent 32 H&R Magnum.

These loads are for use only in handguns known to be safe with smokeless powder.

With an 86-grain bullet, seated normally, usable capacity is about 17.1 grains of water. H110, No.9 and A1680 are good choices for 32-20 revolver loads.

32-20 WINCHESTER LOADING DATA (Revolver Specific Loads)

Lead 100 Lyman 313631 (SWC-GC)

Powder	—STARTING— Grs.	MV (fps)	—MAXIMUM— Grs.	MV (fps)	Press. (CUP/psi)	Comments
A1680	12.2	888	12.8	945	15,100C	1.585″/CCI 400
No.9	6.7	869	7.0	924	15,500C	1.585″/CCI 400
No.7	5.8	869	6.1	924	16,000C	1.585″/CCI 400
XMP5744			9.3	900	16,000C	1.585″/CCI 400
No.5	4.6	813	4.8	865	14,400C	1.585″/CCI 400
A2015BR	13.3	795	14.0	846	16,000C	1.585″/CCI 400/(C)

85

Powder	—STARTING— Grs.	MV (fps)	—MAXIMUM— Grs.	MV (fps)	Press. (CUP/psi)	Comments
H110	15.5	1617	17.5	1783		JHP (.312″)
H4227	15.0	1490	17.0	1750		JHP (.312″)
HS7	7.5	1134	8.0	1205		JHP (.312″)
HS6	6.5	1071	7.0	1182		JHP (.312″)
HP38	3.3	781	4.5	1050		JHP (.312″)

90

Powder	—STARTING— Grs.	MV (fps)	—MAXIMUM— Grs.	MV (fps)	Press. (CUP/psi)	Comments
H110	15.1	1545	17.1	1728		JHP (.312″)
H4227	14.6	1482	16.6	1680		JHP (.312″)
HS7	7.3	1091	7.8	1172		JHP (.312″)
HS6	6.2	1011	6.8	1081		JHP (.312″)
HP38	3.3	811	4.3	1023		JHP (.312″)
A1680	13.7	977	14.4	1039	13,700C	Sra JHC/1.565″/CCI 400
No.9	6.9	927	7.3	986	13,600C	Sra JHC/1.565″/CCI 400
No.7	5.8	881	6.1	937	13,400C	Sra JHC/1.565″/CCI 400
XMP5744			9.7	920	15,000C	Sra JHC/1.565″/CCI 400
No.5	4.8	852	5.0	906	14,200C	Sra JHC/1.565″/CCI 400
A2015BR	14.3	823	15.0	875	12,700C	Sra JHC/1.565″/CCI 400/(C)

>>>>>>>>>>>>>>>>>>>>>>>>>>>>>>>

Never exceed maximum load nor use any load exhibiting signs of excessive pressure. Begin at suggested starting load and work up carefully.

100

Powder	—STARTING— Grs.	MV (fps)	—MAXIMUM— Grs.	MV (fps)	Press. (CUP/psi)	Comments
H110	14.9	1468	16.5	1627		Spr Plink (.308″)
H4227	14.3	1375	16.0	1546		Spr Plink (.308″)
HS7	7.1	904	7.6	993		Spr Plink (.308″)
HS6	5.6	849	6.6	992		Spr Plink (.308″)
A1680	11.9	917	12.5	975	15,600C	Hdy XTP/1.565″/ CCI 400
XMP5744			9.5	930	15,500C	Hdy XTP/1.565″/ CCI 400
No.9	6.7	871	7.0	927	15,500C	Hdy XTP/1.565″/ CCI 400
HP38	3.7	838	4.1	922		Spr Plink (.308″)
No.7	5.5	834	5.8	887	14,800C	Hdy XTP/1.565″/ CCI 400
A2015BR	14.0	824	14.7	877	15,400C	Hdy XTP/1.565″/ CCI 400/(C)
No.5	4.5	793	4.7	844	15,200C	Hdy XTP/1.565″/ CCI 400

110

Powder	—STARTING— Grs.	MV (fps)	—MAXIMUM— Grs.	MV (fps)	Press. (CUP/psi)	Comments
H110	14.5	1380	16.2	1561		Spr JRN (.308″)
H4227	13.8	1311	15.5	1475		Spr JRN (.308″)
HS7	6.9	863	7.5	998		Spr JRN (.308″)
HS6	5.4	803	6.5	988		Spr JRN (.308″)
HP38	3.6	770	4.0	869		Spr JRN (.308″)

Caution: Loads exceeding SAAMI OAL Maximum must be verified for bullet-to-rifling clearance and magazine functioning. Where a specific primer or bullet is indicated those components must be used, no substitutions! Where only a maximum load is shown, reduce starting load 10%, unless otherwise specified.

Key: (C) = compressed charge; C = CUP; p = psi; Plink = Plinker; Bns = Barnes; Hdy = Hornady; Lap = Lapua; Nos = Nosler; Rem = Remington; Sra = Sierra; Spr = Speer; Win = Winchester.

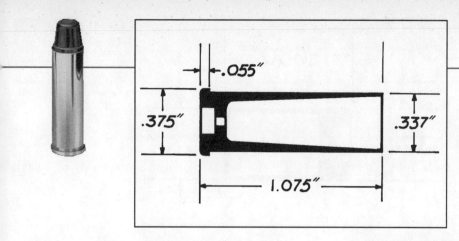

Case: Federal
Primer: Small Pistol
Barrel: 10″ Accurate/5″ Hodgdon
Bullet Diameter: 0.312″

Maximum Case Length: 1.075″
Trim to Length: 1.065″
Maximum Cartridge OAL: 1.350″
Minimum Cartridge OAL: 1.300″

Introduced in 1984, this cartridge resulted from a joint venture of Federal and Harrington & Richardson. The case is simply a stretched version of the 32 S&W Long. Both the 32 S&W Long and the 32 S&W can be fired in 32 H&R Magnum-chambered guns.

For reasons that this author cannot understand, chamber pressures for this modern "magnum" cartridge suggest introduction in the blackpowder era. Performance is necessarily extremely limited. Adding the magnum moniker to a chambering offering performance that is no better than the 1873-vintage 32-20 seems a bit silly.

Typical loads do not come anywhere near matching 38 Special muzzle energy, and other than minimal recoil and use for small game hunting, the round has little to recommend it. As a self-defense option, the 380 Automatic is almost certainly a far superior choice and the 38 Special is in an entirely different class!

With an 86-grain bullet, seated normally, usable capacity is about 14.8 grains of water. H4227, No. 7 and No. 5 are good performers in the 32 H&R Magnum.

32 HARRINGTON & RICHARDSON MAGNUM LOADING DATA

Powder	—STARTING— Grs.	MV (fps)	—MAXIMUM— Grs.	MV (fps)	Press. (CUP/psi)	Comments
Lead 90-95						
H4227	8.2	906	9.0	1043	20,900C	
HS7	5.4	886	5.9	1017	20,100C	
HS6	4.6	829	5.0	982	19,500C	
Trap100	3.3	818	3.8	973	20,800C	
HP38	3.0	801	3.6	956	19,700C	
Universal			3.2	908	11,500C	SWC (90-gr.)
Lead 100 Lyman 313631 (SWC)						
No.7	5.4	1126	6.0	1279	20,200C	1.31″/CCI 500
No.5	4.2	1110	4.7	1261	21,000C	1.31″/CCI 500
N100	3.0	1048	3.3	1191	20,800C	1.31″/CCI 500
No.2	3.2	1021	3.6	1160	18,700C	1.31″/CCI 500
85 (5″ Barrel)						
H4227	8.5	989	9.5	1151	21,000C	JHP
Universal			4.3	1123	19,000C	JHP
HS7	6.2	952	6.6	1095	20,900C	JHP
HS6	5.2	902	5.6	1046	20,200C	JHP
Trap100	3.4	837	4.0	1023	20,900C	JHP
HP38	3.2	785	3.8	1003	20,700C	JHP

Powder	—STARTING— Grs.	MV (fps)	—MAXIMUM— Grs.	MV (fps)	Press. (CUP/psi)	Comments
85 (10″ Barrel)						
No.7	5.9	1200	6.5	1364	20,300C	Hdy JHP/1.325″/CCI 500
No.5	4.8	1176	5.3	1336	20,100C	Hdy JHP/1.325″/CCI 500
No.2	3.6	1117	4.0	1269	20,800C	Hdy JHP/1.325″/CCI 500
N100	3.2	1082	3.5	1229	19,800C	Hdy JHP/1.325″/CCI 500
90						
No.7	5.7	1149	6.3	1306	19,800C	Sra JHC/1.34″/CCI 500
No.5	4.8	1137	5.3	1292	20,000C	Sra JHC/1.34″/CCI 500
No.2	3.6	1096	4.0	1245	21,000C	Sra JHC/1.34″/CCI 500
N100	3.2	1058	3.5	1202	20,300C	Sra JHC/1.34″/CCI 500
100						
No.5	4.5	1077	5.0	1224	21,000C	Spr JHP/1.335″/CCI 500
No.7	5.5	1075	6.0	1222	20,200C	Spr JHP/1.335″/CCI 500
No.2	3.3	1008	3.7	1146	20,700C	Spr JHP/1.335″/CCI 500
N100	3.0	985	3.3	1119	20,200C	Spr JHP/1.335″/CCI 500

Never exceed maximum load nor use any load exhibiting signs of excessive pressure. Begin at suggested starting load and work up carefully.

380 Automatic

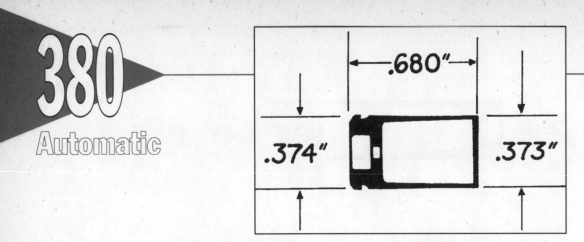

.680"
.374" **.373"**

Case: Federal
Primer: Small Pistol
Barrel: 3″ Accurate (Obermeyer)
3¹/₅″ Hodgdon (PPK-S)
3″ Vihtavuori

Bullet Diameter: 0.355″
Maximum Case Length: 0.680″
Trim to Length: 0.675″
Maximum Cartridge OAL: 0.984″
Minimum Cartridge OAL: 0.940″

Introduced in 1912 by John M. Browning and chambered in one of his numerous pistols, the 380 easily adapts to all but the smallest of blowback pistols. This cartridge offers substantial performance, compared to lesser "pocket pistol" chamberings.

The most recent factory high-performance loadings bring 380 performance very close to typical 38 Special levels—the two cartridges work at similar pressures. The 380 large-ly makes up for a deficit in usable case capacity through its lack of a velocity robbing barrel-cylinder gap.

Widely used as a backup self-defense gun, the 380 is also useful for short-range small game hunting.

With a 100-grain bullet, seated normally, usable capacity is about 7.5 grains of water. No. 5, N320, Unique, SR4756 and Universal all work well in the 380.

380 AUTOMATIC LOADING DATA

Powder	STARTING Grs.	MV (fps)	MAXIMUM Grs.	MV (fps)	Press. (CUP/psi)	Comments
Lead 100 SAECO 371						
No.2	3.2	830	3.6	943	17,000C	0.95″/CCI 500
No.5	4.1	811	4.5	922	16,900C	0.95″/CCI 500
90						
N320			3.6	1097	20,400p	Hdy XTP/0.98″
N310			2.9	1035	20,400p	Hdy XTP/0.98″
N320			3.0	980	19,200p	Win HP/0.955″
Universal			3.6	955	15,700C	JHP
N310			2.5	950	19,200p	Win HP/0.955″
Unique	3.7	869	4.0	944		
Red Dot	2.9	866	3.1	930		
No.2	3.3	818	3.7	930	17,000C	Hdy XTP/0.96″/ CCI 500
Bullseye	2.7	858	3.0	929		
HP38	3.2	841	3.5	927		JHP
W231	3.2	839	3.5	920		
No.5	4.3	810	4.8	920	16,700C	Hdy XTP/0.96″/ CCI 500
IMR700-X	2.6	844	2.9	890		
Green Dot	3.0	857	3.2	888		
IMR-PB	2.7	840	3.0	886		
SR4756	3.3	829	3.6	882		
SR7625	3.0	834	3.2	877		

Powder	STARTING Grs.	MV (fps)	MAXIMUM Grs.	MV (fps)	Press. (CUP/psi)	Comments
95						
N320			3.7	1089	20,400p	Spr TMJ/0.98″
N310			3.0	1017	20,400p	Spr TMJ/0.98″
No.2	3.3	822	3.7	934	14,600C	Sra FMJ/0.945″/ CCI 500
Universal			3.5	901	15,500C	
No.5	4.3	784	4.8	891	14,000C	Sra FMJ/0.945″/ CCI 500

Caution: Loads exceeding SAAMI OAL Maximum must be verified for bullet-to-rifling clearance and magazine functioning. Where a specific primer or bullet is indicated those components must be used, no substitutions! Where only a maximum load is shown, reduce starting load 10%, unless otherwise specified.

Key: (C) = compressed charge; C = CUP; p = psi; Plink = Plinker; Bns = Barnes; Hdy = Hornady; Lap = Lapua; Nos = Nosler; Rem = Remington; Sra = Sierra; Spr = Speer; Win = Winchester.

Never exceed maximum load nor use any load exhibiting signs of excessive pressure. Begin at suggested starting load and work up carefully.

100

Powder	STARTING Grs.	MV (fps)	MAXIMUM Grs.	MV (fps)	Press. (CUP/psi)	Comments
N320			3.4	1031	20,400p	Hdy FMJ/0.98"
N310			2.6	936	20,400p	Hdy FMJ/0.98"
No.5	4.4	788	4.9	895	17,000C	Hdy FMJ/0.975"/ CCI 500
Unique	3.6	822	3.8	894		
Universal			3.4	889	16,100C	FMJ
HP38	2.9	819	3.1	878		FMJ
SR4756	3.1	811	3.5	871		
W231	2.9	810	3.1	870		
Green Dot	2.9	828	3.1	862		
SR7625	2.7	804	3.0	852		
Red Dot	2.7	814	2.9	846		
IMR700-X	2.5	819	2.7	842		
Bullseye	2.6	819	2.8	840		
IMR-PB	2.5	809	2.8	837		
No.2	3.1	698	3.4	793	16,300C	Hdy FMJ/0.975"/ CCI 500

115

Powder	STARTING Grs.	MV (fps)	MAXIMUM Grs.	MV (fps)	Press. (CUP/psi)	Comments
Unique	3.3	800	3.5	832		
SR4756	3.0	792	3.2	824		
IMR-PB	2.4	755	2.6	802		
SR7625	2.6	746	2.8	797		
IMR700-X	2.3	740	2.6	788		
Green Dot	2.5	737	2.7	779		
HP38	2.5	749	2.7	778		JHP
W231	2.5	744	2.7	774		
Red Dot	2.2	727	2.5	768		
Bullseye	2.1	724	2.4	757		

124

Powder	STARTING Grs.	MV (fps)	MAXIMUM Grs.	MV (fps)	Press. (CUP/psi)	Comments
SR4756	2.6	710	2.9	764		
Unique	2.7	689	3.0	748		
SR7625	2.5	729	2.6	747		
Green Dot	2.2	666	2.4	718		
HP38	2.3	674	2.4	714		FMJ
IMR-PB	2.0	656	2.3	711		
Red Dot	2.0	680	2.1	705		
W231	2.2	651	2.4	700		
IMR700-X	2.0	639	2.2	698		
Bullseye	1.8	629	2.0	698		

Never exceed maximum load nor use any load exhibiting signs of excessive pressure. Begin at suggested starting load and work up carefully.

9x18
Makarov

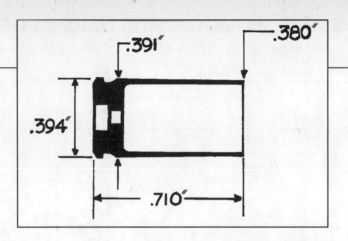

Case: Starline
Primer: Winchester WSP
Barrel: 3³/₄″ Accurate (HS)
(Unknown) Vihtavuori
Bullet Diameter: 0.364″-0.365″

Maximum Case Length: 0.710″
Trim to Length: 0.700″
Maximum Cartridge OAL: 0.970″
Minimum Cartridge OAL: Bullet and
Magazine Dependent

Introduced almost immediately after the end of WWII, this chambering was developed by the Soviets for use in the Makarov pistol. Performance, while not up to 9mm Luger levels, is very similar to standard 38 Special loadings. There is, however, a paucity of bullets designed to work properly in the Makarov's 0.365″ nominal bore.

Makarov cases are easily formed from 9mm Luger cases.

Simply run an expander into the case mouth after trimming to proper length.

Operating pressure is similar to the 38 Special. With modern light expanding bullets, which tend to limit expansion and hold together properly, the Makarov has a lot to offer. No. 5 and No. 7 are good Makarov choices.

9x18mm MAKAROV LOADING DATA

	—STARTING—		—MAXIMUM—			
Powder	Grs.	MV (fps)	Grs.	MV (fps)	Press. (CUP/psi)	Comments

Lead 95 Lyman 364653 (RN)

Powder	Grs.	MV (fps)	Grs.	MV (fps)	Press. (CUP/psi)	Comments
No.5	4.7	931	5.2	1058	17,200C	0.955″
No.7	6.5	921	7.2	1047	16,300C	0.955″
No.2	3.6	900	4.0	1023	17,200C	0.955″

95

Powder	Grs.	MV (fps)	Grs.	MV (fps)	Press. (CUP/psi)	Comments
No.5	5.0	936	5.6	1064	19,000C	Hdy XTP/0.965″
No.5	5.0	934	5.6	1061	19,400C	Sra JHP/0.965″
No.7	6.5	919	7.2	1044	18,200C	Sra JHP/0.965″
No.2	3.8	918	4.2	1043	19,500C	Hdy XTP/0.965″
No.7	6.5	915	7.2	1040	18,100C	Hdy XTP/0.965″
No.2	3.8	895	4.2	1017	17,900C	Sra JHP/0.965″
N320			3.2	990	23,500p	Hdy HP/0.94″
N310			2.7	970	23,000p	Hdy HP/0.94″

100

Powder	Grs.	MV (fps)	Grs.	MV (fps)	Press. (CUP/psi)	Comments
No.7	6.5	907	7.2	1031	18,500C	Sra FPJ/0.965″
No.2	3.7	869	4.1	987	18,800C	Sra FPJ/0.965″
No.5	4.7	853	5.2	969	16,600C	Sra FPJ/0.965″

Caution: Loads exceeding SAAMI OAL Maximum must be verified for bullet-to-rifling clearance and magazine functioning. Where a specific primer or bullet is indicated those components must be used, no substitutions! Where only a maximum load is shown, reduce starting load 10%, unless otherwise specified.

Key: (C) = compressed charge; C = CUP; p = psi; Plink = Plinker; Bns = Barnes; Hdy = Hornady; Lap = Lapua; Nos = Nosler; Rem = Remington; Sra = Sierra; Spr = Speer; Win = Winchester.

Never exceed maximum load nor use any load exhibiting signs of excessive pressure. Begin at suggested starting load and work up carefully.

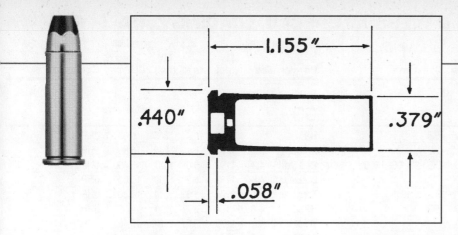

Smith & Wesson Special & Special +P

Case: Hornady
Primer: Small Pistol
Barrel: 8³/₈″ Accurate (S&W K-38)
  7″ Hodgdon
  6¹/₂″ Vihtavuori
  4″ Winchester (Vented Test)
Bullet Diameter: 0.357″-0.358″

Maximum Case Length: 1.155″
Trim to Length: 1.145″
Maximum Cartridge OAL: 1.550″
Minimum Cartridge OAL: 1.145″
  (Listed Wadcutter Loads Only);
  1.400″ (+P)

An original U.S. military chambering, the 38 Special was standardized in 1902. It immediately garnered a strong following and has never looked back. It has long been noted for its accuracy potential. For many decades, it was the standard police-issue chambering in the U.S. and in many other countries.

Usable capacity is generous, and working pressure, while mild, allows considerable performance. Many today consider the 38 Special to be passé because of "limited performance." We must note, however, that the vaunted 9mm, 147-grain sub-sonic load largely duplicates 38 Special +P performance.

The 38 Special is still a favorite target chambering, and with the best modern bullets it offers very impressive performance as a self-defense round.

The +P loads listed here should not be regularly used in any aluminum framed—or aluminum cylindered—gun or any other lightweight revolver. Many larger guns are specifically +P designated by the manufacturer.

Lighter guns are not apt to disintegrate if such loads are used. However, regular use of +P ammunition will loosen those up rather fast. Obviously, this practice is not recommended excepting one purpose: For familiarity and for use in a carry gun for self-defense. For that purpose, considerations of shooter longevity might take precedence over considerations of gun longevity.

Generally, to provide assured expansion, only jacketed bullets lighter than 150 grains should be used. Those should be loaded to near top velocities.

Jacketed bullets should never be used with loads reduced below those shown. That practice could result in either a squib load or a bullet jacket separating from its core and stopping in the bore.... Firing a second shot into a bullet or a bullet jacket lodged in a gun's bore is certain to wreck the barrel, at the very least. So many powders work well in the 38 Special that it is impractical to offer a reasonable list.

38 SMITH & WESSON SPECIAL LOADING DATA

Lead 124 Intercast SWC

Powder	STARTING Grs.	MV (fps)	MAXIMUM Grs.	MV (fps)	Press. (CUP/psi)	Comments
N350	5.6	1048	6.3	1141	16,200p	1.437″
3N37	5.9	1023	6.5	1124	16,200p	1.437″
N340	5.4	1003	5.9	1113	16,200p	1.437″
N320	4.2	954	4.8	1067	16,200p	1.437″

Lead 145 Intercast SWC

Powder	STARTING Grs.	MV (fps)	MAXIMUM Grs.	MV (fps)	Press. (CUP/psi)	Comments
N350	5.0	909	5.7	1031	16,200p	1.476″
N340	4.7	906	5.3	1022	16,200p	1.476″
3N37	5.1	884	5.6	990	16,200p	1.476″
N320	3.5	835	4.0	929	16,200p	1.476″

Lead 148 HBWC

Powder	STARTING Grs.	MV (fps)	MAXIMUM Grs.	MV (fps)	Press. (CUP/psi)	Comments
Universal			3.8	940	15,600C	
Clays			2.5	836	13,200C	
No.5	3.6	710	4.0	807	16,200p	Hdy/1.152″/CCI 500
W231	2.9	690	3.3	770	16,100C	
W231	3.0	690	3.4	760	16,400C	BBWC
No.2	2.6	634	2.9	720	15,500p	Hdy/1.152″/CCI 500

Lead 148 WC

Powder	—STARTING— Grs.	MV (fps)	—MAXIMUM— Grs.	MV (fps)	Press. (CUP/psi)	Comments
Clays	2.5	799	3.2	950	15,800C	BB
HS6	5.0	822	6.0	924	14,400C	BB
No.5	4.5	803	5.0	912	16,500p	DE/1.252"/CCI 500
Trap100	3.1	828	3.5	891	15,600C	BB
N350	3.9	783	4.3	882	16,200p	Sako/1.181"
HP38	3.2	830	3.8	879	14,800C	BB
Red Dot	2.8	781	3.3	871	14,400C	
Bullseye	2.7	772	3.1	864	14,200C	
Unique	3.5	774	4.0	854	12,800C	
SR7625	3.0	757	3.6	854	14,200C	
N340	3.5	764	3.9	853	16,200p	Sako/1.181"
No.2	3.2	748	3.5	850	16,000p	DE/1.252"/CCI 500
IMR-PB	2.8	770	3.4	849	15,000C	
IMR700-X	2.5	761	3.1	828	15,200C	
N330	3.2	731	3.6	828	16,200p	Sako/1.181"
N320	2.8	730	3.2	810	16,200p	Sako/1.181"
N320	2.4	660	2.7	730	16,000p	Hdy DE/1.165"
N310	2.0	610	2.3	700	15,200p	Hdy DE/1.165"

Lead 158 Bull-X (SWC)

Powder	Grs.	MV (fps)	Grs.	MV (fps)	Press.	Comments
No.5	5.3	827	5.9	940	16,100p	1.481"/CCI 500
No.2	3.6	764	4.0	868	14,100p	1.481"/CCI 500

Lead 158 SWC

Powder	Grs.	MV (fps)	Grs.	MV (fps)	Press.	Comments
W231	4.0	745	4.5	830	15,800C	SWC

Lead 158-160

Powder	Grs.	MV (fps)	Grs.	MV (fps)	Press.	Comments
Universal			4.5	974	16,700C	RN
HS6			6.5	966	14,400C	
H4227			10.0	956	15,600C	
Clays			3.1	871	15,100C	RN
HP38	3.1	782	3.7	834	14,600C	
Trap100	3.0	766	3.3	832	14,400C	

Lead 173 Lyman 358429 (SWC)

Powder	Grs.	MV (fps)	Grs.	MV (fps)	Press.	Comments
No.5	4.9	766	5.4	870	16,500p	1.515"/CCI 500
No.2	3.6	721	4.0	819	16,300p	1.515"/CCI 500

Lead 160 Intercast (FN)

Powder	Grs.	MV (fps)	Grs.	MV (fps)	Press.	Comments
N340	4.8	916	5.3	1021	16,200p	1.476"
N350	5.2	910	5.7	1003	16,200p	1.476"
3N37	4.9	844	5.6	963	16,200p	1.476"

Lead 200

Powder	Grs.	MV (fps)	Grs.	MV (fps)	Press.	Comments
H4227			8.5	819	15,900C	
HS6	4.5	749	5.0	794	15,900C	
Trap100	2.6	630	2.8	688	15,000C	
HP38	2.8	636	3.2	681	14,900C	

90

Powder	—STARTING— Grs.	MV (fps)	—MAXIMUM— Grs.	MV (fps)	Press. (CUP/psi)	Comments
HS6			10.0	1305	15,000C	JHP
Unique	5.5	1204	6.1	1249	15,800C	JHP
Red Dot	4.3	1199	5.0	1237	15,400C	JHP
Bullseye	4.6	1169	5.2	1219	15,000C	JHP
Trap100	4.8	1124	5.8	1211	14,800C	JHP
HP38	4.7	1164	5.7	1201	14,300C	JHP
W231	4.8	1175	5.6	1194	15,400C	JHP
SR7625	5.2	1084	5.7	1122	15,300C	JHP
IMR-PB	5.0	1030	5.4	1102	15,900C	JHP

110 (Revolver)

Powder	Grs.	MV (fps)	Grs.	MV (fps)	Press.	Comments
No.5	6.6	959	7.3	1090	16,600p	Hdy XTP/1.435"/CCI 500
No.2	5.0	953	5.6	1083	16,800p	Hdy XTP/1.435"/CCI 500

110

Powder	Grs.	MV (fps)	Grs.	MV (fps)	Press.	Comments
N350	6.2	1104	7.0	1216	16,200p	Hdy XTP/1.437"
3N37	7.0	1090	7.6	1210	16,200p	Hdy XTP/1.437"
HS6	7.5	1117	8.5	1180	15,700C	JHP
Bullseye	4.4	990	5.0	1150	14,900C	JHP
Universal			5.6	1143	16,700C	JHP
SR7625	5.1	1009	5.5	1117	16,000C	JHP
IMR-PB	4.6	977	5.0	1081	16,000C	JHP
Unique	4.8	955	5.6	1075	14,700C	JHP
Trap100	4.2	940	5.2	1062	15,400C	JHP
W231	4.6	998	5.2	1058	15,200C	JHP
Red Dot	3.5	940	4.0	1055	15,400C	JHP
IMR700-X	4.0	959	4.4	1052	15,900C	JHP
HP38	4.2	959	5.2	1043	14,800C	JHP
N340	5.9	1067	6.5	1177	16,200p	Hdy XTP/1.437"
N320	5.2	1054	5.7	1174	16,200p	Hdy XTP/1.437"

125 (Revolver)

Powder	Grs.	MV (fps)	Grs.	MV (fps)	Press.	Comments
No.2	4.8	871	5.3	990	16,800p	Spr JHP/1.445"/CCI 500
No.5	6.1	757	6.8	860	16,300p	Spr JHP/1.445"/CCI 500

125

Powder	Grs.	MV (fps)	Grs.	MV (fps)	Press.	Comments
HS6	6.8	932	7.8	1169	15,800C	JHP
N340	5.8	992	6.5	1137	16,200p	Hdy FP-XTP/1.437"
N350	6.1	988	6.9	1117	16,200p	Hdy FP-XTP/1.437"
3N37	6.6	978	7.1	1101	16,200p	Hdy FP-XTP/1.437"
N320	4.7	921	5.2	1031	16,200p	Hdy FP-XTP/1.437"
Universal			5.2	1019	17,000C	JHP
Unique	4.5	907	5.2	1004	14,800C	JHP
Bullseye	4.0	899	4.4	980	14,200C	JHP
SR7625	4.8	877	5.2	960	15,800C	JHP
Red Dot	3.5	868	4.0	947	14,000C	JHP
Trap100	3.8	824	4.8	930	15,500C	JHP
IMR-PB	4.2	848	4.7	930	15,700C	JHP
HP38	3.8	829	4.8	914	14,100C	JHP
W231	4.1	833	4.7	899	14,400C	JHP

Never exceed maximum load nor use any load exhibiting signs of excessive pressure. Begin at suggested starting load and work up carefully.

130

Powder	STARTING Grs.	MV (fps)	MAXIMUM Grs.	MV (fps)	Press. (CUP/psi)	Comments
HS6	6.2	878	7.2	1077	14,900C	JHP
Trap100	3.5	809	4.5	910	15,100C	JHP
HP38	3.5	811	4.5	900	15,000C	JHP

137-140

Powder	STARTING Grs.	MV (fps)	MAXIMUM Grs.	MV (fps)	Press. (CUP/psi)	Comments
Unique	4.2	811	5.0	975	14,900C	JHP (140-gr.)
HS6	6.0	874	7.0	969	15,800C	
Universal			4.8	939	15,400C	
Bullseye	3.9	856	4.2	929	13,900C	JHP (140-gr.)
Red Dot	3.0	774	3.8	927	14,200C	JHP (140-gr.)
SR7625	4.5	829	4.9	924	16,000C	JHP (140-gr.)
IMR-PB	4.2	806	4.6	888	15,800C	JHP (140-gr.)
IMR700-X	3.2	776	3.7	866	15,400C	JHP (140-gr.)
HP38	3.4	822	4.0	862	15,100C	
W231	3.5	830	4.0	858	15,000C	JHP (140-gr.)
Trap100	3.4	810	4.0	840	15,200C	
Clays			3.4	761	16,200C	JHP

140 (Revolver)

Powder	STARTING Grs.	MV (fps)	MAXIMUM Grs.	MV (fps)	Press. (CUP/psi)	Comments
No.2	4.2	781	4.7	888	16,700p	Spr JHP/1.445"/CCI 500
No.5	5.8	757	6.4	860	16,700p	Spr JHP/1.445"/CCI 500

140

Powder	STARTING Grs.	MV (fps)	MAXIMUM Grs.	MV (fps)	Press. (CUP/psi)	Comments
3N37	5.8	855	6.5	993	16,200p	Spr HP/1.437"
N350	5.8	854	6.3	988	16,200p	Spr HP/1.437"
N340	5.2	839	5.7	967	16,200p	Spr HP/1.437"
N320	4.4	807	4.9	938	16,200p	Spr HP/1.437"

146-150

Powder	STARTING Grs.	MV (fps)	MAXIMUM Grs.	MV (fps)	Press. (CUP/psi)	Comments
HS6			7.0	1011	14,900C	JHP
Unique	3.8	805	4.5	919	15,800C	JHP
H4227			10.5	909	15,500C	JHP
Bullseye	3.6	828	4.0	888	14,200C	JHP
W231	3.4	820	3.9	879	16,000C	JHP
Red Dot	2.9	752	3.5	870	14,800C	JHP
SR7625	4.2	809	4.6	869	15,800C	JHP
Trap100	3.2	829	3.6	868	14,600C	JHP
HP38	3.3	814	3.8	856	15,000C	JHP
IMR-PB	3.8	788	4.2	851	16,100C	JHP
IMR700-X	3.2	799	3.5	840	15,800C	JHP

146

Powder	STARTING Grs.	MV (fps)	MAXIMUM Grs.	MV (fps)	Press. (CUP/psi)	Comments
N350	4.9	811	5.5	920	16,200p	Spr JHP/1.378"
3N37	5.1	798	5.7	917	16,200p	Spr JHP/1.378"
N340	4.3	800	4.9	909	16,200p	Spr JHP/1.378"

150 (Revolver)

Powder	STARTING Grs.	MV (fps)	MAXIMUM Grs.	MV (fps)	Press. (CUP/psi)	Comments
No.2	4.2	751	4.7	853	17,000p	Nos JHP/1.45"/CCI 500
No.5	5.9	715	6.5	813	16,600p	Nos JHP/1.45"/CCI 500

158 (Revolver)

Powder	STARTING Grs.	MV (fps)	MAXIMUM Grs.	MV (fps)	Press. (CUP/psi)	Comments
No.5	5.2	740	5.8	841	16,500p	Hdy XTP/1.445"/CCI 500
No.2	3.6	665	4.0	756	16,500p	Hdy XTP/1.445"/CCI 500

158-160

Powder	STARTING Grs.	MV (fps)	MAXIMUM Grs.	MV (fps)	Press. (CUP/psi)	Comments
HS6			6.5	914	14,600C	JSP (160-gr.)
N350	5.1	792	5.8	912	16,200C	Spr HP/1.437"
H4227			10.0	872	15,100C	JSP (160-gr.)
N340	4.5	723	5.1	862	16,200C	Spr HP/1.437"
SR7625	4.0	810	4.4	860	16,000C	JSP
IMR-PB	3.6	790	3.9	834	15,900C	JSP
Trap100	3.0	771	3.4	823	15,100C	JSP (160-gr.)
IMR700-X	3.1	784	3.4	820	16,000C	JSP
HP38	3.1	783	3.7	819	14,900C	JSP (160-gr.)
Bullseye	3.4	791	3.8	812	15,400C	JSP
W231	3.1	779	3.6	809	15,000C	JSP
Unique	3.5	701	4.1	798	16,100C	JSP
N320	3.6	652	4.1	780	16,200p	Spr HP/1.437"
Universal			4.4	778	16,200C	JHP (158-gr.)
Red Dot	2.8	657	3.2	722	15,000C	JSP

170

Powder	STARTING Grs.	MV (fps)	MAXIMUM Grs.	MV (fps)	Press. (CUP/psi)	Comments
H4227			9.3	859	15,600C	
HS7	6.5	788	7.0	840	15,600C	
HS6	5.1	772	6.1	836	15,400C	
HP38	3.0	753	3.6	802	15,100C	
Trap100	2.9	749	3.3	794	14,900C	

180

Powder	STARTING Grs.	MV (fps)	MAXIMUM Grs.	MV (fps)	Press. (CUP/psi)	Comments
N110	7.5	741	8.3	852	16,200p	Lapua Tera/1.476"

Caution: **Loads exceeding SAAMI OAL Maximum must be verified for bullet-to-rifling clearance and magazine functioning. Where a specific primer or bullet is indicated those components must be used, no substitutions! Where only a maximum load is shown, reduce starting load 10%, unless otherwise specified.**

Key: (C) = compressed charge; C = CUP; p = psi; Plink = Plinker; Bns = Barnes; Hdy = Hornady; Lap = Lapua; Nos = Nosler; Rem = Remington; Sra = Sierra; Spr = Speer; Win = Winchester.

Never exceed maximum load nor use any load exhibiting signs of excessive pressure. Begin at suggested starting load and work up carefully.

38 SMITH & WESSON SPECIAL +P LOADING DATA

Lead 158 SWC

Powder	Grs.	MV (fps)	Grs.	MV (fps)	Press. (CUP/psi)	Comments
No.5	5.6	880	6.2	1000	18,400p	1.481"/CCI 500
No.2	4.2	879	4.7	999	18,500p	1.481"/CCI 500

Lead 158 RN

Powder	Grs.	MV (fps)	Grs.	MV (fps)	Press. (CUP/psi)	Comments
Universal			4.8	1018	19,100C	

Lead 173 Lyman 358429 (SWC)

Powder	Grs.	MV (fps)	Grs.	MV (fps)	Press. (CUP/psi)	Comments
No.5	5.0	792	5.6	900	17,900p	1.515"/CCI 500
No.2	3.8	748	4.2	850	18,000p	1.515"/CCI 500

110 (Revolver)

Powder	Grs.	MV (fps)	Grs.	MV (fps)	Press. (CUP/psi)	Comments
No.5	6.8	1046	7.5	1189	17,400p	Hdy XTP/1.435"/CCI 500
No.2	5.2	996	5.8	1132	17,800p	Hdy XTP/1.435"/CCI 500

110

Powder	Grs.	MV (fps)	Grs.	MV (fps)	Press. (CUP/psi)	Comments
HS7			11.2	1319	20,000C	
HS6			9.8	1300	20,600C	
IMR4227			14.0	1290	17,900C	JHP
Universal			6.0	1204	18,700C	JHP
SR4756			6.4	1169	18,000C	JHP
Blue Dot			8.7	1154	19,400C	JHP
HP38			6.0	1146	19,460C	
W231			5.9	1134	19,200C	JHP
Her2400			10.1	1132	19,000C	JHP
Unique			6.0	1129	19,200C	JHP
Clays			4.5	1110	19,220C	

125 (Revolver)

Powder	Grs.	MV (fps)	Grs.	MV (fps)	Press. (CUP/psi)	Comments
No.2	5.0	899	5.5	1022	17,700p	Spr JHP/1.445"/CCI 500
No.5	6.4	810	7.1	920	17,300p	Spr JHP/1.445"/CCI 500

125

Powder	Grs.	MV (fps)	Grs.	MV (fps)	Press. (CUP/psi)	Comments
H4227			14.0	1277	18,900C	
HS7			9.5	1244	20,000C	
IMR4227			13.5	1239	18,600C	JHP
HS6			8.5	1220	20,200C	
Universal			5.4	1072	18,900C	JHP
Her2400			9.8	1071	19,400C	JHP
Blue Dot			7.6	1068	19,800C	JHP
HP38			5.8	1067	19,200C	
W231			5.6	1064	19,100C	JHP
SR4756			6.0	1022	18,400C	JHP
Unique			5.9	1019	19,900C	JHP
Clays			4.3	1012	19,700C	

140 (Revolver)

Powder	Grs.	MV (fps)	Grs.	MV (fps)	Press. (CUP/psi)	Comments
No.5	6.0	778	6.7	884	17,800p	Spr JHP/1.445"/CCI 500
No.2	4.4	775	4.9	881	18,300p	Spr JHP/1.445"/CCI 500

140

Powder	Grs.	MV (fps)	Grs.	MV (fps)	Press. (CUP/psi)	Comments
H4227			13.6	1198	19,900C	
IMR4227			13.2	1166	19,400C	JHP
HS7			9.2	1137	20,800C	
HS6			7.9	1091	19,400C	
Blue Dot			8.4	1034	19,600C	JHP
Her2400			9.5	1028	19,400C	JHP
Universal			5.1	1022	19,100C	JHP
HP38			5.7	1019	20,100C	
W231			5.3	1009	19,400C	JHP
SR4756			5.7	984	19,100C	JHP
Unique			5.4	981	19,400C	JHP
Clays			4.2	953	19,400C	

146-150

Powder	Grs.	MV (fps)	Grs.	MV (fps)	Press. (CUP/psi)	Comments
HS7			8.9	1118	21,900C	
H4227			13.2	1103	21,000C	
IMR4227			12.8	1088	20,900C	JHP
HS6			7.6	1071	19,000C	
Blue Dot			8.0	1038	19,800C	JHP
Her2400			8.5	998	19,600C	JHP
HP38			5.5	973	19,800C	
Unique			5.0	964	19,000C	JHP
SR4756			5.5	944	19,600C	JHP
W231			5.1	941	19,000C	JHP

150 (Revolver)

Powder	Grs.	MV (fps)	Grs.	MV (fps)	Press. (CUP/psi)	Comments
No.2	4.4	791	4.9	899	17,600p	Nos JHP/1.45"/CCI 500
No.5	6.0	757	6.7	860	18,200p	Nos JHP/1.45"/CCI 500

Caution: Loads exceeding SAAMI OAL Maximum must be verified for bullet-to-rifling clearance and magazine functioning. Where a specific primer or bullet is indicated those components must be used, no substitutions! Where only a maximum load is shown, reduce starting load 10%, unless otherwise specified.

Key: (C) = compressed charge; C = CUP; p = psi; Plink = Plinker; Bns = Barnes; Hdy = Hornady; Lap = Lapua; Nos = Nosler; Rem = Remington; Sra = Sierra; Spr = Speer; Win = Winchester.

Never exceed maximum load nor use any load exhibiting signs of excessive pressure. Begin at suggested starting load and work up carefully.

158 (Revolver)

Powder	Grs.	MV (fps)	Grs.	MV (fps)	Press. (CUP/psi)	Comments
No.5	5.4	792	6.0	900	18,500p	Hdy XTP/1.445"/CCI 500
No.2	3.8	702	4.2	798	17,800p	Hdy XTP/1.445"/CCI 500

158-160

Powder	Grs.	MV (fps)	Grs.	MV (fps)	Press. (CUP/psi)	Comments
H4227			12.5	1052	20,600C	
IMR4227			12.2	1029	20,200C	JSP
HS7			8.5	1009	19,000C	
HS6			7.3	995	19,200C	
HP38			5.2	948	20,400C	
Her2400			8.0	925	19,800C	JHP
Blue Dot			6.4	917	19,200C	JHP
W231			4.8	909	19,400C	JSP
Unique			4.5	904	19,400C	JHP
SR4756			5.2	880	19,900C	JSP
Universal			4.7	837	19,200C	JHP (158-gr.)

170

Powder	Grs.	MV (fps)	Grs.	MV (fps)	Press. (CUP/psi)	Comments
HS7			7.9	979	26,200C	
H4227			11.5	977	19,800C	
IMR4227			11.3	959	19,400C	JHP
HS6			7.0	943	19,400C	
HP38			4.8	891	19,000C	
Blue Dot			6.1	891	19,800C	FMJ
Her2400			7.4	877	20,000C	FMJ
W231			4.6	870	19,000C	FMJ
Unique			4.0	860	19,600C	FMJ

180

Powder	Grs.	MV (fps)	Grs.	MV (fps)	Press. (CUP/psi)	Comments
H4227			11.0	890	21,200C	
HS7			7.6	885	21,600C	
HS6			6.7	870	20,200C	
Her2400			6.9	848	79,800C	JHP
IMR4227			10.7	844	21,000C	JHP
Blue Dot			5.6	824	19,700C	JHP
HP38			4.5	809	19,800C	
Unique			3.7	801	19,400C	JHP
W231			4.4	800	19,600C	FMJ

38 Special +P loads are for use in modern arms in good condition. These loads should not be used in small frame or aluminum frame revolvers, nor are they intended for use in automatic pistols. Where only maximum loads are shown, no reduction in charge is recommended.

9mm
Luger

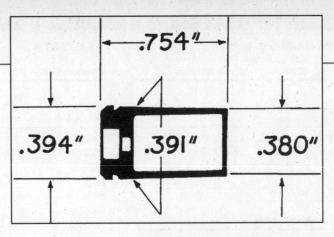

.754″

.394″ .391″ .380″

Case: Federal
Primer: Small Pistol
Barrel: 4″ Accurate (Obermeyer)
4″ Hodgdon
4″ Vihtavuori
4″ Winchester

Bullet Diameter: 0.355″
Maximum Case Length: 0.754″
Trim to Length: 0.749″
Maximum Cartridge OAL: 1.169″
Minimum Cartridge OAL: 1.095″

The German navy claims credit for initial military adoption of this cartridge in 1904. In 1908, the German army followed suit and cemented the 9mm Luger's future. With compact dimensions and high working pressures, the 9mm Luger offers significant performance for military and self-defense purposes.

Best loads with lighter bullets come very near to duplicating 357 Magnum revolver performance. With heavier bullets, the 9mm compares well to top 38 Special +P loads. The debate will never settle—many consider this and similar chamberings as simply too light, regardless of load

used—but the 9mm has much to offer for serious self-defense use.

Among its best features is limited recoil. All but the most sensitive shooters find typical 9mm-chambered pistols manageable. Increased magazine capacity is perhaps of military value. This feature is of little value in most self-defense situations—it has been said that "high-capacity" 9mm pistols give poor marksmen more shots to miss with.

Case capacity with a 100-grain bullet, seated normally, is about 11.4 grains of water. No.7 was specifically designed for the 9mm Luger, and its performance is most impressive.

9mm LUGER LOADING DATA

Lead 114-115

Powder	—STARTING— Grs.	MV (fps)	—MAXIMUM— Grs.	MV (fps)	Press. (CUP/psi)	Comments
No.7	7.8	1078	8.7	1225	33,000C	SWC/1.1″/Win WSP
No.5	5.7	1040	6.3	1182	33,000C	SWC/1.1″/Win WSP
WAP	4.8	1040	5.7	1160	33,200p	
No.2	4.4	1008	4.9	1146	32,900C	SWC/1.1″/Win WSP

Lead 124-125 Intercast (SWC)

Powder	Grs.	MV (fps)	Grs.	MV (fps)	Press. (CUP/psi)	Comments
3N37	5.2	1135	6.0	1230	33,300p	SWC/1.142″
N340	4.5	1112	5.2	1224	33,300p	SWC/1.142″
N350	4.8	1112	5.5	1201	33,300p	SWC/1.142″
N330	4.3	1113	4.9	1183	33,300p	SWC/1.142″
No.7	7.5	1017	8.3	1156	32,500C	RN/1.1″/Win WSP
N320	3.7	1055	4.3	1136	33,300p	SWC/1.142″
No.5	5.6	997	6.2	1133	32,800C	RN/1.1″/Win WSP
WAP	4.4	955	5.1	1080	33,200p	
No.2	4.1	935	4.5	1063	30,100C	RN/1.1″/Win WSP

Lead 130 RN

Powder	Grs.	MV (fps)	Grs.	MV (fps)	Press. (CUP/psi)	Comments
No.7	7.4	1030	8.2	1170	33,000C	1.095″/Win WSP
No.5	5.4	1018	6.0	1157	33,000C	1.095″/Win WSP
No.2	3.6	895	4.0	1017	31,100C	1.095″/Win WSP

Lead 145-147 RN

Powder	Grs.	MV (fps)	Grs.	MV (fps)	Press. (CUP/psi)	Comments
No.7	6.5	926	7.2	1052	29,500C	1.14″/Win WSP
WAP	3.9	845	4.7	985	33,100p	
No.5	4.6	866	5.1	984	26,800C	1.14″/Win WSP
No.2	3.3	786	3.7	893	24,100C	1.14″/Win WSP

Caution: Loads exceeding SAAMI OAL Maximum must be verified for bullet-to-rifling clearance and magazine functioning. Where a specific primer or bullet is indicated those components must be used, no substitutions! Where only a maximum load is shown, reduce starting load 10%, unless otherwise specified.

Key: (C) = compressed charge; C = CUP; p = psi; Plink = Plinker; Bns = Barnes; Hdy = Hornady; Lap = Lapua; Nos = Nosler; Rem = Remington; Sra = Sierra; Spr = Speer; Win = Winchester.

88-90

Powder	STARTING Grs.	MV (fps)	MAXIMUM Grs.	MV (fps)	Press. (CUP/psi)	Comments
3N37	6.2	1381	7.3	1518	33,300p	Hdy XTP/1.063"
N340	5.3	1331	6.3	1495	33,300p	Hdy XTP/1.063"
N330	5.3	1336	6.1	1444	33,300p	Hdy XTP/1.063"
HS6	7.9	1366	8.2	1419	28,900C	
N320	4.6	1269	5.4	1384	33,300p	Hdy XTP/1.063"
No.5	6.8	1209	7.5	1374	33,000p	PMC JHP/1.095"/ Win WSP
HP38	5.5	1312	5.8	1349	30,100C	
SR7625	5.2	1238	5.6	1348	30,200C	JHP
W231	5.5	1288	5.9	1344	31,000C	JHP
Unique	5.6	1218	6.1	1341	31,300C	JHP
IMR-PB	5.1	1230	5.5	1322	30,100C	JHP
IMR700-X	5.0	1234	5.3	1318	30,000C	JHP
No.7	8.6	1158	9.5	1316	31,200C	PMC JHP/1.095"/ Win WSP
Red Dot	4.8	1209	5.2	1315	29,600C	JHP
Trap100	5.6	1249	5.9	1314	27,600C	
No.2	4.8	1133	5.3	1287	33,000C	PMC JHP/1.095"/ Win WSP
Bullseye	4.7	1184	5.1	1285	29,400C	JHP
Universal			5.5	1266	30,100C	FMJ (90-gr.)
N310	3.8	1171	4.3	1262	33,300p	Hdy XTP/1.063"

95

Powder	STARTING Grs.	MV (fps)	MAXIMUM Grs.	MV (fps)	Press. (CUP/psi)	Comments
WAP	5.6	1140	6.4	1285	33,000p	FMJ
No.5	6.5	1110	7.2	1261	30,700C	IMI FMJ/1.08"/Win WSP
No.2	4.8	1110	5.3	1261	33,000C	IMI FMJ/1.08"/Win WSP
No.7	8.2	1096	9.1	1246	29,100C	IMI FMJ/1.08"/Win WSP

100

Powder	STARTING Grs.	MV (fps)	MAXIMUM Grs.	MV (fps)	Press. (CUP/psi)	Comments
3N37	6.2	1269	7.5	1444	33,300p	Spr HP/1.083"
N340	5.4	1249	6.6	1428	33,300p	Spr HP/1.083"
N330	5.2	1264	6.0	1380	33,300p	Spr HP/1.083"
N320	4.5	1194	5.2	1322	33,300p	Spr HP/1.083"
HS6	7.2	1270	7.5	1313	28,600C	
HP38	5.1	1218	5.5	1282	28,400C	
W231	5.2	1220	5.5	1278	28,800C	JHP
No.7	8.1	1103	9.0	1253	29,800C	Hdy FMJ/1.095"/ Win WSP
Unique	5.4	1122	6.0	1248	30,600C	JHP
No.5	6.3	1091	7.0	1240	29,800C	Hdy FMJ/1.095"/ Win WSP
SR7625	4.8	1152	5.2	1220	31,100C	JHP
Trap100	5.1	1167	5.5	1218	27,400C	
IMR-PB	4.8	1148	5.2	1217	31,600C	JHP
No.2	4.9	1067	5.4	1213	33,000C	Hdy FMJ/1.095"/ Win WSP
Universal			5.3	1212	31,500C	FMJ
Red Dot	4.6	1138	4.9	1209	31,000C	JHP
Bullseye	4.5	1116	4.9	1182	31,100C	JHP
IMR700-X	4.4	1066	4.9	1171	32,000C	JHP

115

Powder	STARTING Grs.	MV (fps)	MAXIMUM Grs.	MV (fps)	Press. (CUP/psi)	Comments
3N37	5.8	1182	6.9	1322	33,300p	Hdy HP-XTP/1.083"
N340	5.1	1164	6.1	1321	33,300p	Hdy HP-XTP/1.083"
N350	5.7	1199	6.5	1313	33,300p	Hdy HP-XTP/1.083"
N330	4.7	1136	5.5	1266	33,300p	Hdy HP-XTP/1.083"
HS6	6.7	1171	7.0	1234	29,400C	
N320	4.0	1084	4.8	1211	33,300p	Hdy HP-XTP/1.083"
Unique	5.0	1060	5.4	1199	30,700C	JHP
No.7	7.9	1052	8.8	1196	29,700C	Hdy FMJ/1.095"/ Win WSP
No.5	6.3	1049	7.0	1192	31,400C	Hdy FMJ/1.095"/ Win WSP
W231	4.7	1071	5.2	1170	29,000C	JHP
HP38	4.7	1075	5.1	1167	28,100C	
Red Dot	4.0	1090	4.5	1166	31,400C	JHP
Bullseye	4.0	1081	4.4	1160	31,100C	JHP
WAP	5.3	1055	6.0	1155	33,100p	FMJ
WAP	5.3	1065	5.8	1150	33,200p	JHP
Universal			5.0	1149	31,200C	JHP
Trap100	4.8	1049	5.2	1121	25,700C	
SR7625	4.5	1032	5.0	1111	32,800C	JHP
IMR-PB	4.5	1022	5.0	1108	33,000C	JHP
Clays			3.9	1095	32,600C	JHP
No.2	4.0	961	4.4	1092	29,900C	Hdy FMJ/1.095"/ Win WSP
IMR700-X	4.0	890	4.5	1004	33,200C	JHP

124-125

Powder	STARTING Grs.	MV (fps)	MAXIMUM Grs.	MV (fps)	Press. (CUP/psi)	Comments
3N37	5.8	1149	6.6	1248	33,300p	Hdy FMJ-FP/1.142"
N350	5.3	1120	6.1	1228	33,300p	Hdy FMJ-FP/1.142"
N340	5.1	1113	5.7	1227	33,300p	Hdy FMJ-FP/1.142"
No.5	5.8	1069	6.4	1200	33,000C	Hdy RN/1.095"/ Win WSP
N330	4.7	1084	5.3	1192	33,300p	Hdy FMJ-FP/1.142"
HS6	6.4	1131	6.8	1169	27,100C	
No.7	7.2	1026	8.0	1166	29,800C	Hdy RN/1.095"/ Win WSP
N320	4.1	1035	4.7	1140	33,300p	Hdy FMJ-FP/1.142"
Universal			4.9	1118	30,600C	FMJ (124-gr.)
WAP	4.9	1005	5.6	1105	33,300p	FMJ (124-gr.)
Unique	4.8	1059	5.1	1104	29,800C	FMJ
W231	4.5	1018	4.9	1102	29,900C	FMJ
HP38	4.4	1009	4.8	1088	28,800C	
SR7625	4.3	969	4.8	1084	33,400C	FMJ
IMR-PB	4.2	960	4.7	1080	33,600C	FMJ
IMR700-X	4.0	987	4.5	1077	33,000C	FMJ
Trap100	4.6	994	5.0	1064	26,900C	
No.2	3.7	930	4.1	1057	29,500C	Hdy RN/1.095"/ Win WSP
Clays			3.7	1056	32,500C	FMJ (24-gr.)
Bullseye	3.8	904	4.2	1051	29,900C	FMJ
Red Dot	3.9	911	4.3	1029	28,800C	FMJ

Never exceed maximum load nor use any load exhibiting signs of excessive pressure. Begin at suggested starting load and work up carefully.

130

Powder	STARTING Grs.	MV (fps)	MAXIMUM Grs.	MV (fps)	Press. (CUP/psi)	Comments
No.7	7.3	1004	8.1	1141	31,500C	PMC FMJ/1.095"/ Win WSP
HS6	6.3	981	6.6	1090	26,900C	
Unique	4.6	949	5.0	1088	30,400C	FMJ
No.5	5.3	929	5.9	1060	33,000C	PMC FMJ/1.095"/ Win WSP
Universal			4.7	1058	30,400C	FMJ
HP38	4.3	978	4.6	1050	28,200C	
W231	4.2	959	4.6	1042	28,100C	FMJ
Trap100	4.5	973	4.8	1032	27,100C	
No.2	4.2	906	4.7	1029	30,900C	PMC FMJ/1.095"/ Win WSP
Red Dot	3.4	829	3.8	1002	30,700C	FMJ
Bullseye	3.2	824	3.7	988	30,000C	FMJ
SR7625	4.0	888	4.4	929	32,600C	FMJ
IMR-PB	3.9	860	4.3	919	32,200C	FMJ
IMR700-X	3.6	844	4.1	889	32,400C	FMJ

135

Powder	STARTING Grs.	MV (fps)	MAXIMUM Grs.	MV (fps)	Press. (CUP/psi)	Comments
No.5	5.5	974	6.1	1110	33,000C	Elite FMJ/1.095"/ Win WSP
No.7	6.8	958	7.5	1089	31,000C	Elite FMJ/1.095"/ Win WSP
No.2	4.0	858	4.4	975	27,500C	Elite FMJ/1.095"/ Win WSP

147

Powder	STARTING Grs.	MV (fps)	MAXIMUM Grs.	MV (fps)	Press. (CUP/psi)	Comments
N350	4.4	964	5.1	1084	33,300p	Hdy BTHP/1.142"
3N37	4.5	953	5.2	1066	33,300p	Hdy BTHP/1.142"
No.7	6.5	921	7.2	1047	31,900C	Spr TMJ/1.095"/ Win WSP
N330	3.9	938	4.4	1044	33,300p	Hdy BTHP/1.142"
N340	3.9	923	4.4	1027	33,300p	Hdy BTHP/1.142"
No.5	4.8	872	5.3	991	30,900C	Spr TMJ/1.095"/ Win WSP
HS6	5.5	881	6.0	973	32,700C	FMJ
HP38	4.2	865	4.5	959	34,000C	FMJ
Trap100	4.4	900	5.0	949	34,000C	FMJ
SR4756	5.0	905	5.2	948	33,800C	FMJ
WAP	4.2	880	4.6	940	33,200p	FMJ
IMR-PB	3.5	740	4.1	935	34,800C	FMJ
WAP	4.0	865	4.4	920	33,300p	JHP
W231	4.0	839	4.3	911	31,900C	FMJ
Herco	4.5	844	4.9	904	34,000C	FMJ
Green Dot	4.0	788	4.3	894	31,600C	FMJ
Unique	4.3	832	4.7	889	34,400C	FMJ
SR7625	3.4	792	4.0	889	34,700C	FMJ
No.2	3.6	781	4.0	888	29,200C	Spr TMJ/1.095"/ Win WSP
Universal			3.7	851	26,000C	JHP

Caution: **Loads exceeding SAAMI OAL Maximum must be verified for bullet-to-rifling clearance and magazine functioning. Where a specific primer or bullet is indicated those components must be used, no substitutions! Where only a maximum load is shown, reduce starting load 10%, unless otherwise specified.**

Key: (C) = compressed charge; C = CUP; p = psi; Plink = Plinker; Bns = Barnes; Hdy = Hornady; Lap = Lapua; Nos = Nosler; Rem = Remington; Sra = Sierra; Spr = Speer; Win = Winchester.

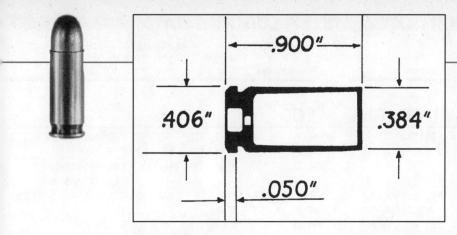

Case: PMC
Primer: Small Pistol
Barrel: 5″ Accurate
      5″ Hodgdon
      5½″ Vihtavuori
      5″ Winchester

Bullet Diameter: 0.355″
Maximum Case Length: 0.900″
Trim to Length: 0.895″
Maximum Cartridge OAL: 1.280″
Minimum Cartridge OAL: 1.220″

In 1929, manufacturers recognized that the 38 Automatic was severely handicapped by a very low pressure standard and that newer guns with stronger designs and better steel could utilize loads generating significantly higher pressures. (The recent bastardization of the name, addition of the +P designation, signifies nothing other than a continued attempt to keep foolish shooters from chambering ammunition in the wrong gun—an endless, and likely fruitless, endeavor.)

Rather than develop an entirely new, albeit similar, chambering, the standard 38 Automatic was reintroduced as the 38 Super Automatic. There was a 45-percent increase in chamber pressure, but there were no dimensional changes. This began an unending reign of confusion.

Unlike other +P designations (38 Special, 9mm Luger, 45 Automatic), this one suggests genuine safety concerns. It is unlikely that firing a few +P loads in even the weakest of guns chambered for any of those cartridges would seriously damage the gun or injure the shooter. Conversely, the 38 Super, with its huge pressure increase, far exceeds the limit of what many older 38 Automatic-chambered guns can safely handle.

Never fire any 38 Super load or any unknown handload using 38 Automatic, 38 Super Automatic or 38 Super Automatic +P cases in any gun marked for the 38 Automatic. These guns are still commonly used. Many simply cannot safely handle the pressures of normal 38 Super loads.

Loaded with heavy bullets, the 38 Super can meet IPSC Major Power Factor requirements, without exceeding SAAMI pressure specifications. This is the smallest commonly available pistol cartridge that can do so.

With a 100-grain bullet, seated normally, usable capacity is about 15.5 grains of water. Blue Dot, Unique, No. 9, 3N37 and No. 5 are among the best choices for the 38 Super.

38 SUPER AUTOMATIC +P LOADING DATA

Powder	—STARTING— Grs.	MV (fps)	—MAXIMUM— Grs.	MV (fps)	Press. (CUP/psi)	Comments

Lead 115 Lane (SWC)

Powder	Grs.	MV (fps)	Grs.	MV (fps)	Press. (CUP/psi)	Comments
No.9	11.3	1209	12.5	1374	32,400C	1.285″/CCI 500/(C)/*
No.7	8.8	1162	9.8	1320	33,000C	1.285″/CCI 500/*
No.5	6.8	1115	7.6	1267	32,600C	1.285″/CCI 500/*
No.2	4.3	992	4.8	1133	33,000C	1.285″/CCI 500/*

Lead 125 CP (RN)

Powder	Grs.	MV (fps)	Grs.	MV (fps)	Press. (CUP/psi)	Comments
No.9	10.8	1177	12.0	1338	31,200C	1.22″/CCI 500/(C)
No.7	8.6	1133	9.6	1287	33,000C	1.22″/CCI 500
No.5	6.5	1100	7.2	1260	33,000C	1.22″/CCI 500
No.2	4.6	1030	5.1	1171	33,000C	1.22″/CCI 500

*Exceeds SAAMI maximum OAL.

Lead 130 Clements (RN)

Powder	Grs.	MV (fps)	Grs.	MV (fps)	Press. (CUP/psi)	Comments
No.9	10.4	1106	11.5	1257	29,100C	1.22″/CCI 500/(C)
No.7	8.1	1095	9.0	1244	32,000C	1.22″/CCI 500
No.5	6.3	1043	7.0	1185	31,900C	1.22″/CCI 500
No.2	4.0	970	4.4	1102	33,000C	1.22″/CCI 500

Lead 140 CP (SWC)

Powder	Grs.	MV (fps)	Grs.	MV (fps)	Press. (CUP/psi)	Comments
No.9	9.9	1079	11.0	1226	30,400C	1.34″/CCI 500/(M)/(C)/*
No.7	7.8	1033	8.7	1180	33,000C	1.34″/CCI 500/*
No.5	6.2	1015	6.9	1158	33,000C	1.34″/CCI 500/*
No.2	4.3	948	4.8	1077	32,500C	1.34″/CCI 500/*

(M) USPSA/IPSC Major Power Factor.

Never exceed maximum load nor use any load exhibiting signs of excessive pressure. Begin at suggested starting load and work up carefully.

Lead 145 Intercast (SWC)/CP (RN)

Powder	Grs.	MV (fps)	Grs.	MV (fps)	Press. (CUP/psi)	Comments
3N37	5.6	1085	6.3	1211	34,700p	1.26"/SWC
No.9	9.5	1062	10.5	1207	30,700C	1.25"/CCI 500/RN/ (M)/(C)/*
N350	5.2	1051	6.0	1180	34,700p	1.26"/SWC
No.5	6.1	1028	6.8	1168	33,000C	1.25"/CCI 500/RN/*
No.7	7.7	1025	8.5	1165	31,400C	1.25"/CCI 500/RN/*
No.2	4.3	949	4.8	1078	33,000C	1.25"/CCI 500/RN/*

*Exceeds SAAMI maximum OAL.

Lead 158-160

Powder	Grs.	MV (fps)	Grs.	MV (fps)	Press. (CUP/psi)	Comments
Blue Dot	6.5	1019	7.0	1123	35,700C	
No.9	8.6	982	9.5	1116	29,500C	1.25"/CCI 500/RN/ (M)/(C)
No.7	7.2	981	8.0	1115	32,800C	1.25"/CCI 500/RN/(M)
HS7	6.6	966	7.2	1083	35,100C	
HS6	5.8	939	6.2	1064	34,200C	
No.5	5.4	922	6.0	1048	33,000C	1.25"/CCI 500/RN
WAP	4.6	930	5.5	1035	34,200p	(160-gr.)
SR7625	3.5	898	3.9	1030	35,400C	(158-gr.)
No.2	4.1	902	4.5	1025	32,500C	1.25"/CCI 500/RN
IMR-PB	3.6	914	4.1	1011	32,900C	(158-gr.)
Unique	4.6	826	5.1	975	33,400C	
HP38	4.1	828	4.5	904	34,000C	
Universal			4.1	901	25,400C	
IMR700-X	3.2	828	3.6	900	34,400C	(158-gr.)
W231	4.0	818	4.4	898	34,100C	
Trap100	4.4	832	4.8	896	33,400C	
Bullseye	3.9	780	4.2	834	34,000C	
Universal			4.1	811	27,400C	JHP

(M) USPSA/IPSC Major Power Factor.

88

Powder	Grs.	MV (fps)	Grs.	MV (fps)	Press. (CUP/psi)	Comments
No.5	8.6	1370	9.6	1557	33,000C	Spr JHP/1.195"/CCI 500
No.7	10.2	1324	11.3	1504	31,800C	Spr JHP/1.195"/CCI 500
No.2	5.2	1200	5.8	1379	33,000C	Spr JHP/1.195"/CCI 500

90

Powder	Grs.	MV (fps)	Grs.	MV (fps)	Press. (CUP/psi)	Comments
Unique	6.8	1354	7.4	1494	31,000C	JHP
Trap100	7.0	1324	7.4	1474	32,300C	JHP
Bullseye	5.7	1288	6.3	1449	31,600C	JHP
HP38	6.5	1287	7.0	1448	34,600C	JHP
W231	6.4	1280	6.9	1436	34,200C	JHP
Universal			7.0	1379	32,000C	JHP
IMR700-X	5.1	1279	5.6	1378	35,100C	JHP

95

Powder	Grs.	MV (fps)	Grs.	MV (fps)	Press. (CUP/psi)	Comments
No.7	10.3	1294	11.4	1471	31,700C	IMI FMJ/1.225"/CCI 500
No.5	8.2	1262	9.1	1434	31,500C	IMI FMJ/1.225"/CCI 500
No.2	5.1	1161	5.7	1323	33,000C	IMI FMJ/1.225"/CCI 500

100

Powder	Grs.	MV (fps)	Grs.	MV (fps)	Press. (CUP/psi)	Comments
No.7	9.9	1270	11.0	1450	33,000C	Hdy FMJ/1.24"/CCI 500
Blue Dot	9.9	1329	10.5	1438	30,400C	FMJ
No.9	12.2	1256	13.5	1427	29,300C	Hdy FMJ/1.24"/ CCI 500/(C)
No.5	7.8	1252	8.7	1423	33,000C	Hdy FMJ/1.24"/CCI 500
HP38	6.1	1248	6.6	1374	32,300C	JHP
W231	6.1	1240	6.5	1372	33,600C	FMJ
Unique	5.8	1236	6.5	1367	31,400C	FMJ
Trap100	6.7	1244	7.1	1361	32,900C	JHP
Universal			6.6	1342	33,000C	FMJ
Bullseye	5.5	1189	5.9	1314	32,000C	FMJ
No.2	5.3	1148	5.9	1300	33,000C	Hdy FMJ/1.24"/CCI 500
IMR700-X	4.8	1171	5.2	1279	32,300C	
IMR-PB	5.6	1190	6.2	1276	30,000C	

115

Powder	Grs.	MV (fps)	Grs.	MV (fps)	Press. (CUP/psi)	Comments
3N37	6.5	1270	8.0	1436	34,700p	Hdy HP-XTP/1.24"
N340	6.0	1255	7.0	1401	34,700p	Hdy HP-XTP/1.24"
No.9	11.7	1228	13.0	1395	32,800C	Hdy FMJ/1.24"/ CCI 500/(C)
N350	5.6	1178	7.2	1368	34,700p	Hdy HP-XTP/1.24"
No.7	9.3	1186	10.3	1340	33,000C	Hdy FMJ/1.24"/CCI 500
WAP	6.6	1190	7.8	1340	34,300p	JHP
No.5	7.5	1162	8.3	1321	33,000C	Hdy FMJ/1.24"/CCI 500
N320	5.1	1193	5.9	1321	34,700p	Hdy HP-XTP/1.24"
Blue Dot	8.7	1128	9.2	1244	31,600C	JHP
Universal			6.0	1229	32,800C	JHP
IMR-PB	5.5	1147	6.0	1220	31,600C	
IMR700-X	4.5	1154	4.9	1219	33,400C	
HP38	5.7	1096	6.1	1213	34,000C	JHP
HS6	8.0	1142	8.5	1207	32,300C	JHP
No.2	5.1	1056	5.7	1200	32,200C	Hdy FMJ/1.24"/CCI 500
Trap100	6.0	1114	6.4	1196	32,700C	JHP
W231	5.6	1089	6.0	1192	32,900C	JHP
Unique	5.8	1099	6.2	1188	30,400C	JHP
Bullseye	5.1	1054	5.5	1161	28,000C	JHP

Caution: Loads exceeding SAAMI OAL Maximum must be verified for bullet-to-rifling clearance and magazine functioning. Where a specific primer or bullet is indicated those components must be used, no substitutions! Where only a maximum load is shown, reduce starting load 10%, unless otherwise specified.

Key: (C) = compressed charge; C = CUP; p = psi; Plinker = Plinker; Bns = Barnes; Hdy = Hornady; Lap = Lapua; Nos = Nosler; Rem = Remington; Sra = Sierra; Spr = Speer; Win = Winchester.

124-125

Powder	STARTING Grs.	MV (fps)	MAXIMUM Grs.	MV (fps)	Press. (CUP/psi)	Comments
3N37	7.2	1267	8.0	1411	34,700p	Hdy FMJ-FP/1.26"
N340	6.1	1214	7.1	1360	34,700p	Hdy FMJ-FP/1.26"
N350	6.4	1205	7.5	1354	34,700p	Hdy FMJ-FP/1.26"
No.9	11.3	1184	12.5	1346	33,000C	IMI FMJ/1.245"/CCI 500/(C)
WAP	6.2	1150	7.3	1270	34,300p	FMJ (124-gr.)
No.7	8.6	1111	9.6	1263	31,700C	IMI FMJ/1.245"/CCI 500
HS6	7.6	1116	8.2	1237	34,400C	FMJ
No.5	6.8	1079	7.6	1230	33,000C	IMI FMJ/1.245"/CCI 500
Blue Dot	8.5	1187	9.0	1209	31,900C	FMJ
Bullseye	4.9	1119	5.2	1180	32,000C	FMJ
Unique	5.5	1082	6.0	1177	31,600C	FMJ
Universal			5.7	1177	31,800C	FMJ (124-gr.)
No.2	4.9	1023	5.4	1163	32,200C	IMI FMJ/1.245"/CCI 500
IMR-PB	5.4	999	5.8	1131	33,400C	
SR7625	5.4	1060	5.8	1124	35,000C	
W231	5.2	980	5.6	1111	32,000C	FMJ
HP38	5.1	984	5.6	1109	31,600C	FMJ
Trap100	5.4	996	6.0	1107	31,100C	FMJ
IMR700-X	4.4	937	4.8	1012	33,400C	

130

Powder	STARTING Grs.	MV (fps)	MAXIMUM Grs.	MV (fps)	Press. (CUP/psi)	Comments
No.9	10.7	1148	11.9	1305	33,000C	PMC FMJ/1.25"/CCI 500/(C)
WAP	6.3	1120	7.3	1250	34,600p	FMJ
No.7	8.3	1060	9.2	1209	33,000C	PMC FMJ/1.25"/CCI 500
No.5	6.6	1057	7.3	1201	33,000C	PMC FMJ/1.25"/CCI 500
Blue Dot	7.9	1132	8.4	1194	32,000C	FMJ
HS6	6.7	1028	7.1	1169	33,600C	FMJ
Universal			5.5	1142	32,400C	FMJ
Bullseye	4.4	1009	4.9	1128	29,000C	FMJ
No.2	4.7	978	5.2	1116	33,000C	PMC FMJ/1.25"/CCI 500
Unique	5.4	1040	5.8	1111	27,600C	FMJ
IMR-PB	5.2	974	5.6	1111	34,200C	FMJ
SR7625	5.1	969	5.5	1100	34,900C	FMJ
HP38	4.8	889	5.3	1004	32,300C	FMJ
W231	4.8	878	5.3	1000	32,100C	FMJ
Trap100	5.0	867	5.4	989	31,600C	FMJ
IMR700-X	4.1	856	4.5	986	33,100C	FMJ

135

Powder	STARTING Grs.	MV (fps)	MAXIMUM Grs.	MV (fps)	Press. (CUP/psi)	Comments
No.9	9.6	1055	10.7	1199	27,100C	CP FMJ/1.25"/CCI 500
No.7	8.3	1045	9.0	1190	33,000C	CP FMJ/1.25"/CCI 500
No.5	6.3	1003	7.0	1140	31,400C	CP FMJ/1.25"/CCI 500
No.2	4.9	1000	5.2	1140	33,000C	CP FMJ/1.25"/CCI 500

147-150

Powder	STARTING Grs.	MV (fps)	MAXIMUM Grs.	MV (fps)	Press. (CUP/psi)	Comments
No.9	9.9	1082	11.0	1229	33,000C	Sra FMJ/1.28"/CCI 500/(M)
3N37	5.9	1099	6.9	1224	34,700p	Hdy HP-XTP/1.26"
N350	5.7	1078	6.6	1197	34,700p	Hdy HP-XTP/1.26"
No.9	9.2	1034	10.2	1175	29,400C	Spr TMJ/1.23"/CCI 500
No.7	7.7	1010	8.5	1148	32,700C	FMJ/1.25"/CCI 500
No.7	7.8	1008	8.7	1146	31,500C	Spr TMJ/1.23"/CCI 500
Blue Dot	6.9	1045	7.3	1142	35,300C	
Unique	5.3	1056	5.5	1116	33,300C	
No.7	7.6	975	8.5	1115	33,000C	Sra FMJ/1.28"/CCI 500
HS7	7.4	1012	8.1	1114	33,000C	
No.9	8.7	978	9.7	1111	27,900C	FMJ/1.25"/CCI 500
WAP	5.5	990	6.3	1110	34,500p	JHP (147-gr.)
No.5	6.1	970	6.8	1100	33,000C	Spr TMJ/1.23"/CCI 500
No.5	5.8	970	6.5	1100	33,000C	Sra FMJ/1.28"/CCI 500
No.5	5.9	946	6.5	1075	30,100C	FMJ/1.25"/CCI 500
SR7625	4.0	880	4.7	1063	34,700C	
No.2	4.8	932	5.3	1059	32,400C	Sra FMJ/1.28"/CCI 500
IMR-PB	4.4	862	4.7	1040	32,000C	
HS6	6.4	954	7.0	1040	32,700C	
No.2	4.3	913	4.8	1038	32,300C	FMJ/1.25"/CCI 500
No.2	4.4	913	4.9	1038	33,000C	Spr TMJ/1.23"/CCI 500
Trap100	4.7	856	5.1	968	34,000C	
HP38	4.8	871	5.0	967	33,800C	
Universal			4.5	961	28,800C	JHP (147-gr.)
Bullseye	4.2	848	4.5	938	34,000C	
IMR700-X	4.0	834	4.3	937	34,800C	
W231	4.6	869	4.9	924	33,800C	

158

Powder	STARTING Grs.	MV (fps)	MAXIMUM Grs.	MV (fps)	Press. (CUP/psi)	Comments
No.9	8.7	986	9.7	1121	31,000C	Hdy JHP/1.25"/CCI 500/(M)
No.7	7.2	936	8.0	1064	31,000C	Hdy JHP/1.25"/CCI 500
No.5	5.6	903	6.2	1026	31,400C	Hdy JHP/1.25"/CCI 500
No.2	3.9	850	4.3	970	33,000C	Hdy JHP/1.25"/CCI 500

(M) USPSA/IPSC Major Power Factor.

Never exceed maximum load nor use any load exhibiting signs of excessive pressure. Begin at suggested starting load and work up carefully.

357 SIG

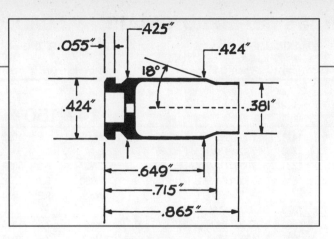

Case: Federal
Primer: Small Pistol
Barrel: 4″ Accurate
    (Unknown) Vihtavuori

Maximum Case Length: 0.865″
Trim to Length: 0.860″
Maximum Cartridge OAL: 1.140″
Minimum Cartridge OAL: 1.130″

Based on the 40 S&W case, the 357 SIG was intended to offer 357 Magnum ballistics from a 35-caliber pistol with the same dimensions of the compact 40 S&W guns. Reviews are mixed. Some labs report serious problems getting consistent ballistics with this chambering; others say it is a breeze.

It remains to be seen if there is sufficient demand for a compact pistol chambering offering slightly less recoil than the 40 S&W but with no other notable advantages.

357 SIG LOADING DATA

Powder	—STARTING— Grs.	MV (fps)	—MAXIMUM— Grs.	MV (fps)	Press. (CUP/psi)	Comments
Lead 115 Lane (SWC)						
No.9			13.5	1430	39,000p	1.14″/(C)
No.7			11.0	1344	37,800p	1.14″
No.5			9.0	1319	38,500p	1.14″
No.2			6.2	1249	38,200p	1.14″
Lead 122 CP (FN)						
No.9			13.0	1383	36,100p	1.14″/(C)
No.7			10.7	1321	37,900p	1.14″
No.5			8.8	1300	37,100p	1.14″
No.2			5.8	1217	38,100p	1.14″
Lead 147 Lane						
No.7			9.6	1218	40,000p	1.14″
No.5			7.5	1170	39,600p	1.14″
No.2			4.7	1049	36,800p	1.14″
88						
No.5			11.1	1616	39,000p	Spr JHP/1.13″
No.7			13.1	1601	39,300p	Spr JHP/1.13″
No.9			15.0	1545	32,100p	Spr JHP/1.13″/(C)
95						
No.5			11.0	1572	39,200p	Sra FMJ/1.135″
No.7			13.0	1562	38,900p	Sra FMJ/1.135″
No.9			15.0	1530	32,600p	Sra FMJ/1.135″/(C)

Powder	—STARTING— Grs.	MV (fps)	—MAXIMUM— Grs.	MV (fps)	Press. (CUP/psi)	Comments
100						
No.9			14.5	1516	35,100p	Hdy FMJ/1.14″/(C)
No.5			10.5	1496	38,800p	Hdy FMJ/1.14″
No.7			12.2	1490	38,500p	Hdy FMJ/1.14″
115						
No.9			13.5	1434	36,900p	Hdy XTP/1.14″/(C)
N350			8.7	1400		Hdy XTP/1.135″
No.7			11.3	1385	39,100p	Hdy XTP/1.14″
No.5			9.4	1354	37,900p	Hdy XTP/1.14″
124						
No.9			13.0	1387	39,100p	Hdy XTP/1.14″/(C)
N350			8.2	1330		Hdy XTP/1.135″
No.5			9.2	1325	39,600p	Hdy XTP/1.14″
No.7			11.0	1320	37,100p	Hdy XTP/1.14″
130						
No.9			12.0	1285	35,900p	Sra FMJ/1.135″/(C)
No.7			10.4	1278	39,300p	Sra FMJ/1.135″
No.5			8.8	1253	38,300p	Sra FMJ/1.135″
147						
N350			6.9	1170		Hdy XTP/1.135″
No.7			9.2	1160	38,600p	Hdy XTP/1.14″
No.5			7.9	1159	38,400p	Hdy XTP/1.14″

Never exceed maximum load nor use any load exhibiting signs of excessive pressure. Begin at suggested starting load and work up carefully.

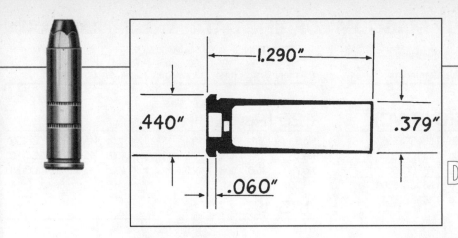

Case: Frontier
Primer: Small Pistol (Mag & Target)
CCI 500 (DE)
Small Pistol Magnum (T/C)
Barrel: 6″ Accurate (S&W 686)
10″ Accurate (T/C)
7″ Hodgdon

10″ Hodgdon (T/C)
7″ Vihtavuori
Bullet Diameter: 0.357″-0.358″
Maximum Case Length: 1.290″
Trim to Length: 1.280″
Maximum Cartridge OAL: 1.590″
Minimum Cartridge OAL: 1.540″

Introduced in 1935 and chambered in the recently discontinued Model 27 S&W revolver, the 357 Magnum was originally factory loaded to very high pressures. In the 8³/₈″ S&W, early 158-grain lead SWC loads often generated an honest 1500 fps muzzle velocity.

In recent decades, pressures have been reduced considerably, nay vastly. Even with the best of modern powders, it is impossible to achieve anything approaching original load performance from any revolver. Nevertheless, the 357 Magnum can still deliver substantial performance. It is generally considered a fully adequate self-defense cartridge. It is also capable for hunting smaller species of big game.

Bullet selection is enormous, and the best modern jacketed bullets offer substantial performance where expansion is desired.

Case capacity with a 158-grain bullet, seated normally, is about 17.8 grains of water. For target loads, at reduced velocity, use faster powders for best results. H110, W296, No. 9 and N110 are good 357 Magnum choices.

357 MAGNUM LOADING DATA

Lead 124 Intercast (LSWC)

Powder	STARTING Grs.	MV (fps)	MAXIMUM Grs.	MV (fps)	Press. (CUP/psi)	Comments
N110	15.0	1492	17.0	1668	33,300p	1.614″
N350	8.0	1352	9.1	1460	33,300p	1.614″
N340	7.6	1338	8.6	1450	33,300p	1.614″

Lead 145 Intercast (LSWC)

Powder	STARTING Grs.	MV (fps)	MAXIMUM Grs.	MV (fps)	Press. (CUP/psi)	Comments
N110	13.4	1428	15.0	1566	33,300p	1.614″
3N37	7.2	1231	8.3	1349	33,300p	1.614″
N350	6.5	1187	7.8	1319	33,300p	1.614″

Lead 150 SWC

Powder	STARTING Grs.	MV (fps)	MAXIMUM Grs.	MV (fps)	Press. (CUP/psi)	Comments
No.9	11.9	1182	13.2	1343	34,100p	1.595″/*
No.7	9.5	1142	10.6	1298	34,500p	1.595″/*
No.5	7.6	1098	8.4	1248	34,300p	1.595″/*

*Exceeds SAAMI maximum OAL.

Lead 158 SWC

Powder	STARTING Grs.	MV (fps)	MAXIMUM Grs.	MV (fps)	Press. (CUP/psi)	Comments
No.9	11.0	1126	12.2	1280	32,400p	1.58″/CCI 500
No.5	7.4	1090	8.2	1239	33,800p	1.58″/CCI 500
No.7	9.5	1090	10.5	1239	34,400p	1.58″/CCI 500

Lead 158-160

Powder	STARTING Grs.	MV (fps)	MAXIMUM Grs.	MV (fps)	Press. (CUP/psi)	Comments
N110	12.7	1363	14.1	1492	33,300p	1.575″/Intercast FN
H4227	13.0	1223	15.0	1396	32,600C	
HS7	9.0	1162	10.0	1299	25,600C	
Universal			6.7	1297	34,600C	RN
3N37	6.9	1141	7.8	1254	33,300p	1.575″/Intercast FN
N350	6.4	1160	7.4	1253	33,300p	1.575″/Intercast FN
N340	6.1	1152	6.9	1230	33,300p	1.575″/Intercast FN
HS6	7.0	1100	8.0	1161	21,400C	
Trap100	3.3	788	4.0	864	17,100C	
HP38	3.4	796	3.9	846	15,700C	

▶▶▶▶▶▶▶▶▶▶▶▶▶▶▶▶▶▶▶▶▶▶▶▶▶

Caution: Loads exceeding SAAMI OAL Maximum must be verified for bullet-to-rifling clearance and magazine functioning. Where a specific primer or bullet is indicated those components must be used, no substitutions! Where only a maximum load is shown, reduce starting load 10%, unless otherwise specified.

Key: (C) = compressed charge; C = CUP; p = psi; Plink = Plinker; Bns = Barnes; Hdy = Hornady; Lap = Lapua; Nos = Nosler; Rem = Remington; Sra = Sierra; Spr = Speer; Win = Winchester.

Never exceed maximum load nor use any load exhibiting signs of excessive pressure. Begin at suggested starting load and work up carefully.

Lead 174 Lyman 358429 (SWC)

Powder	Grs.	MV (fps)	Grs.	MV (fps)	Press. (CUP/psi)	Comments
XMP5744			14.5	1361	34,400p	1.66″/CCI 500/*
No.9	11.0	1138	12.5	1293	35,000p	1.66″/CCI 500/*
No.7	9.2	1072	10.2	1218	34,400p	1.66″/CCI 500/*
No.5	7.2	1025	8.0	1170	35,000p	1.66″/CCI 500/*
No.2	5.9	985	6.5	1119	34,600p	1.66″/CCI 500/*

*Exceeds SAAMI maximum OAL.

Lead 200

Powder	Grs.	MV (fps)	Grs.	MV (fps)	Press. (CUP/psi)	Comments
H110	9.5	1106	11.5	1212	31,200C	
W296	9.5	1089	11.5	1209	32,000C	
Her2400	10.0	1088	11.0	1189	37,990C	
H4227	10.5	1062	12.0	1174	31,800C	
IMR4227	10.5	1050	12.0	1169	33,100C	
HS7	7.5	1041	8.5	1142	29,600C	
HS6	5.2	822	6.8	1073	30,600C	
Trap100	3.4	721	4.2	829	28,800C	
W231	3.4	700	4.2	825	28,400C	
HP38	3.4	709	4.2	821	28,100C	

90

Powder	Grs.	MV (fps)	Grs.	MV (fps)	Press. (CUP/psi)	Comments
HS6	11.0	1725	11.5	1855	32,400C	JHP
Bullseye	7.4	1422	8.8	1690	35,600C	JHP
HP38	6.9	1382	8.4	1668	27,100C	JHP
Trap100	6.5	1369	8.5	1627	28,200C	JHP
W231	6.8	1344	8.2	1610	26,800C	JHP
SR4756	9.5	1364	10.5	1610	32,200C	JHP
IMR700-X	7.5	1393	8.5	1577	33,000C	JHP

110 (Revolver)

Powder	Grs.	MV (fps)	Grs.	MV (fps)	Press. (CUP/psi)	Comments
No.7	11.7	1253	13.0	1424	34,100p	Spr JHP/1.575″/CCI 500
No.5	9.7	1179	10.8	1340	34,500p	Spr JHP/1.575″/CCI 500
No.2	7.9	1165	8.8	1324	34,400p	Spr JHP/1.575″/CCI 500

110

Powder	Grs.	MV (fps)	Grs.	MV (fps)	Press. (CUP/psi)	Comments
N110			17.6	1910	32,400p	Hdy XTP/1.57″
H4227	18.0	1634	19.5	1816	34,200C	JSP
IMR4227	17.5	1544	19.0	1666	32,000C	JHP
HS7	12.0	1569	13.0	1646	29,800C	JSP
HS6	9.0	1492	10.6	1612	31,800C	JSP
3N37			9.1	1600	32,200p	Hdy XTP/1.57″
N350			9.1	1565	32,000p	Hdy XTP/1.57″
N340			7.1	1500	32,100p	Hdy XTP/1.57″
Blue Dot	11.0	1398	12.5	1480	37,200C	JHP
SR4756	9.2	1309	10.4	1449	29,800C	JHP
Trap100	6.0	1182	8.0	1432	29,400C	JSP
HP38	5.9	1167	7.9	1414	27,600C	JSP
W231	5.8	1150	7.8	1396	27,200C	JHP
IMR700-X	7.0	1261	8.0	1394	28,900C	JHP
Unique	7.2	1188	8.6	1312	38,600C	JHP
N320			6.0	1300	31,200C	Hdy XTP/1.57″

125 (Revolver)

Powder	Grs.	MV (fps)	Grs.	MV (fps)	Press. (CUP/psi)	Comments
No.5	9.1	1163	10.1	1322	35,000p	Hdy XTP/1.57″/CCI 500
No.2	7.4	1155	8.2	1312	34,400p	Hdy XTP/1.57″/CCI 500
No.7	10.8	1088	12.0	1236	33,400p	Hdy XTP/1.57″/CCI 500

125

Powder	Grs.	MV (fps)	Grs.	MV (fps)	Press. (CUP/psi)	Comments
H110			19.0	1822	34,200C	JHP
W296	18.5	1770	19.0	1820	34,000C	JHP
N110	16.5	1571	18.1	1738	33,300p	Hdy XTP/1.575″
H4227	16.0	1634	17.8	1683	34,600C	JHP
HS7	11.5	1511	12.5	1604	31,500C	JHP
HS6	8.5	1222	10.0	1542	34,800C	JHP
IMR4227	17.0	1366	18.0	1510	33,400C	JHP
Her2400	14.5	1344	16.0	1472	38,600C	JHP
Universal			8.8	1435	43,700C	JHP
3N37			8.4	1420	31,500p	Hdy XTP/1.57″
Blue Dot	10.5	1229	12.0	1366	36,600C	JHP
SR4756	8.0	1160	10.0	1360	34,800C	JHP
N340			6.9	1325	31,000p	Hdy XTP/1.57″
W231	5.0	1002	7.0	1321	27,600C	JHP
HP38	5.0	1007	7.0	1319	27,200C	JHP
IMR700-X	6.8	1229	7.5	1309	33,000C	JHP
Unique	7.0	1172	8.4	1294	37,700C	JHP
Trap100	5.0	952	7.0	1292	26,000C	JHP

130

Powder	Grs.	MV (fps)	Grs.	MV (fps)	Press. (CUP/psi)	Comments
H110	17.0	1670	18.5	1759	33,600C	JSP
H4227	15.5	1529	17.5	1648	33,600C	JSP
HS7	11.0	1439	12.0	1579	30,800C	JSP
HS6	8.2	1208	9.8	1503	33,600C	JSP
HP38	4.8	947	6.8	1267	28,800C	JSP
Trap100	4.8	919	6.8	1218	27,600C	JSP

140 (Revolver)

Powder	Grs.	MV (fps)	Grs.	MV (fps)	Press. (CUP/psi)	Comments
No.9	13.0	1187	14.4	1349	33,600p	Spr JHP/1.575″/CCI 500
No.7	10.4	1069	11.6	1215	33,600p	Spr JHP/1.575″/CCI 500
No.5	8.7	1060	9.7	1205	34,900p	Spr JHP/1.575″/CCI 500
No.2	7.0	1055	7.8	1199	34,400p	Spr JHP/1.575″/CCI 500

137-140

Powder	Grs.	MV (fps)	Grs.	MV (fps)	Press. (CUP/psi)	Comments
H110	16.5	1609	17.0	1687	33,600C	
W296	16.5	1596	17.0	1678	33,400C	JHP (140-gr.)
N110	15.6	1473	16.8	1620	33,300p	Spr HP/1.575″
H4227	15.0	1426	16.0	1574	34,600C	
Universal			8.5	1487	43,800C	JHP (140-gr.)
HS7	10.0	1243	11.0	1465	32,200C	
Her2400	13.5	1288	14.8	1458	39,600C	JHP (140-gr.)
Blue Dot	9.5	1204	10.5	1440	39,900C	JHP (140-gr.)
IMR4227	15.5	1384	16.5	1438	32,000C	JHP (140-gr.)
HS6	8.2	1097	9.6	1404	32,400C	
3N37	8.1	1239	9.1	1364	33,300p	Spr HP/1.575″

137-140 con't

Powder	STARTING Grs.	MV (fps)	MAXIMUM Grs.	MV (fps)	Press. (CUP/psi)	Comments
N350	7.9	1242	9.0	1361	33,300p	Spr HP/1.575″
N340	7.4	1215	8.2	1321	33,300p	Spr HP/1.575″
Unique	6.5	1128	8.0	1286	38,600C	JHP (140-gr.)
SR4756	8.0	1160	9.0	1274	33,600C	JHP (140-gr.)
IMR700-X	6.0	1044	6.5	1214	34,400C	JHP (140-gr.)
W231	4.5	875	6.5	1209	29,600C	JHP (140-gr.)

146-150

Powder	STARTING Grs.	MV (fps)	MAXIMUM Grs.	MV (fps)	Press. (CUP/psi)	Comments
H110	15.0	1450	15.5	1517	33,000C	JHP
W296	15.0	1444	15.5	1515	32,960C	JHP
Her2400	12.0	1230	14.0	1411	39,000C	JHP
Blue Dot	9.0	1179	10.0	1404	39,400C	JHP
Universal			7.7	1396	43,100C	JHP (146-gr.)
H4227	13.0	1244	15.0	1382	34,700C	JHP
IMR4227	14.0	1292	15.0	1371	33,800C	JHP
HS7	9.5	1222	10.5	1359	29,700C	JHP
Unique	6.2	1104	7.8	1340	36,500C	JHP
SR4756	7.8	1119	8.5	1259	34,000C	JHP
IMR700-X	5.3	944	6.0	1138	34,400C	JHP

150 (Revolver)

Powder	STARTING Grs.	MV (fps)	MAXIMUM Grs.	MV (fps)	Press. (CUP/psi)	Comments
No.9	12.5	1142	13.9	1298	33,400p	Nos JSP/1.59″/CCI 500
No.2	6.8	1040	7.5	1182	34,200p	Nos JSP/1.59″/CCI 500
No.7	10.0	1030	11.1	1171	33,300p	Nos JSP/1.59″/CCI 500
No.5	8.3	979	9.2	1112	34,000p	Nos JSP/1.59″/CCI 500

158 (Revolver)

Powder	STARTING Grs.	MV (fps)	MAXIMUM Grs.	MV (fps)	Press. (CUP/psi)	Comments
No.9	11.7	1110	13.0	1261	34,000p	Hdy XTP/1.58″/CCI 500
No.7	9.5	1002	10.5	1139	34,100p	Hdy XTP/1.58″/CCI 500
No.2	6.2	957	6.9	1088	33,500p	Hdy XTP/1.58″/CCI 500
No.5	7.7	950	8.6	1080	32,900p	Hdy XTP/1.58″/CCI 500

158-160

Powder	STARTING Grs.	MV (fps)	MAXIMUM Grs.	MV (fps)	Press. (CUP/psi)	Comments
N110	13.7	1321	15.1	1475	33,300p	Spr HP/1.575″
H110	14.0	1373	14.5	1456	35,400C	JSP
N110			12.8	1450	33,300p	Hdy XTP/1.57″
W296	14.0	1366	14.5	1441	35,600C	JSP
Her2400	11.5	1200	13.8	1388	37,000C	
H4227	12.5	1172	14.5	1377	34,100C	JSP
IMR4227	13.5	1239	14.5	1359	35,000C	JHP
Blue Dot	8.0	1148	9.8	1340	38,800C	
HS7	9.0	1157	10.0	1304	29,300C	JSP
Universal			7.5	1299	41,100C	JHP (158-gr.)
Unique	6.0	1090	7.6	1277	39,000C	
N350	7.4	1169	8.3	1259	33,300p	Spr HP/1.575″
HS6	8.5	1150	9.0	1240	29,000C	JSP
3N37	7.1	1114	8.2	1232	33,300p	Spr HP/1.575″
SR4756	7.5	1060	8.2	1220	35,200C	JHP
N340	6.5	1086	7.3	1182	33,300p	Spr HP/1.575″
N320	5.5	990	6.2	1096	33,300p	Spr HP/1.575″

170 (Revolver)

Powder	STARTING Grs.	MV (fps)	MAXIMUM Grs.	MV (fps)	Press. (CUP/psi)	Comments
No.9	11.0	1030	12.2	1170	33,700p	Sra FMJ/1.565″/CCI 500
No.2	5.8	932	6.4	1059	33,200p	Sra FMJ/1.565″/CCI 500
No.5	7.2	930	8.0	1057	33,700p	Sra FMJ/1.565″/CCI 500
No.7	8.6	916	9.6	1041	32,800p	Sra FMJ/1.565″/CCI 500

170

Powder	STARTING Grs.	MV (fps)	MAXIMUM Grs.	MV (fps)	Press. (CUP/psi)	Comments
H110	12.5	1214	13.5	1349	34,800C	
Her2400	11.5	1211	13.0	1344	39,800C	FMJ
W296	12.5	1219	13.5	1340	34,700C	FMJ
H4227	12.5	1184	13.5	1283	39,800C	
IMR4227	12.0	1129	13.5	1280	39,000C	FMJ
Blue Dot	8.5	1130	9.4	1214	39,100C	FMJ
Unique	5.8	1040	6.8	1150	39,700C	FMJ
HS7	8.2	989	9.2	1139	32,400C	
HS6	6.5	940	7.5	1084	28,400C	
HP38	4.2	904	5.2	1030	27,900C	
W231	4.0	878	5.0	1004	27,000C	FMJ

180 (Revolver)

Powder	STARTING Grs.	MV (fps)	MAXIMUM Grs.	MV (fps)	Press. (CUP/psi)	Comments
XMP5744			13.0	1196	34,900p	Hdy XTP/1.575″/CCI 500
No.9	10.5	1003	11.7	1140	35,000p	Hdy XTP/1.575″/CCI 500
No.5	7.2	915	8.0	1040	35,000p	Hdy XTP/1.575″/CCI 500
No.7	8.5	900	9.4	1023	34,900p	Hdy XTP/1.575″/CCI 500

180

Powder	STARTING Grs.	MV (fps)	MAXIMUM Grs.	MV (fps)	Press. (CUP/psi)	Comments
N110	12.5	1229	13.8	1368	33,300p	Spr TMJ/1.677″
H110	13.0	1268	13.5	1304	37,600C	
Her2400	11.0	1184	12.5	1303	38,400C	FMJ
W296	12.0	1194	13.5	1294	37,400C	FMJ
N110			11.1	1250	32,000C	Hdy XTP-HP/1.57″
H4227	12.0	1120	13.0	1240	37,200C	
IMR4227	12.0	1178	13.0	1234	38,000C	FMJ
Blue Dot	8.0	1121	9.0	1209	39,000C	FMJ
3N37	6.6	972	7.7	1096	33,300p	Spr TMJ/1.677″
N350	6.2	924	7.3	1062	33,300p	Spr TMJ/1.677″
N340	6.1	937	6.9	1049	33,300p	Spr TMJ/1.677″
W231	3.8	834	4.5	890	27,300C	FMJ

Caution: **Loads exceeding SAAMI OAL Maximum must be verified for bullet-to-rifling clearance and magazine functioning. Where a specific primer or bullet is indicated those components must be used, no substitutions! Where only a maximum load is shown, reduce starting load 10%, unless otherwise specified.**

Key: (C) = compressed charge; C = CUP; p = psi; Plink = Plinker; Bns = Barnes; Hdy = Hornady; Lap = Lapua; Nos = Nosler; Rem = Remington; Sra = Sierra; Spr = Speer; Win = Winchester.

Never exceed maximum load nor use any load exhibiting signs of excessive pressure. Begin at suggested starting load and work up carefully.

357 MAGNUM TARGET LOADING DATA

Powder	STARTING Grs.	MV (fps)	MAXIMUM Grs.	MV (fps)	Press. (CUP/psi)	Comments
Lead 148 DEWC						
No.2	3.0	746	4.0	919	20,300p	1.37"/CCI 500
Lead 148 HBWC						
Universal			4.0	989	17,700C	
Trap100	3.4	842	4.4	970	19,400C	
No.2	2.5	645	4.0	913	22,700p	1.32"/CCI 500
Lead 148 HBWC con't						
HP38	3.6	869	4.3	962	18,800C	
W231	3.6	841	4.5	960	19,600C	
Bullseye	3.5	830	4.0	904	17,100C	
IMR700-X	4.2	829	5.0	900	23,600C	
Lead 158 SWC						
No.2	4.0	864	5.0	1008	25,500p	1.51"/CCI 500

Minor reductions in powder charge might improve accuracy.

357 MAGNUM DESERT EAGLE SPECIFIC LOADING DATA

Powder	STARTING Grs.	MV (fps)	MAXIMUM Grs.	MV (fps)	Press. (CUP/psi)	Comments
150						
No.9	12.5	1163	13.9	1345	33,400p	Nos JSP/1.59"
158						
No.9	11.7	1077	13.0	1252	34,000p	Hdy XTP/1.58"
170						
No.9	11.0	1030	12.2	1159	33,700p	Sra FMJ/1.565"
180						
No.9	10.5	988	11.7	1126	35,000p	Hdy XTP/1.575"

357 MAGNUM T/C SPECIFIC LOADING DATA

Powder	STARTING Grs.	MV (fps)	MAXIMUM Grs.	MV (fps)	Press. (CUP/psi)	Comments
Lead 180 RCBS (TC-GC)						
No.9	10.3	1160	11.5	1330	35,000p	1.675"/CCI 500/*
XMP5744			13.0	1231	33,500p	1.675"/CCI 500/*
No.7	8.6	1074	9.5	1220	34,200p	1.675"/CCI 500/*
No.5	6.5	990	7.2	1122	35,000p	1.675"/CCI 500/*
No.2	5.2	877	5.8	997	32,400p	1.675"/CCI 500/*
125						
H110	18.0	1728	19.0	1914		
H4227	17.0	1710	18.0	1809		
HS7	12.0	1612	13.0	1722		
140						
H110	17.0	1711	18.0	1790		
H4227	16.0	1669	17.0	1719		
HS7	11.0	1527	12.0	1584		
146-150						
H110	15.0	1594	16.5	1689		
H4227	15.0	1613	16.0	1677		
146-150 con't						
HS7	10.0	1392	11.0	1522		
158-160						
H110	15.0	1539	16.0	1618		
H4227	14.0	1455	15.5	1550		
170						
H110	14.0	1324	15.0	1394		
H4227	13.0	1233	14.0	1280		
180						
H110	13.0	1222	14.0	1284		
H4227	12.0	1144	13.5	1261		
200						
N110	10.9	1068	12.1	1183	33,300p	Spr TMJ/1.697"
3N37	6.1	858	7.0	971	33,300p	Spr TMJ/1.697"
N350	5.9	802	6.9	941	33,300p	Spr TMJ/1.697"

* Exceeds SAAMI maximum OAL.

Never exceed maximum load nor use any load exhibiting taigns of excessive pressure. Begin at suggested starting load and work up carefully.

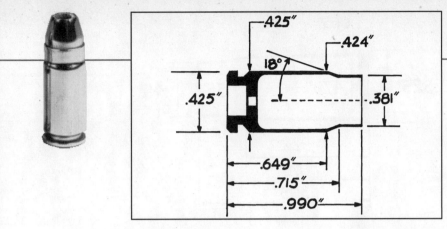

Case: Norma
Primer: CCI 350
Barrel: 10³/₄″ HP White
Bullet Diameter: 0.355″-0.356″

Maximum Case Length: 0.990″
Trim to Length: 0.987″
Maximum Cartridge OAL: 1.250″
Minimum Cartridge OAL: 1.190″

Developed by Randy Shelley in 1988, while he was employed at Dillon Precision, the 9x25mm Dillon, as it has come to be called, is based on the 10mm Automatic and offers IPSC shooters a superior choice for achieving Major Power Factor without resorting to extremely high pressures. The 9x25mm can safely launch light bullets fast enough to meet IPSC momentum requirements. This is the smallest cartridge that can do so.

Several manufacturers currently offer pistols chambered for the 9x25mm, and this cartridge seems likely to achieve commercial standardization in the near future.

9x25mm DILLON LOADING DATA

Powder	STARTING Grs.	MV (fps)	MAXIMUM Grs.	MV (fps)	Press. (CUP/psi)	Comments
Lead 115						
H110			17.9	2000	29,500p	RN/1.265″
115						
H110			17.5	1970	30,500p	Win JHP/1.252″

Caution: **Loads exceeding SAAMI OAL Maximum must be verified for bullet-to-rifling clearance and magazine functioning. Where a specific primer or bullet is indicated those components must be used, no substitutions! Where only a maximum load is shown, reduce starting load 10%, unless otherwise specified.**

Key: (C) = compressed charge; C = CUP; p = psi; Plink = Plinker; Bns = Barnes; Hdy = Hornady; Lap = Lapua; Nos = Nosler; Rem = Remington; Sra = Sierra; Spr = Speer; Win = Winchester.

38-40

Winchester (WCF)
(Revolver)

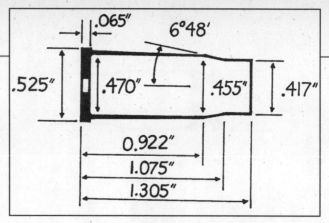

Case: Winchester
Primer: Winchester WLP
Barrel: 6½" Accurate (Ruger)
Bullet Diameter: 0.401"-0.403"

Maximum Case Length: 1.305" (Very Rare)
Trim to Length: 1.295" (Rare)
Maximum Cartridge OAL: 1.593"
Minimum Cartridge OAL: 1.560"

Introduced by Winchester in 1874, chambered in the Model 73 lever-action, the 38-40 is very likely the first of a long pedigree of factory wildcat centerfire cartridges. This number was created by necking down the 44-40 to accept 40-caliber bullets.

Colt wasted little time, soon the 38-40 was also chambered in their famous single-action revolver. Several companies are currently importing reproduction revolvers chambered for the 38-40.

Those interested in a Colt SAA chambering with substantial punch but with reduced recoil should find the 38-40 an interesting choice. For various reasons, loading is temperamental—thin and short case necks, huge usable capacity and low working pressures—good results require a bit of patience.

Interestingly, it seems at least possible the 38-40 was named in the following manner: 38, for the original charge of blackpowder, 40 for bullet diameter. The facts? The orig-

inal blackpowder charge was 38 grains, not 40 as is often reported, and designed bullet diameter is 0.401". Oversize bores are common—for best results measure cylinder throats and size cast bullets accordingly.

Although the 38-40 is denigrated by many today, it has to be noted that original 38-40 loads fired from a revolver were ballistically indistinguishable from the 180-grain loading in the 40 S&W! Top loads listed here are serious medicine.

These loads leave a huge amount of unburned powder behind. Faster powders have been extensively tested by the author. Those are extremely sensitive to powder position. Intermediate powders are dirty *and* unduly sensitive to powder position!

These loads are for use only in guns known to be safe with smokeless powder.

Usable case capacity with a 180-grain bullet, seated normally, is about 32.9 grains of water. Also note, cases are typically short.

38-40 WINCHESTER (WCF) LOADING DATA (Revolver Specific Loads)

Lead 155 Colorado Cast Bullet (RN)

Powder	STARTING Grs.	MV (fps)	MAXIMUM Grs.	MV (fps)	Press. (CUP/psi)	Comments
XMP5744			16.5	1013	12,700C	

Lead 185 Colorado Cast Bullet (FP-BB)

Powder	STARTING Grs.	MV (fps)	MAXIMUM Grs.	MV (fps)	Press. (CUP/psi)	Comments
A1680	21.2	964	23.5	1095	14,000C	1.58"
A2015BR	22.5	821	25.0	933	13,800C	1.58"
XMP5744			14.5	900	13,600C	1.58"

150

Powder	STARTING Grs.	MV (fps)	MAXIMUM Grs.	MV (fps)	Press. (CUP/psi)	Comments
A1680	24.8	1096	27.5	1246	13,200C	Sra HP/1.575"
A2015BR	27.0	994	30.0	1130	13,900C	Sra HP/1.575"
XMP5744			17.5	1039	13,200C	Sra HP/1.574"

180

Powder	STARTING Grs.	MV (fps)	MAXIMUM Grs.	MV (fps)	Press. (CUP/psi)	Comments
A1680	23.0	1052	25.5	1196	14,000C	Spr HP/1.585"
A2015BR	24.3	864	27.0	982	14,000C	Spr HP/1.585"
XMP5744			16.5	961	13,700C	Spr HP/1.585"

Caution: Loads exceeding SAAMI OAL Maximum must be verified for bullet-to-rifling clearance and magazine functioning. Where a specific primer or bullet is indicated those components must be used, no substitutions! Where only a maximum load is shown, reduce starting load 10%, unless otherwise specified.

Key: (C) = compressed charge; C = CUP; p = psi; Plink = Plinker; Bns = Barnes; Hdy = Hornady; Lap = Lapua; Nos = Nosler; Rem = Remington; Sra = Sierra; Spr = Speer; Win = Winchester.

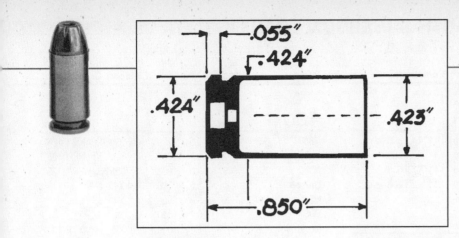

Case: Hornady
Primer: Small Pistol
Barrel: 4″ Accurate/4″ Hodgdon
5½″ Vihtavuori
4″ Winchester

Bullet Diameter: 0.400″-0.401″
Maximum Case Length: 0.850″
Trim to Length: 0.845″
Maximum Cartridge OAL: 1.135″
Minimum Cartridge OAL: 1.095″

By modern standards, the 40 S&W was a unique development. In this era of committees and grinding analysis, it is hard to imagine that Winchester and Smith & Wesson could team up to take this cartridge from concept to introduction in six months. Nevertheless, that is exactly what happened.

As the FBI was looking for a way to back out of their evidently disastrous decision to retire the 45 Automatic in lieu of the 9mm Luger, it was decided the 10mm bore offered a good compromise. The cartridge used in those trials, the 10mm Automatic, was deemed overly powerful. A lower velocity, lower pressure 10mm loading was standardized.

It took no genius to realize a shortened full-pressure 10mm

cartridge could achieve FBI-stipulated performance, and offer superior intrinsic accuracy and a smaller grip frame.

The 40 S&W works at about the same pressure as the 9mm Luger. With greater usable capacity and more bore area, the 40 S&W can launch substantially heavier bullets just as fast. This cartridge easily achieves IPSC Major Power Factor.

The meteoric rise to popularity of the 40 S&W is nothing short of amazing. Introduced in early 1990, this has already become a dominant chambering for all self-defense applications.

Usable case capacity with a 180-grain bullet, seated normally, is about 10.6 grains of water. Universal, 3N37, WAP, N350 and No. 9 are good choices for the 40 S&W.

40 SMITH & WESSON LOADING DATA

Powder	—STARTING— Grs.	MV (fps)	—MAXIMUM— Grs.	MV (fps)	Press. (CUP/psi)	Comments
Lead 145 Bull-X						
No.5	7.2	1038	8.0	1179	34,900p	1.115″/CCI 500
No.7	9.0	1030	10.0	1171	33,700p	1.115″/CCI 500
No.2	5.9	1016	6.6	1155	33,400p	1.115″/CCI 500
No.9	10.8	988	12.0	1123	29,200p	1.115″/CCI 500
Lead 155 Master Cast (SWC)						
No.5	6.8	1019	7.5	1158	35,000p	1.13″/CCI 500/(M)
No.7	8.7	1008	9.7	1146	34,600p	1.13″/CCI 500/(M)
No.9	10.8	1005	12.0	1142	32,100p	1.13″/CCI 500/(M)
No.2	5.7	982	6.3	1116	34,100p	1.13″/CCI 500
Lead 170						
WAP	5.7	980	6.4	1075	33,400p	
Lead 175 CP (SWC)						
No.7	7.6	892	8.4	1014	35,000p	1.115″/CCI 500/(M)
No.9	9.2	878	10.2	998	34,900p	1.115″/CCI 500

Powder	—STARTING— Grs.	MV (fps)	—MAXIMUM— Grs.	MV (fps)	Press. (CUP/psi)	Comments
Lead 175 CP (SWC) con't						
No.5	5.5	868	6.1	986	35,000p	1.115″/CCI 500
No.2	4.8	858	5.3	975	34,200p	1.115″/CCI 500
Lead 185 Colorado Custom (FN)						
No.7	7.4	871	8.2	990	35,000p	1.12″/CCI 500/(M)
No.5	5.4	858	6.0	975	35,000p	1.12″/CCI 500/(M)
No.9	8.7	841	9.7	956	33,500p	1.12″/CCI 500
No.2	4.6	829	5.1	942	33,000p	1.12″/CCI 500
Lead 195 Clements (FN)						
No.9	8.1	812	9.0	923	35,000p	1.11″/CCI 500/(M)
No.5	4.8	798	5.3	907	35,000p	1.11″/CCI 500/(M)
No.7	6.1	777	6.8	883	34,800p	1.11″/CCI 500
No.2	4.1	774	4.6	880	34,900p	1.11″/CCI 500
Lead 200						
WAP	4.2	795	4.9	900	33,000p	

(M) USPSA/IPSC Major Power Factor.

➤➤➤➤➤➤➤➤➤➤➤➤➤➤➤➤➤➤➤➤➤➤➤➤➤➤➤

Never exceed maximum load nor use any load exhibiting signs of excessive pressure. Begin at suggested starting load and work up carefully.

Lead 205 Clements (FN)

Powder	—STARTING— Grs.	MV (fps)	—MAXIMUM— Grs.	MV (fps)	Press. (CUP/psi)	Comments
No.9	7.8	774	8.7	880	35,000p	1.11"/CCI 500/(M)
No.7	5.9	744	6.6	845	33,700p	1.11"/CCI 500
No.2	3.9	737	4.3	838	32,400p	1.11"/CCI 500
No.5	4.5	736	5.0	836	32,600p	1.11"/CCI 500

135

Powder	Grs.	MV (fps)	Grs.	MV (fps)	Press. (CUP/psi)	Comments
Universal			7.5	1324	32,500C	JHP
No.5	8.4	1114	9.3	1266	34,900p	Nos JHP/1.125"/CCI 500
No.2	6.8	1097	7.6	1247	34,700p	Nos JHP/1.125"/CCI 500
No.7	10.1	1089	11.2	1237	33,900p	Nos JHP/1.125"/CCI 500

150

Powder	Grs.	MV (fps)	Grs.	MV (fps)	Press. (CUP/psi)	Comments
WAP	7.0	1110	7.5	1190	32,800p	JHP
No.5	7.5	1030	8.3	1170	35,000p	Nos JHP/1.12"/CCI 500/(M)
No.2	6.3	1016	7.0	1155	34,200p	Nos JHP/1.12"/CCI 500
No.7	9.2	1000	10.2	1136	34,300p	Nos JHP/1.12"/CCI 500

155

Powder	Grs.	MV (fps)	Grs.	MV (fps)	Press. (CUP/psi)	Comments
3N37	7.2	1152	8.0	1267	33,300p	Hdy XTP/1.126"
N350	6.5	1131	7.5	1247	33,300p	Hdy XTP/1.126"
N340	5.8	1113	6.8	1231	33,300p	Hdy XTP/1.126"
N330	5.9	1125	6.6	1220	33,300p	Hdy XTP/1.126"
Universal			6.6	1186	33,200C	JHP
N320	5.1	1091	5.8	1178	33,300p	Hdy XTP/1.126"
HS7	9.0	1057	9.8	1174		JHP
WAP	6.9	1103	7.4	1170	33,500p	JHP
SR7625	6.0	1027	6.4	1106		JHP
HS6	8.0	1005	9.0	1103		JHP
W540	8.6	989	9.3	1094		JHP
W231	5.7	970	6.3	1074		JHP
Unique	6.6	964	7.3	1073		JHP

170

Powder	Grs.	MV (fps)	Grs.	MV (fps)	Press. (CUP/psi)	Comments
3N37	5.8	1037	6.8	1148	33,300p	Hdy HP/1.126"
N350	5.7	1038	6.6	1145	33,300p	Hdy HP/1.126"
N340	5.2	1009	6.0	1118	33,300p	Hdy HP/1.126"
HS6	7.3	942	8.0	1097		JHP
HS7	7.8	969	8.5	1094		JHP
WAP	6.2	1020	6.7	1085	33,500p	JHP
No.7	8.4	923	9.3	1049	34,400p	Nos JHP/1.125"/CCI 500/(M)
No.2	5.6	916	6.2	1041	35,000p	Nos JHP/1.125"/CCI 500/(M)
SR7625	5.3	913	5.9	1035		JHP
No.5	6.5	911	7.2	1035	34,000p	Nos JHP/1.125"/CCI 500/(M)
No.9	10.2	902	11.3	1025	30,800p	Nos JHP/1.125"/CCI 500/(C)
W540	7.6	926	8.3	1009		JHP

180

Powder	—STARTING— Grs.	MV (fps)	—MAXIMUM— Grs.	MV (fps)	Press. (CUP/psi)	Comments
N350	5.8	1029	6.6	1126	33,300p	Spr HP/1.126"
3N37	5.6	972	6.7	1097	33,300p	Spr HP/1.126"
N340	5.3	982	6.0	1093	33,300p	Spr HP/1.126"
Universal			5.8	1046	33,400C	JHP
HS7	7.0	865	8.0	1028		JHP
WAP	5.5	920	6.2	1020	33,200p	JHP
No.9	9.9	897	11.0	1019	35,000p	Hdy XTP/1.135"/CCI 500/(M)
HS6	6.5	849	7.3	994		JHP
W540	7.0	920	7.4	994		JHP
No.9	9.9	875	11.0	994	32,100p	Spr JHP/1.125"/CCI 500/(M)
No.5	6.3	873	7.0	992	35,000p	Spr JHP/1.125"/CCI 500/(M)
SR7625	5.0	830	5.8	986		JHP
No.7	7.9	866	8.8	984	34,400p	Spr JHP/1.125"/CCI 500/(M)
No.7	7.7	861	8.5	978	34,600p	Hdy XTP/1.135"/CCI 500/(M)
No.2	5.0	851	5.6	967	35,000p	Hdy XTP/1.135"/CCI 500
No.5	5.9	849	6.6	965	32,500p	Hdy XTP/1.135"/CCI 500

190

Powder	Grs.	MV (fps)	Grs.	MV (fps)	Press. (CUP/psi)	Comments
No.9	9.9	877	11.0	997	32,700p	Spr TMJ/1.125"/CCI 500/(M)
No.7	7.7	848	8.6	964	34,300p	Spr TMJ/1.125"/CCI 500/(M)
No.5	6.0	828	6.7	950	35,000p	Spr TMJ/1.125"/CCI 500/(M)
No.2	5.0	819	5.6	931	32,000p	Spr TMJ/1.125"/CCI 500/(M)

200

Powder	Grs.	MV (fps)	Grs.	MV (fps)	Press. (CUP/psi)	Comments
N350	5.2	878	5.9	974	33,300p	Spr TMJ/1.126"
SR7625	4.7	819	5.5	973		JHP
3N37	4.9	850	5.8	969	33,300p	Spr TMJ/1.126"
N340	4.6	857	5.3	961	33,300p	Spr TMJ/1.126"
No.9	9.5	838	10.6	952	34,500p	Spr TMJ/1.135"/CCI 500/(M)
No.7	7.5	819	8.3	931	35,000p	Spr TMJ/1.135"/CCI 500/(M)
HS7	5.8	862	6.7	927		FMJ
HS6	5.2	764	6.1	916		FMJ
Universal			4.7	903	33,600C	JHP
No.2	4.9	791	5.4	899	34,800p	Spr TMJ/1.135"/CCI 500/(M)
W540	6.1	800	6.8	894		JHP
No.5	5.7	777	6.3	883	33,100p	Spr TMJ/1.135"/CCI 500/(M)
W231	4.1	741	4.7	877		JHP
Green Dot	4.5	814	4.9	864		FMJ
No.9	8.3	759	9.2	863	35,000p	Hdy XTP/1.13"/CCI 500

(M) USPSA/IPSC Major Power Factor.

Never exceed maximum load nor use any load exhibiting signs of excessive pressure. Begin at suggested starting load and work up carefully.

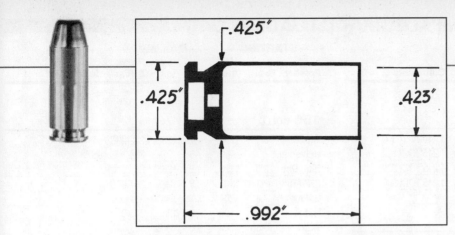

Case: Hornady
Primer: Large Pistol
Barrel: 5″ Accurate
　　　5″ Hodgdon
　　　5″ Vihtavuori

Bullet Diameter: 0.400″-0.401″
Maximum Case Length: 0.992″
Trim to Length: 0.987″
Maximum Cartridge OAL: 1.260″
Minimum Cartridge OAL: 1.240″

Introduced with the Bren Ten semi-automatic pistol in 1983, this chambering was enthusiastically embraced by gun writers. Others seemed a bit less taken with this hard-kicking, ear-shattering combination.

Some early loads generated truly rifle-like chamber pressures. Nevertheless, chronographs clearly demonstrated that few of those could offer a significant muzzle-energy advantage over the best factory 45 Automatic loads. Evidently, few shooters could justify the added noise for such a modest increase in actual performance—as measured by actual muzzle energy.

Chamber pressures of current loads are considerably sub-dued, yet with the best current powders, performance is impressive. One of the better loads launches a 200-grain Hornady XTP faster than any factory 185-grain 45 Automatic load. Lighter 10mm bullets can be launched at rather surprising velocities.

Nevertheless, popularity is still limited. Evidently, few shooters see any significant advantage over the 45 Automatic for self-defense, and this chambering is not really suitable for any other purpose.

Usable case capacity with a 180-grain bullet, seated normally, is about 14.6 grains of water. No. 9 is a singularly good choice for top 10mm loads.

10mm AUTOMATIC LOADING DATA

Powder	—STARTING— Grs.	MV (fps)	—MAXIMUM— Grs.	MV (fps)	Press. (CUP/psi)	Comments
Lead 145 Bull-X FN						
No.9	13.5	1251	15.0	1422	32,500p	1.25″/CCI 300
No.7	10.8	1203	12.0	1367	33,700p	1.25″/CCI 300
No.5	8.7	1190	9.7	1352	33,400p	1.25″/CCI 300
No.2	6.8	1138	7.5	1293	32,200p	1.25″/CCI 300
Lead 165 Clements SWC						
No.9	12.6	1174	14.0	1334	32,900p	1.25″/CCI 300
No.7	9.9	1120	11.0	1273	35,500p	1.25″/CCI 300
No.5	7.8	1085	8.7	1233	31,800p	1.25″/CCI 300
No.2	6.4	1082	7.1	1230	36,000p	1.25″/CCI 300

Powder	—STARTING— Grs.	MV (fps)	—MAXIMUM— Grs.	MV (fps)	Press. (CUP/psi)	Comments
Lead 170						
WAP	7.4	1180	8.4	1270	35,300p	
Lead 175 CP SWC						
No.9	12.2	1131	13.6	1285	34,900p	1.245″/CCI 300
No.7	9.4	1055	10.4	1199	35,200p	1.245″/CCI 300
No.2	6.0	1027	6.7	1167	35,300p	1.245″/CCI 300
No.5	7.5	1026	8.3	1166	31,500p	1.245″/CCI 300
Lead 185 Colorado Custom FN						
No.9	11.7	1098	13.0	1248	34,700p	1.245″/CCI 300
No.7	9.2	1032	10.2	1173	34,500p	1.245″/CCI 300
No.5	7.5	1030	8.3	1171	35,800p	1.245″/CCI 300
No.2	5.9	1000	6.6	1136	35,900p	1.245″/CCI 300

Caution: Loads exceeding SAAMI OAL Maximum must be verified for bullet-to-rifling clearance and magazine functioning. Where a specific primer or bullet is indicated those components must be used, no substitutions! Where only a maximum load is shown, reduce starting load 10%, unless otherwise specified.

Key: (C) = compressed charge; C = CUP; p = psi; Plink = Plinker; Bns = Barnes; Hdy = Hornady; Lap = Lapua; Nos = Nosler; Rem = Remington; Sra = Sierra; Spr = Speer; Win = Winchester.

Lead 195 Clements FN

Powder	Grs.	MV (fps)	Grs.	MV (fps)	Press. (CUP/psi)	Comments
No.9	10.7	1050	11.9	1193	35,600p	1.245"/CCI 300
No.7	8.6	998	9.5	1134	35,400p	1.245"/CCI 300
No.5	6.6	965	7.3	1097	34,900p	1.245"/CCI 300
No.2	5.2	928	5.8	1055	35,500p	1.245"/CCI 300

Lead 200

Powder	Grs.	MV (fps)	Grs.	MV (fps)	Press. (CUP/psi)	Comments
WAP	5.8	975	6.9	1080	35,200p	

Lead 205 Clements FN

Powder	Grs.	MV (fps)	Grs.	MV (fps)	Press. (CUP/psi)	Comments
No.9	10.6	1018	11.8	1157	36,200p	1.25"/CCI 300
No.7	8.4	960	9.3	1091	35,900p	1.25"/CCI 300
No.5	6.3	935	7.0	1063	35,700p	1.25"/CCI 300
No.2	4.7	862	5.2	979	33,800p	1.25"/CCI 300

135

Powder	Grs.	MV (fps)	Grs.	MV (fps)	Press. (CUP/psi)	Comments
No.9	15.8	1326	17.5	1507	29,200p	Nos JHP/1.25"/CCI 300
No.5	10.3	1323	11.4	1503	36,900p	Nos JHP/1.25"/CCI 300
No.7	12.2	1299	13.6	1476	34,900p	Nos JHP/1.25"/CCI 300
No.2	8.2	1271	9.1	1444	36,300p	Nos JHP/1.25"/CCI 300

150

Powder	Grs.	MV (fps)	Grs.	MV (fps)	Press. (CUP/psi)	Comments
No.9	15.0	1284	16.7	1459	33,000p	Nos JHP/1.245"/CCI 300
No.7	11.7	1236	13.0	1405	36,400p	Nos JHP/1.245"/CCI 300
No.5	9.5	1229	10.6	1397	36,900p	Nos JHP/1.245"/CCI 300
WAP	8.7	1290	9.8	1395	35,500p	JHP
No.2	7.6	1182	8.4	1343	36,700p	Nos JHP/1.245"/CCI 300

155

Powder	Grs.	MV (fps)	Grs.	MV (fps)	Press. (CUP/psi)	Comments
No.9	14.3	1244	15.9	1414	32,700p	Hdy JHP/1.25"/CCI 300
No.7	11.4	1214	12.7	1379	37,500p	Hdy JHP/1.25"/CCI 300
WAP	8.8	1265	9.7	1355	35,400p	JHP
No.5	9.0	1174	10.0	1334	35,300p	Hdy JHP/1.25"/CCI 300
N350	7.3	1192	8.6	1331	35,700p	Hdy XTP/1.256"
3N37	7.3	1193	8.8	1330	35,700p	Hdy XTP/1.256"
HS7	11.0	1173	11.4	1307	28,000C	
N340	6.7	1177	7.7	1299	35,700p	Hdy XTP/1.256"
No.2	7.2	1140	8.0	1296	35,700p	Hdy JHP/1.25"/CCI 300

155 con't

Powder	Grs.	MV (fps)	Grs.	MV (fps)	Press. (CUP/psi)	Comments
IMR800-X	8.4	1280	8.7	1289	28,400C	
Universal			7.5	1279	35,200C	JHP
Blue Dot	9.5	1190	9.9	1266	28,200C	
SR4756	8.1	1207	8.5	1260	28,500C	
Unique	7.4	1204	7.7	1240	28,000C	
HS6	9.5	1192	10.0	1280	27,700C	
W231	6.3	1179	6.6	1212	28,000C	
Trap100	6.2	1141	6.5	1207	27,700C	
HP38	6.4	1188	6.9	1194	28,000C	
SR7625	6.2	1090	6.4	1179	28,000C	
Green Dot	6.0	1070	6.4	1177	27,700C	
IMR700-X	5.2	1062	5.6	1174	28,000C	
Bullseye	5.5	1096	5.8	1154	28,000C	

170

Powder	Grs.	MV (fps)	Grs.	MV (fps)	Press. (CUP/psi)	Comments
No.9	13.5	1180	15.0	1341	34,100p	Nos HP/1.25"/CCI 300
No.7	10.8	1148	12.0	1305	37,500p	Nos HP/1.25"/CCI 300
WAP	7.9	1165	9.1	1285	34,600p	JHP
No.5	8.7	1122	9.7	1275	36,200p	Nos HP/1.25"/CCI 300
Blue Dot	9.0	1153	9.4	1270	28,100C	
IMR800-X	8.2	1195	8.4	1242	28,400C	
No.2	6.9	1074	7.7	1220	36,400p	Nos HP/1.25"/CCI 300
HS7	10.2	1158	10.5	1206	27,700C	
Trap100	6.0	1044	6.8	1193	27,700C	
HS6	9.0	1085	9.3	1190	28,000C	
Universal			6.7	1187	36,100C	JHP
Unique	7.0	1054	7.3	1156	28,000C	
SR4756	7.8	1100	8.0	1138	28,000C	
SR7625	5.6	995	5.9	1124	28,100C	
HP38	6.0	966	6.8	1118	28,000C	
W231	6.0	960	6.4	1098	28,800C	
Green Dot	6.0	1033	6.2	1090	27,700C	
IMR700-X	5.0	992	5.4	1088	27,700C	
Bullseye	5.2	994	5.6	1082	28,400C	

180

Powder	Grs.	MV (fps)	Grs.	MV (fps)	Press. (CUP/psi)	Comments
No.9	13.1	1135	14.5	1290	32,600p	Spr JHP/1.25"/CCI 300
No.9	12.2	1093	13.5	1242	34,100p	Hdy XTP/1.25"/CCI 300
No.7	10.3	1084	11.4	1232	36,600p	Spr JHP/1.25"/CCI 300
Blue Dot	8.8	1129	9.1	1218	28,200C	
No.5	8.3	1069	9.2	1215	37,000p	Spr JHP/1.25"/CCI 300
3N37	6.8	1104	7.9	1212	35,700p	Spr HP/1.256"
WAP	7.5	1110	8.4	1210	34,400p	JHP
No.5	7.8	1053	8.7	1197	36,800p	Hdy XTP/1.25"/CCI 300
N350	6.1	1088	7.4	1195	35,700p	Spr HP/1.256"
No.7	9.6	1041	10.7	1183	35,300p	Hdy XTP/1.25"/CCI 300

Never exceed maximum load nor use any load exhibiting signs of excessive pressure. Begin at suggested starting load and work up carefully.

180 con't

Powder	—STARTING— Grs.	MV (fps)	—MAXIMUM— Grs.	MV (fps)	Press. (CUP/psi)	Comments
No.2	6.7	1037	7.4	1178	36,700p	Spr JHP/1.25"/ CCI 300
N340	6.1	1038	6.9	1167	35,700p	Spr HP/1.256"
HS7	9.9	1089	10.3	1143	28,200C	
IMR800-X	7.7	1070	8.0	1129	28,000C	
Universal			6.4	1122	32,200C	JHP
No.2	6.1	986	6.8	1120	34,300p	Hdy XTP/1.25"/ CCI 300
Unique	6.8	1048	7.2	1119	28,000C	
SR7625	5.4	998	5.9	1111	28,400C	
HS6	8.5	1071	8.7	1109	27,000C	
SR4756	7.5	1041	7.7	1106	27,700C	
Bullseye	5.1	971	5.4	1077	28,400C	
Trap100	6.0	991	6.7	1069	27,400C	
HP38	6.2	984	6.5	1065	26,900C	
Green Dot	5.9	988	6.1	1063	27,000C	
IMR700-X	4.9	980	5.3	1062	27,000C	
W231	5.9	955	6.3	1054	28,600C	

190

Powder	—STARTING— Grs.	MV (fps)	—MAXIMUM— Grs.	MV (fps)	Press. (CUP/psi)	Comments
No.9	12.8	1115	14.2	1267	35,800p	Spr TMJ/1.25"/ CCI 300
No.7	10.1	1054	11.2	1198	36,000p	Spr TMJ/1.25"/ CCI 300
No.5	8.2	1044	9.1	1186	36,800p	Spr TMJ/1.25"/ CCI 300
WAP	7.4	1100	8.3	1185	34,700p	JFP
No.2	6.5	991	7.2	1126	34,400p	Spr TMJ/1.25"/ CCI 300

200

Powder	—STARTING— Grs.	MV (fps)	—MAXIMUM— Grs.	MV (fps)	Press. (CUP/psi)	Comments
No.9	12.2	1056	13.5	1200	36,300p	Spr TMJ/1.25"/ CCI 300
No.9	11.3	1030	12.5	1170	38,000p	Hdy XTP/1.25"/ CCI 300
No.7	9.6	1007	10.7	1144	36,200p	Spr TMJ/1.25"/ CCI 300
No.5	7.8	1003	8.7	1140	37,100p	Spr TMJ/1.25"/ CCI 300
HS7	9.7	1073	10.0	1130	28,500C	
SR4756	7.2	1010	7.4	1102	27,700C	
Blue Dot	8.4	1088	8.8	1102	28,000C	
HS6	8.4	1051	8.7	1094	28,000C	
No.7	8.8	960	9.8	1091	36,500p	Hdy XTP/1.25"/ CCI 300
No.2	6.3	959	7.0	1090	37,500p	Spr TMJ/1.25"/ CCI 300
SR7625	5.3	981	5.8	1089	28,800C	
3N37	6.0	967	6.9	1084	35,700p	Hdy FMJ-FP/1.256"
Unique	6.7	1036	7.1	1081	27,700C	
IMR700-X	4.8	979	5.1	1081	28,300C	
No.5	7.0	938	7.8	1066	35,100p	Hdy XTP/1.25"/ CCI 300
Bullseye	5.0	980	5.2	1060	28,000C	
N350	5.4	945	6.4	1059	35,700p	Hdy FMJ-FP/1.256"
Trap100	5.8	941	6.5	1050	28,100C	
IMR800-X	7.0	1019	7.5	1045	28,200C	
HP38	5.8	934	6.4	1044	27,700C	
Green Dot	5.7	989	6.0	1042	28,400C	
No.2	5.7	916	6.3	1041	36,700p	Hdy XTP/1.25"/ CCI 300
W231	5.7	949	6.2	1031	28,000C	
N340	5.0	890	5.8	1027	35,700p	Hdy FMJ-FP/1.256"
Universal			5.9	1015	36,900C	FMJ

Caution: Loads exceeding SAAMI OAL Maximum must be verified for bullet-to-rifling clearance and magazine functioning. Where a specific primer or bullet is indicated those components must be used, no substitutions! Where only a maximum load is shown, reduce starting load 10%, unless otherwise specified.

Key: (C) = compressed charge; C = CUP; p = psi; Plink = Plinker; Bns = Barnes; Hdy = Hornady; Lap = Lapua; Nos = Nosler; Rem = Remington; Sra = Sierra; Spr = Speer; Win = Winchester.

41

Remington Magnum & Desert Eagle

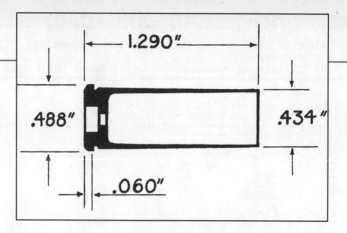

Case: Winchester
Primer: Large Pistol
CCI 300 (DE)
Barrel: 6″ Accurate (DE)
9″ Accurate
6″ Hodgdon (Ruger)

Bullet Diameter: 0.410″
Maximum Case Length: 1.290″
Trim to Length: 1.285″
Maximum Cartridge OAL: 1.590″
Minimum Cartridge OAL: 1.540″

Introduced in June of 1964 in Smith & Wesson's Model 57 revolver, the 41 Magnum was the result of long-time badgering of ammunition and handgun manufacturers by famous handgunners such as Bill Jordan and Elmer Keith. Their goal was a superior revolver chambering for police use—the 357 Magnum was considered marginal, especially in short-barreled guns, and standard 44 Magnum loads are considered "too much" by most shooters.

There is nothing wrong with the 41 Magnum. However, by the time S&W and Remington got around to offering it, the revolver was rapidly losing favor for police use. For many others, especially the average handloader, the 41 Magnum seems less than useless. It is offered in the same size revolvers as the 44 Magnum and cannot be loaded to match 44 Magnum ballistics. Factory loads of 44 Special, mid-range factory loads of 44 Magnum and an entire genre of useful handloads offer the handloader levels of performance milder than, similar to, and superior to anything the 41 Magnum can accomplish.

Nevertheless, the 41 Magnum is a fine cartridge and can be loaded to offer substantial hunting or self-defense performance. The originators believed a 210-grain SWC bullet at about 1000 fps would be an ideal 41-caliber self-defense load.

Usable case capacity with a 210-grain bullet, seated normally, is about 20.8 grains of water. No. 9, W296 and H110 are superior choices for full-power 41 Magnum loads.

41 REMINGTON MAGNUM LOADING DATA

Lead 210 Lyman 410459 (SWC)

Powder	STARTING Grs.	MV (fps)	MAXIMUM Grs.	MV (fps)	Press. (CUP/psi)	Comments
No.9	16.2	1392	18.0	1582	38,600C	1.675″/CCI 300/*
No.7	13.1	1269	14.5	1442	37,000C	1.675″/CCI 300/*
No.5	11.3	1264	12.5	1436	36,700C	1.675″/CCI 300/*
XMP5744			21.5	1431	38,000C	1.675″/CCI 300/*
No.2	8.3	1157	9.2	1315	40,000C	1.675″/CCI 300/*

*Exceeds SAAMI maximum OAL.

Lead 240 Lyman 410426 (RN)

Powder	STARTING Grs.	MV (fps)	MAXIMUM Grs.	MV (fps)	Press. (CUP/psi)	Comments
No.9	15.5	1305	17.2	1483	39,300C	1.71″/CCI 300
No.7	12.6	1197	14.0	1360	37,800C	1.71″/CCI 300
No.5	10.8	1194	12.0	1357	40,000C	1.71″/CCI 300
XMP5744			20.0	1334	38,100C	1.71″/CCI 300
No.2	7.4	1047	8.2	1190	39,700C	1.71″/CCI 300

Lead 250

Powder	STARTING Grs.	MV (fps)	MAXIMUM Grs.	MV (fps)	Press. (CUP/psi)	Comments
H110	19.0	1254	20.5	1342		
H4227	19.0	1186	20.0	1255		

Lead 295-300

Powder	STARTING Grs.	MV (fps)	MAXIMUM Grs.	MV (fps)	Press. (CUP/psi)	Comments
H110	17.5	1165	19.0	1267		
H4227	17.5	1134	18.5	1201		

170 (Revolver)

Powder	STARTING Grs.	MV (fps)	MAXIMUM Grs.	MV (fps)	Press. (CUP/psi)	Comments
Universal			10.3	1488	38,700C	
Blue Dot	14.0	1338	15.0	1480		
H110	22.0	1311	24.0	1466		
Her2400	18.0	1279	20.0	1460		
W296	22.0	1308	24.0	1449		
H4227	21.5	1330	23.0	1437		
IMR4227	21.0	1309	23.0	1429		
SR4756	12.0	1324	13.5	1419		
Unique	10.0	1221	11.5	1409		
Bullseye	7.0	1119	8.0	1280		
HS7	12.5	1030	14.5	1269		
IMR700-X	7.5	1122	8.2	1259		
HS6	10.5	916	12.5	1065		

Never exceed maximum load nor use any load exhibiting signs of excessive pressure. Begin at suggested starting load and work up carefully.

170 (Revolver) con't

Powder	—STARTING— Grs.	MV (fps)	—MAXIMUM— Grs.	MV (fps)	Press. (CUP/psi)	Comments
HP38	6.4	854	7.4	929		
Trap100	6.5	872	7.5	928		
W231	6.2	831	7.2	914		

170

Powder	Grs.	MV (fps)	Grs.	MV (fps)	Press. (CUP/psi)	Comments
No.9	17.7	1500	19.7	1705	37,800C	Sra JHC/1.565"/CCI 300
XMP5744			24.0	1577	40,000C	Sra JHC/1.565"/CCI 300
No.7	14.0	1368	15.5	1555	37,000C	Sra JHC/1.565"/CCI 300
No.5	10.8	1314	12.0	1493	37,900C	Sra JHC/1.565"/CCI 300
No.2	9.0	1277	10.0	1451	39,600C	Sra JHC/1.565"/CCI 300

200

Powder	Grs.	MV (fps)	Grs.	MV (fps)	Press. (CUP/psi)	Comments
No.9	16.2	1338	18.0	1521	40,000C	Hdy XTP/1.57"/CCI 300
XMP5744			22.0	1422	39,800C	Spr HP/CCI 300
No.7	12.8	1214	14.2	1379	39,600C	Hdy XTP/1.57"/CCI 300
XMP5744			20.5	1326	36,800C	Hdy XTP/1.57"/CCI 300
No.5	10.4	1163	11.5	1322	39,200C	Hdy XTP/1.57"/CCI 300
No.2	8.6	1096	9.5	1245	40,000C	Hdy XTP/1.57"/CCI 300

200-210 (Revolver)

Powder	Grs.	MV (fps)	Grs.	MV (fps)	Press. (CUP/psi)	Comments
H110	19.0	1263	21.0	1448		
W296	19.5	1289	21.0	1431		
H4227	19.0	1169	21.0	1319		
IMR4227	19.0	1174	21.0	1307		
Her2400	16.0	1094	18.0	1277		
Unique	8.0	1028	10.5	1271		
Blue Dot	12.0	1100	13.5	1260		
Universal			8.9	1243	37,700C	
SR4756	11.0	1103	12.5	1218		
HS7	11.5	1003	13.5	1217		
IMR700-X	6.4	1068	7.4	1190		
Bullseye	6.5	1019	7.5	1166		
HS6	9.5	923	11.5	1084		
Trap100	6.0	831	7.0	911		
HP38	5.9	837	6.9	903		
W231	5.8	817	6.8	900		

220 (Revolver)

Powder	Grs.	MV (fps)	Grs.	MV (fps)	Press. (CUP/psi)	Comments
H110	18.0	1273	20.0	1401		
W296	18.0	1270	20.0	1396		
H4227	18.0	1207	20.0	1293		
IMR4227	18.0	1194	20.0	1269		
Her2400	15.5	1070	17.5	1256		
Blue Dot	11.5	1066	12.5	1224		
Unique	7.5	989	9.5	1189		
HS7	11.0	926	13.0	1185		
Universal			8.5	1178	38,600C	
SR4756	10.0	1054	11.5	1172		
Bullseye	5.5	947	7.0	1108		
HS6	9.0	904	11.0	1069		
IMR700-X	5.5	862	6.5	907		
Trap100	6.0	814	7.0	890		
HP38	5.9	812	6.9	887		
W231	5.7	800	6.7	877		

220

Powder	Grs.	MV (fps)	Grs.	MV (fps)	Press. (CUP/psi)	Comments
No.9	16.2	1316	18.0	1496	37,700C	Sra SIL-FPJ/1.56"/ CCI 300
No.7	12.8	1200	14.2	1364	39,400C	Sra SIL-FPJ/1.56"/ CCI 300
XMP5744			20.0	1311	37,700C	Sra SIL-FPJ/1.56"/ CCI 300
No.5	10.4	1153	11.5	1310	39,400C	Sra SIL-FPJ/1.56"/ CCI 300
No.2	8.3	1081	9.2	1228	40,000C	Sra SIL-FPJ/1.56"/ CCI 300

Caution: Loads exceeding SAAMI OAL Maximum must be verified for bullet-to-rifling clearance and magazine functioning. Where a specific primer or bullet is indicated those components must be used, no substitutions! Where only a maximum load is shown, reduce starting load 10%, unless otherwise specified.

Key: (C) = compressed charge; C = CUP; p = psi; Plink = Plinker; Bns = Barnes; Hdy = Hornady; Lap = Lapua; Nos = Nosler; Rem = Remington; Sra = Sierra; Spr = Speer; Win = Winchester.

41 REMINGTON MAGNUM DESERT EAGLE SPECIFIC LOADING DATA

210

Powder	—STARTING— Grs.	MV (fps)	—MAXIMUM— Grs.	MV (fps)	Press. (CUP/psi)	Comments
No.9	16.2	1204	18.0	1295	40,000C	Hdy XTP/1.57"

220

Powder	—STARTING— Grs.	MV (fps)	—MAXIMUM— Grs.	MV (fps)	Press. (CUP/psi)	Comments
No.9	16.2	1176	18.0	1288	37,700C	Sra SIL-FPJ/1.56"

44-40

Winchester (WCF) (Revolver)

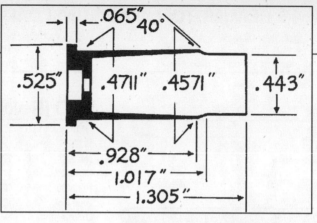
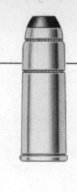

Case: Remington
Primer: CCI 300
Barrel: 7½″ Accurate
Bullet Diameter: 0.427″ (Cast bullets of 0.429″ can sometimes be used, see text.)

Maximum Case Length: 1.305″ (Very Rare)
Trim to Length: 1.300″ (Rare)
Maximum Cartridge OAL: 1.592″
Minimum Cartridge OAL: 1.540″

Co-introduced in 1873 with Winchester's wildly successful lever-action rifle, this chambering has persisted. It is still chambered in both revolvers and shoulder guns. Colt's adoption for chambering in their Single Action Army revolver probably was more responsible for the cartridge's survival than any other factor. The 44-40 is currently offered in several single-action revolvers, both modern and reproduction.

Typical of cartridges introduced in that era, this is not a true 44-caliber. Like the more modern 44 S&W Special and 44 Magnum, this is a 42-caliber cartridge. Somehow 42 just does not roll off the tongue. It is not surprising that something a bit more sexy was chosen. However, it is also possible, nay likely, that such early chamberings were named for another dimension...the diameter of the case neck!

To understand this, it is necessary to discuss cartridge conversions of cap-and-ball revolvers. That process centered on the simple expedient of boring holes completely through the chambers and facing off the back of the cylinder so that self-contained metallic cartridges could be used in those revolvers.

Note that most such conversions used cylinder holes that were bigger than bore diameter. This accommodated case wall thickness, allowing a bore-diameter bullet to be inserted into the case. For example, the original "38-caliber" conversion cartridges were actually adapted to 36-caliber guns.

Performance of the 44-40 in a handgun is impressive even by modern self-defense standards. The original black-powder load launched a 200-grain bullet at about 1000 fps from the Colt. With the proper smokeless powders, it is no trick to launch 215-grain cast bullets just as fast.

These loads are for use only in guns known to be safe with smokeless powder.

Proper bullet diameter is usually smaller than standard 44-caliber—0.429″/0.430″—but some guns will chamber and shoot these bullets very accurately. For best results, slug the cylinder throats and size cast bullets accordingly.

Usable case capacity with a 200-grain bullet, seated normally, is about 32.0 grains of water. No.5 and No.7 are noted 44-40 performers.

44-40 WINCHESTER (WCF) LOADING DATA (Revolver Specific Loads)

Powder	STARTING Grs.	MV (fps)	MAXIMUM Grs.	MV (fps)	Press. (CUP/psi)	Comments
Lead 200 Lyman 42798 (FN)						
XMP5744			17.0	1035	12,300C	1.575″
No.7			11.2	1004	11,300C	1.575″
No.5			9.2	983	11,900C	1.575″
No.2			6.3	961	12,800C	1.575″
N100			5.3	922	12,800C	1.575″
Lead 215 Lyman 429434 (FN)						
No.9			13.0	1022	12,200C	1.56″
No.5			8.8	949	12,800C	1.56″
No.7			10.5	945	11,600C	1.56″
N100			5.2	874	13,200C	1.56″
No.2			5.5	846	11,300C	1.56″

Powder	STARTING Grs.	MV (fps)	MAXIMUM Grs.	MV (fps)	Press. (CUP/psi)	Comments
180						
No.7			13.0	1086	13,200C	1.51″
No.5			10.5	989	11,700C	1.51″
No.2			6.7	890	11,800C	1.51″
N100			6.0	860	12,600C	1.51″
200						
No.7			12.0	1034	13,200C	Nos JHP/1.6″/*
No.5			10.0	1010	13,300C	Nos JHP/1.6″/*
N100			5.5	832	12,500C	Nos JHP/1.6″/*
No.2			6.0	826	11,600C	Nos JHP/1.6″/*

* Exceeds SAAMI maximum OAL.

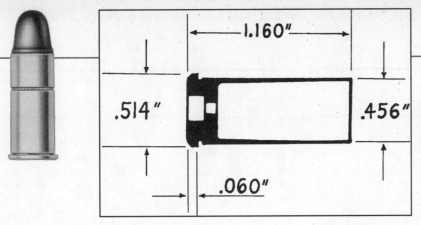

Case: Midway
Primer: Large Pistol
Barrel: 7½" Accurate
7" Hodgdon
6" Vihtavuori

Bullet Diameter: 0.429"-0.430"
Maximum Case Length: 1.160"
Trim to Length: 1.155"
Maximum Cartridge OAL: 1.615"
Minimum Cartridge OAL: 1.560"

Based on the 44 Smith & Wesson Russian, the 44 Special was introduced about 1907 expressly to accommodate the bulky smokeless powders of that era. With limited case capacity, and more consistent chamber and barrel dimensions than were typical of other big bore chamberings of the era, the 44 Special soon gained a reputation as the most accurate big-bore revolver cartridge. There is nothing magical about this—in a properly fitted gun the 45 Colt can do just as well, especially with heavy cast bullets.

For various reasons, Elmer Keith and others chose the 44 Special over the larger 45 Colt for their development of a high-pressure handloaded hunting cartridge. (Semi-balloon-head 45 Colt cases were comparatively common and 45 Colt chambered guns also have considerably thinner chamber walls.) This work led to the introduction of the 44 Magnum in 1955.

By modern standards, Keith's pet 44 Special load—18 grains of Hercules 2400 behind a 250-grain cast bullet—is a gross overload. Nevertheless, he used it in dozens of fine S&W revolvers firing tens of thousands of shots with nary a hitch. This is testimony to the strength of those guns, and it cannot be assumed that all 44 Special-chambered guns are strong enough to safely handle such loads....If you want magnum performance, please, buy a magnum-chambered gun.

Despite mild pressures, the 44 Special can safely launch a 250-grain cast lead SWC at sufficient velocity to suggest it as a formidable hunting round. For self-defense, the better light JHP bullets loaded to top velocity are perhaps a better choice—but don't ever let the late Elmer Keith's spirit know I suggested that! Like the 38 Special, many powders work well with this cartridge.

44 SMITH & WESSON SPECIAL LOADING DATA

Lead 200 Rucker (SWC)

Powder	STARTING Grs.	MV (fps)	MAXIMUM Grs.	MV (fps)	Press. (CUP/psi)	Comments
No.9	10.4	898	11.5	1020	13,900C	1.465"/CCI 300
No.7	8.6	873	9.5	992	14,000C	1.465"/CCI 300
No.5	6.4	876	7.4	959	14,000C	1.465"/CCI 300
N100	4.3	822	4.8	914	14,000C	1.465"/CCI 300
No.2	4.7	827	5.2	905	14,000C	1.465"/CCI 300
XMP5744			12.5	737	12,600C	1.465"/CCI 300

Lead 215 Lyman 429215 (SWC)

Powder	STARTING Grs.	MV (fps)	MAXIMUM Grs.	MV (fps)	Press. (CUP/psi)	Comments
H4227			17.0	1151	14,900C	
HS6	8.0	821	10.0	1100	14,400C	
No.9	10.3	869	11.4	988	13,800C	1.535"/CCI 300
No.5	7.0	844	7.8	959	14,000C	1.535"/CCI 300
No.7	8.6	839	9.5	953	14,000C	1.535"/CCI 300
No.2	4.8	790	5.3	900	14,000C	1.535"/CCI 300
N100	4.3	780	4.8	890	14,000C	1.535"/CCI 300
HP38	4.8	779	5.8	879	14,100C	
Trap100	4.8	786	5.8	874	14,900C	

Lead 245 Lyman 429383 (RN)

Powder	STARTING Grs.	MV (fps)	MAXIMUM Grs.	MV (fps)	Press. (CUP/psi)	Comments
No.9	9.7	818	10.8	930	14,000C	1.6"/CCI 300
No.7	7.8	792	8.7	900	14,000C	1.6"/CCI 300
No.5	6.1	757	6.8	860	14,000C	1.6"/CCI 300
No.2	4.2	721	4.7	819	14,000C	1.6"/CCI 300
N100	3.9	720	4.3	818	14,000C	1.6"/CCI 300

▶▶▶▶▶▶▶▶▶▶▶▶▶▶▶▶▶▶▶▶▶▶▶▶▶▶▶▶

Caution: **Loads exceeding SAAMI OAL Maximum must be verified for bullet-to-rifling clearance and magazine functioning. Where a specific primer or bullet is indicated those components must be used, no substitutions! Where only a maximum load is shown, reduce starting load 10%, unless otherwise specified.**

Key: (C) = compressed charge; C = CUP; p = psi; Plink = Plinker; Bns = Barnes; Hdy = Hornady; Lap = Lapua; Nos = Nosler; Rem = Remington; Sra = Sierra; Spr = Speer; Win = Winchester.

Never exceed maximum load nor use any load exhibiting signs of excessive pressure. Begin at suggested starting load and work up carefully.

Lead 250 Lyman 429421 (SWC)

Powder	STARTING Grs.	MV (fps)	MAXIMUM Grs.	MV (fps)	Press. (CUP/psi)	Comments
H4227			16.5	1109	17,600C	
HS6	7.0	708	9.0	1011	13,100C	
No.9	10.4	832	11.5	946	14,000C	1.575"/CCI 300
No.7	8.1	779	9.0	885	14,000C	1.575"/CCI 300
No.5	6.3	760	7.0	864	14,000C	1.575"/CCI 300
No.2	4.5	711	5.0	808	13,900C	1.575"/CCI 300
N100	4.0	700	4.4	800	14,000C	1.575"/CCI 300
HP38	3.9	715	4.9	775	13,900C	
Trap100	3.8	682	4.8	769	14,400C	

Lead 267 Intercast (FN)

Powder	STARTING Grs.	MV (fps)	MAXIMUM Grs.	MV (fps)	Press. (CUP/psi)	Comments
N350	7.5	867	8.2	942	14,700p	1.89"
N330	6.5	870	7.2	937	14,700p	1.89"
N340	6.6	857	7.3	926	14,700p	1.89"
N320	5.5	807	6.1	874	14,700p	1.89"

180

Powder	STARTING Grs.	MV (fps)	MAXIMUM Grs.	MV (fps)	Press. (CUP/psi)	Comments
H4227			18.5	1285	16,100C	JHP
HS6	9.5	1024	11.5	1264	15,900C	JHP
IMR4227	17.0	1149	18.0	1229	16,400C	JHP
N350	10.0	1065	10.7	1173	14,700p	Hdy XTP/1.469"
N340	9.0	1069	9.7	1168	14,700p	Hdy XTP/1.469"
N330	7.9	1032	8.8	1130	14,700p	Hdy XTP/1.469"
N320	6.9	958	7.7	1054	14,700p	Hdy XTP/1.469"
Blue Dot	13.0	980	13.5	1024	13,200C	JHP
No.5	7.8	878	8.7	1000	14,000C	Hdy JHP/1.485"/CCI 300
No.7	9.9	880	10.5	1000	14,000C	Hdy JHP/1.485"/CCI 300
Unique	8.6	914	9.2	1000	13,400C	JHP
SR7625	8.0	839	9.0	964	14,400C	JHP
Trap100	5.5	841	6.5	954	14,800C	JHP
HP38	5.6	858	6.6	941	14,200C	JHP
W231	5.5	840	6.5	934	14,400C	JHP
N100	4.6	807	5.2	920	14,000C	Hdy JHP/1.485"/CCI 300
IMR700-X	5.4	828	6.4	914	15,600C	JHP
No.2	5.3	802	5.9	911	14,000C	Hdy JHP/1.485"/CCI 300
Bullseye	5.5	812	6.5	907	12,400C	JHP

200

Powder	STARTING Grs.	MV (fps)	MAXIMUM Grs.	MV (fps)	Press. (CUP/psi)	Comments
IMR4227	15.5	1094	16.5	1130	15,800C	JHP
N350	9.3	995	10.1	1104	14,700p	Hdy XTP/1.469"
N340	8.5	984	9.2	1091	14,700p	Hdy XTP/1.469"
N330	7.9	962	8.6	1056	14,700p	Hdy XTP/1.469"
N320	6.5	902	7.1	983	14,700p	Hdy XTP/1.469"
No.7	9.0	825	10.0	938	13,800C	Nos JHP/1.49"/CCI 300
Blue Dot	11.0	820	12.0	909	14,400C	JHP
SR7625	7.5	822	8.5	909	15,400C	JHP
Unique	6.8	811	7.4	890	14,100C	JHP
W231	5.2	801	6.0	889	14,400C	JHP
No.5	7.2	766	8.0	871	13,000C	Nos JHP/1.49"/CCI 300
IMR700-X	5.2	788	5.8	844	14,900C	JHP
N100	4.5	740	5.0	840	14,000C	Nos JHP/1.49"/CCI 300
Bullseye	5.0	744	5.8	834	13,600C	JHP
No.2	4.9	708	5.4	805	14,000C	Nos JHP/1.49"/CCI 300

210

Powder	STARTING Grs.	MV (fps)	MAXIMUM Grs.	MV (fps)	Press. (CUP/psi)	Comments
H4227			16.5	1142	15,800C	JHP
HS6	9.5	944	10.5	1086	15,600C	JHP
HP38	5.2	806	6.2	909	14,600C	JHP
Trap100	5.0	801	6.0	888	15,800C	JHP

225

Powder	STARTING Grs.	MV (fps)	MAXIMUM Grs.	MV (fps)	Press. (CUP/psi)	Comments
W296	15.0	1180	15.5	1219	15,000C	JHP
H4227			15.0	1148	18,400C	JHP
IMR4227	14.0	1019	15.0	1128	16,200C	JHP
SR7625	7.0	791	8.0	870	15,100C	JHP
Blue Dot	9.5	804	10.0	861	14,200C	JHP
Trap100	4.3	741	5.3	832	15,800C	JHP
W231	4.5	749	5.5	829	15,900C	JHP
HP38	4.5	757	5.5	827	15,800C	JHP
Unique	6.0	730	6.8	808	14,600C	JHP
IMR700-X	5.0	782	5.5	807	14,600C	JHP
Bullseye	4.9	733	5.6	792	13,600C	JHP

Caution: Loads exceeding SAAMI OAL Maximum must be verified for bullet-to-rifling clearance and magazine functioning. Where a specific primer or bullet is indicated those components must be used, no substitutions! Where only a maximum load is shown, reduce starting load 10%, unless otherwise specified.

Key: (C) = compressed charge; C = CUP; p = psi; Plink = Plinker; Bns = Barnes; Hdy = Hornady; Lap = Lapua; Nos = Nosler; Rem = Remington; Sra = Sierra; Spr = Speer; Win = Winchester.

240

Powder	—STARTING— Grs.	MV (fps)	—MAXIMUM— Grs.	MV (fps)	Press. (CUP/psi)	Comments
W296	14.5	1174	15.0	1190	15,400C	JHP
H4227			14.0	1002	18,600C	JSP
IMR4227	13.0	911	14.0	984	17,400C	JSP
SR7625	6.8	777	7.8	888	15,000C	JSP
Her2400	11.5	781	12.0	868	15,400C	JHP
Blue Dot	8.8	764	9.3	830	14,000C	JHP
No.9	9.0	714	10.0	811	14,000C	IMI JSP/1.485"/ CCI 300
Trap100	4.0	712	5.0	794	15,900C	JSP
HP38	4.0	718	5.2	790	13,800C	JSP
W231	4.2	727	5.1	788	14,100C	JHP
Bullseye	4.2	664	5.0	777	15,500C	JHP
IMR700-X	4.7	740	5.2	774	14,200C	JSP
No.7	7.2	689	8.0	745	14,000C	IMI JSP/1.485"/ CCI 300
No.5	5.8	640	6.5	730	14,000C	IMI JSP/1.485"/ CCI 300
N100	4.0	580	4.4	659	14,000C	IMI JSP/1.485"/ CCI 300
No.2	4.1	532	4.5	604	13,900C	IMI JSP/1.485"/ CCI 300

250

Powder	—STARTING— Grs.	MV (fps)	—MAXIMUM— Grs.	MV (fps)	Press. (CUP/psi)	Comments
W296	14.0	1119	14.5	1149	17,800C	JSP
H4227	13.0	890	13.5	952	17,700C	JSP
IMR4227	12.5	854	13.5	949	17,900C	JSP
HS6	8.0	833	8.5	892	14,400C	JSP
Her2400	11.0	760	11.5	847	15,800C	JSP
SR7625	6.6	747	7.4	839	16,400C	JSP
HP38	4.0	717	5.0	788	14,200C	JSP
Blue Dot	8.4	734	9.0	788	16,000C	JSP
W231	4.0	719	5.0	782	14,400C	JSP
Bullseye	4.4	711	4.8	742	16,100C	JSP
IMR700-X	4.5	713	4.9	726	15,400C	JSP

260-265

Powder	—STARTING— Grs.	MV (fps)	—MAXIMUM— Grs.	MV (fps)	Press. (CUP/psi)	Comments
W296	13.0	953	13.5	981	16,000C	JSP
H4227	12.0	831	13.0	929	15,700C	JSP
IMR4227	12.0	819	13.0	909	16,100C	JSP
HS6	6.5	765	7.0	833	14,700C	JSP
Her2400	10.0	717	11.0	825	16,100C	JSP
SR7625	6.0	714	7.0	812	16,600C	JSP
Blue Dot	7.2	715	8.5	760	15,200C	JSP

275

Powder	—STARTING— Grs.	MV (fps)	—MAXIMUM— Grs.	MV (fps)	Press. (CUP/psi)	Comments
W296	11.5	774	12.5	877	17,500C	JSP
H4227	11.5	769	12.5	852	17,700C	JSP
IMR4227	11.2	740	12.2	812	18,000C	JSP
IMR800-X	6.5	711	7.0	769	17,700C	JSP
Her2400	9.5	685	10.5	763	16,400C	JSP
Blue Dot	7.5	679	8.0	705	15,700C	JSP

300

Powder	—STARTING— Grs.	MV (fps)	—MAXIMUM— Grs.	MV (fps)	Press. (CUP/psi)	Comments
W296	10.5	720	11.0	794	17,700C	JSP
H4227	10.5	680	11.5	752	18,600C	JSP
IMR4227	10.5	688	11.5	732	18,400C	JSP
IMR800-X	5.8	667	6.4	721	18,800C	JSP
Her2400	9.0	649	9.6	711	18,000C	JSP
Blue Dot	7.0	612	7.5	648	16,800C	JSP

Never exceed maximum load nor use any load exhibiting signs of excessive pressure. Begin at suggested starting load and work up carefully.

Automatic Magnum (44 AMP/44 Auto Mag)

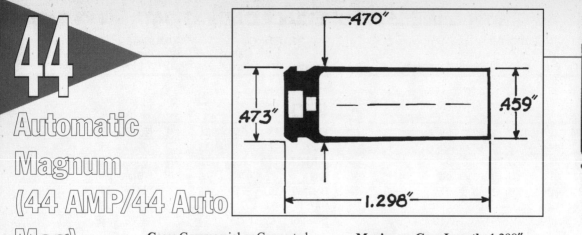

Case: Commercial or Converted 308 Winchester
Primer: Large Pistol Magnum
Barrel: 6″ Hodgdon (TDE)
Bullet Diameter: 0.429″

Maximum Case Length: 1.298″
Trim to Length: 1.296″
Maximum Cartridge OAL: NA
Minimum Cartridge OAL: NA

Based on the standard 30-06 family of cases, the 44 Auto Mag was created by cutting a 308 case to 1.3″ and reaming the interior to achieve normal pistol-cartridge wall thickness. The ill-fated Auto Mag pistol never got very far off the ground, and the cartridge soon faltered, for lack of a commercially chambered gun.

The designers intended the cartridge to duplicate 44 Magnum revolver ballistics in a semi-automatic pistol. Current loads do not quite achieve that goal. Nevertheless, the 44 Auto Mag is a formidable chambering and offers serious hunting and self-defense performance. Introduction of the similar 45 Winchester Magnum likely doomed the 44 Auto Mag to an early obsolescence.

■ 44 AUTOMATIC MAGNUM LOADING DATA (44 AMP/44 AUTO MAG) ■

Powder	—STARTING— Grs.	MV (fps)	—MAXIMUM— Grs.	MV (fps)	Press. (CUP/psi)	Comments
180						
H110	25.0	1483	27.0	1564		
H4227	25.0	1316	27.0	1478		
HS7	17.0	1240	18.0	1390		
200						
H110	23.0	1415	25.0	1485		
H4227	25.0	1379	26.0	1427		
HS7	16.0	1175	17.0	1302		

Powder	—STARTING— Grs.	MV (fps)	—MAXIMUM— Grs.	MV (fps)	Press. (CUP/psi)	Comments
225						
H110	19.0	1243	22.0	1358		
H4227	20.0	1126	22.0	1269		
240						
H110	19.0	1182	21.0	1241		
H4227	20.0	1125	21.0	1183		

Caution: Loads exceeding SAAMI OAL Maximum must be verified for bullet-to-rifling clearance and magazine functioning. Where a specific primer or bullet is indicated those components must be used, no substitutions! Where only a maximum load is shown, reduce starting load 10%, unless otherwise specified.

Key: (C) = compressed charge; C = CUP; p = psi; Plink = Plinker; Bns = Barnes; Hdy = Hornady; Lap = Lapua; Nos = Nosler; Rem = Remington; Sra = Sierra; Spr = Speer; Win = Winchester.

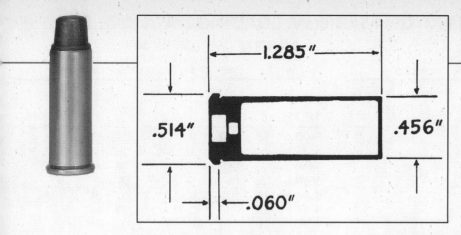

Case: Winchester
Primer: Large Pistol; CCI 300 (DE);
    Large Pistol Magnum (T/C)
Barrel: 7½" Accurate (Redhawk) (DE)
    7" Hodgdon
    14" Hodgdon (T/C)
    7" Vihtavuori

Bullet Diameter: 0.429"-0.430";
    0.429" (T/C)
Maximum Case Length: 1.285"
Trim to Length: 1.280"
Maximum Cartridge OAL: 1.610"
Minimum Cartridge OAL: 1.535"

Developed through the efforts of independent handgunners—Elmer Keith and others—this revolver chambering was introduced in 1955 as a joint effort of Remington and Smith & Wesson. Several manufacturers offer handguns chambered for the 44 Magnum. It continues to garner a high level of popularity.

Elmer always maintained that factory loads went wildly overboard. He might have been right. In the late '50s and early '60s, the various ammunition manufacturers seem to have engaged in a velocity war. No self-respecting 44 Magnum load would fail to launch a 240-grain lead gas-check bullet from a typical revolver at less than 1500 fps! With the powders then available, pressures were predictably high.

Several handgunners reported factory loads that required a wood dowel and a mallet for extraction! H.P. White labs pressure-tested several lots of factory 44 Magnum ammunition that exceeded 60,000 CUP when fired from pressure barrels—that greatly exceeds the highest current SAAMI pressure specification for any cartridge! If you have any early factory 44 Magnum ammunition, the best bet is to sell it to a collector—along with a warning label. The stuff is just not safe to use in some later and potentially weaker handguns and rifles.

The advent of improved powders has allowed current 44 Magnum loads largely to duplicate those early ballistics while staying within a more reasonable pressure limit. Elmer would be pleased. He always advocated a 240/250-grain cast SWC at about 1300 fps as the ideal 44 Magnum load for all uses. Such a load is easily achieved.

The best jacketed-bullet hunting combinations depend entirely on the game at hand. For smaller species of deer, the lighter modern expanding bullets can deliver instantaneous kills when placed through the lungs on broadside shots. These will do the same thing on elk, if the shot is properly placed. However, if heavy bone might be struck, 300-grain bullets are a better choice.

Usable case capacity with a 240-grain bullet, seated normally, is about 25.2 grains of water. W296, H110, N110 and especially No.9 are excellent 44 Magnum powders. **NOTE:** The Redhawk revolver used by Accurate Arms gave higher velocity than most pressure barrels!

44 REMINGTON MAGNUM LOADING DATA

Lead 215 Penney's (SWC)

Powder	STARTING Grs.	MV (fps)	MAXIMUM Grs.	MV (fps)	Press. (CUP/psi)	Comments
No.9	21.2	1456	23.6	1655	40,000C	1.56"
No.7	16.5	1336	18.3	1518	40,000C	1.56"
No.5	13.3	1293	14.8	1469	38,900C	1.56"
No.2	9.2	1155	10.2	1313	39,300C	1.56"

Lead 215 GC

Powder	STARTING Grs.	MV (fps)	MAXIMUM Grs.	MV (fps)	Press. (CUP/psi)	Comments
H110	25.0	1441	26.0	1630	33,300C	
H4227	25.0	1490	26.0	1592	34,500C	
HS7	15.0	1316	17.0	1541	24,400C	
HS6	11.0	1065	13.0	1240	20,200C	

Lead 215 GC con't

Powder	STARTING Grs.	MV (fps)	MAXIMUM Grs.	MV (fps)	Press. (CUP/psi)	Comments
HP38	5.9	832	6.9	954	15,600C	
Trap100	6.0	837	7.0	949	16,800C	

Lead 240 SWC

Powder	STARTING Grs.	MV (fps)	MAXIMUM Grs.	MV (fps)	Press. (CUP/psi)	Comments
No.9	19.5	1364	21.7	1550	39,600C	1.56"
No.7	15.8	1283	17.5	1458	39,700C	1.56"
XMP5744			24.0	1446	34,500C	1.56"
No.5	12.6	1235	14.0	1400	40,000C	1.56"
No.2	9.0	1126	10.0	1280	40,000C	1.56"

Never exceed maximum load nor use any load exhibiting signs of excessive pressure. Begin at suggested starting load and work up carefully.

Lead 250

Powder	STARTING Grs.	MV (fps)	MAXIMUM Grs.	MV (fps)	Press. (CUP/psi)	Comments
H110	22.0	1460	23.0	1602	35,000C	
H4227	22.0	1355	24.0	1476	34,800C	
HS7	11.0	1082	13.0	1237	27,800C	
HS6	10.0	1001	12.0	1176	24,000C	
HP38	5.4	766	6.4	881	16,900C	
Trap100	5.5	776	6.5	877	17,300C	

Lead 267 Intercast (FN)

Powder	Grs.	MV (fps)	Grs.	MV (fps)	Press. (CUP/psi)	Comments
N110	19.6	1337	21.2	1443	34,200p	1.681"/*
3N37	11.2	1155	12.7	1254	34,200p	1.681"/*
N350	10.8	1142	12.2	1233	34,200p	1.681"/*
N340	10.0	1142	11.2	1211	34,200p	1.681"/*

Lead 280 American (SWC)

Powder	Grs.	MV (fps)	Grs.	MV (fps)	Press. (CUP/psi)	Comments
No.9	17.1	1202	19.0	1350	40,000C	1.695"/*
No.7	14.0	1137	15.5	1277	34,800C	1.695"/*
No.5	10.6	1013	11.8	1151	29,400C	1.695"/*
No.2	8.9	1002	9.5	1139	36,500C	1.695"/*

Lead 300 SSK (Penney's)

Powder	Grs.	MV (fps)	Grs.	MV (fps)	Press. (CUP/psi)	Comments
No.9	16.6	1175	18.5	1320	40,000C	1.72"/*
No.7	13.5	1100	15.0	1245	34,000C	1.72"/*
No.5	10.4	1003	11.6	1140	32,300C	1.72"/*
No.2	8.6	1001	9.5	1138	38,800C	1.72"/*

Lead 325 SWC

Powder	Grs.	MV (fps)	Grs.	MV (fps)	Press. (CUP/psi)	Comments
XMP5744			18.0	1082	27,800C	1.69"

180

Powder	Grs.	MV (fps)	Grs.	MV (fps)	Press. (CUP/psi)	Comments
H110	28.0	1782	29.0	1873	33,000C	JHP
W296	28.0	1775	29.0	1866	32,900C	JHP
N110	25.9	1667	28.4	1837	34,200p	Hdy XTP/1.602"
No.7	18.5	1502	20.5	1707	40,000C	Hdy JHP/1.56"
H4227	27.0	1604	28.0	1701	30,600C	JHP
HS7	17.0	1462	19.0	1694	29,000C	JHP
W571	17.0	1349	19.0	1691	29,400C	JHP
HS6	14.0	1356	16.5	1663	35,200C	JHP
Her2400	22.0	1544	23.5	1639	34,600C	JHP
W540	14.0	1350	16.0	1634	34,600C	JHP
IMR4227	24.0	1493	27.0	1632	30,200C	
No.5	14.8	1421	16.4	1615	38,100C	Hdy JHP/1.56"
Blue Dot	16.0	1498	17.5	1594	34,100C	JHP
IMR800-X	14.0	1502	15.0	1566	36,200C	
N350	13.1	1416	14.8	1539	34,200p	Hdy XTP/1.602"
Universal			12.5	1519	38,200C	JHP
N340	12.3	1385	13.7	1509	34,200p	Hdy XTP/1.602"
Herco	11.0	1344	13.0	1480	32,600C	JHP
Unique	11.2	1351	13.2	1480	32,600C	JHP
Green Dot	9.5	1269	11.5	1454	34,100C	JHP

*Exceeds SAAMI maximum OAL.

180 con't

Powder	STARTING Grs.	MV (fps)	MAXIMUM Grs.	MV (fps)	Press. (CUP/psi)	Comments
Red Dot	9.0	1240	11.0	1448	34,200C	JHP
No.2	10.0	1271	11.1	1444	36,500C	Hdy JHP/1.56"
N320	10.1	1289	11.4	1398	34,200p	Hdy XTP/1.602"
SR4756	12.5	1284	13.5	1390	35,500C	
Bullseye	8.5	1152	10.5	1380	31,800C	JHP
HP38	8.0	1118	10.0	1307	26,200C	JHP
W231	8.0	1110	10.0	1289	26,000C	JHP
SR7625	10.0	1202	11.0	1282	36,600C	
IMR-PB	10.0	1192	11.0	1274	36,700C	
Trap100	8.0	1111	10.0	1260	24,200C	JHP
IMR700-X	7.0	1009	9.0	1169	37,000C	

200

Powder	Grs.	MV (fps)	Grs.	MV (fps)	Press. (CUP/psi)	Comments
N110	23.5	1561	25.7	1698	34,200p	Hdy XTP/1.602"
No.9	22.5	1475	25.0	1676	37,800C	Nos JHP/1.595"
No.7	16.8	1353	18.7	1538	37,500C	Nos JHP/1.595"
No.5	14.2	1348	15.8	1532	40,000C	Nos JHP/1.595"
3N37	13.0	1373	14.7	1483	34,200p	Hdy XTP/1.602"
N350	12.0	1304	14.0	1444	34,200p	Hdy XTP/1.602"
N340	11.2	1299	12.6	1403	34,200p	Hdy XTP/1.602"
No.2	9.9	1181	11.0	1342	39,500C	Nos JHP/1.595"
N320	9.5	1207	10.9	1308	34,200p	Hdy XTP/1.602"

200-210

Powder	Grs.	MV (fps)	Grs.	MV (fps)	Press. (CUP/psi)	Comments
H110	26.0	1666	27.0	1848	36,000C	JHP
W296	26.0	1664	27.0	1838	35,900C	JHP (200-gr.)
H4227	25.0	1488	27.0	1648	35,400C	JHP
IMR4227	24.0	1444	27.0	1594	33,800C	(200-gr.)
HS7	15.0	1348	17.0	1582	29,800C	JHP
W571	15.0	1339	17.0	1575	30,000C	JHP (200-gr.)
Her2400	19.0	1310	21.5	1560	35,100C	JHP (200-gr.)
Blue Dot	14.0	1284	16.0	1529	36,000C	JHP (200-gr.)
IMR800-X	13.5	1434	14.5	1529	36,600C	(200-gr.)
HS6	13.0	1197	15.5	1516	32,400C	JHP
W540	13.0	1200	15.0	1477	31,700C	JHP (200-gr.)
Herco	11.0	1244	12.5	1456	34,400C	JHP (200-gr.)
Unique	10.5	1229	12.0	1420	33,900C	JHP (200-gr.)
Universal			12.0	1409	37,300C	JHP (200-gr.)
Green Dot	9.0	1192	11.0	1397	34,000C	JHP (200-gr.)
Red Dot	8.5	1175	10.5	1378	33,700C	JHP (200-gr.)
Bullseye	8.0	1149	10.0	1354	34,000C	JHP (200-gr.)
SR4756	12.0	1262	13.0	1354	35,900C	(200-gr.)
SR7625	9.5	1129	10.5	1227	35,400C	(200-gr.)
W231	7.5	1034	9.5	1225	25,000C	JHP (200-gr.)
HP38	7.4	1029	9.4	1220	24,200C	JHP
IMR-PB	9.0	1118	10.0	1198	35,000C	(200-gr.)
Trap100	7.5	1037	9.5	1188	23,100C	JHP
IMR700-X	7.5	1129	8.5	1187	35,600C	(200-gr.)

225

Powder	Grs.	MV (fps)	Grs.	MV (fps)	Press. (CUP/psi)	Comments
H110	23.0	1452	24.0	1596	39,200C	JHP

Never exceed maximum load nor use any load exhibiting signs of excessive pressure. Begin at suggested starting load and work up carefully.

225 con't

Powder	Grs.	MV (fps)	Grs.	MV (fps)	Press. (CUP/psi)	Comments
W296	23.0	1444	24.0	1581	39,000C	JHP
H4227	23.0	1414	24.0	1529	36,300C	JHP
Her2400	18.5	1272	20.5	1479	35,100C	JHP
IMR800-X	13.0	1333	14.0	1434	34,600C	
Blue Dot	13.0	1219	15.0	1411	33,400C	JHP
Universal			11.5	1356	37,600C	JHP
IMR4227	22.0	1261	23.0	1352	32,000C	
Herco	11.0	1220	12.0	1348	32,600C	JHP
Unique	10.0	1224	11.5	1340	33,500C	JHP
W571	13.0	1199	15.0	1311	30,100C	JHP
Green Dot	9.0	1171	10.5	1290	33,800C	JHP
Red Dot	8.0	1154	10.0	1288	34,000C	JHP
HS7	12.5	1197	14.5	1282	28,800C	JHP
SR4756	11.5	1209	12.5	1280	36,100C	
Bullseye	7.5	1081	9.5	1240	32,800C	JHP
HS6	11.5	1150	13.5	1239	27,900C	JHP
W540	12.0	1189	13.5	1228	28,000C	JHP
SR7625	9.0	1091	10.0	1177	35,400C	
IMR-PB	8.5	1050	9.5	1144	36,600C	
IMR700-X	7.0	1057	8.0	1129	36,900C	
HP38	6.4	896	8.4	1090	24,400C	JHP
W231	6.5	904	8.5	1088	24,800C	JHP
Trap100	6.5	911	8.5	1086	23,800C	JHP

240

Powder	Grs.	MV (fps)	Grs.	MV (fps)	Press. (CUP/psi)	Comments
H110	23.0	1411	24.0	1548	39,300C	JSP
N110	19.6	1369	21.5	1500	34,200p	Hdy JTC-SIL/1.602"
No.9	19.1	1320	21.3	1500	40,000C	IMI JHP/1.56"
H4227	22.0	1319	24.0	1444	36,900C	JSP
W296	21.5	1284	23.5	1429	36,400C	JSP
No.7	15.6	1245	17.3	1415	40,000C	IMI JHP/1.56"
XMP5744			24.0	1413	34,900C	Hdy XTP
Her2400	18.0	1270	19.5	1411	36,000C	JSP
No.5	13.0	1217	14.4	1383	39,800C	IMI JHP/1.56"
Blue Dot	13.0	1168	15.0	1328	34,900C	JSP
IMR800-X	12.5	1244	13.5	1328	38,000C	
IMR4227	21.0	1235	22.0	1298	33,900C	
3N37	11.3	1173	12.9	1284	34,200p	Hdy JTC-SIL/1.602"
Herco	10.5	1166	11.5	1282	34,000C	JSP
N350	11.3	1190	12.4	1279	34,200p	Hdy JTC-SIL/1.602"
Unique	9.5	1100	11.0	1273	34,200C	JSP
Universal			10.8	1257	36,400C	JHP
No.2	9.0	1100	10.0	1250	38,600C	IMI JHP/1.56"
HS7	11.0	1149	13.0	1223	28,000C	JSP
N340	9.8	1138	11.1	1221	34,200p	Hdy JTC-SIL/1.602"
W571	11.0	1138	13.0	1220	28,000C	JSP
HS6	10.0	1134	12.0	1211	26,600C	JSP
SR4756	11.0	1174	12.0	1210	35,600C	
W540	10.0	1122	12.0	1198	26,400C	JSP
Green Dot	8.5	1140	9.5	1191	32,400C	JSP
Red Dot	8.0	1133	9.0	1182	33,900C	JSP
Bullseye	7.0	1019	9.0	1178	34,000C	JSP
N320	8.6	1046	9.5	1135	34,200p	Hdy JTC-SIL/1.602"

240 con't

Powder	Grs.	MV (fps)	Grs.	MV (fps)	Press. (CUP/psi)	Comments
SR7625	8.5	1039	9.5	1122	34,800C	
IMR-PB	8.0	1012	9.0	1069	33,000C	
W231	5.5	844	7.5	1040	24,000C	JSP
HP38	5.4	845	7.4	1032	23,400C	JSP
Trap100	5.5	851	7.5	1012	22,900C	JSP

250

Powder	Grs.	MV (fps)	Grs.	MV (fps)	Press. (CUP/psi)	Comments
H110	22.0	1396	23.0	1492	34,600C	
W296	21.0	1249	23.0	1469	35,100C	JSP
No.9	18.9	1275	21.0	1449	39,200C	Sra FPJ/1.6"
H4227	21.0	1224	23.0	1400	34,800C	
IMR4227	21.0	1230	23.0	1389	35,200C	
Her2400	17.5	1260	19.0	1377	35,400C	JSP
No.5	13.1	1198	14.5	1361	39,700C	Sra FPJ/1.6"
No.7	15.3	1170	17.0	1330	37,700C	Sra FPJ/1.6"
IMR800-X	12.0	1229	13.0	1320	39,800C	
Blue Dot	13.0	1162	14.5	1295	33,400C	JSP
No.2	9.5	1083	10.5	1231	38,400C	Sra FPJ/1.6"
Herco	10.0	1067	11.0	1204	31,600C	JSP
W571	11.0	1119	13.0	1200	28,200C	JSP
Unique	9.0	1044	10.5	1184	34,000C	JSP
SR4756	11.2	1071	11.8	1180	33,000C	
W540	10.0	998	12.0	1134	25,200C	JSP
Green Dot	8.0	1003	9.0	1069	30,000C	JSP
SR7625	8.0	932	9.0	1042	33,000C	
IMR-PB	7.5	880	8.5	983	34,800C	
HP38	5.5	751	7.0	944	19,600C	JSP
W231	6.0	790	7.0	941	19,400C	JSP

260-265

Powder	Grs.	MV (fps)	Grs.	MV (fps)	Press. (CUP/psi)	Comments
H110	19.0	1300	22.0	1507	34,200C	JSP
W296	19.0	1284	22.0	1496	34,900C	JSP
H4227	19.0	1163	22.0	1368	35,400C	JSP
Her2400	17.5	1244	18.5	1335	34,600C	JSP
Blue Dot	12.0	1221	14.0	1302	36,000C	JSP
HS7	12.0	1178	14.0	1295	31,900C	JSP
IMR4227	19.0	1060	21.0	1288	34,400C	
HS6	10.0	1061	13.5	1287	33,600C	JSP
W571	12.0	1166	14.0	1279	32,000C	JSP
IMR800-X	11.5	1139	12.5	1279	36,700C	
W540	10.0	966	13.0	1244	31,900C	JSP
Universal			10.0	1160	35,600C	JHP

▶▶▶▶▶▶▶▶▶▶▶▶▶▶▶▶▶▶▶▶▶▶▶▶▶▶▶▶▶

Caution: Loads exceeding SAAMI OAL Maximum must be verified for bullet-to-rifling clearance and magazine functioning. Where a specific primer or bullet is indicated those components must be used, no substitutions! Where only a maximum load is shown, reduce starting load 10%, unless otherwise specified.

Key: (C) = compressed charge; C = CUP; p = psi; Plink = Plinker; Bns = Barnes; Hdy = Hornady; Lap = Lapua; Nos = Nosler; Rem = Remington; Sra = Sierra; Spr = Speer; Win = Winchester.

Never exceed maximum load nor use any load exhibiting signs of excessive pressure. Begin at suggested starting load and work up carefully.

319

44 REMINGTON MAGNUM LOADING DATA

Powder	STARTING Grs.	MV (fps)	MAXIMUM Grs.	MV (fps)	Press. (CUP/psi)	Comments
275						
H110	18.5	1198	20.5	1341	34,800C	JSP
W296	18.5	1211	20.5	1340	35,100C	JSP
H4227	18.5	1094	20.5	1311	37,700C	JSP
Her2400	16.5	1224	17.5	1273	36,000C	JSP
IMR4227	18.5	1064	20.5	1262	36,900C	JSP
IMR800-X	11.0	1188	12.0	1241	36,600C	JSP
Blue Dot	11.5	1161	13.5	1240	34,000C	JSP
300						
H110	18.0	1153	20.0	1303	34,800C	
W296	18.0	1166	20.0	1290	35,400C	JSP
No.9	15.9	1121	17.7	1274	38,320C	Hdy XTP/1.595"
N110	17.1	1161	18.6	1271	34,200p	Sra JSP/1.717"
No.9	17.1	1106	19.0	1257	40,000C	Sra JSP/1.735"
H4227	18.0	1047	20.0	1244	36,800C	

Powder	STARTING Grs.	MV (fps)	MAXIMUM Grs.	MV (fps)	Press. (CUP/psi)	Comments
300 con't						
Her2400	16.0	1161	17.0	1242	35,700C	JSP
IMR4227	18.0	1056	20.0	1238	37,700C	JSP
No.5	12.6	1080	14.0	1227	40,000C	Sra JSP/1.735"
No.7	14.6	1074	16.2	1221	40,000C	Sra JSP/1.735"
No.5	11.7	1074	13.0	1220	39,000C	Hdy XTP/1.595"
Blue Dot	10.0	1019	12.0	1209	36,600C	JSP
IMR800-X	10.5	1077	11.5	1194	38,000C	JSP
XMP5744			20.0	1191	31,400C	Hdy XTP/1.595"
No.7	13.1	1047	14.5	1190	38,000C	Hdy XTP/1.595"
No.2	8.8	975	9.8	1108	39,400C	Hdy XTP/1.595"
No.2	8.7	933	9.7	1060	38,700C	Sra JSP/1.735"
3N37	9.5	954	10.8	1057	34,200p	Sra JSP/1.717"
Universal			9.5	1048	33,700C	JHP
N350	9.3	924	10.6	1036	34,200p	Sra JSP/1.717"
N340	8.9	934	9.9	1019	34,200p	Sra JSP/1.717"

44 REMINGTON MAGNUM DESERT EAGLE SPECIFIC LOADING DATA

Powder	STARTING Grs.	MV (fps)	MAXIMUM Grs.	MV (fps)	Press. (CUP/psi)	Comments
240						
No.9	19.1	1226	21.3	1312	40,000C	IMI JHP/1.56"
No.7	15.6	1063	17.3	1224	40,000C	IMI JHP/1.56"
250						
No.9	18.9	1206	21.0	1299	39,200C	Sra FPJ/1.6"
No.7	15.3	1050	17.0	1210	37,700C	Sra FPJ/1.6"

Powder	STARTING Grs.	MV (fps)	MAXIMUM Grs.	MV (fps)	Press. (CUP/psi)	Comments
300						
No.9	15.9	1162	17.7	1222	38,300C	Hdy XTP/1.595"
No.7	13.1	934	14.5	1041	38,000C	Hdy XTP/1.595"

44 REMINGTON MAGNUM T/C SPECIFIC LOADING DATA

Powder	STARTING Grs.	MV (fps)	MAXIMUM Grs.	MV (fps)	Press. (CUP/psi)	Comments
180						
H110	28.0	1910	29.0	1984		
HS7	17.0	1627	19.0	1881		
H4227	27.0	1754	28.0	1840		
200						
H110	26.0	1810	27.0	1977		
H4227	25.0	1634	27.0	1758		
225						
H110	24.0	1643	25.0	1790		
H4227	23.0	1591	25.0	1687		

Powder	STARTING Grs.	MV (fps)	MAXIMUM Grs.	MV (fps)	Press. (CUP/psi)	Comments
240						
H110	23.0	1594	24.0	1720		
H4227	22.0	1514	24.0	1686		
260-265						
H110	20.0	1322	22.0	1571		
H4227	20.0	1264	22.0	1459		
300						
H110	18.0	1219	20.0	1411		
H4227	18.0	1161	20.0	1359		

Never exceed maximum load nor use any load exhibiting signs of excessive pressure. Begin at suggested starting load and work up carefully.

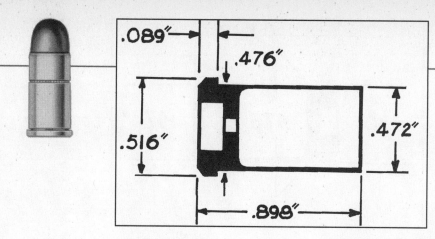

Case: Remingon
Primer: CCI 300
Barrel: 6½″ Accurate (S&W 25-2)
Bullet Diameter: 0.451″-0.454″

Maximum Case Length: 0.898″
Trim to Length: 0.893″
Maximum Cartridge OAL: 1.275″
Minimum Cartridge OAL: 1.225″

U.S. involvement in WWI found this country with neither sufficient issue sidearms nor the manufacturing facilities to produce enough Model 1911s to meet the needs of the burgeoning Army. As a military expedient, both Smith & Wesson and Colt produced special versions of their large-frame double-action revolvers. These were chambered for the 45 Automatic. This expedient simplified battlefield ammunition supply.

To facilitate extraction of rimless 45 Automatic cases, these guns were designed to use half-moon clips. These clips inserted into the extractor grooves and assembled three cartridges. The gun's extractor pushed on these clips, which pulled the spent cases from the cylinder. While sufficient for military wartime needs, this was never particularly handy.

After the treaty, which temporarily ended our European military involvement, thousands of these revolvers were sold to the U.S. public. Peters Cartridge Company solved

the extraction problem and the half-moon-clip nuisance by introducing the oddly named 45 Automatic Rim cartridge. The cartridge is identical to the 45 Automatic in every way excepting inclusion of an extra-thick rim—to equal the thickness of the original 45 Auto rim and the half-moon clip combined. Factory loads used only lead bullets.

More recently, Smith & Wesson offered a modified version of their large-frame double-action revolver chambered to use the 45 Auto or 45 Auto Rim. With a shorter cylinder and a barrel that extended appreciably into the cylinder housing of the frame, this revolver looks a bit odd. However, accuracy is dramatically improved owing to the reduced bullet jump to the bore.

The 45 AR allows use of a crimp. This is a good revolver cartridge. Not surprisingly, performance is similar to the 45 Auto.

45 AUTOMATIC RIM LOADING DATA

Lead 200 H&G 130 (SWC)

Powder	STARTING Grs.	MV (fps)	MAXIMUM Grs.	MV (fps)	Press. (CUP/psi)	Comments
No.2	5.6	863	6.2	981	14,600C	1.175″/*
N100	5.0	849	5.5	965	13,900C	1.175″/*
No.5	7.7	848	8.6	964	15,000C	1.175″/*

Lead 235 RCBS (RN)

Powder	STARTING Grs.	MV (fps)	MAXIMUM Grs.	MV (fps)	Press. (CUP/psi)	Comments
No.2	5.2	769	5.8	874	14,700C	1.265″/*
N100	4.8	765	5.3	869	15,000C	1.265″/*
No.5	7.2	730	8.0	830	13,900C	1.265″/*

* 0.454″ bullet diameter

Lead 255 Lyman 452424 (SWC)

Powder	STARTING Grs.	MV (fps)	MAXIMUM Grs.	MV (fps)	Press. (CUP/psi)	Comments
No.9	10.8	769	12.0	874	14,400C	1.25″
No.7	8.6	744	9.5	846	13,600C	1.25″
No.5	6.2	733	6.9	833	15,000C	1.25″
No.2	4.7	710	5.2	807	14,800C	1.25″
N100	4.2	699	4.7	794	14,400C	1.25″

Caution: Loads exceeding SAAMI OAL Maximum must be verified for bullet-to-rifling clearance and magazine functioning. Where a specific primer or bullet is indicated those components must be used, no substitutions! Where only a maximum load is shown, reduce starting load 10%, unless otherwise specified.

Key: (C) = compressed charge; C = CUP; p = psi; Plink = Plinker; Bns = Barnes; Hdy = Hornady; Lap = Lapua; Nos = Nosler; Rem = Remington; Sra = Sierra; Spr = Speer; Win = Winchester.

Never exceed maximum load nor use any load exhibiting signs of excessive pressure. Begin at suggested starting load and work up carefully.

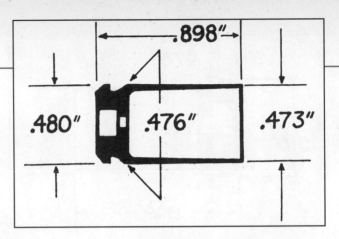

Case: Remington
Primer: Large Pistol
Barrel: 5″ Accurate (1911-A1)
6½″ Accurate (S&W 25-2)
5″ Hodgdon
6″ Vihtavuori
5″ Winchester

Bullet Diameter: 0.451″-0.452″
Maximum Case Length: 0.898″
Trim to Length: 0.893″
Maximum Cartridge OAL: 1.275″
Minimum Cartridge OAL: 1.150″;
(Listed Match Loads Only!)

Developed to meet a purpose—the delivery of a bullet of a specified size, weight and shape at a specified velocity—the 45 Automatic has been with us since its adoption in 1911, as the official service cartridge for U.S. military sidearms. It became a common chambering in submachine guns for military, police and civilian(!) markets.

With comparatively generous powder capacity, by pistol standards, the 45 Automatic can generate substantial performance without the necessity of high chamber pressures—not significantly different from typical blackpowder cartridge pressures. The more recent +P standard produces pressures similar to the original military load, providing a worthwhile increase in performance.

A quick comparison of this +P data with that for all smaller caliber pistol chamberings is quite revealing. Using the best powders, the 1911 Colt 45 easily pushes the 185-grain bullet to almost 1200 fps, and the 200-grain can safely exceed 1100 fps! The vaunted 10mm Automatic, despite working at 60-percent higher chamber pressures, can only manage a modest 100 fps increase with similar-weight bullets—bullet diameter and usable capacity make a difference!

The 45 Automatic cannot be considered a big game cartridge, and it certainly lacks the velocity necessary for varmints except at the shortest ranges. Primarily a serious self-defense chambering, it has also won an amazing share of target pistol matches and is still a favorite among competitors.

Usable case capacity with a 230-grain bullet, seated normally, is about 17.6 grains of water. It is impossible to single out any reasonable list of superior 45 Auto powders...too many work too well.

45 AUTOMATIC LOADING DATA

Lead 154-155 SWC

Powder	STARTING Grs.	MV (fps)	MAXIMUM Grs.	MV (fps)	Press. (CUP/psi)	Comments
N340	7.8	1156	8.5	1274	20,000p	1.24″/Intercast
No.7	12.0	1076	13.3	1223	20,200p	1.24″/Rem 2½/Behn
No.2	6.8	1060	7.5	1204	20,600p	1.24″/Rem 2½/Behn
No.5	9.0	1046	10.0	1189	18,500p	1.24″/Rem 2½/Behn
N320	6.0	1059	6.7	1181	20,000p	1.24″/Intercast
N100	5.9	1010	6.5	1148	17,600p	1.24″/Rem 2½/Behn
WAP	8.2	1035	9.0	1135	19,700p	

Lead 155-160

Powder	STARTING Grs.	MV (fps)	MAXIMUM Grs.	MV (fps)	Press. (CUP/psi)	Comments
Universal			7.6	1795	18,200C	SWC (155-gr.)
Trap100	7.0	1130	7.8	1239	19,900C	
HP38	7.5	1122	8.0	1179	19,900C	
Bullseye	6.2	1051	6.7	1164	19,300C	
SR4756	9.5	982	10.4	1155	19,700C	
W231	7.1	1040	7.7	1144	19,200C	

Lead 155-160 con't

Powder	STARTING Grs.	MV (fps)	MAXIMUM Grs.	MV (fps)	Press. (CUP/psi)	Comments
Unique	7.7	1044	8.2	1130	18,400C	
IMR700-X	5.5	1044	6.0	1104	19,900C	
Clays			5.2	1082	17,700C	SWC (155-gr.)

Lead 170 SWC

Powder	STARTING Grs.	MV (fps)	MAXIMUM Grs.	MV (fps)	Press. (CUP/psi)	Comments
No.7	11.3	1031	12.5	1172	20,800p	1.13″/Rem 2½
No.2	5.9	950	6.5	1079	19,400p	1.13″/Rem 2½
No.5	8.1	945	9.0	1074	17,800p	1.13″/Rem 2½
N100	5.4	943	6.0	1072	19,400p	1.13″/Rem 2½

Lead 180 SWC

Powder	STARTING Grs.	MV (fps)	MAXIMUM Grs.	MV (fps)	Press. (CUP/psi)	Comments
N340	6.9	1047	7.8	1167	20,000p	1.244″/Intercast
N320	5.6	998	6.4	1116	20,000p	1.244″/Intercast
WAP	7.5	940	8.3	1055	20,000p	

Never exceed maximum load nor use any load exhibiting signs of excessive pressure. Begin at suggested starting load and work up carefully.

Powder	—STARTING— Grs.	MV (fps)	—MAXIMUM— Grs.	MV (fps)	Press. (CUP/psi)	Comments

Lead 200 SWC

Powder	Grs.	MV (fps)	Grs.	MV (fps)	Press. (CUP/psi)	Comments
N340	6.3	990	7.0	1095	20,000p	1.24"/Intercast
No.5	7.8	902	8.7	1025	19,400p	1.19"/Rem 2½/Hdy
No.7	10.4	899	11.5	1022	18,700p	1.19"/Rem 2½/Hdy
N320	4.8	912	5.5	1010	20,000p	1.24"/Intercast
Universal			6.7	981	16,600C	
WAP	6.6	850	7.6	970	19,700p	
N100	5.0	838	5.5	952	18,100p	1.19"/Rem 2½/Hdy
No.2	5.2	826	5.8	939	17,400p	1.19"/Rem 2½/Hdy
HP38	4.4	771	5.6	914	16,900C	
HS6	8.2	860	8.4	907	16,300C	
Clays			4.3	888	17,000C	

Lead 220

Powder	Grs.	MV (fps)	Grs.	MV (fps)	Press. (CUP/psi)	Comments
HP38	4.3	764	5.4	886	16,400C	
HS6	8.1	849	8.3	885	16,400C	
Trap100	4.4	749	5.2	830	15,000C	

Lead 230 Hdy (RN)

Powder	Grs.	MV (fps)	Grs.	MV (fps)	Press. (CUP/psi)	Comments
No.7	9.9	862	11.0	979	19,400p	1.23"/Rem 2½
No.5	7.7	852	8.5	968	19,800p	1.23"/Rem 2½
WAP	6.6	845	7.3	915	19,600p	
N100	4.8	790	5.3	898	18,800p	1.23"/Rem 2½
No.2	5.0	766	5.6	870	17,200p	1.23"/Rem 2½

Lead 250 Clements (SWC)/6½" S&W 25-2

Powder	Grs.	MV (fps)	Grs.	MV (fps)	Press. (CUP/psi)	Comments
No.9	10.8	766	12.0	870	20,600p	1.26"/Rem 2½
No.7	8.6	732	9.5	832	17,100p	1.26"/Rem 2½
No.5	6.4	722	7.1	820	18,300p	1.26"/Rem 2½
No.2	4.7	711	5.2	808	19,400p	1.26"/Rem 2½
N100	4.3	709	4.8	806	18,600p	1.26"/Rem 2½

185

Powder	Grs.	MV (fps)	Grs.	MV (fps)	Press. (CUP/psi)	Comments
N340	7.3	1022	8.1	1149	20,000p	Spr TMJ-SWC/1.268"
No.5	9.2	970	10.2	1102	19,900p	Hdy XTP/1.21"/Rem 2½
No.7	11.7	962	13.0	1093	18,000p	Hdy XTP/1.21"/Rem 2½
No.5	8.6	952	9.5	1082	20,500p	Hdy Target/1.135"/Rem 2½
No.2	6.8	948	7.5	1077	20,400p	Hdy XTP/1.21"/Rem 2½
No.7	10.8	938	12.0	1066	20,600p	Hdy Target/1.135"/Rem 2½
N320	5.8	937	6.5	1047	20,000p	Spr TMJ-SWC/1.268"
WAP	8.3	970	8.9	1045	19,900p	JHP
N100	5.9	919	6.6	1044	19,800p	Hdy XTP/1.21"/Rem 2½
WAP	7.2	865	8.1	1000	20,000p	JSWC
No.2	5.9	876	6.5	996	18,700p	Hdy Target/1.135"/Rem 2½
N100	5.2	876	5.8	995	19,600p	Hdy Target/1.135"/Rem 2½
Universal			7.2	993	17,000C	JHP
IMR800-X	7.0	851	8.3	990	18,600C	JHP
Clays			4.9	981	17,400C	JHP
Clays	3.9	816	4.9	974	17,409C	JSP
IMR700-X	4.5	811	5.5	956	17,700C	JHP

185 con't

Powder	Grs.	MV (fps)	Grs.	MV (fps)	Press. (CUP/psi)	Comments
Blue Dot	9.0	892	9.5	949	14,800C	JHP
Unique	6.0	869	7.0	928	16,000C	JHP
HS6	8.3	872	8.6	917	15,100C	JSP
Bullseye	4.8	844	5.3	914	15,900C	JHP

200

Powder	Grs.	MV (fps)	Grs.	MV (fps)	Press. (CUP/psi)	Comments
N350	6.9	943	7.9	1057	20,000p	Hdy FMJ-CT/1.24"
No.5	8.7	924	9.7	1050	20,600p	Hdy XTP/1.225"/Rem 2½
N340	6.4	933	7.1	1048	20,000p	Hdy FMJ-CT/1.24"
No.7	10.8	912	12.0	1036	19,200p	Hdy XTP/1.225"/Rem 2½
N320	5.1	878	5.8	983	20,000p	Hdy FMJ-CT/1.24"
WAP	7.0	825	8.0	965	19,400p	FMJ
WAP	7.0	855	7.7	965	20,100p	JHP
No.2	5.9	847	6.5	963	19,700p	Hdy XTP/1.225"/Rem 2½
N100	5.4	827	6.0	940	17,500p	Hdy XTP/1.225"/Rem 2½
IMR800-X	6.6	791	8.1	938	17,700C	JHP
Universal			6.7	930	17,200C	
IMR700-X	4.3	788	5.2	924	17,900C	JHP
Unique	5.9	848	6.6	921	16,200C	JHP
Bullseye	4.4	810	5.1	911	15,600C	JHP
Blue Dot	8.5	880	9.0	904	15,800C	JHP
W231	5.0	762	5.5	889	16,400C	JHP

225-230

Powder	Grs.	MV (fps)	Grs.	MV (fps)	Press. (CUP/psi)	Comments
N350	6.9	870	7.6	978	20,000p	Hdy FMJ-RN/1.26"
N340	6.0	856	6.8	974	20,000p	Hdy FMJ-RN/1.26"
No.5	7.8	816	8.7	927	19,300p	Sra FMJ/1.25"/Rem 2½
No.7	9.9	811	11.0	922	17,800p	Sra FMJ/1.25"/Rem 2½
Unique	5.0	794	6.0	898	16,200C	
N320	4.9	807	5.5	898	20,000p	Hdy FMJ-RN/1.26"
Blue Dot	7.5	822	8.5	894	16,000C	
N100	5.0	779	5.6	885	19,100p	Sra FMJ/1.25"/Rem 2½
WAP	6.8	820	7.4	885	19,600p	FMJ (230-gr.)
Bullseye	4.0	801	4.8	884	15,400C	
IMR800-X	6.2	766	7.2	859	17,800C	
Universal			6.0	853	16,900C	FMJ (230-gr.)
WAP	6.1	760	6.6	835	20,200p	JHP (230-gr.)
IMR700-X	4.2	757	5.0	834	17,400C	
Trap100	4.2	726	5.1	828	15,800C	(230-gr.)
HS6	8.0	790	8.2	825	15,400C	(230-gr.)
W231	4.6	750	5.2	824	17,100C	
No.2	5.5	769	6.1	814	19,200p	Sra FMJ/1.25"/Rem 2½

>>>>>>>>>>>>>>>>>>>>>>>>>>>>>>

Caution: Loads exceeding SAAMI OAL Maximum must be verified for bullet-to-rifling clearance and magazine functioning. Where a specific primer or bullet is indicated those components must be used, no substitutions! Where only a maximum load is shown, reduce starting load 10%, unless otherwise specified.

Key: (C) = compressed charge; C = CUP; p = psi; Plink = Plinker; Bns = Barnes; Hdy = Hornady; Lap = Lapua; Nos = Nosler; Rem = Remington; Sra = Sierra; Spr = Speer; Win = Winchester.

Never exceed maximum load nor use any load exhibiting signs of excessive pressure. Begin at suggested starting load and work up carefully.

45 AUTOMATIC LOADING DATA

Powder	—STARTING— Grs.	MV (fps)	—MAXIMUM— Grs.	MV (fps)	Press. (CUP/psi)	Comments
240/6½" S&W 25-2						
No.7	9.5	793	10.5	901	20,100p	Sra JHP/1.215"/Rem 2½
No.9	11.3	774	12.5	879	18,200p	Sra JHP/1.215"/Rem 2½
No.5	7.5	769	8.3	874	20,300p	Sra JHP/1.215"/Rem 2½
N100	4.9	732	5.4	832	19,600p	Sra JHP/1.215"/Rem 2½
No.2	5.1	714	5.7	811	19,600p	Sra JHP/1.215"/Rem 2½
250/6½" S&W 25-2						
No.7	9.5	790	10.5	898	20,900p	Nos JHP/1.23"/Rem 2½
No.9	11.3	780	12.5	886	20,800p	Nos JHP/1.23"/Rem 2½
No.5	7.2	752	8.0	854	19,100p	Nos JHP/1.23"/Rem 2½
N100	4.9	705	5.4	801	20,500p	Nos JHP/1.23"/Rem 2½
No.2	5.1	697	5.7	792	20,000p	Nos JHP/1.23"/Rem 2½

Powder	—STARTING— Grs.	MV (fps)	—MAXIMUM— Grs.	MV (fps)	Press. (CUP/psi)	Comments
260						
HS7	8.8	816	9.3	853	15,900C	JHP
HS6	7.5	801	8.0	849	16,800C	JHP
Trap100	4.5	714	5.0	806	16,600C	JHP
HP38	4.5	696	5.1	800	16,400C	JHP
IMR800-X	5.8	730	6.4	790	17,100C	JHP
W231	4.4	681	5.0	788	16,600C	JHP
Blue Dot	7.5	721	8.0	764	15,400C	JHP
Unique	5.0	694	5.8	755	15,100C	JHP
IMR700-X	4.2	714	4.6	746	17,400C	JHP
Bullseye	4.2	668	4.6	729	15,800C	JHP

45 AUTOMATIC TARGET LOADING DATA

Powder	—STARTING— Grs.	MV (fps)	—MAXIMUM— Grs.	MV (fps)	Press. (CUP/psi)	Comments
Lead 200 Hornady SWC						
No.5	6.3	720	7.0	818	13,100p	1.19"
No.2	3.6	616	4.0	700	11,500p	1.19"
N100	3.2	612	3.5	696	11,400p	1.19"

Powder	—STARTING— Grs.	MV (fps)	—MAXIMUM— Grs.	MV (fps)	Press. (CUP/psi)	Comments
185						
No.5	6.8	726	7.5	825	14,200p	Hdy Target/1.135"
N100	3.6	638	4.0	725	12,000p	Hdy Target/1.135"
No.2	4.1	629	4.5	715	11,900p	Hdy Target/1.135"

45 AUTOMATIC +P LOADING DATA

Powder	—STARTING— Grs.	MV (fps)	—MAXIMUM— Grs.	MV (fps)	Press. (CUP/psi)	Comments
185						
No.5	9.7	1049	10.8	1192	22,400p	Hdy XTP/1.21"/Rem 2½
No.7	12.2	1039	13.5	1181	21,700p	Hdy XTP/1.21"/Rem 2½(C)
HS6			10.0	1162	19,900C	
No.2	7.2	1016	8.0	1155	23,000p	Hdy XTP/1.21"/Rem 2½
HP38			6.6	1143	19,500C	
N100	6.2	923	6.9	1049	21,500p	Hdy XTP/1.21"/Rem 2½
200						
No.7	11.5	979	12.8	1112	23,000p	Hdy XTP/1.225"/Rem 2½
No.5	9.0	951	10.0	1081	22,600p	Hdy XTP/1.225"/Rem 2½
HS6			9.7	1056	19,500C	
HP38			6.4	1049	19,300C	
No.2	6.3	900	7.0	1023	23,000p	Hdy XTP/1.225"/Rem 2½
N100	5.9	880	6.5	1000	23,000p	Hdy XTP/1.225"/Rem 2½

Powder	—STARTING— Grs.	MV (fps)	—MAXIMUM— Grs.	MV (fps)	Press. (CUP/psi)	Comments
225						
HS6			9.4	1040	19,900C	
HP38			6.1	975	19,300C	
230						
HS6			9.3	981	19,700C	
HP38			6.0	970	19,100C	
260						
HS7			10.0	891	19,700C	
HS6			8.9	880	19,400C	
HP38			5.6	847	19,900C	

Never exceed maximum load nor use any load exhibiting signs of excessive pressure. Begin at suggested starting load and work up carefully

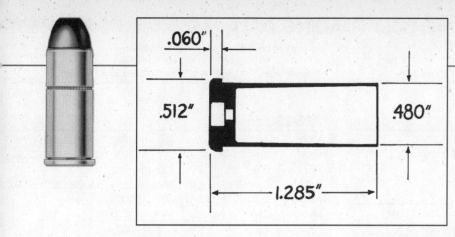

Case: Winchester
Primer: Large Pistol
Barrel: 7½″ Accurate
7″ Hodgdon
6″ Vihtavuori

Bullet Diameter: 0.451″-0.452″
(0.454″ for pre-WWII revolvers)
Maximum Case Length: 1.285″ (Rare)
Trim to Length: 1.280″
Maximum Cartridge OAL: 1.600″
Minimum Cartridge OAL: 1.550″

Co-introduced in 1873 with Colt's Single Action Army revolver, this—along with the 45-70—is perhaps one of the two most successful centerfire chamberings dating from the first years of self-contained cartridges. Others have survived, but none are nearly so popular anywhere in the world.

(Since there was never any other 45 Colt chambering, and since, obviously, there is no 45 Short Colt chambering, the moniker 45 Long Colt is senseless and has no *logical* historical basis. Nevertheless, none other than Colt at one time marketed ammunition under that very name! This confusion arises from the existence of the similar but shorter 45 Smith & Wesson cartridge, which could also be used in some 45 Colt-chambered guns.)

Cases of 45 Colt were originally the balloon-head design, those were followed by semi-balloon-head cases. Both types hold considerably more powder, but are also comparatively weak. The earliest cases were made of 100-percent copper and were very weak. In recent decades, all cases have been the solid-head type and are strong. Nevertheless, there is a general prohibition against using high pressure loads in the 45 Colt—for a very good reason.

The problem is not with the (modern) cases, as some

have suggested. The problem is with the existence of 120-year-old revolvers that inevitably will still be shot. Our advice is to have any old 45 Colt checked by a competent gunsmith before firing it with any load, and if in doubt, make a wall hanger out of it—better safe than sorry. These loads should not be fired in any blackpowder gun.

Even modern Colt and Colt replica revolvers have limited strength, owing to thin chamber walls. The Ruger revolver has much thicker chamber walls and does allow a useful increase in performance. For those guns, we have listed separate loads.

With substantial capacity, the 45 Colt can easily duplicate 45 Automatic performance despite modest pressures. Until the advent of the 357 Magnum, in 1935, the 45 Colt was the most powerful factory-chambered handgun cartridge, generating well over 800 fps with a 255-grain bullet—impressive self-defense performance, even by today's standards.

Usable case capacity with a 250-grain bullet, seated normally, is about 29.8 grains of water. HS7, HS6, Unique, N320, N100 and N340 are good 45 Colt powders.

45 COLT LOADING DATA

Powder	STARTING Grs.	MV (fps)	MAXIMUM Grs.	MV (fps)	Press. (CUP/psi)	Comments
Lead 180 SWC						
N350	11.0	1130	12.2	1247	13,300p	1.594″/Intercast
N340	10.2	1140	11.0	1233	13,300p	1.594″/Intercast
N330	9.7	1137	10.5	1229	13,300p	1.594″/Intercast
N320	8.2	1072	8.9	1158	13,300p	1.594″/Intercast
N310	5.2	930	6.2	1030	12,700p	1.525″/Starline
Lead 200 Hornady (SWC)						
N340	10.4	1080	11.2	1156	13,300p	1.594″
N320	8.3	1031	9.0	1102	13,300p	1.594″

Powder	STARTING Grs.	MV (fps)	MAXIMUM Grs.	MV (fps)	Press. (CUP/psi)	Comments
Lead 210 Starline						
N320	5.5	840	6.5	970	12,700p	1.525″
N310	4.5	820	5.5	930	13,400p	1.525″

➤➤➤➤➤➤➤➤➤➤➤➤➤➤➤➤➤➤➤➤➤➤➤➤➤

Caution: Loads exceeding SAAMI OAL Maximum must be verified for bullet-to-rifling clearance and magazine functioning. Where a specific primer or bullet is indicated those components must be used, no substitutions! Where only a maximum load is shown, reduce starting load 10%, unless otherwise specified.

Key: (C) = compressed charge; C = CUP; p = psi; Plink = Plinker; Bns = Barnes; Hdy = Hornady; Lap = Lapua; Nos = Nosler; Rem = Remington; Sra = Sierra; Spr = Speer; Win = Winchester.

Never exceed maximum load nor use any load exhibiting signs of excessive pressure. Begin at suggested starting load and work up carefully.

Lead 215 CP (SWC)

Powder	Grs.	MV (fps)	Grs.	MV (fps)	Press. (CUP/psi)	Comments
No.5	10.9	904	12.1	1027	12,500C	1.575″
N100	6.3	846	7.0	961	14,000C	1.575″

Lead 225 CP (FN)

Powder	Grs.	MV (fps)	Grs.	MV (fps)	Press. (CUP/psi)	Comments
No.5	10.9	909	12.1	1033	13,800C	1.62″/CCI 300/*
N100	6.2	821	6.9	933	13,600C	1.62″/CCI 300/*

*Exceeds SAAMI Maximum OAL.

Lead 240 Clements (SWC)

Powder	Grs.	MV (fps)	Grs.	MV (fps)	Press. (CUP/psi)	Comments
No.5	10.2	869	11.3	988	14,000C	1.57″/CCI 300
N100	5.9	799	6.6	908	14,000C	1.57″/CCI 300

Lead 255 Lyman 454424/Starline (FP)

Powder	Grs.	MV (fps)	Grs.	MV (fps)	Press. (CUP/psi)	Comments
No.5	9.4	846	10.4	961	13,400C	1.6″/CCI 300
N340	7.0	810	7.8	920	13,600p	1.6″/FP
N100	5.6	780	6.2	886	13,400C	1.6″/CCI 300
N320	5.6	830	6.1	870	13,100C	1.6″/FP
XMP5744			17.8	860	13,100p	1.6″/CCI 300
N310	4.2	730	5.2	830	13,300p	1.6″/FP

Cast Lead 340 SSK

Powder	Grs.	MV (fps)	Grs.	MV (fps)	Press. (CUP/psi)	Comments
Universal			6.8	805	14,000C	

185

Powder	Grs.	MV (fps)	Grs.	MV (fps)	Press. (CUP/psi)	Comments
HS6	12.0	949	14.0	1140	16,000C	
N320	8.3	1051	9.1	1137	13,300p	Hdy XTP/1.594″
HP38	8.5	979	9.5	1135	16,200C	
W231	8.0	949	9.0	1104	15,500C	
IMR-PB	8.0	989	9.0	1100	16,500C	
No.5	10.8	946	12.0	1075	12,200C	Sra JHP/1.575″/CCI 300
N100	6.8	944	7.6	1073	14,000C	Sra JHP/1.575″/CCI 300
IMR700-X	6.5	961	7.5	1066	15,900C	
Unique	8.5	912	9.5	1001	14,000C	

200

Powder	Grs.	MV (fps)	Grs.	MV (fps)	Press. (CUP/psi)	Comments
N320	7.6	999	8.5	1079	13,300p	Hdy FMJ-CT/1.594″
IMR-PB	7.0	929	8.5	1072	16,000C	
No.5	10.4	908	11.5	1032	13,400C	Hdy XTP/1.595″/CCI 300
N100	6.4	878	7.1	998	13,900C	Hdy XTP/1.595″/CCI 300
Bullseye	5.5	821	6.5	892	15,000C	
HP38	8.0	782	9.0	884	15,200C	
Unique	8.0	838	9.0	883	14,400C	
IMR700-X	6.0	812	7.0	873	15,000C	
HS6	12.0	810	13.5	870	14,400C	

225-230

Powder	Grs.	MV (fps)	Grs.	MV (fps)	Press. (CUP/psi)	Comments
N340	9.3	938	10.0	1032	13,300p	Sra FMJ-Match/1.594″
Universal			9.3	1000	14,200C	JHP

225-230 con't

Powder	Grs.	MV (fps)	Grs.	MV (fps)	Press. (CUP/psi)	Comments
N320	7.1	904	7.9	970	13,300p	Sra FMJ-Match/1.594″
No.5	9.9	853	11.0	969	14,000C	Hdy XTP/1.595″/CCI 300
HS7	15.0	887	16.0	960	15,900C	
N100	6.1	793	6.8	901	14,000C	Hdy XTP/1.595″/CCI 300
HS6	12.0	777	13.5	860	15,400C	
IMR-PB	7.0	792	8.0	847	15,100C	
HP38	7.5	744	8.5	830	15,000C	

240-250

Powder	Grs.	MV (fps)	Grs.	MV (fps)	Press. (CUP/psi)	Comments
No.5	9.5	854	10.5	970	14,000C	Sra JHP/1.59″/CCI 300
HS7	13.0	822	14.0	900	16,000C	
N100	6.0	774	6.7	880	14,000C	Sra JHP/1.59″/CCI 300
Universal			8.5	856	14,200C	
IMR800-X	8.5	769	9.5	849	15,900C	
HS6	11.5	744	12.5	836	14,300C	
Green Dot	6.5	729	7.5	800	15,600C	
HP38	7.0	714	8.0	790	15,200C	
Unique	7.0	720	8.0	788	14,900C	

250

Powder	Grs.	MV (fps)	Grs.	MV (fps)	Press. (CUP/psi)	Comments
No.5	9.9	704	11.0	800	14,000C	Hdy XTP/1.57″/CCI 300
N100	6.0	616	6.7	700	14,000C	Hdy XTP/1.57″/CCI 300

260

Powder	Grs.	MV (fps)	Grs.	MV (fps)	Press. (CUP/psi)	Comments
HS7	12.5	788	13.5	871	16,100C	
IMR800-X	8.0	729	9.0	810	15,700C	
HS6	11.0	709	12.0	804	14,500C	
HP38	6.0	697	7.5	797	15,900C	
Unique	7.0	709	8.0	770	15,500C	
No.5	9.5	671	10.5	762	14,000C	Spr JHP/1.6″/CCI 300
Green Dot	6.0	698	7.0	756	15,000C	
W231	6.5	699	7.5	749	15,400C	
IMR-PB	6.5	648	7.0	698	16,000C	

275

Powder	Grs.	MV (fps)	Grs.	MV (fps)	Press. (CUP/psi)	Comments
HS7	12.0	749	13.0	828	15,900C	
HS6	10.0	666	11.5	799	16,000C	
IMR800-X	8.0	711	8.5	761	15,500C	
HP38	6.0	639	7.0	740	15,700C	
W231	6.0	654	7.0	740	15,900C	
Green Dot	5.5	636	6.5	711	16,000C	
Unique	7.0	667	7.5	705	15,200C	

300

Powder	Grs.	MV (fps)	Grs.	MV (fps)	Press. (CUP/psi)	Comments
HS7	11.0	694	12.0	771	16,000C	
IMR800-X	7.0	637	8.0	738	15,500C	
HS6	9.5	632	10.5	712	16,200C	
Universal			7.3	700	13,700C	JHP
W231	5.5	592	6.5	698	15,800C	
Unique	6.0	634	7.0	689	16,000C	

Never exceed maximum load nor use any load exhibiting signs of excessive pressure. Begin at suggested starting load and work up carefully.

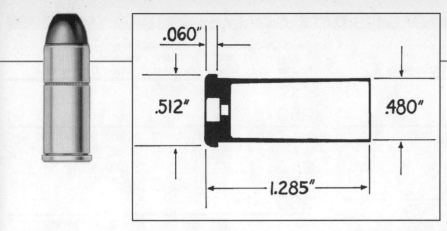

Case: Winchester
Primer: CCI 300
Barrel: 7½″ Accurate
Bullet Diameter: 0.451″-0.452″

Maximum Case Length: 1.285 (Rare)
Trim to Length: 1.280″
Maximum Cartridge OAL: 1.600″
Minimum Cartridge OAL: 1.550″

These loads are for use in Ruger revolvers, but they are also safe in the T/C Contender. They generate 45 Auto +P pressures, and while similar loads have sometimes been suggested for more recent Colt revolvers, prudence requires that such loads never be used in any Colt or replica revolver.

Using these loads with heavier cast bullets brings the Ruger 45 Colt-chambered revolver very close to 44 Magnum performance. This is certainly a fully capable hunting gun for deer-sized species.

Usable case capacity with a 250-grain bullet, seated normally, is about 29.8 grains of water. No.7 and No.9 are good 45 Colt choices for these Ruger and T/C specific loads.

45 COLT +P LOADING DATA (Ruger & T/C Specific Loads)

Lead 215 CP (SWC GC)

Powder	STARTING Grs.	MV (fps)	MAXIMUM Grs.	MV (fps)	Press. (CUP/psi)	Comments
No.7	14.9	1104	16.6	1254	20,900C	1.55″
No.5	12.2	1090	13.6	1239	20,800C	1.55″
N100	8.1	1023	9.0	1162	20,700C	1.55″

Lead 225 CP (SWC)

Powder	Grs.	MV (fps)	Grs.	MV (fps)	Press. (CUP/psi)	Comments
No.7	14.8	1087	16.4	1235	21,000C	1.575″
No.5	12.2	1076	13.6	1223	21,400C	1.575″
N100	7.9	1005	8.8	1142	20,800C	1.575″

Lead 230 CP (RN)

Powder	Grs.	MV (fps)	Grs.	MV (fps)	Press. (CUP/psi)	Comments
No.5	12.2	1065	13.5	1210	20,900C	1.6″
No.7	14.6	1062	16.2	1207	20,600C	1.6″
N100	7.7	965	8.6	1097	20,300C	1.6″

Lead 240 Clements (SWC)

Powder	Grs.	MV (fps)	Grs.	MV (fps)	Press. (CUP/psi)	Comments
No.7	14.1	1052	15.7	1196	20,600C	1.57″
No.5	11.1	1010	12.3	1148	20,000C	1.57″
N100	7.6	954	8.4	1084	20,300C	1.57″

Lead 255 Lyman 454424 (SWC)

Powder	Grs.	MV (fps)	Grs.	MV (fps)	Press. (CUP/psi)	Comments
No.9	15.8	1038	17.6	1180	20,100C	1.6″
No.7	13.6	1010	15.1	1148	19,700C	1.6″
No.5	10.6	950	11.8	1080	18,200C	1.6″
N100	7.3	928	8.1	1055	20,200C	1.6″

Lead 280 LBT (T/C)

Powder	Grs.	MV (fps)	Grs.	MV (fps)	Press. (CUP/psi)	Comments
No.9	15.8	998	17.5	1134	19,300C	1.65″/*
No.7	12.6	940	14.0	1068	19,000C	1.65″/*
No.5	9.9	891	11.0	1012	18,300C	1.65″/*
N100	6.9	865	7.7	983	19,100C	1.65″/*

*Exceeds SAAMI maximum OAL.

> *Caution:* Loads exceeding SAAMI OAL Maximum must be verified for bullet-to-rifling clearance and magazine functioning. Where a specific primer or bullet is indicated those components must be used, no substitutions! Where only a maximum load is shown, reduce starting load 10%, unless otherwise specified.
>
> *Key:* (C) = compressed charge; C = CUP; p = psi; Plink = Plinker; Bns = Barnes; Hdy = Hornady; Lap = Lapua; Nos = Nosler; Rem = Remington; Sra = Sierra; Spr = Speer; Win = Winchester.

45 COLT +P LOADING DATA (Ruger & T/C Specific Loads)

Lead 300 FN

Powder	Grs.	MV (fps)	Grs.	MV (fps)	Press. (CUP/psi)	Comments
No.7	11.7	804	13.0	914	19,200C	1.585"
No.9	13.5	798	15.0	907	17,600C	1.585"

200

Powder	Grs.	MV (fps)	Grs.	MV (fps)	Press. (CUP/psi)	Comments
No.5	13.1	1120	14.6	1273	20,000C	Sra FPJ/1.56"
No.7	14.8	1055	16.4	1199	15,300C	Sra FPJ/1.56"
N100	8.3	1021	9.2	1160	19,300C	Sra FPJ/1.56"

230

Powder	Grs.	MV (fps)	Grs.	MV (fps)	Press. (CUP/psi)	Comments
No.7	13.9	1018	15.4	1157	18,500C	Hdy RN-FMJ/1.6"
No.5	11.7	1000	13.0	1136	18,600C	Hdy RN-FMJ/1.6"
N100	7.8	933	8.7	1060	19,600C	Hdy RN-FMJ/1.6"

240

Powder	Grs.	MV (fps)	Grs.	MV (fps)	Press. (CUP/psi)	Comments
No.7	14.0	1010	15.5	1148	20,400C	Sra JHC/1.57"
No.5	11.7	970	13.0	1102	18,300C	Sra JHC/1.57"
N100	7.7	920	8.5	1045	20,100C	Sra JHC/1.57"

250

Powder	Grs.	MV (fps)	Grs.	MV (fps)	Press. (CUP/psi)	Comments
No.7	13.7	971	15.2	1103	19,600C	Nos JHP/1.585"
No.5	10.9	902	12.1	1025	18,100C	Nos JHP/1.585"
N100	7.5	887	8.3	1008	19,300C	Nos JHP/1.585"

260

Powder	Grs.	MV (fps)	Grs.	MV (fps)	Press. (CUP/psi)	Comments
No.7	13.5	953	15.0	1083	19,400C	Spr JHP/1.595"
No.5	10.7	900	11.9	1023	19,300C	Spr JHP/1.595"
N100	7.3	862	8.1	980	19,700C	Spr JHP/1.595"

300

Powder	Grs.	MV (fps)	Grs.	MV (fps)	Press. (CUP/psi)	Comments
No.9	13.5	745	15.0	847	19,200C	Spr SP/1.585"
No.7	11.7	730	13.0	830	20,300C	Spr SP/1.585"
No.9	13.5	710	15.0	807	19,500C	Hdy XTP/1.58"
No.7	11.7	693	13.0	788	20,700C	Hdy XTP/1.58"

Caution: Loads exceeding SAAMI OAL Maximum must be verified for bullet-to-rifling clearance and magazine functioning. Where a specific primer or bullet is indicated those components must be used, no substitutions! Where only a maximum load is shown, reduce starting load 10%, unless otherwise specified.

Key: (C) = compressed charge; C = CUP; p = psi; Plink = Plinker; Bns = Barnes; Hdy = Hornady; Lap = Lapua; Nos = Nosler; Rem = Remington; Sra = Sierra; Spr = Speer; Win = Winchester.

Never exceed maximum load nor use any load exhibiting signs of excessive pressure. Begin at suggested starting load and work up carefully.

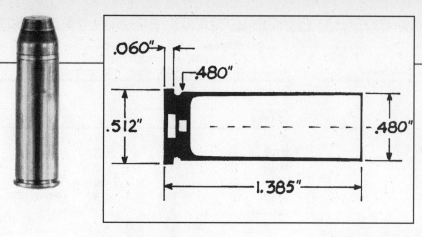

Case: Freedom Arms
Primer: Small Rifle (Remington
7½ is highly recommended
for all loads.)
Barrel: 7½″ Accurate
7½″ Hodgdon (Freedom Arms)
8″ Vihtavuori (Freedom Arms)

Bullet Diameter: 0.451″-0.452″
Maximum Case Length: 1.385″
Trim to Length: 1.380″
Maximum Cartridge OAL: 1.795″
Minimum Cartridge OAL:
Bullet dependent

This proprietary cartridge, developed by Dick Casull, is chambered by Freedom Arms in a five-shot single-action revolver. Most shooters agree that subjective recoil of typical 454 loads fired from Freedom Arms' revolvers is similar to top 44 Magnum loads fired from a Super Blackhawk. This is most impressive when one compares these similar-weight guns and realizes that the 454 generates about twice the muzzle energy!

The 454 case is a stretched version of the 45 Colt case, but uses small primers. Other primers can be used, but Remington's 7½ is preferred for all high-performance 454 loads. For target loads and for general plinking, cast bullets, faster powders and milder primers can be used to advantage.

The 454 is a premier choice for a companion sidearm for those hunting in country where genuinely dangerous game might be found. Special cautions are in order, though. First, with truly high recoil levels, bullet pull is a critical concern.

Make certain your sizing die adequately reduces case neck diameter and that your expander plug does not open the neck too large. Best results are likely obtained with an expander of 0.448″, or even smaller! Further, understand that, with some of the slower powders listed, maximum loads can be highly compressed. Extreme powder compression can create a situation where the bullet might be driven from the case by the compressed charge. The combination of recoil pulling the case back and the powder pushing the bullet forward can get the job done. This can tie up a revolver.

Usable case capacity with a 250-grain bullet, seated normally, is about 33.8 grains of water. Accurate No. 9 is the powder of choice for all 454 loads. For the above cited reasons, No. 9 is an especially good choice in all dangerous game loadings. Slower powders can provide good ballistics, but require entirely too much compression to achieve top velocities.

◼ 454 CASULL LOADING DATA ◼

Powder	STARTING Grs.	MV (fps)	MAXIMUM Grs.	MV (fps)	Press. (CUP/psi)	Comments	Powder	STARTING Grs.	MV (fps)	MAXIMUM Grs.	MV (fps)	Press. (CUP/psi)	Comments
185							**200 con't**						
Unique			14.0	1580	18,700C		Unique			16.0	1591	38,200C	
IMR800-X			13.0	1392	18,000C		HS7			21.0	1519	34,400C	
Bullseye			7.5	1067	15,200C		HS6			19.0	1489	34,700C	
IMR700-X			7.0	958	13,400C		W571			20.5	1488	34,000C	
HP38			10.0	945	21,400C		W540			18.5	1449	32,400C	
W231			10.0	940	20,900C		IMR800-X			13.0	1314	18,400C	
							Bullseye			7.0	1003	14,000C	
200							IMR700-X			7.0	977	15,800C	
H110			37.5	2042	39,400C		HP38			10.0	924	23,600C	
W296			37.0	2011	38,800C		W231			9.5	904	21,800C	
Her2400			28.0	1769	35,100C								
Blue Dot			24.0	1749	36,900C								
IMR4227			32.0	1690	31,700C								
H4227			32.0	1670	31,100C								

▶▶▶▶▶▶▶▶▶▶▶▶▶▶▶▶▶▶▶▶▶▶▶▶▶▶▶▶

Never exceed maximum load nor use any load exhibiting signs of excessive pressure. Begin at suggested starting load and work up carefully.

225-230

Powder	STARTING Grs.	MV (fps)	MAXIMUM Grs.	MV (fps)	Press. (CUP/psi)	Comments
H110			37.0	1928	41,400C	
W296			36.5	1892	40,400C	
Blue Dot			23.0	1737	38,800C	
Her2400			27.0	1711	34,400C	
IMR4227			31.0	1647	31,000C	
H4227			30.0	1510	32,000C	
Unique			15.0	1477	37,100C	
HS6			18.0	1449	34,400C	
W540			18.0	1437	34,900C	
HS7			20.0	1426	32,800C	
W571			20.0	1420	33,000C	
IMR800-X			14.0	1339	24,400C	
Bullseye			7.0	921	15,100C	

240

Powder	STARTING Grs.	MV (fps)	MAXIMUM Grs.	MV (fps)	Press. (CUP/psi)	Comments
H110	36.0	1889	39.0	2090	54,100C	JHP
W296	36.0	1874	38.0	2004	53,400C	JHP
No.9	27.9	1686	31.0	1916	54,100C	JHP/1.78"/CCI 400
Blue Dot	21.0	1588	25.0	1896	55,100C	JHP
Her2400	26.0	1639	30.0	1886	53,700C	JHP
N110	27.0	1655	31.0	1877	48,040p	1.76"
IMR800-X	14.0	1371	20.0	1794	50,700C	JHP
H4227	29.0	1421	34.0	1792	41,400C	JHP
IMR4227	30.0	1477	34.0	1769	44,400C	JHP
A1680	34.2	1557	38.0	1769	46,500C	JHP/1.78"/CCI 400/(C)
No.9	25.2	1543	28.0	1753	39,800C	Sra JHP/1.705"/CCI 400
HS7	19.0	1352	25.5	1746	50,100C	JHP
W571	19.0	1359	25.5	1740	50,600C	JHP
A1680	32.4	1498	36.0	1702	42,200C	SraJHP/1.705"/CCI400/(C)
HS6	17.0	1277	21.5	1641	44,600C	JHP
W540	17.0	1274	21.5	1629	44,200C	JHP
Unique	14.0	1367	16.5	1580	49,700C	JHP
N350	13.0	1280	17.2	1564	48,660p	JHP/1.76"

250

Powder	STARTING Grs.	MV (fps)	MAXIMUM Grs.	MV (fps)	Press. (CUP/psi)	Comments
H110			35.0	1799	43,200C	
W296			35.0	1784	42,900C	
No.9	25.2	1558	28.0	1770	45,800C	Hdy XTP/1.7"/CCI 400
A1680	33.3	1547	37.0	1758	49,100C	Hdy XTP/1.7"/CCI 400/(C)
N110	22.0	1400	25.3	1610	28,720p	Hdy XTP/1.695"
Her2400			25.0	1560	34,400C	
N350	13.5	1335	16.4	1525	48,600p	Hdy XTP/1.695"
Blue Dot			19.0	1444	35,100C	
H4227			29.0	1384	34,400C	
IMR4227			29.0	1379	34,100C	
IMR800-X			13.5	1320	24,800C	
W571			18.0	1284	35,800C	
HS7			18.0	1277	35,500C	
N320	9.9	1195	11.0	1262	38,440p	Hdy XTP/1.695"
W540			17.0	1244	35,700C	
HS6			17.0	1240	35,400C	
Unique			13.0	1233	32,900C	

260

Powder	STARTING Grs.	MV (fps)	MAXIMUM Grs.	MV (fps)	Press. (CUP/psi)	Comments
H110	34.0	1790	37.0	2005	53,800C	JHP
W296	34.0	1789	37.0	1977	53,100C	JHP
No.9	27.0	1615	30.0	1835	52,800C	JFP/1.765"/CCI 400
N110	26.0	1575	30.4	1816	48,820p	JFP/1.76"
A1680	34.7	1566	38.5	1780	50,800C	JFP/1.765"/CCI 400/(C)
Her2400	25.0	1538	29.0	1780	51,800C	JHP
H4227	28.0	1309	33.0	1759	41,000	
Blue Dot	18.0	1429	22.0	1704	53,700C	JHP
HS7	17.0	1228	24.0	1701	51,700C	JHP
W571	17.0	1234	24.0	1689	51,400C	JHP
IMR4227	29.0	1349	33.0	1688	43,200C	JHP
No.9	24.1	1458	26.8	1657	38,600C	Spr JHP/1.71"/CCI 400
A1680	31.5	1448	35.0	1646	42,500C	Spr JHP/1.71"/CCI 400
HS6	16.0	1181	20.5	1562	44,200C	JHP
W540	16.0	1188	20.0	1522	43,400C	JHP
Unique	12.0	1220	15.0	1452	46,600C	JHP
Bullseye	7.0	829	10.5	1255	32,900C	JHP
HP38	8.5	811	12.5	1248	36,600C	JHP
W231	8.5	815	12.5	1244	36,700C	JHP
IMR700-X	7.0	829	9.5	1127	33,600C	JHP

300

Powder	STARTING Grs.	MV (fps)	MAXIMUM Grs.	MV (fps)	Press. (CUP/psi)	Comments
H110	28.5	1589	31.5	1780	55,000C	JHP
W296	28.0	1537	31.0	1750	54,800C	JHP
Her 2400	24.0	1461	27.0	1656	55,000C	JHP
N110	24.0	1505	26.6	1634	49,380p	JFP/1.76"
H4227	27.0	1494	30.0	1634	53,700C	JHP
N110	24.0	1485	26.5	1631	48,080p	Hdy XTP/1.76"
No.9	23.4	1428	26.0	1623	50,000C	Hdy XTP/1.765"/CCI 400
A1680	31.1	1427	34.5	1622	54,500C	JFP/1.755"/CCI 400
No.9	23.4	1404	26.0	1596	46,200C	Spr JSP/1.765"/CCI 400
A1680	30.2	1403	33.5	1594	49,600C	Hdy XTP/1.765"/CCI 400
A1680	30.2	1400	33.5	1591	48,500C	Spr JSP/1.765"/CCI 400
No.9	22.5	1386	25.0	1575	49,500C	JFP/1.755"/CCI 400
IMR4227	26.0	1368	29.0	1540	54,400C	JHP
Blue Dot	16.0	1240	19.0	1534	54,000C	JHP
HS7	16.0	1111	22.0	1501	50,200C	JHP
W571	16.0	1107	22.0	1494	50,700C	JHP
N120	27.0	1290	31.0	1491	43,760p	JFP/1.76"
IMR800-X	11.0	1031	16.0	1457	53,100C	JHP
HS6	15.0	1084	19.0	1450	46,200C	JHP
W540	15.0	1100	19.0	1440	46,000C	JHP
N350	13.5	1229	15.2	1342	48,600C	Hdy XTP/1.76"
N340	12.2	1200	13.5	1281	48,980p	Hdy XTP/1.76"
Unique	10.0	1049	14.0	1275	38,600C	JHP
HP38	8.5	820	11.5	1076	43,200C	JHP
Bullseye	6.5	804	9.5	1062	33,400C	JHP
W231	8.5	824	11.5	1062	42,400C	JHP

Note: Seating bullets to their cannelure resulted in loaded overall lengths exceeding Freedom Arms' recommendation.

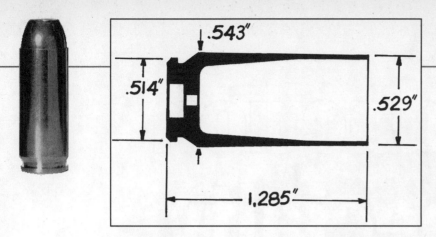

Case: Speer
Primer: CCI 350
Barrel: Accurate (Desert Eagle)
Bullet Diameter: 0.510″

Maximum Case Length: 1.285″
Trim to Length: 1.280″
Maximum Cartridge OAL: 1.610″
Minimum Cartridge OAL: 1.560″

A development of Action Arms, Magnum Research and Israel Military Industries, this is the largest commercial, and legal, handgun chambering—a larger caliber chambering would require a special permit in the U.S.

The case is an interesting design. First, it features a 44 Magnum rim size, to accommodate adaptation to 44 Magnum bolt faces. Second, it is slightly tapered, similar to the 9mm Luger. Evidently this was deemed a worthwhile feature. This might improve semi-automatic functioning, but it burdens the handloader who must lubricate such cases regardless of a carbide sizer die. Finally, pressures are held to levels only slight-

ly lower than the 44 Magnum.

Performance is just about intermediate between the 44 Magnum and the 454 Casull. With about 28-percent more frontal area than a 45, no doubt, the 50 AE can generate considerable impact trauma.

With impressive accuracy and energy, the 50 AE-chambered Desert Eagle is an excellent pistol for those who want to hunt big game with a handgun. However, this gun is a bit large for many to handle properly.

Usable case capacity with a 300-grain bullet, seated normally, is about 35.4 grains of water.

50 ACTION EXPRESS LOADING DATA (50 AE)

Powder	—STARTING— Grs.	MV (fps)	—MAXIMUM— Grs.	MV (fps)	Press. (CUP/psi)	Comments
325						
A1680	34.0	1157	37.8	1305	32,000p	Spr U-C/1.575″/(C)/*
No.9	22.6	1157	23.8	1247	32,000p	Spr U-C/1.575″/*

* Speer data.

Caution: Loads exceeding SAAMI OAL Maximum must be verified for bullet-to-rifling clearance and magazine functioning. Where a specific primer or bullet is indicated those components must be used, no substitutions! Where only a maximum load is shown, reduce starting load 10%, unless otherwise specified.

Key: (C) = compressed charge; C = CUP; p = psi; Plink = Plinker; Bns = Barnes; Hdy = Hornady; Lap = Lapua; Nos = Nosler; Rem = Remington; Sra = Sierra; Spr = Speer; Win = Winchester.

Introduction To Specialty Handgun Data

HERE, WE LIST data for 12 specialty pistol cartridges or special handloads for standard cartridges. **These loads are intended only for use in single shot handguns capable of handling high pressures such as Thompson/Center's Contender and Remington's XP-100.**

We have omitted several chamberings that are reasonably common and are being handloaded. Besides the limitations of space, lack of pressure-tested data has limited their inclusion.

Barrel length variations can have profound effects on specialty handgun ballistics. To get a reasonable estimate of expected variations, compare the data to a similar rifle cartridge load. For example: A 150-grain bullet in a 15″ barreled 7mm-08 generates about 2450 fps; in a 24″ barrel the same loads will generate about 2650 fps. This suggests about a 22 fps loss per inch of barrel. However, as the barrel gets shorter, the per-inch velocity loss increases. Not surprisingly, the only way to know what any given load does in any given barrel is to chronograph it.

Caution: The maximum charge for your firearms will depend, in part, on the specific components you use, and your specific assembly methods and equipment, as well as your specific firearm.

In that neither the publisher nor the author has any control over the manufacture, assembly, and storage of components, or the method of assembling a handload, the condition of the firearm in which it is used, or the degree of knowledge of the handloader, we cannot assume any responsibility, either expressed or implied, for the use of this data. While this data was safe in the original test firearm, it could prove otherwise in your gun with your components. Use of this data is entirely at the risk of the handloader.

No warranty or guarantee is expressed or implied. The publisher and author assume no responsibility for any use of this data. It is offered solely as a comparison to other such data.

SPECIALTY HANDGUN CARTRIDGE DATA

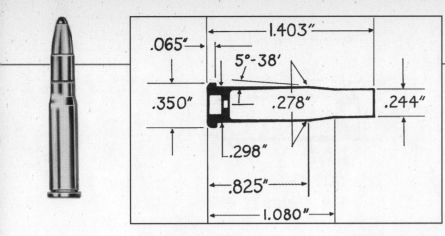

Case: Winchester
Primer: CCI 500
Barrel: 10″ Accurate (T/C)
Bullet Diameter: 0.223″-0.224″

Maximum Case Length: 1.403″
Trim to Length: 1.383″
Maximum Cartridge OAL: 1.723″
Minimum Cartridge OAL: 1.660″

This circa 1920's cartridge was derived from the black-powder 22 Winchester Center Fire (WCF) cartridge, introduced in 1885. Names like Wotkyns and Whelen figure in the domestic development of the smokeless-powder, high-pressure version called the 22 Hornet.

Europeans beat them to the punch. A modernized version of the 22 WCF was introduced in Germany long before the Hornet was standardized. The German 22 Veirling is practically interchangeable with the 22 Hornet.

With comparatively small case capacity, the Hornet is a fine choice for chambering in handguns. Handgun performance is quite close to that of much larger 22-caliber chamberings—this is especially true with shorter barrels.

Even when limited by a 10″ barrel, Hornet performance surpasses 22 Winchester Magnum Rimfire rifle ballistics by a wide margin. In the right gun and with the proper load, the Hornet can achieve 125-yard hits on varmints and delivers all the punch necessary to get the job done.

Winchester produced the first commercial factory ammunition in 1930. All modern Hornet handguns are bored to use standard 0.224″ bullets.

Owing to limited velocity potential, best results are obtained with lighter rapid-expansion bullets. There is currently a paucity of powders offering optimum Hornet performance. We have listed the best here.

With a standard 45-grain bullet, seated normally, usable case capacity is about 12.2 grains of water. A1680, A2015BR and N110 are the only good choices for loading the Hornet.

22 HORNET LOADING DATA

Lead 44 Lyman 225438 (RN-GC)

Powder	STARTING Grs.	MV (fps)	MAXIMUM Grs.	MV (fps)	Press. (CUP/psi)	Comments
A1680	10.4	1802	11.5	2048	31,100C	1.665″
A2015BR	11.3	1621	12.5	1842	29,700C	1.665″
N100	2.7	1321	3.0	1501	32,600C	1.665″

40

Powder	STARTING Grs.	MV (fps)	MAXIMUM Grs.	MV (fps)	Press. (CUP/psi)	Comments
A1680	12.6	2109	14.0	2397	43,000C	Sra Hornet/1.715″
A2015BR	11.3	1590	12.5	1807	26,900C	Sra Hornet/1.715″/(C)

45

Powder	STARTING Grs.	MV (fps)	MAXIMUM Grs.	MV (fps)	Press. (CUP/psi)	Comments
A1680	11.1	1909	12.3	2169	40,700C	Nos Hornet/1.72″
A2015BR	11.3	1646	12.5	1870	32,100C	Nos Hornet/1.72″/(C)

50

Powder	STARTING Grs.	MV (fps)	MAXIMUM Grs.	MV (fps)	Press. (CUP/psi)	Comments
A1680	10.4	1831	11.5	2081	42,400C	Hdy SX/1.78″
A2015BR	10.8	1566	12.0	1780	35,000C	Hdy SX/1.78″/(C)

Caution: **Loads exceeding SAAMI OAL Maximum must be verified for bullet-to-rifling clearance and magazine functioning. Where a specific primer or bullet is indicated those components must be used, no substitutions! Where only a maximum load is shown, reduce starting load 10%, unless otherwise specified.**

Key: (C) = compressed charge; C = CUP; p = psi; Plink = Plinker; Bns = Barnes; Hdy = Hornady; Lap = Lapua; Nos = Nosler; Rem = Remington; Sra = Sierra; Spr = Speer; Win = Winchester.

221
Remington Fireball

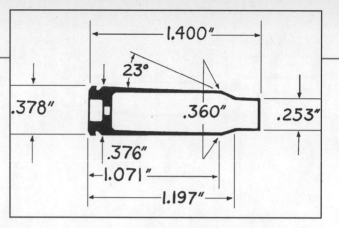

Case: Remington
Primer: Small Rifle
Barrel: 14″ Accurate (T/C)
        10³/₄″ Hodgdon (XP-100)
Bullet Diameter: 0.224″

Maximum Case Length: 1.400″
Trim to Length: 1.390″
Maximum Cartridge OAL: 1.830″
Minimum Cartridge OAL: 1.780″

Developed more than a decade after its parent cartridge—the 222 Remington—the Fireball was designed specifically to give optimal 22-caliber handgun performance. From the XP-100, originally with a 10¹³/₁₆″ barrel, it lived up to its billing. Performance is even better in the 14″ T/C Contender. Using about 30-percent less powder and working at somewhat higher pressures than the 222 Remington, the Fireball produces 95 percent of 222 velocity.

An efficient cartridge, the Fireball has a shorter powder column than the 222 or 223. This implies superior intrinsic accuracy. The 221 can be suggested as a superior handgun chambering for varmint hunting at intermediate ranges—to perhaps 200 yards.

With a 52-grain bullet, seated normally, usable case capacity is about 22.0 grains of water. There is currently a genuine paucity of useful powders. Only A1680 has been noted as an excellent 221 Fireball performer.

221 REMINGTON FIREBALL LOADING DATA

Powder	—STARTING— Grs.	MV (fps)	—MAXIMUM— Grs.	MV (fps)	Press. (CUP/psi)	Comments
Lead 45 GC						
HS6			4.5	1374		
40						
H4227	15.5	2925	17.0	3033		
H110	13.0	2714	14.0	2933		
W296	13.0	2692	14.0	2918		
W680	17.0	2680	17.5	2808		
Her2400	14.5	2592	15.5	2702		

Powder	—STARTING— Grs.	MV (fps)	—MAXIMUM— Grs.	MV (fps)	Press. (CUP/psi)	Comments
45 (10³/₄″ barrel)						
W680	16.5	2544	17.3	2777		
Her2400	13.8	2580	14.8	2764		
RL-7	17.0	2578	18.0	2744		
W296	13.0	2552	14.0	2720		
H110	13.0	2553	14.0	2714		
H4227	15.0	2592	16.0	2697		
IMR4227	15.0	2577	16.0	2689		
IMR4198	17.0	2569	18.0	2657		
H4198	16.0	2451	17.0	2632		
SR4756	7.0	1904	8.0	2110		
SR7625	6.0	1844	7.0	2003		
IMR700-X	5.0	1757	5.7	1814		
45 (14″ barrel)						
A1680	16.5	2593	18.3	2947	51,300C	Nos SP/1.765″/Rem 7½
A2015BR	18.0	2420	20.0	2750	47,100C	Nos SP/1.765″/ Rem 7½/(C)
A2230	18.9	2393	21.0	2719	49,500C	Nos SP/1.765″/ Rem 7½/(C)

Caution: Loads exceeding SAAMI OAL Maximum must be verified for bullet-to-rifling clearance and magazine functioning. Where a specific primer or bullet is indicated those components must be used, no substitutions! Where only a maximum load is shown, reduce starting load 10%, unless otherwise specified.

Key: (C) = compressed charge; C = CUP; p = psi; Plink = Plinker; Bns = Barnes; Hdy = Hornady; Lap = Lapua; Nos = Nosler; Rem = Remington; Sra = Sierra; Spr = Speer; Win = Winchester.

Powder	STARTING Grs.	MV (fps)	MAXIMUM Grs.	MV (fps)	Press. (CUP/psi)	Comments

50 (10³/₄" barrel)

Powder	Grs.	MV (fps)	Grs.	MV (fps)	Press. (CUP/psi)	Comments
H4227	15.0	2582	16.0	2672		
W680	16.1	2504	17.0	2661		
H110	12.5	2520	13.5	2637		
W296	12.5	2494	13.5	2611		
RL-7	16.6	2488	17.6	2608		
Her2400	13.2	2464	14.0	2580		
H4198	15.5	2412	16.5	2539		
IMR4198	15.5	2409	16.5	2531		
IMR4227	14.0	2418	15.0	2522		
SR4756	6.5	1843	7.5	1987		
SR7625	6.2	1838	6.8	1933		
IMR700-X	4.8	1626	5.6	1774		

50 (14" barrel)

Powder	Grs.	MV (fps)	Grs.	MV (fps)	Press. (CUP/psi)	Comments
A1680	16.0	2475	17.8	2813	51,500C	Nos SP/1.825"/Rem 7½
A2230	18.9	2352	21.0	2673	49,500C	Nos SP/1.825"/Rem 7½/(C)
A2015BR	17.6	2327	19.5	2644	45,600C	Nos SP/1.825"/Rem 7½/(C)

52-53

Powder	Grs.	MV (fps)	Grs.	MV (fps)	Press. (CUP/psi)	Comments
H110	12.0	2492	13.0	2619		
W680	16.0	2482	16.8	2611		
H4227	15.0	2449	16.0	2603		
W296	12.0	2479	13.0	2590		
RL-7	16.5	2469	17.5	2587		
Her2400	13.5	2398	14.0	2577		
H4198	15.5	2343	16.5	2537		
IMR4198	15.5	2409	16.5	2521		
IMR4227	14.0	2390	15.0	2460		
SR4756	6.3	1818	7.3	1966		
SR7625	6.0	1800	6.6	1884		
IMR700-X	4.8	1594	5.5	1751		

55 (10³/₄" barrel)

Powder	Grs.	MV (fps)	Grs.	MV (fps)	Press. (CUP/psi)	Comments
H4227	14.5	2418	15.5	2503		
W680	15.5	2366	16.2	2499		
IMR4198	15.0	2289	16.0	2483		
H4198	15.0	2261	16.0	2441		
IMR4227	13.8	2360	14.8	2439		
W296	12.0	2314	13.0	2429		
SR4756	6.0	1770	7.0	1927		

55 (14" barrel)

Powder	Grs.	MV (fps)	Grs.	MV (fps)	Press. (CUP/psi)	Comments
A1680	15.3	2380	17.0	2700	52,000C	Nos SBT/1.85"/Rem 7½
A2015BR	17.1	2268	19.0	2577	48,700C	Nos SBT/1.85"/Rem 7½
A2230	18.0	2245	20.0	2551	51,600C	Nos SBT/1.85"/Rem 7½/(C)

60-63

Powder	Grs.	MV (fps)	Grs.	MV (fps)	Press. (CUP/psi)	Comments
H4227	14.0	2328	15.0	2414		
RL-7	15.6	2223	16.6	2412		
H4198	15.0	2251	16.0	2399		
IMR4227	13.5	2220	14.5	2358		(60-gr.)
W680	14.0	2264	15.0	2292		
IMR4198	14.5	2162	15.5	2265		(60-gr.)
W748	18.5	2062	19.3	2215		
Her2400	11.5	2042	12.5	2212		

Never exceed maximum load nor use any load exhibiting signs of excessive pressure. Begin at suggested starting load and work up carefully.

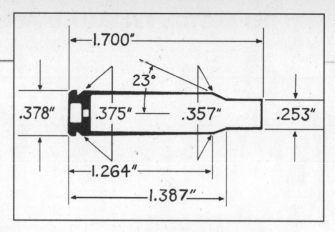

Case: Remington
Primer: Remington 7½
Barrel: 14″ Accurate (T/C)
Bullet Diameter: 0.224″

Maximum Case Length: 1.700″
Trim to Length: 1.680″
Maximum Cartridge OAL: 2.130″
Minimum Cartridge OAL: 2.040″

If ever any factory research and development effort got anything right, the 222 Remington is a shining example! Introduced in 1950 in the Model 722 rifle—and still available in the Model 700—the "triple deuce" was an instant success. Chambered in a 14″ handgun, and with careful handloading, this cartridge will deliver all the accuracy necessary to cleanly dispatch any varmint to 200 yards—perhaps a bit farther in especially competent hands. In the field, the 222 easily out-shoots most handgunners, even on their best days.

The smaller, higher-pressure 221 Fireball uses considerably less powder and nearly duplicates 222 performance, while likely offering superior intrinsic handgun accuracy.

With a 52-grain bullet, seated normally, usable case capacity is about 26.0 grains of water. A2230 and A2015BR have been noted as excellent choices in the 222 Remington.

222 REMINGTON LOADING DATA

Powder	—STARTING— Grs.	MV (fps)	—MAXIMUM— Grs.	MV (fps)	Press. (CUP/psi)	Comments
45						
A2230	24.3	2790	27.0	3171	47,400p	Nos SB/2.065″/(C)
A2015BR	22.1	2769	24.5	3147	49,300p	Nos SB/2.065″
A2460	24.3	2757	27.0	3133	45,900p	Nos SB/2.065″/(C)
A1680	18.9	2698	21.0	3066	48,500p	Nos SB/2.065″
A2495BR	21.6	2526	24.0	2870	39,900p	Nos SB/2.065″/(C)
A2520	22.5	2499	25.0	2840	34,200p	Nos SB/2.065″/(C)
50						
A2015BR	21.2	2625	23.5	2983	45,800p	Hdy SX/2.15″/Win Case
A2230	22.1	2613	24.5	2969	48,200p	Hdy SX/2.15″/Win Case/(C)
A2460	22.1	2594	24.5	2948	46,000p	Hdy SX/2.15″/Win Case/(C)
A1680	16.8	2442	18.5	2778	50,000p	Hdy SX/2.15″/Win Case
A2520	22.5	2440	25.0	2773	38,300p	Hdy SX/2.15″/Win Case/(C)
A2495BR	21.6	2437	24.0	2769	41,100p	Hdy SX/2.15″/Win Case/(C)
53						
A2015BR	21.2	2604	23.5	2950	50,000p	Hdy HP Match/2.19″
A2230	22.1	2526	24.5	2870	46,400p	Hdy HP Match/2.19″/(C)
A2460	22.1	2519	24.5	2862	45,500p	Hdy HP Match/2.19″/(C)
A2495BR	21.6	2460	24.0	2795	46,300p	Hdy HP Match/2.19″/(C)
A2520	22.5	2441	25.0	2774	40,900p	Hdy HP Match/2.19″/(C)
A1680	17.1	2409	19.0	2737	47,400p	Hdy HP Match/2.19″

Powder	—STARTING— Grs.	MV (fps)	—MAXIMUM— Grs.	MV (fps)	Press. (CUP/psi)	Comments
55						
A2230	22.1	2521	24.5	2865	46,200p	Nos SB/2.155″/ Win Case
A2460	22.1	2494	24.5	2834	45,000p	Nos SB/2.155″/ Win Case
A2015BR	20.3	2482	22.5	2820	46,100p	Nos SB/2.155″/ Win Case
A1680	17.1	2370	19.0	2693	44,200p	Nos SB/2.155″/ Win Case
A2520	22.1	2335	24.5	2653	36,300p	Nos SB/2.155″/ Win Case/(C)
A2495BR	21.2	2328	23.5	2645	42,100p	Nos SB/2.155″/ Win Case/(C)
60						
A2015BR	20.0	2407	22.2	2735	47,800p	Hdy SP/2.2″
A2230	21.6	2384	24.0	2709	48,100p	Hdy SP/2.2″
A2460	21.5	2380	23.9	2704	46,100p	Hdy SP/2.2″
A2495BR	21.2	2350	23.5	2670	49,400p	Hdy SP/2.2″/(C)
A2520	22.1	2325	24.5	2642	43,900p	Hdy SP/2.2″
A1680	17.1	2294	19.0	2607	50,000p	Hdy SP/2.2″

Never exceed maximum load nor use any load exhibiting signs of excessive pressure. Begin at suggested starting load and work up carefully.

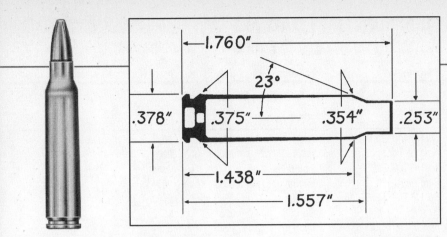

Case: Remington
Primer: Small Rifle
Barrel: 14″ Accurate
            14″ Hodgdon
Bullet Diameter: 0.224″

Maximum Case Length: 1.760″
Trim to Length: 1.740″
Maximum Cartridge OAL: 2.260″
Minimum Cartridge OAL: 2.165″

After considerable research and development, by several NATO allies, the 5.56mm Ball Cartridge M193 was adopted in 1964 for standardization by all NATO forces. It is unlikely anyone at Remington ever dreamed this chambering would someday become popular in handguns!

Because of relatively large capacity, this cartridge does not perform consistently in shorter-barreled handguns. This data is for 14″ barrels, but we strongly suggest 16″ barrels for their superior performance.

Military 5.56mm Ball ammunition does not necessarily meet current SAAMI ammunition specifications. For these reasons, we advise against firing any military ammunition in any commercial chamber.

Military cases are common and inexpensive, so their use is inevitable. Should you choose to use those thicker and softer cases, we recommend a reduction in charge of a full

10 percent. Such loads will produce similar velocity to these listed loads using commercial cases. Maximum listed loads used in military cases could generate dangerous pressures.

Chambered in a 14″ handgun and with careful handloading, this cartridge will deliver all the accuracy necessary to cleanly dispatch any varmint to 200 yards—farther in especially competent hands. Best loads can outshoot most handgunners. However, this chambering is not as easy to load for in a handgun as the smaller 22s. Consistent combinations—and the accuracy they generate—are not so easy to find.

With a 52-grain bullet, seated normally, usable case capacity is about 28.8 grains of water. As is typical of middle-of-the-road chamberings, the 223 Remington delivers good performance with a wide range of propellants. H322, A2460, H335, H4895 and BL-C(2) have all been noted as good 223 performers.

223 REMINGTON LOADING DATA

Powder	STARTING Grs.	MV (fps)	MAXIMUM Grs.	MV (fps)	Press. (CUP/psi)	Comments
40						
H322	23.0	2614	25.0	3040		
H4895	24.0	2627	26.0	3022		
BL-C(2)	26.0	2631	28.0	3011		
H4198	20.5	2741	22.5	2993		
H335	25.0	2530	27.0	2907		
H4227	15.0	2174	17.0	2468		
45						
A2015BR	23.4	2840	26.0	3227	49,100C	Nos SB/2.115″/Rem 7½
A2460	24.8	2814	27.5	3198	49,300C	Nos SB/2.115″/Rem 7½
A2230	24.3	2798	27.0	3180	50,500C	Nos SB/2.115″/Rem 7½
A2520	23.9	2712	28.5	3082	42,000C	Nos SB/2.115″/Rem 7½/(C)
A1680	18.5	2673	20.5	3038	48,200C	Nos SB/2.115″/Rem 7½
A2495BR	24.8	2660	26.5	3023	47,000C	Nos SB/2.115″/Rem 7½/(C)

Powder	STARTING Grs.	MV (fps)	MAXIMUM Grs.	MV (fps)	Press. (CUP/psi)	Comments
45 con't						
H335	24.0	2504	26.0	2869		
BL-C(2)	24.5	2474	26.5	2861		
H4895	23.0	2351	25.0	2766		
H4198	20.0	2501	21.5	2760		
H322	21.5	2442	23.5	2759		
H4227	14.5	2042	16.5	2388		

➤➤➤➤➤➤➤➤➤➤➤➤➤➤➤➤➤➤➤➤➤➤➤➤➤➤➤

Caution: **Loads exceeding SAAMI OAL Maximum must be verified for bullet-to-rifling clearance and magazine functioning. Where a specific primer or bullet is indicated those components must be used, no substitutions! Where only a maximum load is shown, reduce starting load 10%, unless otherwise specified.**

Key: (C) = compressed charge; C = CUP; p = psi; Plink = Plinker; Bns = Barnes; Hdy = Hornady; Lap = Lapua; Nos = Nosler; Rem = Remington; Sra = Sierra; Spr = Speer; Win = Winchester.

Never exceed maximum load nor use any load exhibiting signs of excessive pressure. Begin at suggested starting load and work up carefully.

50

Powder	Grs.	MV (fps)	Grs.	MV (fps)	Press. (CUP/psi)	Comments
A2015BR	23.0	2712	25.5	3082	46,400C	Spr HP TNT/2.235″/ Rem 7½
A2520	25.7	2709	28.5	3078	42,200C	Spr HP TNT/2.235″/ Rem 7½/(C)
A2230	23.4	2706	26.0	3075	49,800C	Spr HP TNT/2.235″/ Rem 7½
A2460	23.4	2695	26.0	3063	47,100C	Spr HP TNT/2.235″/ Rem 7½
A1680	18.5	2547	20.5	2894	47,900C	Spr HP TNT/2.235″/ Rem 7½
A2495BR	23.9	2541	26.5	2888	44,400C	Spr HP TNT/2.235″/ Rem 7½/(C)
H380	26.5	2579	28.5	2740		
H414	27.0	2511	29.0	2705		
H4895	22.0	2454	24.0	2690		
H4198	19.0	2581	21.0	2663		
H322	21.0	2418	23.0	2622		
BL-C(2)	23.5	2424	25.5	2619		
H335	23.0	2409	25.0	2614		
H4227	14.0	2031	16.0	2346		

52-53

Powder	Grs.	MV (fps)	Grs.	MV (fps)	Press. (CUP/psi)	Comments
A2230	23.4	2633	26.0	2992	49,900C	Hdy HP Match/2.225″/ Rem 7½
A2460	23.0	2618	25.5	2975	47,300C	Hdy HP Match/2.225″/ Rem 7½
A2015BR	22.1	2617	24.5	2974	47,800C	Hdy HP Match/2.225″/ Rem 7½
A2520	24.8	2610	27.5	2966	43,300C	Hdy HP Match/2.225″/ Rem 7½
A2495BR	23.4	2530	26.0	2875	48,800C	Hdy HP Match/2.225″/ Rem 7½
A1680	18.0	2467	20.0	2803	49,600C	Hdy HP Match/2.225″/ Rem 7½
H380	26.5	2564	28.5	2732		
H414	27.0	2527	29.0	2704		
H4895	22.0	2407	24.0	2640		
H4198	18.5	2544	20.5	2627		
BL-C(2)	23.0	2410	25.0	2611		
H335	23.0	2392	25.0	2604		
H322	20.5	2388	22.5	2591		
H4227	14.0	2011	16.0	2329		

55

Powder	Grs.	MV (fps)	Grs.	MV (fps)	Press. (CUP/psi)	Comments
A2015BR	22.5	2628	25.0	2986	49,800C	Nos SPBT/2.23″/Rem 7½
A2460	23.9	2616	26.5	2973	49,200C	Nos SPBT/2.23″/Rem 7½
A2520	24.8	2610	27.5	2966	43,300C	Nos SPBT/2.23″/ Rem 7½/(C)
A2230	23.4	2604	26.0	2959	50,300C	Nos SPBT/2.23″/Rem 7½
A2495BR	23.6	2530	26.2	2875	51,100C	Nos SPBT/2.23″/ Rem 7½/(C)
A1680	18.5	2475	20.5	2813	50,000C	Nos SPBT/2.23″/Rem 7½

55 con't

Powder	Grs.	MV (fps)	Grs.	MV (fps)	Press. (CUP/psi)	Comments
H380	25.5	2421	27.5	2614		
H414	26.0	2400	28.0	2609		
H4895	21.5	2377	23.5	2554		
H4198	18.0	2389	20.0	2534		
H322	20.0	2368	22.0	2522		
BL-C(2)	23.0	2333	25.0	2512		
H335	22.5	2325	24.5	2494		
H4227	13.5	1981	15.5	2253		

60

Powder	Grs.	MV (fps)	Grs.	MV (fps)	Press. (CUP/psi)	Comments
A2520	24.8	2554	27.5	2902	45,600C	Hdy SP/2.235″/Rem 7½/(C)
A2015BR	21.6	2532	24.0	2877	49,100C	Hdy SP/2.235″/Rem 7½
A2230	22.1	2497	24.5	2838	49,200C	Hdy SP/2.235″/Rem 7½
A2460	22.7	2490	25.2	2829	49,400C	Hdy SP/2.235″/Rem 7½
A2495BR	22.2	2359	24.7	2681	46,300C	Hdy SP/2.235″/Rem 7½/100% density

60-63

Powder	Grs.	MV (fps)	Grs.	MV (fps)	Press. (CUP/psi)	Comments
H414	25.0	2352	27.0	2520		
H380	24.5	2330	26.5	2513		
H335	21.5	2310	23.5	2473		
BL-C(2)	22.0	2324	24.0	2469		
H322	19.0	2286	21.0	2435		
H4895	20.5	2272	22.5	2417		
H4198	17.0	2179	19.0	2366		
H450	25.0	2009	27.0	2223		
H4227	13.0	1947	15.0	2213		
H4831	24.0	1919	26.0	2115		

70

Powder	Grs.	MV (fps)	Grs.	MV (fps)	Press. (CUP/psi)	Comments
H380	23.5	2280	25.5	2451		
H414	24.5	2251	26.5	2422		
BL-C(2)	20.5	2207	22.5	2421		
H335	20.0	2188	22.0	2403		
H4895	19.5	2202	21.5	2354		
H322	18.0	2182	20.0	2322		
H4198	16.5	2162	18.5	2306		
H450	25.0	2067	27.0	2256		
H4831	24.0	1839	26.0	2045		
H4227	12.0	1741	14.0	1991		

Caution: **Loads exceeding SAAMI OAL Maximum must be verified for bullet-to-rifling clearance and magazine functioning. Where a specific primer or bullet is indicated those components must be used, no substitutions! Where only a maximum load is shown, reduce starting load 10%, unless otherwise specified.**

Key: (C) = compressed charge; C = CUP; p = psi; Plink = Plinker; Bns = Barnes; Hdy = Hornady; Lap = Lapua; Nos = Nosler; Rem = Remington; Sra = Sierra; Spr = Speer; Win = Winchester.

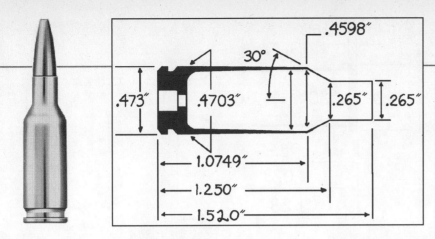

Case: Remington
Primer: Rem 7½
Barrel: 14½″ Accurate (XP-100)
Bullet Diameter: 0.243″

Maximum Case Length: 1.520″
Trim to Length: 1.515″
Maximum Cartridge OAL: 2.200″
Minimum Cartridge OAL: 2.080″

A standard chambering in the recently discontinued XP-100 handgun, the 6mm BR is based on the more popular 7mm BR. XP-100 14½″ barrel ballistics are most impressive. The 6mm BR is a good handgun choice for varmint hunting to 200 yards or a bit farther. It is an excellent handgun choice for hunting the smallest species of big game.

Primarily, though, the 6mm BR has been used in handgun silhouette competition. With limited recoil and superb intrinsic accuracy, this is a good cartridge for that purpose.

Do not attempt to convert any standard 30-06 family case

to 6mm BR. The thicker case walls and large (usually hotter) primers are certain to dramatically increase pressures—not the thing you want to see in a cartridge working at the top end of rifle pressures! We can make no recommendation for loading data based on any such conversion case. Stick to factory 7mm BR cases for conversion to 6mm BR.

Usable case capacity depends on case and chamber, but with lighter bullets, it would be about 35.0 grains of water. A2460 and A2520 are noted choices for accurate loads.

6mm BENCHREST REMINGTON LOADING DATA (6mm BR)

Powder	STARTING Grs.	MV (fps)	MAXIMUM Grs.	MV (fps)	Press. (CUP/psi)	Comments
60						
A2460	31.1	2774	34.5	3152	51,600p	Sra HP/2.125″
A2015BR	27.5	2750	30.5	3125	52,700p	Sra HP/2.125″
A2520	31.5	2742	35.0	3116	50,500p	Sra HP/2.125″/(C)
A2230	30.2	2707	33.5	3076	49,400p	Sra HP/2.125″
A2495BR	29.7	2685	33.0	3051	46,700p	Sra HP/2.125″/(C)
A2700	33.3	2621	35.0	2788	37,900p	Sra HP/2.125″/(C)
70						
A2520	30.6	2600	34.0	2955	51,900p	Sra HP/2.17″/(C)
A2015BR	27.5	2599	30.5	2953	52,900p	Sra HP/2.17″
A2460	29.7	2594	33.0	2948	51,600p	Sra HP/2.17″
A2495BR	28.4	2584	31.5	2936	50,500p	Sra HP/2.17″/(C)
A2230	29.3	2578	32.5	2930	52,500p	Sra HP/2.17″
A2700	33.3	2495	35.0	2654	37,900p	Sra HP/2.17″/(C)
80						
A2460	28.8	2475	32.0	2812	51,200p	Spr SP/2.12″
A2520	29.7	2472	33.0	2809	51,200p	Spr SP/2.12″
A2495BR	27.0	2436	30.0	2768	53,400p	Spr SP/2.12″
A2015BR	26.1	2411	29.0	2740	50,200p	Spr SP/2.12″

Powder	STARTING Grs.	MV (fps)	MAXIMUM Grs.	MV (fps)	Press. (CUP/psi)	Comments
80 con't						
A2230	27.9	2405	31.0	2733	49,700p	Spr SP/2.12″
A2700	33.3	2482	35.0	2640	46,700p	Spr SP/2.12″/(C)
87						
A2700	33.3	2472	35.0	2630	53,000p	Hdy HPBT/2.225″/(C)
A2520	27.0	2291	30.0	2603	51,800p	Hdy HPBT/2.225″
A2495BR	25.2	2287	28.0	2599	51,200p	Hdy HPBT/2.225″
A2460	26.6	2285	29.5	2597	50,700p	Hdy HPBT/2.225″
A2230	26.1	2262	29.0	2570	50,500p	Hdy HPBT/2.225″
A2015BR	24.3	2262	27.0	2570	52,000p	Hdy HPBT/2.225″
100						
A2230	25.2	2131	28.0	2422	52,400p	Spr SBT/2.21″
A2520	25.7	2125	28.5	2415	52,000p	Spr SBT/2.21″
A2460	25.2	2121	28.0	2410	50,900p	Spr SBT/2.21″
A2700	30.4	2238	32.0	2381	50,100p	Spr SBT/2.21″
A2495BR	23.4	2093	26.0	2378	54,000p	Spr SBT/2.21″
A2015BR	22.5	2069	25.0	2351	51,900p	Spr SBT/2.21″

Never exceed maximum load nor use any load exhibiting signs of excessive pressure. Begin at suggested starting load and work up carefully.

339

256
Winchester
Magnum

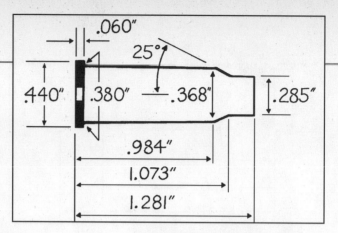

Case: Winchester
Primer: Small Rifle
Barrel: 10″ Hodgdon (T/C)
Bullet Diameter: 0.257″

Maximum Case Length: 1.281″
Trim to Length: 1.275″
Maximum Cartridge OAL: 1.590″
Minimum Cartridge OAL: 1.540″

This represents one of those interesting little oddities in the cartridge world. The 256 Win. Mag. was introduced in 1960, as a handgun cartridge, but there were no commercial guns then chambered for it! This is simply the 357 Magnum necked down, and cases are easily converted.

Ruger soon offered an innovative adaptation of their single-action revolver, called the Hawkeye, chambered for the 256 Win. Mag. The anticipated Ruger and Smith & Wesson revolver chamberings were never commercially offered because case setback problems could not be solved.

As with any tapered or necked revolver cartridge, the cylinder is easily jammed. In response to chamber pressures,

the case backs out of the chamber when the round is fired. At the same time, the case shoulder is pushed forward—any trace of lubrication on the case or in the chamber exacerbates this case body lengthening.

The best varmint bullets for the 256 Win. Mag. are probably Hornady's 60-grain flatnose and Speer's 75-grain flatnose. Heavier bullets offer limited expansion and lack the velocity necessary to achieve useful trajectories for longer shots.

Usable case capacity with a 60-grain bullet, seated normally, is about 18.1 grains of water. H4198, IMR4198 and H110 are probably the best powder choices.

256 WINCHESTER MAGNUM LOADING DATA

60

Powder	STARTING Grs.	MV (fps)	MAXIMUM Grs.	MV (fps)	Press. (CUP/psi)	Comments
H4227	15.0	2156	16.0	2386		
IMR4227	15.0	2140	16.0	2374		
H110	15.0	2264	16.0	2369		
Her2400	14.0	2236	15.0	2360		
W296	15.0	2220	16.0	2339		
W680	15.5	2160	16.5	2249		
H4198			18.0	1704		
IMR4198	17.0	1624	18.0	1702		

75

Powder	STARTING Grs.	MV (fps)	MAXIMUM Grs.	MV (fps)	Press. (CUP/psi)	Comments
H110	14.0	2115	15.0	2180		
W296	14.0	2089	15.0	2174		
W680	14.5	2043	15.5	2144		
H4227	14.0	2026	15.0	2120		
IMR4198	15.0	1982	16.0	2110		
IMR4227	13.5	1947	14.5	2037		
Her2400	12.0	1890	13.0	2027		

87

Powder	STARTING Grs.	MV (fps)	MAXIMUM Grs.	MV (fps)	Press. (CUP/psi)	Comments
H110	12.5	1883	13.5	2049		
W296	12.5	1878	13.5	2043		
H4227	13.0	1798	14.0	2040		
W680	13.0	1811	14.0	2029		
H4198			15.0	2007		
IMR4198	14.0	1840	15.0	1981		
Her2400	11.0	1748	12.0	1965		
IMR4227	12.0	1676	13.0	1897		

Caution: **Loads exceeding SAAMI OAL Maximum must be verified for bullet-to-rifling clearance and magazine functioning. Where a specific primer or bullet is indicated those components must be used, no substitutions! Where only a maximum load is shown, reduce starting load 10%, unless otherwise specified.**

Key: (C) = compressed charge; C = CUP; p = psi; Plink = Plinker; Bns = Barnes; Hdy = Hornady; Lap = Lapua; Nos = Nosler; Rem = Remington; Sra = Sierra; Spr = Speer; Win = Winchester.

Never exceed maximum load nor use any load exhibiting signs of excessive pressure. Begin at suggested starting load and work up carefully.

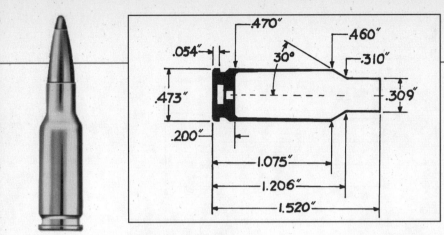

Case: Remington
Primer: Small Rifle
Barrel: 15″ Accurate/14″ Vihtavuori
Bullet Diameter: 0.284″
Maximum Case Length: 1.520″

Trim to Length: 1.510″
Maximum Cartridge OAL:
    Chamber Dependent
Minimum Cartridge OAL:
    Bullet Dependent

Originally, the 7mm BR was offered as a factory chambering, but the ammunition was in the "roll your own" category. Remington now offers a 140-grain PSP loading at 2215 fps. With a wide selection of bullets available and sufficient capacity, the 7mm BR is a fine choice for recoil-sensitive shooters who want to hunt big game with a handgun.

The 7mm BR was introduced as a metallic silhouette chambering and performs admirably in that application.

For hunting, it can deliver more energy to targets past about 50 yards than typical 30-30 Winchester rifle loads. It is capable for hunting game to the size of mule deer. In competent hands,

it would be a good choice up to the size of elk. This chambering offers the necessary accuracy for shots to 200 yards.

Do not attempt to convert any standard 30-06 family case to 7mm BR. The thicker case walls and large (usually hotter) primers are certain to dramatically increase pressures—not the thing you want to see in a cartridge working at the top end of rifle pressures! We can make no recommendation for loading data based on any such conversion case. Stick to factory 7mm BR cases.

With a 120-grain bullet, seated normally, usable case capacity is about 33.7 grains of water.

7mm BENCHREST REMINGTON LOADING DATA (7mmBR)

Powder	STARTING Grs.	MV (fps)	MAXIMUM Grs.	MV (fps)	Press. (CUP/psi)	Comments
100						
N130	29.2	2449	32.4	2748	50,800p	Hdy HP/2.205″
N120	26.8	2418	29.8	2721	50,800p	Hdy HP/2.205″
120						
N133	29.4	2298	32.6	2529	50,800p	Hdy SPSS/2.228″
N130	26.8	2191	29.9	2454	50,800p	Hdy SPSS/2.228″
A2495BR	29.3	2142	32.5	2434	41,900C	Hdy SSP/2.225″/Rem 7½/(C)
N120	24.9	2171	27.8	2421	50,800p	Hdy SPSS/2.228″
A2520	28.8	2109	32.0	2397	43,600C	Hdy SSP/2.225″/Rem 7½
A2460	28.4	2089	31.5	2374	42,900C	Hdy SSP/2.225″/Rem 7½
139-140						
A2495BR	28.4	1996	31.5	2268	42,200C	Hdy SP/2.305″/Rem 7½/(C)
A2460	27.9	1977	31.0	2247	45,900C	Hdy SP/2.305″/Rem 7½
A2520	27.9	1947	31.0	2212	41,700C	Hdy SP/2.305″/Rem 7½
N133	25.6	1993	28.4	2202	50,800p	Nos BT/2.374″
A2015BR	25.2	1928	28.0	2191	40,400C	Hdy SP/2.305″/Rem 7½
A2230	27.0	1925	30.0	2188	43,900C	Hdy SP/2.305″/Rem 7½
150						
A2495BR	27.9	1981	31.0	2251	45,100C	Sra SBT/2.255″/Rem 7½/(C)
A2520	27.5	1917	30.5	2178	43,100C	Sra SBT/2.255″/Rem 7½
A2460	26.6	1892	29.5	2150	44,100C	Sra SBT/2.255″/Rem 7½
A2015BR	24.8	1887	27.5	2144	41,300C	Sra SBT/2.255″/Rem 7½
N135	26.0	1916	28.8	2132	50,800p	Nos BT/2.374″
A2230	26.1	1868	29.0	2123	43,200C	Sra SBT/2.255″/Rem 7½
N133	24.7	1926	27.3	2107	50,800p	Nos BT/2.374″
160						
N135	24.8	1862	27.7	2066	50,800p	Sra HPBT/2.35″
N133	23.5	1838	26.1	2030	50,800p	Sra HPBT/2.35″
N130	21.6	1812	23.9	1975	50,800p	Sra HPBT/2.35″
168						
A2520	27.0	1828	30.0	2077	44,600C	Sra HPBT/2.31″/Rem 7½/(C)
A2460	25.7	1776	28.5	2018	45,000C	Sra HPBT/2.31″/Rem 7½/(C)
A2230	25.2	1746	28.0	1984	43,600C	Sra HPBT/2.31″/Rem 7½/(C)
A2495BR	25.7	1744	28.5	1982	39,600C	Sra HPBT/2.31″/Rem 7½/(C)

Never exceed maximum load nor use any load exhibiting signs of excessive pressure. Begin at suggested starting load and work up carefully.

341

7·30
Waters

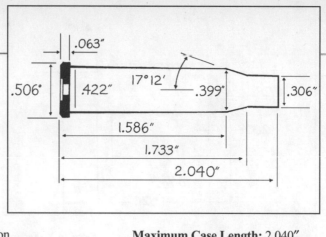

Case: Remington
Primer: Remington 9½
Barrel: 14″ Accurate
Bullet Diameter: 0.284″

Maximum Case Length: 2.040″
Trim to Length: 2.030″
Maximum Cartridge OAL: 2.550″
Minimum Cartridge OAL: 2.480″

Ken Waters, well-known ballistics expert, designed this cartridge specifically to flatten the trajectory available from typical lever-action rifles without appreciably increasing recoil levels. Cases are easily formed from standard 30-30 cases.

SAAMI pressure standards for the 7-30 Waters are about 5-percent higher than for the 30-30, and performance is just a bit better. The 7-30 will launch a 140-grain bullet as much as 150 fps faster than the 30-30 will launch a 150-grain bullet. The 7-30 produces considerably more energy and a flatter trajectory.

Chambered in the T/C Contender, the 7-30 has become a very popular handgun hunting cartridge. With a 14″ barrel, the 7-30 very nearly duplicates rifle 30-30 muzzle energy. With spitzer bullets, which can be used safely in the Contender, delivered energy surpasses typical 30-30 rifle loads beyond a few dozen yards. The 7-30 is a good hunting choice for smaller species of big game.

Case capacity with a 139-grain bullet, seated normally, is about 40.0 grains of water. A2495BR, A2230 and A2460 are noted performers in Water's little 7-30.

▰ 7-30 WATERS LOADING DATA ▰

Powder	STARTING Grs.	MV (fps)	MAXIMUM Grs.	MV (fps)	Press. (CUP/psi)	Comments
100						
A2230	34.2	2393	38.0	2719	37,800C	Sra HP/2.665″/*
A2495BR	35.1	2391	39.0	2717	32,700C	Sra HP/2.665″/(C)/*
A2015BR	32.4	2377	36.0	2701	37,600C	Sra HP/2.665″/*
A2460	34.2	2349	38.0	2669	37,900C	Sra HP/2.665″/*
A2520	35.1	2326	39.0	2643	36,300C	Sra HP/2.665″/*
A2700	37.8	2167	42.0	2462	37,900C	Sra HP/2.665″/(C)/*
120						
A2230	32.0	2189	35.5	2487	37,400C	Hdy SSP/2.755″/*
A2495BR	32.4	2179	36.0	2476	36,400C	Hdy SSP/2.755″/*
A2460	32.4	2174	36.0	2471	37,300C	Hdy SSP/2.755″/*
A2520	32.4	2126	36.0	2416	35,500C	Hdy SSP/2.755″/*
A2015BR	29.7	2109	33.0	2397	35,700C	Hdy SSP/2.755″/*
A2700	36.0	2078	40.0	2361	39,000C	Hdy SSP/2.755″/*
145						
A2495BR	30.6	2024	34.0	2300	38,700C	Spr HPBT/2.74″/*
A2230	29.7	1994	33.0	2266	39,000C	Spr HPBT/2.74″/*
A2460	29.7	1969	33.0	2237	38,500C	Spr HPBT/2.74″/*
A2520	30.6	1955	34.0	2222	38,800C	Spr HPBT/2.74″/*
A2015BR	27.5	1925	30.5	2188	39,000C	Spr HPBT/2.74″/*

Powder	STARTING Grs.	MV (fps)	MAXIMUM Grs.	MV (fps)	Press. (CUP/psi)	Comments
150						
A2495BR	30.6	2006	34.0	2280	38,400C	Nos BT/2.795″/*
A2460	29.7	1934	33.0	2198	39,500C	Nos BT/2.795″/*
A2230	29.3	1933	32.5	2197	37,600C	Nos BT/2.795″/*
A2520	30.2	1900	33.5	2159	37,000C	Nos BT/2.795″/*
A2700	33.8	1857	37.5	2110	38,800C	Nos BT/2.795″/*
168						
A2495BR	29.7	1902	33.0	2161	38,700C	Sra HPBT/2.77″/*
A2460	28.8	1857	32.0	2110	39,800C	Sra HPBT/2.77″/*
A2230	27.9	1834	31.0	2084	38,500C	Sra HPBT/2.77″/*
A2520	28.8	1814	32.0	2061	38,800C	Sra HPBT/2.77″/*
A2015BR	25.7	1767	28.5	2008	38,700C	Sra HPBT/2.77″/*
175						
A2495BR	29.7	1800	33.0	2045	39,100C	Hdy SP/2.79″/*
A2460	28.8	1765	32.0	2006	39,700C	Hdy SP/2.79″/*
A2230	27.9	1764	31.0	2004	38,700C	Hdy SP/2.79″/*
A2700	31.5	1675	35.0	1903	36,200C	Hdy SP/2.79″/*
A2520	27.9	1673	31.0	1901	36,100C	Hdy SP/2.79″/*

* These loads are intended for use in the T/C Contender only. They exceed SAAMI OAL maximum. Since these are spitzer bullets, they do not touch the rifling. Do not use in tubular magazine guns!

Never exceed maximum load nor use any load exhibiting signs of excessive pressure. Begin at suggested starting load and work up carefully.

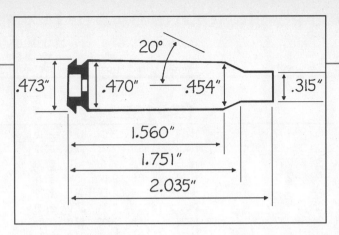

Case: Remington
Primer: Large Rifle
Barrel: 15″ Accurate (XP-100)
    14″ Hodgdon
Bullet Diameter: 0.284″

Maximum Case Length: 2.035″
Trim to Length: 2.025″
Maximum Cartridge OAL: 2.800″
Minimum Cartridge OAL: 2.530″

This was originally a wildcat chambering developed for Metallic Silhouette shooting competition. The 7mm-08 was created by the simple expedient of necking down the standard 308 Winchester to 7mm. Excepting the headstamp, there are no other differences in the cases. To make 7mm-08 cases, simply run 308 cases into the 7mm-08 full-length sizing die.

In 1980, Remington offered the 7mm-08 as a factory chambering. Chambered in Remington's recently discontin-ued XP-100, this cartridge became popular among International Handgun Metallic Silhouette Association (IHMSA) competitors and handgun hunters.

Loaded with the proper bullet and with careful shot placement, the 7mm-08 is capable as a handgun elk cartridge at closer ranges.

Case capacity with a 145-grain bullet, seated normally, is about 51.2 grains of water. H414, H380, H4895, H335 and A2460 have all been noted as good 7mm-08 performers.

7mm-08 REMINGTON LOADING DATA

Powder	STARTING Grs.	MV (fps)	MAXIMUM Grs.	MV (fps)	Press. (CUP/psi)	Comments
100						
A2460	38.7	2567	43.0	2917	49,500C	Sra HP/2.665″
A2520	40.1	2559	44.5	2908	48,400C	Sra HP/2.665″
A2230	38.3	2557	42.5	2906	49,800C	Sra HP/2.665″
A2015BR	36.5	2502	40.5	2843	48,500C	Sra HP/2.665″
H322	37.0	2650	39.0	2784		
H4895	39.0	2657	41.0	2771		
BL-C(2)	40.0	2644	42.0	2763		
A2495BR	38.3	2411	42.5	2740	48,500C	Sra HP/2.665″
H335	39.0	2640	41.0	2739		
A2700	45.6	2573	48.0	2737	50,700C	Sra HP/2.665″
H4198	32.0	2494	34.0	2641		
A4350	42.8	2227	47.5	2531	44,200C	Sra HP/2.665″/(C)
A3100	42.8	1978	47.5	2248	40,600C	Sra HP/2.665″/(C)
115-120						
A2460	36.6	2365	40.7	2688	48,800C	Nos SP/2.765″
A2230	36.3	2337	40.3	2656	48,900C	Nos SP/2.765″
A2520	37.3	2327	41.4	2644	47,700C	Nos SP/2.765″
H380	44.0	2461	46.0	2628		
A2015BR	34.4	2312	38.2	2627	49,000C	Nos SP/2.765″
H414	45.0	2443	47.0	2618		
H4895	37.0	2479	39.0	2618		
115-120 con't						
H322	35.0	2481	37.0	2599		
A2700	44.2	2429	46.5	2584	49,200C	Nos SP/2.765″
A2495BR	36.0	2268	40.0	2577	49,000C	Nos SP/2.765″
H450	48.0	2414	50.0	2567		
BL-C(2)	38.0	2452	40.0	2567		
H335	37.0	2439	39.0	2552		
H4350	46.0	2409	48.0	2509		
H4831	46.0	2391	48.0	2507		
H4198	30.0	2360	32.0	2459		
A4350	42.8	2164	47.5	2459	45,500C	Nos SP/2.765″/(C)
A3100	42.8	1934	47.5	2198	41,500C	Nos SP/2.765″/(C)

▶▶▶▶▶▶▶▶▶▶▶▶▶▶▶▶▶▶▶▶▶▶▶▶▶▶▶▶

Caution: **Loads exceeding SAAMI OAL Maximum must be verified for bullet-to-rifling clearance and magazine functioning. Where a specific primer or bullet is indicated those components must be used, no substitutions! Where only a maximum load is shown, reduce starting load 10%, unless otherwise specified.**

Key: (C) = compressed charge; C = CUP; p = psi; Plink = Plinker; Bns = Barnes; Hdy = Hornady; Lap = Lapua; Nos = Nosler; Rem = Remington; Sra = Sierra; Spr = Speer; Win = Winchester.

Never exceed maximum load nor use any load exhibiting signs of excessive pressure. Begin at suggested starting load and work up carefully.

130

Powder	—STARTING— Grs.	MV (fps)	—MAXIMUM— Grs.	MV (fps)	Press. (CUP/psi)	Comments
A2460	35.8	2284	39.8	2595	52,000C	Spr SP/2.77″
A2230	35.4	2270	39.3	2580	51,800C	Spr SP/2.77″
A2015BR	33.8	2236	37.6	2541	52,000C	Spr SP/2.77″
A2520	35.6	2229	39.6	2533	51,400C	Spr SP/2.77″
BL-C(2)	37.0	2391	39.0	2506		
A2700	42.8	2351	45.0	2501	50,500C	Spr SP/2.77″
A4350	42.8	2197	47.5	2497	48,600C	Spr SP/2.77″/(C)
H450	47.0	2377	49.0	2491		
H380	43.0	2378	45.0	2489		
H414	44.0	2364	46.0	2484		
H4895	36.0	2332	38.0	2473		
H335	36.0	2340	38.0	2462		
H322	34.0	2357	36.0	2460		
A2495BR	35.1	2152	39.0	2446	49,800C	Spr SP/2.77″
H4350	45.0	2292	47.0	2409		
H4831	45.0	2220	47.0	2353		

139-140

Powder	—STARTING— Grs.	MV (fps)	—MAXIMUM— Grs.	MV (fps)	Press. (CUP/psi)	Comments
A2460	36.0	2241	40.0	2547	51,900C	Sra SBT/2.8″
A2230	35.1	2195	39.0	2494	49,600C	Sra SBT/2.8″
A2520	35.6	2186	39.5	2484	50,800C	Sra SBT/2.8″
A4350	42.8	2171	47.5	2467	49,800C	Sra SBT/2.8″
A2015BR	33.3	2161	37.0	2456	49,300C	Sra SBT/2.8″
H380	42.0	2331	44.0	2433		
A2700	42.3	2284	44.5	2430	49,500C	Sra SBT/2.8″
H450	46.0	2301	48.0	2414		
H4350	45.0	2280	47.0	2411		
A2495BR	34.7	2094	38.5	2379	49,200C	Sra SBT/2.8″
H4831	45.0	2240	47.0	2367		
BL-C(2)	35.0	2247	37.0	2364		
H4895	34.0	2258	36.0	2362		
H414	43.0	2249	45.0	2356		
H335	34.0	2242	36.0	2337		
H322	33.0	2209	35.0	2329		

145-150

Powder	—STARTING— Grs.	MV (fps)	—MAXIMUM— Grs.	MV (fps)	Press. (CUP/psi)	Comments
A2460	34.5	2125	38.3	2415	50,200C	Sra SBT/2.8″
A2230	34.2	2121	38.0	2410	51,000C	Sra SBT/2.8″
A4350	41.9	2115	46.5	2403	51,100C	Sra SBT/2.8″
A2520	35.1	2115	39.0	2403	51,600C	Sra SBT/2.8″
A2700	41.3	2230	43.5	2372	51,900C	Sra SBT/2.8″
H380	41.0	2244	43.0	2369		
A2015BR	32.4	2064	36.0	2346	50,300C	Sra SBT/2.8″
H414	42.0	2233	44.0	2344		
H450	45.0	2229	47.0	2341		
H4350	44.0	2202	46.0	2321		
BL-C(2)	34.0	2222	36.0	2316		
H335	33.0	2193	35.0	2296		
A2495BR	33.6	2018	37.3	2293	50,300C	Sra SBT/2.8″
H4831	44.0	2202	46.0	2292		
H322	32.0	2200	34.0	2286		
H4895	33.0	2169	35.0	2267		

154-162

Powder	—STARTING— Grs.	MV (fps)	—MAXIMUM— Grs.	MV (fps)	Press. (CUP/psi)	Comments
H414	41.0	2204	43.0	2319		
H450	45.0	2237	47.0	2312		
H4350	43.0	2178	45.0	2296		
H380	40.0	2194	42.0	2281		
H4831	44.0	2169	46.0	2272		
BL-C(2)	33.0	2111	35.0	2209		
H322	31.0	2099	33.0	2201		
H335	32.0	2096	34.0	2194		

160

Powder	—STARTING— Grs.	MV (fps)	—MAXIMUM— Grs.	MV (fps)	Press. (CUP/psi)	Comments
A4350	41.4	2036	46.0	2314	49,400C	Nos SP Part./2.8″/(C)
A2520	34.2	1988	38.0	2259	48,500C	Nos SP Part./2.8″
A2460	33.3	1985	37.0	2256	48,500C	Nos SP Part./2.8″
A2230	32.9	1971	36.5	2240	47,300C	Nos SP Part./2.8″
A2015BR	31.5	1954	35.0	2220	48,500C	Nos SP Part./2.8″
A2700	39.9	2079	42.0	2212	45,600C	Nos SP Part./2.8″

168

Powder	—STARTING— Grs.	MV (fps)	—MAXIMUM— Grs.	MV (fps)	Press. (CUP/psi)	Comments
H450	44.0	2184	46.0	2299		
H4350	42.0	2177	44.0	2290		
A4350	41.4	2011	46.0	2285	50,400C	Sra HPBT/2.8″
H4831	43.0	2147	45.0	2260		
H414	40.0	2141	42.0	2259		
A2460	33.3	1986	37.0	2257	50,100C	Sra HPBT/2.8″
H380	39.0	2138	41.0	2242		
A2230	33.3	1954	37.0	2220	49,500C	Sra HPBT/2.8″
A2520	33.3	1947	37.0	2212	49,400C	Sra HPBT/2.8″
A2700	37.8	1941	42.0	2206	47,300C	Sra HPBT/2.8″
A2495BR	34.2	1938	38.0	2202	52,000C	Sra HPBT/2.8″
A2015BR	31.5	1936	35.0	2200	49,300C	Sra HPBT/2.8″
H322	30.0	2050	32.0	2159		
H4895	31.0	2042	33.0	2152		
BL-C(2)	32.0	2027	34.0	2147		

170-175

Powder	—STARTING— Grs.	MV (fps)	—MAXIMUM— Grs.	MV (fps)	Press. (CUP/psi)	Comments
A4350	41.0	1937	45.5	2201	49,400C	Rem PSPCL/2.795″
H450	43.0	2085	45.0	2198		
A2230	33.3	1921	37.0	2183	49,600C	Rem PSPCL/2.795″
A2460	33.3	1916	37.0	2177	49,800C	Rem PSPCL/2.795″
A2520	34.2	1914	38.0	2175	51,200C	Rem PSPCL/2.795″
A2700	39.9	2019	42.0	2148	47,400C	Rem PSPCL/2.795″
H4831	42.0	2026	44.0	2145		
H4350	41.0	2021	43.0	2136		
H414	39.0	2030	41.0	2134		
A2015BR	31.5	1855	35.0	2108	47,700C	Rem PSPCL/2.795″
H380	37.0	1974	39.0	2090		
A2495BR	34.2	1823	38.0	2072	47,900C	Rem PSPCL/2.795″
A3100	42.3	1778	47.0	2070	42,600C	Rem PSPCL/2.795″/(C)
BL-C(2)	31.0	1951	33.0	2049		
H335	30.0	1932	32.0	2036		

Never exceed maximum load nor use any load exhibiting signs of excessive pressure. Begin at suggested starting load and work up carefully.

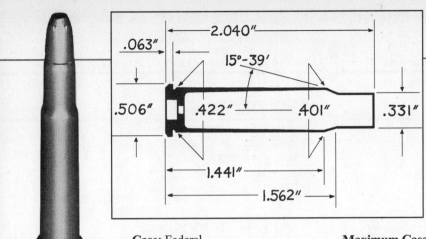

Case: Federal
Primer: Large Rifle
Barrel: 14″ Accurate (T/C)
       10″ Hodgdon (T/C)
Bullet Diameter: 0.308″

Maximum Case Length: 2.040″
Trim to Length: 2.035″
Maximum Cartridge OAL: 2.550″
Minimum Cartridge OAL: 2.450″

When Winchester designed the 30-30 for chambering in a smokeless-powder version of John M. Browning's now famous Model 94 rifle, they could never have envisioned it would still be around in 1995, and that it would be more popular than ever and also be a common handgun chambering! Nevertheless, that is the current situation.

The 30-30 shines in 14″ and 16″ handguns. Safely encasing spitzer bullets, handgun loads deliver substantially more energy to game targets at 50 yards and beyond, compared to any standard rifle 30-30 load, the ballistics being limited by the necessity of using flatpoint bullets.

With proper shot placement, the 30-30 handgun is a capable elk cartridge because it can deliver more energy at maximum usable range. The 30-30 rifle is, at best, a marginal choice—ballistic coefficient does matter.

Case capacity with a 170-grain bullet, seated normally, is about 37.8 grains of water. A2700, A2520 and A2015BR are good choices in the 30-30. As data becomes available, VarGet and N550 promise to be genuinely superior 30-30 performers.

30-30 WINCHESTER LOADING DATA

Lead 152 Lyman 311466 (RN-GC)

Powder	Grs.	MV (fps)	Grs.	MV (fps)	Press. (CUP/psi)	Comments
A2700	32.3	1801	34.0	1916	28,100p	2.45″/CCI 200
A2015BR	23.0	1642	25.5	1866	27,700p	2.45″/CCI 200
A2520	24.8	1628	27.5	1850	25,700p	2.45″/CCI 200
A2460	24.3	1617	27.0	1838	26,400p	2.45″/CCI 200
A2230	23.4	1614	26.0	1834	27,800p	2.45″/CCI 200
A2495BR	25.7	1476	28.5	1677	28,400p	2.45″/CCI 200

Lead 173 Lyman 31141 (FNGC)

Powder	Grs.	MV (fps)	Grs.	MV (fps)	Press. (CUP/psi)	Comments
A2520	25.7	1662	28.5	1889	29,300p	2.55″/CCI 200
A2015BR	23.4	1645	26.0	1869	29,000p	2.55″/CCI 200
A2700	31.4	1747	33.0	1859	32,800p	2.55″/CCI 200
A2460	24.8	1633	27.5	1856	28,300p	2.55″/CCI 200
A2230	23.4	1599	26.0	1817	27,400p	2.55″/CCI 200
A2495BR	24.8	1453	27.5	1651	35,100p	2.55″/CCI 200

100

Powder	Grs.	MV (fps)	Grs.	MV (fps)	Press. (CUP/psi)	Comments
A2015BR	33.8	2230	37.5	2534	39,900p	Spr Plink/2.345″/ CCI 200
A2230	35.1	2212	39.0	2514	39,500p	Spr Plink/2.345″/ CCI 200
A2460	35.1	2181	39.0	2478	37,200p	Spr Plink/2.345″/ CCI 200
A2520	34.2	2075	38.0	2358	30,600p	Spr Plink/2.345″/ CCI 200
A2700	38.0	2175	40.0	2314	30,700p	Spr Plink/2.345″/ CCI 200/(C)
A2495BR	33.3	1934	37.0	2198	34,800p	Spr Plink/2.345″/ CCI 200

> *Caution:* **Loads exceeding SAAMI OAL Maximum must be verified for bullet-to-rifling clearance and magazine functioning. Where a specific primer or bullet is indicated those components must be used, no substitutions! Where only a maximum load is shown, reduce starting load 10%, unless otherwise specified.**
>
> *Key:* (C) = compressed charge; C = CUP; p = psi; Plink = Plinker; Bns = Barnes; Hdy = Hornady; Lap = Lapua; Nos = Nosler; Rem = Remington; Sra = Sierra; Spr = Speer; Win = Winchester.

Never exceed maximum load nor use any load exhibiting signs of excessive pressure. Begin at suggested starting load and work up carefully.

110 (10" barrel)

Powder	Grs.	MV (fps)	Grs.	MV (fps)	Press. (CUP/psi)	Comments
H4895	32.0	1946	35.0	2229		
H322	30.0	1906	33.0	2210		
H4198	25.0	1910	28.0	2194		
H4227	18.0	1688	20.0	1796		

110 (14" barrel)

Powder	Grs.	MV (fps)	Grs.	MV (fps)	Press. (CUP/psi)	Comments
A2015BR	32.0	2110	35.5	2398	40,900p	Hdy RN/2.44"/CCI 200
A2460	33.3	2085	37.0	2369	37,400p	Hdy RN/2.44"/CCI 200
A2520	34.2	2082	38.0	2366	35,700p	Hdy RN/2.44"/CCI 200
A2230	32.4	2059	36.0	2340	37,000p	Hdy RN/2.44"/CCI 200
A2700	38.0	2153	40.0	2290	33,300p	Hdy RN/2.44"/CCI 200/(C)
A2495BR	33.3	1947	37.0	2213	41,000p	Hdy RN/2.44"/CCI 200

125-130

Powder	Grs.	MV (fps)	Grs.	MV (fps)	Press. (CUP/psi)	Comments
H335	34.0	1988	37.0	2144		
H4198	24.0	1808	27.0	2090		
H4895	31.0	1819	34.0	2074		
H322	29.0	1783	32.0	1980		
H4227	17.0	1534	19.0	1701		

130

Powder	Grs.	MV (fps)	Grs.	MV (fps)	Press. (CUP/psi)	Comments
A2520	33.3	1998	37.0	2270	40,730p	Hdy SSP/2.625"/CCI 200/(C)
A2015BR	28.8	1908	32.0	2168	39,700p	Hdy SSP/2.625"/CCI 200
A2460	31.5	1905	35.0	2165	39,700p	Hdy SSP/2.625"/CCI 200
A2230	30.6	1903	34.0	2162	39,900p	Hdy SSP/2.625"/CCI 200
A2700	36.1	1977	38.0	2103	34,500p	Hdy SSP/2.625"/CCI 200/(C)
A2495BR	29.7	1734	33.0	1971	40,300p	Hdy SSP/2.625"/CCI 200

150 (10" barrel)

Powder	Grs.	MV (fps)	Grs.	MV (fps)	Press. (CUP/psi)	Comments
H4198	23.0	1620	26.0	1864		
H4895	30.0	1677	33.0	1818		
H335	30.0	1684	33.0	1807		
H322	27.0	1592	30.0	1796		
H4227	16.0	1352	18.0	1539		

150 (14" barrel)

Powder	Grs.	MV (fps)	Grs.	MV (fps)	Press. (CUP/psi)	Comments
A2520	30.2	1800	33.5	2046	38,800p	Spr FN/2.54"/CCI 200
A2700	35.2	1916	37.0	2038	39,300p	Spr FN/2.54"/CCI 200
A2460	29.3	1773	32.5	2015	40,200p	Spr FN/2.54"/CCI 200
A2230	28.5	1760	31.7	2000	41,300p	Spr FN/2.54"/CCI 200
A2015BR	26.1	1698	29.0	1929	38,400p	Spr FN/2.54"/CCI 200
A2495BR	27.5	1607	30.5	1826	40,600p	Spr FN/2.54"/CCI 200

165-170

Powder	Grs.	MV (fps)	Grs.	MV (fps)	Press. (CUP/psi)	Comments
H335	29.0	1709	32.0	1819		
H4895	27.0	1654	30.0	1729		
H322	25.0	1620	28.0	1727		
H4198	22.0	1569	25.0	1716		
H4227	15.0	1237	17.0	1401		

170

Powder	Grs.	MV (fps)	Grs.	MV (fps)	Press. (CUP/psi)	Comments
A2700	33.3	1775	35.0	1888	39,700p	Nos FN/2.545"/CCI 200
A2520	28.4	1649	31.5	1874	38,400p	Nos FN/2.545"/CCI 200
A2230	27.0	1645	30.0	1869	42,000p	Nos FN/2.545"/CCI 200
A2460	27.2	1640	30.2	1864	39,900p	Nos FN/2.545"/CCI 200
A2015BR	24.3	1578	27.0	1793	38,600p	Nos FN/2.545"/CCI 200
A2495BR	26.6	1512	29.5	1718	40,200p	Nos FN/2.545"/CCI 200

Caution: Loads exceeding SAAMI OAL Maximum must be verified for bullet-to-rifling clearance and magazine functioning. Where a specific primer or bullet is indicated those components must be used, no substitutions! Where only a maximum load is shown, reduce starting load 10%, unless otherwise specified.

Key: (C) = compressed charge; C = CUP; p = psi; Plink = Plinker; Bns = Barnes; Hdy = Hornady; Lap = Lapua; Nos = Nosler; Rem = Remington; Sra = Sierra; Spr = Speer; Win = Winchester.

Never exceed maximum load nor use any load exhibiting signs of excessive pressure. Begin at suggested starting load and work up carefully.

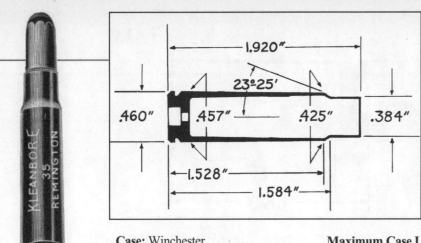

Case: Winchester
Primer: Large Rifle
Barrel: 14″ Accurate (T/C)
      14″ Hodgdon (T/C)
Bullet Diameter: 0.357″-0.358″

Maximum Case Length: 1.920″
Trim to Length: 1.910″
Maximum Cartridge OAL: 2.525″
Minimum Cartridge OAL: 2.460″

Originally introduced by Remington in 1906, chambered in their Model 8 semi-automatic rifle, the 35 Remington rapidly developed a strong following. Recently, the 35 Remington has become a popular handgun chambering.

In handguns with barrels of 14″ or 16″, the 35 Remington has found an entirely new following. It is rapidly becoming a favorite of hunters and silhouette shooters. The lack of lighter spitzer bullets in 35-caliber limits long-range performance.

The 35 Remington shines with cast bullets, which can provide inexpensive and effective loads.

Case capacity with a 200-grain bullet, seated normally, is about 44.0 grains of water. H322 and A2520 are on the short list of good 35 Remington choices.

35 REMINGTON LOADING DATA

Lead 200 RCBS 35-200 (FN-GC)

Powder	STARTING Grs.	MV (fps)	MAXIMUM Grs.	MV (fps)	Press. (CUP/psi)	Comments
A2520	36.1	1763	38.0	1875	30,900p	2.41″/CCI 200
A2495BR	38.0	1700	40.0	1809	24,000p	2.41″/CCI 200
A2460	32.3	1604	34.0	1706	30,300p	2.41″/CCI 200
A2230	30.9	1560	32.5	1660	29,700p	2.41″/CCI 200
A2015BR	30.9	1529	32.5	1627	30,800p	2.41″/CCI 200

Lead 250 RCBS 35-250 (SP-GC)

Powder	STARTING Grs.	MV (fps)	MAXIMUM Grs.	MV (fps)	Press. (CUP/psi)	Comments
A2460	30.4	1614	32.0	1717	32,200p	2.685″/CCI 200/*
A2495BR	33.3	1595	35.0	1697	26,100p	2.685″/CCI 200/*
A2520	30.4	1550	32.0	1649	30,700p	2.685″/CCI 200/*
A2230	27.6	1543	29.0	1641	33,500p	2.685″/CCI 200/*
A2015BR	25.7	1451	27.0	1544	31,800p	2.685″/CCI 200/*

158-160

Powder	STARTING Grs.	MV (fps)	MAXIMUM Grs.	MV (fps)	Press. (CUP/psi)	Comments
H322	40.0	2190	43.0	2277		
H4198	30.0	2110	33.0	2248		
H4227	26.0	2065	29.0	2239		

170-180

Powder	STARTING Grs.	MV (fps)	MAXIMUM Grs.	MV (fps)	Press. (CUP/psi)	Comments
H322	39.0	2072	42.0	2215		
H4198	29.0	2021	32.0	2209		
H4227	25.0	1961	28.0	2142		

170-180 con't

Powder	STARTING Grs.	MV (fps)	MAXIMUM Grs.	MV (fps)	Press. (CUP/psi)	Comments
A2520	36.1	1751	38.0	1863	28,100p	Hdy SSP/2.56″/ CCI 200/*
A2495BR	38.0	1727	40.0	1837	27,400p	Hdy SSP/2.56″/ CCI 200/*
A2460	34.2	1678	36.0	1785	27,500p	Hdy SSP/2.56″/ CCI 200/*
A2230	33.7	1666	35.5	1772	28,100p	Hdy SSP/2.56″/ CCI 200/*
A2015BR	33.7	1646	35.5	1751	28,600p	Hdy SSP/2.56″/ CCI 200/*

200

Powder	STARTING Grs.	MV (fps)	MAXIMUM Grs.	MV (fps)	Press. (CUP/psi)	Comments
H322	38.0	1947	41.0	2120		
H4198	28.0	1825	30.0	1964		
H4227	24.0	1796	26.0	1914		
A2520	37.1	1754	39.0	1866	27,800p	Sra RN/2.47″/CCI 200
A2495BR	38.0	1715	40.0	1824	25,500p	Sra RN/2.47″/CCI 200
A2015BR	33.3	1663	35.0	1769	31,000p	Sra RN/2.47″/CCI 200
A2460	35.2	1649	37.0	1754	27,200p	Sra RN/2.47″/CCI 200
A2230	33.3	1621	35.0	1724	30,900p	Sra RN/2.47″/CCI 200

* Exceeds SAAMI maximum OAL.

Never exceed maximum load nor use any load exhibiting signs of excessive pressure. Begin at suggested starting load and work up carefully.

347

45

Winchester Magnum

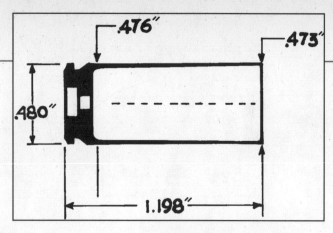

Case: Winchester
Primer: Large Pistol (Magnum for all Hodgdon powder loads)
Barrel: 8″ Accurate/5″ Hodgdon
10″ Hodgdon (T/C)
12″ Vihtavuori

Bullet Diameter: 0.451″-0.452″
Maximum Case Length: 1.198″
Trim to Length: 1.193″
Maximum Cartridge OAL: 1.575″
Minimum Cartridge OAL: 1.545″

Introduced in 1979 by Winchester and chambered in the Wildey gas-operated semi-automatic pistol, this chambering has more recently been offered in T/C Contender and L.A.R. Grizzly Magnum handguns. Performance is quite similar to the 44 Magnum.

Drawing on a tradition of stretching handgun cartridges to introduce higher-pressure versions, Winchester lengthened the 45 Automatic case from 0.898″ to 1.198″ and increased overall cartridge length similarly. The result is a case that holds about the same amount of powder as the 44 Magnum and, since working pressure is the same, can gen-

erate a bit more energy from the same-length barrel. The rimless design is much more amenable to chambering in semi-auto pistols.

Anything the standard 44 Magnum can do the 45 Winchester Magnum can do. The only disadvantage of note is that there are fewer heavy cast bullets commercially available in 45-caliber.

Usable case capacity with a 250-grain bullet, seated normally, is about 29.3 grains of water. If there is one powder that performs particularly well in the 45 Win. Mag., it is Accurate Arms excellent No.9.

45 WINCHESTER MAGNUM LOADING DATA

Powder	STARTING Grs.	MV (fps)	MAXIMUM Grs.	MV (fps)	Press. (CUP/psi)	Comments

185 (5″ Test)

Powder	Grs.	MV (fps)	Grs.	MV (fps)	Press. (CUP/psi)	Comments
HS7	18.0	1349	19.0	1489	38,400C	
HS6	17.0	1323	18.0	1472	38,700C	
HP38	9.5	1114	11.6	1362	37,000C	
Trap100	10.0	1090	12.2	1291	36,800C	

185

Powder	Grs.	MV (fps)	Grs.	MV (fps)	Press. (CUP/psi)	Comments
No.9	27.0	1662	30.0	1889	35,200C	Sra JHP/1.555″/Win WLP/(C)
3N37	14.4	1678	16.2	1766	38,000p	Hdy XTP/1.516″
H110	26.0	1524	27.0	1698		
No.7	18.9	1452	21.0	1650	35,800C	Sra JHP/1.555″/Win WLP
H4227	25.0	1460	27.0	1644		
HS7	19.0	1510	21.0	1624		
No.5	15.3	1426	17.0	1620	36,200C	Sra JHP/1.555″/Win WLP
No.2	12.6	1379	14.0	1567	37,800C	Sra JHP/1.555″/Win WLP

200 (5″ Test)

Powder	Grs.	MV (fps)	Grs.	MV (fps)	Press. (CUP/psi)	Comments
HS7	17.0	1261	18.6	1423	36,400C	
HS6	16.0	1244	17.5	1409	37,000C	
HP38	9.0	1084	11.2	1289	37,000C	
Trap100	9.5	1049	11.4	1201	36,600C	

200

Powder	Grs.	MV (fps)	Grs.	MV (fps)	Press. (CUP/psi)	Comments
N110	23.4	1757	25.6	1911	38,000p	Spr TMJ/1.516″
No.9	26.6	1632	29.5	1854	38,400C	Hdy XTP/1.57″Win WLP
3N37	14.2	1612	15.5	1698	38,000p	Spr TMJ/1.516″
No.7	18.5	1404	20.5	1595	34,700C	Hdy XTP/1.57″Win WLP
H110	24.0	1352	26.0	1590		
No.5	15.3	1398	17.0	1589	36,600C	Hdy XTP/1.57″Win WLP
HS7	17.0	1397	19.0	1549		
H4227	24.0	1389	26.0	1522		
No.2	12.2	1332	13.5	1514	40,000C	Hdy XTP/1.57″Win WLP

Never exceed maximum load nor use any load exhibiting signs of excessive pressure. Begin at suggested starting load and work up carefully.

225-230 (5" Test)

Powder	Grs.	MV (fps)	Grs.	MV (fps)	Press. (CUP/psi)	Comments
H110	27.5	1356	28.0	1410	29,000C	
HS7	17.0	1219	18.3	1320	37,100C	
HS6	15.0	1137	17.0	1296	36,600C	
H4227	24.0	1160	25.0	1259	29,400C	
HP38	9.0	994	10.8	1191	37,100C	
Trap100	9.0	989	11.0	1175	37,600C	

225-230

Powder	Grs.	MV (fps)	Grs.	MV (fps)	Press. (CUP/psi)	Comments
N110	22.2	1646	24.3	1765	38,000p	Hdy FMJ-RN/1.555"
No.9	24.8	1529	27.5	1738	38,700C	Nos FMJ/1.575"/ Win WLP
H110	22.0	1390	24.0	1550		
HS7	16.0	1310	17.0	1522		
3N37	12.9	1366	14.4	1502	38,000p	Hdy FMJ-RN/1.555"
No.7	17.1	1294	19.0	1470	34,400C	Nos FMJ/1.575"/ Win WLP
No.5	14.0	1258	15.5	1430	35,200C	Nos FMJ/1.575"/ Win WLP
H4227	22.0	1352	24.0	1419		
No.2	11.3	1194	12.5	1357	38,200C	Nos FMJ/1.575"/ Win WLP

240 (5" Test)

Powder	Grs.	MV (fps)	Grs.	MV (fps)	Press. (CUP/psi)	Comments
H110	26.5	1359	27.0	1411	37,400C	
HS7	16.0	1152	17.8	1323	37,600C	
HS6	14.0	1077	16.0	1300	38,800C	
H4227	24.6	1164	25.0	1266	33,000C	
HP38	8.6	950	10.3	1160	36,800C	
Trap100	8.8	969	10.4	1129	38,700C	

240

Powder	Grs.	MV (fps)	Grs.	MV (fps)	Press. (CUP/psi)	Comments
No.9	21.6	1413	24.0	1606	40,000C	Sra JHP/1.49"/Win WLP
No.7	17.1	1274	19.0	1448	34,800C	Sra JHP/1.49"/Win WLP
No.5	13.0	1225	14.5	1400	40,000C	Sra JHP/1.49"/Win WLP
No.2	9.9	1060	11.0	1205	38,500C	Sra JHP/1.49"/Win WLP

250 (5" Test)

Powder	Grs.	MV (fps)	Grs.	MV (fps)	Press. (CUP/psi)	Comments
H110	25.5	1344	26.0	1380	37,400C	
HS7	15.0	1103	17.0	1276	38,300C	
H4227	23.0	1141	24.0	1239	37,100C	
HS6	13.5	1024	15.4	1220	37,700C	
HP38	7.8	871	9.8	1100	38,400C	
Trap100	8.0	888	10.1	1060	38,800C	

250

Powder	Grs.	MV (fps)	Grs.	MV (fps)	Press. (CUP/psi)	Comments
No.9	19.3	1315	21.5	1500	40,000C	Hdy XTP/1.48"/Win WLP
No.7	16.9	1280	18.8	1454	39,600C	Hdy XTP/1.48"/Win WLP
H110	21.0	1304	23.0	1396		
H4227	21.0	1288	23.0	1384		
No.5	13.1	1184	14.5	1345	39,000C	Hdy XTP/1.48"/Win WLP
HS7	15.0	1194	16.0	1274		
No.2	9.0	971	10.0	1103	40,000C	Hdy XTP/1.48"/Win WLP

260 (5" Test)

Powder	Grs.	MV (fps)	Grs.	MV (fps)	Press. (CUP/psi)	Comments
H110	24.5	1290	25.0	1339	37,400C	
HS7	14.5	1041	16.5	1251	37,600C	
HS6	13.0	1004	15.0	1219	37,000C	
H4227	22.0	1148	23.0	1209	35,400C	
HP38	7.4	833	9.6	1066	37,200C	
Trap100	7.5	824	9.7	1032	36,900C	

260

Powder	Grs.	MV (fps)	Grs.	MV (fps)	Press. (CUP/psi)	Comments
No.9	20.7	1331	23.0	1512	37,100C	Spr SP/1.515"/Win WLP
No.7	17.1	1268	19.0	1441	38,500C	Spr SP/1.515"/Win WLP
A1680	27.0	1209	30.0	1374	31,300C	Spr SP/1.515"/ Win WLP/(C)
H110	20.0	1201	22.0	1359		
H4227	20.0	1180	22.0	1347		
No.5	13.1	1140	14.5	1295	38,800C	Spr SP/1.515"/Win WLP
HS7	14.0	1116	15.0	1234		
No.2	9.9	1000	11.0	1136	39,100C	Spr SP/1.515"/Win WLP

300

Powder	Grs.	MV (fps)	Grs.	MV (fps)	Press. (CUP/psi)	Comments
No.9	19.4	1234	21.5	1402	37,900C	Spr SP/1.565"/Win WLP
A1680	25.2	1164	28.0	1323	39,900C	Spr SP/1.565"/ Win WLP/(C)
No.7	15.8	1110	17.5	1261	38,200C	Spr SP/1.565"/Win WLP
No.5	12.2	1005	13.5	1142	38,800C	Spr SP/1.565"/Win WLP
No.2	9.0	854	10.0	970	37,400C	Spr SP/1.565"/Win WLP

Caution: **Loads exceeding SAAMI OAL Maximum must be verified for bullet-to-rifling clearance and magazine functioning. Where a specific primer or bullet is indicated those components must be used, no substitutions! Where only a maximum load is shown, reduce starting load 10%, unless otherwise specified.**

Key: (C) = compressed charge; C = CUP; p = psi; Plink = Plinker; Bns = Barnes; Hdy = Hornady; Lap = Lapua; Nos = Nosler; Rem = Remington; Sra = Sierra; Spr = Speer; Win = Winchester.

Manufacturers' Directory of the Reloading Trade

A

A-Square Co., Inc., One Industrial Park, Bedford, KY 40006-9667/502-255-7456; FAX: 502-255-7657

Acadian Ballistic Specialties, P.O. Box 61, Covington, LA 70434

Accuracy Den, The, 25 Bitterbrush Rd., Reno, NV 89523/702-345-0225

Accurate Arms Co., Inc., 5891 Hwy. 230 West, McEwen, TN 37101/615-729-4207, 800-416-3006; FAX 615-729-4211

Action Bullets, Inc., 1811 W. 13th Ave., Denver, CO 80204/303-595-9636; FAX: 303-595-4413

Advance Car Mover Co., Rowell Div., P.O. Box 1, 240 N. Depot St., Juneau, WI 53039/414-386-4464; FAX: 414-386-4416

Alaska Bullet Works, P.O. Box 54, Douglas, AK 99824/907-789-3834

Alex, Inc., Box 3034, Bozeman, MT 59772/406-282-7396; FAX: 406-282-7396

Allred Bullet Co., 932 Evergreen Drive, Logan, UT 84321/801-752-6983

Alpha LaFranck Enterprises, P.O. Box 81072, Lincoln, NE 68501/402-466-3193

American Gas & Chemical Co., Ltd., 220 Pegasus Ave., Northvale, NJ 07647/201-767-7300

Ames Metal Products, 4324 S. Western Blvd., Chicago, IL 60609/312-523-3230; FAX: 312-523-3854

Armfield Custom Bullets, 4775 Caroline Drive, San Diego, CA 92115/619-582-7188; FAX: 619-287-3238

Arms Corporation of the Philippines, Bo. Parang Marikina, Metro Manila, PHILIPPINES/632-941-6243, 632-941-6244; FAX: 632-942-0682

B

B-Square Company, Inc., P.O. Box 11281, 2708 St. Louis Ave., Ft. Worth, TX 76110/817-923-0964, 800-433-2909; FAX: 817-926-7012

Bald Eagle Precision Machine Co., 101 Allison St., Lock Haven, PA 17745/717-748-6772; FAX: 717-748-4443

Ballard Built, P.O. Box 1443, Kingsville, TX 78364/512-592-0853

Ballisti-Cast, Inc., Box 383, Parshall, ND 58770/701-862-3324; FAX: 701-862-3331

Barnes Bullets, Inc., P.O. Box 215, American Fork, UT 84003/801-756-4222, 800-574-9200; FAX: 801-756-2465

Bear Reloaders, P.O. Box 1613, Akron, OH 44309-1613/216-920-1811

Beartooth Bullets, P.O. Box 491, Dept. HLD, Dover, ID 83825-0491/208-448-1865

Beeline Custom Bullets Limited, P.O. Box 85, Yarmouth, Nova Scotia CANADA B5A 4B1/902-648-3494; FAX: 902-648-0253

Bell Reloading, Inc., 1725 Harlin Lane Rd., Villa Rica, GA 30180

Berger Bullets, Ltd., 5342 W. Camelback Rd., Suite 200, Glendale, AZ 85301/602-842-4001; FAX: 602-934-9083

Berry's, Div. of Berry's Mfg., Inc., 401 N. 3050 E., St. George, UT 84770-9004

Berry's Mfg., Inc., 401 North 3050 East St., St. George, UT 84770/801-634-1682; FAX: 801-634-1683

Bertram Bullet Co., P.O. Box 313, Seymour, Victoria 3660, AUSTRALIA/61-57-922912; FAX: 61-57-991650

Big Bore Bullets of Alaska, P.O. Box 872785, Wasilla, AK 99687/907-373-2673; FAX: 907-373-2673

Bitterroot Bullet Co., Box 412, Lewiston, ID 83501-0412/208-743-5635

Black Belt Bullets, Big Bore Express Ltd., 7154 W. State St., Suite 200, Boise, ID 83703

Black Hills Shooters Supply, P.O. Box 4220, Rapid City, SD 57709/800-289-2506

Blackhawk East, Box 2274, Loves Park, IL 61131

Blackhawk West, Box 285, Hiawatha, KS 66434

Blount, Inc., Sporting Equipment Div., 2299 Snake River Ave., P.O. Box 856, Lewiston, ID 83501/800-627-3640, 208-746-2351; FAX: 208-799-3904

Blue Mountain Bullets, HCR 77, P.O. Box 231, John Day, OR 97845/503-820-4594

Blue Ridge Machinery & Tools, Inc., P.O. Box 536, Hurricane, WV 25526/800-872-6500; FAX: 304-562-5311

Brass and Bullet Alloys, P.O. Box 1238, Sierra Vista, AZ 85636/602-458-5321; FAX: 602-458-9125

Brass-Tech Industries, P.O. Box 521-v, Wharton, NJ 07885/201-366-8540

Break-Free, Inc., P.O. Box 25020, Santa Ana, CA 92799/714-953-1900; FAX: 714-953-0402

Briese Bullet Co., Inc., RR1, Box 108, Tappen, ND 58487/701-327-4578; FAX: 701-327-4579

British Antiques, P.O. Box 7, Latham, NY 12110/518-783-0773

British Arms Co. Ltd. (See British Antiques)

Brown Co., E. Arthur, 3404 Pawnee Dr., Alexandria, MN 56308/612-762-8847

Brownells, Inc., 200 S. Front St., Montezuma, IA 50171/515-623-5401; FAX: 515-623-3896

BRP, Inc. High Performance Cast Bullets, 1210 Alexander Rd., Colorado Springs, CO 80909/719-633-0658

Bruno Shooters Supply, 106 N. Wyoming St., Hazleton, PA 18201/717-455-2211; FAX: 717-455-2211

Buck Stix—SOS Products Co., Box 3, Neenah, WI 54956

Buckeye Custom Bullets, 6490 Stewart Rd., Elida, OH 45807/419-641-4463

Buckskin Bullet Co., P.O. Box 1893, Cedar City, UT 84721/801-586-3286

Buffalo Arms, 123 S. Third, Suite 6, Sandpoint, ID 83864/208-263-6953; FAX: 208-265-2096

Buffalo Bullet Co., Inc., 12637 Los Nietos Rd., Unit A, Santa Fe Springs, CA 90670/310-944-0322; FAX: 310-944-5054

Bull Mountain Rifle Co., 6327 Golden West Terrace, Billings, MT 59106/406-656-0778

Bull-X, Inc., 520 N. Main, Farmer City, IL 61842/309-928-2574, 800-248-3845 orders only; FAX: 309-928-2130

Bullet Mills, P.O. Box 102, Port Carbon, PA 17965/717-622-0657

Bullet, Inc., 3745 Hiram Alworth Rd., Dallas, GA 30132

Bullseye Bullets, 1610 State Road 60, No. 12, Valrico, FL 33594/813-654-6563

Buzztail Brass (See Grayback Wildcats)

C

C-H Tool & Die Corp. (See 4-D Custom Die Co.)

C.W. Cartridge Co., 71 Hackensack St., Wood Ridge, NJ 07075

C.W. Cartridge Co., 242 Highland Ave., Kearney, NJ 07032/201-998-1030

Calhoon Varmint Bullets, James, Shambo Rt., Box 304, Havre, MT 59501/406-395-4079

Canons Delcour, Rue J.B. Cools, B-4040 Herstal, BELGIUM/+32.(0)41.40.61.40; FAX: +32(0)412.40.22.88

Canyon Cartridge Corp., P.O. Box 152, Albertson, NY 11507/FAX: 516-294-8946

Carbide Die & Mfg. Co., Inc., 15615 E. Arrow Hwy., Irwindale, CA 91706/818-337-2518

Carnahan Bullets, 17645 110th Ave. SE, Renton, WA 98055

Carroll Bullets (See Precision Reloading, Inc.)

Cascade Bullet Co., Inc., 2355 South 6th St., Klamath Falls, OR 97601/503-884-9316

CCI, Div. of Blount, Inc., 2299 Snake River Ave., P.O. Box 856, Lewiston, ID 83501/800-627-3640, 208-746-2351; FAX: 208-746-2915

Champion's Choice, Inc., 201 International Blvd., LaVergne, TN 37086/615-793-4066; FAX: 615-793-4070

Chem-Pak, Inc., 11 Oates Ave., P.O. Box 1685, Winchester, VA 22604/800-336-9828, 703-667-1341; FAX: 703-722-3993

CheVron Bullets, RR1, Ottawa, IL 61350/815-433-2471

Chronotech, 1655 Siamet Rd. Unit 6, Mississauga, Ont. L4W 1Z4 CANADA/905-625-5200; FAX: 905-625-5190

Clark Custom Guns, Inc., 336 Shootout Lane, Princeton, LA 71067/318-949-9884; FAX: 318-949-9829

Classic Brass, 14 Grove St., Plympton, MA 02367/FAX: 617-585-5673

Clymer Manufacturing Co., Inc., 1645 W. Hamlin Rd., Rochester Hills, MI 48309-1530/810-853-5555, 810-853-5627; FAX: 810-853-1530

Colorado Shooter's Supply, 1163 W. Paradise Way, Fruita, CO 81521/303-858-9191

Competition Electronics, Inc., 3469 Precision Dr., Rockford, IL 61109/815-874-8001; FAX: 815-874-8181

Competitor Corp., Inc., Appleton Business Center, 30 Tricnit Road, Unit 16, New Ipswich, NH 03071-0508/603-878-3891; FAX: 603-878-3950

CONKKO, P.O. Box 40, Broomall, PA 19008/215-356-0711

Cook Engineering Service, 891 Highbury Rd., Vermont VICT 3133 AUSTRALIA

Cooper-Woodward, 3800 Pelican Rd., Helena, MT 59601/406-458-3800

Cor-Bon Bullet & Ammo Co., 1311 Industry Rd., Sturgis, SD 57785/800-626-7266; FAX: 800-923-2666

Corbin, Inc., 600 Industrial Circle, P.O. Box 2659, White City, OR 97503/541-826-5211; FAX: 541-826-8669

Crane & Crane Ltd., 105 N. Edison Way 6, Reno, NV 89502-2355/702-856-1516; FAX: 702-856-1616

Creative Cartridge Co., 56 Morgan Rd., Canton, CT 06019/203-693-2529

Cummings Bullets, 1417 Esperanza Way, Escondido, CA 92027

Curtis Gun Shop, Dept. ST, 119 W. College, Bozeman, MT 59715/406-587-4934

Custom Bullets by Hoffman, 2604 Peconic Ave., Seaford, NY 11783

Custom Products (See Jones Custom Products, Neil)

Cutsinger Bench Rest Bullets, RR 8, Box 161-A, Shelbyville, IN 46176/317-729-5360

D

D&H Precision Tooling, 7522 Barnard Mill Rd., Ringwood, IL 60072/815-653-4011

D&J Bullet Co. & Custom Gun Shop, Inc., 426 Ferry St., Russell, KY 41169/606-836-2663; FAX: 606-836-2663

D.C.C. Enterprises, 259 Wynburn Ave., Athens, GA 30601

Dakota Arms, Inc., HC 55, Box 326, Sturgis, SD 57785/605-347-4686; FAX: 605-347-4459

Davis Products, Mike, 643 Loop Dr., Moses Lake, WA 98837/509-765-6178, 509-766-7281 orders only

Davis, Don, 1619 Heights, Katy, TX 77493/713-391-3090

Del Rey Products, P.O. Box 91561, Los Angeles, CA 90009/213-823-0494

Denver Instrument Co., 6542 Fig St., Arvada, CO 80004/800-321-1135, 303-431-7255; FAX: 303-423-4831

DeSantis Holster & Leather Goods, Inc., P.O. Box 2039, 149 Denton Ave., New Hyde Park, NY 11040-0701/516-354-8000; FAX: 516-354-7501

Dever Co., Jack, 8590 NW 90, Oklahoma City, OK 73132/405-721-6393

Dewey Mfg. Co., Inc., J., P.O. Box 2014, Southbury, CT 06488/203-264-3064; FAX: 203-598-3119

Dillon Precision Products, Inc., 8009 East Dillon's Way, Scottsdale, AZ 85260/602-948-8009, 800-762-3845; FAX: 602-998-2786

DKT, Inc., 14623 Vera Drive, Union, MI 49130-9744/616-641-7120; FAX: 616-641-2015

Dohring Bullets, 100 W. 8 Mile Rd., Ferndale, MI 48220

Double A Ltd., Dept. ST, Box 11306, Minneapolis, MN 55411

Dutchman's Firearms, Inc., The, 4143 Taylor Blvd., Louisville, KY 40215/502-366-0555

Dynamit Nobel-RWS, Inc., 81 Ruckman Rd., Closter, NJ 07624/201-767-7971; FAX: 201-767-1589

Dyson & Son Ltd., Peter, 29-31 Church St., Honley, Huddersfield, W. Yorkshire HDL7 2AH, ENGLAND/0484-661062; FAX: 0484 663709

E

E-Z-Way Systems, Box 4310, Newark, OH 43058-4310/614-345-6645, 800-848-2072; FAX: 614-345-6600

Eagan, Donald V., P.O. Box 196, Benton, PA 17814/717-925-6134

Eezox, Inc., P.O. Box 772, Waterford, CT 06385-0772/203-447-8282, 800-462-3331; FAX: 203-447-3484

Eichelberger Bullets, Wm., 158 Crossfield Rd., King of Prussia, PA 19406

Elkhorn Bullets, P.O. Box 5293, Central Point, OR 97502/503-826-7440

Essex Metals, 1000 Brighton St., Union, NJ 07083/800-282-8369

F

Federal Cartridge Co., 900 Ehlen Dr., Anoka, MN 55303/612-323-2300; FAX: 612-323-2506

Federated-Fry, 6th Ave., 41st St., Altuna, PA 16602/814-946-1611

Firearms Supplies Inc., 514 Quincy St., Hancock, MI 49930/906-482-1673; FAX: 906-482-3822

First, Inc., Jack, 1201 Turbine Dr., Rapid City, SD 57701/605-343-9544; FAX: 605-343-9420

Fitz Pistol Grip Co., P.O. Box 610, Douglas City, CA 96024/916-623-4019

Flambeau Products Corp., 15981 Valplast Rd., Middlefield, OH 44062/216-632-1631; FAX: 216-632-1581

Flitz International Ltd., 821 Mohr Ave., Waterford, WI 53185/414-534-5898; FAX: 414-534-2991

Forgett, Jr., Valmore J., 689 Bergen Blvd., Ridgefield, NJ 07657/201-945-2500; FAX: 201-945-6859

Forgreens Tool Mfg., Inc., P.O. Box 990, 723 Austin St., Robert Lee, TX 76945/915-453-2800

Forkin, Ben, 20 E. Tamarack St., Bozeman, MT 59715-2913

Forster Products, 82 E. Lanark Ave., Lanark, IL 61046/815-493-6360; FAX: 815-493-2371

4-D Custom Die Co., 711 N. Sandusky St., P.O. Box 889, Mt. Vernon, OH 43050-0889/614-397-7214; FAX: 614-397-6600

Fowler Bullets, 806 Dogwood Dr., Gastonia, NC 28054/704-867-3259

Foy Custom Bullets, 104 Wells Ave., Daleville, AL 36322

Freedom Arms, Inc., P.O. Box 1776, Freedom, WY 83120/307-883-2468, 800-833-4432 (orders only); FAX: 307-883-2005

Fremont Tool Works, 1214 Prairie, Ford, KS 67842/316-369-2327

Fusilier Bullets, 10010 N. 6000 W., Highland, UT 84003/801-756-6813

G

G&C Bullet Co., Inc., 8835 Thornton Rd., Stockton, CA 95209/209-477-6479; FAX: 209-477-2813

Gage Manufacturing, 663 W. 7th St., San Pedro, CA 90731

Gehmann, Walter (See Huntington Die Specialties)

Gner's Hard Cast Bullets, 1107 11th St., LaGrande, OR 97850/503-963-8796

Goddard, Allen, 716 Medford Ave., Hayward, CA 94541/510-276-6830

Golden Bear Bullets, 3065 Fairfax Ave., San Jose, CA 95148/408-238-9515

Gonic Bullet Works, P.O. Box 7365, Gonic, NH 03839

Gonzalez Guns, Ramon B., P.O. Box 370, Monticello, NY 12701/914-794-4515

Gotz Bullets, 7313 Rogers St., Rockford, IL 61111

"Gramps" Antique Cartridges, Box 341, Washago, Ont. L0K 2B0 CANADA/705-689-5348

Granite Custom Bullets, Box 190, Philipsburg, MT 59858/406-859-3245

Graphics Direct, P.O. Box 372421, Reseda, CA 91337-2421/818-344-9002

Graves Co., 1800 Andrews Ave., Pompano Beach, FL 33069/800-327-9103; FAX: 305-960-0311

Grayback Wildcats, 5306 Bryant Ave., Klamath Falls, OR 97603/541-884-1072

Green Bay Bullets, 1638 Hazelwood Dr., Sobieski, WI 54171/414-826-7760

Green, Arthur S., 485 S. Robertson Blvd., Beverly Hills, CA 90211/310-274-1283

Greenwood Precision, P.O. Box 468, Nixa, MO 65714-0468/417-725-2330

Grizzly Bullets, 322 Green Mountain Rd., Trout Creek, MT 59874/406-847-2627

Group Tight Bullets, 482 Comerwood Court, San Francisco, CA 94080/415-583-1550

Guardsman Products, 411 N. Darling, Fremont, MI 49412/616-924-3950

Gun City, 212 W. Main Ave., Bismarck, ND 58501/701-223-2304

Gun Works, The, 236 Main St., Springfield, OR 97477/503-741-4118

Guns, 81 E. Streetsboro St., Hudson, OH 44236/216-650-4563

H

Hammets VLD Bullets, P.O. Box 479, Rayville, LA 71269/318-728-2019

Hanned Line, The, P.O. Box 2387, Cupertino, CA 95015-2387

Hardin Specialty Dist., P.O. Box 338, Radcliff, KY 40159-0338/502-351-6649

Harrell's Precision, 5756 Hickory Dr., Salem, VA 24133/703-380-2683

Harris Enterprises, P.O. Box 105, Bly, OR 97622/503-353-2625

Harrison Bullets, 6437 E. Hobart St., Mesa, AZ 85205

Hart & Son, Inc., Robert W., 401 Montgomery St., Nescopeck, PA 18635/717-752-3655, 800-368-3656; FAX: 717-752-1088

Hawk Laboratories, Inc., P.O. Box 1689, Glenrock, WY 82637/307-436-5561

Haydon Shooters' Supply, Russ, 15018 Goodrich Dr. NW, Gig Harbor, WA 98329/206-857-7557

HEBB Resources, P.O. Box 999, Mead, WA 99021-09996/509-466-1292

Heidenstrom Bullets, Urds GT 1 Heroya, 3900 Porsgrunn, NORWAY

Hensley & Gibbs, Box 10, Murphy, OR 97533/503-862-2341

Hercules, Inc., Hercules Plaza, 1313 N Market St., Wilmington, DE 19894/800-276-9337, 302-594-5000; FAX: 302-594-5305

Hirtenberger Aktiengesellschaft, Leobersdorferstrasse 31, A-2552 Hirtenberg, AUSTRIA/43(0)2256 81184; FAX: 43(0)2256 81807

Hobson Precision Mfg. Co., Rt. 1, Box 220-C, Brent, AL 35034/205-926-4662

Hoch Custom Bullet Moulds (See Colorado Shooter's Supply)

Hodgdon Powder Co., Inc., P.O. Box 2932, 6231 Robinson, Shawnee Mission, KS 66202/913-362-9455; FAX: 913-362-1307

Hoehn Sales, Inc., 75 Greensburg Ct., St. Charles, MO 63304/314-441-4231

Hollywood Engineering, 10642 Arminta St., Sun Valley, CA 91352/818-842-8376

Hornady Mfg. Co., P.O. Box 1848, Grand Island, NE 68802/800-338-3220, 308-382-1390; FAX: 308-382-5761

Howell Machine, 815½ D St., Lewiston, ID 83501/208-743-7418

HT Bullets, 244 Belleville Rd., New Bedford, MA 02745/508-999-3338

Huntington Die Specialties, 601 Oro Dam Blvd., Oroville, CA 95965/916-534-1210; FAX: 916-534-1212

I

IMI Services USA, Inc., 2 Wisconsin Circle, Suite 420, Chevy Chase, MD 20815/301-215-4800; FAX: 301-657-1446

Imperial Magnum Corp., P.O. Box 249, Oroville, WA 98844/604-495-3131; FAX: 604-495-2816

IMR Powder Co., 1080 Military Turnpike, Suite 2, Plattsburgh, NY 12901/518-563-2253; FAX: 518-563-6916

Iosso Products, 1485 Lively Blvd., Elk Grove Village, IL 60007/708-437-8400; FAX: 708-437-8478

J

J&D Components, 75 East 350 North, Orem, UT 84057-4719/801-225-7007

J&J Products, Inc., 9240 Whitmore, El Monte, CA 91731/818-571-5228, 800-927-8361; FAX: 818-571-8704

J&L Superior Bullets (See Huntington Die Specialties)

Javelina Products, P.O. Box 337, San Bernardino, CA 92402/714-882-5847; FAX: 714-434-6937

Jensen Bullets, 86 North, 400 West, Blackfoot, ID 83221/208-785-5590

Jester Bullets, Rt. 1 Box 27, Orienta, OK 73737

JGS Precision Tool Mfg., 1141 S. Summer Rd., Coos Bay, OR 97420/503-267-4331; FAX:503-267-5996

JLK Bullets, 414 Turner Rd., Dover, AR 72837/501-331-4194

Jones Custom Products, Neil, RD 1, Box 483A, Saegertown, PA 16433/814-763-2769; FAX: 814-763-4228

Jones Moulds, Paul, 4901 Telegraph Rd., Los Angeles, CA 90022/213-262-1510

Jones, J.D. (See SSK Industries)

K

K&M Services, 5430 Salmon Run Rd., Dover, PA 17315/717-764-1461

K&S Mfg., 2611 Hwy. 40 East, Inglis, FL 34449/904-447-3571

Kasmarsik Bullets, 152 Crstler Rd., Chehalis, WA 98532

Kaswer Custom, Inc., 13 Surrey Drive, Brookfield, CT 06804/203-775-0564; FAX: 203-775-6872

Keith's Bullets, 942 Twisted Oak, Algonquin, IL 60102/708-658-3520

Ken's Kustom Kartridges, 331 Jacobs Rd., Hubbard, OH 44425/216-534-4595

Keng's Firearms Specialty, Inc., 875 Wharton Dr. SW, Atlanta, GA 30336/404-691-7611; FAX: 404-505-8445

Kent Cartridge Mfg. Co. Ltd., Unit 16, Branbridges Industrial Estate, East, Peckham/Tonbridge, Kent, TN12 5HF ENGLAND 622-872255; FAX: 622-872645

King & Co., P.O. Box 1242, Bloomington, IL 61701/309-473-3964

KJM Fabritek, Inc., P.O. Box 162, Marietta, GA 30061/404-426-8251

KLA Enterprises, P.O. Box 2028, Eaton Park, FL 33840/813-682-2829; FAX: 813-682-2829

Kodiak Custom Bullets, 8261 Henry Circle, Anchorage, AK 99507/907-349-2282

Kolpin Mfg., Inc., P.O. Box 107, 205 Depot St., Fox Lake, WI 53933/414-928-3118; FAX: 414-928-3687

L

Lakewood Products, Inc., 275 June St., P.O. Box 230, Berlin, WI 54923/800-US-BUILT; FAX: 414-361-5058

Lapua Ltd., P.O. Box 5, Lapua, FINLAND SF-62101/64-310111; FAX: 64-4388951

Lathrop's, Inc., 5146 E. Pima, Tucson, AZ 85712/602-881-0226, 800-875-4867

LBT, HCR 62, Box 145, Moyie Springs, ID 83845/208-267-3588

Lead Bullets Technology (See LBT)

Lee Precision, Inc., 4275 Hwy. U, Hartford, WI 53027/414-673-3075

Liberty Metals, 2233 East 16th St., Los Angeles, CA 90021/213-581-9171; FAX: 213-581-9351

Liberty Shooting Supplies, P.O. Box 357, Hillsboro, OR 97123/503-640-5518

Lindsley Arms Cartridge Co., P.O. Box 757, 20 College Hill Rd., Henniker, NH 03242/603-428-3127

Lithi Bee Bullet Lube, 1885 Dyson St., Muskegon, MI 49442/616-726-3400

Loadmaster, P.O. Box 1209, Warminster, Wilts. BA12 9XJ ENGLAND/01044 1985 218544; FAX: 01044 1985 214111

Lomont Precision Bullets, 4236 W. 700 South, Poneto, IN 46781/219-694-6792; FAX: 219-694-6797

Lortone, Inc., 2856 NW Market St., Seattle, WA 98107/206-789-3100

Loweth, Richard, 29 Hedgegrow Lane, Kirby Muxloe, Leics. LE9 9BN ENGLAND

Luch Metal Merchants, Barbara, 48861 West Rd., Wixon, MI 48393/800-876-5337

Lyman Instant Targets, Inc. (See Lyman Products Corp.)

Lyman Products Corp., 475 Smith Street, Middletown, CT 06457-1541/860-632-2020, 800-22-LYMAN; FAX: 860-632-1699

M

M&D Munitions Ltd., 127 Verdi St., Farmingdale, NY 11735/800-878-2788, 516-752-1038; FAX: 516-752-1905

M&N Bullet Lube, P.O. Box 495, 151 NE Jefferson St., Madras, OR 97741/503-255-3750

Magma Engineering Co., P.O. Box 161, 20955 E. Ocotillo Rd., Queen Creek, AZ 85242/602-987-9008; FAX: 602-987-0148

Magnus Bullets, P.O. Box 239, Toney, AL 35773/205-828-5089; FAX: 205-828-7756

Maine Custom Bullets, RFD 1, Box 1755, Brooks, ME 04921

Marchmon Bullets, 8191 Woodland Shore Dr., Brighton, MI 48116

Marmik Inc., 2116 S. Woodland Ave., Michigan City, IN 46361-7508/219-872-7231

Marquart Precision Co., Inc., Rear 136 Grove Ave., Box 1740, Prescott, AZ 86302/602-445-5646

MAST Technology, 4350 S. Arville, Suite 3, Las Vegas, NV 89103/702-362-5043; FAX: 702-362-9554

Master Class Bullets, 4209-D West 6th, Eugene, OR 97402/503-687-1263, 800-883-1263

McKillen & Heyer, Inc., 35535 Euclid Ave. Suite 11, Willoughby, OH 44094/216-942-2044

MCRW Associates Shooting Supplies, R.R. 1 Box 1425, Sweet Valley, PA 18656/717-864-3967; FAX: 717-864-2669

MCS, Inc., 34 Delmar Dr., Brookfield, CT 06804/203-775-1013; FAX: 203-775-9462

Men-Metallwerk Elisenhuette, GmbH, P.O. Box 1263, D-56372 Nassau/Lahn, GERMANY/2604-7819

MI-TE Bullets, R.R. 1 Box 230, Ellsworth, KS 67439/913-472-4575

Michaels of Oregon Co., P.O. Box 13010, Portland, OR 97213/503-255-6890; FAX: 503-255-0746

Midway Arms, Inc., 5875 W. Van Horn Tavern Rd., Columbia, MO 65203/800-243-3220, 314-445-6363; FAX: 314-446-1018

Miller Engineering, P.O. Box 6342, Virginia Beach, VA 23456/804-468-1402

Miller Enterprises, Inc., R.P., 1557 E. Main St., P.O. Box 234, Brownsburg, IN 46112/317-852-8187

Mitchell Bullets, R.F., 430 Walnut St., Westernport, MD 21562

MKL Service Co., 610 S. Troy St., P.O. Box D, Royal Oak, MI 48068/810-548-5453

Mo's Competitor Supplies (See MCS, Inc.)

MoLoc Bullets, P.O. Box 2810, Turlock, CA 95381-2810/209-632-1644

Montana Precision Swaging, P.O. Box 4746, Butte, MT 59702/406-782-7502

Monte Kristo Pistol Grip Co., P.O. Box 85, Whiskeytown, CA 96095/916-623-4019

Mt. Baldy Bullet Co., 12981 Old Hill City Rd., Keystone, SD 57751-6623/605-666-4725

MTM Molded Products Co., Inc., 3370 Obco Ct., Dayton, OH 45414/513-890-7461; FAX: 513-890-1747

Mulhern, Rick, Rt. 5, Box 152, Rayville, LA 71269/318-728-2688

Mushroom Express Bullet Co., 601 W. 6th St., Greenfield, IN 46140/317-462-6332

N

Nagel's Bullets, 9 Wilburn, Baytown, TX 77520

National Bullet Co., 1585 E. 361 St., Eastlake, OH 44095/216-951-1854; FAX: 216-951-7761

Naval Ordnance Works, Rt. 2, Box 919, Sheperdstown, WV 25443/304-876-0998

NECO, 1316-67th St., Emeryville, CA 94608/510-450-0420

Necromancer Industries, Inc., 14 Communications Way, West Newton, PA 15089/412-872-8722

Niemi Engineering, W.B., Box 126 Center Road, Greensboro, VT 05841/802-533-7180 days, 802-533-7141 evenings

Noble Co., Jim, 1305 Columbia St., Vancouver, WA 98660/206-695-1309

Norma Precision AB (See U.S. importers—Dynamit Nobel-RWS Inc.; Paul Co. Inc., The)

North American Shooting Systems, P.O. Box 306, Osoyoos, B.C. V0H 1V0 CANADA/604-495-3131; FAX: 604-495-2816

North Devon Firearms Services, 3 North St., Braunton, EX33 1AJ ENGLAND/01271 813624; FAX: 01271 813624

Northern Precision Custom Swaged Bullets, 329 S. James St., Carthage, NY 13619/315-493-1711

Nosler, Inc., P.O. Box 671, Bend, OR 97709/800-285-3701, 503-382-3921; FAX: 503-388-4667

O

October Country, P.O. Box 969, Dept. GD, Hayden Lake, ID 83835/208-772-2068; FAX: 208-772-2068

Oehler Research, Inc., P.O. Box 9135, Austin, TX 78766/512-327-6900, 800-531-5125

OK Weber, Inc., P.O. Box 7485, Eugene, OR 97401/503-747-0458; FAX: 503-747-5927

Oklahoma Ammunition Co., 4310 W. Rogers Blvd., Skiatook, OK 74070/918-396-3187; FAX: 918-396-4270

Old Wagon Bullets, 32 Old Wagon Rd., Wilton, CT 06897

Old West Bullet Moulds, P.O. Box 519, Flora Vista, NM 87415/505-334-6970

Old Western Scrounger, Inc., 12924 Hwy. A-l2, Montague, CA 96064/916-459-5445; FAX: 916-459-3944

Ordnance Works, The, 2969 Pidgeon Point Road, Eureka, CA 95501/707-443-3252

P

P.A.C.T., Inc., P.O. Box 531525, Grand Prairie, TX 75053/214-641-0049

Pace Marketing, Inc., P.O. Box 2039, Stuart, FL 34995/407-223-2189; FAX: 407-286-9547

Paco's (See Small Custom Mould & Bullet Co.)

Page Custom Bullets, P.O. Box 25, Port Moresby Papua, NEW GUINEA

Paragon Sales & Services, Inc., P.O. Box 2022, Joliet, IL 60434/815-725-9212; FAX: 815-725-8974

Patrick Bullets, P.O. Box 172, Warwick QSLD 4370 AUSTRALIA

Pattern Control, 114 N. Third St., P.O. Box 462105, Garland, TX 75046/214-494-3551; FAX: 214-272-8447

Paul Co., The, 27385 Pressonville Rd., Wellsville, KS 66092/913-883-4444; FAX: 913-883-2525

Pease Accuracy, Bob, P.O. Box 310787, New Braunfels, TX 78131/210-625-1342

Pedersoli Davide & C., Via Artigiani 57, Gardone V.T., Brescia, ITALY 25063/030-8912402; FAX: 030-8911019

Peerless Alloy, Inc., 1445 Osage St., Denver, CO 80204/303-825-6394, 800-253-1278

PEM's Mfg. Co., 5063 Waterloo Rd., Atwater, OH 44201/216-947-3721

Pendleton Royal, 4/7 Highgate St., Birmingham, ENGLAND B12 0X5/44 121 440 3060; FAX: 44 121 446 4165

Phillippi Custom Bullets, Justin, P.O. Box 773, Ligonier, PA 15658/412-238-9671

Pinetree Bullets, 133 Skeena St., Kitimat BC, CANADA V8C 1Z1/604-632-3768; FAX: 604-632-3768

Plum City Ballistic Range, N2162 80th St., Plum City, WI 54761-8622/715-647-2539

Policlips North America, 59 Douglas Crescent, Toronto, Ont. CANADA M4W 2E6/800-229-5089, 416-924-0383; FAX: 416-924-4375

Pomeroy, Robert, RR1, Box 50, E. Corinth, ME 04427/207-285-7721

Ponsness/Warren, P.O. Box 8, Rathdrum, ID 83858/208-687-2231; FAX: 208-687-2233

Powell & Son (Gunmakers) Ltd., William, 35-37 Carrs Lane, Birmingham B4 7SX ENGLAND/21-643-0689; FAX: 21-631-3504

Precision Cast Bullets, 101 Mud Creek Lane, Ronan, MT 59864/406-676-5135

Precision Components, 3177 Sunrise Lake, Milford, PA 18337/717-686-4414

Precision Reloading, Inc., P.O. Box 122, Stafford Springs, CT 06076/203-684-7979; FAX: 203-684-6788

Prescott Projectile Co., 1808 Meadowbrook Road, Prescott, AZ 86303

Price Bullets, Patrick W., 16520 Worthley Drive, San Lorenzo, CA 94580/510-278-1547

Prime Reloading, 30 Chiswick End, Meldreth, Royston SG8 6LZ UK/0763-260636

Pro-Shot Products, Inc., P.O. Box 763, Taylorville, IL 62568/217-824-9133; FAX: 217-824-8861

Professional Hunter Supplies (See Star Custom Bullets)

Protector Mfg. Co., Inc., The, 443 Ashwood Place, Boca Raton, FL 33431/407-394-6011

Q

Quinetics Corp., 5731 Kenwick, P.O. Box 13237, San Antonio, TX 78238/512-684-8561; FAX: 512-684-2912

R

R.E.I., P.O. Box 88, Tallevast, FL 34270/813-755-0085

R.I.S. Co., Inc., 718 Timberlake Circle, Richardson, TX 75080/214-235-0933

R.M. Precision, Inc., Attn. Greg F. Smith Marketing, P.O. Box 210, LaVerkin, UT 84745/801-635-4656; FAX: 801-635-4430

Radical Concepts, P.O. Box 1473, Lake Grove, OR 97035/503-636-6686

Rainier Ballistics Corp., 4500 15th St. East, Tacoma, WA 98424/800-638-8722, 206-922-7589; FAX: 206-922-7854

Ranger Products, 2623 Grand Blvd., Suite 209, Holiday, FL 34609/813-942-4652, 800-407-7007; FAX: 813-942-6221

Rapine Bullet Mould Mfg. Co., 9503 Landis Lane, East Greenville, PA 18041/215-679-5413; FAX: 215-679-9795

Ravell Ltd., 289 Diputacion St., 08009, Barcelona SPAIN

Raytech, Div. of Lyman Products Corp., 475 Smith Street, Middletown, CT 06457-1541/860-632-2020; FAX: 860-632-1699